NOTES

ON THE

OLD TESTAMENT

EXPLANATORY AND PRACTICAL

BY

ALBERT BARNES

ENLARGED TYPE EDITION

EDITED BY

ROBERT FREW, D.D.

PSALMS

VOL. II

BAKER BOOK HOUSE
Grand Rapids, Michigan

Library of Congress Catalog Card Number: 55-11630

ISBN: 0-8010-0536-1

First Printing, March 1950
Second Printing, June 1956
Third Printing, April 1959
Fourth Printing, March 1961
Fifth Printing, February 1963
Sixth Printing, September 1964
Seventh Printing, April 1968
Eighth Printing, January 1970
Ninth Printing, June 1971
Tenth Printing, May 1973
Eleventh Printing, March 1974
Twelfth Printing, August 1975

PHOTOLITHOPRINTED BY CUSHING - MALLOY, INC.
ANN ARBOR, MICHIGAN, UNITED STATES OF AMERICA
1975

THE BOOK OF PSALMS.

PSALM XLII.

The *title* of this psalm is, "To the chief Musician, Maschil, for the sons of Korah." On the phrase "To the chief Musician," see Notes on the title to Ps. iv. On the term *Maschil*, see Notes on the title to Ps. xxxii. This title is prefixed to eleven psalms. It properly means, as in the margin, *giving instruction.* But why such a title was prefixed to these psalms rather than to others is unknown. So far as appears, the title, in that sense, would be applicable to many other psalms as well as to these, whether understood in the signification of "giving instruction" in general, or of "giving instruction" on any particular subject. It is not easy to give an account of the origin of such titles long after the occasion for affixing them has passed away. The phrase "for the sons of Korah" is rendered in the margin "of the sons," etc. The Hebrew may mean *for* the sons of Korah; *of* the sons of Korah; or *to* the sons of Korah, as it is here rendered by Prof. Alexander. The LXX. render the title "*For the end*—εἰς τὸ τέλος: —*for understanding*, εἰς σύνεσιν: —*to the sons of Kore*, τοῖς υἱοῖς Κορέ." So the Latin Vulgate. De Wette renders it, "A poem of the sons of Korah." The psalms to which this title is prefixed are the xlii., xliv., xlv., xlvi., xlvii., xlviii., xlix., lxxxiv., lxxxv., lxxxvii., lxxxviii. So far as the *title* is concerned, it may mean either that the psalms were dedicated to them, or that they were submitted to them for arranging the music; or that they were designed to be employed by them as leaders of the music; or that they were the authors of these psalms, that is, that the psalms thus indicated emanated from their body, or were composed by one of their number. *Which* of these is the true idea must be determined, if determined at all, from some other source than the mere title. The sons of Korah were a family of Levitical singers. Korah was a great-grandson of Levi, (Num. xvi. 1). He was united with Dathan and Abiram in opposition to Moses, and was the leader of the conspiracy, Num. xvi. 2; Jude 11. Korah had three sons, Assir, Elkanah, and Abiasaph (Ex. vi. 24); and of their descendants David selected a number to preside over the music of the sanctuary, 1 Chron. vi. 22, 23, 31; and they continued in this service until the time of Jehoshaphat, 2 Chron. xx. 19. One of the most eminent of the descendants of Korah, who was employed especially in the musical service of the sanctuary, was Heman: 1 Chron. vi. 33, "Of the sons of the Kohathites; Heman, a singer." The sons of Heman were appointed by David, in connexion with the sons of Asaph, and of Jeduthun, to preside over the music: 1 Chron. xxv. 1, 4, 6; 2 Chron. v. 12; xxix. 14; xxxv. 15. See Notes on the title to Ps. xxxix. The general appellation, the "sons of Korah," seems to have been given to this company or class of singers. Their office was to preside over the music of the sanctuary; to arrange tunes for the music; to distribute the parts; and *possibly* to furnish compositions for that service. Whether, however, they actually *composed* any of the psalms is uncertain. It would seem that the usual custom was for the author of a psalm or hymn designed for public service to deliver it, when composed, into the hands of these leaders of the music, to be employed by them in the public devotions of the people. Thus, in 1 Chron. xvi. 7, it is said, "Then on that day David delivered first this psalm, to thank the Lord, *into the hand of Asaph and his brethren.*" Comp. 2 Chron. xxix. 30. See also Notes on the title of Ps. l.

It is not absolutely certain, therefore, who composed this psalm. If it was written by David, as seems most probable, it was with some reference to the "sons of Korah;" that is, to those who presided over the music of the sanctuary. In other words, it was prepared *especially* to be used by them in the sanctuary, in contradistinction from psalms which had a more general reference, or which were composed for no such specific design. If it was written *by* the sons of Korah, that is, by any one of their number, it was intended by the author, undoubtedly, to illustrate the feelings of a man of God in deep trials; and the language and the allusions were probably drawn from the history of David, as furnishing the best historical instance for such an illustration of feeling. In this case, the language would be that of one placing himself in imagination in such circumstances, and giving in poetic form a description of the emotions which would pass through his mind, *as if* they were his own,—unless it be supposed that one of the sons of Korah, the author of the psalm, had actually experienced such trials himself. I regard the former as the most probable supposition, and consider that the psalm was composed *by* David specifically for the use of the leaders of the music in the sanctuary. The *name* of the author may have been omitted because it was so well understood who he was that there was no need to designate him.

There is a very marked resemblance between this psalm and the forty-third. They were composed on a similar, if not on the same occasion; and the two might be united so as to constitute one connected psalm. In fact, they *are* thus united in thirty-seven codices of Kennicott, and in nine of De Rossi. The structure of both is the same, though they are separated in most of the Hebrew MSS., in the Septuagint and Latin Vulgate, in the Chaldee Paraphrase, and in the Syriac and Arabic versions.

The forty-second psalm consists of two parts, marked by the *burden* or *refrain* in vers. 5 and 11; and if Psalm xliii. were regarded as a part of the same composition, the two would be divided into three parts, marked by the same *burden* or *refrain*, in Ps. xlii. 5, 11, and xliii. 5. Of these parts the general structure is similar, containing (*a*) an expression of trouble, sorrow, despondency; and then (*b*) a solemn appeal of the author to his own soul, asking why he should be cast down, and exhorting himself to put his trust in God.

The occasion on which the psalm was composed by David, if he wrote it,—or the occasion which was supposed by the author, if that author was one of the sons of Korah,—is not certainly known. The psalm agrees best with the supposition that it was in the time of the rebellion of Absalom, when David was driven from his throne, and from the place which he had appointed for the worship of God after he had removed the ark to Mount Zion, and when he was an exile and a wanderer beyond the Jordan, 2 Samuel xv.-xviii.

The psalm records the feelings of one who had been driven away from the place where he had been accustomed to worship God, and his recollections of those sad days when he endeavoured to comfort himself in his despondency by looking to God, and by dwelling on his promises.

I. In the first part (vers. 1-5) there is

(1) An expression of his desire to hold communion with God—the panting of his soul after God, vers. 1, 2.

(2) His tears under the reproaches of his enemies, while they said, "Where is thy God?" ver. 3.

(3) His remembrance of the former days when he had gone with the multitude to the house of God; and the expression of a firm belief, implied in the language used, that he *would* go again to the house of God, and with them would keep "holyday," ver. 4. See Notes on that verse.

(4) Self-remonstrance for his despondency, and an exhortation to himself to arouse and to trust in God, with the confident assurance that he would yet be permitted to praise Him, ver. 5.

II. The second part contains a series of similar reflections, vers. 6-11.

(1) A description of his desponding feelings under these circumstances; under the troubles which had rolled over him like waters, vers. 6, 7.

(2) An assurance that God would yet manifest His loving-kindness to him; and, on the ground of that, an earnest appeal to God as his God, vers. 8, 9.

(3) A further statement of his troubles, as derived from the reproaches of his enemies, as if a sword penetrated even to his bones, ver. 10.

(4) Self-remonstrance again for his despondency, and an exhortation to himself to trust in God (in the same language with which the former part of the psalm closes), ver. 11.

The idea of the whole is, that we

PSALM XLII.

To the chief Musician, [1] Maschil, for the sons of Korah.

[1] Or, A Psalm *giving instruction to the sons, etc.*

AS the hart [2] panteth after the water-brooks, so panteth my soul after thee, O God.

[2] *brayeth.*

should *not* be overwhelmed or cast down in trouble; that we should confide in God; that we should be cheerful, not desponding; that we should go to God, whatever may happen; and that we should feel that all will yet be well, that all will be overruled for good, and that brighter and happier days will come. How often have the people of God occasion to use the language of this psalm! In a world of trouble and sorrow such as ours is; in a world where the friends of God have often been, and may again be, persecuted; in the anguish which is felt from the ingratitude of children, kindred, and friends; in the distress which springs up in the heart when, from sickness or from any other cause, we are long deprived of the privileges of public worship—in *exile* as it were from the sanctuary — how imperfect would be a book professing to be a revelation from God, if it did *not* contain some such psalm as this, so accurately describing the feelings of those who are in such circumstances; so adapted to their wants; so well fitted to direct to the true source of consolation! It is this *adaptedness* of the Bible to the actual requirements of mankind,—this accurate description of the feelings which pass through our own mind and heart,—this constant direction to God as the true source of support and consolation—which so much endears the Bible to the hearts of the people of God, and which serves, more than any arguments from miracle and prophecy—valuable as those arguments are — to keep up in their minds the conviction that the Bible *is* a Divine revelation. Psalms like this make the Bible a *complete* book, and show that He who gave it "knew what is in man," and what man needs in this vale of tears.

1. *As the hart panteth after the water-brooks.* Marg., *brayeth.* The word rendered *hart* — אַיָּל, *ayyal*— means commonly a stag, hart, male deer: Deut. xii. 15; xiv. 5; Isa. xxxv. 6. The word is masculine, but in this place is joined with a feminine verb, as words of the common gender may be, and thus denotes a *hind*, or female deer. The word rendered in the text *panteth*, and in the margin *brayeth*—עָרַג, *arag*—occurs only in this place and in Joel i. 20, where it is applied to the beasts of the field as "crying" to God in a time of drought. The word properly means to rise; to ascend; and then, to look up towards anything; to long for. It refers here to the intense desire of the hind, in the heat of day, for water; or, in Joel, to the desire of the cattle for water in a time of drought. Luther renders it "cries;" the Septuagint and Vulgate render it simply "desires." Neither the idea of *panting* nor *braying* seems to be in the original word. It is the idea of looking for, longing for, desiring, that is expressed there. By *water-brooks* are meant the streams that run in vallies. Dr. Thomson (Land and the Book, vol. i., p. 253) says, "I have seen large flocks of these panting harts gather round the water-brooks in the great deserts of Central Syria, so subdued by thirst that you could approach quite near them before they fled." There is an idea of tenderness in the reference to the word *hart* here—female deer, gazelle—which would not strike us if the reference had been to any other animal. These are so timid, so gentle, so delicate in their structure, so much the natural objects of love and compassion, that our feelings are drawn towards them as to all other animals in similar circumstances. We sympathize with them; we pity them; we love them; we feel deeply for them when they are pursued, when they fly away in fear, when they are in want. The following engraving will help us more to appreciate the comparison employed by the psalmist. Nothing could more beautifully or appropriately describe the earnest longing of a soul after God, in the circumstances of the psalmist, than this image. ¶ *So*

2 My soul[a] thirsteth for God, for the living God: when [b] shall I come and appear before God?

a Ps. lxiii. 1; John vii. 37. b Job xxiii. 3.

panteth my soul after thee, O God. So earnest a desire have I to come before thee, and to enjoy thy presence and thy favour. So sensible am I of want; so much does my soul need something that can satisfy its desires. This was at first applied to the case of one who was cut off from the privileges of public worship, and

GAZELLES.

who was driven into exile far from the place where he had been accustomed to unite with others in that service (ver. 4); but it will also express the deep and earnest feelings of the heart of piety at all times, and in all circumstances, in regard to God. There is no desire of the soul more intense than that which the pious heart has for God; there is no want more deeply felt than that which is experienced when one who loves God is cut off by any cause from communion with him.

2. *My soul thirsteth for God.* That is, as the hind thirsts for the running stream. ¶ *For the living God.* God, not merely as God, without anything more definitely specified, but God considered as *living*, as himself *possessing* life, and as having the power of *imparting* that life to the soul. ¶ *When shall I come and appear before God?* That is, as I have been accustomed to do in the sanctuary. When shall I be restored to the privilege of again uniting with his people in public prayer and praise? The psalmist evidently expected that this would be; but to one who loves public worship the time seems long

3 My tears have been my meat day and night, while they continually say unto me, Where *is* thy God?

4 When I remember these *things*, I pour out my soul in me: for I had gone with the multitude; I went with them to

when he is prevented from enjoying that privilege.

3. *My tears have been my meat.* The word rendered *tears* in this place is in the singular number, and means literally *weeping*. Comp. Ps. xxxix. 12. The word *meat* here means literally *bread,* and is used in the general signification of *food,* as the word *meat* is always used in the English version of the Bible. The English word *meat,* which originally signified *food,* has been changed gradually in its signification, until it now denotes in common usage animal food, or flesh. The idea here is, that instead of *eating,* he had *wept.* The state described is that which occurs so often when excessive sorrow takes away the appetite, or destroys the relish for food, and occasions fasting. This was the foundation of the whole idea of fasting,—that sorrow, and especially sorrow for sin, takes away the desire for food for the time, and leads to involuntary abstinence. Hence arose the correlative idea of abstaining from food with a view to *promote* that deep sense of sin, or to produce a condition of the body which would be favourable to a proper recollection of guilt. ¶ *Day and night.* Constantly; without intermission. See Notes on Ps. i. 2. ¶ *While they continually say unto me.* While it *is* constantly said to me; that is, by mine enemies. See ver. 10. ¶ *Where is thy God?* See Ps. iii. 2; xxii. 8. The meaning here is, "He seems to be utterly forsaken or abandoned by God. He trusted in God. He professed to be his friend. He looked to him as his protector. But he is now forsaken, as if he had no God; and God is treating him as if he were none of his; as if he had no love for him, and no concern about his welfare."

4. *When I remember these* things. These sorrows; this banishment from the house of God; these reproaches of my enemies. The verb here used is in the future tense, and would be appropriately rendered "I *will* remember these things, and I *will* pour out my soul within me." That is, it is not a mere recollection of the past, but it indicates a state or purpose of mind—a solemn resolution to bear these things ever in remembrance, and to allow them to produce a proper impression on his mind and heart that would not be effaced by time. Though the future tense is used as denoting what the state of his mind *would* be, the immediate reference is to the past. The sorrows and afflictions which *had* overwhelmed him were the things he would remember. ¶ *I pour out my soul in me.* Heb., *upon me.* See Notes on Job xxx. 16. The idea is derived from the fact that the soul in grief seems to be *dissolved,* or to lose all firmness, consistency, or power, and to be like water. We speak now of the soul as being *melted, tender, dissolved,* with sympathy or grief, or as *overflowing* with joy. ¶ *For I had gone with the multitude.* The word here rendered *multitude*—סָךְ, *sach*—occurs nowhere else in the Scriptures. It is supposed to denote properly a thicket of trees; a thick wood; and then, a crowd of men. The LXX. render it, "I will pass on to the place of the wonderful tabernacle,"—σκηνῆς θαυμαστῆς. So the Latin Vulgate. Luther translates it, "multitude," *Haufen.* The Hebrew verb is in the future—"I shall pass," or "when I pass," indicating a confident expectation of a favourable issue of his present trials, and referring not to the fact that he *had* gone with the multitude in time past, but to the fact that he *would* be permitted to go with them in solemn procession

the house of God, with the voice of [c]joy and praise, with a multitude that kept holyday.
5 Why art thou [1]cast down, O

c Ps. cxxii. 1.

1 *bowed down.*

to the house of God, and that then he *would* recall these things, and pour out his soul in the fulness of his emotions. The Septuagint renders this in the future; so also the Latin Vulgate, De Wette, and Prof. Alexander. Luther renders it, "For I would gladly go hence with the multitude." It seems clear, therefore, that this does not refer to what *had been* in the past, but to what he confidently hoped and expected *would be* in the future. He expected again to go with the multitude to the house of God. Even in his exile, and in his sorrows, he confidently anticipated this, and he says that he would then pour forth the full expression of gratitude—his whole soul—in view of all these things which had occurred. He was *now* in exile: his heart was overwhelmed with sorrow; he was away from the place of worship—the house of God; he no longer went with others with solemn steps to the sanctuary, but he hoped and expected again to be permitted to do so; and, in view of this, he calls on his soul (ver. 5) not to be cast down. This interpretation, referring it to the future, also brings this part of the psalm into harmony with the subsequent part (ver. 8), where the author of the psalm confidently expresses the same hope. ¶ *I went with them to the house of God.* The tabernacle; the place of public worship. See Notes on Ps. xxiii. 6. The Hebrew verb here is also in the future tense, and, in accordance with the interpretation above, the meaning is, "I *will* go," etc. The word occurs only here, and in Isa. xxxviii. 15, "I shall go softly all my years." See the word explained in the Notes on that passage. It seems here to be used with reference to a movement in a slow and solemn procession, as in the usual processions connected with public worship among the Hebrews. The meaning is, that he would go with the multitude with seriousness and solemnity, as they went up to the house of God to worship. ¶ *With the voice of joy and praise.* Chanting hymns to God. ¶ *With a multitude that kept holyday.* The word here rendered *multitude*—הָמוֹן, *hamon*—is different from that which is employed in the former part of the verse. This is the *usual* word to denote a multitude. It literally means a noise or sound, as of rain, 1 Kings xviii. 41; then, a multitude or crowd *making* a noise, as of nations, or of an army, Isa. xiii. 4; Judges iv. 7; Dan. xi. 11, 12, 13. The word rendered "that kept holyday"—חוֹגֵג, *hhogaig*—from חָגַג, *hhagag*, to dance—means literally *dancing;* dancing in a circle; and then, keeping a festival, celebrating a holyday, as this was done formerly by leaping and dancing, Ex. v. 1; Lev. xxiii. 41. The meaning is, that he would join with the multitude in the joyful celebrations of public worship. This was the bright anticipation before him in exile; this cheered and sustained his heart when sinking in despair.

5. *Why art thou cast down, O my soul?* Marg., *bowed down.* The Hebrew word means to bow down, to incline oneself; then, usually, to prostrate oneself as in public worship; and then, to sink down under the weight of sorrow; to be depressed and sad. The LXX. render it, "Why art thou grieved?"—περίλυπος. So the Vulgate. This is an earnest remonstrance addressed by himself *to his own soul,* as if there were really no occasion for this excessive depression; as if he cherished his grief improperly. There was a brighter side, and he *ought* to turn to that, and take a more cheerful view of the matter. He had allowed his mind to rest on the dark side, to look at the discouraging things in his condition. He now felt

my soul? and *why* art thou disquieted in me? Hope thou in God; for I shall yet [1] praise him [2] *for* the help of his countenance.

[1] Or, *give thanks.*

[2] Or, *his presence* is *salvation.*

that this was in some measure voluntary, or had been indulged too freely, and that it was wrong: that it was *proper* for a man like him to seek for comfort in brighter views; that it was a *duty* which he owed to himself and to the cause of religion to take brighter views. We may remark, (1.) That there are two sides to the events which occur, and which seem so discouraging to us—a *dark* side and a *bright* side. (2.) That in certain states of mind, connected often with a diseased nervous system, we are prone to look only on the *dark* side, to see only what is gloomy and discouraging. (3.) That this often becomes in a sense *voluntary*, and that we find a melancholy satisfaction in *being* miserable, and in *making* ourselves more unhappy, as if we had been wronged, and as if there were a kind of virtue in dejection and gloom —in "refusing," like Rachel, "*to be comforted*" (Jer. xxxi. 15);—perhaps also feeling as if by this we were *deserving* of the Divine approbation, and laying the foundation for some *claim* to favour on the score of merit. (4.) That in this we are often eminently *guilty*, as putting away those consolations which God has provided for us; as if a man, under the influence of some morbid feeling, should find a kind of melancholy pleasure in starving himself to death in the midst of a garden full of fruit, or dying of thirst by the side of a running fountain. And (5) that it is the *duty* of the people of God to look at the bright side of things; to think of the past mercies of God; to survey the blessings which surround us still; to look to the future, in this world and the next, with hope; and to come to God, and cast the burden on him. It is a part of religious duty to be *cheerful;* and a man may often do more real good by a cheerful and submissive mind in times of affliction, than he could by much active effort in the days of health, plenty, and prosperity. Every sad and desponding Christian *ought* to say to his soul, "*Why* art thou thus cast down?" ¶ *And* why *art thou disquieted in me?* Troubled, sad. The word means literally, (1) to growl as a bear; (2) to sound, or make a noise, as a harp, rain, waves; (3) to be agitated, troubled, or anxious in mind: *to moan internally.* See Notes on Isa. xvi. 11; comp. Jer. xlviii. 36. ¶ *Hope thou in God.* That is, trust in him, with the hope that he will interpose and restore thee to the privileges and comforts heretofore enjoyed. The soul turns to God when all other hope fails, and finds comfort in the belief that he can and will aid us. ¶ *For I shall yet praise him.* Marg., *give thanks.* The idea is, that he would yet have occasion to give him thanks for his merciful interposition. This implies a strong assurance that these troubles would not last always. ¶ For *the help of his countenance.* Literally, "the salvations of his face," or his presence. The original word rendered *help* is in the plural number, meaning *salvations;* and the idea in the use of the plural is, that his deliverance would be complete or entire —as if double or manifold. The meaning of the phrase "help of his *countenance*" or "*face,*" is that God would look favourably or benignly upon him. Favour is expressed in the Scriptures by lifting up the light of the countenance on one. See Notes on Ps. iv. 6; comp. Ps. xi. 7; xxi. 6; xliv. 3; lxxxix. 15. This closes the first part of the psalm, expressing the confident belief of the psalmist that God would yet interpose, and that his troubles would have an end; reposing entire confidence in God as the only ground of hope; and expressing the feeling that when that confidence exists the soul should *not* be dejected or cast down.

6 O my God, my soul [d] is cast down within me: therefore will I remember thee from the land of Jordan, and of the Hermonites, from [1] the hill Mizar.

d Ps. lxxvii. 3--10.
1 Or, *the little hill*, Ps. cxxxiii. 3.

6. *O my God, my soul is cast down within me.* This is the utterance of a soul in anguish, notwithstanding the purpose *not* to be cast down, and the conviction that hope *ought* to be cherished. The psalmist cannot but say that, despite all this, he *is* sad. His troubles come rushing over his soul; they all return at once; his heart is oppressed, and he is constrained to confess that, notwithstanding his solemn purpose *not* to be sad, and the conviction that he *ought* to be cheerful, and his wish to be and to appear so, yet his sorrows get the mastery over all this, and his heart is filled with grief. What sufferer has not felt thus? When he really wished to trust in God; when he hoped that things would be better; when he saw that he ought to be calm and cheerful, his sorrows have returned like a flood, sweeping all these feelings away for the time, filling his soul with anguish, compelling him to form these resolutions anew, and driving him afresh to the throne of grace, to beat back the returning tide of grief, and to bring the soul to calmness and peace. ¶ *Therefore will I remember thee.* I will look to thee; I will come to thee; I will recall thy former merciful visitations. In this lone land; far away from the place of worship; in the midst of these privations, troubles, and sorrows; surrounded as I am by taunting foes, and having no source of consolation *here*, I will remember my God. Even here, amidst these sorrows, I will lift up my heart in grateful remembrance of him, and will think of him alone. The words which follow are designed merely to give an idea of the desolation and sadness of his condition, and of the fact of his exile. ¶ *From the land of Jordan.* Referring probably to the fact he was then *in* that "land." The phrase would denote the region adjacent to the Jordan, and through which the Jordan flowed, as we speak of "the valley of the Mississippi," *i. e.* the region through which that river flows. The lands adjacent to the Jordan on either side were covered with underbrush and thickets, and were, in former times, the favourite resorts of wild animals: Jer. xlix. 19; l. 44. The psalmist was on the eastern side of the Jordan. ¶ *And of the Hermonites.* The land of the Hermonites. The region in which Mount Hermon is situated. This was on the north-east of Palestine, beyond the Jordan. Mount Hermon was a ridge or spur of Antilibanus: Josh. xi. 3, 17. This spur or ridge lies near the sources of the Jordan. It consists of several summits, and is therefore spoken of here in the plural number, *Hermonim*, the Hebrew plural of Hermon. These mountains were called by the Sidonians, *Sirion.* See Notes on Ps. xxix. 6. Different names were given to different parts of these summits of the mountain-ranges. The principal summit, or Mount Hermon properly so called, rises to the height of ten or twelve thousand feet, and is covered with perpetual snow; or rather, as Dr. Robinson says (Biblical Researches, iii. 344), the snow is perpetual in the *ravines*, so that the top presents the appearance of radiant stripes around and below the summit. The word is used here with reference to the mountain-region to which the general name of Hermon was given on the north-east of Palestine, and on the east of the sources of the Jordan. It would seem not improbable that after passing the Jordan the psalmist had gone in that direction in his exile. ¶ *From the hill Mizar.* Marg., *the little hill.* So the LXX., the Latin Vulgate, and Luther. De Wette renders it as a proper name. The word *Mizar*, or *Mitzar* (Heb.), means properly *smallness;* and thus, anything small or little. The word seems

7 Deep calleth unto deep at the noise of thy waterspouts: all thy waves [c] and thy billows are gone over me.

c Ps. lxxxviii. 7.

here, however, to be used as a proper name, and was probably applied to some part of that mountain-range, though to what particular portion is now unknown. This would seem to have been the place where the psalmist took up his abode in his exile. As no such name is now known to be given to any part of that mountain-range, it is impossible to identify the spot. It would seem from the following verse, however, that it was not far from the Jordan.

7. *Deep calleth unto deep.* The language used here would seem to imply that the psalmist was near some floods of water, some rapid river or water-fall, which constituted an appropriate illustration of the waves of sorrow that were rolling over his soul. It is not possible to determine exactly *where* this was, though, as suggested in the verse above, it would seem most probable that it was in the vicinity of the upper portion of the Jordan; and doubtless the Jordan, if swollen, would suggest all that is conveyed by the language used here. The word rendered *deep*—תְּהוֹם, *tehom* —means properly a wave, billow, surge, and then, a mass of waters; a flood—the deep; the sea. In this latter sense it is used in Deut. viii. 7; Ezek. xxxi. 4; Gen. vii. 11; Job xxviii. 14; xxxviii. 16, 30; Ps. xxxvi. 6. Here it would seem to mean merely a wave or billow, perhaps the waves of a rapid stream dashing on one shore, and then driven to the opposite bank, or the torrents pouring over rocks in the bed of a stream. It is not necessary to suppose that this was the ocean, nor that there was a *cataract* or *water-fall.* All that is meant here would be met by the roaring waters of a swollen river. The word "*calleth,*" here means that one wave seemed to speak to another, or one wave responded to another. See a similar expression in Ps. xix. 2, "Day unto day uttereth speech." Comp. Notes on that verse. ¶ *At the noise of thy water-spouts.* Literally, *at the voice.* That is, "water-spouts" make a noise, or seem to give forth a voice; and this *appears* to be as if one part of the "deep" were speaking to another, or as if one wave were calling with a loud voice to another. The word *water-spouts* — צִנּוֹר, *tzinnor* — occurs only here and in 2 Sam. v. 8, where it is rendered *gutter.* It properly means a cataract, or a water-fall, or a water-course, as in 2 Sam. Any pouring of water—as from the clouds, or in a swollen river, or in a "water spout," properly so called—would correspond with the use of the word here. It *may* have been rain pouring down; or it may have been the Jordan pouring its floods over rocks, for it is well known that the descent of the Jordan in that part is rapid, and especially when swollen; or it may have been the phenomena of a "water-spout," for these are not uncommon in the East. There are two forms in which "waterspouts" occur, or to which the name is given in the east, and the language here would be applicable to either of them. One of them is described in the following manner by Dr. Thomson, Land and the Book, vol. i., pp. 498, 499:—"A small black cloud traverses the sky in the latter part of summer or the beginning of autumn, and pours down a flood of rain that sweeps all before it. The Arabs call it *sale;* we, a waterspout, or the bursting of a cloud. In the neighbourhood of Hermon I have witnessed it repeatedly, and was caught in one last year, which in five minutes flooded the whole mountain side, washed away the fallen olives —the food of the poor—overthrew

stone walls, tore up by the roots large trees, and carried off whatever the tumultuous torrents encountered, as they leaped madly down from terrace to terrace in noisy cascades. Every summer threshing-floor along the line of its march was swept bare of all precious food, cattle were drowned,

WATERSPOUT.

flocks disappeared, and the mills along the streams were ruined in half an hour by this sudden deluge." The other is described in the following language, and the above engraving will furnish an illustration of it.—Land and the Book, vol. ii., pp. 256, 257:—"Look at those clouds which hang like a heavy pall of sackcloth over the sea along the western horizon. From them, on such windy days as these, are formed *waterspouts*, and I have already noticed several incipient "spouts" drawn down from the clouds toward the sea, and ... seen to be in violent agitation, whirling round on themselves as they are driven along by the wind. Directly beneath them the surface of the sea is also in commotion by a whirlwind, which travels onward in concert with the spout above. I have

8 *Yet* the LORD will command his loving-kindness in the daytime, and in the night his song *shall be* with me, *and* my prayer unto the God of my life.

9 I will say unto God my rock, Why hast thou forgotten me? why go I mourning because of the oppression of the enemy?

---

often seen the two actually unite in mid air, and rush toward the mountains, writhing, and twisting, and bending like a huge serpent with its head in the clouds, and its tail on the deep." We cannot now determine to which of these the psalmist refers, but either of them would furnish a striking illustration of the passage before us. ¶ *All thy waves and thy billows are gone over me.* The waves of sorrow; anguish of soul; of which rolling floods would be an emblem. The rushing, and heaving, and restless waters furnished the psalmist with an illustration of the deep sorrows of his soul. So we speak of "*floods* of grief," "*floods* of tears," "*oceans* of sorrows," *as if* waves and billows swept over us. And so we speak of being "*drowned* in grief," or "in tears." Comp. Ps. cxxiv. 4, 5.

8. Yet *the* LORD *will command his loving-kindness in the daytime.* Literally, "By day the Lord will command his mercy;" that is, he will so order or direct his mercy or his favour. The word "*daytime*" here refers evidently to prosperity; and the expectation of the psalmist was that a time of prosperity would return; that he might hope for better days; that the loving-kindness of God would again be manifested to him. He did not wholly despair. He expected to see better times (comp. Notes on ver. 5); and, in view of this, and in the confident assurance of it, he says in the subsequent part of the verse that even in the night—the season of calamity—his song should be unto God, and he would praise Him. Some, however, as De Wette, have understood the words "daytime" and "night" as synonymous with "day and night;" that is, at all times; implying an assurance that God would *always* show his loving-kindness. But it seems to me that the above is the most correct interpretation. ¶ *And in the night his song* shall be *with me.* I will praise him, even in the dark night of calamity and sorrow. God will even then give me such views of himself, and such manifest consolations, that my heart will be full of gratitude, and my lips will utter praise. See Notes on Job xxxv. 10; comp. Acts xvi. 25. ¶ And *my prayer unto the God of my life.* To God, who has given me life, and who preserves my life. The meaning is, that in the dark night of sorrow and trouble he would not cease to call on God. Feeling that he had given life, and that he was able to sustain and to defend life, he would go to him and supplicate his mercy. He would not allow affliction to drive him *from* God, but it should lead him the more earnestly and fervently to implore his aid. Afflictions, God's apparently severe dealings, which it might be supposed would have a tendency to turn men *from* God, are the very means of leading them *to* him.

9. *I will say unto God my rock.* I will appeal to God as my defence, my helper, my Saviour. On the word *rock*, as applied to God, see Notes on Ps. xviii. 2. ¶ *Why hast thou forgotten me?* See Notes on Ps. xxii. 1. He had *seemed* to forget and forsake him, for He did not come to interpose and save him. This is a part of the prayer which he says (ver. 8) that he would use. ¶ *Why go I mourning?* On the meaning of the word here used—קֹדֵר, *kodair*—see Notes on Ps. xxxv. 14; xxxviii. 6. The idea is that of being bowed down, made sad, deeply afflicted, as one forsaken. ¶ *Because of the oppression of the enemy. In* the oppression of the enemy; that is, during its continuance,

10 *As* with a [1]sword in my
bones, mine enemies reproach
me; while they say daily unto
me, Where *is* thy God?
11 Why art thou cast down, O
my soul? and why art thou disquieted within me? Hope thou
in God; for I shall yet praise
him, *who is* the health of my
countenance, and my God.

[1] Or, *killing*.

---

or on account of it. The word here rendered *oppression* means *distress, affliction, straits,* Job xxxvi. 15; 1 Kings xxii. 27; Isa. xxx. 20. The "enemy" here referred to may have been Absalom, who had driven him from his throne and kingdom.

10. As *with a sword in my bones.* Marg., *killing.* The treatment which I receive in their reproaches is like *death.* The word rendered *sword*—רֶצַח, *retzahh*—means properly *killing, slaying, breaking in pieces, crushing.* It occurs only here and in Ezek. xxi. 22, where it is rendered *slaughter.* The LXX. render it, "In the bruising of my bones they reproach me." The Vulgate, "While they break my bones they reproach me." Luther, "It is as death in my bones, that my enemies reproach me." The idea in the Hebrew is, that their reproaches were like breaking or crushing his very bones. The idea of the "sword" is not in the original. ¶ *Mine enemies reproach me.* That is, as one forsaken of God, and as suffering justly under his displeasure. Their argument was, that if he was truly the friend of God, he would not leave him thus; that the fact of his *being* thus abandoned proved that he was not a friend of God. ¶ *While they say daily unto me.* They say this constantly. I am compelled to hear it every day. ¶ *Where* is *thy God?* See Notes on ver. 3.

11. *Why art thou cast down, O my soul?* This closes the second strophe of the psalm, and, with one or two slight and immaterial variations, is the same as that which closes the first (ver. 5). In this latter the word "why" is inserted, and the expression "the salvation of *my* countenance" occurs instead of "salvations of *his* countenance," with the addition of the words "and my God" at the close. The sense, however, is the same; and the verse contains, as before, self-reproof for being thus cast down, and self-exhortation to put trust in God. In the former part of the psalm (ver. 5) he had addressed this language to himself, as designed to impress his own mind with the guilt of thus yielding to discouragement and sorrow; but he had then almost immediately admitted that his mind *was* distressed, and that he *was* cast down; here he rallies again, and endeavours to arouse himself to the conviction that he ought *not* to be thus depressed and dejected. He exhorts himself, therefore; he charges his own soul to hope in God. He expresses again the assurance that he *would* yet be permitted to praise him. He regards God now as the "salvation of *his* countenance," or as his Deliverer and Friend, and expresses the conviction that he would yet make such manifestations of himself as *to clear up* and *illuminate* his countenance, at present made dark and saddened by affliction; and he appeals to him now as "*his* God." He has reached the true source of comfort to the afflicted and the sad,—the living God as *his* God; and his mind is calm. Why should a man be sorrowful when he feels that he has a God? Why should his heart be sad when he can pour out his sorrows before Him? Why should he be cast down and gloomy when he can *hope*:—hope for the favour of God here; hope for immortal life in the world to come!

PSALM XLIII.

This psalm is without a title. The name of the author is unknown, and, of course, it is not known on what occasion the psalm was composed. It bears, how-

PSALM XLIII.

JUDGE me, O God, and plead my cause against an [1] ungodly nation: O deliver me from [2] the deceitful and unjust man.

2 For thou *art* the God of my

[1] Or, *unmerciful.*

[2] *a man of deceit and iniquity.*

ever, a very strong resemblance, in its general spirit and in its structure, to Ps. xlii., and was, beyond doubt, composed by the same author, and in reference to the same occasion. The resemblance between the two psalms is so striking that many have supposed that they are parts of the same psalm, and as this one terminates with the same language (ver. 5) as that which occurs at the close of the two parts of Ps. xlii. (vers. 5, 11), it has been conjectured by many that this is the third part or strophe of the psalm, and that they have been separated by mistake of the transcribers. See introd. to Ps. xlii. It would be impossible to account for the fact that they had become separated in the majority of Hebrew MSS. if they had originally constituted one psalm; while the fact of their being found united in a small number of Hebrew MSS. is easily accounted for, as the resemblance of the two may have led the transcribers to suppose that they were parts of one composition. The probability is, that this psalm was composed by the same author, as a kind of *supplement* to the former psalm, or as expressing, in a slightly different form, the emotions which passed through his mind on that same occasion.

The psalm contains (1) an earnest appeal to God to assist the suffering author, and to protect him from the efforts of an ungodly nation, and from the designs of the deceitful and unjust man, ver. 1; (2) an appeal to God as his strength, with the language of anxious inquiry why he had cast him off, and had suffered him to go mourning because of the oppression of his enemy, ver. 2; (3) an earnest prayer that God would interpose, and would send out his light and his truth, and would permit him to go again to his holy hill, to the tabernacles, and to the altar, vers. 3, 4; and (4), as in Ps. xlii. 5, 11, self-reproach that he is thus dejected and dispirited, and an appeal to his own soul to arouse itself, and to put its trust in God. It is a psalm, like the former, of great practical value to those who, in affliction, are sad and desponding.

1. *Judge me, O God.* This does not mean, Pronounce sentence upon me; but, Undertake my cause; interpose in my behalf; do justice in the case. He regarded his own cause as right; he felt that he was greatly wronged by the treatment which he received from men, and he asks to have it shown that he was not guilty of what his enemies charged on him; that he was an upright man, and a friend of God. See Notes on Ps. vii. 8; xxvi. 1. ¶ *And plead my cause.* See Notes on Ps. xxxv. 1. ¶ *Against an ungodly nation.* Marg., *unmerciful.* Literally, "from a nation not merciful," or not religious. The idea is, that the nation or people referred to manifested none of the spirit of religion in their conduct towards him; that he was treated with severity and injustice. This entire description would agree well with the state of things in the time of the rebellion of Absalom, when David was driven from his home and his throne: 2 Sam. xv., *seq.* ¶ *O deliver me from the deceitful and unjust man.* Marg., as in Heb., *from a man of deceit and iniquity.* This would apply well to the case and character of Absalom, or perhaps more directly and properly to the character and counsel of Ahithophel, among the leading conspirators in the rebellion of Absalom, to whose counsels much of the rebellion was owing: 2 Sam. xv. 31; comp. xvi. 23; xvii. 14, 23.

2. *For thou* art *the God of my strength.* See Notes on Ps. xviii. 2; xxviii. 7. ¶ *Why dost thou cast me off?* As if I were none of thine; as if I were wholly abandoned. Comp. Notes on Ps. xxii. 1. The word rendered *cast off*—זָנַח, *zanahh*—is a word which implies strong disgust or loathing:—"Why dost thou cast me off as a loathsome or disgusting object?" Comp. Rev. iii. 16. The Hebrew word means properly to be

strength: why dost thou cast me off? why go I mourning because of the oppression of the enemy?
3 O send out thy light and thy truth: let them lead me; let them bring me unto thy holy hill, and to thy tabernacles.
4 Then will I go unto the altar of God, unto God [1] my exceeding

[1] *the gladness of my joy.*

foul, to be rancid, to stink: then, to be loathsome or abominable; and then, to treat or regard anything as such. Comp. Hosea viii. 3, 5; Isa. xix. 6. ¶ *Why go I mourning*, etc. See Notes on Ps. xlii. 9. This expression, with others of a similar character, renders it morally certain that this psalm was composed by the same person, and with reference to the same circumstances, as the former.

3. *O send out thy light and thy truth.* Send them forth as from thy presence; or, let them be made manifest. The word *light* here is equivalent to favour or mercy, as when one prays for the "*light* of God's countenance" (see Notes on Ps. iv. 6); and the idea is, that now, in the time of darkness and trouble, when the light of God's countenance seemed to be withdrawn or hidden, he prays that God would impart light; that he would restore his favour; that he would conduct him back again to his former privileges. The word *truth* here is equivalent to *truthfulness* or *faithfulness;* and the prayer is, that God would manifest his faithfulness to him as one of his own people, by restoring him to the privileges and blessings from which he had been unjustly driven. Comp. Notes on Ps. xxv. 5. ¶ *Let them lead me.* That is, Let them lead me back to my accustomed privileges; let me go under their guidance to the enjoyment of the blessings connected with the place of public worship. ¶ *Let them bring me unto thy holy hill.* Mount Zion; the place where the worship of God was then celebrated, and hence called the "holy hill" of God. ¶ *And to thy tabernacles.* The *tabernacle* was the sacred tent erected for the worship of God (see Notes on Ps. xv. 1), and was regarded as the place where Jehovah had his abode. The tabernacle was divided, as the temple was afterwards, into two parts or rooms, the holy and the most holy place (see Notes on Heb. ix. 1–5); and hence the *plural* term, *tabernacles,* might be employed in speaking of it. The language here implies, as in Ps. xlii., that the author of the psalm was now exiled or banished from this, and hence also it may be inferred that the two psalms were composed by the same author, and with reference to the same occasion. If the reference here, moreover, is to Mount Zion as the "holy hill," it may be observed that this would fix the composition of the psalm to the time of David, as *before* his time that was not the place of the worship of God, but was made "holy" by his removing the ark there. *After* his time the place of worship was removed to Mount Moriah, where the temple was built. It cannot be *demonstrated,* however, with absolute certainty that the reference here is to Mount Zion, though that seems in every way probable. Comp. Notes on Ps. ii. 6; iii. 4; comp. 2 Sam. v. 7–9; vi. 17.

4. *Then will I go unto the altar of God.* The altar on Mount Zion, where sacrifices were offered: 2 Sam. vi. 17. The meaning is, that he would again unite with others in the public and customary worship of God. Comp. Notes on Ps. xlii. 4. ¶ *Unto God.* Into the immediate presence of God; the place where he was worshipped. ¶ *My exceeding joy.* Marg., *the gladness of my joy.* The LXX. render this, "who makes my youth joyous:" or, "the joy of my youth," (*Thompson.*) The Hebrew is, *the gladness of my joy;* meaning, that God was the source of his joy, so that he found all his happiness in Him. ¶ *Yea, upon the harp will I praise thee.* Comp. Notes on Ps. xxxiii. 2, 3. Instru-

joy: yea, upon the harp will I praise thee, O God, my God.

5 Why [f]art thou cast down, O my soul? and why art thou disquieted within me? Hope in God; for I shall yet praise him, *who is* the health of my countenance, and my God.

f Ps. xlii. 5, 11.

ments of music were commonly used in the worship of God, and David is represented as excelling in the music of the harp. Comp. 1 Sam. xvi. 16–23. ¶ *O God, my God.* It was not merely God as such that he desired to worship, or to whom he now appealed, but God *as his God*, the God to whom he had devoted himself, and whom he regarded as his God even in affliction and trouble. Comp. Notes on Ps. xxii. 1.

5. *Why art thou cast down?* etc. See Notes on Ps. xlii. 5, 11. The sameness of this verse with vers. 5 and 11 of Ps. xlii. proves, as has been already remarked, that this psalm was composed by the same writer, and with reference to the same subject as the former. The doctrine which is taught is the same—that we should not be dejected or cast down in the troubles of life, but should hope in God, and look forward to better times, if not in this world, certainly in the world to come. If we are his children, we *shall* "yet praise him;" we shall acknowledge him as the "health" or the *salvation* (Heb.) of our countenance; as one who by giving "salvation" diffuses joy over our countenance; as one who will manifest himself as our God. He who has an eternity of blessedness before him,—he who is to dwell for ever in a world of peace and joy,—he who is soon to enter an abode where there will be no sin, no sadness, no tears, no death,—he who is to commence a career of glory which is never to terminate and never to change,—should *not* be cast down,—should *not* be overwhelmed with sorrow.

PSALM XLIV.

The *title* of this psalm, "To the chief Musician for the sons of Korah, Maschil," is the same as the title prefixed to Ps. xlii., except with a slight transposition. See Notes on the title to Ps. xlii. This does not, however, prove that the psalm was by the same author; or that it was composed on the same occasion; or that the design and the contents of the two resemble each other; but merely that they were alike submitted, for the same purpose, to those descendants of the family of Korah who were employed in regulating the music of the sanctuary. It may be true, indeed, that the psalm was composed *by* one of the descendants of Korah, or one who had the charge of the music, but that is not made certain by the title.

There is no way in which the authorship can be determined. It does not belong to the general division of the book of Psalms which is ascribed to David (Ps. i.–xli.); and though there can be no doubt that a large number of the psalms in the other portions of the book were composed by him, yet it is impossible now to ascertain which were his, except as his *name* is prefixed to a psalm; while the fact that his name is *not* so prefixed may be regarded as a proof that, in the belief of those who arranged the collection, it was not his composition. That he *may* have been the author of some of those which are ascribed to no particular writer is unquestionable, but there is nothing *in* this psalm which would indicate particularly that it was a psalm of David. We cannot hope, therefore, now to ascertain the name of the author.

The occasion on which the psalm was composed is also wholly unknown, and conjecture is useless. There are no circumstances mentioned in the psalm which will enable us to determine with certainty when it was composed. Many occasions, however, occurred in the history of the Jews to which the sentiments contained in it are applicable; but there is no one of those occasions to which the psalm is so *peculiarly and exclusively* applicable that it can be assigned to that with undoubted certainty. The consequence is, that different expositors have assigned the composition of it to very different occasions. Not a few have referred it to the time of Antiochus

Epiphanes, and to the persecutions which occurred under him. Calvin, Venema, Dathe, and Rosenmüller adopt this view. De Wette supposes that the reference is to the time before the Babylonian exile, either in the reign of Jehoiakim, when Nebuchadnezzar first invaded the land (2 Kings xxiv. 1), or in the reign of Jehoiachin, when the land was again invaded by him, 2 Kings xxiv. 10. Tholuck supposes that it refers either to the time of Jehoiachin (2 Chron. xxxvi. 9), or to the time of Zedekiah (2 Chron. xxxvi. 11), when the land was invaded by the Babylonians, and when the Captivity commenced. Prof. Alexander supposes that there is nothing in the psalm which makes it necessary to suppose that it refers to a later period than the time of David.

What is manifest in the psalm itself in regard to the occasion of its composition is, (1) that it was a season of defeat and disaster, when the armies of Israel were discomfited, vers. 9, 10; (2) that their armies and people were scattered among the heathen, and that the people were "sold" among them, vers. 11, 12; (3) that they were made a reproach and a by-word among surrounding nations, vers. 13, 14; (4) that this discomfiture and disgrace had befallen them in some place which might be called "the place of dragons," ver. 19; and (5) that this had occurred at some time when the author of the psalm, speaking in the name of the people, could say that it was not on account of prevailing idolatry, or because, as a people, they had "stretched out their hands to a strange god," vers. 17, 18, 20.

Perhaps it will be found, on an examination of the psalm, that all the circumstances accord better with the time of Josiah, and especially the close of his reign (2 Kings xxiii. 26-30; 2 Chron. xxxv. 20-27), and the commencement of the reign following (2 Kings xxiii. 31-37; xxiv. 1), than with any other period of the history of the Hebrew people. This was the beginning of the calamities that came upon the nation in the period immediately preceding the Babylonish captivity; it was a time when the nation was free, as far as the efforts of a pious king could accomplish it, from prevailing idolatry; and yet it was a time when that series of disasters commenced which resulted in the entire removal of the nation to Babylon. There is not the slightest internal evidence that the psalm has reference to the times of the Maccabees; there were no historical facts in the time of David to which it can be easily applied; but all the circumstances in the psalm would find a fulfilment in the events which just preceded the Babylonish captivity, and in the series of national disasters which commenced with the defeat and death of Josiah.

The psalm is an earnest appeal to God to interpose amid the calamities of the nation, and to arise for their defence and deliverance. It consists of the following parts:—

I. An allusion to former national blessings in the tradition which had come down from ancient times respecting the Divine interposition in behalf of the nation when it was in danger, and when God delivered it from its foes, vers. 1-8. This reference to the past is evidently designed to be an argument or a reason for expecting and imploring the Divine interposition in the present period of national darkness and calamity. The fact that God *had* interposed in similar circumstances was an argument which might be urged why he should do so again.

II. The condition of the nation described, vers. 9-16. It was a time of national calamity. God had cast the nation off, and went forth no more with their hosts. Their armies were turned back and plundered; the people were sold into slavery, they were made a reproach and a by-word among the nations of the earth.

III. The statement that whatever might be the reason why all this had come upon them, it was not on account of national defection, or the prevalence of idolatry, or because they had forgotten God, vers. 17-22. The idea is that there was a prevailing desire in the nation to serve God, and that this was to be regarded as a calamity coming upon the people of God *as such;* their sufferings were endured in the cause of true religion, or because they *were* the people of God. This furnishes a ground of appeal that God would interpose in their behalf; or that he would vindicate them and his own cause.

IV. An earnest appeal to God to aid and save them, vers. 23-26.

PSALM XLIV.

To the chief Musician for the sons of Korah. Maschil.

WE have heard with our ears, O God, our fathers have told us, *what* work thou didst in their days, in the times of old.

2 *How* thou didst drive out the heathen with thy hand, and plantedst them; *how* thou didst afflict the people, and cast them out.

---

1. *We have heard with our ears.* That is, it has been handed down by tradition. ¶ *Our fathers have told us.* Our ancestors. They have delivered it down from generation to generation. The word rendered *"told"* means properly to grave, or to insculp on a stone; and thence, to write. Then it comes to mean to number, to count, to recount, to tell, to declare. The *word* would be applicable to any method of making the thing known, either by hieroglyphic figures in sculpture, by writing, or by oral tradition, though it seems probable that the latter mode is particularly referred to here. Comp. Ex. x. 2; xii. 26, 27. ¶ What *work thou didst in their days.* The great work which thou didst accomplish for them; or, how thou didst interpose in their behalf. The reference is to what God accomplished for them in delivering them from Egyptian bondage, and bringing them into the land of Canaan. ¶ *In the times of old.* In ancient times; in the beginning of our history. The idea here is, that we may properly appeal to the past—to what God has done in former ages—as an argument for his interposition in similar circumstances now; for, (*a*) His former interposition showed his *power* to save; (*b*) it was such an illustration of his *character* that we may appeal to that as a reason for asking him to interpose again.

2. How *thou didst drive out the heathen with thy hand.* The word rendered *heathen* means simply *nations* without necessarily conveying the idea of *heathenism*, as that word is now understood. It means the *nations*, to wit, of the land of Canaan, or the Canaanites; and as these nations were *in fact* idolaters, or strangers to the true religion, the word came in time to have that idea attached to it. It is in that sense that we use the term now, though the word *nations* would accurately express the meaning of the original. The word rendered *drive out*—יָרַשׁ, *yarash*—means properly to take, seize, or take possession of; and then, in the form here used (*Hiphil*), it means to cause to possess; to give possession of; and then, to *take* possession of, to drive out of a possession, to *dispossess*, to *disinherit*. The meaning here is, he dispossessed them of their country; he disinherited them. This, the psalmist says, God had done "by his hand;" that is, it was by his own power. ¶ *And plantedst them.* That is, planted *his people*—the children of Israel. He put them in the place of those whom he had disinherited or dispossessed. The word is properly applicable to a tree, but it is also used with reference to a nation, and means that he assigned them a fixed and permanent residence. Thus we say in English, "to plant a colony." Comp. Amos ix. 15; Jer. xxiv. 6; xxxii. 41; Ps. lxxx. 8; 2 Sam. vii. 10. ¶ How *thou didst afflict the people.* That is, the people of the land of Canaan; the nations that dwelt there. The word means to bring evil or calamity upon any one. ¶ *And cast them out.* The word here used may be taken in the sense of sending out or expelling, as in Gen. iii. 23; 1 Kings ix. 7,—and then it would be applicable to the *Canaanites*, as meaning that God had expelled or *driven them out*—as it is understood by our translators; or it may be used to denote the sending out of shoots or branches by a tree or vine, as in Ps. lxxx. 11; Jer. xvii. 8; Ezek. xvii. 6, 7,—and then it would refer here to the *Israelites*, and would mean that God *caused them to in-*

3 For [g] they got not the land in possession by their own sword, neither did their own arm save them; but thy right hand, and thine arm, and the light of thy countenance, because [h] thou hadst a favour unto them.

4 Thou art my King, O God: command deliverances for Jacob.

5 Through thee will we push down our enemies; through thy

g Jos. xxiv. 12. h Deut. iv. 37.

---

crease; multiplied them; spread them over the land, as a vine spreads, Ps. lxxx. 8–11. The parallelism here clearly demands the latter interpretation. So it is understood by Luther, De Wette, Tholuck, and Prof. Alexander.

3. *For they got not the land in possession.* The land of Canaan. The design of this verse is to illustrate the sentiment in the previous verse, that they owed their establishment in the promised land wholly to God. The fact that *He* had interposed in their behalf; that *He* had shown that he was able to discomfit their enemies, is appealed to as a reason why he should now interpose in a time of national danger and calamity. He who had driven out the nations in the days of their fathers; he who had established his people peaceably in the land from which the former inhabitants had been expelled, was able to interpose now and save them. The prominent thought in all this is, that it was *God* who had accomplished all that had been done. That same God was able to save them again. ¶ *By their own sword.* That is, it was not owing to their valour, but to the Divine power: Deut. viii. 10–18; ix. 3–6; Josh. xxiv. 12. ¶ *Neither did their own arm save them.* Not their own strength or prowess. ¶ *But thy right hand.* The right hand is mentioned because it is that which is employed in wielding the sword or the spear in battle. ¶ *And the light of thy countenance.* Thy favour. It was because thou didst lift upon them the light of thy countenance, or because thou didst favour them. See Notes on Ps. iv. 6. ¶ *Because thou hadst a favour unto them.* Thou didst desire to show them favour; thou hadst pleasure in them. The idea in the Hebrew word is that of delighting in anything, or having pleasure in it.

4. *Thou art my King, O God.* Literally, "Thou art He, my King, O God;" that is, Thou art the same:—the same King, and the same God, who didst interpose in the time of the fathers, and thou art he whom *I* recognise as King, as the Sovereign Ruler of thy people. The psalmist here uses the singular number, "*my* King," as expressive of his own feelings, though he doubtless means also to speak in the name of the people. It would seem not improbable from this, that the author of the psalm was the reigning monarch in the time of the troubles referred to. If not, it was evidently one who personated him, and who meant to represent his feelings. The language shows the strong confidence of the author of the psalm in God, and perhaps also is designed to express his personal responsibility at the time, and his consciousness that his only refuge in conducting the troubled affairs of the nation was God. ¶ *Command deliverances for Jacob.* As if all was under His command, and He had only to give direction, and salvation would come. The word *Jacob* here is used to denote the descendants of Jacob, or the people of God. See Notes on Ps. xxiv. 6.

5. *Through thee.* By thy help. ¶ *Will we push down our enemies.* The word here rendered *push down* means literally to strike or push with the horns, spoken of horned animals, Ex. xxi. 28, 31, 32. Then it is applied to a conqueror prostrating nations before him: Deut. xxxiii. 17; 1 Kings xxii. 11. ¶ *Through thy name.* That is, acting under thine authority and by thy help. If he gave the commandment (ver. 4), it would be certain that they would be

name will we tread them under
that rise up against us.
6 For [i] I will not trust in my
bow, neither shall my sword save
me.
7 But thou hast saved us from
our enemies, and hast put them
to [k] shame that hated us.
8 In God we boast all the day
long, and praise thy name for
ever. Selah.
9 But thou hast cast [l] off, and

i Hos. i. 7. *k* Ps. cxxxii. 18. *l* Ps. lxxiv. 1; Lam. iii. 31, 32.

able to overcome their adversaries. ¶ *Will we tread them under.* Will we conquer or subdue them. The language is taken from the custom of treading on a prostrate foe. See Notes on Ps. vii. 5; xviii. 40; comp. Notes on Job xl. 12; Isa. x. 6; lxiii. 3; Dan. vii. 23. ¶ *That rise up against us.* Our enemies that have mustered their strength for war. The language would *properly* denote those who had rebelled against a government; but it seems here to be used in a more general sense, as referring to those who had waged war against them. See Ps. xviii. 39.

6. *For I will not trust in my bow.* The author of the psalm himself again speaks as expressing his own feelings, and stating the grounds of his confidence and hope. Comp. ver. 4. At the same time he doubtless expresses the feelings of the people, and speaks in their name. He had said (ver. 3) that the ancestors of the Jewish people had not obtained possession of the promised land by any strength or skill of their own, and he now says that he, and those who were connected with him, did not depend on their own strength, or on the weapons of war which they might employ, but that their only ground of trust was God.

7. *But thou hast saved us from our enemies.* That is, Thou hast done it in times past. Thou hast interposed in behalf of our nation in periods of danger and trial, and hast delivered us. This is stated as a reason for what is said by the psalmist in ver. 6,—that he would not trust in his sword and in his bow,—and for the earnest appeal which he now makes to God. He and his people did not rely on their own strength and prowess, but on that God who had often interposed to save the nation. ¶ *And hast put them to shame that hated us.* In former times. That is, he had caused them to be discomfited. He had turned them back. He had covered them with confusion. On the meaning of the words *shame* and *ashamed*, see Notes on Job vi. 20; Ps. xxxiv. 5.

8. *In God we boast all the day long.* That is, continually or constantly. It is not a momentary or temporary expression of our feelings, but it is our habitual and constant employment. We have no other ground of reliance, and we express that reliance constantly. The word rendered *boast* here rather more literally means *praise:* "In God we *praise* all the day long." The *idea* is, that he was their only ground of confidence. They ascribed all their former successes to him; they had no other reliance now. ¶ *And praise thy name for ever.* We do it now; we shall never cease to do it. ¶ *Selah.* On the meaning of this word, see Notes on Ps. iii. 2.

9. *But thou hast cast off.* The author of the psalm now commences a description of the existing circumstances of the nation, so strongly in contrast with what had existed in former times when God interposed in their behalf, and when he gave them success. This is properly the commencement of the second part of the psalm, and the description is continued to ver. 16. The Hebrew word here rendered "hast cast off" implies disgust and abhorrence, as the casting away of that which is loathsome. See the word explained in the Notes on Ps. xliii. 2. The reference is to what had occurred at the time when the psalm was written. See introduction to this psalm. The allu-

put us to shame; and goest not forth with our armies.

10 Thou makest us to turn back [m] from the enemy; and they which hate us spoil for themselves.

11 Thou hast given us [1] like sheep *appointed* for meat; and hast scattered us among the heathen.

12 Thou sellest [n] thy people

m Lev. xxvi. 17; Deut. xxviii. 25, 64.

1 *as sheep of meat.* *n* Deut. xxxii. 30.

sion is to the invasion of the land by foreigners; their own discomfiture in their wars; and the calamities consequent on these invasions and defeats. ¶ *And put us to shame.* By defeat and disgrace. See the word explained above, ver. 7. For the defeat and discomfiture supposed to be referred to, see 2 Chron. xxxv. 20–27; xxxvi. 5, 6. ¶ *And goest not forth with our armies.* See the places referred to above. Thus Josiah was defeated and slain; and thus the land was conquered by the invaders.

10. *Thou makest us to turn back from the enemy.* Instead of giving us the victory. That is, we are defeated. ¶ *And they which hate us spoil for themselves.* They plunder us; they take our property as spoil, and carry it away. That this was *done* at the time referred to in the introduction as the time of the composition of the psalm, is apparent from the narrative in the Book of Chronicles. 2 Chron. xxxvi. 7, "Nebuchadnezzar also carried of the vessels of the house of the Lord to Babylon, and put them in his temple at Babylon." Comp. 2 Kings xxiii. 33; xxiv. 13–16; xxv. 13–17.

11. *Thou hast given us like sheep* appointed *for meat.* Marg., as in Heb., *as sheep of meat.* That is, as sheep are killed for food, so thou hast allowed us to be put to death. ¶ *And hast scattered us among the heathen.* Among the surrounding nations. See Notes on ver. 2. That is, they had been discomfited in war; many had fled into surrounding countries; many had been carried away captive. All this undoubtedly occurred at the time at which I have supposed that the psalm was written—the time immediately preceding the Babylonish captivity.

12. *Thou sellest thy people for nought.* Marg., *without riches.* Without gain, or advantage; that is, for no price that would be an equivalent. The people were given up to their enemies, but there was nothing in return that would be of equal value. The loss was in no way made up. They were taken away from their country and their homes. They were withdrawn from useful labour in the land; there was a great diminution of the national strength and of the national wealth; but there was no *return* to the land, no advantage, no valuable result, that would be an *equivalent* for thus withdrawing them from their country and their homes. It was as though they had been *given away.* A case *may* be supposed where the exile of a part of a people might be an advantage to a land, or where there would be a full equivalent for the loss sustained, as when soldiers go forth to defend their country, and to repel a foe, rendering a higher service than they could by remaining at home; or as when colonists go forth and settle in a new region, producing valuable returns in commerce; or as when missionaries go forth among the heathen, often producing, by a reflex influence, effects on the piety and prosperity of the churches at home, more important, and more widely diffused, than would have been produced by their remaining to labour in their own country. But no such valuable results occurred here. The idea is that they were *lost* to their homes; to their country; to the cause of religion. It is not *necessary* to suppose that the psalmist here means to say that the people had been literally *sold* into slavery, although it is not in itself improbable that this had occurred. All that the words necessarily imply would be that the effect was *as if* they were sold into bondage. In Deut. xxxii. 30; Judges ii. 14; iii. 8; iv. 2,

[1] for nought, and dost not increase *thy wealth* by their price.

13 Thou makest us a reproach [o] to our neighbours, a scorn and a derision to them that are round about us.

14 Thou makest us a byword among the heathen, a shaking of the head among the people.

15 My confusion *is* continually before me, and the shame of my face hath covered me,

[1] *without riches.* [o] Jer. xxiv. 9.

9; x. 7, the word here used is employed to express the fact that God delivered his people into the hand of their enemies. Any *removal* into the territories of the heathen would be a fact corresponding with all that is conveyed by the language used. There can be little doubt, however, that (at the time referred to) those who were made captives in war were *literally* sold as slaves. This was a common custom. Comp. Notes on Isa. lii. 3. ¶ *And dost not increase* thy wealth *by their price.* The words "thy wealth" are supplied by the translators; but the idea of the psalmist is undoubtedly expressed with accuracy. The meaning is, that no good result to the cause of religion, no corresponding returns had been the consequence of thus giving up the people into the hand of their enemies. This *may*, however, be rendered, as De Wette translates it, "thou hast not enhanced their price;" that is, God had not set a high price on them, but had sold them for too little, or had given them away for nothing. But the former idea seems better to suit the connexion, and to convey more exactly the meaning of the original. So it is rendered in the Chaldee, and by Luther.

13. *Thou makest us a reproach to our neighbours.* Comp. Notes on Ps. xxxix. 8. The word *neighbours* here refers to surrounding people or nations. They were reproached, scorned, and derided as forsaken by God, and given up to their foes. They no longer commanded the admiration of mankind as a prosperous, favoured, happy people. Surrounding nations treated them with contempt as inspiring no fear, and as having nothing to entitle them to respect.

14. *Thou makest us a byword among the heathen.* The word rendered byword — מָשָׁל, *mashal*—means properly a similitude or parable; then, a sententious saying, and apophthegm; then, a proverb; then, a song or verse, particularly a satirical song, or a song of derision. The idea here is, that they were made a *proverb*, or were referred to as a striking instance of the Divine abandonment, or as something marked to which the nations might and did refer as an *example* of calamity, judgment, misfortune, failure; a warning to all. See Deut. xxviii. 37. ¶ *A shaking of the head among the people.* An *occasion* for the shaking of the head, in derision and scorn. Comp. Notes on Ps. xxii. 7.

15. *My confusion* is *continually before me.* My shame; the conviction and the evidence of my disgrace is constantly present with me. Literally, "all the day my shame is before me." That is, the evidences of disgrace, defeat, and disaster, rendering him a reproach to the nations, were everywhere around him, and he could not conceal them from himself. The psalmist here is represented as the head of the people, and expresses the sense of disgrace which the sovereign of a people would feel in a time of national calamity; identifying himself with the people, he speaks of the national disgrace as his own. ¶ *And the shame of my face.* The shame that is manifested on the countenance when we blush. ¶ *Hath covered me.* That is, I am suffused with the evidence of my shame; or, as we sometimes say, "he blushed *all over.*" The blush, however—that peculiar rush of blood manifesting itself through the skin—which constitutes the evidence of shame, is confined to the face and the neck;—an arrange-

16 For the voice of him that reproacheth and blasphemeth; by reason of the enemy [p] and avenger.

17 All [q] this is come upon us; yet have we not forgotten thee, neither have we dealt falsely in thy covenant.

p Ps. viii. 2.

q Dan. ix. 13.

ment which none can explain, except on the supposition that there is a God; that he is a moral governor; and that, as it was designed that the body should be covered or clothed, he *meant* that the evidence of guilt should manifest itself on the parts of the person which are most exposed to view, or where others could *see* it. The idea here is, that he could not conceal the proofs of his shame and disgrace; he was compelled to exhibit them to all around.

16. *For the voice of him*, etc. That is, Because I hear the voice of him that reproaches and blasphemes. The word rendered *blasphemeth*, means properly to use cutting words; then, to reproach or revile. It may be applied either to men or to God. In the former case, it means reproach or reviling; in the latter, blasphemy in the usual sense of that term, denoting reproachful words concerning God. The word *may* be used here in both these senses, as it is evident that not only were the *people* the subject of reproach, but that *God* was also. ¶ *By reason of the enemy.* That is, the foreign enemies, or those who had invaded the land. ¶ *And avenger.* Of him who had come to take vengeance. Here the word refers to the foreign enemies of the nation, and to the spirit by which they were actuated; their purposes to avenge themselves of what they regarded as wrongs, or take vengeance on a nation which they had long hated. Comp. Notes on Ps. viii. 2.

17. *All this is come upon us.* All these calamities. The connecting thought here is, that *although* all these things had come upon them, yet they could not be traced to their own infidelity or unfaithfulness to God. There was nothing in the national character, there were no circumstances at that time existing, there was no peculiar unfaithfulness among the people, there was no such general forgetfulness of God, and no such general prevalence of idolatry as would account for what had occurred, or as would explain it. The nation was not then more deeply depraved than it had been at other times; but, on the contrary, there was among the people a prevalent regard for God and for his service. It was, therefore, a mystery to the author of the psalm, that these calamities had been suffered to come upon them at that time; it was an event the cause of which he desired to search out, ver. 21. ¶ *Yet have we not forgotten thee.* As a nation. That is, there was nothing peculiar in the circumstances of the nation at that time which would call down the Divine displeasure. We cannot suppose that the psalmist means to claim for the nation entire perfection, but only to affirm that the nation at that time was not characterised by any *peculiar* forgetfulness of God, or prevalence of wickedness. All that is here said was true at the time when, as I have supposed, the psalm was written—the closing part of the reign of Josiah, or the period immediately following. ¶ *Neither have we dealt falsely in thy covenant.* We have not been unfaithful to thy covenant; to the covenant which thou didst make with our fathers; to the commandments which thou hast given us. This can only mean that there was no such *prevailing* departure from the principles of that covenant as could account for this. The psalmist could not connect the existing state of things—the awful and peculiar discomfitures and calamities which had come upon the nation—with anything peculiar in the character of the people, or in the religious condition of the nation.

18 Our heart is not turned
back, [r] neither have our [1] steps
declined from thy way;
19 Though thou hast sore
broken us in the place of
dragons,[s] and covered us with
the shadow[t] of death.
20 If we have forgotten the
name of our God, or [u] stretched
out our hands to a strange god;

r Job xxiii. 11, 12; Ps. cxix. 157.
1 Or, *goings*.

s Isa. xxxv. 7. t Ps. xxiii. 4.
u Job xxxi. 26—28.

18. *Our heart is not turned back.* That is, We have not turned away from thy service; we have not apostatized from thee; we have not fallen into idolatry. This must mean that such was not at that time the *characteristic* of the nation; it was not a *prominent* thing among the people; there was no such general and pervading iniquity as to explain the fact that these calamities had come upon them, or to be properly the *cause* of these troubles. ¶ *Neither have our steps declined from thy way.* Marg., *goings.* The idea as expressed by our translators is, that the people had not departed from the path prescribed by God; that is, from what he required in his law. The LXX. and the Vulgate render it, "Thou hast turned our steps from thy way;" that is, though our heart is not turned back, and we have not revolted from thee, yet thou hast turned our steps from thy way, or hast turned us from the way of thy favour and from prosperity. The rendering in the common version, however, is more in conformity with the idea in the original.

19. *Though thou hast sore broken us in the place of dragons.* Or rather, "That thou hast crushed us in the place of dragons." The connexion is continued from the previous verse: "Our heart is not so turned back, nor have our steps so declined from thy path, that thou shouldst crush us in the place of dragons." That is, we have been guilty of no such apostasy and infidelity as to account for the fact that thou hast dealt with us in this manner, or make it necessary and proper that we should thus be crushed and overthrown. The word rendered *dragons*—תַּנִּם, *tannim*—means either a great fish; a sea monster; a serpent; a dragon; or a crocodile. See Notes on Isa. xiii. 22. It may also mean a jackal, a fox, or a wolf. De Wette renders it here *jackals.* The *idea* in the passage is essentially the same, whichever interpretation of the word is adopted. The "*place* of dragons" would denote the place where such monsters are found, or where they had their abode;—that is to say, in desolate places; wastes; deserts; old ruins; depopulated towns. See Notes, as above, on Isa. xiii. 19-22; comp. Jer. ix. 11. The meaning here would be, therefore, that they had been vanquished; that their cities and towns had been reduced to ruins; that their land had been laid waste; that the place where they had been "sore broken" was in fact a fit abode for wild beasts and monsters. ¶ *And covered us with the shadow of death.* Our land has been covered with a dark and dismal shade, as if *Death* had cast his image or shadow over it. See Notes on Job iii. 5 and Ps. xxiii. 4. There could be no more striking illustration of calamity and ruin.

20. *If we have forgotten the name of our God.* That is, if we have apostatized from him. ¶ *Or stretched out our hands to a strange god.* Or have been guilty of idolatry. The act of stretching out the hands, or spreading forth the hands, was significant of worship or prayer: 1 Kings viii. 22; 2 Chron. vi. 12, 13; see Notes on Isa. i. 15. The *idea* here is, that this was *not* the cause or reason of their calamities; that if this had occurred, it *would have been* a sufficient reason for what had taken place; but that no such cause actually existed, and therefore the reason must

21 Shall not God search this out? for he knoweth the secrets of the heart.

22 Yea, [v] for thy sake are we killed all the day long; we are counted as sheep for the slaughter.

23 Awake, why sleepest thou,

v Rom. viii. 36.

be found in something else. It was the fact of such calamities having come upon the nation when no such cause existed, that perplexed the author of the psalm, and led to the conclusion in his own mind (ver. 22) that these calamities were produced by the malignant designs of the enemies of the true religion, and that, instead of their suffering for their national sins, they were really *martyrs* in the cause of God, and were suffering for his sake.

21. *Shall not God search this out?* That is, If this had been the case, it would be known to God. If, as a nation, we had been given to idolatry, or if our hearts had been secretly alienated from the true God, though there had been no open manifestation of apostasy, yet that could not have been concealed from him. The question here asked implies a solemn declaration on the part of the psalmist that this was not so; or that there was no such national apostasy from God, and no such prevalence of idolatry in the land as to account for what had occurred. The reason for the calamities which had come upon them, therefore, must be found in something else. ¶ *For he knoweth the secrets of the heart.* What is in the heart: what is concealed from the world. If there were any such alienation from him in the hearts of the people, he would know it. The fact that God knows the heart, or that he understands all the secret thoughts, purposes, and motives of men, is one that is everywhere affirmed in the Scriptures. See 1 Chron. xxviii. 9; Rom. viii. 27; comp. Notes on Rev. ii. 23.

22. *Yea, for thy sake are we killed all the day long.* That is, we are *continually* or *constantly* subjected to these calamities. It is not a single defeat, but it is a continued slaughter. This verse contains, in the apprehension of the psalmist, the true cause of the calamities which had come upon the nation. The emphasis in the passage lies in the phrase "*for thy sake.*" The meaning is, It is on thy account; it is in thy cause; it is because we are thy friends, and because we worship thee. It is not on account of our national sins; it is not because there is any prevalent idolatry, but it is *because* we are the worshippers of the true God, and we are, therefore, *martyrs.* All these calamities have come upon us in consequence of our attachment to thee. There is no evidence that there was any self-glorying in this, or any intention to blame God as if he were unjust or severe, but it is the feeling of martyrs as suffering in the cause of religion. This passage is applied by the apostle Paul to Christians in his time, as fitly describing their sufferings, and the cause of the calamities which came upon them. See Notes on Rom. viii. 36. ¶ *We are counted as sheep for the slaughter.* We are *reckoned* like sheep designed for the slaughter. That is, It is not because we are *guilty*, but we are regarded and treated *as innocent sheep* who are driven to be slaughtered. See Notes on Rom. viii. 36. Their attachment to the true religion,—their devotion to Jehovah as the true God,—was the secret cause of all the calamities which had come upon them. As a nation they were his friends, and as such they were opposed by the worshippers of other gods.

23. *Awake, why sleepest thou?* This is a solemn and earnest appeal to God to interpose in their behalf, *as if* he were "asleep," or were regardless of their sufferings. Comp.

O Lord? arise, cast [w] *us* not off for ever.

24 Wherefore hidest thou thy face, *and* forgettest our affliction and our oppression?

25 For our soul is bowed down to the dust; our belly cleaveth unto the earth.

26 Arise [1] for our help, and redeem us for thy mercies' sake.

w ver. 9.

1 *a help for us.*

Notes on Ps. iii. 7; vii. 6; xxxv. 23. ¶ *Arise, cast* us *not off for ever.* Do not forsake us always. Comp. ver. 9. He had *seemed* to have cast them off; to have forgotten them; to have forsaken them utterly, and the psalmist, in the name of the people, calls on him not entirely to abandon them.

24. *Wherefore hidest thou thy face?* See Notes on Ps. xiii. 1. Why dost thou turn away from us, and refuse to aid us, and leave us to these unpitied sufferings? ¶ And *forgettest our affliction and our oppression.* Our trials, and the wrongs that are committed against us. These are earnest appeals. They are the pleadings of the oppressed and the wronged. The language is such as man would use in addressing his fellow-men; and, when applied to God, it must be understood *as* such language. As used in the Psalms it denotes earnestness, but not irreverence; it is solemn petition, not dictation; it is affectionate pleading, not complaint. It indicates depth of suffering and distress, and is the strongest language which could be employed to denote entire helplessness and dependence. At the same time, it is language which implies that the cause for which they suffered was the cause of God, and that they might *properly* call on him to interfere in behalf of his own friends.

25. *For our soul is bowed down to the dust.* That is, We are overborne with calamity, so that we sink to the earth. The expression is one that denotes great affliction. ¶ *Our belly cleaveth unto the earth.* We are like animals that are prone upon the earth, and that cannot rise. The allusion may be to reptiles that cannot stand erect. The figure is intended to denote great prostration and affliction.

26. *Arise for our help.* Marg., as in Heb., *a help for us.* That is, Deliver us from our present calamities and troubles. ¶ *And redeem us.* Save us; deliver us. See Notes on Ps. xxv. 22; xxxi. 5; Isa. i. 27; lii. 3. ¶ *For thy mercies' sake.* On account of thy mercies. That is, in order that thy mercy may be manifested; or that thy character, as a God of mercy, may be made known. It was not primarily or mainly on their own account that the psalmist urges this prayer; it was that the character of God might be made known, or that it might be seen that he was a merciful Being. The proper manifestation of the Divine character, as showing what God *is*, is in itself of more importance than our personal salvation,—for the welfare of the universe depends on *that;* and the highest ground of appeal and of hope which we can have, as sinners, when we come before him, is that he would glorify himself in his mercy. To that we may appeal, and on that we may rely. When that is urged as an argument for our salvation, and when that is the sole ground of our confidence, we may be assured that he is ready to hear and to save us. In the New Testament he has told us *how* that mercy has been manifested, and *how* it may be made available to us,—to wit, through the Lord Jesus, the great Mediator; and hence we are directed to come in his name, and to make mention of what he has done and suffered in order that the Divine mercy may be *consistently* manifested to men. From the beginning of the world,—from the time when man apostatized from God,—through all dispensations, and in all ages and lands, the only hope of men

for salvation has been the fact that God *is* a merciful Being; the true ground of successful appeal to him has been, is, and ever will be, that his own name might be glorified and honoured in the salvation of lost and ruined sinners—in the displays of his MERCY.

PSALM XLV.

This psalm is entitled "To the chief Musician upon Shoshannim, for the sons of Korah, Maschil. A song of love." On the phrase "To the chief Musician," see Notes on the title to Ps. iv. The words "Upon Shoshannim" occur also, as a title, or part of a title, in Ps. lxix., lxxx.; and, in a different form, in the title to Ps. lx., "Shushan-eduth." The word *Shoshan*—שׁוֹשָׁן—occurs in 1 Kings vii. 22, 26; Cant. ii. 16; iv. 5; v. 13; vi. 2, 3; vii. 2; and, in a modified form—שׁוֹשַׁנָּה, *Shoshannah*—in 2 Chron. iv. 5; Cant. ii. 1, 2; Hos. xiv. 5; in all which it is rendered *lily*, or *lilies*. The word, therefore, probably means a lily; and then it came to denote, probably, a musical instrument that had a *resemblance* to a lily, or that was shaped like a lily. It is not known to what kind of musical instrument there is a reference, but it would seem probable that something like the trumpet or the cymbal was intended. The special reference here would seem to be to the chief musician who presided over *this part* of the musical instruments employed in public worship,—as it would seem not improbable that each of the different parts, as trumpets, horns, viols, harps, etc., would have a special leader. On the portion of the title, "for the sons of Korah,"—and on the word "*Maschil*,"—see Notes on the title to Ps. xlii. The portion of the title, "A Song of Loves," would properly denote a song devoted to love, or in celebration of love; that is, in which love would be the main idea. The phrase "a lovely song," or "a charming song," as Gesenius renders it here, would not, it seems to me, express the meaning of the original. An author would hardly prefix such a title to a psalm himself, as indicating that the psalm had special beauty, or was specially adapted to please; and if we suppose that the titles were prefixed by some other person than the author, or by common usage, it would be difficult to see why such a title should be prefixed to *this* psalm rather than to many others. It has, indeed, great beauty; but so have very many of the rest. If we suppose, however, that the title was prefixed as indicating the general subject of the psalm, or as indicating the feelings of the author towards the main persons referred to in it, the title is eminently appropriate. In this sense the title would be proper whether we regard the psalm as having reference to the Messiah, or as an epithalamium—a bridal or marriage hymn.

The author of the psalm is wholly unknown, and nothing can be determined on the subject, unless it be supposed that the portion of the title "for the sons of Korah," or "of the sons of Korah," conveys the idea that it was the composition of one of that family. On that point, see Notes on the title to Ps. xlii. That it *may* have been written by David no one can disprove, but there is no certain evidence that he was the author, and as his name is not mentioned, the presumption is that it is not his.

Very various opinions have been entertained in regard to the *reference* of the psalm, and the occasion on which it was composed. A very material question is, To whom does the psalm refer? And especially, Has it reference to the Messiah, and is it to be classed with the Messianic Psalms?

Nearly all the older Christian interpreters, without hesitation, suppose that it refers to the Messiah. This opinion has been held, also, by a large part of the modern interpreters of the Bible, among others by Michaelis, Lowth, Dathe, Rosenmüller (in his second edition), Hengstenberg, Tholuck, Professor Alexander. Many, however, have defended the opposite opinion, though they have not been agreed on the question *to whom* the psalm refers. Grotius, Dereser, and Kaiser suppose it to have been sung at the marriage of Solomon with a foreign princess, probably the daughter of the king of Egypt. Doederlein supposes the king whose praises are sung to be an Israelite. Augusti thinks that it was sung at the nuptials of a Persian king. This last opinion De Wette adopts.

On this question it may be remarked, (1.) There is no evidence that the psalm refers to David; and, indeed, from the psalm itself it is evident that it *could* not have such a reference. The term "O

God" (ver. 6) could not be applied to him, nor the expression "Thy throne is for ever and ever," *ibid.* In the life of David, moreover, there was no marriage with a foreign princess that would correspond with the statement here; and no occasion on which the "daughter of Tyre" was present with a gift, ver. 12.

(2.) It seems equally clear that the psalm does not refer to Solomon. In addition to the considerations already suggested as reasons why it does not refer to David, and which are as applicable in the main to Solomon as to him, it may be added that Solomon was never a warlike prince, and was never distinguished for conquests. But the "hero" of the psalm is a warrior—a prince who goes forth to conquest, and who would be distinguished for his victories over the enemies of the king, vers. 3-5.

(3.) For stronger reasons still the psalm cannot be supposed to refer to a Persian prince. Such a supposition is a mere conjecture, with not even the pretence that there are any historical facts that would justify such an application, and without even the suggestion as to a particular case to which it could be applicable. It is, moreover, wholly improbable that a nuptial ode designed to celebrate the marriage of a Persian king—a foreigner—would have been introduced into a book of sacred poetry among the Hebrews.

(4.) The remaining opinion, therefore, is, that the psalm had original and exclusive reference to the Messiah. For this opinion the following reasons may be assigned:—(*a*) The authority of the New Testament. If the Bible is an inspired book, then one part of it may properly be regarded as an authoritative interpretation of another; or a statement in one part must be admitted to be proof of what is meant in another, since the entire book has one *Author* only—the Holy Spirit. But there can be no doubt that the author of the Epistle to the Hebrews meant to quote this psalm as having reference to the Messiah, or as containing an *intended* statement in regard to him which might be appealed to as *proof* that he was divine. Thus, in ch. i. 8, 9, he quotes vers. 6, 7, of the psalm, "Thy throne, O God, is for ever and ever," etc., *in proof* that the Son of God is superior to the angels. See Notes on the Epistle to the Hebrews, on the passage referred to, where this point is considered at length. There can be no doubt that the author of the Epistle to the Hebrews *meant* to quote the passage as having original reference to the Messiah; and his argument would have no force whatever on the supposition that the psalm had original reference to David, or to Solomon, or to a Persian prince.

(*b*) The testimony of tradition, or of early interpretation, is in favour of this supposition. Thus, the Chaldee Paraphrase (ver. 3) applies the psalm expressly to the Messiah: "Thy beauty, king Messiah—מַלְכָּא מְשִׁיחָא—is more excellent than the sons of men." This may not improperly be understood as representing the current opinion of the Hebrews at the time when the Chaldee interpretation was made, in regard to the design and reference of the psalm. The two eminent Jewish interpreters, Aben-Ezra and Kimchi, explain the psalm in the same manner, and may be supposed also to represent the prevailing mode of explaining it away among the Hebrews. On this point, also, the Epistle to the Hebrews may be referred to, as showing that such was the current explanation up to the time when that was written. I have referred to the fact that the author of that epistle quotes the psalm as an inspired man, and as thus furnishing the authority of inspiration in favour of this interpretation. I now refer to it as showing that this must have been the prevailing and well-understood opinion in regard to the design of the psalm. The author of the epistle was establishing by *argument*, not by *authority*, the claims of the Messiah to a rank above that of the angels. He made use of an argument which he evidently believed would have force among those who regarded the Old Testament as of Divine origin. But the argument which he used, and on which he relied, would have no weight with those for whom he wrote unless they admitted that the psalm *had* reference to the Messiah, and that this point might be assumed without further proof. The fact, therefore, that he thus quotes and applies the psalm demonstrates that such was its current and admitted interpretation in his time.

(*c*) The internal evidence may be referred to. This will be further illustrated in the Notes. At present it is necessary only to remark—(1.) That there are passages in this psalm which cannot be applied to any man—to any created being—and which can be applied only to one who may properly be called God, ver. 6.—(2.) The characteristics of the principal personage in the psalm are such as accurately describe the Messiah. These points will be illustrated in the Notes.

(*d*) The psalm, on the supposition that it refers to the Messiah, is in accordance with a prevailing mode of writing in the Old Testament. See Notes on Heb. i. 8; comp. Introd. to Isaiah, § 7; and Introd. to Ps. xl. It is to be remembered that the expectation of a Messiah was the peculiar hope of the Jewish people. He is really the "*hero*" of the Old Testament,—more so than Achilles is of the Iliad, or Æneas of the Æneid. The sacred poets were accustomed to employ their most magnificent imagery in describing him, that they might present him in every form that was beautiful in conception, and that would be gratifying to the pride and the hopes of the nation. Everything that is gorgeous and splendid in description is lavished upon him. And they were never under any apprehension of attributing to him too high a rank, too great perfection of moral character, or too wide an extent of dominion. They freely applied to him language which would be a magnificent description of an earthly monarch; and the terms which usually denote splendid conquests, or a wide and permanent reign, are freely given to him. Under this view, and in this style, this psalm was evidently composed; and although the *language* may have been taken from the magnificence of the court of David or Solomon, or even from the splendour of a Persian king, yet there can be no reason to doubt that the description is that of the Messiah, and not of David or Solomon, or any Persian prince. The writer in the psalm imagines to himself a magnificent and beautiful prince,—a prince riding prosperously to his conquests; swaying a permanent sceptre over a wide empire; clothed in rich and splendid vestments; eminently upright and pure; and scattering blessings on every hand. That prince was the Messiah. He describes the queen—the bride of such a prince—as attended by the daughters of kings; as clad in the gold of Ophir; as greatly beloved by the prince; as glorious in her appearance and character; as having on robes of wrought gold and raiment of needlework; as followed by a numerous retinue; and as brought to the king in his palace. That queen is the "bride of the Lamb"—the church. All this is in the magnificent style of the Orientals, but all accords with the custom of the sacred writers in speaking of the Messiah.

(*e*) It may be added that this is in harmony with the constant language of the sacred writers in the New Testament, who speak of the Messiah as the "husband" of the church, and of the church as his "bride." Comp. Notes on Eph. v. 23—32; 2 Cor. xi. 2; Rev. xxi. 2, 9; xxii. 17.

The proof, therefore, seems to me to be conclusive that the psalm had original and sole reference to the Messiah.

The contents of the psalm are as follows:—

I. A statement of the purpose or design of the psalm. It is to speak of the things which the psalmist had meditated on respecting the "king;" some one in his view to whom that title was applicable, and whose praises he intended particularly to set forth, ver. 1.

II. A description of the king, vers. 2-9.

- (*a*) He is the fairest among men: distinguished for grace and beauty, ver. 2.
- (*b*) He is a warrior—a conqueror. He will go forth to conquest, and will be successful in overcoming his enemies, vers. 3-5.
- (*c*) His throne is the throne of God, and will endure for ever, ver. 6.
- (*d*) His character is eminently righteous, vers. 6, 7.
- (*e*) He is clad in robes of beauty; his garments are rich with perfumes; his attendants are the daughters of kings, vers. 8, 9.

III. A description of the queen, the bride, vers. 9-17.

- (*a*) She is clad in robes of gold,—the gold of Ophir, ver. 9.
- (*b*) She is entreated to forget her own people, and her father's house,—to become wholly devoted to him who had espoused her, assured that thus she would secure his heart, and be certain of his love, vers. 10, 11.
- (*c*) She would be honoured with the favour of the rich, and the attendance of foreign princesses, represented by the "daughter of Tyre;" Tyre, distinguished for wealth and splendour; Tyre, the representative of the commercial world, ver. 12.
- (*d*) The daughter of the king—the bride—is glorious and beautiful,

PSALM XLV.

To the chief Musician upon *x* Shoshannim, for the sons of Korah, [1] Maschil. A song of loves.

MY heart [2] is inditing a good matter: I speak of the things which I have made touching the king; my tongue *is* the pen of a ready writer.

2 Thou art fairer *y* than the

x Ps. lxix., lxxx. [1] Or, *of instruction.* [2] *boileth,* or, *bubbleth up,* *y* S. Song v. 9—16.

as seen "within" her own palace or dwelling, ver. 13.

(*e*) Her raiment is of wrought gold; of needlework of delicate finish and taste, vers. 13, 14.

(*f*) She is attended by virgins, her companions, who with her shall enter into the palace of the king, vers. 14, 15.

IV. An address to the king. He is to be honoured by his children, who will be more to him than even his ancestors. His praise will spring from those children rather than from the lustre and fame of his great progenitors. He will be remembered in all coming generations, and praised for ever and ever, vers. 16, 17. See Notes, ver. 16.

Such is the outline or substance of this exquisite specimen of sacred song,—this very beautiful Hebrew ode. It must be apparent, I think, at once, that it cannot be applied with propriety to either David, or Solomon, or to a Persian prince. How far it is applicable to the Messiah and the church; to him as the bridegroom, and to the church as a bride,—will be made apparent in the exposition of its particular words and phrases.

1. *My heart is inditing.* That is, *I* am engaged in inditing a good matter; though implying at the same time that it was a work of the *heart*—a work in which the heart was engaged. It was not a mere production of the intellect; not a mere work of skill; not a mere display of the beauty of song, but a work in which the *affections* particularly were engaged, and which would express the feelings of the heart:—the result or effusion of sincere *love.* The word rendered *is inditing*—רָחַשׁ, *rahhash*—is rendered in the margin, *boileth* or *bubbleth up.* It means properly to boil up or over, as a fountain; and the idea here is that his heart boiled over with emotions of love; it was full and overflowing; it found expression in the words of this song. The Hebrew word does not occur elsewhere in the Bible. ¶ *A good matter.* Literally, *a good word;* that is, it was something which he was about to say which was *good;* something interesting, pure, important; not only a subject on which his heart was engaged, but also which was worthy of attention. ¶ *I speak of the things which I have made.* Literally, "I say my works to the king." That is, My work—that which I meditate and am about to compose—pertains to the king. ¶ *Touching the king. He* is to be the main subject of my song. Comp. Notes on Isa. v. 1. If the remarks made in the introduction to the psalm are correct, then the "king" here referred to was the future Messiah—the great personage to whom all the writers of the Old Testament looked forward, and whose glory they were so anxious to see and to describe. Comp. Notes on 1 Peter i. 10–12. ¶ *My tongue* is *the pen of a ready writer.* Let my tongue in speaking of him be as the pen of a rapid writer. That is, let my tongue rapidly and freely express my thoughts and feelings. The word rendered *pen*—עֵט, *ait*—means a *stylus,* usually made of iron, used for the purpose of inscribing letters on lead or wax. See Notes on Job xix. 24. The idea is that the psalmist's mind was full of his subject, and that he desired to express his thoughts in warm, free, gushing language—the language of overflowing emotion.

2. *Thou art fairer than the children of men.* That is, Thou art more fair and comely than men; thy comeliness is greater than that which is found among men. In other words, Thou art beautiful

children of men; grace [z] is poured into thy lips: therefore God hath blessed thee for ever.

z Luke iv. 22.

3 Gird thy sword [a] upon *thy* thigh, O *most* mighty, with thy glory and thy majesty.

a Heb. iv. 12; Rev. i. 16.

beyond any human standard or comparison. The language, indeed, would not necessarily imply that he was *not* a man, but it means that among all who dwell upon the earth there was none to be found that could be compared with him. The Hebrew word rendered "thou art fairer"—יָפְיָפִיתָ, *Yoph-ya-phitha*—is a very unusual term. It is properly a *reduplication* of the word meaning "beautiful," and thus means *to be very beautiful.* It would be well expressed by the phrase "Beautiful—beautiful—art thou above the children of men." It is the language of surprise,—of a sudden impression of beauty—beauty as it strikes at the first glance—such as the eye had never seen before. The impression here is that produced by the general appearance or aspect of him who is seen as king. Afterwards the attention is more particularly directed to the "grace that is poured into his lips." The *language* here would well express the emotions often felt by a young convert when he is first made to see the beauty of the character of the Lord Jesus as a Saviour: "Beautiful; beautiful, above all men." ¶ *Grace is poured into thy lips.* The word here rendered *is poured* means properly to pour, to pour out as liquids,—water, or melted metal: Gen. xxviii. 18; 2 Kings iv. 4. The meaning here is, that grace seemed to be *spread over* his lips; or that this was strikingly manifest on his lips. The word *grace* means properly favour; and then it is used in the general sense of benignity, kindness, mildness, gentleness, benevolence. The reference here is to his manner of speaking, as corresponding with the beauty of his person, and as that which particularly attracted the attention of the psalmist:—the mildness; the gentleness; the kindness; the persuasive eloquence of his words. It is hardly necessary to remark that this, in an eminent degree, was applicable to the Lord Jesus. Thus it is said (Luke iv. 22), "And all bare him witness, and wondered at the GRACIOUS words which proceeded out of his mouth." So John vii. 46: "Never man spake like this man." See also Matt. vii. 29; xiii. 54; Luke ii. 47. ¶ *Therefore God hath blessed thee for ever.* In connexion with this moral beauty—this beauty of character—God will bless thee to all eternity. Since he has endowed thee with such gifts and graces, he will continue to bless thee for ever. In other words, it is impossible that one who is thus endowed should ever be an object of the Divine displeasure.

3. *Gird thy sword upon* thy *thigh.* That is, Arm or prepare thyself for battle and conquest. The Messiah is introduced here as a conquering king; as about to go forward to subdue the nations to himself; as about to set up a permanent kingdom. ¶ *O* most *mighty.* That is, Hero; Warrior; Conqueror. ¶ *With thy glory and thy majesty.* With the glory and majesty appropriate to thee; or which properly belong to thee. This is at the same time the expression of a *wish* on the part of the author of the psalm, and a *prophetic description.* The psalmist *desired* that he would thus go forth to the conquest of the world; and saw that he *would* do it. Comp. vers. 5, 6. It is needless to remark that this is easily and naturally applicable to the Messiah—the Lord Jesus—as going forth for the subjugation of the world to the authority of God. Comp. 1 Cor. xv. 25, 28. See also, in reference to the figure here used, Isa. xlix. 2; Heb. iv. 12; Rev. i. 16; xix. 15.

4 And in thy majesty [1] ride [b] prosperously because of truth and meekness *and* righteousness; and thy right hand shall teach thee terrible [c] things.

5 Thine arrows [d] *are* sharp in

[1] *prosper thou, ride thou.* *b* Rev. vi. 2. *c* Ps. lxv. 5. *d* Ps. xxxviii. 2.

4. *And in thy majesty ride prosperously.* Marg., *Prosper thou, ride thou.* The *majesty* here referred to is the glory or magnificence which became a prince of such rank, and going forth to such deeds. The prayer is, that he would go forth with the pomp and glory becoming one in that station. The word here used, rendered in the margin, "prosper thou," means properly to go over or through, to pass over, and may be correctly rendered here, *pass on;* that is, move forward to conquest. The word *ride* refers to the way in which warriors usually went forth to conquest in a chariot of war. The idea is that of one caparisoned for war, and with the glory appropriate to his rank as king, going forth to victory. This language is such as is often employed in the Scriptures to describe the Messiah as a conquering king. ¶ *Because of truth.* On account of truth; or in the cause of truth. That is, the great purpose of his conquests would be to establish a kingdom based on truth, in contradistinction from the existing kingdom of darkness as based on error and falsehood. The *object* of his conquests was to secure the reign of truth over the minds of men. Comp. John xviii. 37. ¶ *And meekness* and *righteousness.* Literally, *humility-righteousness;* or, humble right. It would be a kingdom or a conquest of righteousness, *not* established, as most kingdoms are, by pride and arrogance and mere power, but a dominion where humility, meekness, gentleness would be at the foundation—that on which the whole superstructure would be reared. Its characteristic would be *righteousness* or *justice,*—a righteousness and justice, however, not asserted and established by mere power, or by the pride of conquest, but which would be established and maintained by meekness or gentleness:—a kingdom not of outward pomp and power, but the reign of the gentle virtues in the heart. ¶ *And thy right hand.* The instrument of martial power and success; that which, in war, wields the sword and the spear. ¶ *Shall teach thee.* Shall guide thee, or lead thee to the performance of terrible things. ¶ *Terrible things.* Fearful deeds; things that are fitted to excite astonishment or wonder. They were such things as would be regarded as distinguished achievements in war, indicating extraordinary valour; such conquests as would strike the world with amazement. We have here, therefore, a description of the Messiah as going forth to the great conquest of the world; and at the same time we have this intimation of the nature of his kingdom, that however great the *power* which would be exerted in securing its conquests, it would be founded on *truth:*—it would be a kingdom where righteousness would prevail, and whose essential characteristic would be gentleness and peace.

5. *Thine arrows* are *sharp in the heart,* etc. Literally, *Thine arrows are sharp,—the people under thee shall fall,—in the heart of the enemies of the king.* The process of *thought* in the verse seems to be this: First. The *arrows* are seen as sharp or penetrating. Second. The *people* are seen falling as those arrows are shot forth. Third. It is seen that those who fall are the *enemies of the king,* and that the arrows have pierced the *heart.* The word *sharp* is applied to the arrows as denoting that they were adapted to *pierce.* Sometimes arrows are blunted, or with a thick head, rather adapted to smite with force than to wound by penetrating. The bow and the arrow were common instruments in ancient wars, and

the heart of the king's enemies;
whereby the people fall under
thee.
6 Thy throne, [e] O God, *is* for
ever and ever: the sceptre of
thy kingdom *is* a right sceptre.

7 Thou lovest righteousness,
and hatest wickedness: therefore
[1] God, thy God, hath [f] anointed
thee with the oil of [g] gladness
above thy fellows.
8 All [h] thy garments *smell* of

e Ps. xciii. 2; Heb. i. 8.
1 Or, *O God.*
f Isa. lxi. 1. g 1 Kings i. 39, 40.
h S. Song i. 3.

were mainly used by those who went forth to battle in a chariot. Comp. 1 Kings xxii. 34; 2 Kings ix. 21–24. As pertaining to the Messiah, the reference here is, of course, to the *truth,* and to the power of that truth in penetrating the hearts of men. Comp. Notes on Heb. iv. 12. ¶ *In the heart of the king's enemies.* That is, the *truths* stated by the Messiah, the conquering king, would penetrate deep into the soul, and slay the sinner, the enemy of the king, that is, of the Messiah. The idea is, that truth would produce an effect in regard to the hopes of the sinner—his self-confidence—his life *as* a sinner—like that which the arrow does when it penetrates the heart. Comp. Rom. vii. 9: "For I was alive without the law once, but when the commandment came, sin revived and I died." See also *ibid.*, vers. 10, 11. ¶ Whereby *the people fall under thee.* As the effect of the arrows; as the effect of truth. The representation is that of victory. As here represented, it is the victory of truth; a conquest by subjecting men to the authority and reign of God.

6. *Thy throne, O God,* is *for ever and ever.* This passage is quoted by the author of the Epistle to the Hebrews in proof that the Messiah is exalted above the angels, and it is, beyond all question, adduced by him as having original reference to the Messiah. See the passage explained at length in the Notes on Heb. i. 8. I do not perceive, after an interval of nearly twenty years since those Notes were written, that it is necessary to alter or to add anything to what is there said in explanation of the passage. It is undoubtedly an address to the "king" here referred to as *God*—as one to whom the name *God*—אֱלֹהִים, *Elohim*—may be properly applied; and, as applied to the Messiah by the author of the Epistle to the Hebrews, it clearly proves that Christ is Divine.

7. *Thou lovest righteousness,* etc. See this verse explained in the Notes on Heb. i. 9, where it is applied to the Messiah. The word "God" is rendered in the margin "O God:"—"O God, thy God, hath anointed thee," etc. According to this construction, the thought would be carried on which is suggested in ver. 6, of a direct address to the Messiah as God. This construction is not necessary, but it is the most obvious one. The Messiah—the Lord Jesus—though he is described as God himself (John i. 1, *et al.*), yet addresses God as *his* God, John xx. 17. As Mediator, as appearing in human form, as commissioned to perform the work of redemption, and to subdue the world to the Divine authority, it was proper thus to address his Father as *his* God, and to acknowledge Him as the source of all authority and law.

8. *All thy garments* smell *of myrrh.* The word *smell* is not in the original. The literal translation would be, "Myrrh, and aloes,—cassia,—all thy garments;" that is, they were so impregnated with perfumes that these seemed to constitute his very clothing. The mention of the "anointing" in the previous verse may have suggested the idea of these perfumes, as the anointing with a richly perfumed unguent seemed to have spread over, and to have pervaded all his raiment. Comp. Ps. cxxxiii. 2. It was common, however, for Orientals to use much perfumery, particularly

myrrh, and aloes, *and* cassia, out of the ivory palaces, whereby they have made thee glad.

on festive occasions. Myrrh—מֹר, *mor*, or *mur*—is an article which exudes from a tree found in Arabia, and still more extensively in Abyssinia. It is obtained by making an incision in the bark. It constituted one of the earliest articles of commerce (Gen. xliii. 11), and was highly esteemed by the Egyptians and Jews, as well as by the Greeks and the Romans. It is mentioned in Esther ii. 12 as an article used in the purification of women; and as a perfume, Cant. iv. 6; v. 5. It was used among the ancients, not only as a perfume, but as a fumigator, and as an article of medicine, and was employed in embalming the bodies of the dead. Herodotus, speaking of the practice of embalming among the Egyptians, says, "They then fill the body with powder of pure myrrh, cassia, and other perfumes, except frankincense," ii. 86. Comp. Ex. xxx. 23; Matt. ii. 11; Mark xv. 23; John xix. 39. Of the tree which produces the myrrh, however, we have as yet no very accurate accounts. See Kitto's Encyc., art. *Mor*. ¶ *And aloes*. The word rendered *aloes*—אֲהָלוֹת, *ahaloth*—occurs four times in the Old Testament: Numb. xxiv. 6, where it is rendered *lign-aloes;* and here, as in Prov. vii. 17; Cant. iv. 14, where it is rendered *aloes*. The reference is, undoubtedly, to some odoriferous substance, well known in ancient times. Why the word *aloes* has been used as a translation of the original word, in the English and in the older versions, it is not easy to ascertain, but it is certain that the substance referred to is not to be confounded with the bitter and nauseous aloes known as a medicine. It is now generally understood that the reference in the word as used in the Scriptures, is to a species of odoriferous tree growing in India, and which anciently doubtless constituted part of the valuable commerce of the East. It is not a *fruit* or a *gum*, but the tree itself. It is a species of sweet-smelling *wood*, and was valued on account of its fragrance. It is produced still in India. The tree is believed to be a native of the mountainous tracts east and south-east of Silhet, in about 24 degrees of north latitude. See Kitto's Encyc., art. *Ahalim*. ¶ And *cassia*. Cassia — קְצִיעוֹת, *ketzioth*—is better known. It is a bark resembling cinnamon, but less aromatic. It is mentioned in two other places in the Scriptures, Ex. xxx. 24; Ezek. xxvii. 19. This, as well as "aloes," is a production of India and its islands. See Kitto's Encyc., art. *Ketzioth*. ¶ *Out of the ivory palaces*. That is, As thou comest out of the ivory palaces. The representation is that of the king as coming out of the palace where he dwelt, and as clad in apparel appropriate to his station, and surrounded by his attendants, diffusing joy all around them. The imagery has *changed* from what it was in vers. 3–5, where he goes forth as a conqueror, with his sword on his "thigh," and ascending his war-chariot. Here he appears clothed, indeed, in regal splendour, in the magnificence of state, but as the husband of the bride, and as encircled with the attendants of an Oriental court. Ivory palaces are palaces adorned with ivory, or where ivory constituted a prominent and striking part of the ornaments. It cannot be supposed that the palace was constructed entirely of ivory. Kitto supposes that this refers to the interior decorations, or that the walls were *inlaid* with ivory, gold, etc., as constituting a part of the decorations of the building. *Ivory*, it would seem, was so abundant and conspicuous that the name might be given to the whole structure. Such a palace was that built by Ahab: 1 Kings xxii. 39. ¶ *Whereby they have made thee glad*. Hebrew, "from them (or thence) they have gladdened thee."

9 Kings' daughters [i] *were* among thy honourable women:
upon thy right [k] hand did stand the queen in gold of Ophir.
10 Hearken, O daughter, and

i S. Song vi. 8. *k* 1 Kings ii. 19.

That is, They, the attendants referred to more particularly in the following verses, have gladdened thee; have diffused around a general joy; have contributed to make thee happy. He was clad in robes that became his station, and was accompanied and surrounded by attendants who diffused around a general joy, and who made his own heart glad. The *idea* may be, that the Redeemer, the Messiah, is made happy by the affection and the companionship of the redeemed, his people.

9. *Kings' daughters* were *among thy honourable women.* Those who were in attendance on him and on the bride were from the most elevated ranks; among the most honourable of the earth. The word rendered "honourable women," means properly, precious, costly; and then, dear, beloved; and this might be rendered "kings' daughters are among thy beloved ones;" that is, in the number of thy maidens, or of those attending on thee. The allusion is to a marriage, and the description is drawn from the usual accompaniments of a marriage in the east. The design, as applicable to the Messiah and to his union with the Church, his bride, is to describe him as accompanied with every circumstance of distinction and honour, to throw around him all that constituted beauty and splendour in an Oriental marriage ceremony. Nothing of earth could be too rich or beautiful to illustrate the glory of the union of the Redeemer with his redeemed Church. ¶ *Upon thy right hand did stand the queen.* The right hand is the place of honour, and that idea is intended here: 1 Kings ii. 19; Mark xiv. 62; xvi. 19; Heb. i. 3; Acts vii. 55. The idea here is, that the Church, the bride of the Lamb of God, as seen in the vision, is exalted to the highest post of honour. That Church has the place in his affections which the newly-married bride has in the affections of her husband. ¶ *In gold of Ophir.* In garments decked or ornamented with the finest gold. On the phrase "the gold of Ophir," see Notes on Isa. xiii. 12.

10. *Hearken, O daughter, and consider.* This is probably to be understood as the language of the psalmist, in vision, as uttering counsel and advice which would be appropriate to the new condition of the bride. Some have understood it as the language of the father of the bride, uttering appropriate counsel to his daughter on entering upon her new relationship; exhorting her to affection and obedience in that relationship; charging her to feel that she is his, that she is to go with him, that she is to identify herself with his interests, and to "forget,"—that is, not improperly to long for her own people and her father's house. All this would be good advice for a father to give to his daughter in such circumstances; but the most natural interpretation is to regard the language here as that of the psalmist, or as inspired wisdom, in regard to the proper feeling in entering on such a relation. If this be the meaning, the word "daughter" may be used as a term of affection or kindness, as the word *son* often is, to denote one who is a disciple or learner. The *thought* suggested here is, that counsel or advice in regard to the manner in which she should demean herself to secure the continual confidence of her husband, may be very properly given to a newly-married bride. The counsel here suggested, considered with reference only to that relation, would be eminently wise. ¶ *And incline thine ear.* Attend to what is now said. The address is *repeated*—"Hearken;" "consider;" "incline thine ear;" as if the matter were of great importance. On the phrase "incline thine ear," see

consider, and incline thine ear;
forget [l] also thine own people,
and thy father's house;
11 So [m] shall the king greatly

[l] Deut. xxxiii. 9; Matt. x. 37.

[m] S. Song iv. 9, etc.

Notes on Ps. xxxi. 2; comp. Ps. lxxviii. 1. ¶ *Forget also thine own people.* This is said on the supposition that the bride was a foreign princess. As such, it is to be supposed that she had been trained under other customs, under other forms of religion, and with reference to other interests than those which would now pertain to her. The counsel is, that she must now forget all these, and identify herself with her husband, and with his interests. The word "forget" cannot denote absolute forgetfulness, or that she was to cast off all affection for those who had trained her up; but the meaning is, that she was not to pine after them; that she was not to be dissatisfied with her new home and her new relations; that she was not to carry the institutions of her native country with her; that she was not to make use of her new position to promote the ends of her native country if they were adverse to, or hostile to, the interests of her husband and his country. As applied to a bride now, the advice would mean that she is not to pine for her old home; that she is not to make complaining and unfavourable comparison between that and her new home; that she is not to divert her husband from his plans, and the proper pursuits of his life, by endeavouring to induce him to forsake his friends, and to abandon his position, in order that she may be restored to the society of her earlier friends; that she is not to introduce habits, customs, amusements, modes of living into her husband's arrangements, derived from her former habits and modes of life, which would interfere with what is the proper economy of his house, and which would be inconsistent with his principles, and with his means of living. When she marries, she should make up her mind, while she cherishes a proper regard for her old friends, and a proper memory of her past life, to identify her interests with his; to go where he goes; to live as he lives; and to die, if such be the will of God, where he dies, and to be buried by his side. As applied to the Church—the bride of the Lamb—the idea here is that which we find so often enforced in the New Testament, that they who become the followers of the Saviour must be willing to forsake all for him, and to identify themselves with him and his cause. See Notes on Matt. x. 37; Luke xiv. 26. We are to forsake the world, and devote ourselves to him; we are to break away from all worldly attachments, and to consecrate all to him; we are to bid adieu to worldly companions as our chosen friends, and make the friends of Christ our friends: we are not to pine after the world, to seek to return to it, to pant for its pleasures; we are not to take advantage of our position in the church to promote the objects which we had pursued before we entered it; we are not to introduce the customs, the habits, the plans which we before pursued, *into* the church. We are in all things to become identified with him to whom we have become "espoused" (2 Cor. xi. 2); we are to live with him; to go with him; to die with him; to be his for ever. ¶ *And thy father's house.* The home of thy childhood; the house where thy father dwells. The strongest earthly ties are to be made subservient to a higher and stronger tie, if we would become true followers of the Saviour. See Luke ix. 59—62.

11. *So shall the king greatly desire thy beauty.* That is, in consequence of your love to him, and your entire devotion of yourself to him. The word *desire* here is equivalent to having pleasure in; as meaning that his affection would thus be fixed on her. In this way—by forgetting her own home, and devoting herself to

desire thy beauty; for [n] he *is* thy
Lord; and worship [o] thou him.
12 And the daughter of Tyre
[p] *shall be there* with a gift; *even*
the rich [q] among the people shall
entreat thy [1] favour.
13 The king's daughter *is* all

n Isa. liv. 5. *o* Ps. xcv. 6.
p Isa. xxiii. 18; Acts xxi. 3—6.
q Isa. lx. 3. [1] *face.*

him—she would secure his affection. In the married life, mere *beauty* will not secure permanently the love of a husband. The heart, as given to him, and as faithful to him, will alone secure his love. In like manner, it is nothing but sincere affection—true love on the part of the professed friends of the Saviour—the forgetting and forsaking of all else—that will secure his love, or make the church to him an object of desire. ¶ *For he is thy Lord.* That is, as a husband he sustains this relation to thee; or, this appellation may be given to him. In what sense this is true in respect to a husband, see Notes on 1 Pet. iii. 6; 1 Cor. xi. 3. In respect to the Saviour, the dominion implied in the word "*Lord*" is absolute and entire. ¶ *And worship thou him.* That is, as applicable to a bride, Show him respect, honour, reverence. See Notes on Eph. v. 33. The word means properly to bow down; then, to show respect, as to a superior; and then, to show proper respect to God, to wit, by worshipping or adoring him. See Notes on Matt. ii. 11; see Matt. viii. 2; xiv. 33; xv. 25; xviii. 26; xxviii. 9; Rev. xix. 10; xxii. 9; comp. Notes on Heb. i. 6.

12. *And the daughter of Tyre* shall be there *with a gift.* On the situation of Tyre, and its ancient splendour, see Notes on Matt. xi. 21; the introduction to Isaiah xxiii.; and the Notes on that chapter. In the time of the psalmist it was probably the most wealthy and luxurious commercial town then existing; and it is referred to here as meaning that persons of highest rank, and of the greatest riches, and those who were surrounded most by affluence and luxury, would come to honour the king. Even the daughter of the magnificent prince of Tyre would deem it an honour to be present with a gift becoming her exalted station, and properly representing the wealth of a king of so much magnificence. This is the imagery. As applied to the Messiah, it is a description of the honour which would be shown to *him* by those of highest rank and largest wealth. Comp. Notes on Isa. lx. 5—7, 9, 11, 13. ¶ Even *the rich among the people.* Rich men scattered among the people. Comp. Notes on Ps. xxii. 29. ¶ *Shall entreat thy favour.* Marg., as in Heb., *thy face.* Shall desire thy smile; the light of thy countenance; thy friendship. The word rendered "entreat"— חָלָה, *hhalah*—means properly to be rubbed; then, to be polished; and then, in the form used here (Piel) to rub, or stroke the face of any one; to soothe or caress; to flatter, to court; and the idea is literally that of one who caresses or soothes, or seeks to conciliate. The sense here is, *the richest of the nations shall make court to thee with gifts.* Gesenius, *Lex.* Ultimately this will be true in regard to the Messiah. Comp. as above, Isa. lx. The wealth of the world will yet be laid at his feet, and placed at his disposal. The effect of true conversion is *always* to make men willing to consecrate to the Saviour *all* that they possess.

13. *The king's daughter.* This evidently refers to the bride, the daughter of the foreign king. The verse contains a description of her beauty—her splendour of attire—before she is brought to the king, her future husband. She is represented here as in the palace or home of her father, before she is conducted forth to be given to her future husband in marriage. Is *all glorious.* Is all splendour or beauty; is *altogether* splendour. There is nothing that is

glorious within; her clothing [r] *is* of wrought gold.

14 She shall be brought [s] unto the king in raiment of needlework: the virgins her companions that follow her shall be brought unto thee.

15 With gladness [t] and re-

r Isa. lxi. 10; Rev. xix. 7, 8. *s* S. Song i. 4. *t* Isa. xxxv. 10; Jude 24.

not splendid, rich, magnificent in her appearance, or in her apparel. As seen in ver. 9, she is clad in gold; she is surrounded by honourable women—the daughters of kings (ver. 9), and encompassed with the rich, ver. 12. As seen here, she is in her father's house, adorned for the marriage, and to be brought to the king, her future husband, attired in all that could give grace and beauty to her person. The allusion here, as referring to the church—the "bride of the Lamb"—*may be* to that church considered as redeemed, and about to be received to heaven, to dwell with its Husband and Saviour. Comp. Notes on Rev. xix. 7, 8; xxi. 2, 9. ¶ *Within.* This does not refer to herself, as if she was not merely splendid in her attire, but holy and pure—glorious and lovely—in *heart;* it refers to her as seen while yet "*within*" the palace or home of her father, in her own dwelling. The Hebrew word—פְּנִימָה, *penimah*—means properly, "at or by the inner wall of a house, room, or court; that is, opposite to or in front of the door, and of those entering." Gesenius, *Lex.* As seen in her dwelling—within the palace—in the most honoured place—she is arrayed in gorgeous apparel, and adorned as becomes a king's daughter about to be married. ¶ *Her clothing* is *of wrought gold.* Gold embroidery. See ver. 9. That is, she is arrayed in the richest apparel.

14. *She shall be brought unto the king.* She shall be conducted to the king in the marriage procession, and be presented to him, clad in this magnificent raiment. The entire imagery is that of an Oriental marriage procession, where the bride is conducted forth to her future husband, attended by her virgin companions, or (as we should say) *bridesmaids.* ¶ *In raiment of needlework.* The word here used means properly *something variegated* or *versicoloured,* and would here denote a garment of divers colours, or *versicoloured raiment.* The word—רִקְמָה, *rikmah*—occurs in the following places: Judges v. 30, twice, where (as here) it is rendered *needlework;*—1 Chron. xxix. 2; Ezek. xvii. 3, rendered *divers colours;*—and Ezek. xvi. 10, 13, 18; xxvi. 16; xxvii. 7, 16, 24, where it is rendered *broidered work.* It has reference probably to embroidery or needlework, though the particular idea is rather that of the variegated *appearance* of the garment than to the manner in which it is made. ¶ *The virgins her companions that follow her shall be brought unto thee.* Literally, "virgins after her, her companions, brought unto thee." That is, they will be brought to the king. They will come in the same state as the queen herself; they, her companions, will be of so illustrious rank and birth, and apparelled with so much richness, that even *they* will be regarded as worthy to be treated as queens, or in the manner of queens. The design of the whole is to show the rank, the dignity, the splendour of the bride; herself gorgeously apparelled, and attended with companions so exalted as to be worthy of being treated as queens themselves. If this is to be regarded as applicable to the church, "the Lamb's wife" (Rev. xxi. 9), it is designed to describe that church as beautiful and glorious, and as worthy of the affection of its Saviour. Comp. Eph. v. 27.

15. *With gladness and rejoicing shall they be brought.* They shall come forth, attending the bride, with music and songs; the procession will be one of hilarity and joy. ¶ *They shall enter into the king's palace.*

joicing shall they be brought: they shall enter into the king's palace.

16 Instead [u] of thy fathers shall be thy children, whom thou mayest make princes [v] in all the earth.

17 I will make thy name [w] to be remembered in all genera-

u Psa. xxii. 30.

v Rev. i. 6. w Mal. i. 11.

That is, Moving from the palace of the royal father of the bride, or from her home, they will enter the palace of her husband, her future home. If this is designed to refer to the church, it is a beautiful description of what will occur when the church redeemed shall enter heaven, the home—the palace—the glorious abode—of the great king its Saviour, and of the joy that will attend its triumphant admission into those everlasting abodes. Comp. Notes on Rev. xxi.

16. *Instead of thy fathers shall be thy children.* Instead of thy fame—thy celebrity—thy distinction—being derived from thine illustrious predecessors, it will be derived hereafter rather from thy sons; from the fact that they will be made princes and rulers in the earth. In our translation, this would seem to be an address to the bridal-queen, as if to console her for leaving the home of her illustrious ancestors, by the assurance that she would have children of her own, who would be still more illustrious. The connexion, however, and the original, at least, in the Masoretic pointing, demands that this should be understood as an address to the king himself—the main subject in the poem, as in vers. 2–9. The idea is, that he would derive his dignity and honour ultimately, not so much from his ancestors as his descendants; that those who would be born unto him would be more illustrious, and would have a wider dominion, than any who had gone before him in the line in which he was descended. It is not easy or practicable to apply this to Solomon, or to any other Hebrew prince; it is not difficult to apply it to the Messiah, and to the fact that those who would be descended spiritually from him, and who would ultimately be regarded as deriving true rank and honour from him, would far surpass in dignity all those who, in the line of kings, had been his predecessors. ¶ *Whom thou mayest make princes in all the earth.* Not merely assigning to them provinces, to be governed as a part of the empire, but in all lands, or where thy dominion shall be acknowledged all over the world. The image here is derived, undoubtedly, from the custom prevailing among kings of assigning portions of an empire as provinces to their sons. The meaning, however, considered as referring to the Messiah, is, that his lustre and dignity on earth would not be derived from a distinguished earthly ancestry, or from an illustrious line of kings from whom he was descended, but from the fact that those who would derive their authority from him would yet possess the world, and that this their authority under him would extend to all lands. Comp. Notes on Dan. vii. 14, 27.

17. *I will make thy name to be remembered in all generations.* The psalmist here evidently speaks as an inspired man, and the idea is that his thus singing the praises of the "king"—the Messiah—would be among the means of causing His name to be celebrated in all future ages. This song would go down to future times, and would serve to keep up the true knowledge of the Messiah in the far distant ages of the world. No one can doubt that this has been thus far accomplished; no one has any reason to doubt that this psalm *will be* among the means of keeping up the true knowledge of the Messiah, and of securing the remembrance of him upon the earth in all future periods of the world's history. This psalm has been on millions of lips, in

tions; therefore shall the people praise thee for ever and ever.

praise of the Messiah; it will be on hundreds of millions more in future times, as expressive of tender love for the Redeemer. ¶ *Therefore shall the people praise thee for ever and ever.* Thy praise will never cease to be celebrated. The time will never come on earth when that praise will die away; and in all the eternity beyond the termination of this world's history there never will arrive a period when thy name will not be honoured, and when thy praises shall cease to be sung. Comp. Notes on Rev. iv. 10; v. 9–13. Happy are they who join in that song on earth; happy they who will unite in it in the heavenly world!

PSALM XLVI.

This psalm has been called *Luther's Psalm*. It was that which he was accustomed to sing in trouble. When the times were dark; when the enemies of truth appeared to triumph; when disaster seemed to come over the cause in which he was engaged, and the friends of the Reformation were dispirited, disheartened, and sad, he was accustomed to say to his fellow-labourers, "Come, let us sing the 46th Psalm."

The author of the psalm is unknown. It is not ascribed to David, but to "the Sons of Korah," and there are no indications *in* the psalm that David was the author, or that it refers to his times. There is reason to believe that most of the psalms attributed to the "Sons of Korah" were composed subsequent to the time of David.

The *title* of the psalm is, "To the chief Musician, for the Sons of Korah, a song upon Alamoth." On the phrase "To the chief Musician," see Notes on the title to Ps. iv. On the phrase "For the Sons of Korah," see Notes on the title to Ps. xlii. The word "*song*" in the title occurs also in that to Ps. xxx. (see Notes on that title), and also in the titles to Psalms xlv., xlviii., lxv., lxvi., lxvii., lxviii., lxxv., lxxvi., lxxxiii., lxxxvii., lxxxviii., xcii., cviii., and from Ps. cxx. to Ps. cxxxiv. inclusive. Nothing seems to be indicated by it in regard to the nature and character of the psalms where it is found. The word *Alamoth* occurs only here and in 1 Chron. xv. 20, where it is found in connexion with the mention of certain singers or musicians, evidently referring to some kind of musical instruments which those who are mentioned used; "so the singers" (ver. 19), "Heman, Asaph, and Ethan, *to sound with cymbals of brass*; and Zechariah, and Aziel, and Shemiramoth, etc., *with psalteries on Alamoth*." The *word* from which this is derived—עַלְמָה, *Almah*—means properly *a virgin*, or a youthful spouse (comp. Notes on Isa. vii. 14); and the phrase here, and in 1 Chron. xv. 20, would seem properly to denote *after the manner of virgins*; that is, with the female voice, answering to our treble or soprano, as opposed to the deep bass or baritone voice of men. Then the reference might be to some musical instruments that were fitted to accompany that voice, or whose tones resembled that voice, as distinguished from cymbals, trumpets, harps, etc. The form of the instrument is now unknown.

It is not possible now to ascertain the occasion on which the psalm was written. It was evidently in view of trouble, or of some impending calamity; apparently some national calamity, or some time when the nation was in danger, and when it was felt that their only refuge—their last hope—was in God. It would seem to be not improbable that the psalm was composed when wars were raging abroad in the earth; when the nations were convulsed; and when Jerusalem itself was besieged and threatened with ruin. The main thought of the psalm—the central idea in it—is, that, amidst these general and far-spreading agitations and convulsions among the nations of the earth, the people of God were safe. They had nothing to fear, even though those convulsions and agitations should be multiplied and increased; even though they should be carried so far that the very foundations of the earth should be shaken, and the mountains removed and carried into the midst of the sea. There was to them an Infinite Protector; there were unfailing sources of peace; they had nothing to dread. It was their duty, therefore, to be calm, still, confiding, for God would be exalted among the nations of the earth. It is *possible* that the psalm refers to the invasion of the land of Israel by Sennacherib, and to the miraculous destruction of his

PSALM XLVI.

To the chief Musician [1] for the sons of Korah. A Song *x* upon *y* Alamoth.

GOD *is* our refuge and strength, a very present help in trouble.

[1] Or, *of*. *x* Ps. xlviii., lxvi. *y* 1 Chron. xv. 20.

host, as recorded in 2 Kings xix. and Isa. xxxvi., xxxvii. All the circumstances in that invasion,—the tumultuous hosts summoned for the war (Isa. xxxvi. 2); the overthrow of numerous nations by their armies (Isa. xxxvi. 18-21); the siege of Jerusalem itself (Isa. xxxvi. 2); the confidence of Hezekiah and of his people in God when the city was besieged (Isa. xxxvii. 14-20); and the final overthrow of the Assyrian host by the angel of the Lord (Isa. xxxvii. 36), agree well with all the statements in the psalm, and seem well to *illustrate* the psalm, though it be impossible now to determine with precise accuracy to what particular historical occasion it has reference. The circumstances in that invasion, however, are so similar to those supposed in the psalm, that, perhaps, we shall not be likely to err in supposing that the psalm *had* reference to that occasion.

The psalm is divided into three parts or strophes, the close of each of which is indicated by the word *Selah*, in vers. 3, 7, 11.

I. The first strophe, vers. 1-3. In this there is the general statement that God is a refuge and strength, and that the people of God would have nothing to fear though the earth should be removed, and though the raging waters of the ocean should shake the very mountains.

II. The second, vers. 4-7. In this there is the statement that the people of God had an unfailing source of consolation, like an ever-flowing river, making glad the city of God; that God himself was in that city as its Protector; that though the nations raged, and the kingdoms were moved, he had only to utter his voice and even the earth would be dissolved; that they had nothing to fear while the God of hosts—the God of mightier armies than those which had invaded the land—was with them.

III. *The third strophe*, vers. 8-11. In this we have a reference to the mighty power of God as actually put forth in the desolations, which *he* had made in the earth. He had shown that power by making wars to cease; by breaking the bow, and cutting the spear in sunder; and by causing the war-chariot to be burned in the fire. They had, therefore, nothing to fear while such a God was their Protector, and it was their duty calmly to confide in him, and leave the whole issue with him, for it was his purpose to exalt himself among the nations of the earth.

1. *God is our refuge and strength.* God is for us as a place to which we may flee for safety; a source of strength to us in danger. The first word, *refuge*, from a verb meaning *to flee*, and then *to flee to*—חָסָה, *hhasah*—or to take shelter in—denotes a place to which one would flee in time of danger—as a lofty wall; a high tower; a fort; a fortress. See Notes on Ps. xviii. 2. The idea here is, that the people of God, in time of danger, may find him to be what such a place of refuge would be. Comp. Prov. xviii. 10. The word *strength* implies that God is the *source* of strength to those who are weak and defenceless; or that we may rely on his strength *as if* it were our own; or that we may feel as safe in his strength as though we had that strength ourselves. We may make it the basis of our confidence as really as though the strength resided in our own arm. See Notes on Ps. xviii. 2. ¶ *A very present help.* The word *help* here means aid, assistance. The word *trouble* would cover all that can come upon us which would give us anxiety or sorrow. The word rendered *present*—נִמְצָא, *nimtza*—means rather, *is found*, or *has been found;* that is, he has *proved* himself to be a help in trouble. The word *present*, as if he were near to us, or close by us, does not accurately express the idea, which is rather, that he *has been found* to be such, or that he has always *proved* himself to be such a help, and that, therefore, we may now confide in him. The word *very*, or *exceedingly*, is added to qualify the whole proposition, as if this were *emphatically* true. It was true in the most eminent

2 Therefore will not we fear, though the earth be removed, and though the mountains be carried into the [1]midst of the sea;

3 *Though* the waters thereof roar *and* be troubled, *though* the mountains shake with the swelling thereof. Selah.

[1] *heart of the seas.*

sense that God had always been found to be such a helper, and, *therefore*, there was nothing to fear in the present distress. Ver. 2.

2. *Therefore will not we fear.* Our confidence in God shall be unshaken and abiding. Having Him for our refuge and strength (ver. 1), we can have nothing to fear. Comp. Ps. lvi. 3. ¶ *Though the earth be removed.* Literally, "in the changing of the earth;" that is, though the earth should be changed. This may either mean, Though the earth should change its place or its very structure in these convulsions; or, though it should perish altogether. Comp. Ps. cii. 26. The idea is, that they would not be afraid, though the convulsions then occurring in the world should be continued, and should be extended so far as to destroy the very earth itself. God would remain their friend and protector, and they would have nothing to fear. ¶ *And though the mountains be carried into the midst of the sea.* Marg., as in Heb., *into the heart of the seas.* This may either be understood literally, as implying that they would *not* be afraid though the mountains, the most fixed and firm things of earth, should be uprooted and sunk in the ocean—implying that nothing earthly was stable; or, the mountains here may be referred to as emblems of that which seemed to be most settled and established on earth—the kingdoms of the world. The idea is, that in any convulsion — any change — any threatened danger—they would place confidence in God, who ruled over all, and who could not change. It will be seen at once that this entire description of trust and confidence in God is applicable to the time of Hezekiah, and to the feelings which he manifested when the land was invaded by the hosts of Sennacherib, and when wars and commotions were abroad among the kingdoms of the earth. See the introduction to the psalm. It was, also, eminently fitted to console the mind in the circumstances to which Luther so often applied the psalm—the agitations, convulsions, wars, dangers in Europe, in the time of the Reformation. It is fitted to *any* time of trouble, when commotions and revolutions are occurring in the earth, and when everything sacred, true, and valuable seems to be in danger.

3. Though *the waters thereof roar* and *be troubled.* The waters of the sea. The idea is, that they would not be afraid though everything should be in commotion, and be as unsettled as the restless waves of the ocean. The earth might be changed, the mountains removed, the agitated sea roar and dash against the shore, but their minds would be calm. The word rendered *be troubled* means to boil; to ferment; to foam; and here it refers to the ocean as agitated and lashed into foam. Nothing is more sublime and fearful than the ocean in a storm; nothing furnishes a better illustration of the peace produced by confidence in God amid the agitations which occur in the world, than the mind of a seaman that is calm when the ocean is heaved in wild commotion. ¶ Though *the mountains shake with the swelling thereof.* The rolling ocean breaking against the sides of the mountains on its shore, and seeming to shake them to their foundation. The word rendered *swelling* means properly majesty, glory; then pride, haughtiness, insolence. Literally, "though the mountains tremble *through their pride.*" Comp. Ps. cxxiv. 5. On the word *Selah,* see Notes on Ps. iii. 2.

4 *There is* a river, [z] the streams whereof shall make glad the city [a] of God, the holy *place* of the tabernacles of the Most High.

z Ezek. xlvii. 1—12. *a* Rev. xxi. 2, 3.

5 God *is* in the midst of her; she shall not be moved: God shall help her, [1] *and that* right early.

[1] *when the morning appeareth.*

4. There is *a river.* There is no allusion here to any particular stream or river, but the image is designed to represent a state of peace and calm security in contrast with the rough and troubled ocean. While the ocean rages, and foams, and dashes against the mountains as if it would overturn them, the state of Jerusalem, the city of God, was well represented by a calm and gently-flowing river;—a river of full banks, diffusing joy and fertility and beauty wherever it flowed. This image, to represent happiness, abundance, peace, joy, is one that is often employed in the Scriptures. Comp. Isa. xxxii. 2; xxxiii. 21; xli. 18; Ps. i. 3; Rev. xxii. 1; Ps. xxxvi. 8. The *idea* here is simply that Jerusalem would be calm and serene amidst all the external agitations in the world—calm as a gently-flowing stream. The streams—the canals—the water-courses of such a river flowing around each dwelling and along each garden, would diffuse happiness and beauty everywhere. ¶ *The streams. whereof.* The allusion here is undoubtedly to the canals, water-courses, or rivulets that were led off from the main stream for the purpose of supplying fountains and watering gardens. Thus the city of Damascus is watered by streams or canals cut from the river Barrady, that flows down from the regions of Anti-Libanus. The greenness—the beauty—the fertility—of Damascus is owing wholly to the waters of the river thus conducted to every house and garden in the city. Comp. introduction to Isa. xvii. So here, the flowing river of Divine mercy and goodness is conveyed, as in smaller canals or streams, to each home and heart, producing peace, calmness, joy,—while the world around is full of commotion and trouble. ¶ *Shall make glad the city of God.* Jerusalem, considered as the place where God was worshipped, and where he was supposed peculiarly to dwell: Ps. xlviii. 1. ¶ *The holy* place *of the tabernacles of the Most High.* Of the *tent* where the Most High is supposed to abide. The word is applicable to any habitation or dwelling-place; but in the Scriptures it is applied peculiarly to the sacred tent erected by Moses in the wilderness, and ultimately removed to Mount Zion by David, as the Divine abode on earth. It is sometimes, also, applied to the temple; and if this psalm was written, as I have supposed, in the time of Hezekiah, it would be applicable to that. Comp. Ps. lxxxiv. 2; cxxxii. 5. The tabernacle and the temple were alike divided into two parts—the holy and the most holy place—and hence the *plural* term is sometimes applied to them. Comp. Notes on Heb. ix. 2, 3.

5. *God* is *in the midst of her.* God is in the midst of the *city* referred to above—the "city of God." That is, (*a*) he dwelt there by the visible symbol of his presence, the Shekinah; (*b*) he was there *actually* as a help and a protector. It was his chosen abode, and as long as such a Being dwelt in the city, they had nothing to fear. ¶ *God shall help her.* That is, in her danger, he will interpose to save her. This is language such as would be used in reference to a place that was besieged, and would well apply to the state of things when Jerusalem was besieged by the armies of Assyria under Sennacherib. The language expresses the confidence of the people in the time of the impending danger. ¶ And that *right early.* Marg., *when the morning appeareth.* Literally, *in the faces of the morning*, as the word is commonly used; or, more literally, in the *turning* of

6 The heathen raged, the kingdoms were moved: he uttered his voice, the earth melted.
7 The LORD of hosts *is* with us; the God of Jacob *is*[1] our refuge. Selah.
8 Come, behold the works of

[1] *an high place for us.*

the morning,—for the verb from which the word is derived means properly *to turn*, and then *to turn to or from any one*. The noun is applied to the face or countenance, because the person is *turned to* us when we see his countenance. The poetic idea here seems to refer to the day as having turned away *from* us at night, and then as turning about *towards* us in the morning, after having gone, as it were, to the greatest distance from us. *Possibly* there may be an allusion here to what occurred in the camp of the Assyrians, when the discovery that the angel of the Lord had smitten them was made early in the morning, or when men arose in the morning:—"The angel of the Lord went forth, and smote in the camp of the Assyrians an hundred and fourscore and five thousand: and when they arose in the morning" [that is, when men arose in the morning], "behold, they were all dead corpses," Isa. xxxvii. 36.

6. *The heathen raged.* The nations were in commotion, or were agitated like the waves of the sea. This language would well describe the consternation of the nations when the Assyrians went forth to conquest, and when, having subdued so many other kingdoms, they made war on Jerusalem. Comp. Isa. xxxvi. 18–20. ¶ *The kingdoms were moved.* That is, those who were invaded, as well as those that made the invasion. There was a general convulsion or shaking among the nations of the earth. ¶ *He uttered his voice.* God spoke; he gave command; he expressed his will. Comp. Gen. i. 3; Hab. iii. 6. ¶ *The earth melted.* The very earth seemed to melt or dissolve before him. Every thing became still. The danger passed away at his command, and the raging world became calm. The Bible abounds in language of this kind, showing the absolute power of God, or his power to control all the raging elements on land and ocean by a word. Comp. Notes on Ps. xxxiii. 9. See also Ps. cvii. 25, 29; Matt. viii. 26.

7. *The* LORD *of hosts.* The God commanding, ordering, marshalling the hosts of heaven,—the angels, and the starry worlds. See Notes on Isa. i. 9. Comp. Ps. xxiv. 10. The reference here is to God considered as having control over all *armies*, or all that can be regarded and described as a marshalled host, in earth and in heaven. Having such a Being, therefore, for a protector, they had nothing to fear. See ver. 11. ¶ Is *with us.* Is on our side; is our defender. The Hebrew phrase here used is employed in Isa. vii. 14; viii. 8, to describe the Messiah. See Notes on those passages. ¶ *The God of Jacob.* See Notes on Ps. xxiv. 6. The meaning is, The God whom Jacob acknowledged, and whom he found to be his friend, is with us. ¶ Is *our refuge.* Literally, a high place, as a tower, far above the reach of enemies. See Notes on Ps. ix. 9; xviii. 2. So the margin, *an high place for us.*

8. *Come, behold the works of the* LORD. Go forth and see what the Lord has done. See, in what his hand has accomplished, how secure we are if we put our trust in him. ¶ *What desolations he hath made in the earth.* Or, in the land. The word *desolations* might refer to any *ruin* or *overthrow*, which he had brought upon the land of Israel, or on the nations abroad—the destruction of cities, towns, or armies, as proof of his power, and of his ability to save those who put their trust in him. But if this be supposed to refer to the invasion of the land of Israel by Sennacherib, it may point to what occurred to his armies when the angel of the Lord went forth and smote them in their

the LORD, what desolations he hath made in the earth.

9 He maketh wars to cease unto the end of the earth; he breaketh the bow, and cutteth the spear in sunder: he burneth [b] the chariot in the fire.

10 Be still, and know that I *am* God; I will be exalted among

b Ezek. xxxix. 9, 10.

camp (Isa. xxxvii. 36), and to the consequent deliverance of Jerusalem from danger. Without impropriety, perhaps, this may be regarded as an appeal to the inhabitants of Jerusalem to go forth and see for themselves how complete was the deliverance; how utter the ruin of their foes; how abundant the proof that God was able to protect his people in times of danger. It adds great beauty to this psalm to suppose that it *was* composed on that occasion, or in view of that invasion, for every part of the psalm may receive a beautiful, and an ample illustration from what occurred at that memorable period. Nothing *could* furnish a clearer proof of the power of God to save, and of the propriety of putting confidence in him in times of national danger, than a survey of the camp of the Assyrians, where an hundred and eighty-five thousand men had been smitten down in one night by the angel of God. Comp. 2 Kings xix. 35; 2 Chron. xxxii. 21; Isa. xxxvii. 36.

9. *He maketh wars to cease unto the end of the earth.* Either in all the land, or in all the world. The overthrow of the Assyrian army would probably put an end to all the wars then raging in the world. The Assyrian empire was then the most mighty on the globe; it was engaged in wide schemes of conquest; it had already overrun many of the smaller kingdoms of the world (Isa. xxxvii. 18–20); and it hoped to complete its conquests, and to secure the ascendancy over the entire earth, by the subjugation of India and Egypt. When the vast army of that empire, engaged in such a purpose, was overthrown, the consequence would be that the nations would be at rest, or that there would be universal peace. Comp. Notes on Isa. xiv. 6, 7. ¶ *He breaketh the bow, and cutteth the spear in sunder.* That is, he makes them useless, as a bow that is broken is of no value, or a spear that is cut into parts. ¶ *He burneth the chariot in the fire.* The war-chariot, that which was employed in battle. See Notes on Isa. ii. 7; Ps. xx. 7. The expression here may refer to a custom of collecting the spoils of war into a heap, and setting them on fire. This was particularly done when the victors were unable to remove them, or so to secure them as to preclude all danger of their being taken again and used against themselves. This custom is alluded to by Virgil, *Æn.* viii. 561, 562,

> "Qualis eram, cùm primam aciem Præneste sub ipsâ
> Stravi, scutorumque incendi victor acervos."

The idea here is, that God had wholly overthrown the foe, and had prevented all danger of his returning again for purposes of conquest.

10. *Be still.* The word here used—from רָפָה, *raphah*—means properly to cast down; to let fall; to let hang down; then, to be relaxed, slackened, especially the hands. It is also employed in the sense of *not* making an effort; *not* putting forth exertion; and then would express the idea of leaving matters with God, or of being without anxiety about the issue. Comp. Ex. xiv. 13, "Stand still, and see the salvation of God." In this place the word seems to be used as meaning that there was to be no anxiety; that there was to be a calm, confiding, trustful state of mind in view of the displays of the Divine presence and power. The mind was to be calm, in view of the fact that God had interposed, and had shown that he was able to defend his people when surrounded by dangers. If this is understood as having reference to

the heathen, I will be exalted [e] in the earth.

[e] Isa. ii. 11, 17.

11 The LORD of hosts *is* with us; the God of Jacob *is* our refuge. Selah.

the Divine interposition when Jerusalem was threatened by the armies of the Assyrians under Sennacherib, the force and beauty of the expression will be most clearly seen. ¶ *And know that I* am *God.* See, in what I have done, the evidence that I am God. See a work accomplished which none *but* God could effect. Comp. Isa. xxxvii. 36. ¶ *I will be exalted among the heathen.* That is, among the *nations.* The nations abroad that do not worship me, but worship idols, shall see in these deeds full proof that I am the true God, and that I am worthy of universal adoration. Comp. Notes on Daniel iii. 28, 29; iv. 1–3, 37. See also Ex. ix. 16; Rom. ix. 17. ¶ *I will be exalted in the earth.* In the lands abroad; all over the world. The defeat and destruction of the armies of Sennacherib were eminently fitted to make a deep impression on the world that the God of the Hebrew people was the true God.

11. *The* LORD *of hosts is with us,* etc. See ver. 7. This is the conclusion, or the result of the whole. As applied to the invasion of Sennacherib, this would be clearly seen, for all that occurred in that invasion was adapted to leave the impression that Jehovah, God of hosts, was with the Hebrew people. He had interposed in time of danger; he had saved his city and nation; he had overthrown one of the most mighty armies that had ever been assembled; he had caused the boasting conqueror himself to retrace his steps to his capital; he had wholly delivered the nation from all danger; and he had shown how easy it was, in ways which they could not have anticipated, to bring deliverance. The truth thus conveyed was adapted to the people of God in all lands and at all times, as showing that God has power to defend his people against the most formidable enemies, and that all their interests are safe in his hands.

PSALM XLVII.

This psalm is entitled, "To the chief Musician, a psalm for [marg., of] the sons of Korah." On the phrase "To the chief Musician," see Notes on the title to Ps. iv. On the phrase "For the sons of Korah," see Notes on the title to Ps. xlii.

The occasion on which the psalm was composed, and the name of the author, are alike unknown. It is a triumphal psalm, and was composed apparently on some occasion of *victory* over enemies, and with reference to a triumphal procession. Professor Alexander supposes that it was composed to commemorate the victory of Jehoshaphat over the Ammonites and Edomites, recorded in 2 Chron. xx. It is, as he remarks, a coincidence of some importance, that there is express mention made of the presence of the "Kohathites" on that occaion, as among those who "stood up to praise the Lord," 2 Chron. xx. 19. This is not, however, decisive, as they might have been present on other similar occasions, and as it is probable, in fact, that they usually took part in celebrations of this kind. All that can be expressed with any certainty in regard to the occasion on which the psalm was composed is, that it was on an occasion of victory.

The psalm consists of two parts, quite similar in structure and in design. Each part consists of an exhortation to praise God, followed by a statement of reasons why it should be done.

I. The first part comprises the first five verses:

(1) An exhortation to praise God—to celebrate the joy of the soul by a clapping of hands, and by a shout of triumph, ver. 1.

(2) Reasons for doing this, vers. 2–5. These reasons are that he is terrible; that he is king over all the earth; that he will subdue the nations, and make them subject to his own people; and that, in anticipation of this, and in proof of this, he had now achieved a signal victory, and had gone up as from that victory to his own abode in heaven.

PSALM XLVII.

To the chief Musician. A Psalm [1] for the sons of Korah.

O CLAP your hands, all ye people; shout unto God with the voice of triumph.

[1] Or, *of*.

2 For the LORD most high *is* terrible; *he is* a great King over all the earth.

3 He shall subdue the people under us, and the nations under our feet.

II. The second part embraces the last four verses of the psalm:

(1) An exhortation, as before, to praise God, ver. 6.

(2) Reasons for this, vers. 7-9. These reasons are, as before, that God is king over all the earth; that he now sits upon the throne of his holiness, and that (ver. 9) the princes of the nations—the subdued kings and rulers—are borne along in triumph to the people of the God of Abraham; and that in this victory it has been shown that the shields of the earth belong to God. See Notes, ver. 9.

The psalm, therefore, is a triumphal ode, and was probably composed to be sung on occasion of some military triumph—some solemn procession on a return from battle, with captive princes marching in the procession, and with a display of the "shields" and other implements of war taken from the foe. All this is celebrated as indicative of the interposing power of God in victory, and as evidence of his purpose to protect his chosen people in time of peril. The psalm may yet be used in a higher sense by the church at large, when all the foes of God on earth shall be subdued, and when his kingdom shall be in fact set up over all the world.

1. *O clap your hands, all ye people.* A common way of expressing joy, or indicating applause. Comp. Notes on Isa. lv. 12. The *people* here referred to are probably the Jewish people, and the call on them is to rejoice, with the customary marks of joy, in view of the great victory which God had gained over their enemies. ¶ *Shout unto God.* Make a joyful noise in praise of God; that is, in acknowledgment that this victory has been gained by his interposition. ¶ *With a voice of triumph.* With such a shout as is usually raised when a victory is obtained; such a shout as occurs in a triumphal procession. Comp. 2 Sam. vi. 15; 1 Chron. xv. 28; Job xxxix. 25; Zech. iv. 7; Ex. xxxii. 18; Isa. xii. 6; xlii. 11; xliv. 23; Jer. l. 15. There are doubtless times when loud shouts, as expressive of joy, are proper.

2. *For the* LORD *most high.* Jehovah, the Most High God; that is, who is exalted above all other beings. Comp. Ex. xviii. 11; 1 Chron. xvi. 25 (Ps. xcvi. 4); 2 Chron. ii. 5; Ps. xcv. 3. ¶ Is *terrible.* Literally, is to be *feared;* that is, reverenced and adored. There is an idea in the words *terrible* and *terror* which is not contained in the original, as if there were something harsh, severe, stern, in his character. The word in the original does not go beyond the notion of inspiring reverence or awe, and is the common word by which the worship of God is designated in the Scriptures. The meaning is, that he is worthy of profound reverence or adoration. ¶ He is *a great king over all the earth.* He rules the world. He is a universal Sovereign. The immediate *occasion* of saying this, when the psalm was composed, was evidently some victory (which had been achieved over the enemies of the people of God) so decided, and so immediately by the Divine power, as to prove that he has absolute control over all nations.

3. *He shall subdue the people under us.* Comp. Notes on Ps. xviii. 39, 47. The word rendered "*subdue*" is that which commonly means *to speak.* The idea in the use of this word here is that he has only to *speak* and it is done (comp. Ps. xxxiii. 9), or that he could do it by a word. Comp., however, on the use of the word here, Gesenius (*Lex.*), on the word—דָּבַר, 2, Hiph. ¶ *And the nations under*

4 He shall choose our inheritance for us, the excellency of
Jacob whom he loved. Selah.
5 God is gone up [f] with a shout,
the LORD with the sound of a
trumpet.
6 Sing praises to God, sing
praises; sing praises unto our
King, sing praises.
7 For [g] God *is* the King of all

f Ps. lxviii. 18, 33; Acts i. 11.

g Zech. xiv. 9.

our feet. That is, they shall be entirely or effectually subdued. See Notes on Ps. vii. 5; xliv. 5. As God would enable them to do this, it was an occasion for thankfulness and triumph.

4. *He shall choose our inheritance for us.* He has chosen or selected the land which we inherit. Of all the countries which compose the world, he has chosen *this* to be the inheritance of his own people, or the place where they should dwell. The thought in this verse is based on the idea so common in the writings of the Hebrews, that their country was the glory of all lands—the place of all on earth most desirable to dwell in. It is in view of this fact that they are here called on to praise God, and to rejoice in him. ¶ *The excellency of Jacob.* Literally, "*the pride*—גָּאוֹן, *gaon* — of Jacob." LXX., *beauty*—καλλονὴν. So the Vulgate, *speciem.* The meaning is, that it was a land of which Jacob, the ancestor of the people, might be proud, or which he did boast of. It was ever regarded as an honour among the Jews that they dwelt in a land which had been the abode of the prophets; and especially was anything regarded as of value that could be traced to Jacob; that had been once in his possession; or that could be regarded as his gift. Comp. John iv. 12. ¶ *Whom he loved.* As one of the patriarchs. Perhaps special allusion is here made to *Jacob* rather than to Abraham and Isaac, because the land came actually into the possession of the Hebrew people in the time of Jacob's sons. It was divided among the descendants of his sons, the twelve tribes, bearing their names; and thus Jacob was most naturally referred to as having been in possession of the land. Abraham and Isaac dwelt in the land as strangers and pilgrims (Heb. xi. 9, 10, 13), having no possession there, not even of a burying-place except as they purchased it (comp. Gen. xxiii. 12–16); and the land actually came into the possession of the nation only in the family of Jacob.

5. *God is gone up with a shout.* That is, he has ascended to heaven, his home and throne, after having secured the victory. He is represented as having come down to aid his people in the war by the overthrow of their enemies, and (having accomplished this) as returning to heaven, accompanied by his hosts, and amidst the shouts of triumph. All this is, of course, poetical, and is not to be regarded as literal in any sense. Comp. Notes on Ps. vii. 7. ¶ *The* LORD *with the sound of a trumpet.* Jehovah, accompanied with the notes of victory. All this is designed to denote triumph, and to show that the victory was to be traced solely to God.

6. *Sing praises to God, sing praises.* This commences the *second* part of the psalm. The *repetition* shows that the heart was full, or was overflowing with joy. It is a call on all to celebrate the praises of God, especially as he had enabled his people to triumph over their enemies. ¶ *Sing praises unto our King.* Unto God, who has shown himself to be the *King* of his people,—one who rules in their behalf, and who has interposed for their deliverance in danger.

7. *For God* is *the King of all the earth.* He has shown himself to be a universal sovereign. All nations are subject to him, and he has a claim to universal praise. ¶ *Sing ye praises with understanding.* Marg., Every one *that hath understanding.* Neither

the earth; sing ye praises [1] with
[h] understanding.

8 God reigneth over the heathen: God sitteth upon the throne of his holiness.

9 [2] The princes of the people are gathered together, *even* the people of the God of Abraham: for the shields [i] of the earth *be-*

[1] Or, every one *that hath understanding.*
h 1 Cor. xiv. 15; Col. iii. 16.

[2] Or, *The voluntary of the people are gathered unto the people of*, etc. 2 Cor. viii. 5.
i Ps. lxxvi. 3.

the text here, however, nor the margin, expresses the true idea of the original. The Hebrew is, "Sing a *Maschil*"—מַשְׂכִּיל; that is, Sing, or play, a didactic psalm or tune; that is, a song or ode adapted to convey valuable lessons of instruction. See the word explained in the Notes on the title to Ps. xxxii. The idea is, that the occasion was one on which *such* a psalm or song would be peculiarly appropriate; an occasion on which great *lessons* or *truths* had been taught by the dealings of God, which it became his people now to set forth in a becoming manner. Those lessons or truths pertained to the fact that God is the great King over all the earth, or that he is a sovereign among the nations:—a truth of immense importance to mankind, and a truth which the occasion on which the psalm was composed was peculiarly adapted to bring to view.

8. *God reigneth over the heathen.* Over the *nations;* not over the "heathen" in the sense in which that term is understood now. It does not mean that God reigns, or that he has set up his throne over the people that have not the true religion, but that he is exalted over the *nations* of the earth as such; or, that he has universal dominion. See Notes on Ps. xlvi. 10. ¶ *God sitteth upon the throne of his holiness.* Upon his holy throne. The idea is, that his government is established in holiness or justice.

9. *The princes of the people are gathered together.* The marginal reading is, *The voluntary of the people are gathered unto the people of the God of Abraham.* The word rendered *princes*—נָדִיב, *nadhib*—means properly, voluntary, ready, prompt; then, generous, liberal; then, those of noble birth, princes, nobles. It is evidently used here in this latter sense. The word *people* here may mean either the people of Israel, or the people of other lands; but in this place it seems evidently to denote the latter. The words "are gathered together" may refer either to a voluntary or an involuntary assembling; meaning either that they came in chains as prisoners of war, subdued by the arms of the people of God, and thus rendering an involuntary tribute to their power and their religion; or that they came in a voluntary manner, and submitted themselves, acknowledging the God of Israel to be the true God. It seems to me that the connexion requires that we should understand this in the former sense, as referring to the subjugation of the enemies of the people of God, and to their being led along as captives, assembled thus from distant parts of the world as proof that the God of Israel reigned. ¶ Even *the people of the God of Abraham.* The word *even* is not in the original. The meaning is, "*to* the people of the God of Abraham;" that is, they come and mingle with the people of the God of Abraham; or, they come as captives in war *to* that people, and confess in this manner that their God is the true God. The image is that of the assemblage of great numbers of foreign princes and nobles as furnishing either a voluntary or involuntary acknowledgment of the fact that the God of Abraham was the true God, and that the people of Israel were his people. ¶ *For the shields of the earth belong unto God.* Are of right his. This would seem to have been suggested by the marching in triumph of subdued and vanquished princes and

long unto God: he is greatly exalted.

warriors, their shields or weapons of war being borne along in the procession, demonstrating that Jehovah was King among the nations. It was seen in such a march that all those weapons of war *belonged* to him, or that he had a right to dispose of them, and to use them as he pleased. ¶ *He is greatly exalted.* That is, one who can thus subdue nations, and lead along captive princes and warriors, *must* be a Being greatly exalted; a Being that has dominion over the nations of the earth. This completes the imagery in the psalm, and gives occasion for the shouts and the joys of triumph. God had shown that he was a great King over the earth. Princes and armies were subdued to his will. They were led along as captives, and were gathered together to the people of God, as if to acknowledge their own inferiority; and in this solemn manner the nations thus subdued owned Jehovah to be the true God. In a higher sense this will be true when all the earth shall be subdued by the power of truth, and when kings, and princes, and people everywhere shall come and acknowledge God, reigning through the Messiah, to be the King of all nations. Comp. Isa. lx.

PSALM XLVIII.

The title of the psalm is, "A song *and* psalm for the sons of Korah." The *two* appellations, *song* and *psalm*, would seem to imply that it was intended to *combine* what was implied in both these words; that is, that it embraced what was usually understood by the word *psalm*, and that it was intended also specifically to be *sung*. Comp. Notes on the titles to Ps. iii., xviii., xxx. In Ps. xxx the two are combined as they are here. On the phrase "For the sons of Korah," see Notes on the title to Ps. xlii.

The *occasion* on which the psalm was composed cannot be ascertained. Prof. Alexander and some others suppose that it was composed on the same occasion, or with reference to the same event, as the previous psalm,—the overthrow of the enemies of Judah, under Jehoshaphat, 2 Chron. xx. Others, as De Wette, suppose that it was on occasion of the overthrow of the army of Sennacherib, 2 Kings xix. 35. The circumstances of the case best agree with the former of these suppositions, though it is not possible to ascertain this with absolute precision.

The contents of the psalm are as follows:—

I. An ascription of praise to God, especially as dwelling in a city which was, for its beauty and strength, an appropriate dwelling-place of such a God, vers. 1-3. The psalmist *begins* with a statement that God is worthy to be praised, (ver. 1); he then, in the same verse, refers to the abode of God, the city where he dwelt, as a holy mountain; he describes the beauty of that city (ver. 2); and he then adverts to the fact that God is "known in her palaces," or that he dwells in that city as its protector. Its beauty, and its security in having God as a dweller there, are the first things to which the attention is directed.

II. A reference to the danger of the city on the occasion referred to, and the fact and the manner of its deliverance, vers. 4-7. The psalmist represents the "kings" as assembling with a view to take it, but as being awe-struck with its appearance and as hastening away in consternation,—driven away as the ships of Tarshish are broken with an east wind.

III. The psalmist sees in these events a confirmation of what had been before affirmed of Jerusalem, that it would stand for ever, or that God would be its protector, vers. 8-10. There were on this subject ancient records, the truth of which the present event confirmed (ver. 8), and the psalmist says (ver. 9) that those records were now called to remembrance, and (ver. 10) that the effect would be that the name of God would be made known to the ends of the earth.

IV. A call on Jerusalem to rejoice, and a call on all persons to walk around and see the matchless beauty and strength of the city thus favoured by God, vers. 11-14. Its towers, its bulwarks, its palaces, were all such as to show its strength; the certainty of its permanence was such that one generation should proclaim it to another. God's interposition had been such as to furnish proof that he would be their God for

PSALM XLVIII.

A Song *and* Psalm [1] for the sons of Korah.

GREAT *is* the LORD, and greatly to be praised in [k] the city of our God, *in* the mountain of his holiness.

2 Beautiful [l] for situation, the joy of the whole earth, *is* mount Zion, *on* the sides of the [m] north, the city [n] of the great King.

[1] Or, *of*.

k Ps. lxv. 1. *l* Ps. l. 2; Lam. ii. 15. *m* Isa. xiv. 13. *n* Matt. v. 35.

ever and ever, and that even unto death he would be the guide of those that trusted in Him.

1. *Great* is *the* LORD. That is, he is high and exalted; he is a Being of great power and glory. He is not weak and feeble, like the idols worshipped by other nations. He is able to defend his people; he has shown his great power in overthrowing the mighty forces that were gathered together against the city where he dwells. ¶ *And greatly to be praised.* Worthy to be praised. In his own nature, he is worthy of adoration; in interposing to save the city from its foes, he has shown that he is worthy of exalted praise. ¶ *In the city of our God.* Jerusalem. In the city which he has chosen for his abode, and where his worship is celebrated. See Notes on Ps. xlvi. 4. This praise was peculiarly appropriate there, (*a*) because it was a place set apart *for* his worship; (*b*) because he had now interposed to save it from threatened ruin. ¶ In *the mountain of his holiness.* His holy mountain;—either Mount Zion, if the psalm was composed before the building of the temple,—or more probably here Mount Moriah, on which the temple was reared. The names Zion, and Mount Zion, however, were sometimes given to the entire city. Comp. Notes on Isa. ii. 2, 3.

2. *Beautiful for situation.* The word rendered *situation*—נוֹף, *noph*—means properly *elevation, height,* (Ges. *Lex.*); and the idea here is, that the mountain referred to is *beautiful for elevation;* that is, it rises gracefully. The allusion here is to Jerusalem as it would appear to one approaching it, and especially as it appeared to the "kings" (ver. 4) who came to invest it, and who were so impressed with its marvellous beauty and strength, that they were afraid to attack it, and turned away (ver. 5). ¶ *The joy of the whole earth.* Either the whole *land* of Palestine, or the whole world. Most probably the former is the meaning; and the idea is that, as a place of beauty and strength, and as a place where the worship of God was celebrated, and where the people of the land were accustomed to assemble, it was a source of national joy. ¶ Is *Mount Zion.* The term here used would seem to denote the whole city, Jerusalem, as it often does. Mount Zion was the most conspicuous object in the city, the residence of the king, and for a long time, until the temple was built, the place where the ark reposed, and where the worship of God was celebrated, and hence the term came to be used to denote the whole city. ¶ On *the sides of the north.* That is, probably, the houses, the palaces, on the north sides of the Mount Zion. These were eminently beautiful; they struck one in approaching the city from that quarter, as impressive and grand. The natural and usual approach to the city was from the north, or the north-west. On the west was the valley of Gihon, on the south the valley of Hinnom; and on the east the valley of Jehoshaphat and of the brook Kidron; and it was only as the city was approached from the north that there would be a complete view of it; or, that was the only quarter from which it could be assailed. The "kings," therefore (ver. 8), may be supposed to have approached it from that quarter; and thus approaching it, they would have a clear and impressive view of its beauty, and of the sources of its strength,—of the walls,

3 God is known in her palaces
for a refuge.
4 For, lo, the kings [o] were
assembled, they passed by together.
5 They saw *it, and* so they

o Ps. lxviii. 12.

towers, and bulwarks which defended it, and of the magnificence of the buildings on Mount Zion. Dr. Thomson (Land and the Book, vol. ii., p. 476), says of the situation of Mount Zion, "What is there or was there about Zion to justify the high eulogium of David: 'Beautiful for situation, the joy of the whole earth, is Mount Zion, on the sides of the north, the city of the great King?' The situation is indeed eminently adapted to be the platform of a magnificent citadel. Rising high above the deep valley of Gihon and Hinnom on the west and south, and the scarcely less deep one of the Cheesemongers on the east, it could only be assailed from the north-west; and then 'on the sides of the north' it was magnificently beautiful, and fortified by walls, towers, and bulwarks, the wonder and terror of the nations: 'For the kings were assembled; they passed by together. They saw it, and so they marvelled; they were troubled, and hasted away.' At the thought of it the royal psalmist again bursts forth in triumph: 'Walk about Zion, and go round about her; tell the towers thereof; mark ye well her bulwarks; consider her palaces, that ye may tell it to the generation following.' Alas! her towers have long since fallen to the ground, her bulwarks have been overthrown, her palaces have crumbled to dust, and we who now walk about Zion can tell no other story than this to the generation following." It was actually on the northern side of Mount Zion that most of the edifices of the city were erected. (Reland, Pales., p. 847.) ¶ *The city of the great King.* That is, of God; the place where he has taken up his abode. Comp. Notes on Ps. xlvi. 4.

3. *God is known in her palaces.* The word rendered *palaces* here means properly a fortress, castle, or palace, so called from its height, from a verb, אָרַם, *aram*, meaning to elevate, to lift up. It may be applied to any fortified place, and would be particularly applicable to a royal residence, as a castle or stronghold. The word *known* here means that it was well understood, or that the point had been fully tested and determined that God had chosen those abodes as his peculiar residence—as the place where he might be found. ¶ *For a refuge.* See Notes on Ps. xlvi. 1. That is, there was safety or security in the God who had chosen Jerusalem as his peculiar abode.

4. *For, lo, the kings were assembled.* There is evidently allusion here to some fact that had occurred; some gathering together of kings and their armies, with a view to besiege or attack Jerusalem. The kings referred to, if the allusion here is, as is supposed, to the time of Jehoshaphat, were the kings of Ammon and of Moab, and of Mount Seir, and perhaps others, not particularly mentioned, who came up against Jehoshaphat, 2 Chron. xx. 1, 10. ¶ *They passed by together.* That is, they were smitten with consternation; they were so impressed with the beauty, the majesty, the strength of the city, that they passed along without venturing to attack it. Or, perhaps, the meaning may be, that they were discomfited and overthrown as suddenly *as if* the mere sight of the city had filled their minds with dread, and had made them desist from their intended assault. Comp. 2 Chron. xx. 22—25.

5. *They saw* it. That is, they looked on it; they contemplated it; they were struck with its beauty and strength, and fled. ¶ And *so they marvelled.* It surpassed their expectations of its strength, and they saw with wonder that any attempt to conquer it was hopeless. ¶ *They were*

marvelled; they were troubled *and* hasted away.
6 Fear *p* took hold upon them there, *and* pain, as of a woman in travail.
7 Thou breakest the ships *q* of Tarshish with an east wind.

p Ps. xiv. 5. *q* Ezek. xxvii. 25.

troubled. They were filled with anxiety and confusion. They even began to have apprehensions about their own safety. They saw that their preparations had been made in vain, and that all hopes of success must be abandoned. ¶ And *hasted away.* They fled in confusion. The idea in the whole verse is that of a *panic,* leading to a disorderly flight. This *may* have occurred in the time of Jehoshaphat (2 Chron. xx.), when the kings of Moab, Edom, and others, came up to attack Jerusalem, though the immediate cause of their overthrow was a conflict among themselves (2 Chron. xx. 22–25). It may have been, however, that they approached the city, and were dismayed by its strength, so that they turned away before the internal conflict occurred which ended in their ruin. But it is not *necessary* to adjust these accounts one to another, or even to suppose that this was the event referred to in the psalm, though the general ideas in it accord well with all which occurred on that occasion.

6. *Fear took hold upon them there.* Trembling seized them; they were filled with sudden consternation. That is, as soon as they saw the city, or had a distinct view of it, they became alarmed. ¶ And *pain.* Distress; anguish. The distress arising from disappointed hopes, and perhaps from the apprehension of their own safety. They were filled with dismay. ¶ *As of a woman in travail.* This comparison is often used in the Scriptures to denote the severest kind of pain. Comp. Jer. iv. 31; vi. 24; xiii. 21; xxii. 23; xxx. 6; xlix. 24; Mic. iv. 9, 10; Isa. liii. 11.

7. *Thou breakest the ships of Tarshish.* On the ships of Tarshish, see notes on Isa. ii. 16. The allusion to these ships here may have been to illustrate the power of God; the ease with which he destroys that which man has made. The ships so strong—the ships made to navigate distant seas, and to encounter waves and storms—are broken to pieces with infinite ease when God causes the wind to sweep over the ocean. With so much ease God overthrows the most mighty armies, and scatters them. His power in the one case is strikingly illustrated by the other. It is not necessary, therefore, to suppose that there was any actual occurrence of this kind particularly in the eye of the psalmist; but it is an interesting fact that such a disaster did befall the navy of Jehoshaphat himself, 1 Kings xxii. 48: "Jehoshaphat made *ships of Tarshish* to go to Ophir for gold; but they went not: *for the ships were broken* at Ezion-geber." Comp. 2 Chron. xx. 36, 37. This coincidence would seem to render it not improbable that the discomfiture of the enemies of Jehoshaphat *was* particularly referred to in this psalm, and that the overthrow of his enemies when Jerusalem was threatened called to remembrance an important event in his own history, when the power of God was illustrated in a manner not less unexpected and remarkable. If this was the allusion, may not the reference to the "breaking of the ships of Tarshish" have been *designed* to show to Jehoshaphat, and to the dwellers in Zion, that they should not be proud and self-confident, by reminding them of the ease with which God had scattered and broken their own mighty navy, and by showing them that what he had done to their enemies he could do to them also, notwithstanding the strength of their city, and that their *real* defence was not in walls and bulwarks reared by human hand, any more than it could be in the natural strength of their position only, but in God.

8 As we have heard, so have we seen in the city of the LORD of hosts, in the city of our God; God will establish [r] it for ever. Selah.

9 We have thought of thy loving-kindness, O God, in the midst of thy temple.

10 According to thy name, [s] O God, so *is* thy praise unto the ends of the earth; thy right hand is full of righteousness.

r Isa. ii. 2.

s Jos. vii. 9; Ps. cxiii. 3.

8. *As we have heard, so have we seen.* That is, What has been told us, or handed down by tradition, in regard to the strength and safety of the city—what our fathers have told us respecting its sacredness and its being under the protection of God—we have found to be true. It *has* been shown that God is its protector; that he dwells in the midst of it; that it is safe from the assaults of man; that it is permanent and abiding. All that had ever been said of the city in this respect had been found, in this trial when the kings assembled against it, to be true. ¶ *In the city of the* LORD *of hosts.* The city where the Lord of hosts has taken up his abode, or which he has chosen for his dwelling-place on earth. See Notes on Isa. i. 24; Ps. xxiv. 10. ¶ *In the city of our God.* Of Him who has shown himself to be our God; the God of our nation. ¶ *God will establish it for ever.* That is, this had been told them; this is what they had heard from their fathers; this they now saw to be verified in the Divine interposition in the time of danger. They had seen that these combined armies could not take the city; that God had mercifully interposed to scatter their forces; and they inferred that it could be taken by no human power, and that God intended that it should be permanent and abiding. What is here said of Jerusalem is true in a sense more strict and absolute of the Church—that nothing can prevail against it, but that it will endure to the end of the world. See Notes on Matt. xvi. 18.

9. *We have thought of thy loving-kindness, O God.* We have reflected on, or meditated on. The word used here literally means *to compare, to liken;* and this idea is perhaps always implied when it is used in the sense of thinking on, or meditating on. Perhaps the meaning here is, that they had *compared* in their own minds what they had heard from their fathers with what they had now seen; they had called all these things up to their remembrance, and had compared the one with the other. ¶ *In the midst of thy temple.* See Notes on Ps. v. 7. The allusion here most probably is to the *temple,* properly so called, as these transactions are supposed to have occurred after the building of the temple by Solomon. The expression here also would make it probable that the psalm was composed after the defeat and overthrow of the armies referred to, in order that it might be used in the temple in celebrating the deliverance.

10. *According to thy name, O God, so* is *thy praise.* That is, as far as thy name is known, it will be praised; or, the effect of knowing it will be to inspire praise. A just view of thy character and doings will lead men to praise thee as far as thy name is known. This seems to have been said in view of what had occurred. Events so remarkable, and so fitted to show that God was a just, a powerful, and a merciful Being, would claim universal praise and adoration. ¶ *Unto the ends of the earth.* In every part of the world. The earth is frequently represented in the Scriptures as an extended plain, having ends, corners, or limits. See Notes on Isa. xi. 12; Rev. vii. 1. ¶ *Thy right hand is full of righteousness.* The right hand is the instrument by which we accomplish anything. The idea here is, that in what God had done it seemed as if his hand—the instrument by

11 Let mount Zion rejoice, let the daughters of Judah be glad, because of thy judgments.

12 Walk about Zion, and go round about her: tell the towers thereof.

13 [1] Mark ye well her bulwarks, [2] consider her palaces; that ye may tell *it* to the generation following.

[1] *Set your heart to.*

[2] Or, *raise up.*

---

which this had been accomplished—had been *filled* with justice. All that had been manifested had been righteousness, and that had been in abundance.

11. *Let mount Zion rejoice.* Let Jerusalem, the holy city, rejoice or be glad. Mount Zion is evidently used here to designate the city; and the idea is, that the city of God—the holy city—had occasion for joy and gladness in view of the manifestation of the Divine favour. ¶ *Let the daughters of Judah be glad.* The phrase "daughters of Judah" *may* denote the smaller *cities* in the tribe of Judah, that surrounded Jerusalem as the "mother" city—in accordance with an usage quite common in the Hebrew Scriptures. See Notes on Isa. i. 8. Perhaps, however, the more obvious interpretation is the correct one, as meaning that the women of Judah had special occasion to rejoice on account of their deliverance from so great danger, and from the horrors which usually attended the siege or the conquest of the city—the atrocities which commonly befall the female sex when a city is captured in war. The "daughters of Judah" are those descended from Judah, or connected with the tribe of Judah. Jerusalem was in the bounds of that tribe, and the name Judah was given to all those that remained after the removal of the ten tribes. ¶ *Because of thy judgments.* Thy righteous interposition in delivering the city and people.

12. *Walk about Zion.* This is a call on all persons to go round the city; to take a survey of it; to see how beautiful and how strong it was—how it had escaped all danger, and was uninjured by the attempt to destroy it—how capable it was of resisting an attack. The word *walk* here means simply to go around or surround. The other word used has a more direct reference to a solemn procession. ¶ *And go round about her.* The word here used—from נָקַף, *nakaph*—to fasten together, to join together, means to move round in a circle, as if persons joined together (see Notes on Job i. 5), and would refer here properly to a solemn procession moving round the city, and taking a deliberate survey of its entire circuit. ¶ *Tell the towers thereof.* That is, Take the number of the towers. See how numerous they are; how firm they remain; what a defence and protection they constitute. Cities, surrounded by walls, had always *towers* or elevated portions as posts of observation, or as places from which missiles might be discharged with advantage on those who should attempt to scale the walls. Comp. Gen. xi. 4, 5; 2 Chron. xxvi. 9, 10; Isa. ii. 15.

13. *Mark ye well her bulwarks.* Marg. as in Heb., *Set your heart to her bulwarks.* That is, Pay close attention to them; make the investigation with care, not as one does whose heart is not in the thing, and who does it negligently. The word rendered *bulwarks*—חֵיל, *hhail*—means, properly, a host or army, and then a fortification or entrenchment, especially the *ditch* or *trench,* with the low wall or breastwork which surrounds it: 2 Sam. xx. 15; Isa. xxvi. 1. (Gesenius, *Lex.*) The LXX. translate it here δύναμις, power; the Vulgate, *virtus,* courage; Luther, *Mauern*—walls. ¶ *Consider her palaces.* The word *palaces* here refers to the royal residences; and, as these were usually fortified and guarded, the expression here is equivalent to this: "Consider the *strength* of the city; its power to

defend itself; its safety from the danger of being taken." The word rendered *consider* — פַּסְּגוּ, *passegu* —is rendered in the margin *raise up*. The word occurs nowhere else in the Bible. According to Gesenius (*Lex.*), it means to *divide up*; that is, to walk through and survey them; or, to consider them accurately, or in detail, one by one. The Vulgate renders it *distribute*; the LXX., *take a distinct view of* (*Thompson*); Luther, *lift up*. The idea is, *examine attentively* or *carefully*. ¶ *That ye may tell* it *to the generation following*. That you may be able to give a correct account of it to the next age. The *object* of this is to inspire the next generation with a belief that God is the protector of the city; that it is so strong that it cannot be vanquished; that there is safety in such a city as that. As applied to the church now, or at any time, it means that we are to take such views of its being a true church of God; of its being fixed on firm foundations; of its being so able to resist all the assaults of Satan, and of its being so directly under the Divine protection, that it has nothing to fear. It will and must stand to all coming time, a place of absolute safety to all who seek protection and safety within it. The following remarks of Dr. Thomson (Land and the Book, vol. ii., 474, 475), with the above cut, may furnish an illustration of what the ancient defences in the city may have been, and especially of the word *towers* in this passage in the Psalms:—"The only castle of any particular importance is that at

TOWER OF DAVID.

14 For this God *is* our God for ever and ever; he will be our guide [t] *even* unto death.

t Ps. lxxiii. 24; Isa. lviii. 11.

---

the Jaffa Gate, commonly called the Tower of David. The lower part of it is built of huge stones, roughly cut, and with a deep *bevel* round the edges. They are undoubtedly ancient, but the interspersed patch-work proves that they are not in their original positions. I have been within it, and carefully explored all parts of it that are now accessible, but found nothing which could cast any light upon its history. It is believed by many to be the Hippicus of Josephus, and to this idea it owes its chief importance, for the historian makes that the point of departure in laying down the line of the ancient walls of Jerusalem. Volumes have been written in our day for and against the correctness of this identification, and the contest is still undecided; but, interesting as may be the result, we may safely leave it with those who are now conducting the controversy, and turn to matters more in unison with our particular inquiries. Everything that can be said about this grand old tower will be found in the voluminous works of Williams, Robinson, Schultz, Wilson, Fergusson, and other able writers on the topography of the Holy City."

14. *For this God* is *our God for ever and ever.* The God who has thus made his abode in the city, and who has manifested himself as its protector. It is our comfort to reflect that such a God is *our* God; that he has manifested himself as our friend; that we may habitually feel that he is our own. And he is not only our God now, but he will be such for ever and ever. A feeling that the true God is *our* God,—that he is ours and that we are his,—always carries with it the idea that this is to be *for ever;* that what is true now in this respect, will be true to all eternity. He is not a God for the present only, but for all time to come; not merely for this world, but for that unending duration which awaits us beyond the tomb. ¶ *He will be our guide* even *unto death.* The LXX. and the Vulgate render this "he will rule or govern (ποιμανεῖ—*reget*) for ever." The more correct rendering, however, is that in our version, which is a literal translation of the Hebrew. Some have translated it *upon* death, עַל־מוּת; others, *beyond* death; but the true idea is that he will be our guide, or will conduct us all along through life; that he will never forsake us until the close has come; that he will accompany us faithfully to the end. The thought does not, of course, *exclude* the idea that he will be our guide—our protector—our friend—*beyond* death; but it is simply that as long as we live on the earth, we may have the assurance that he will lead and guide us. This he will do in behalf of those who put their trust in him (*a*) by the counsels of His word; (*b*) by the influences of His Spirit; (*c*) by His providential interpositions; (*d*) by special help in special trials; (*e*) by shedding light upon our path when in perplexity and doubt; and (*f*) by support and direction when we tread that dark and to us unknown way which conducts to the grave. Man needs nothing more for this life than the confident assurance that he has the Eternal God for his guide, and that he will never be left or forsaken by Him in any possible situation in which he may be placed. If God, by His own hand, will conduct me through this world, and lead me safely through the dark valley—that valley which lies at the end of every traveller's path—I have nothing to fear beyond.

PSALM XLIX.

The *title* to this psalm is the same essentially as the title to Ps. xlii., xliv., xlv., xlvi., xlvii. On the meaning of the terms occurring in the title, see Notes on the title to Ps. xlii.

PSALM XLIX.

To the chief Musician. A Psalm [1] for the sons of Korah.

HEAR this, all *ye* people; give ear, all *ye* inhabitants of the world.

[1] Or, *of*.

The *author* of the psalm is unknown. There is no evidence that it was composed by David; and, in fact, the presumption is that he was not the author, as his name is not prefixed to it.

It is, of course, impossible to ascertain the *occasion* on which it was composed. It would seem from the psalm itself (see Notes on ver. 5) that it was written in view of some evil or wrong which the author was suffering from rich oppressors, and that he sought consolation in his trials from the reflections which he makes in the psalm,—to wit, from the fact that wealth constitutes no security,—that it gives no permanence to the projects of its owners—and that it really possesses no *power* in carrying out the plans of those who abuse it to purposes of oppression and wrong. The wealthy man, no matter how great his possessions may be, cannot redeem a brother from the grave; he cannot save himself from the tomb; he cannot make his possessions permanent in his family; he cannot take his riches with him when he dies. There is really, therefore, nothing to *fear* from the man of wealth, for whatever such a man can do must be temporary. The higher interests of the soul cannot be affected permanently by anything so uncertain and transitory as riches. It is not improbable that this train of thought was suggested by an actual occurrence in the life of the psalmist, whoever he was; but the reflections are of universal importance in regard to riches considered as a means of power, and to their real value as it respects the great interests of man.

The contents of the psalm are as follows:—

I. An introduction, calling attention to the general subject as worthy of the consideration of all classes of persons, both low and high; as conveying lessons of wisdom; and as being the result of much reflection, vers. 1-4.

II. The main subject in the psalm, or the point to be illustrated; to wit, *that the righteous have no reason to be afraid when rich oppressors compass them around; or when the rich oppress and wrong them*, ver. 5.

III. Reasons for this; or, reasons why those who are possessed of wealth, and who glory in the self-importance derived from wealth, should not be feared, vers. 6-20.

(1) No one can by his riches save another—not even his own brother—from the grave, for all (whatever may be their condition) must die, and leave their wealth to others, vers. 6-10.

(2) They cannot, by any wisdom or skill make their possessions *permanent*, or *secure*, vers. 11, 12.

(3) They will not learn wisdom on this subject from the experience of the past, but the coming generation is as foolish as the one that went before, ver. 13.

(4) All must go down to the grave, however rich they may be, ver. 14.

(5) There is a better hope for the righteous, and though he goes down to the grave, he will live hereafter, ver. 15.

(6) The rich can carry none of their wealth with them when they go to the grave. All must be left behind, and pass into the hands of others, vers. 16-20. The conclusion from the whole, therefore, is, that we should not be "afraid" when one is made rich—when the glory of his house is increased; for the possession of wealth by another, though an enemy, gives him no such permanent power as to make him an object of dread. In our real, our highest interests, we must be safe, whatever the rich oppressor may do.

1. *Hear this, all* ye *people.* That is, What I am about to utter is worthy of universal attention; it pertains equally to all mankind. The psalmist therefore calls on all the *nations* to attend to what he is about to say. Comp. Notes on Isa. i. 2. ¶ *Give ear.* Incline your ear; attend. Comp. Notes on Ps. xvii. 6. See also Isa. xxxvii. 17; lv. 3; Dan. ix. 18; Prov. ii. 2. ¶ *All* ye *inhabitants of the world.* The truth to be declared does not pertain exclusively to any one nation, or any one class of men. All are interested in it. The term here rendered *world*—חֶלֶד, *hheled*—means properly *dura-*

2 Both low and high, rich and poor, together.
3 My mouth shall speak of wisdom; and the meditation of my heart *shall be* of understanding.
4 I will incline mine ear to a

---

tion of life, lifetime; then, *life, time, age;* and then it comes to denote the world, considered as made up of the living, or the passing generations.

2. *Both low and high.* Those alike of humble and those of exalted rank, for it pertains equally to all. On the meaning of the *terms* employed here, see Notes on Isa. ii. 9. These truths pertained to the "low;" that is, to those of humble rank, as teaching them not to envy the rich, and not to fear their power; and they pertained to those of exalted rank, as teaching them not to trust in their riches, and not to suppose that they could permanently possess and enjoy them. ¶ *Rich and poor together.* As equally interested in these truths; that is, What the psalmist was about to say was adapted to impart useful lessons to both classes. Both needed instruction on the subject; and the same class of truths was adapted to furnish that instruction. The class of truths referred to was derived from the powerlessness of wealth in regard to the things of most importance to man, and from the fact that all which a man can gain must soon be left:—teaching those of one class that they should not set their heart on wealth, and should not pride themselves on possessing it, and teaching the other class that they should not envy or fear the possessor of riches.

3. *My mouth shall speak of wisdom.* That is, I will utter sentiments that are wise, or that are of importance to all; sentiments that will enable all to take a just view of the subject on which I speak. This indicates *confidence* in what he was about to utter, as being eminently deserving of attention. ¶ *And the meditation of my heart* shall be *of understanding.* What I reflect on, and what I give utterance to, in the matter under consideration. The idea is, that he had meditated on the subject, as to what was real wisdom in the matter, and that he would now give utterance to the result of his meditations. It was not wisdom in general, or intelligence or understanding as such, on which he designed to express the results of his thoughts, but it was only in respect to the proper value to be attached to wealth, and as to the fact of its causing fear (ver. 5) in those who were not possessed of it, and who might be subjected to the oppressive acts of those who were rich.

4. *I will incline mine ear to a parable.* The phrase "I will incline mine ear" means that he would listen or attend to,—as we incline our ear towards those whom we are anxious to hear, or in the direction from which a sound seems to come. Comp. Ps. v. 1; xvii. 1; xxxix. 12; Isa. i. 2. On the word rendered *parable* here —מָשָׁל, *mashal*—see Notes on Isa. xiv. 4. Comp. Notes on Job xiii. 12; xxvii. 1. The word properly means similitude; then, a sentence, sententious saying, apophthegm; then, a proverb; then, a song or poem. There is usually found in the word some idea of *comparison,* and hence usually something that is to be illustrated *by* a comparison or a story. The reference here would seem to be to some dark or obscure subject which needed to be illustrated; which it was not easy to understand; which had given the writer, as well as others, perplexity and difficulty. He proposed now, with a view to understand and explain it, to place his ear, as it were, *close to the matter,* that he might clearly comprehend it. The matter was difficult, but he felt assured he could explain it,—as when one unfolds the meaning of an enigma. The *problem*—the "parable"—the

parable; I will open my dark saying upon the harp.

5 Wherefore [u] should I fear in the days of evil, *when* the iniquity of my heels shall compass [v] me about?

u Rom. viii. 33, 34.

v Ps. cxviii. 11.

difficult point—related to the right use, or the proper value, of wealth, or the estimate in which it should be held by those who possessed it, and by those who did not. It was very evident to the author of the psalm that the views of men were not right on the subject; he therefore proposed to examine the matter carefully, and to state the exact truth. ¶ *I will open.* I will explain; I will communicate the result of my careful inquiries. ¶ *My dark saying.* The word here used—חִידָה, *Hhidāh*—is rendered *dark speeches* in Num. xii. 8; *riddle*, in Judges xiv. 12, 13, &c., to 19; Ezek. xvii. 2; *hard questions* in 1 Kings x. 1; 2 Chron. ix. 1; *dark* saying (as here) in Ps. lxxviii. 2; Prov. i. 6; *dark sentences*, in Dan. viii. 23; and *proverb* in Hab. ii. 6. It does not elsewhere occur. It means properly *something entangled, intricate;* then, a trick or stratagem; then an intricate speech, a riddle; then, a sententious saying, a maxim; then a parable, a poem, a song, a proverb. The idea here is, that the point was intricate or obscure; it was not well understood, and he purposed *to lay it open*, and to make it plain. ¶ *Upon the harp.* On the meaning of the word here used, see Notes on Isa. v. 12. The idea here is, that he would accompany the explanation with music, or would so express it that it might be accompanied with music; that is, he would give it a poetic form—a form such that the sentiment might be used in public worship, and might be impressed upon the mind by all the force and power which music would impart. Sentiments of purity and truth, and sentiments of pollution and falsehood also, are always most deeply imbedded in the minds of men, and are made most enduring and effective, when they are connected with music. Thus the sentiments of patriotism are perpetuated and impressed in song; and thus sentiments of sensuality and pollution owe much of their permanence and power to the fact that they are expressed in corrupt verse, and that they are perpetuated in exquisite poetry, and are accompanied with song. Scenes of revelry, as well as acts of devotion, are kept up by song. Religion proposes to take advantage of this principle in our nature by connecting the sentiments of piety with the sweetness of verse, and by impressing and perpetuating those sentiments through associating them with all that is tender, pure, and inspiriting in music. Hence music, both vocal and that which is produced by instruments, has always been found to be an invaluable auxiliary in securing the proper impression of truth on the minds of men, as well as in giving utterance to the sentiments of piety in devotion.

5. *Wherefore should I fear in the days of evil.* This verse is designed evidently to state the main subject of the psalm; the result of the reflections of the author on what had been to him a source of perplexity; on what had seemed to him to be a dark problem. He *had* evidently felt that there was occasion to dread the power of wicked rich men; but he now felt that he had no ground for that fear and alarm. He saw that their power was short-lived; that all the ability to injure, arising from their station and wealth, must soon cease; that his own highest interests could not be affected by anything which they could do. The "days of evil" here spoken of are the times which are referred to in the following phrase, "when the iniquity of my heels," etc. ¶ When *the iniquity of my heels shall compass me about.* It would be difficult to make any sense out of this expression,

6 They that trust in their wealth, and boast themselves in the multitude of their riches;

7 None *of them* can by any means redeem his brother, [w] nor give to God a ransom for him;

w Job xxxvi. 18.

though it is substantially the same rendering which is found in the Vulgate and the Septuagint. Luther renders it "when the iniquity of my oppressors encompasses me." The Chaldee Paraphrase renders it, "why should I fear in the days of evil, unless it be when the guilt of my sin compasses me about?" The Syriac renders it, "the iniquity *of my enemies.*" The Arabic, "when my enemies surround me." De Wette renders it as Luther does. Rosenmüller, "when the iniquity of those who lay snares against me shall compass me around." Prof. Alexander, "when the iniquity of my oppressors (or supplanters) shall surround me." The word rendered *heels* here—עָקֵב, *âkaib*—means properly *heel*, Gen. iii. 15; Job xviii. 9; Judges v. 22; then, the rear of an army, Josh. viii. 13; then, in the plural, *footsteps*, prints of the heel or foot, Ps. lxxvii. 19; and then, according to Gesenius (*Lex.*) *a lier in wait, insidiator*. Perhaps there is in the word the idea of craft; of lying in wait; of taking the advantage—from the verb עָקַב, *akab*, to be behind, to come from behind; and hence to supplant; to circumvent. So in Hos. xii. 3, "in the womb he held his brother by the heel" (comp. Gen. xxv. 26). Hence the word is used as meaning to supplant; to circumvent, Gen. xxvii. 36; Jer. ix. 4 (Heb., ver. 3.) This is, undoubtedly, the meaning here. The true idea is, when I am exposed to the crafts, the cunning, the tricks, of those who lie in wait for me; I am liable to be attacked suddenly, or to be taken unawares; but what have I to fear? The psalmist refers to the evil conduct of his enemies, as having given him alarm. They were rich and powerful. They endeavoured in some way to supplant him—perhaps, as we should say, to "trip him up"—to overcome him by art, by power, by trick, or by fraud. He *had been* afraid of these powerful foes; but on a calm review of the whole matter, he came to the conclusion that he had really no cause for fear. The reasons for this he proceeds to state in the following part of the psalm.

6. *They that trust in their wealth.* The first reason why there was no cause of alarm is drawn (vers. 6—10) from the *powerlessness* of wealth, as illustrated by the fact that it can do nothing to save life or to prevent death. He refers to those who possess it as *trusting* in their wealth, or *relying on* that as the source of their power. ¶ *And boast themselves*; pride themselves; or feel conscious of safety and strength because they are rich. It is the *power* which wealth is supposed to confer, that is alluded to here. ¶ *In the multitude of their riches.* The abundance of their wealth.

7. *None* of them *can by any means redeem his brother.* None of those who are rich. This verse might be literally rendered, "a brother cannot by redeeming redeem; a man cannot give to God his own ransom." The passage, therefore, may mean either, as in our version, that no one, however rich, can redeem a brother—his own brother—by his wealth; or, that a brother—one who sustains the relation of a brother—cannot rescue another from death. On the word *redeem*, see Notes on Ps. xxv. 22; Isa. xliii. 3. It means here that he could not rescue him, or save him from the grave; he could not by his wealth preserve him in life. The whole expression is emphatic: "redeeming he cannot redeem;" that is—according to Hebrew usage—he cannot *possibly* do it; it *cannot* be done. There is here no particular reference to the *means* to be employed,

8 (For the redemption of their soul *is* precious, and [x] it ceaseth for ever);

[x] Zeph. i. 18.

but only an emphatic statement of the fact that *it cannot by any possibility be done.* The object is to show how powerless and valueless is wealth in regard to the things that most pertain to a man's welfare. It can do literally *nothing* in that which most deeply affects man, and in which he most needs help. There is no allusion here to the redemption of the soul, or to the great work of redemption, as that term is commonly understood; but it *is* true, in the highest sense, that if wealth cannot "redeem" life, or keep our best and nearest friend from the grave, much less can it avail in that which is so much more important, and so much more difficult, the redemption of the soul from eternal ruin. Here, also, as in the matter of saving from the grave, it is absolutely true that wealth can do *nothing*—literally, *nothing*—in saving the soul of its possessor, or in enabling its possessor to save his best friend. Nothing but the blood of the cross can avail then; and the wealth of the richest can do no more here than the poverty of the poorest. ¶ *Nor give to God a ransom for him.* This would be more literally rendered, "a man cannot give to God his ransom;" that is, he cannot, though in the possession of the most ample wealth, give to God that which would purchase his own release from the grave. On the word *ransom,* see as above, the Notes on Isa. xliii. 3. Comp. Matt. xvi. 26.

8. *For the redemption of their soul is precious.* The word *soul* here means *life,* and not the immortal part. The only question which the psalmist here considers is the value of wealth in preserving *life,* or in saving man from the grave. The phrase, "*their* soul," refers doubtless to the man and his brother, as alluded to in the previous verse. The idea is, that neither can the man of wealth ransom his own life from the grave, nor the life of his brother. Wealth can save neither of them. The word "precious" means *costly, valuable.* The word is applied (1 Kings x. 2, 10, 11) to gems, and then to the costlier kinds of stones employed in building, as marble and hewn-stones, 2 Chron. iii. 6. Comp. Notes on Ps. xxxvi. 7. The idea here is, that the rescue of the life, or the saving from the grave, would be too *costly;* it would be beyond the power of all wealth to purchase it; no amount of silver or gold, or raiment, or precious stones, could constitute a sufficient *price* to secure it. ¶ *And it ceaseth for ever.* That is, Wealth for ever comes short of the power necessary to accomplish this. It has always been insufficient; it always *will* be. There is no hope that it *ever* will be sufficient; that by any increase in the amount,—or by any change in the conditions of the bargain,—property or riches can avail for this. The whole matter is perfectly *hopeless* as to the power of wealth in saving one human being from the grave. It must always *fail* in saving a man from death. The word rendered *ceaseth*—חָדַל, *hhadal*—means *to leave off, to desist, to fail,* Gen. xi. 8; Ex. ix. 34; Isa. ii. 22. As there is no allusion here to the redemption of the *soul*—the immortal part—this passage affirms nothing in regard to the fact that the work of redemption by the Saviour is completed or finished, and that an atonement cannot be made again, which is true; nor to the fact that when salvation through that atonement is rejected, all hope of redemption is at an end, which is also true. But though there is, originally, no such reference here, the *language* is such as is *adapted* to express that idea. In a much higher and more important sense than any which pertains to the power of wealth in saving from the grave, it is true that the work of the atonement ceased for ever when the Redeemer expired on the cross, and

9 That he should still live for ever, *and* not see corruption.

10 For [y] he seeth *that* wise men die, likewise the fool and the brutish person perish, and leave their wealth to others.

11 Their inward thought *is, that* their houses *shall continue* for ever, *and* their dwelling-

y Ecc. ii. 16—21.

that all hope of salvation ceases for ever when the atonement is rejected, and when man refuses to be saved by his blood; nothing then can save the soul. No other sacrifice will be made, and when a man has finally rejected the Saviour, it may be said in the highest sense of the term, that the redemption of the soul is too costly to be effected by any other means, and that all hope of its salvation *has ceased* FOR EVER.

9. *That he should still live for ever.* That his brother whom he could not redeem—or that he himself—should not die, ver. 8. The idea is, that the price of life is so great that no wealth can rescue it so that a man shall not die. ¶ And *not see corruption.* Should not return to dust, or moulder away in the grave. See Notes on Ps. xvi. 10.

10. *For he seeth* that *wise men die.* He must see this; he does see it. He perceives that no one can be saved from death. It comes on all alike—the wise and the unwise. Nothing saves from it. The allusion is here especially to the *rich,* whether *they* are wise or whether they are fools and "brutish." The simple fact, as stated, is that no matter what may be the character of the man of wealth, whether wise or foolish, he must certainly die. His wealth cannot save him from the grave. The possessor of wealth himself *sees* this. It cannot be concealed from him. ¶ *Likewise the fool.* The rich man who is a fool, or who is destitute of wisdom. He who is rich and who is wise—wise in the things of this life and wise unto salvation—(or who is gifted with a high degree of intelligence and who evinces wisdom in respect to the higher matters of existence)—and the rich man who is a fool—(who is regardless of his highest interests, and who evinces no special intelligence, though possessed of wealth),—all, all die alike. ¶ *And the brutish person.* The rich man who is stupid and dull; who lives like a brute; who lives to eat and drink; who lives for gross sensuality—*he* dies as well as he who is wise. Wealth cannot in either case save from death. Whether connected with wisdom or folly—whether carefully husbanded or lavishly spent—whether a man employs it in the highest and noblest manner in which it can be devoted, or in the indulgence of the most low and debasing enjoyments—it is alike powerless in saving men from the grave. ¶ *And leave their wealth to others.* It all passes into other hands. It *must* be so left. It cannot be carried away by its possessor when he goes into the eternal world. It not only cannot save him from the grave, but he cannot even take it with him. All his houses, his lands, his title-deeds, his silver, his gold, his parks, gardens, horses, hounds—all that he had accumulated with so much care, and worshipped with so idolatrous an affection, is not even his own in the sense that he can take it with him. The title passes absolutely into other hands, and even if he could come back to earth again, he could no longer claim it, for when he dies it ceases to be his for ever. How powerless, then, is wealth in reference to the great purposes of human existence!

11. *Their inward thought* is. Their secret expectation and feeling is that they have secured permanency for their wealth in their own families, though they themselves may pass away. The essential thought in this verse is, that the rich men referred to in the foregoing verses imagine that their possessions will be perpetuated in their own families. The word ren-

places to [1] all generations: they call *their* lands [z] after their own names.

[1] *generation and generation.*
z 2 Sam. xviii. 18.

12 Nevertheless, man *being* in honour abideth [a] not: he is like the beasts *that* perish.
13 This their way *is* their

a Ps. xxxix. 5.

dered *inward thought*—קֶרֶב, *kereb*—means properly *the midst, the middle, inner part;* and hence it comes to mean the heart, or the mind, as the seat of thought and affection: Ps. v. 9; lxiv. 6. It means here, their hope, their calculation, their secret expectation; and the whole verse is designed to show the value or importance which they attach to wealth as being, in their apprehension, fitted to build up their families for ever. ¶ That *their houses* shall continue *for ever.* Either the dwellings which they rear, or—more probably—their families. ¶ And *their dwelling-places to all generations.* Marg., as in Heb., *to generation and generation.* That is, for ever. They expect that their possessions will always remain in the family, and be transmitted from one generation to another. ¶ *They call* their *lands after their own names.* They give their own names to the farms or grounds which they own, in the hope that, though they must themselves pass away, their *names* may be handed down to future times. This practice, which is not uncommon in the world, shows how intense is the desire of men not to be forgotten; and at the same time illustrates the main thought in the psalm—the importance attached to wealth by its possessor, as if it could carry his *name* down to future times, when he shall have passed away. In this respect, too, wealth is commonly as powerless as it is in saving its possessor from the grave. It is not very far into future times that mere wealth can carry the name of a man after he is dead. Lands and tenements pass into other hands, and the future owner soon ceases to have any concern about the *name* of the former occupier, and the world cares nothing about it. A man must have some other claim to be remembered than the mere fact of his having been rich, or he will be soon forgotten. Comp. Notes on Isa. xxii. 15—19.

12. *Nevertheless, man* being *in honour abideth not.* No matter to what rank he may rise, no matter how much wealth he may accumulate, no matter how fixed and secure he may seem to make his possessions, he cannot make them permanent and enduring. He must pass away and leave all this to others. The word rendered *abideth* — יָלִין, *yalin* — means properly to pass the night; to remain over night; to lodge, as one does for a night; and the idea is, that he is not to lodge or remain permanently in that condition; or, more strictly, he will not lodge there even for a night; that is, he will soon pass away. It is possible that the Saviour had his eye on this passage in the parable of the rich fool, and especially in the declaration, "This night thy soul shall be required of thee," Luke xii. 20. ¶ *He is like the beasts* that *perish.* He is like the beasts; they perish. This does not mean that in all respects he is like them, but only in this respect, that he must die as they do; that he cannot by his wealth make himself immortal. He must pass away just as if he were an animal of the inferior creation, and had no power of accumulating wealth, or of laying plans that stretch into the future. The squirrel and the beaver—animals that *lay up* something, or that, like men, have the power of *accumulating*, die just like other animals. So the rich *man.* His intelligence, his high hopes, his far-reaching schemes, make no difference between him and his fellow-men and the brute in regard to death. They all die alike.

13. *This their way* is *their folly.* This might be rendered, "This is

folly: yet their posterity [1] approve their sayings. Selah.

14 Like sheep they are laid in the grave; death shall feed on them; and the upright shall have dominion [b] over them in the

[1] *delight in their mouth.*

[b] Dan. vii. 22; Rev. ii. 26, 27.

---

their way or course of life. It is their folly;" or, such is their folly. On the word *way*, see Notes on Ps. i. 6. The idea is, that it is folly for a man to cherish these hopes; to feel that wealth is of so much importance; to imagine that it can deliver from the grave; to suppose that he can perpetuate his own name, and secure his possessions in his own family upon the earth. And yet the world is still full of men as foolish as were those in the time of the psalmist; men who will not be admonished by the suggestions of reason, or by the experience of six thousand years in the past. This is one thing in which the world makes no progress—in which it learns nothing from the experience of the past; and as the beaver under the influence of instinct builds his house and his home now in the same way that the first beaver did his, and as the brutes all act in the same manner from generation to generation, accumulating no knowledge, and making no advances from the experience of the past, so it is with men in their desire to grow rich. On other points the world accumulates knowledge, and profits from experience, garnering up the lessons taught by past experiment and observation, and thus becoming wiser in all other respects; but in regard to the desire of wealth, it makes no progress, gains no knowledge, derives no advantage, from the generations of fools that have lived and died in past ages. They now engage in the pursuit of gold with the same zeal, and the same expectation and hope which were evinced in the first ages of the world, and *as if* their own superior skill and wisdom could set at nought all the lessons taught by the past. ¶ *Yet their posterity.* The coming generation is as confident and as foolish as the one that went before. ¶ *Approve their sayings.* Margin, *delight in their mouth.* That is, they delight or take pleasure in what proceeds from their mouth; in what they say; in their views of things. They adopt *their* principles, and act on *their* maxims; and, attaching the same importance to wealth which *they* did, seek as *they* sought to perpetuate their names upon the earth.

14. *Like sheep they are laid in the grave.* The allusion here is to a flock as *driven* forward by the shepherd; and the meaning is that they are driven forward to the grave, as it were, in flocks, or as a flock of sheep is driven by a shepherd. The word rendered "are laid"—שַׁתּוּ, *shattu*—is not probably derived from the verb שׁוּת, *shuth*, or שִׁית, *shith*, as our translators seem to have supposed, but from שָׁתַת, *shathath*, to set, or place; and the meaning is, "Like sheep they put them in Sheol, or the grave;" that is, they thrust or drive them down thither. In other words, this is *done*, without intimating by whom it is done. They are urged forward; they are driven towards the tomb as a flock of sheep is driven forward to the slaughter. Some influence or power is pressing them in masses down to the grave. The word rendered *grave* is *Sheol.* It is sometimes used in the sense of the grave, and sometimes as referring to the abode of departed spirits. See Notes on Job x. 21, 22; Ps. vi. 5. It seems here to be used in the former sense. ¶ *Death shall feed on them.* The word rendered *feed* here—רָעָה, *raah*—means properly to feed a flock; to pasture; then, to perform the office of a shepherd. The idea here is not, as in our translation, "death shall feed *on* them;" but, death shall rule over them as the shepherd rules his flock. The

morning: and their [1] beauty shall consume [2] in the grave from their dwelling.

[1] Or, *strength.*

[2] Or, *the grave* being *an habitation to every one of them.*

allusion to the *flock* suggested this. They are driven down to the grave, or to Sheol. The shepherd, the ruler, he who does this, is *death;* and the idea is not that death is a hungry monster, devouring them *in* the grave, but that the shepherd over *that* flock, instead of being a kind and gentle friend and protector (as the word "shepherd" naturally suggests), is *death*—a fearful and grim Ruler of the departed. The idea, therefore, is not that of *feeding,* specifically, but it is that of ruling, controlling, guiding. So the Septuagint, *θάνατος ποιμανεῖ αὐτούς.* The Vulgate, however, renders it, *mors depascet eos;* and Luther, *der Tod naget sie;* death gnaws or feeds on them. ¶ *And the upright.* The just; the righteous. The meaning of this part of the verse undoubtedly is, that the just or pious would have some kind of ascendancy or superiority over them at the period here referred to as the "morning." ¶ *Shall have dominion over them.* Or rather, as De Wette renders it, shall *triumph* over them. That is, will be exalted over them; or shall have a more favoured lot. Though depressed now, and though crushed by the rich, yet they will soon have a more exalted rank, and a higher honour than those who, though once rich, are laid in the grave under the dominion of death. ¶ *In the morning.* That is, very soon; to-morrow; when the morning dawns after the darkness of the present. See Notes on Ps. xxx. 5. There is a time coming—a brighter time—when the relative condition of the two classes shall be changed, and when the upright—the pious—though poor and oppressed now, shall be exalted to higher honours than *they* will be. There is no certain evidence that this refers to the "morning" of the resurrection; but it is language which well expresses the idea when connected with that doctrine, and which can be best explained on the supposition that that doctrine was referred to, and that the hope of such a resurrection was cherished by the writer. Indeed, when we remember that the psalmist expressly refers to the "*grave*" in regard to the rich, it is difficult to explain the language on any other supposition than that he refers here to the resurrection—certainly not as well as on this supposition—and especially when it is remembered that death makes no distinction in cutting down men, whether they are righteous or wicked. Both are laid in the grave alike, and *any* prospect of distinction or triumph in the case must be derived from scenes beyond the grave. This verse, therefore, may belong to that class of passages in the Old Testament which are founded on the belief of the resurrection of the dead without always expressly affirming it, and which are best explained on the supposition that the writers of the Old Testament were acquainted with that doctrine, and drew their hopes as well as their illustrations from it. Comp. Dan. xii. 2; Isa. xxvi. 19; Ps. xvi. 9, 10. ¶ *And their beauty.* Marg., *strength.* The Hebrew word means *form, shape, image;* and the idea here is, that their form or figure will be changed, or disappear, to wit, by consuming away. The idea of *beauty,* or *strength,* is not necessarily in the passage, but the meaning is, that the form or figure which was so familiar among men will be dissolved, and disappear in the grave. ¶ *Shall consume in the grave.* Heb., *in Sheol.* The word probably means here *the grave.* The original word rendered *consume,* means literally to make old; to wear out; to waste away. The entire form of the *man* will disappear. ¶ *From their dwelling.* Marg., *the grave being a habitation to every one of them.* LXX., "and their help shall grow old in the grave from their glory." So the Latin Vulgate. The whole expression

15 But God will redeem my soul from the [1]power of [2]the grave; for he shall receive me. Selah.

16 Be not thou afraid when one is made rich, when the glory of his house is increased;

[1] *hand.* [2] Or, *hell.*

is obscure. The most probable meaning is, "they shall consume in the grave, *from its being a dwelling to him;*" that is, to each of them. Sheol, or the grave, becomes a dwelling to the rich man, and *in* that gloomy abode—that which is now his dwelling—he consumes away. It appertains to that dwelling, or it is one of the conditions of residing there, that all consume away and disappear. Others render it, "so that there is no dwelling or habitation for them." Others, and this is the more common interpretation, "their form passes away, the underworld is their habitation." See De Wette *in loc.* This last rendering requires a slight change in the punctuation of the original. DeWette, Note, p. 339. The *general* idea in the passage is plain, that the possessors of wealth are soon to find their home in the grave, and that their forms, with all on which they valued themselves, are soon to disappear.

15. *But God will redeem my soul from the power of the grave.* Literally, *from the hand of Sheol;* that is, from the dominion of death. The hand is an emblem of power, and it here means that death or Sheol holds the dominion over all those who are in the grave. The control is absolute and unlimited. The grave or Sheol is here personified as if reigning there, or setting up an empire there. Comp. Notes on Isa. xiv. 9. On the word *redeem*, see the references in the Notes on ver. 7. ¶ *For he shall receive me.* Literally, *he shall take me.* That is, either, He will take me *from* the grave; or, He will take me *to* himself. The general idea is, that God would take hold of him, and save him from the dominion of the grave; from that power which death exercises over the dead. This would either mean that he would be preserved from going down to the grave and returning to corruption there; or, that he would hereafter be rescued from the power of the grave in a sense which would not apply in respect to the rich man. The former evidently cannot be the idea, since the psalmist could not hope to escape death; yet there might be a hope that the dominion of death would not be permanent and enduring, or that there would be a future life, a resurrection from the grave. It seems to me, therefore, that this passage, like the expression in ver. 14, "in the morning," and the passages referred to in the Notes on that verse, is founded on the belief that death is not the end of a good man, but that he will rise again, and live in a higher and better state. It was this consideration which gave such comfort to the psalmist in contemplating the whole subject; and the idea, thus illustrated, is substantially the same as that stated by the Saviour in Matt. x. 28, "Fear not them which kill the body, but are not able to kill the soul."

16. *Be not thou afraid when one is made rich.* Do not dread the power derived from wealth; do not fear anything which a man can do merely because he is rich. The original is, "when *a man* becomes rich." The allusion is not necessarily to a bad man, though that is implied in the whole passage, since there is no reason for fearing a *good* man, whether he is rich or poor. The only thing that seems to have been apprehended in the mind of the psalmist was that power of doing injury to others, or of employing means to injure others, which wealth confers on a bad man. The psalmist here changes the form of the expression, no longer referring to himself, and to his own feelings, as in the former part of the psalm, but making an application of the whole

17 For when he dieth, he shall carry nothing [c] away; his glory shall not descend after him.

c Luke xii. 20. 1 in his life.

18 Though, [1] while he lived, he blessed his soul: (and *men* will praise thee when thou doest well to thyself:)

course of thought to others, showing them, as the result of his own reflection and observation, that no man had any real cause for dread and alarm when riches increased in the hands of the wicked. The reasons why this power should not be feared are stated in the following verses. ¶ *When the glory of his house is increased.* Rich men often lavish much of their wealth on their dwellings;—on the dwelling itself; on the furniture; on the grounds and appendages of their habitation. This is evidently referred to here as "the *glory* of their house;" as that which would be adapted to make an impression of the power and rank of its possessor.

17. *For when he dieth.* He must die. His wealth cannot save him from the grave. It is always to be *assumed* of rich men, as of all other men, that they *will* have to die. The point is not one which is to be argued; not one about which there can be any doubt. Of all men, whatever else may be said of them, it may always be affirmed that they must *die,* and important inferences may be always drawn from that fact. ¶ *He shall carry nothing away.* It is not improbable that the apostle Paul had this passage in his eye in what he says in 1 Tim. vi. 7, "For we brought nothing into this world, and it is certain that we can carry nothing out." See Notes on that passage. Comp. Job xxvii. 16–19. ¶ *His glory shall not descend after him.* His wealth, and those things which have been procured by wealth, as indicating station and rank, cannot accompany him to the other world. This is said to show that he is not to be "feared" on account of his wealth. The argument is, that whatever there is in wealth that *seems* to give power, and to afford the means of doing injury, must soon be separated from him. In respect to wealth, and to all the power derived from wealth, he will be like the most poor and penniless of mortals. All that he possesses will pass into other hands, and whether for good or for evil, it will no longer be in his power to use it. As this *must* occur soon,—as it *may* occur in a moment,—there is no reason to "fear" such a man, or to suppose that he can do permanent injury by any power derived from wealth. Comp. Notes on Isa. xiv. 6, 7, 10, 11.

18. *Though while he lived.* Marg., as in Heb., *in his life.* More literally, *in his lives.* The idea is, as long as he lived. ¶ *He blessed his soul.* That is, he blessed himself; he congratulated himself; he regarded his condition as desirable and enviable. He "took airs" upon himself; he felt that his was a happy lot; he expected and demanded respect and honour from others on account of his wealth. He commended himself as having evinced sagacity in the means by which he acquired wealth—thus imparting honour to himself; and he congratulated himself on the result, as placing him in a condition above want, and in a condition that entitled him to honour. A striking illustration of this feeling is found in the parable of the rich fool, Luke xii. 19, "And I will say to my soul, Soul, thou hast much goods laid up for many years; take thine ease, eat, drink, and be merry." ¶ *And* men *will praise thee.* Others will praise thee. He not only blessed or commended himself, but he might expect that others would praise and congratulate him also. They would regard him as a happy man;—happy, because he had been thus successful; happy, because he had accumulated that which was the object of so universal desire among men. Success,

19 [1] He shall go to the generation of his fathers; they shall never see light.

[1] The soul *shall go*.

20 Man *that is* in honour, and understandeth not, is like the beasts [d] *that* perish.

d Eccles. iii. 18, 19.

though founded on that which is entitled to no praise, and which is even the result of unprincipled conduct, often secures the temporary praise of men, while a want of success, though connected with the strictest, sternest virtue, is often followed by neglect, or is even regarded as proof that he who fails has no claim to honour. ¶ *When thou doest well to thyself.* Well, in reference to success in life, or in the sense that thou art prospered. Your industry, your sagacity, your prosperity will be the theme of commendation. To a certain extent, where this does not lead to self-flattery and pride, it is proper and right. The virtues which ordinarily contribute to prosperity *are* worthy of commendation, and should be held up to the example of the young. But what is evil and wrong in the matter here referred to is that the man's commendation of himself, and the commendation by others, all tends to foster a spirit of pride and self-confidence; to make the soul easy and satisfied with the condition; to produce the feeling that all is gained which needs to be gained; to make the possessor of wealth arrogant and haughty; and to lead him to neglect the higher interests of the soul.

19. *He shall go to the generation of his fathers.* To be gathered to one's own people, or to his fathers, is a common expression in the Old Testament in speaking of death. See Gen. xxv. 8, 17; xxxv. 29; xlix. 29, 33; Numb. xx. 24, 26; xxvii. 13; xxxi. 2; Deut. xxxii. 50; Judges ii. 10. It means that they were united again with those who had gone before them, in the regions of the dead. Death had indeed separated them, but by death they were again united. ¶ *They shall never see light.* He and the "generation" to which he has gone to be united, would no more see the light of this world; no more walk among the living: Job xxxiii. 30. Comp. Notes on Isa. xxxviii. 11; Ps. xxvii. 13. The meaning is, that the rich sinner will die as others have done before him, leaving all his earthly possessions, and will no more be permitted to revisit the world where his forsaken possessions are, and will not even be permitted to *look* on what before had been to him such a source of self-confidence, self-gratulation, and pride.

20. *Man* that is *in honour.* Man that is in possession of wealth, or that occupies an exalted rank. See Notes on ver. 12. ¶ *And understandeth not.* That is, who has no proper appreciation of what it is to be a man; of what is his true rank *as* a man; of his relations to God; of his condition as an immortal being,—man that values himself only on the fact that he is rich; that lives for this world alone; that regards it as a sufficient distinction that he *is* rich; that degrades his nobler nature in the mere enjoyment of the pleasures of sense,—is like the beasts,—is in no way elevated above them. ¶ *Is like the beasts* that *perish.* They live only for this life. They have no higher nature than that which pertains to the senses, and they live accordingly. The man who, though of exalted rank, lives for this life alone, herein resembles them. See Notes on ver. 12. Alas! what multitudes there are who thus live,—whose only aim is to secure the wealth and the honours of this life,—who have no more thought of a future state, and who form no more plans in regard to a future world, than do the brutes! For many there are in exalted stations, who are surrounded by all that wealth can give, yet who no more admit the thought of a future world into their hopes and plans than if

they had no other endowment than the camel or the ox, and whose conduct in this respect would not be changed if all the higher endowments which constitute the nature of *man* were withdrawn, and they were at once reduced to the condition of a brute. While, therefore, the main purpose of this psalm is to show that wealth confers no *power* which is to be dreaded,—that its possessor, though wicked, cannot permanently injure us, since he must soon pass away by death,—the course of thought at the same time teaches us that we should not *desire* wealth as our portion; that we should not live for this, as the main object of life. The possessor of the most ample fortune must soon be laid in the grave. All that he has acquired will pass into other hands, and will be his no more. But he *has* a higher nature. He *may* live in a manner different from the brute that perishes. He *may* act with reference to a higher—an eternal—state of existence; and, when he dies, he *may* leave his earthly inheritance, whether great or small, only to enter on an inheritance that shall be permanent and eternal. "What shall it profit a man, if he shall gain the whole world, and lose his own soul?" Mark viii. 36.

PSALM L.

This psalm purports to be a "psalm of Asaph." This is the first of the psalms ascribed to him. Twelve in all are attributed to him, viz., Ps. l., and lxxiii.-lxxxiii. Asaph was a Levite, a son of Berachiah, 1 Chron. vi. 39; xv. 17. He was eminent as a musician, Neh. xii. 46; 1 Chron. xvi. 7, and was appointed by "the chief of the Levites," at the command of David, with two others, Heman and Ethan, to preside over a part of the sacred choral services of public worship, 1 Chron. xv. 16-19. They had charge particularly of the worship as conducted with "cymbals of brass," 1 Chron. xv. 19. The "sons of Asaph" are afterwards mentioned among the choristers of the temple (1 Chron. xxv. 1, 2; 2 Chron. xx. 14; xxix. 13; Ezra ii. 41; iii. 10; Neh. vii. 44; xi. 22); and this office appears to have been hereditary in his family, 1 Chron. xxv. 1, 2. Asaph was celebrated in after times as a prophet and a poet, 2 Chron xxix. 30; Neh. xii. 46. The title, rendered in the margin, "*for* Asaph," *may* mean either that the psalm was composed *by* Asaph himself, or that it was composed especially *for* him, by David or by some one else, and that it was committed to him to be set to music, or to be sung by that band of musicians over which he was appointed to preside. Comp. Notes on the title to Ps. xlii. The presumption is, that it was composed *by* Asaph, as this is the most natural explanation of the title, and as there is nothing in the circumstances of the case to render this improbable.

Of the *occasion* on which the psalm was composed we have no information. There is nothing in the title to indicate this, nor is there anything in the psalm itself which would connect it with any known events in the Jewish history. There are no local allusions, there are no names mentioned, there are no circumstances referred to, which enable us to determine the time of its composition.

The *object* of the psalm seems to be to set forth *the value and importance of spiritual religion as compared with a mere religion of forms.* It is one among numerous portions of the Old Testament which show that the Jewish religion *contemplated* and *required* spirituality in its worshippers, and that it was not designed to be merely formal. There was, indeed, great tendency among the Jewish people to rely on the forms of religion, and it must be admitted that there was not a little in their modes of worship which went to foster this unless there was constant vigilance on the part of the worshipper, and on the part of the public teachers of religion. At the time when this psalm was composed, it would seem that there was a general reliance on the mere ceremonies of public worship; that much of the spirituality of religion had vanished; and that under the forms of religion, and connected with a decent and even scrupulous attention to them, there was a great, if not general, prevalence, of moral corruption among the people. See vers. 16-21.

In the composition of the psalm, therefore, the author represents a scene of solemn judgment; describes God as coming with pomp, and amidst fire and

PSALM L.

A Psalm [1] of Asaph.

THE [e] mighty God, *even* the LORD, hath spoken, and called the earth from the rising of the sun unto the going down thereof.

[1] Or, *for*. [e] Isa. ix. 6.

tempests, to pronounce a sentence on man; and then, as in his presence, and as amidst these solemn scenes, shows what will be found to be true piety; what will meet with the approbation, and what will incur the disapprobation, of God.

The psalm may be regarded as composed of the following parts.

I. A solemn representation of the scenes of judgment; of God as coming to judge his professed people, assembling together those who had avowed themselves to be his friends, and who had pledged themselves to be his amidst the solemn scenes of sacrifice, vers. 1-6.

In this part of the psalm there are the following things:

(*a*) A general summons to the world, from the rising to the setting sun, ver. 1.

(*b*) The statement that the great principles on which all would be determined would proceed out of Zion, or would be such as were inculcated there in the worship of God, ver. 2.

(*c*) A description of God as coming to judgment amidst fire and tempest, ver. 3.

(*d*) A general call to the heavens and the earth, that His people might be summoned from all quarters with reference to the final sentence, vers. 4, 5.

(*e*) A statement that perfect justice would be done, which the very heavens would reveal, for that God was himself the judge, ver. 6.

II. A declaration of the great principles on which the judgment would proceed, and by which the issue would be determined. It would not be by an observance of the mere external forms of devotion, but by spiritual religion; by a sincere worship of God; by a holy life, vers. 7-23.

This portion of the psalm is divided into two parts: the *first*, showing that it is not by mere outward forms that acceptance can be found with God, but that there must be, under these forms, pure and spiritual religion, vers. 7-15; and the *second*, that the wicked cannot hope to meet with the favour of God though they do observe these forms, vers. 16-23.

First. It is not by mere external forms that acceptance can be found with God, vers. 7-15.

(*a*) A statement of the fact, and of the grounds of the fact, that God will testify against them, vers. 7, 8.

(*b*) The mere offering of sacrifices cannot be acceptable to Him. He does not *need* their sacrifices, as all the beasts of the world are His, vers. 9-13.

(*c*) Only praise—spiritual worship—humble trust in him—can be admitted as true righteousness; as that which will be acceptable to him, vers. 14, 15.

Second. The wicked cannot be accepted and approved though they do observe the forms of religion, vers. 16-23.

(*a*) Such men, though in the priestly office, cannot be regarded as appointed by God to declare his will, or to represent him on earth, vers. 16, 17.

(*b*) A description of the actual conduct of many of those who professed to be His friends; who were rigid in their observances of the external forms of religion, and who were even in the priestly office, vers. 18-21.

(*c*) As before (vers. 14, 15);—only the righteous—the spiritually minded—the upright—can in such a solemn trial meet with the approbation of God, vers. 22, 23.

This psalm, therefore, is one of the most instructive portions of the Old Testament, as setting forth the necessity of spiritual religion, and the fact that a mere observance of forms can never constitute that righteousness which will make men acceptable to God.

1. *The mighty God*, even *the* LORD. Even *Jehovah*,—for this is the original word. The Septuagint and Vulgate render this "The God of gods, the Lord." De Wette renders it, "God, God Jehovah, speaks." Prof. Alexander, "The Almighty, God,

2 Out [f] of Zion, the perfection of beauty, God hath shined.
3 Our God shall come, [g] and shall not keep silence; a [h] fire shall devour before him, and it shall be very tempestuous round about him.

[f] Ps. lxviii. 24. [g] Rev. xxii. 20. [h] Dan. vii. 10.

Jehovah, speaks;" and remarks that the word "mighty" is not an adjective agreeing with the next word (*the mighty God*), but a substantive in apposition with it. The idea is, that he who speaks is the true God; the Supreme Ruler of the universe. It is *that* God who has a right to call the world to judgment, and who has power to execute his will. ¶ *Hath spoken.* Or rather, *speaks.* That is, the psalmist represents him as now speaking, and as calling the world to judgment. ¶ *And called the earth.* Addressed all the inhabitants of the world; all dwellers on the earth. ¶ *From the rising of the sun unto the going down thereof.* From the place where the sun seems to rise, to the place where it seems to set;—that is, all the world. Comp. Notes on Isa. lix. 19. See also Mal. i. 11; Ps. cxiii. 3. The call is made to all the earth; to all the human race. The scene is imaginary as represented by the psalmist, but it is founded on a true representation of what will occur—of the universal judgment, when all nations shall be summoned to appear before the final Judge. See Matt. xxv. 32; Rev. xx. 11–14.

2. *Out of Zion.* The place where God was worshipped, and where he dwelt. Comp. Notes on Isa. ii. 3. ¶ *The perfection of beauty.* See Notes on Ps. xlviii. 2. ¶ *God hath shined.* Has shined forth, or has caused light and splendour to appear. Comp. Deut. xxxiii. 2; Ps. lxxx. 2; xciv. 1 (see *marg.*) The meaning here is, that the great principles which are to determine the destiny of mankind in the final judgment are those which proceed from Zion; or, those which are taught in the religion of Zion; they are those which are inculcated through the church of God. God has there made known his law; he has stated the principles on which he governs, and on which he will judge the world.

3. *Our God shall come.* That is, he will come to judgment. This language is derived from the supposition that God *will* judge the world, and it shows that this doctrine was understood and believed by the Hebrews. The New Testament has stated the fact that this will be done by the coming of his Son Jesus Christ to gather the nations before him, and to pronounce the final sentence on mankind: Matt. xxv. 31; Acts xvii. 31; x. 42; John v. 22. ¶ *And shall not keep silence.* That is, he will come forth and *express* his judgment on the conduct of mankind. See Notes on Ps. xxviii. 1. He *seems* now to be silent. No voice is heard. No sentence is pronounced. But this will not always be the case. The time is coming when he will manifest himself, and will no longer be silent as to the conduct and character of men, but will pronounce a sentence, fixing their destiny according to their character. ¶ *A fire shall devour before him.* Comp. Notes on 2 Thess. i. 8; Heb. x. 27. The *language* here is undoubtedly taken from the representation of God as he manifested himself at Mount Sinai. Thus, in Ex. xix. 16, 18, it is said, "And it came to pass on the third day in the morning, that there were thunders and lightnings, and a thick cloud upon the mount, and the voice of a trumpet exceeding loud; and Mount Sinai was altogether on a smoke, because the Lord descended upon it in fire: and the smoke thereof ascended as the smoke of a furnace, and the whole mount quaked greatly. ¶ *And it shall be very tempestuous round about him.* The word here used—שָׂעַר, *saar*—means properly to shudder; to shiver; and then

4 He shall call to the heavens from above, and to the earth, that he may judge his people.

5 Gather[i] my saints together unto me; those that have made a covenant[k] with me by sacrifice.

i Matt. xxiv. 31.

k Heb. xii. 24.

it is employed to denote the commotion and raging of a tempest. The allusion is doubtless to the descent on Mount Sinai (Ex. xix. 16), and to the storm accompanied by thunder and lightning which beat upon the mountain when God descended on it to give his law. The whole is designed to represent God as clothed with appropriate majesty when judgment is to be pronounced upon the world.

4. *He shall call to the heavens from above.* He will call on all the universe; he will summon all worlds. The meaning here is, not that he will gather those who are in heaven to be judged, but that he will call on the inhabitants of all worlds to be his witnesses; to bear their attestation to the justice of his sentence. See ver. 6. The phrase "from above" does not, of course, refer to the heavens as being above *God*, but to the heavens as they appear to men to be above themselves. ¶ *And to the earth.* To all the dwellers upon the earth; *to the whole universe.* He makes this universal appeal with the confident assurance that his final sentence will be approved; that the universe will see and admit that it is just. See Rev. xv. 3; xix. 1–3. There can be no doubt that the universe, as such, will approve the ultimate sentence that will be pronounced on mankind. ¶ *That he may judge his people.* That is, all these arrangements—this coming with fire and tempest, and this universal appeal—will be preparatory to the judging of his people, or in order that the judgment may be conducted with due solemnity and propriety. The idea is, that an event so momentous should be conducted in a way fitted to produce an appropriate impression; so conducted, that there would be a universal conviction of the justice and impartiality of the sentence. The reference here is particularly to his professed "*people,*" that is, to determine whether they were truly his, for that is the main subject of the psalm, though the *language* is derived from the solemnities appropriate to the universal judgment.

5. *Gather my saints together unto me.* This is an address to the messengers employed for assembling those who are to be judged. Similar language is used by the Saviour (Matt. xxiv. 31): "And he [the Son of Man] shall send his angels with a great sound of a trumpet, and they shall gather together his elect from the four winds, from one end of heaven to the other." The idea is, that God will bring them, or assemble them together. All this is language derived from the notion of a universal judgment, *as if* the scattered people of God were thus gathered together by special messengers sent out for this purpose. The word "saints" here refers to those who are truly his people. The object—the purpose—of the judgment is to assemble in heaven those who are sincerely his friends; or, as the Saviour expresses it (Matt. xxiv. 31), his "*elect.*" Yet in order to this, or in order to determine who *are* his true people, there will be a larger gathering—an assembling of all the dwellers on the earth. ¶ *Those that have made a covenant with me by sacrifice.* Ex. xxiv. 6, 7. Comp. Notes on Heb. ix. 19–22. The idea here is, that they are the professed people of God; that they have entered into a solemn covenant-relation to him, or have bound themselves in the most solemn manner to be his; that they have done this in connexion with the sacrifices which accompany their worship; that they have brought their sacrifices or bloody offerings as a pledge that they mean to be his, and will be his. Over

6 And the heavens shall declare his righteousness: for God [l] *is* judge himself. Selah.

7 Hear, [m] O my people, and I will speak; O Israel, and I will testify against thee: I *am* God, *even* thy God.

l Rev. xx. 12. *m* Micah vi. 1—8.

---

these solemn sacrifices made to him, they have bound themselves to be the Lord's; and the purpose of the judgment now is, to determine whether this was sincere, and whether they have been faithful to their vows. As applied to professed believers under the Christian system, the *idea* here presented would be, that the vow to be the Lord's has been made over the body and blood of the Redeemer once offered as a sacrifice, and that by partaking of the memorials of that sacrifice they have entered into a solemn "covenant" to be his. Nothing more solemn can be conceived than a "covenant" or pledge entered into in such a manner; and yet nothing is more painfully certain than that the process of a judgment will be necessary to determine in what cases it is genuine; for the mere outward act, no matter how solemn, does not of necessity decide the question whether he who performs it will enter into heaven.

6. *And the heavens shall declare his righteousness.* Shall make it known, or announce it. That is, the heavens—the heavenly inhabitants—will bear witness to the justness of the sentence, or will approve the sentence. See Notes on ver. 4. Comp. Ps. xcvii. 6. ¶ *For God* is *judge himself.* The judgment is not committed to mortal men, or even to angels. Creatures, even the most exalted and pure, might err in such a work as that of judging the world. That judgment, to be correct, must be founded on a perfect knowledge of the heart, and on a clear and complete understanding of all the thoughts, the motives, the words, the deeds of all men. It cannot be supposed that any created being, however exalted, could possess all this knowledge, and it cannot be supposed that any created being, however pure, could be so endowed as to be secure against error in pronouncing a judgment on the countless millions of men. But God combines all these in himself;—a perfect knowledge of all that has ever occurred on earth, and of the motives and feelings of every creature,—and, at the same time, absolute purity and impartiality; therefore his judgment must be such that the universe will see that it is just. It may be added here that as the New Testament has stated (see Notes on ver. 3) that the judgment of the world in the last day will be committed to the Lord Jesus Christ, the considerations just suggested prove that he is Divine. The immediate point in the passage before us is, that the fact that *God* will preside in the judgment, demonstrates that the acts of judgment will be *right*, and will be such as the "heavens"—the universe—will approve; such, that all worlds will proclaim them to be right. There is no higher evidence that a thing is right, and that it ought to be done, than the fact that God has done it. Comp. Gen. xviii. 25; Ps. xxxix. 9.

7. *Hear, O my people, and I will speak.* God himself is now introduced as speaking, and as stating the principles on which the judgment will proceed. The previous verses are introductory, or are designed to bring the scene of the judgment before the mind. The solemn scene now opens, and God himself speaks, especially as rebuking the disposition to rely on the mere forms of religion, while its spirituality and its power are denied. The purpose of the whole is, by asking how these things will appear in the judgment, to imply the vanity of *mere* forms of religion now. The particular address is made to the "people" of God, or to "Israel," because the purpose of the psalmist was to rebuke the prevailing tendency

8 I will not reprove thee for thy sacrifices or thy burnt-offerings, *to have been* continually before me.

9 I [n] will take no bullock out of thy house, *nor* he-goats out of thy folds:

n Acts xvii. 25; Heb. x. 4, 6.

to rely on outward forms. ¶ *O Israel, and I will testify against thee.* In the judgment. In view of those scenes, and as *at* that time, I will *now* bear this solemn testimony against the views which you entertain on the subject of religion, and the practices which prevail in your worship. ¶ *I am God, even thy God.* I am the true God, and therefore I have a right to speak; I am *thy* God—the God who has been the Protector of thy people,—acknowledged as the God of the nation,—and therefore I claim the right to declare the great principles which pertain to true worship, and which constitute true religion.

8. *I will not reprove thee for thy sacrifices or thy burnt-offerings.* On the words *sacrifices* and *burnt-offerings* here used, see Notes on Isa. i. 11. The meaning is, "I do not reprove or rebuke you in respect to the withholding of sacrifices. I do not charge you with neglecting the offering of such sacrifices. I do not accuse the nation of indifference in regard to the external rites or duties of religion. It is not on this ground that you are to be blamed or condemned; for that duty is outwardly and publicly performed. I do not say that such offerings are wrong; I do not say that there has been any failure in the external duties of worship. The charge—the reproof—relates to other matters; to the want of a proper spirit, to the withholding of the heart, in connexion with such offerings." ¶ To have been *continually before me.* The words "to have been" are inserted by the translators, and weaken the sense. The simple idea is, that their offerings *were* continually before him; that is, they were constantly made. He had no charge of neglect in this respect to bring against them. The insertion of the words "to have been" would seem to imply that though they had neglected this external rite, it was a matter of no consequence; whereas the simple meaning is, that they were *not* chargeable with this neglect, or that there was *no* cause of complaint on this point. It was on other grounds altogether that a charge was brought against them. It was, as the following verses show, because they supposed there was special *merit* in such offerings; because they supposed that they laid God under obligation by so constant and so expensive offerings, as if they did not already belong to him, or as if he needed them; and because, while they did this, they withheld the very offering which he required, and without which all other sacrifices would be vain and worthless,—a sincere, humble, thankful heart.

9. *I will take no bullock out of thy house.* Bullocks were offered regularly in the Hebrew service and sacrifice (Ex. xxix. 11, 36; Lev. iv. 4; 1 Kings xviii. 23, 33); and it is with reference to this that the language is used here. In obedience to the law it was right and proper to offer such sacrifices; and the design here is not to express disapprobation of these offerings in themselves considered. On this subject—on the external compliance with the law in this respect—God says (ver. 8) that he had no cause to complain against them. It was only with respect to the design and the spirit with which they did this, that the language in this verse and the following verses is used. The idea which it is the purpose of these verses to suggest is, that God did not *need* such offerings; that they were not to be made *as if* he needed them; and that if he needed such he was not *dependent* on them, for all the beasts of the earth and all the fowls of the mountains were his, and could be taken for that purpose; and that

10 For every beast of the forest *is* mine, *and* the cattle upon a thousand hills.

11 I know all the fowls of the mountains; and the wild beasts of the field *are*[1] mine.

12 If I were hungry, I would not tell thee: for the world *is* mine, and the fulness thereof.

13 Will I eat the flesh of bulls, or drink the blood of goats?

[1] *with me.*

if he took what was claimed to be theirs—the bullocks and the goats—he did not wrong them, for all were his, and he claimed only his own. ¶ Nor *he-goats out of thy folds.* Goats were also offered in sacrifice. Lev. iii. 12; iv. 24; x. 16: Num. xv. 27.

10. *For every beast of the forest* is *mine.* All the beasts that roam at large in the wilderness; all that are untamed and unclaimed by man. The idea is, that even if God *needed* such offerings, he was not dependent on them,—for the numberless beasts that roamed at large as his own would yield an ample supply. ¶ And *the cattle upon a thousand hills.* This may mean either the cattle that roamed by thousands on the hills, or the cattle on numberless hills. The Hebrew will bear either construction. The former is most likely to be the meaning. The allusion is probably to the animals that were pastured in great numbers on the hills, and that were claimed by men. The idea is, that all—whether wild or tame—belonged to God, and he had a right to them, to dispose of them as he pleased. He was not, therefore, in any way dependent on sacrifices. It is a beautiful and impressive thought, that the *property* in all these animals—in all living things on the earth—is in God, and that he has a right to dispose of them as he pleases. What man owns, he owns under God, and has no right to complain when God comes and asserts his superior claim to dispose of it at his pleasure. God has never given to man the absolute proprietorship in *any* thing; nor does he invade our rights when he comes and claims what we possess, or when in any way he removes what is most valuable to us. Comp. Job i. 21.

11. *I know all the fowls of the mountains.* That is, I am fully acquainted with their numbers; their nature; their habits; their residence. I have such a knowledge of them that I could appropriate them to my own use if I were in need of them. I am not, therefore, dependent on men to offer them, for I can use them as I please. ¶ *And the wild beasts of the field* are *mine.* Marg., *with me.* That is, they are before me. They are never out of my presence. At any time, therefore, I could use them as I might need them. The word rendered *wild beasts*—זִיז, *ziz*—means any moving thing; and the idea here is, whatever moves in the field, or roams abroad. Everything is his—whether on the mountains, in the forest, or in the cultivated field.

12. *If I were hungry, I would not tell thee.* I should not have occasion to apply to you; I should not be dependent on you. ¶ *For the world* is *mine.* The earth; all that has been created. ¶ *And the fulness thereof.* All that fills the world; all that exists upon it. The whole is at his disposal; to all that the earth produces he has a right. This language is used to show the absurdity of the supposition that he was in any way dependent on man, or that the offering of sacrifice could be supposed in any way to lay him under obligation.

13. *Will I eat the flesh of bulls, or drink the blood of goats?* This is said to show still further the absurdity of the views which seem to have prevailed among those who offered sacrifices. They offered them *as if* they were needed by God; *as if* they laid him under obligation; *as if* in some way they contributed to his happiness, or were essential to his welfare. The only supposition on which this could be true was, that he

14 Offer unto God thanksgiving; and pay thy vows unto the Most High.

15 And call *o* upon me in the day of trouble; I will deliver

o Ps. cvii. 6.

---

needed the flesh of the one for food, and the blood of the other for drink; or that he was sustained as creatures are. Yet this was a supposition, which, when it was stated in a formal manner, must be at once seen to be absurd; and hence the emphatic question in this verse. It may serve to illustrate this, also, to remark, that, among the heathen, the opinion did undoubtedly prevail that the gods ate and drank what was offered to them in sacrifice; whereas the truth was, that these things were consumed by the priests who attended on heathen altars, and conducted the devotions of heathen temples, and who found that it contributed much to their own support, and did much to secure the liberality of the people, to keep up the impression that what was thus offered was consumed by the gods. God appeals here to his own people in this earnest manner because it was to be presumed that *they* had higher conceptions of him than the heathen had; and that, enlightened as they were, they could not for a moment suppose these offerings necessary for him. This is one of the passages in the Old Testament which imply that God is a Spirit, and that, as such, he is to be worshipped in spirit and in truth. Comp. John iv. 24.

14. *Offer unto God thanksgiving.* The word rendered *offer* in this place —זָבַח, *zebahh* — means properly *sacrifice.* So it is rendered by the LXX., θῦσον,—and by the Vulgate, *immola.* The word is used, doubtless, with design,—to show what was the *kind* of sacrifice with which God would be pleased, and which he would approve. It was not the mere *sacrifice* of animals, as they commonly understood the term; it was not the mere presentation of the bodies and the blood of slain beasts; it was an offering which proceeded from the heart, and which was expressive of gratitude and praise. This is not to be understood as implying that God did not require or approve of the offering of bloody sacrifices, but as implying that a higher sacrifice was necessary; that these would be vain and worthless unless they were accompanied with the offerings of the heart; and that his worship, even amidst outward forms, was to be a spiritual worship. ¶ *And pay thy vows unto the Most High.* To the true God, the most exalted Being in the universe. The word *vows* here—נֶדֶר, *neder*—means properly a vow or promise; and then, a thing vowed; a votive offering, a sacrifice. The idea seems to be, that the true notion to be attached to the sacrifices which were prescribed and required was, that they were to be regarded as expressions of internal feelings and purposes; of penitence; of a deep sense of sin; of gratitude and love; and that the design of such sacrifices was not fulfilled unless the "vows" or pious purposes implied in the very nature of sacrifices and offerings were carried out in the life and conduct. They were not, therefore, to come merely with these offerings, and then feel that all the purpose of worship was accomplished. They were to carry out the true design of them by lives corresponding with the idea intended by such sacrifices—lives full of penitence, gratitude, love, obedience, submission, devotion. This only could be acceptable worship. Comp. Notes on Isa. i. 11–17. See also Ps. lxxvi. 11; Eccles. v. 5.

15. *And call upon me in the day of trouble.* This is a part of real religion as truly as praise is, ver. 14. This is also the duty and the privilege of all the true worshippers of God. To do this shows where the heart is, as really as direct acts of praise and thanksgiving. The purpose of all that is said here is to show that true

thee, and thou shalt glorify me.

16 But unto the wicked God saith, What [p] hast thou to do, to declare my statutes, or *that* thou shouldest take my covenant in thy mouth?

p Isa. i. 11—15; John iv. 24.

religion—the proper service of God—does not consist in the mere offering of sacrifice, but that it is of a spiritual nature, and that the offering of sacrifice is of no value unless it is accompanied by corresponding acts of spiritual religion, showing that the heart has a proper appreciation of the mercies of God, and that it truly confides in him. Such spirituality in religion is expressed by acts of praise (ver. 14); but it is also as clearly expressed (ver. 15) by going to God in times of trouble, and rolling the burdens of life on his arm, and seeking consolation in him. ¶ *I will deliver thee.* I will deliver thee from trouble. This will occur (*a*) either in this life, in accordance with the frequent promises of his word (comp. Notes on Ps. xlvi. 1); or (*b*) wholly in the future world, where all who love God will be completely and for ever delivered from all forms of sorrow. ¶ *And thou shalt glorify me.* That is, Thou wilt honour me, or do me honour, by thus coming to me with confidence in the day of calamity. There is no way in which we can honour God more, or show more clearly that we truly confide in him, than by going to him when everything seems to be dark; when his own ways and dealings are wholly incomprehensible to us, and committing all into his hands.

16. *But unto the wicked God saith.* This commences a second part of the subject. See the introduction. Thus far the psalm had reference to those who were merely external worshippers, or mere formalists, as showing that such could not be approved and accepted in the day of judgment; that spiritual religion—the offering of the *heart* — was necessary in order to acceptance with God. In this part of the psalm the same principles are applied to those who actually *violate* the law which they profess to receive as prescribing the rules of true religion, and which they profess to teach to others. The design of the psalm is not merely to reprove the mass of the people as mere formalists in religion, but especially to reprove the leaders and teachers of the people, who, under the form of religion, gave themselves up to a course of life wholly inconsistent with the true service of God. The address here, therefore, is to those who, while they professed to be teachers of religion, and to lead the devotions of others, gave themselves up to abandoned lives. ¶ *What hast thou to do.* What right hast thou to do this? How can men, who lead such lives, consistently and properly do this? The idea is, that they who profess to declare the law of a holy God should be themselves holy; that they who profess to teach the principles and doctrines of true religion should themselves be examples of purity and holiness. ¶ *To declare my statutes.* My laws. This evidently refers rather to the teaching of others than to the profession of their own faith. The language would be applicable to the priests under the Jewish system, who were expected not only to conduct the outward services of religion, but also to instruct the people; to explain the principles of religion; to be the guides and teachers of others. Comp. Mal. ii. 7. There is a striking resemblance between the language used in this part of the psalm (vers. 16–20) and the language of the apostle Paul in Rom. ii. 17–23; and it would seem probable that the apostle in that passage had this portion of the psalm in his eye. See Notes on that passage. ¶ *Or that thou shouldest take my covenant in thy mouth.* Either as professing faith in it, and a purpose

17 Seeing that thou [q] hatest instruction, and castest my words behind thee.

18 When thou sawest a thief, then thou consentedst with him, and [1] hast been partaker with adulterers.

19 Thou [2] givest thy mouth to evil, and thy tongue frameth deceit.

20 Thou sittest *and* speakest

q Prov. v. 12, 13.

1 *thy portion* was. 2 *sendest.*

---

to be governed by it,—or, more probably, as explaining it to others. The "*covenant*" here is equivalent to the *law* of God, or the principles of his religion; and the idea is, that he who undertakes to explain that to others, should himself be a holy man. He can have no *right* to attempt to explain it, if he is otherwise; he cannot hope to be *able* to explain it, unless he himself sees and appreciates its truth and beauty. This is as true now of the Gospel as it was of the law. A wicked man can have no right to undertake the work of the Christian ministry, nor can he be able to explain to others what he himself does not understand.

17. *Seeing thou hatest instruction.* That is, He is unwilling himself to be taught. He will not learn the true nature of religion, and yet he presumes to instruct others. Comp. Notes on Rom. ii. 21. ¶ *And castest my words behind thee.* He treated them with contempt, or as unworthy of attention. He did not regard them as worthy of being *retained*, but threw them contemptuously away.

18. *When thou sawest a thief.* When you have seen or found one who was intending to commit theft, then (instead of rebuking or exposing him) you have been willing to act with him, and to divide the profits. The words "when thou *sawest*" would seem to imply readiness and willingness to engage with them, as *at first sight*. Whenever there was an opportunity to share in the results of theft, they were ready to engage in it. The main *point* in this is, that they were willing to do so even when observing the outward duties of religion, and when professing to be the true worshippers of God. A similar sentiment occurs in Rom. ii. 21. See Notes on that passage. ¶ *Then thou consentedst with him.* Literally, Thou didst delight in him, or hadst pleasure in him. He was a man after thine own heart. Thou wast at once on good terms with him. ¶ *And hast been partaker with adulterers.* Marg., as in Heb., *thy portion was with adulterers.* This was a common vice among the Jewish people. See Notes on Rom. ii. 22. The idea here is, that they were associated in practice with adulterers; they were guilty of that crime as others were. The point of the remark here is, that they did this under the cloak of piety, and when they were scrupulous and faithful in offering sacrifices, and in performing all the external rites of religion.

19. *Thou givest thy mouth to evil.* Marg., as in Heb., *thou sendest.* That is, they gave it up to evil; they employed it in evil:—in falsehood, malice, deceit, slander, deception, detraction. ¶ *And thy tongue frameth deceit.* The word rendered *frameth* means properly to bind, to fasten; and then, to contrive, to frame. The meaning is, that it was employed in the work of deceit; that is, it was employed in devising and executing purposes of fraud and falsehood.

20. *Thou sittest* and *speakest against thy brother.* To the general character of falsehood and slander there is now added the fact that they were guilty of this in the most aggravated manner conceivable—against their nearest relations, the members of their own families. They were not only guilty of the crime against neighbours—against

against thy brother; thou slanderest thine own mother's son.

21 These *things* hast thou done, and [r] I kept silence; thou thoughtest that I was altogether *such an one* as thyself; *but* I will reprove thee, and set *them* in order before thine eyes.

r Eccles. viii. 11, 12; Rom. ii. 4; 2 Pet. iii. 9.

strangers—against persons to whom they sustained no near relationship; but against those of their own households, — those whose characters, on that account, ought to have been specially dear to them. The words "*thou sittest*" probably refer to the fact that they would do this when enjoying social intercourse with them; in confidential conversation; when words of peace, and not of slander, might be properly expected. The word "brother" *might* be used as denoting any other man, or any one of the same nation; but the phrase which is added, "thine own mother's son," shows that it is here to be taken in the strictest sense. ¶ *Thou slanderest.* Literally, *Thou givest to ruin.* Prof. Alexander renders it, *Thou wilt aim a blow.* The LXX., the Vulgate, Luther, and De Wette understand it of slander. ¶ *Thine own mother's son.* It is to be remembered that where polygamy prevailed there would be many children in the same family who had the same father, but not the same mother. The nearest relationship, therefore, was where there was the same mother as well as the same father. To speak of a brother, in the strictest sense, and as implying the nearest relationship, it would be natural to speak of one as having the same mother. The idea here is, that while professing religion, and performing its external rites with the most scrupulous care, they were guilty of the basest crimes, and showed an entire want of moral principle and of natural affection. External worship, however zealously performed, could not be acceptable in such circumstances to a holy God.

21. *These* things *hast thou done, and I kept silence.* Comp. Notes on Isa. xviii. 4. The meaning is, that while they did these things,—while they committed these abominations, —he did not interfere. He did not come forth in his anger to destroy them. He had borne all this with patience. He had borne this until it was now time that he should interpose (ver. 3), and state the true principles of his government, and warn them of the consequences of such a course of sin and hypocrisy. Comp. Notes on Acts xvii. 30. ¶ *Thou thoughtest that I was altogether* such an one *as thyself.* The idea here is, that they thought or imagined that God was just like themselves in the matter under consideration, and they acted under this impression; or, in other words, the fair interpretation of their conduct was that they thus regarded God. That is, they supposed that *God* would be satisfied with the *forms* of religion, as *they* were; that all he required was the proper offering of sacrifice, according to *their* views of the nature of religion; that he did not regard principle, justice, pure morality, sincerity, even as they themselves did not; and that he would not be strict to punish sin, or to reprove them for it, if these forms were kept up, even as *they* were not disposed to be rigid on the subject of sin. ¶ But *I will reprove thee.* I will rebuke thee alike for thy sins, and for this view of the nature of religion. ¶ *And set* them *in order.* Literally, I will *array* them; that is, I will draw them out to view in their appropriate ranks and orders, as soldiers are drawn up in martial array. They shall be so arranged and classified that they may be seen distinctly. ¶ *Before thine eyes.* So that they may be plainly seen. The meaning is, that they would have a clear and impressive view of them: they would be made to see them as

22 Now consider this, ye that [s]forget God, lest I tear *you* in pieces, and *there be* none to deliver.

s Ps. ix. 17.

23 Whoso offereth praise [t] glorifieth me: and to him that [1] ordereth *his* conversation *aright* will I show the salvation of God.

t 1 Pet. ii. 9. [1] *disposeth* his *way*.

they were. This might be done then, as it is done now, either (*a*) by their being set before their minds and hearts, so that they would see and feel the enormity of sin, to wit, by conviction for it; or (*b*) by sending such punishment on them for their sins that they might *measure* the guilt and the number of their transgressions by the penalties which would be inflicted. In some way all sinners will yet be made to see the nature and the extent of their guilt before God.

22. *Now consider this.* Understand this; give attention to this. The word *now* does not well express the force of the original. The Hebrew word is not an adverb of *time*, but a particle denoting *entreaty*, and would be better rendered by, "Oh, consider this;" or, "Consider this, I beseech you." The matter is presented to them as that which deserved their most solemn attention. ¶ *Ye that forget God.* Who really forget him though you are professedly engaged in his worship; who, amidst the forms of religion, are actually living in entire forgetfulness of the just claims and of the true character of God. ¶ *Lest I tear* you *in pieces.* Language derived from the fury of a ravenous beast tearing his victim from limb to limb. ¶ *And* there be *none to deliver.* As none can do when God rises up in his wrath to inflict vengeance. None would *venture* to interpose; none *could* rescue from his hand. There *is* a point of time in relation to all sinners when no one, not even the Redeemer — the great and merciful Mediator—will interpose to save; when the sinner will be left to be dealt with by simple, pure, unmixed and unmitigated *justice;* when mercy and kindness will have done their work in regard to them in vain; and when they will be left to the *mere desert* of their sins. At that point there is no power that can deliver them.

23. *Whoso offereth praise glorifieth me.* That is, he truly honours me; he is a true worshipper; he meets with my approbation. The word here rendered "*offereth*" is the same which is used in ver. 14, and means *he that sacrifices :*—here meaning, he that presents the sacrifice of praise. So the LXX.: "the sacrifice of praise glorifies me." So the Vulgate. The idea is, that the worship which God requires is *praise;* it is not the mere external act of homage; it is not the presentation of a bloody sacrifice; it is not the mere bending of the knee; it is not a mere outward form :—it is that which proceeds from the heart, and which shows that there is there a spirit of true thankfulness, adoration, and love. ¶ *And to him that ordereth* his *conversation* aright. Marg., as in Heb., *that disposeth his way.* Or, more literally, "To him that *prepares* or *plans* his way;"—that is, to him who is attentive to his going; who seeks to walk in the right path; who is anxious to go in the road that leads to a happier world; who is careful that all his conduct shall be in accordance with the rules which God has prescribed. ¶ *Will I show the salvation of God.* This may mean either, "I, the author of the psalm as a teacher" (comp. Ps. xxxii. 8); or, "I" as referring to God,—as a promise that *He* would instruct such an one. The latter is the probable meaning, as it is God that has been speaking in the previous verse. The "salvation of God" is the salvation of which God is the author; or, which he alone can give. The *idea* here is, that where there is a true

desire to find the way of truth and salvation, God will impart needful instruction. He will not suffer such an one to wander away and be lost. See Notes on Ps. xxv. 9.

The general ideas in the psalm, therefore, are (1) That there is to be a solemn judgment of mankind; (2) that the issues of that judgment will not be determined by the observance of the external forms of religion; (3) that God will judge men impartially for their sins, though they observe those forms of religion; and (4) that no worship of God can be acceptable which does not spring from the heart.

PSALM LI.

This psalm purports to be a psalm of David, and the contents of it accord with this supposition, and with the statement in the title in regard to the occasion on which it was composed. There would be no difficulty on the subject, and no ground for hesitation, in regard to the author and the occasion on which it was composed, if it were not for the prayer in ver. 18, "Do good in thy good pleasure unto Zion; build thou the walls of Jerusalem," which, it has been maintained by De Wette, Rosenmüller, Venema, and others, must have been written in the time of the Babylonish exile. Except this, it is admitted on all hands that the psalm in its composition accords entirely with the statement in the title, that it was composed by David. It has, in fact, been generally admitted that the psalm *was* composed by David, though it is the opinion of Rosenmüller, Venema, and Doederlein, that the last two verses were added by a later hand.

According to the title, the psalm was composed on occasion of the great fault and crime in the life of David, and as an expression of his penitence in view of his sin. On the phrase "To the chief Musician," see Notes on the title to Ps. iv. We are not to suppose that this title was prefixed to the psalm by David himself, but the use to be made of it by committing it to the "chief Musician," or to the overseer of the music in the public worship of God, shows that the psalm was considered as designed to be used in public, and was not a mere expression of the private feelings of the author. It was, doubtless, commonly understood (and was probably so intended by David himself) that it was to be used as a *public* expression of his penitence in view of his crime; and both the fact of its composition, and the manner in which it was to be used, were to be interpreted as indicating his willingness that the widest publicity should be given to his confession, and that the memory of the crime and of his penitence should be perpetuated in all ages of the world. The phrase in the title, "A *Psalm* of David," denotes that it was to be used for public worship, or as connected with praise. It was designed not merely to express his private feelings, but was intended to be employed in the solemn services of public devotion. See introd. to Ps. iii.

The phrase "when Nathan the prophet came unto him," refers to the fact recorded in 2 Sam. xii. 1-13. It means that the psalm was the *result* of the visit of Nathan to him; or that it records the feelings of the author, when the sense of his sin had been brought to his mind by the faithful message of the prophet. We may suppose that the record of his feelings was made without delay, for the psalm bears all the marks of having been composed under the deepest feeling, and not of being the result of calm reflection. On the phrase "after he had gone in to Bath-sheba," see the sad record in 2 Sam. xi. 1–5.

De Wette, however, maintains that the psalm could not have been composed by David, but that it must have been written in the time of the Babylonish exile. The only argument which he adduces in favour of this opinion is the prayer in ver. 18, "Build thou the walls of Jerusalem," which, he says, could not have been a prayer offered by David, as there was in his time nothing which would make this prayer proper. Jerusalem was not then in ruins. It had been strongly fortified by David himself, and required no particular interposition of God as if to *restore* walls that had been thrown down; whereas, in the time of the exile, such a prayer would have been eminently proper, and would be a natural petition for one who loved his country, and who, as an expression of his own penitence, was desirous of doing all he could for the cause of religion. The difficulty will be more appropriately met in the Notes on those verses. It may be observed here, however, that possibly the expression "Build thou the

PSALM LI.

To the chief Musician. A Psalm of David, when *u* Nathan the prophet came unto him, after he had gone in to *v* Bath-sheba.

HAVE mercy upon me, O God, according to thy loving-kind-

u 2 Sam. xii. 1, etc. *v* 2 Sam. xi. 2, 4.

walls of Jerusalem," *may* be used in a figurative or spiritual sense, expressive of a desire that God would bless his people; that he would interpose in their behalf; that he would be their protector and friend; that he would do for them what would be well expressed by building strong and secure walls around a city. But it may be asked, also, Is it absolutely certain that when the psalm was composed the work of enclosing the city of Jerusalem with walls had been completed? May it not have been, in fact, that at that very time David was engaged in *carrying out* his design of rendering the city impregnable by walls and towers, and that in the midst of his intense sorrow for his own sin, though so heinous and aggravated, his heart may have turned to that which was so dear to him as an object to be accomplished, and that even then, in connexion with his bitter repentance for his sin, he may have prayed that God would favour that great design? It is no evidence that our sorrow for sin is not deep and genuine, that, even in our expressions of penitence, our heart turns to Zion—to the Church—to the great work which the Church is accomplishing,—and that, though our prayers *began* with a reference to our own sin, they should *close* with a petition that God would bless his people, and fulfil the great purposes so near to the heart of piety in reference to the progress of true religion in the world. Indeed, from the very narrative in 2 Sam. (chap. vi.-xii.) it would seem probable that the work of fortifying the city of Jerusalem, contemplated by David, was not yet completed, when he committed the crime for which this psalm is the expression of penitence. It was a work of years to do this: and it is not improbable that the guilty transaction to which this psalm refers occurred in the very midst of his design for the defence and protection of the capital of his kingdom.

The psalm consists of two parts:—

I. In the first (vers. 1-12), the psalmist confesses his guilt, and prays for pardon. He begins with an earnest plea for mercy (vers. 1-2); he humbly acknowledges his offence, without any attempt to vindicate himself, or to apologise for it (vers. 3-6); he pleads with God to cleanse him, to pardon him, to create in him a new heart, and not to cast him off or to take his Holy Spirit from him (vers. 7-12).

II. In the second part (vers. 13-19) he shows how he would manifest his sense of the Divine mercy if he was forgiven:—expressing the purpose to lead a new life; to devote himself to the duties of religion; to do all in his power to repair the evils of his conduct, and especially to induce others to avoid the way of sin, warning them by his example. He says that he would teach transgressors the true ways of God, and that sinners would be converted to Him, ver. 13; that he would sing aloud the praise of God, vers. 14, 15; that he would offer to God the sacrifice of a broken heart and a contrite spirit, vers. 16, 17; and he then pleads (vers. 18, 19), that God would interpose and bless Zion, that the great work might be completed in which he had been engaged in defending the city, and in preparing a place which would be secure, where God might be worshipped, and where sacrifices and offerings might perpetually ascend on his altar.

1. *Have mercy upon me, O God.* This is the utterance of a full heart; a heart crushed and broken by the consciousness of sin. The psalmist had been made to see his great guilt; and his first act is to cry out for mercy. There is no attempt to excuse his sin, or to apologise for it; there is no effort to vindicate his conduct; there is no complaint of the righteousness of that holy law which condemned him. It was *guilt* that was before his mind; guilt only; deep and dreadful guilt. The appeal properly expresses the state of a mind that is overwhelmed at the remembrance of crime, and that comes with earnestness to God to plead for pardon. The only hope of a sinner when crushed with the consciousness of sin is the mercy of God; and the plea for that mercy will be urged in

ness; according unto the multitude of thy tender mercies [w] blot out my transgressions.

2 Wash [x] me throughly from mine iniquity, and cleanse me from my sin.

3 For I acknowledge [y] my

w Isa. xliii. 25; xliv. 22; Acts iii. 19.
x Rev. i. 5.
y Prov. xxviii. 13.

the most earnest and impassioned language that the mind can employ. ¶ *According to thy lovingkindness.* On the meaning of the word here used, see Notes on Ps. xxxvi. 7. (*a*) The *ground* of his hope was the compassion of God: (*b*) the *measure* of that hope was His boundless beneficence; or, in other words, he felt that there was need of *all* the compassion of a God. His sin was so great, his offence was so aggravated, that he could have no hope but in a Being of infinite compassion, and he felt that the need of mercy in his case could be measured and covered *only* by that infinite compassion. ¶ *According unto the multitude of thy tender mercies.* The same idea occurs here also. The psalmist fixed his eye on the *vastness* of the Divine mercy; on the numberless *acts* of that mercy toward the guilty; here he found his hope, and here alone. Every instance of extraordinary mercy which had occurred in the world furnished him now with an argument in his appeal to God;—was an encouragement to him *in* that appeal;—was a ground of hope that his appeal would not be rejected. So to us: every instance in which a great sinner has been forgiven is evidence that we may be forgiven also, and is an encouragement to us to come to God for pardon. See Notes on 1 Tim. i. 16. ¶ *Blot out my transgressions.* In allusion to an account that is kept, or a charge made, when such an account is wiped away, erased, or blotted out. Comp. Ex. xxxii. 32, 33; see Notes on Isa. xliii. 25; xliv. 22; Col. ii. 14. Never was a more earnest appeal made by a sinner than that which is made in this verse; never was there a more sincere cry for mercy. It shows us where we should *begin* in our prayers when we are pressed down with the consciousness of sin,—with a cry for *mercy*, and not an appeal to *justice*; it shows us what is to be the *ground* and the *measure* of our hope—the mere compassion of an infinitely benevolent God; it shows us the place which we must take, and the argument on which we must rely—a place among sinners, and an argument that God has been merciful to great sinners, and that therefore he may be merciful to us.

2. *Wash me throughly from mine iniquity.* Literally, "*Multiply* to wash me." The word rendered *throughly* is a verb, either in the infinitive or imperative mood, and suggests the idea of *multiplying* or *increasing.* The reference is to that which might need constant or repeated washings in order to remove a stain. The word is used, however, adverbially to denote intensity, or thoroughness. On the word *wash* as applicable to sin, see Notes on Isa. i. 16. ¶ *And cleanse me from my sin.* Remove it entirely. Make me wholly pure. See Notes on Isa. i. 16. In what manner he hoped that this would be done is shown in the following portions of the psalm. It was (*a*) by forgiveness of the past, ver. 9; and (*b*) by making the heart pure and holy through the renewing and sanctifying influences of the Holy Spirit, vers. 10, 11.

3. *For I acknowledge my transgressions.* Literally, I know, or make known. That is, he knew that he was a sinner, and he did not seek to cloak or conceal that fact. He came with the knowledge of it himself; he was willing to make acknowledgment of it before God. There was no attempt to conceal it; to excuse it. Comp. Notes on Ps. xxxii. 5. The word "*for*" does not imply that

transgressions; and my sin *is* ever before me.

4 Against [z] thee, thee only, have I sinned, and done *this* evil in thy [a] sight; that thou mightest be justified when thou speakest, *and* be clear when thou judgest.

z 2 Sam. xii. 13.

a Luke xv. 21.

he referred to his willingness to confess his sins as an act of merit, but it indicates a state of mind which was necessary to forgiveness, and without which he could not hope for pardon. ¶ *And my sin* is *ever before me.* That is, It is now constantly before my mind. It had not been so until Nathan brought it vividly to his recollection (2 Sam. xii. 1, seq.); but after that it was continually in his view. He could not turn his mind from it. The memory of his guilt followed him; it pressed upon him; it haunted him. It was no wonder that this was so. The only ground of wonder in the case is that it did not occur *before* Nathan made that solemn appeal to him, or that he could have been for a moment insensible to the greatness of his crime. The whole transaction, however, shows that men *may* be guilty of enormous sins, and have for a long time no sense of their criminality; but that *when* the consciousness of guilt is made to come home to the soul, nothing will calm it down. Everything reminds the soul of it; and nothing will drive away its recollection. In such a state the sinner has no refuge—no hope of permanent peace—but in the mercy of God.

4. *Against thee, thee only, have I sinned.* That is, the sin, considered as an offence against God, now appeared to him so enormous and so aggravated, that, for the moment, he lost sight of it considered in any other of its bearings. It *was* a sin, as all other sins are, primarily and mainly against God; it derived its chief enormity from that fact. We are not to suppose that David did not believe and notice that he had done wrong to men, or that he had offended against human laws, and against the well-being of society. His crime against Uriah and his family was of the deepest and most aggravated character, but still the offence derived its chief heinousness from the fact that it was a violation of the law of God. The state of mind here illustrated is that which occurs in every case of true penitence. It is not merely because that which has been done is a violation of human law; it is not that it brings us to poverty or disgrace; it is not that it exposes us to punishment on earth from a parent, a teacher, or civil ruler; it is not that it exposes us to punishment in the world to come:—it is that it is of itself, and apart from all other relations and consequences, *an offence against God*; a violation of his pure and holy law; a wrong done against him, and in his sight. Unless there is this feeling there can be no true penitence; and unless there is this feeling there can be no hope of pardon, for God forgives offences only as committed against himself; not as involving us in dangerous consequences, or as committed against our fellow-men. ¶ *And done* this *evil in thy sight.* Or, When thine eye was fixed on me. Comp. Notes on Isa. lxv. 3. God saw what he had done; and David knew, or might have known, that the eye of God was upon him in his wickedness. It was to him then a great aggravation of his sin that he had *dared* to commit it when he *knew* that God saw everything. The presence of a child—or even of an idiot—would restrain men from many acts of sin which they would venture to commit if alone; how much more should the fact that God is always present, and always sees all that is done, restrain us from open and from secret transgression. ¶ *That thou mightest be justified when thou speakest.* That thy character might be vindicated in

5 Behold, [b] I was shapen in iniquity; and in sin did my mother [1] conceive me.

b Eph. ii. 3. [1] *warm.*

all that thou hast said;—in the law which thou hast revealed; in the condemnation of the sin in that law; and in the punishment which thou mayest appoint. That is, he acknowledged his guilt. He did not seek to apologise for it, or to vindicate it. God was right, and he was wrong. The sin deserved all that God in his law *had* declared it to deserve; it deserved all that God by any sentence which he might pass upon him *would* declare it to deserve. The sin was so aggravated that *any* sentence which God might pronounce would not be beyond the measure of its ill-desert. ¶ And *be clear when thou judgest.* Be regarded as right, holy, pure, in the judgment which thou mayest appoint. See this more fully explained in the Notes on Rom. iii. 4.

5. *Behold, I was shapen in iniquity.* The object of this important verse is to express the deep sense which David had of his depravity. That sense was derived from the fact that this was not a sudden thought, or a mere outward act, or an offence committed under the influence of strong temptation, but that it was the result of an entire corruption of his nature,—of a deep depravity of heart, running back to the very commencement of his being. The idea is, that he could not have committed this offence unless he had been thoroughly corrupt, and always corrupt. The sin was as heinous and aggravated *as if* in his very conception and birth there had been nothing but depravity. He looked at his sin, and he looked back to his own origin, and he inferred that the one demonstrated that in the other there was no good thing, no tendency to goodness, no germ of goodness, but that there was evil, and only evil;—as when one looks at a tree, and sees that it bears sour or poisonous fruit, he infers that it is in the very nature of the tree, and that there is nothing else in the tree, from its origin, but a tendency to produce just such fruit. Of course, the idea here is not to cast reflections on the character of his mother, or to refer to her feelings in regard to his conception and birth, but the design is to express his deep sense of his own depravity; a depravity so deep as to demonstrate that it must have had its origin in the very beginning of his existence. The word rendered *I was shapen*—חוֹלָלְתִּי, *hholalti*—is from a word—חוּל, *hhool*—which means properly, *to turn around, to twist, to whirl;* and then it comes to mean *to twist oneself with pain, to writhe;* and then it is used especially with reference to the pains of childbirth. Isa. xiii. 8; xxiii. 4; xxvi. 18; lxvi. 7, 8; Mic. iv. 10. That is the meaning here. The idea is simply that he was *born* in iniquity; or that he was a sinner when he was born; or that his sin could be traced back to his very birth—as one might say that he was born with a love of music, or with a love of nature, or with a sanguine, a phlegmatic, or a melancholy temperament. There is not in the Hebrew word any idea corresponding to the word "*shapen,*" as if he had been *formed* or *moulded* in that manner by Divine power; but the entire meaning of the word is exhausted by saying that his sin could be traced back to his *very birth;* that it was so deep and aggravated, that it could be accounted for—or that he could express his sense of it—in no other way, than by saying that he was *born a sinner.* How that occurred, or how it was connected with the first apostacy in Adam, or how the fact that he was thus born could be vindicated, is not intimated, nor is it alluded to. There is no statement that the sin of another was *imputed* to him; or that he was *responsible* for the sin of Adam; or that he was guilty *on account of* Adam's sin; for on these points the

6 Behold, thou desirest truth in the inward parts; and in the hidden *part* thou shalt make me to know wisdom.

7 Purge[c] me with hyssop, and

c Lev. xiv. 4—9; Num. xix. 18; Heb. ix. 19.

---

psalmist makes no assertion. It is worthy of remark, further, that the psalmist did not endeavour to *excuse* his guilt on the ground that he was "*born*" in iniquity; nor did he allude to that fact with any purpose of *exculpating* himself. The fact that he was thus born only deepened his sense of his own guilt, or showed the enormity of the offence which was the regular result or outbreak of that early depravity. The points, therefore, which are established by this expression of the psalmist, so far as the language is designed to illustrate how human nature is conceived, are (1) that men are born with a propensity to sin; and (2) that this fact does not excuse us in sin, but rather tends to aggravate and deepen our guilt. The language goes no farther than this in regard to the question of original sin or native depravity. The Septuagint accords with this interpretation—ἰδοὺ γὰρ ἐν ανομίαις συνελήφθην. So the Vulgate: in iniquitatibus conceptus sum. ¶ *And in sin did my mother conceive me.* Marg., as in Heb., *warm me.* This language simply traces his sin back to the time when he began to exist. The previous expression traced it to *his birth;* this expression goes back to the very beginning of *life;* when there were the first indications of life. The idea is, "as soon as I began to exist I was a sinner; or, I had then a propensity to sin—a propensity, the sad proof and result of which is that enormous act of guilt which I have committed."

6. *Behold, thou desirest truth in the inward parts.* The word rendered *desirest,* means to have pleasure in; to delight in; and the idea is that this only is agreeable to God, or this only accords with his own nature. The word rendered *inward parts,* means properly the reins, and is usually employed to denote the seat of the mind, the feelings, the intellect. Comp. Notes on Job xxxviii. 36. The allusion is to the *soul;* and the idea is, that God could be satisfied with nothing *but* purity in the soul. The *connexion* is this: David was deeply conscious of his own pollution; his deep, early, native depravity. This, in his own mind, he contrasted strongly with the nature of God, and with what God must require, and be pleased with. He *felt* that God could not approve of or love such a heart as his, so vile, so polluted, so corrupt; and he felt that it was necessary that he should have a pure heart in order to meet with the favour of a God so holy. But how was that to be obtained? His mind at once adverted to the fact that it could come only from God; and hence the psalm now turns from confession to prayer. The psalmist pleads earnestly (vers. 7-10) that God *would* thus cleanse and purify his soul. ¶ *And in the hidden* part. In the secret part; the heart; the depths of the soul. The cleansing was to begin in that which was hidden from the eye of man; in the soul itself. Wisdom, heavenly, saving wisdom, was to have its seat there; the cleansing needed was not any mere outward purification, it was the purification of the soul itself. ¶ *Thou shalt make me to know wisdom.* Thou only canst enable me to understand what is truly wise. This wisdom, this cleansing, this knowledge of the way in which a guilty man can be restored to favour, can be imparted only by thee; and *thou wilt do it.* There is here, therefore, at the same time a recognition of the truth that this *must* come from God, and an act of faith, or a strong assurance that he *would* impart this.

7. *Purge me with hyssop, and I shall be clean.* On the word hyssop, see Notes on John xix. 29; Heb. ix. 19. The plant or herb was much used by the Hebrews in their sacred

I shall be clean: wash me, and I shall be [d] whiter than snow.

8 Make me to hear joy and gladness; *that* the bones *which* thou hast broken may rejoice.

9 Hide [e] thy face from my sins, and blot out all mine iniquities.

10 Create [f] in me a clean heart,

d Isa, i. 18. *e* Jer. xvi. 17. *f* Ezek. xxxvi. 26.

---

purifications and sprinklings: Exod. xii. 22; Lev. xiv. 4, 6, 49, 51; 1 Kings iv. 33. Under this name the Hebrews seem to have comprised not only the common *hyssop* of the shops, but also other aromatic plants, as mint, wild marjoram, etc.—Gesenius, *Lex.* The idea of the psalmist here evidently is not that the mere sprinkling with hyssop would make him clean; but he prays for that cleansing of which the sprinkling with hyssop was an emblem, or which was designed to be represented by that. The whole structure of the psalm implies that he was seeking an *internal* change, and that he did not depend on any mere outward ordinance or rite. The word rendered "purge" is from the word חָטָא, *hhata*—which means *to sin.* In the Piel form it means to bear the blame (or *loss*) for anything; and then to *atone for, to make atonement, to expiate:* Gen. xxxi. 39; Lev. vi. 26; Num. xix. 19. Here it conveys the notion of cleansing from sin by a sacred rite, or by that which was signified *by* a sacred rite. The idea was that the sin was to be removed or taken away, so that he might be free from it, or that *that* might be accomplished which was represented by the sprinkling with hyssop, and that the soul might be made pure. Luther has rendered it with great force — Entsündige mich mit Ysop—"Unsin me with hyssop." ¶ *Wash me.* That is, cleanse me. Sin is represented as *defiling*, and the idea of *washing* it away is often employed in the Scriptures. See Notes on Isa. i. 16. ¶ *And I shall be whiter than snow.* See Notes on Isa. i. 18. The prayer is, that he might be made *entirely* clean; that there might be no remaining pollution in his soul.

8. *Make me to hear joy and gladness.* That is, the voice of forgiveness, causing joy and rejoicing. What he wished to hear was the kind voice of God in pronouncing his pardon; not the voice of anger and condemnation. God now condemned him. The law condemned him. His own conscience condemned him. The result was anguish and sorrow. The burden was great and overpowering, —such as to crush him; to break all his "bones." He longed to hear the sweet voice of forgiveness, by which he might have peace, and by which his soul might be made to rejoice. Comp. Notes on Ps. xxxii. 1, 2. ¶ That *the bones* which *thou hast broken may rejoice.* That is, which have been crushed or broken by the weight of sin. Comp. Notes on Ps. xxxii. 3. See also Ps. vi. 2; xxii. 14; xxxi. 10; xxxviii. 3. The word "*rejoice*" means here, be free from suffering; the prayer is that the burden which had crushed him might be removed.

9. *Hide thy face from my sins.* That is, Do not look on them; avert thy face from them; do not regard them. Comp. Notes on Ps. xiii. 1. ¶ *And blot out all mine iniquities.* Take them entirely away. Let the account be erased, cancelled, destroyed. See Notes on ver. 1.

10. *Create in me a clean heart, O God.* The word rendered *create,*—בָּרָא, *bera*—is a word which is properly employed to denote an act of *creation;* that is, of causing something to exist where there was nothing before. It is the word which is used in Gen. i. 1,—"In the beginning God *created* the heaven and the earth,"—and which is commonly used to express the act of creation. It is used *here* evidently in the sense of causing that to exist which did not exist before; and there is clearly a

O God; and renew a [1]right spirit within me.

11 Cast me not away from thy presence; and take not [g] thy holy Spirit from me.

[1] Or, *constant*. *g* Luke xi. 13.

recognition of the Divine *power*, or a feeling on the part of David that this could be done by God alone. The idea is, however, not that a new *substance* might be brought into being to which the name "a clean heart" might be given, but that he might *have* a clean heart; that his heart might be made pure; that his affections and feelings might be made right; that he might have what he was conscious that he did *not* now possess,—a clean or a pure heart. This, he felt, could be produced only by the power of God; and the passage, therefore, proves that it is a doctrine of the Old Testament, as it is of the New, that the human heart is changed only by a Divine agency. ¶ *And renew a right spirit within me.* Marg., *a constant spirit.* The Hebrew word — נָכוֹן, *nachon* — means properly, that which is *erect*, or that which is made to stand up, or which is firm or established. It is used to denote (*a*) that which is upright, right, proper: Ex. viii. 26; Job xlii. 8; Ps. v. 9; (*b*) that which is right, true, sincere, Ps. lxxviii. 37; (*c*) that which is firm, constant, fixed. This would seem to be the meaning here. He prays for a heart that would be firm in the purposes of virtue; that would not yield to temptation; that would carry out holy resolutions; that would be stedfast in the service of God. The word *renew* here means to be or to make new; to produce something new. It is also used in the sense of making anew, as applied to buildings or cities in the sense of *rebuilding* or *repairing* them: Isa. lxi. 4; 2 Chron. xv. 8; xxiv. 4. The word here would naturally convey the idea that there had been formerly a right and proper spirit in him, which he prayed might now be restored. The language is that of one who had done right formerly, but who had fallen into sin, and who desired that he might be brought back into his former condition.

11. *Cast me not away from thy presence.* That is, Do not reject me, or cast me off entirely; do not abandon me; do not leave me in my sin and sorrow. The language is derived from the idea that true happiness is to be found in the *presence* of God, and that to be exiled from him is misery. Comp. Notes on Ps. xvi. 11; xxxi. 20. See also Ps. cxl. 13. ¶ *And take not thy holy Spirit from me.* It is not certain that David understood by the phrase "thy Holy Spirit" precisely what is now denoted by it as referring to the third person of the Trinity. The language, as used by him, would denote some influence coming from God producing holiness, *as if* God breathed his own spirit, or his own self, into the soul. The language, however, is appropriate to be used in the higher and more definite sense in which it is now employed, as denoting that sacred Spirit—the Holy Ghost—by whom the heart is renewed, and by whom comfort is imparted to the soul. It is not necessary to suppose that the inspired writers of the Old Testament had a full and complete comprehension of the meaning of the words which they employed, or that they appreciated all that their words might properly convey, or the fulness of signification in which they might be properly used in the times of the Gospel. Comp. Notes on 1 Pet. i. 10–12. The language here used by David—"*take not*"—implies that he had been formerly in possession of that which he now sought. There was still in his heart that which might be regarded as the work of the Spirit of God; and he earnestly prayed that *that* might not be wholly taken away on account of his sin, or that he might not be entirely abandoned to despair.

12 Restore unto me the joy of thy salvation; and uphold me *with thy* free[h] Spirit:
13 *Then*[i] will I teach transgressors thy ways; and sinners shall be converted unto thee.
14 Deliver me from [1] blood-guiltiness, O God, thou God of

h 2 Cor. iii. 17. *i* Zech. iii. 1—8. [1] *bloods.*

12. *Restore unto me the joy of thy salvation.* Literally, "Cause the joy of thy salvation to return." This implies that he had formerly known what was the happiness of being a friend of God, and of having a hope of salvation. That joy had been taken from him by his sin. He had lost his peace of mind. His soul was sad and cheerless. Sin always produces this effect. The only way to enjoy religion is to do that which is right; the only way to secure the favour of God is to obey his commands; the only way in which we can have comforting evidence that we are his children is by doing that which shall be pleasing to him: 1 John ii. 29; iii. 7, 10. The path of sin is a dark path, and in that path neither hope nor comfort can be found. ¶ *And uphold me* with thy *free spirit.* That is, Sustain me; keep me from falling. The words "*with thy*" are not in the original, and there is nothing there to indicate that by the word "spirit" the psalmist refers to the Spirit of God, though it should be observed that there is nothing *against* such a supposition. The word rendered "free"—נָדִיב *nadib*—means properly *willing, voluntary, ready, prompt;* 1 Chron. xxviii. 21; Ex. xxxv. 5. Then the word means liberal, generous, noble-minded; Isa. xxxii. 5, 8; Prov. xvii. 7, 26. It would seem here to mean "a *willing* spirit," referring to David's own mind or spirit; and the prayer is, that God would uphold or sustain him *in* a *willing* spirit or state of mind; that is, a state of mind in which he would be willing and ready to obey all the commands of God, and to serve him faithfully. What he prayed for was grace and strength that he might be kept in a state of mind which would be constant and firm (ver. 10), and a state in which he would always be found *willing* and *ready* to keep the commandments of God. It is a proper object of prayer by all that they may be always *kept* in a state of mind in which they will be *willing* to do all that God requires of them, and to bear all that may be laid on them.

13. Then *will I teach transgressors thy ways.* As an expression of gratitude, and as the result of his own painful experience. He would show them, from that experience, the evil and the bitterness of sin in itself; he would show them with what dreadful consequences sin must always be followed; he would show them the nature of true repentance; he would show them what was required in order that sin might be forgiven; he would encourage them to come to that God who had forgiven him. So the Saviour charged Peter, from his own bitter experience in having fallen under the power of temptation, to strengthen and encourage those who were struggling with the depravity of their own hearts, and who were in danger of falling: "And when thou art converted, strengthen thy brethren," Luke xxii. 32. ¶ *And sinners shall be converted unto thee.* They would see from his case the evil of transgression; they would learn from his example that mercy might be found; they would be persuaded to flee from the wrath to come. The best preparation for success in winning souls to God, and turning them from the error of their ways, is a deep personal experience of the guilt and the danger of sin, and of the great mercy of God in its forgiveness. No man can hope to be successful who has not experienced this in his own soul; no one who has, will labour wholly in vain in such a work.

14. *Deliver me from blood-guilti-*

my salvation; *and* my tongue
shall sing aloud of thy righteousness.

15 O Lord, open thou my
lips; and my mouth shall show
forth thy praise.

16 For [l] thou desirest not sacrifice, [1] else would I give *it:* thou
delightest not in burnt-offering.

k Ps. lxxi. 23, 24.

l Hos. vi. 6; Mic. vi. 7, 8; Heb. x. 4—10.
[1] Or, *that I should.*

ness, O God. Marg., as in Heb., *bloods.* So it is rendered by the Septuagint and the Latin Vulgate. Luther renders it *blood-guilt.* De Wette, *from blood.* Comp. Isa. iv. 4. The *plural* form—*bloods*—is used probably to mark *intensity,* or to denote *great* guilt. The allusion is to the guilt of shedding blood, or taking life (comp. Gen. ix. 5, 6), and the reference is undoubtedly to his guilt in causing Uriah, the husband of Bathsheba, to be slain. 2 Sam. xi. 14–17. It was this which weighed upon his conscience, and filled him with alarm. The guilt of this he prayed might be taken away, that he might have peace. The *fact* of the shedding of that blood could never be changed; the real *criminality* of that fact would always remain the same; the *crime* itself could never be declared to be innocence; his own personal *ill desert* for having caused the shedding of that blood would always remain; but the sin might be pardoned, and his soul could thus find peace. The penalty might be remitted, and, though guilty, he might be assured of the Divine favour. He could not, indeed, repair the evil to Uriah—for *he* had gone beyond the power of David for good or for evil—but he could do much to express his sense of the wrong; he could do much to save others from a similar course; he could do much to benefit society by keeping others from the like guilt. He could not, indeed, recall Uriah from the grave, and repair the evil which he had done to *him,* but he might save others from such a crime, and thus preserve many a useful life from the effects of unrestrained guilty passions. We cannot, indeed, by penitence recall those whom we have murdered; we cannot restore purity to those whom we have seduced; we cannot restore faith to the young man whom we may have made a sceptic; but we may do much to restrain others from sin, and much to benefit the world even when we have been guilty of wrongs that cannot be repaired. ¶ *Thou God of my salvation.* On whom I am dependent for salvation; who art alone the source of salvation to me. ¶ And *my tongue shall sing aloud of thy righteousness.* Comp. Notes on Ps. xxxv. 28.

15. *O Lord, open thou my lips.* That is, by taking away my guilt; by giving me evidence that my sins are forgiven; by taking this burden from me, and filling my heart with the joy of pardon. The original word is in the future tense, but the meaning is well expressed in our common translation. There was, in fact, at the same time a confident expectation that God *would* thus open his lips, and a desire that he *should* do it. ¶ *And my mouth shall show forth thy praise.* Or, I will praise thee. Praise is the natural expression of the feelings when the sense of sin is removed.

16. *For thou desirest not sacrifice,* etc. On the words rendered in this verse *sacrifice* and *burnt-offering,* see Notes on Isa. i. 11. On the main sentiment here expressed—that God did not *desire* such sacrifices—see Notes on Ps. xl. 6—8. The idea here is, that any mere external offering, however precious or costly it might be, was not what God required in such cases. He demanded the expression of deep and sincere repentance; the sacrifices of a contrite heart and of a broken spirit: ver. 17. No offering without this could be acceptable; nothing without this could secure pardon. In mere outward sacrifices,—in bloody offerings themselves, unaccompanied with the expression of

17 The sacrifices of God *are* a broken spirit: a broken [m] and a contrite heart, O God, thou wilt not despise.

18 Do good in thy good pleasure unto Zion: build thou the walls of Jerusalem.

m Isa. lxvi. 2.

genuine penitence, God could have no pleasure. This is one of the numerous passages in the Old Testament which show that the external offerings of the law were valueless unless accompanied by the religion of the heart; or that the Jewish religion, much as it abounded in forms, yet required the offerings of pure hearts in order that man might be acceptable to God. Under all dispensations the real nature of religion is the same. Comp. Notes on Heb. ix. 9, 10. The phrase "else would I give it,"—in the margin, "that I should give it,"—expresses a willingness to make such an offering, if it was required, while, at the same time, there is the implied statement that it would be valueless without the heart.

17. *The sacrifices of God.* The sacrifices which God desires and approves; the sacrifices without which no other offering would be acceptable. David felt that that which he here specified was what was demanded in his case. He had grievously sinned; and the blood of animals offered in sacrifice could not put away his sin, nor could anything remove it unless the heart were itself penitent and contrite. The same thing is true now. Though a most perfect sacrifice, every way acceptable to God, has been made for human guilt by the Redeemer, yet it is as true as it was under the old dispensation in regard to the sacrifices there required, that even that will not avail for us unless we are truly penitent; unless we come before God with a contrite and humble heart. ¶ Are *a broken spirit.* A mind broken or crushed under the weight of conscious guilt. The idea is that of a burden laid on the soul until it is crushed and subdued. ¶ *A broken and a contrite heart.* The word rendered *contrite* means to be broken or crushed, as when the bones are broken, Ps. xliv. 19; li. 8; and then it is applied to the mind or heart as that which is crushed or broken by the weight of guilt. The word does not differ materially from the term *broken.* The two together constitute *intensity* of expression. ¶ *Thou wilt not despise.* Thou wilt not treat with contempt or disregard. That is, God would look upon them with favour, and to such a heart he would grant his blessing. See Notes on Isa. lvii. 15; lxvi. 2.

18. *Do good in thy good pleasure unto Zion.* From himself—his deep sorrow, his conscious guilt, his earnest prayer for pardon and salvation—the psalmist turns to Zion, to the city of God, to the people of the Lord. These, after all, lay nearer to his heart than his own personal salvation; and to these his thoughts naturally turned even in connexion with his own deep distress. Such a prayer as is here offered he would also be more naturally led to offer from the remembrance of the dishonour which he had brought on the cause of religion, and it was natural for him to pray that his own misconduct might not have the effect of hindering the cause of God in the world. The psalms often take this turn. Where they commence with a personal reference to the author himself, the thoughts often terminate in a reference to Zion, and to the promotion of the cause of religion in the world. ¶ *Build thou the walls of Jerusalem.* It is this expression on which De Wette, Doederlein, and Rosenmüller rely in proof that this psalm, or this portion of it, was composed at a later period than the time of David, and that it must have been written in the time of the captivity, when Jerusalem was in ruins. See the introduction to the psalm. But, as was remarked there, it is not necessary to adopt this supposition. There are two other solutions of the diffi-

19 Then shalt thou [n] be pleased with the [o] sacrifices of righteousness, with burnt-offering and whole burnt-offering: then shall they offer bullocks upon thine altar.

n Heb. xiii. 15, 16. o Ps. iv. 5; Rom. xiii. 1.

culty, either of which would meet all that is implied in the language. (*a*) One is, that the walls of Jerusalem, which David had undertaken to build, were not as yet complete, or that the public works commenced by him for the protection of the city had not been finished at the time of the fatal affair of Uriah. There is nothing in the history which forbids this supposition, and the *language* is such as would be used by David on the occasion, if he had been actually engaged in completing the walls of the city, and rendering it impregnable, and if his heart was intensely fixed on the completion of the work. (*b*) The other supposition is, that this is figurative language —a prayer that God would favour and bless his people *as if* the city was to be protected by walls, and thus rendered safe from an attack by the enemy. Such language is, in fact, often used in cases where it could not be pretended that it was designed to be literal. See Jude 20; Rom. xv. 20; 1 Cor. iii. 12; Gal. ii. 18; Eph. ii. 22; Col. ii. 7.

19. *Then shalt thou be pleased with the sacrifices of righteousness.* "Then," that is, when God should have thus showed favour to Zion; when he should have poured out his blessing on Jerusalem; when religion should prosper and prevail; when there should be an increase of the pure worship of God. In such offerings as would *then* be made,—in sacrifices presented not in mere form, but with sincerity, humility, and penitence,—in the outward offering of blood presented with a corresponding sincerity of feeling, and with true contrition, and a proper acknowledgment of the guilt designed to be represented by the shedding of blood in sacrifice,—God would be pleased, and would approve the worship thus rendered to him. Sacrifice would then be acceptable, for it would not be presented as a mere form, but would be *so* offered, that it might be called a "sacrifice *of righteousness*"—a sacrifice offered with a right spirit; in a manner which God would deem right. ¶ *With burnt-offering.* See Notes on Isa. i. 11. ¶ *And whole burnt-offering.* The word here means that which is *wholly* consumed, no part of which was reserved to be eaten by the priests, as was the case in many of the sacrifices. See Deut. xxxiii. 10. Comp. Lev. vi. 9; i. 3—17. ¶ *Then shall they offer bullocks upon thine altar.* That is, then shall bullocks be offered. The meaning is, that all the offerings prescribed in the law would then be brought, and that those sacrifices would be made with a right spirit—a spirit of true devotion—the offering of the heart accompanying the outward form. In other words, there would be manifested the spirit of humble worship; of pure religion.

PSALM LII.

This psalm purports to be "a psalm of David," and there is no reason to doubt that he was the author. The occasion on which it was composed is stated in the title. The correctness of this title has been called in question by De Wette and Rüdinger, on the ground that the contents of the psalm do not seem to them to be so well fitted to that occasion as to the times of Absalom or Ahithophel. There does not, however, appear to be any just reason for doubting the correctness of the title, as all the circumstances referred to in the psalm are susceptible of application to the act of Doeg the Edomite, on the occasion referred to, viz., that mentioned in 1 Sam. xxii. 9, *et seq.* David had fled to Ahimelech the priest at Nob, 1 Sam. xxi. 1. By Ahimelech he had been supplied with bread, and furnished with the sword with which he himself had slain Goliath. On this occasion, an Edomite was present, named Doeg, whose character was, from some cause well known; and David felt that he would not hesitate to betray any one, or do any act of wickedness or meanness, if it would subserve his own purposes (1 Sam. xxii. 22). Apprehensive of danger, therefore, even in the presence and under the protection of Ahimelech, and supposing that his place of retreat could not be concealed from Saul, he fled to Achish, king of Gath (1 Sam. xxi. 10), until in the fear of danger there, he feigned madness, and was driven away as a madman (1 Sam. xxi. 14, 15). He found refuge for a time in the cave of Adullam, where he supposed he would be safe, 1 Sam. xxii. 1, 2. From that cave he went to Mizpeh, in Moab (1 Sam. xxii. 3, 4), and thence, at the suggestion of the prophet Gad, he went into the forest of Hareth, 1 Sam. xxii. 5.

At this time, Doeg the Edomite, in order to secure the favour of Saul, and to show that there was one at least who was friendly to him, and was willing to deliver up to punishment those who had encouraged David in his rebellion, informed Saul of the fact that David had been seen with Ahimelech at Nob, and that Ahimelech had given him food and the sword of Goliath the Philistine. The result was, that Ahimelech and the priests who were with him were summoned before Saul; that they were accused by him of the crime; that Saul commanded those who were around him to fall on Ahimelech and the priests and to put them to death; and when they all hesitated, Doeg himself fell upon them and executed the barbarous order. Eighty-five priests thus perished by the sword, and the city of Nob was destroyed, 1 Sam. xxii. 9–19. It was the conduct of Doeg in this matter that is the subject of this psalm. Doeg is called "the Edomite." He was probably a native of Idumea, who had connected himself with Saul, and who hoped to secure his especial favour by thus informing him of those who were in league with his enemy David. Some have supposed that he was a native-born Jew, and that he is called an Edomite because he may have had his residence in Idumea; but the more obvious supposition is that he was a native of that land. On Idumea, see Notes on Isa. xi. 14; xxxiv. 5, 6; lxiii. 1.

On the phrase in the title, "*To the chief Musician,*" see Notes on the introd. to Ps. iv. The fact that it is thus addressed to the overseer of the public music shows that, though it originally had a private reference, and was designed to record an event which occurred in the life of David, it yet had so much of public interest, and contained truth of so general a nature, that it might properly be employed in the public devotions of the sanctuary.

On the word "*Maschil,*" see introd. to Ps. xxxii. The psalm is divided, in the original, apparently for musical purposes, or to adapt it in some way to the music of the sanctuary, into three parts, which are indicated by the word *Selah*, at the close of verses 3 and 5. These, however, have no reference to the sense, or to the natural divisions of the psalm.

As respects the sense or the contents of the psalm, it is divided into three parts, which are *not* indicated by this musical mark.

I. The first refers to the character of the calumniator and informer, vers. 1-4. He was a man who was confident in himself, and who did not regard the goodness of God, ver. 1; a man whose tongue devised mischiefs like a sharp razor, ver. 2; a man who loved evil more than good, and a lie more than the truth, ver. 3; and a man who loved to utter words that would destroy the character and the happiness of others, ver. 4.

II. The judgment, or punishment that would come upon such a man, vers. 5-7. (*a*) God would destroy and root him out of the land, ver. 5; (*b*) the righteous would see this, and would triumph over him as one who was brought to a proper end,—the proper end of one who did not make God his strength; who trusted in his riches; who strengthened himself in the purposes of wickedness, vers. 6, 7.

III. The security—the preservation—the joy, of the author of the psalm, vers. 8, 9. The aim—the purpose—of the informer referred to in the psalm, namely Doeg, had been really to disclose the place of David's retreat, and to have him delivered into the hands of Saul. This he hoped to accomplish through Ahimelech the priest. He supposed, evidently, that when Saul was informed that David had been with *him*, Ahimelech would be brought before Saul and required to give information as to the place where David might be found, and that thus David would be delivered into the hands of Saul. But in this he had been disappointed. David had fled, and was secure.

Ahimelech was summoned to meet Saul (1 Sam. xxii. 11), and with him were summoned also all "his father's house, the priests that were in Nob." In reply to the charge that he had conspired against Saul; that he had befriended David; that he had "given him," in modern language, "aid and comfort;" that he had assisted him so that he could "rise against Saul," and that he had so befriended him that he could "lie in wait for him" at that time,—he boldly declared his conviction that Saul had not a more faithful subject in his realm than David was;—"And who is so faithful among all thy servants as David, which is the king's son-in-law, and goeth at thy bidding, and is honourable in thine house?" There Ahimelech stood—an example of a bold, firm, independent, honourable, honest man. He maintained the innocence of David, as well as his own. He sought no favour by joining in the clamour against David. He did not seek to avert the blow which he could not but see was impending over himself, by any mean compliance with the prejudices of the king. He did nothing to flatter the offended monarch, or to gratify him in his purpose to arrest David, the fugitive. He made no offer to disclose to him the place of his concealment. Any one of these things—any act in the *line* of that which Doeg had performed—might have saved his life. That he knew the place of David's retreat, is apparent from a circumstance incidentally referred to in the ultimate account of the affair; for, after Ahimelech had been put to death, it is said that one of his sons—Abiathar—fled at once to David (1 Sam. xxii. 20, 21), and disclosed to him the dreadful manner of his father's death; thus showing that the knowledge of the place of his retreat was in the possession of the family, and could easily have been disclosed to Saul, and yet it was not done. Neither Ahimelech, nor any one of his family, even intimated to Saul that they knew where David then was, and that they could put him in possession of the means of securing him. That the fact that they *did* not and *would* not betray the place of his retreat was one cause of the wrath of Saul, is apparent from the reason assigned why the "footmen" were commanded to put them to death;—"And the king said unto the footmen that stood about him, Turn, and slay the priests of the Lord, because their hand also is with David, *and because they knew when he fled, and did not show it to me*," 1 Sam. xxii. 17.

It cannot be doubted, therefore, that if there had been an offer of furnishing the information; if there had been a tender of their services in the case; if there had been evinced a spirit of ready compliance with the prejudices and passions of Saul; if there had been among them the same spirit of mean sycophancy which characterised Doeg,—Ahimelech and the whole family would have been safe. But no such thing was done; no such offer was made; no such spirit was evinced. There they stood—noble-minded men—father, son, all the family, true to honour, to virtue, to religion; true to God, to Saul, to David, and to themselves. They hid the secret in their own bosoms; they neither proffered nor submitted to any mean or dishonourable compliances that they might save their lives. There was, on the one hand, Doeg, *the "mighty" man*, but *the mean informer;* on the other, a noble-minded man standing up in the conscious integrity of what he had done, and maintaining it even at the hazard of life.

The result is well known, and was that which, so far as the fate of Ahimelech was concerned, could easily have been anticipated. Saul, maddened against David, was now equally infuriated against the honest man who had befriended him. He commanded him to be put to death at once. And here, in this remarkable transaction, where so much of meaness and honour, of fidelity and falsehood, of integrity and corruption, of soberness and passion, come so near together, we have another striking instance of firmness and virtue. Saul commanded the "footmen," (marg. the *runners*,) who were about him, to "turn and slay" Ahimelech and his sons. Yet the "footmen" declined to do the bloody work. Noble men, themselves, they saw here an instance of true nobleness of character and of deed in the priests of the Lord; and they refused, even at the peril of the wrath of Saul, to execute an unrighteous sentence on men so noble, so honourable, so true. There *was* one, however, that would do it. There stood the mean, the sycophantic, the base man, Doeg, who had '*informed*' against the priests, and he was ready to do the work. The command was given, and he consummated the work of betrayal and of meanness, by putting at once to the sword, fourscore and five priests of the Lord, and by carrying

PSALM LII.

To the chief Musician, Maschil. *A Psalm* of David, when Doeg *p* the Edomite came and told *q* Saul, and said unto him, David is come to the house of Ahimelech.

WHY boastest thou thyself in mischief, O mighty man? the [r] goodness of God *endureth* continually.

2 Thy tongue deviseth mis-

p 1 Sam. xxi. 7; xxii. 9. *q* Ezek. xxii. 9.

r Ps. cxxxvi. 1, 2.

desolation and death through the city of their habitation, smiting "with the edge of the sword, both men and women, children and sucklings, and oxen, and asses, and sheep;" 1 Sam. xxii. 18, 19.

In the mean time David was safe, and it is this fact which he celebrates when he says in this psalm, "I am like a green olive tree in the house of God," ver. 8; and it is for this that he gives praise, ver. 9.

The psalm refers, therefore, to the character and the conduct of an "*informer*,"—one of the most odious characters among men. In a book claiming to be a revelation from God, as the Bible does—a book designed for all men, and intended to be adapted to all ages, and in a world where such men would be found in all lands and times, it was proper that the character of such should be at least once held up in its true light, that men may see what it really is. Any bad man may make himself more odious by becoming an "informer;" any good man may suffer, as David did, from the acts of such an one; and hence the case in the psalm may suggest useful lessons in every age of the world.

1. *Why boastest thou thyself in mischief?* Why dost thou *exult* in that which is wrong? Why dost thou find pleasure in evil rather than in good? Why dost thou seek to triumph in the injury done to others? The reference is to one who prided himself on schemes and projects which tended to injure others; or who congratulated himself on the success which attended his efforts to wrong other men. ¶ *O mighty man.* De Wette and Luther render this, *tyrant.* The original word would be properly applied to one of rank or distinction; a man of *power*—power derived either from office, from talent, or from wealth. It is a word which is often applied to a hero or warrior: Isa. iii. 2; Ezek. xxxix. 20; 2 Sam. xvii. 10; Ps. xxxiii. 16; cxx. 4; cxxvii. 4; Dan. xi. 3; Gen. vi. 4; Jer. li. 30. So far as the *word* is concerned, it might be applied either to Saul or to any other warrior or man of rank; and Professor Alexander supposes that it refers to Saul himself. The connexion, however, seems to require us to understand it of Doeg, and not of Saul, This appears to be clear (*a*) from the general character here given to the person referred to, a character not particularly applicable to Saul, but applicable to an informer like Doeg (vers. 2—4); and (*b*) from the fact that he derived his power, not from his rank and office, as Saul did, but mainly from his wealth (ver. 7). This would seem to imply that some other was referred to than Saul. ¶ *The goodness of God* endureth *continually.* Literally, *all the day.* That is, the wicked man could not hope to prevent the exercise of the Divine goodness towards him whom he persecuted, and whom he sought to injure. David means to say that the goodness of God was so great and so constant, that he would protect his true friends from such machinations; or that it was so unceasing and watchful, that the informer and accuser could not hope to find an interval of time when God would intermit his care, and when, therefore, he might hope for success. Against the goodness of God, the devices of a wicked man to injure the righteous could not ultimately prevail.

2. *Thy tongue deviseth mischiefs.* The word rendered *mischiefs* means (*a*) desire, cupidity: Prov. x. 3; then (*b*) fall, ruin, destruction, wickedness: Ps. v. 9; xxxviii. 12. The meaning here is, that he made use of his tongue to ruin others. Comp. Ps. l. 19. The particular thing referred to here is the fact that Doeg

chiefs, like a sharp razor, working
deceitfully.
3 Thou lovest evil more than
good, *and* lying[s] rather than to
speak righteousness. Selah.

[s] Jer. ix. 4, 5. [1] Or, and *the*.

4 Thou lovest all devouring
words, [1] O *thou* deceitful tongue.
5 God[t] shall likewise [2] destroy
thee for ever: he shall take thee
away, and pluck thee out of *thy*

[t] Prov. xix. 5, 9. [2] *beat thee down.*

sought the ruin of others by giving *information* in regard to them. He *informed* Saul of what Ahimelech had done; he *informed* him where David had been, thus giving him, also, information in what way he might be found and apprehended. All this was *designed* to bring ruin upon David and his followers. It *actually* brought ruin on Ahimelech and those associated with him, 1 Sam. xxii. 17—19. ¶ *Like a sharp razor.* See Notes on Isa. vii. 20. His slanders were like a sharp knife with which one stabs another. So we say of a slanderer that he "*stabs*" another in the dark. ¶ *Working deceitfully.* Literally, *making deceit.* That is, it was by deceit that he accomplished his purpose. There was no open and fair dealing in what he did.

3. *Thou lovest evil more than good.* Thou dost prefer to do injury to others, rather than to do them good. In the case referred to, instead of aiding the innocent, the persecuted, and the wronged, he had attempted to reveal the place where he might be found, and where an enraged enemy might have an opportunity of wreaking his vengeance upon him. ¶ *And lying rather than to speak righteousness.* He preferred a lie to the truth; and, when he supposed that his own interest would be subserved by it, he preferred a falsehood that would promote that interest, rather than a simple statement of the truth. The *lying* in this case was that which was *implied* in his being desirous of giving up David, or betraying him to Saul,—*as if* David was a bad man, and *as if* the suspicions of Saul were well-founded. He preferred to give his countenance to a falsehood in regard to him, rather than to state the exact truth in reference to his character. His conduct in this was strongly in contrast with that of Ahimelech, who, when arraigned before Saul, declared his belief that David was innocent; his firm conviction that David was true and loyal. *For* that fidelity he lost his life, 1 Sam. xxii. 14. Doeg was willing to lend countenance to the suspicions of Saul, and practically to represent David as a traitor to the king. The word *Selah* here is doubtless a mere musical pause. See Notes on Ps. iii. 2. It determines nothing in regard to the sense of the passage.

4. *Thou lovest all devouring words.* All words that tend to devour or *swallow up* reputation and happiness. Luther, "Thou speakest gladly all things [anything] that will serve to destruction." Anything, everything, that will serve to ruin men. The word rendered "devouring"—בֶּלַע, *bela*—occurs only here and in Jer. li. 44, though the verb from which it is derived occurs frequently: Isa. xxviii. 4; Exod. vii. 12; Jonah ii. 1 [i. 17]; Gen. xli. 7, 24, *et al.* The verb means to swallow; and then, to consume or destroy. ¶ O thou *deceitful tongue.* Marg., *and the deceitful tongue.* The sense is best expressed in the text. It is an address *to* the tongue as loving deceit or fraud.

5. *God shall likewise destroy thee for ever.* Marg., *beat thee down.* The Hebrew word means *to tear, to break down, to destroy:* Lev. xiv. 45; Judges vi. 30. The reference here is not to the *tongue* alluded to in the previous verses, but to Doeg himself. The language in the verse is intensive and emphatic. The main idea is presented in a variety of forms, all designed to denote utter and absolute destruction—a complete and entire sweeping away, so that nothing should be left. The word *here* used would

dwelling-place, and [u] root thee out of the land of the living. Selah.

6 The righteous also shall see, and fear, and shall laugh at him:

7 Lo, *this is* the man *that* made not God his strength; but trusted [v] in the abundance of his riches, *and* strengthened himself in his wickedness.

u Prov. ii. 22.

v 1 Tim. vi. 17. [1] Or, *substance.*

---

suggest the idea of *pulling down*—as a house, a fence, a wall; that is, the idea of completely *demolishing* it; and the meaning is, that destruction would come upon the informer and slanderer *like* the destruction which comes upon a house, or wall, or fence, when it is entirely pulled down. ¶ *He shall take thee away.* An expression indicating in another form that he would be certainly destroyed. The verb here used—חָתָה, *hhatha*—is elsewhere used only in the sense of taking up and carrying fire or coals: Isa. xxx. 14; Prov. vi. 27; xxv. 22. The idea here *may* be that he would be seized and carried away with haste, as when one takes up fire or coals, he does it as rapidly as possible, lest he should be burned. ¶ *And shall pluck thee out of* thy *dwelling-place.* Literally, "out of the *tent.*" The reference is to his abode. The allusion here in the verb that is used—נָסַח, *nasahh*—is to the act of pulling up plants; and the idea is, that he would be plucked up as a plant is torn from its roots. ¶ *And root thee out of the land of the living.* As a tree is torn up from the roots and thus destroyed. He would be no more among the living. Comp. Ps. xxvii. 13. All these phrases are intended to denote that such a man would be utterly destroyed.

6. *The righteous also shall see.* See Notes on Ps. xxxvii. 34. ¶ *And fear.* The effect of such a judgment will be to produce reverence in the minds of good men—a solemn sense of the justice of God; to make them tremble at such fearful judgments; and to fear lest they should violate the law, and bring judgment on themselves. ¶ *And shall laugh at him.* Comp. Notes on Ps. ii. 4. See also Ps. lviii. 10; lxiv. 9, 10; Prov. i. 26. The idea here is not exultation in the *sufferings* of others, or joy that *calamity* has come upon them, or the gratification of selfish and revengeful feeling that an enemy is deservedly punished; it is that of approbation that punishment has come upon those who deserve it, and joy that wickedness is not allowed to triumph. It is not wrong for us to feel a sense of approbation and joy that the laws are maintained, and that justice is done, even though this does involve suffering, for we know that the guilty deserve it, and it is better that they should suffer than that the righteous should suffer through them. All this may be entirely free from any malignant, or any revengeful feeling. It may even be connected with the deepest pity, and with the purest benevolence towards the sufferers themselves.

7. *Lo,* this is *the man* that *made not God his strength.* That is, the righteous (ver. 6) would say this. They would designate him as a man who had not made God his refuge, but who had trusted in his own resources. The result would be that he would be abandoned by God, and that those things on which he had relied would fail him in the day of calamity. He would be pointed out as an instance of what must occur when a man does not act with a wise reference to the will of God, but, confiding in his own strength and resources, pursues his own plans of iniquity. ¶ *But trusted in the abundance of his riches.* See Notes on Ps. xlix. 6. From this it would seem that Doeg was a rich man, and that, as a general thing, in his life, and in his plans of evil, he felt confident in his wealth. He had that spirit of arrogance and self-confidence which springs from the conscious possession of property where there is

8 But I *am* like [w] a green olive-tree in the house of God: I trust in the mercy of God for ever and ever.

w Ps. i. 3; xcii. 12.

9 I will praise thee for ever, because thou hast done *it*: and I will wait [x] on thy name; for [y] *it is* good before thy saints.

x Lam. iii. 25, 26. *y* Ps. lxxiii. 28.

no fear of God; and into all that he did he carried the sense of his own importance as derived from his riches. In the particular matter referred to in the psalm the meaning is, that he would perform the iniquitous work of giving "information" with the proud and haughty feeling springing from wealth and from self-importance—the feeling that he was a man of consequence, and that whatever such a man might do would be entitled to special attention. ¶ And *strengthened himself in his wickedness.* Marg., *substance.* This is the same word which in ver. 1 is rendered *mischief.* The idea is, that he had a malicious pleasure in doing wrong, or in injuring others, and that by every art, and against all the convictions and remonstrances of his own conscience, he endeavoured to confirm himself *in* this unholy purpose and employment.

8. *But I* am *like a green olive-tree in the house of God.* I am safe and happy, notwithstanding the effort made by my enemy, the informer, to secure my destruction. I have been kept unharmed, like a green and flourishing tree—a tree protected in the very courts of the sanctuary—safe under the care and the eye of God. A green tree is the emblem of prosperity. See Notes on Ps. i. 3; xxxvii. 35; comp. Ps. xcii. 12. The "house of God" here referred to is the tabernacle, considered as the place where God was supposed to reside. See Notes on Ps. xv. 1; xxiii. 6; xxvii. 4, 5. The particular allusion here is to the *courts* of the tabernacle. An olive tree would not be cultivated *in* the tabernacle, but it might in the *courts* or *area* which surrounded it. The name "house of God" would be given to the whole area, as it was afterwards to the entire area in which the temple was. A tree thus planted in the very courts of the sanctuary would be regarded as sacred, and would be safe as long as the tabernacle itself was safe, for it would be, as it were, directly under the Divine protection. So David had been, notwithstanding all the efforts of his enemies to destroy him. ¶ *I trust in the mercy of God for ever and ever.* (*a*) I *have* always done it. It has been my constant practice in trouble or danger. (*b*) I *will* always do it. As the result of all my experience, I will still do it; and thus trusting in God, I shall have the consciousness of safety.

9. *I will praise thee for ever, because thou hast done* it. Because thou art the source of my safety. The fact that I have been delivered from the designs of Saul, and saved from the efforts of Doeg to betray me, is to be traced wholly to thee. It has been ordered by thy providence that the purposes alike of Doeg and of Saul have been defeated, and I am still safe. ¶ *And I will wait on thy name.* That is, I will wait on *thee;* the name being often put for the person himself: Ps. xx. 1; lxix. 30; Prov. xviii. 10; Isa. lix. 19. The language here used means that he would trust in God, or confide in him. All his expectation and hope would be in him. There are two ideas essentially in the language;—(1) the expression of a sense of *dependence* on God, as if the only ground of trust was in him; (2) a willingness to *await* his interposition at all times; a belief that, however long such an interposition might be delayed, God *would* interfere at the proper time to bring deliverance; and a purpose calmly and patiently to look to him until the time of deliverance should come. Comp. Ps. xxv. 3, 5, 21; xxvii. 14; xxxvii. 7, 9, 34; lxix. 3; Isa. viii. 17; xl. 31. ¶ *For it is good before thy saints.* God is good;

and I will confess it before his "saints." His mercy has been so marked, that a public acknowledgment of it is proper; and before his assembled people I will declare what he has done for me. So signal an act of mercy, an interposition so fitted to illustrate the character of God, demands more than a private acknowledgment, and I will render him public praise. The same idea occurs in Ps. xxii. 25; xxxv. 18; cxi. 1; Isa. xxxviii. 20. The general thought is, that for great and special mercies it is proper to render special praise to God before his assembled people. It is not that we are to obtrude our private affairs upon the public eye or the public ear; it is not that mercies shown to us have any particular claim to the attention of our fellow-men, but it is that such interpositions illustrate the character of God, and that they may constitute an argument before the world in favour of his benevolent and merciful character. Among the "saints" there is a common bond of union—a common interest in all that pertains to each other; and when special mercy is shown to any one of the great brotherhood, it is proper that all should join in the thanksgiving, and render praise to God.

The importance of the subject considered in this psalm,—the fact that it is not often referred to in books on moral science, or even in sermons,—and the fact that it involves many points of practical difficulty in the intercourse between man and man in the various relations of life—may justify at the close of an exposition of this psalm a consideration of the general question about the morality of giving "*information,*" or, in general, the character of the "*informer.*" Such a departure from the usual method adopted in works designed to be expository would not be ordinarily proper, since it would swell such works beyond reasonable dimensions; but perhaps it may be admitted in a single instance.

In what cases is it our duty to give information which may be in our possession about the conduct of others; and in what cases does it become a moral wrong or a crime to do it?

This is a question of much importance in respect to our own conduct, and often of much difficulty in its solution. It may not be possible to answer all the inquiries which might be made on this subject, or to lay down principles of undoubted plainness which would be applicable to every case which might occur, but a few general principles may be suggested.

The question is one which may occur at any time, and in any situation of life,—Is it never right to give such information? Are we never bound to do it? Are there no circumstances in which it is proper that it should be voluntary? Are there any situations in which we are exempt by established customs or laws from giving such information? Are there any in which we are bound, by the obligations of conscience, not to give such information, whatever may be the penalty? Where and when does guilt begin or end in our volunteering to give information of the conduct or the concealments of others?

These questions often come with much perplexity before the mind of an ingenuous schoolboy, who would desire to do right, and who yet has so much honour that he desires to escape the guilt and the reproach of being a "tell-tale." They are questions which occur to a lawyer (or, rather, which *did* occur before the general principle, which I will soon advert to, had been settled by the courts), in regard to the knowledge of which he has been put in possession under the confidential relation of advocate and client. They are questions which may occur to a clergyman, either in respect to the confidential disclosures made at the confessional of the Catholic priest, or in respect to the confidential statements of the true penitent made to a Protestant pastor, in order that spiritual counsel may be obtained to give relief to a burdened conscience. They are questions which it was necessary should be settled in regard to a fugitive from justice, who seeks protection under the roof of a friend or a stranger. They are questions respecting refugees from oppression in foreign lands—suggesting the inquiry whether they shall be welcomed, or whether there shall be any law by which they shall, on demand, be restored to the dominion of a tyrant. They are questions which the conscience will ask, and does ask, about those who make their escape from slavery, who apply to us for aid in securing their liberty, and who seek an asylum beneath our roof;—questions whether the law of God requires or permits us to render any active assistance in making known the place of their refuge, and returning them to bondage. When, and in what cases, if any, is a man bound to give information in such circumstances as these? It is to be admitted that cases may occur, in regard to these questions, in which there would be great difficulty in determining what are the exact limits of duty, and writers on the subject of morals have not laid down such clear rules as would leave the mind perfectly free from doubt, or be sufficient to guide us on all these points. It will be admitted, also, that some of them are questions of much difficulty, and where instruction would be desirable.

Much may be learned, in regard to the proper estimate of human conduct among men, from the *language* which they employ—language which, in its very structure, often conveys their sentiments from age to age. The ideas of men on many of the subjects of morals, in respect to that which is honourable or dishonourable, right or wrong, manly or mean, became thus *imbedded*—I might almost say *fossilized*—in their modes of speech. Language, in its very structure, thus carries down to future times the sentiments cherished in regard to the morality of actions—as the fossil remains that are beneath the surface of the earth, in the strata of the rocks, bring to us the forms of ancient types of animals, and ferns, and palms, of which there are now no living specimens on the globe. They who have studied Dean Trench's Treatise on "Words" will recollect how this idea is illustrated in that remarkable work; how, without any other information about the views of men in other times, the very *words* which they employed, and which have been transmitted to us, convey to us the estimate which was formed in past ages in regard to the moral quality of an action, as proper or improper—as honourable or dishonourable—as conformed to the noble principles of our nature, or the reverse.

As illustrating the general sentiments of mankind in this respect, I will select *two* words as specimens of many which might be selected, and as words which men have been agreed in applying to some of the acts referred to in the questions of difficulty that I have just mentioned, and which may enable us to do something in determining the morality of an action, so far as those words, in their just application to the subject, indicate the judgment of mankind.

One of these is the word "*meanness*"—a word which a schoolboy would be most *likely* to apply to the act of a tell-tale or an informer, and which we instinctively apply to numerous actions in more advanced periods of life, and which serves to mark the judgment of mankind in regard to certain kinds of conduct. The *idea* in such a case is not so much the *guilt* or the *criminality* of the act considered as a violation of law, as it is that of being opposed to just notions of *honour*, or indicating a base, low, sordid, grovelling spirit—"lowness of mind, want of dignity and elevation; want of honour." (*Webster.*)

The other word is "*sycophant.*" The Athenians had a law prohibiting the exportation of figs. This law, of course, had a penalty, and it was a matter of importance to the magistrate to ascertain who had been guilty of violating it. It suggested, also, a method of securing the favour of such a magistrate, and perhaps of obtaining a reward, by giving *information* of those who had been guilty of violating the law. From these two words—the Greek word *fig*, and the Greek word to *show*, or to *discover*, we have derived the word *sycophant*; and this word has come down from the Greeks, and through the long tract of ages intervening between its first use in Athens to the present time, always bearing in every age the original idea imbedded in the word, as the old fossil that is now dug up bears the form of the fern, the leaf, the worm, or the shell that was imbedded there perhaps millions of ages ago. As such a man would be *likely* to be mean, and fawning, and flattering, so the word has come to describe always a parasite; a mean flatterer; a flatterer of princes and great men; and hence it is, and would be applied as one of the words indicating the sense of mankind in regard to a "tale-bearer," or an "informer."

Words like these indicate the general judgment of mankind on such conduct as that referred to in the psalm before us. Of course, to what particular *actions* of the kind they are properly applicable, would be another point; they are referred to here only as indicating the general judgment of mankind in regard to certain kinds of conduct, and to show how careful men are, in their very language, to express their permanent approbation of that which is *honourable* and *right*, and their detestation of that which is *dishonourable* and *wrong*.

Let us now consider more particularly the subject with respect to *duty*, and to *criminality*. The question is, whether we can find any cases where it is *right*—where it is our *duty* to give such information; or, in what cases, if any, it is right; and in what cases it is malignant, guilty, wrong. The points to be considered are—

(1.) When it is right, or when it may be demanded that we should give information of another; and

(2.) When it becomes guilt.

(1.) When it is right, or when it may be demanded of us.

(*a*) It is to be admitted that there are cases in which the interests of justice demand that men should be *required* to give information of others; or, there are cases where the courts have a right to summon us, to put us upon our oath, and to demand the information which may be in our possession. The courts constantly act on this; and the interests of justice could not be promoted, nor could a cause ever be determined, without exercising this right. If all men were bound in conscience to withhold information simply because they have it in their possession, or because of the mode in which they came in possession of it—or if they withheld it from mere stubbornness and obstinacy—all the departments of justice must stand still, and the officers of justice might be discharged, since it can neither be presumed that *they* would possess all the knowledge necessary to the administration of justice themselves, nor would the law allow them to act on it if they did. The law never presumes that a judge is to decide a case from a knowledge of the facts in his own possession, or simply because *he knows what was done in the case.* The ultimate decision must be made in view of testimony *given*, not of knowledge *possessed.* In most cases, however, there is no difficulty on this point. There is no necessary violation of confidence in giving this information. There have been no improper means used to obtain it. There has been only an observation of that which any other man might have seen. There has been no baseness in *spying* out what was done. There has been no "sycophantic" purpose; there is no voluntariness in betraying what we know; there is no dishonourableness in divulging what *happened* to be known to us. A man may *regret* that he witnessed the act of crime, but he does not blame himself for it; he may feel *pained* that his testimony may consign another man to the gallows, but he does not deem it dishonourable, for he has no mean purpose in it, and the interests of justice demand it.

(*b*) It is an admitted principle that

one employed as counsel in a case—a lawyer—shall *not* be required to give up information which may be in his possession as counsel; information which has been entrusted to him by his client. It is held essential to the interests of justice, that whatever is thus communicated to a professional adviser shall be regarded by the court as strictly confidential, and that the counsel incurs no blame if he does *not* give information on the subject; or, in other words, the true interests of justice do not demand, and the principles of honour will not admit, that he should betray the man who has entrusted his cause to him. How far a man, governed by a good conscience, and by the principles of honour, may undertake a cause which, from the statements of his client in the beginning, he may regard as doubtful, or where in the progress of the case he may become sure that his client is guilty, is a point which does not come under the present inquiry, and which may, in fact, be in some respects a question of difficult solution. It must still, however, even in such a case, be held that he cannot be required to give the information in his possession, and every principle of honour or of right would be understood to be violated, if, abandoning the case, he should become a voluntary "*informer.*"*

(*c*) In like manner, it is understood that the law does not require a juryman to give voluntary "information" of what may be within his own knowledge in the case that may be submitted for trial. The extent of his oath and his obligation is that he shall give a verdict according to the testimony submitted under the proper forms of law. He may not *go back* of that, and found his opinion in the verdict on any private knowledge which he may have in his own possession, and which has not, under the proper forms of law, been laid before the court; nor may what he himself may have seen and heard enter at all into his verdict, or influence it in any manner, unless it has been submitted with the other testimony in the case to the court. The verdict is to be based on evidence *given;* not on what he *has seen.* An accused man has a right to demand that *all* that shall bear on the sentence in the case—*all* that shall enter into the verdict—shall be submitted as testimony, under the solemnities of an oath, and with all proper opportunities of cross-examination, and of rebutting it by counter testimony. A juryman may, indeed, be called as a witness in a case. But then he is to be sworn and examined as any other witness, and when he comes to unite with others in making up the verdict, he is to allow to enter into that verdict *only* that which is in possession of all the members of the jury, and he is not to permit *any* knowledge which he may have, which was *not* obtained from him in giving testimony, to influence his own judgment in the case.†

(*d*) There are cases, however, in which things entrusted to one *as* a secret, or in confidence, may be required to be given up. Such cases may occur in a matter of private friendship, or in a case of professional confidence.‡ In the case of a Presbyterian clergyman, it has been held that he was bound to submit a letter to the court which had been addressed to him by the accused as her pastor, and which was supposed to

* 3 Blackstone p. 370, Book iii., ch. 23.

† 3 Blackstone, p. 375, Book iii., ch. 23. See p. 370. Note.

‡ "The confidence which is placed in a counsel or solicitor, must necessarily be inviolable when the use of advocates and legal assistants is admitted. But the purposes of public justice supersede the delicacy of every other species of confidential communication. In the trial of the Duchess of Kingston, it was determined that a friend might be bound to disclose, if necessary, in a court of justice, secrets of the most sacred nature which one sex could repose in another. And that a surgeon was bound to communicate any information whatever, which he was possessed of, in consequence of his professional attendance. And those secrets only, communicated to a counsel or attorney, are inviolable in a court of justice, which have been entrusted to them whilst acting in their respective characters to the party as their client."—3 *Blackstone*, 370, *Note.*

contain important disclosures in regard to her criminality.* In this case, however, the disclosure was not originally made by the pastor; nor was the fact of the existence of such a letter made known by him. The fact that such a letter had been sent to him, was stated by the party herself; and the court, having this knowledge of it, *demanded* its production in court. It was submitted after taking legal advice, and the community justified the conduct of the pastor. So the principle is regarded as well settled that a minister of religion *may* be required to disclose what has been communicated to him, whether at the "confessional," or as a pastor, which may be necessary to establish the guilt of a party; and that the fact that it had been communicated in confidence, and for spiritual advice, does *not* constitute a reason for refusing to disclose it.

(2.) But the point before us relates rather to the inquiry when the act of giving such information becomes *guilt*, or in what circumstances it is forbidden and wrong.

Perhaps all that need to be said on this point can be reduced to three heads: when it is for base purposes; when the innocent are betrayed; and when professional confidence is violated. The illustration of these points, after what has been said, need not detain us long.

First. When it is for base purposes. This would include all those cases where it is for gain; where it is to secure favour; and where it is from envy, malice, spite, or revenge. The case of Doeg was, manifestly, an instance of this kind, where the motive was not that of promoting public justice, or preserving the peace of the realm, but where it was to ingratiate himself into the favour of Saul, and secure his own influence at court. The parallel case of the Ziphims (Psalm liv.) was another instance of this kind, where, so far as the narrative goes, it is supposable that the only motive was to obtain the favour of Saul, or to secure a reward, by betraying an innocent and a persecuted man who had fled to them for a secure retreat. The case of Judas Iscariot was another instance of this kind. He betrayed his Saviour; he agreed, for a paltry reward, to disclose his place of usual retreat—a place to which he had resorted so often for prayer, that Judas knew that he could be found there. It was for no wrong done to him. It was from no regard to public peace or justice. It was not because he even supposed the Saviour to be guilty. He knew that he was innocent. He even himself confessed this in the most solemn manner, and in the very presence of those with whom he had made the infamous bargain—and with just such a result as the mean and the wicked must always expect, when those for whom they have performed a mean and wicked act have no further use for them.† Such, also, is the case of the "sycophant." That a man *might*, in some circumstances, give information about the exportation of "figs" contrary to law, or might even be required to do it, may be true; but it was equally true that it was not commonly done for any patriotic or honourable ends, but from the most base and ignoble motives; and hence the sense of mankind in regard to the nature of the transaction has been perpetuated in the world itself. So, in a school, there is often no better motive than envy, or rivalship, or malice, or a desire to obtain favour or reward, when information is given by one school-boy of another; and hence the contempt and scorn with which a boy who acts under the influence of these motives is always regarded—emblem of what he is likely to meet in all his subsequent life.

Second. The innocent are never to be betrayed. The Divine law pertaining to this seems to be perfectly plain, and the principles of that law are

* In the "Burch" case, tried in Chicago.

† "I have sinned in that I have betrayed the innocent blood. *And they said, What is that to us?*"—Matt. xxvii. 4.

such as to commend themselves to the consciences of all mankind. Thus, Isaiah xvi. 3, 4, "Take counsel, execute judgment; make thy shadow as the night in the midst of the noonday; hide the outcasts; bewray not him that wandereth. Let mine outcasts dwell with thee, Moab; be thou a covert to them from the face of the spoiler." Also in Deut. xxiii. 15, 16, "Thou shalt not deliver unto his master the servant which is escaped from his master unto thee: he shall dwell with thee, even among you, in that place which he shall choose in one of thy gates, where it liketh him best: thou shalt not oppress him."

On these passages I remark:

1. That they are settled principles of the law of God. There is no ambiguity in them. They have not been repealed. They are, therefore, still binding, and extend to all cases pertaining to the innocent and the oppressed.

2. They accord with the convictions of the human mind—the deep-seated principles which God has laid in our very being, as designed to guide us in our treatment of others.

3. They accord with some of the highest principles of self-sacrifice as illustrated in history—the noblest exhibitions of human nature in giving an asylum to the oppressed and the wronged; instances where life has been perilled, or even given up, rather than that the persecuted, the innocent, and the wronged, should be surrendered or betrayed. How often, in the history of the church has life been thus endangered, because a refuge and a shelter was furnished to the persecuted Christian—the poor outcast, driven from his home under oppressive laws! How honourable have men esteemed such acts to be! How illustrious is the example of those who have at all hazards opened their arms to receive the oppressed, and to welcome the persecuted and the wronged! In the year 1685, by the Revocation of the Edict of Nantz, eight hundred thousand professed followers of the Saviour — Huguenots — were driven from their homes and their country, and compelled to seek safety by flight to other lands. In their own country, fire and the sword spread desolation everywhere, and the voice of wailing filled the land. Those who could flee, did flee. The best men of France—those of noblest blood—fled in every direction, and sought a refuge in other countries. They fled—carrying with them not only the purest form and the best spirit of religion, but the best knowledge of the arts, to all the surrounding nations. Belgium, Holland, England, Scotland, Switzerland, opened their arms to welcome the fugitives. Our own country welcomed them—then, as now, an asylum for the oppressed. In every part of our land they found a home. Thousands of the noblest spirits—the best men of the South and the North, were composed of these exiles and wanderers. But suppose the world had been barred against them. Suppose they had been driven back again to their native land, poor persecuted men and women returned to suffering and to death. How justly mankind would have execrated such an act!

The same principles are applicable to the fugitive from slavery. Indeed, one of the texts quoted relates to this very point, and is designed to guide men on this subject in all ages and in all lands. "Thou shalt not deliver unto his master the servant which is escaped from his master unto thee." No law could possibly be more explicit; none could be more humane, just, or proper; and consequently all those provisions in human laws which require men to aid in delivering up such fugitives are violations of the law of God,—have no binding obligation on the conscience,—and are, at all hazards, to be disobeyed. Acts v. 29; iv. 19.

Third. Professional confidence is not to be betrayed. We have seen, in the remarks before made, that those who are employed as counsellors in the courts, cannot be required to communicate facts which are stated to *them* by their clients, but that confidential communications made to *others* may be demanded in promoting the interests of justice. The point now, however, relates only to the cases where professional confidence is voluntarily violated, or where knowledge thus obtained is made use of in a manner which cannot be sanctioned either by the principles of honour or religion. Two such instances may be referred to as illustrations:

(*a.*) One occurs when a clergyman, to whom such knowledge is imparted *as* a clergyman for spiritual advice, instruction, or comfort, abuses the trust reposed in him, by making use of that information for any other purpose whatever. It is entrusted to him for that purpose alone. It is committed to him as a man of honour. The secret is lodged with him, with the implied understanding that it is there to remain, and to be employed *only* for that purpose. Whether at the "confessional" of the Roman Catholic, or whether made in the confidence reposed in a Protestant pastor, the principle is the same. Whatever advantage may be taken of that secret for the promotion of any other ends; whatever object the minister of religion may propose to secure, based on the fact that he is in possession of it; whatever influence he may choose to exert, founded on the assumption that he *could* divulge it; whatever statement he may make in regard to such a person,—based on the fact that he is in possession of knowledge which he has, but which he is not at liberty to communicate, —and designed to injure the person; whatever use he may make of it as enabling him to form an estimate for his own purposes of what occurs in a family; or, in general, whatever communication he may make of it, of any kind (except under process of law, and because the law demands it), is to be regarded as a betrayal of professional confidence. The interests of religion require that a pastor should be regarded as among the most faithful of confidential friends; and no men, or class of men, should be placed in such circumstances that they may, at the "confessional," or in any other way, have the means of arriving at secrets which may be employed for any purposes of their own whatever.

(*b.*) It is a breach of professional confidence when a lawyer is entrusted with knowledge in one case by a client, which, by being employed in another case, and on another occasion, he uses against him. The secret, whatever it may be, which is entrusted to him by a client, is for that case alone; and is, to all intents, *to die* when that case is determined. It is dishonourable in any way for him to engage as counsel for another party against his former client when, by even the remotest possibility, the knowledge obtained in the former occurrence could come as an element in the determination of the case, or could be made use of to the advantage of his new client. Every sentiment of honesty and honour demands that if there is a *possibility* of this, or if there would be the remotest *temptation* of the kind, he should at once promptly and firmly decline to engage against his former client.

In human nature there are two classes of propensities or principles: —those which are generous, magnanimous, gentle, kind, benevolent, large-hearted, humane, noble; and those which are low, grovelling, sordid, sycophantic, mean, ignoble.

Though man is destitute of holiness, and though, as I believe, not one or all of these things which I have referred to as generous and noble can by cultivation become true religion, or constitute, by mere development, what is needful to secure the salvation of the soul, yet they *are* to be cultivated, for they are invaluable in society, and necessary to the happiness and the progress of mankind. On these, more than on most other things, the happiness of families, and the welfare of the world depend; and whatever may be our views of the necessity and value of religion, we are not required to undervalue "the ornament of a meek and quiet spirit," or those virtues which we connect, in our apprehensions, with that which is manly and honourable, and which tend to elevate and ennoble the race.

Christianity has, if I may so express it, a "natural affinity" for one class of these propensities; it has none for the other. It, too, is generous, humane, gentle, kind, benevolent, noble; it blends easily with these things when it finds them in human nature; and it produces them in the soul which is fully under its influence, where they did not exist before. It has no more affinity for that which is mean, ignoble, morose, sycophantic, than it has for profanity or falsehood; for dishonesty or fraud; for licentiousness or ambition.

That true religion may be found in hearts where these virtues, so generous and noble, are not developed, or where there is not a little that dishonours religion as *not* large, and liberal, and courteous, and gentlemanly, it is, perhaps, impossible to deny. There are souls essentially so mean, so sycophantic, so narrow, so sour, and so morose, that a large part of the work of sanctification *seems* to be reserved for the close of life—for that mysterious and unexplained process by which all who are redeemed are made perfect when they pass "through the valley of the shadow of death." But though there *may* be religion in such a case, it is among the lowest forms of piety. What is mean, ignoble, and narrow, is no part of the Christian religion, and can never be transmuted into it.

There has come down to us as the result of the progress of civilization in this world, and with the highest approbation of mankind, a class of virtues connected with the ideas of honour and honourableness. That the sentiment of honour has been abused among men; that an attempt has been made to set it up as the governing principle in cases where conscience should rule; that in doing this a code has been established which, in many respects, is a departure from the rules of morality, there can be no doubt;—but still there *are* just principles of honour which Christianity does not disdain; which are to be incorporated into our principles of religion, and which we are to endeavour to instil into the hearts of our children. Whatever there is in the world that is "true, and honest, and just, and pure, and lovely, and of good report;" whatever belongs to the name of "virtue," and whatever deserves "praise," is to be blended with our religion, constituting our idea of a Christian man.

It is the blending of these things—the union of Christian principle with what is noble, and manly, and generous, and humane—which, in any case, entitles to the highest appellation that can be given to any of our race,—that of THE CHRISTIAN GENTLEMAN.

PSALM LIII.

There is a remarkable resemblance between this psalm and Ps. xiv. Both are ascribed to the same author, David; and each pursues the same line of thought,—the folly and wickedness of Atheism. They both show that the belief that there is no God is not a harmless idea, or a mere speculation, but that it has important consequences *on* the life, and is naturally connected with a *wicked* life, vers. 3, 4.

The difference in the two compositions is (*a*) in the title; and (*b*) in the psalm itself.

(*a*) In the title. Both psalms are ascribed to David, and both are dedicated to the "Chief Musician." But in the title to the psalm before us, there is this addition: "Upon Mahalath, Maschil." On the meaning of the term *Maschil*, see Introd. to Ps. xxxii. The term here would seem to imply that the psalm was designed to give *instruction* on an important subject, but why it is prefixed to this psalm, and not to the others, we have no means of determining. The word, rendered *Mahalath* — מַחֲלַת — occurs only here and in the title to Ps. lxxxviii. It is supposed by Gesenius to denote a stringed instrument, as a

PSALM LIII.

To the chief Musician upon Mahalath, Maschil. *A Psalm* of David.

THE [w] fool hath said in his heart, *There is* no God. Corrupt [x] are they, and have done [y] abominable iniquity: *there is* none that doeth good.

2 God [z] looked down from heaven upon the children of men, to see if there were *any* that did understand, that did seek God.

3 Every one of them is gone back; they are altogether become

w Ps. xiv. 1, etc. x Gen. vi. 5, 12. y Eph. v. 12. z Ps. xi. 4.

---

lute or guitar, that was designed to be accompanied with the voice. De Wette renders it *flute*. Luther renders it "for a choir, to be sung by one another;" that is, a responsive choir. The Septuagint and the Latin Vulgate retain the original word with no attempt to translate it. Prof. Alexander renders it *disease*, because a form of the word "almost identical" occurs (Ex. xv. 26; Prov. xviii. 14; 2 Chron. xxi. 15) meaning *disease*, and he supposes reference is to "the spiritual malady with which all mankind are infected, and which is really the theme or subject of the composition." It is true that there *is* a word—מַחֲלָה—*similar* to this, meaning *disease;* but it is also true that the word here used is never employed in that sense, and equally true that such a construction here is forced and unnatural. The obvious supposition is that it refers to an instrument of music.

(*b*) The difference in the psalms themselves is mainly that in Ps. liii. the sixth verse of Ps. xiv. is omitted, and that in the other parts of the psalm there are *enlargements* designed to illustrate or to explain more fully the course of thought in the psalm. It is not known by whom these changes were made. They are, as De Wette remarks, such as could not have occurred by an error in transcribing, and they must have been made by design. Whether the changes were made by the author, or by some one who collected and arranged the psalms, and who, adopting the main thoughts of Ps. xiv., inserted additions conveying new phases of thought, though without intending to supersede the use of the original composition, it is not possible now to determine. It is by no means an improbable supposition that the author of the psalm—David—may have revised it himself, and made these changes as expressing more fully his idea, while, as embodying valuable thoughts, it was deemed not undesirable to retain the original psalm in the collection as proper to be used in the service of God. Similar changes occur in Ps. xviii., as compared with 2 Sam. xxii., where that psalm occurs in the original form of composition. There is no *evidence* that the alteration was made by a later writer; we may doubt whether a later writer *would* alter a composition of David, and publish it under his name.

For an analysis of the psalm, see Introd. to Ps. xiv.

1. *The fool hath said in his heart*, etc. For the meaning of this verse, see Notes on Ps. xiv. 1. The only change in this verse—a change which does not affect the sense—is the substitution of the word *iniquity*, in Ps. liii., for *works*, in Ps. xiv.

2. *God looked down from heaven*, etc. See Notes on Ps. xiv. 2. The only change which occurs in this verse is the substitution of the word *Elohim*, rendered *God*, for *Jehovah*, rendered LORD, in Ps. xiv. 2. The same change occurs also in vers. 4, 6. It is to be observed, also, that the word *Jehovah* does not occur in this psalm, but that the term used is uniformly *Elohim*, God. In Ps. xiv. both terms are found,—the word Elohim three times (vers. 1, 2, 5), and the word *Jehovah* four times, vers. 2, 4, 6, 7. It is impossible to account for this change. There is nothing in it, however, to indicate anything in regard to the authorship of the psalm or to the time when it was written, for both these words are frequently used by David elsewhere.

3. *Every one of them is gone back.* See Notes on Ps. xiv. 3. The only variation here in the two psalms is in the substitution of the word—סָג, *sog*, for סָר, *sor*,—words almost identical in form and in sense. The only dif-

filthy: *there is* none that doeth good, no, not one.

4 Have the workers of iniquity no knowledge? who eat up my people *as* they eat bread: they have not called upon God.

5 There [1] were they in great fear, [a] *where* no fear was; for God hath scattered the bones of him

[1] *they feared a fear.* [a] Prov. xxviii. 1.

ference in meaning is, that the former word—the word used here—means *to draw back,* or *to go back;* the other, the word used in Ps. xiv., means *to go off, to turn aside.* Each of them indicates a departure from God; a departure equally fatal and equally guilty, whether men turn *back* from following him, or turn *aside* to something else. Both of these forms of apostasy occur with lamentable frequency.

4. *Have the workers of iniquity no knowledge?* See Notes on Ps. xiv. 4. The only change in this verse is in the omission of the word *all.* This word, as it occurs in Ps. xiv. ("*all* the workers of iniquity"), makes the sentence stronger and more emphatic. It is designed to affirm in the most absolute and unqualified manner that *none* of these workers of iniquity had any true knowledge of God. This has been noticed by critics as the only instance in which the expression in Ps. xiv. is stronger than in the revised form of the psalm before us.

5. *There were they in great fear,* etc. Marg., as in Heb., *they feared a fear.* For the general meaning of the verse, see Notes on Ps. xiv. 5. There is, however, an important change introduced here,—the most important in the psalm. The general sentiment of two verses (5, 6) in Ps. xiv. is here compressed into one, and yet with such an important change as to show that it was by design, and apparently to adapt it to some new circumstance. The solution of this would seem to be that the original form (Ps. xiv.) was suited to some occasion then present to the mind of the writer, and that some new event occurred to which the general sentiment in the psalm might be easily applied (or which would express that as well as could be done by an entirely new composition), but that, in order to adapt it to this new purpose, it would be proper to insert some expression more *particularly* referring to the event. The principal of these additions is found in the verse before us. In Ps. xiv. 5, 6, the language is, "There were they in great fear; for God is in the generation of the righteous; ye have shamed the counsel of the poor, because the Lord is his refuge." In the psalm before us, the language is, "There were they in great fear, where no fear was: for God hath scattered the bones of him that encampeth against thee: thou hast put them to shame, because God hath despised them." ¶ Where *no fear was.* The reference here, as in Ps. xiv. 5, is to the fear or consternation of the people of God on account of the designs and efforts of the wicked. They were apprehensive of being overthrown by the wicked. The design of the psalmist in both cases is to show that there was no occasion for that fear. In Ps. xiv. 5, he shows it by saying that "God is in the congregation of the righteous." In the psalm before us he says expressly that there was no ground for that fear—"where no fear was,"—and he adds, as a reason, that God had "scattered the bones" of them "that encamped against" them. That is, though there *seemed* to be occasion for fear,—though those enemies were formidable in numbers and in power,—yet God was their friend, and he had now *showed* them that they had no real occasion for alarm by dispersing those foes. ¶ *For God hath scattered the bones of him that encampeth against thee.* Of the besieger. This, as already intimated, would seem to have been introduced in order to adapt the psalm to the particular circumstances of the occasion when it

that encampeth *against* thee: thou hast put *them* to shame, because [b] God hath despised them.

6 Oh [1] that the salvation of Israel *were come* out of Zion! When [c] God bringeth back the captivity of his people, Jacob shall rejoice, *and* Israel shall be glad.

b Jer. vi. 30.
1 *Who will give salvations,* etc.

c Ps. cxxvi. 1—3.

was revised. From this clause, as well as others, it appears probable that the particular occasion contemplated in the revision of the psalm was an attack on Jerusalem, or a siege of the city—an attack which had been repelled, or a siege which the enemy had been compelled to raise. That is, they had been overthrown, and their bones had been scattered, unburied, on the ground. The whole language of Ps. xiv., thus modified, would be well suited to such an occurrence. The general description of atheism and wickedness in Ps. xiv. would be appropriate in reference to such an attempt on the city,—for those who made the attack might well be represented as practically saying that there was no God; as being corrupt and abominable; as bent on iniquity; as polluted and defiled; and as attempting to eat up the people of God as they eat bread; and as those who did not call upon God. The verse before us would describe them as discomfited, and as being scattered in slaughtered heaps upon the earth. ¶ *Thou hast put* them *to shame.* That is, they had been put to shame by being overthrown; by being unsuccessful in their attempt. The word "thou" here must be understood as referring to God. ¶ *Because God hath despised them.* He has wholly disapproved their character, and he has "despised" their attempts;—that is, he has shown that they were not formidable or to be feared. They were efforts which might be looked on with contempt, and he had evinced this by showing how easily they could be overthrown.

6. *Oh that the salvation of Israel,* etc. The only change here from Ps. xiv. 7 is that the word *Elohim,* God, is substituted for *Jehovah,* LORD, and that the word rendered *salvation* is here in the plural. On the supposition that the psalm was *adapted* to a state of things when the city had been besieged, and the enemy discomfited, this language would express the deep and earnest desire of the people that the Lord would grant deliverance. Perhaps it may be supposed, also, that at the time of such a siege, and while the Lord interposed to save them *from* the siege, it was also true that there was some general danger hanging over the people; that even the nation might be described as in some sense "captive;" or that some portions of the land were subject to a foreign power. The desire expressed is, that the deliverance might be complete, and that the whole land might be brought to the possession of liberty, and be rescued from all foreign domination. That time, when it should arrive, would be the occasion of universal rejoicing.

PSALM LIV.

This psalm purports to be a psalm of David, and it bears all the internal marks of being his composition. The title suggests, doubtless with accuracy, the occasion on which it was composed, as well as the design for which it was intended. It is addressed or dedicated to the "chief Musician," to be set by him to music, and to be employed in the public service of God. See Introd. to Ps. iv.,—where, also, see the phrase "on Neginoth." The word "Maschil" denotes that it was a *didactic* poem, or a poem designed to set forth important truth. See Introd. to Ps. xxxii. The *occasion* on which the psalm was composed is indicated by the statement that it was "when the Ziphims came and said to Saul, Doth not David hide himself with us?" Such an occurrence is twice recorded; 1 Sam. xxiii. 19; xxvi. 1. It would seem not improbable

PSALM LIV.

To the chief Musician on Neginoth, Maschil. *A Psalm* of David, when the *d* Ziphims came and said to Saul, Doth not David hide himself with us?

SAVE me, O God, by thy name, and judge me by thy strength.
2 Hear my prayer, O God; give ear to the words of my mouth.
3 For strangers are risen up against me, and oppressors seek after my soul: *e* they have not set God before them. Selah.

d 1 Sam. xxiii. 19. *e* Ps. xxxvi. 1.

that they in fact made *two* communications to Saul on the subject at different times, or that David was *twice* in their country, and that they twice endeavoured to betray him to Saul. On the first occasion (1 Sam. xxiii. 19, *et seq.*) Saul, after commending them for their zeal, expressly desired them (ver. 22) to return, and look carefully that they might be sure that he was there, or that he had not escaped into some other place, "for," he adds, "it is told me that he dealeth very subtilly." Before making the attempt himself to seize him, he wished to be certified that he was really there. On their return, the Ziphims found that David *had* escaped to "Maon" (ver. 24), and they came again and informed Saul of that fact. After a vain effort on the part of Saul to find him, and after some other occurrences recorded in 1 Sam. xxiv., xxv., it would seem that David came *again* into the country of the Ziphites, and that they again informed Saul of that fact, 1 Sam. xxvi. 1. Of course, it is not known precisely on *which* of these occasions the psalm was composed.

This psalm is similar in design to Ps. lii.; and is intended, like that, to characterise the base conduct of *informers.* The psalm consists of three parts:—(1) An earnest prayer for deliverance, vers. 1-3; (2) an expression of confident belief that God *would* interpose, and deliver him, vers. 4, 5; (3) a resolution to render sacrifice to God, or to offer the tribute of praise, if he should be thus delivered, ver. 6, 7.

1. *Save me, O God, by thy name.* The word *name* here may include the perfections or attributes properly implied *in* the name. It is a calling on God *as* God, or in view of all that is implied in his name, or that constitutes the idea of "God." That *name* would imply all of power and benevolence that was necessary to secure his salvation or safety. The particular object of the prayer here is that God would save him from the design of the Ziphims to betray him to Saul. In some way David seems to have been apprised of the information which they had given to Saul, or at least to have suspected it so strongly that he felt it was necessary for him to move from place to place in order to find safety. ¶ *And judge me by thy strength.* The word *judge* here is used in the sense of declaring a judgment in his favour, or of vindicating him. See Notes on Ps. vii. 8. Comp. Ps. xviii. 20; xxvi. 1; xliii. 1. The idea is, Vindicate or save me by thy power.

2. *Hear my prayer, O God.* My earnest cry for deliverance from the designs of those who would betray me. ¶ *Give ear to the words of my mouth. Incline* thine ear to me, as one does who wishes to hear. See Notes on Ps. xvii. 6.

3. *For strangers are risen up against me.* That is, foreigners; those of another nation or land. Saul and his friends who sought the life of David were his own countrymen; these persons who sought to betray him were another people. They attempted to gain the favour of Saul, or to secure a reward from him, by betraying to him an innocent man whom he was persecuting. ¶ *And oppressors seek after my soul.* Seek after my life. The word here rendered *oppressors* means men of violence; the proud; the haughty; persecutors; tyrants. The word properly denotes those who exert their power in an arbitrary manner, or not under the sanction of law. ¶ *They have not set God before them.* They do not act as in the presence of God. They do not regard his authority.

4 Behold, God *is* mine helper: the *f* Lord *is* with them that uphold my soul.
5 He shall reward evil unto[1] mine enemies: cut them off in thy truth.
6 I will freely sacrifice unto thee: I will praise thy name, O LORD, for *it is* good.
7 For he hath delivered me

f Ps. cxviii. 7.

[1] *those that observe me.*

See Notes on Ps. xxxvi. 1. The word *Selah* here merely marks a musical pause. It indicates nothing in regard to the sense.

4. *Behold, God* is *mine helper.* That is, God alone *can* aid me in these circumstances, and *to* him I confidently look. ¶ *The Lord* is *with them that uphold my soul.* My friends; those who have rallied around me to defend me; those who comfort me by their presence; those who sustain me in my cause, and who keep me from sinking under the burden of my accumulated troubles.

5. *He shall reward evil unto mine enemies.* Marg., *those that observe me.* The original word here means literally *to twist, to twist together;* then, to press together; then, to *oppress*, or to treat as an enemy. The reference here is to those who pressed upon him as enemies, or who endeavoured to crush him. The idea is that God would recompense them for this conduct, or that he would deal with them as they deserved. ¶ *Cut them off in thy truth.* In thy faithfulness; in thy regard for what is right. This is simply a prayer, or an expression of strong confidence, that God would deal with them as they deserved, or that he would not suffer such conduct to pass without a proper expression of his sense of the wrong. There is no evidence that David in this prayer was prompted by private or vindictive feeling.

6. *I will freely sacrifice unto thee.* The Hebrew words rendered *freely*, mean *with willingness, voluntariness, spontaneousness.* The idea is, that he would do it of a free or willing mind; without constraint or compulsion; voluntarily. The reference is to a free-will or voluntary offering, as distinguished from one that was prescribed by law. See Ex. xxxv. 29; xxxvi. 3; Lev. vii. 16; xxii. 18; Num. xv. 3; xxix. 39. The idea is, that as the result of the Divine interposition which he prayed for, he would bring voluntary offerings to God in acknowledgment of his goodness and mercy. ¶ *I will praise thy name, O* LORD. I will praise thee. See Ps. lii. 9. ¶ *For* it is *good.* That is, God himself is benevolent; and David says that he would express his sense of God's goodness by offering him praise.

7. *For he hath delivered me out of all trouble.* This is spoken either in confident expectation of what *would be*, or as the statement of a general truth that God *did* deliver him from all trouble. It was what he had experienced in his past life; it was what he confidently expected in all time to come. ¶ *And mine eye hath seen* his desire *upon mine enemies.* The words *his desire* are not in the original. A literal translation would be, "And on my enemies hath my eye looked." The *meaning* is, that they had been overthrown; they had been unsuccessful in their malignant attempts against him; and he had had the satisfaction of *seeing* them thus discomfited. Their overthrow had not merely been reported to him, but he had had ocular demonstration of its reality. This is not the expression of *malice*, but of *certainty.* The *fact* on which the eye of the psalmist rested was his own safety. Of that he was assured by what he had witnessed with his own eyes; and in that fact he rejoiced. There is no more reason to charge malignity in this case on David, or to suppose that he rejoiced in the destruction of his enemies *as such*, than there is in our own case when we are rescued from

out of all trouble; and mine eye hath [g] seen *his desire* upon mine enemies.

g Ps. xcii. 11; cxii. 8, 10.

impending danger. It is proper for Americans to rejoice in their freedom, and to give thanks to God for it; nor, in doing this, is it to be supposed that there is a malicious pleasure in the fact that in the accomplishment of this thousands of British soldiers were slain, or that thousands of women and children as the result of their discomfiture were made widows and orphans. We can be thankful for the mercies which we enjoy without having any malignant delight in those woes of others through which our blessings may have come upon us.

PSALM LV.

This psalm is entitled "A Psalm of David," and there is every reason to believe that it is properly ascribed to him. It is addressed to "the chief Musician"—to be by him set to appropriate music, that it might be employed in the public worship of God. See Notes on the title to Ps. iv. On the word *Neginoth* in the title, see also Note in the Introduction of Ps. iv.

The occasion on which the psalm was composed is not indicated in the title, nor can it be with certainty ascertained. The author of the Chaldee Paraphrase refers the psalm to the time of Absalom and to his rebellion, and this is also the opinion of the Jewish expositors in general. They suppose that the psalm was composed on occasion of the departure of David from Jerusalem, when he had heard of the rebellion, and that the psalm has special reference to the time when, having fled from the city, and having come to the ascent of the Mount of Olives, while all was consternation around him, he learned that Ahithophel also was among the conspirators, which was the consummation of his calamity, 2 Sam. xv. 31. Others suppose that the psalm was composed when David was in Keilah, and when, surrounded by foes, he was apprehensive that the inhabitants of that place would deliver him into the hand of Saul, 1 Sam. xxiii. 1-12. Of all the known events in the life of David, the supposition which regards the psalm as composed during the rebellion of Absalom, and at the special time when he learned that the man whom he had trusted—Ahithophel—was among the traitors, is the most probable. All the circumstances in the psalm agree with his condition at that time, and the occasion was one in which the persecuted and much-afflicted king would be *likely* to pour out the desires of his heart before God. Paulus and De Wette have remarked that it is evident from the psalm that the enemies to whom the author refers were inhabitants of the same city with himself, and that the danger was from treason within the walls of the city, ver. 10. This seems not improbable, and this agrees well with the supposition that the scene of the psalm is laid in the time of the rebellion of Absalom.

The contents of the psalm are as follows:

(1) The prayer of the psalmist that God would hear his cry, vers. 1-3.

(2) A general description of his trouble and sorrows, as being so great that he was overwhelmed, and such as to make him wish for the wings of a dove that he might fly away, and be at rest, vers. 4-8.

(3) The causes, or sources of his trouble, vers. 9-14;—

- (*a*) The *general* fact that he was surrounded by enemies; that there were violence, strife, and mischief in the city, vers. 9-11.
- (*b*) The *particular* fact that some one in whom he had put confidence, and who had been his special friend, was, to his surprise, found among his enemies, and had proved himself faithless to him, vers. 12-14.

(4) His earnest prayer for the destruction of his enemies, ver. 15.

(5) His own confidence in God; his reliance on the Divine mercy and protection in the time of trouble and danger; and his assurance that God would interpose in his behalf, vers. 16-21.

(6) A general exhortation, as a practical lesson from all that had occurred, to trust in God,—to cast every burden on him,—with the assurance that the righteous would never be moved, but that the wicked must be subdued, vers. 22, 23.

PSALM LV.

To the chief Musician on Neginoth, Maschil. *A Psalm* of David.

GIVE ear to my prayer, O God; and hide not thyself from my supplication.

2 Attend unto me, and hear me: I mourn in my complaint, and make a noise;

3 Because of the voice of the

1. *Give ear to my prayer.* See Notes on Ps. v. 1; xvii. 6. This is the language of earnestness. The psalmist was in deep affliction, and he pleaded, therefore, that God would not turn away from him in his troubles. ¶ *And hide not thyself from my supplication.* That is, Do not withdraw thyself, or render thyself inaccessible to my prayer. Do not so *conceal* thyself that I may not have the privilege of approaching thee. Comp. Notes on Isa. i. 15. See also Ezek. xxii. 26; Prov. xxviii. 27; Lev. xx. 4; 1 Sam. xii. 3. The same word is used in all these places, and the general meaning is that of "shutting the eyes upon," as implying neglect. So also in Lam. iii. 56, the phrase "to hide the ear" means to turn away so as not to hear. The earnest prayer of the psalmist here is, that God would not, as it were, withdraw or conceal himself, but would give free access to himself in prayer. The language is, of course, figurative, but it illustrates what often occurs when God seems to withdraw himself; when our prayers do not appear to be heard; when God is apparently unwilling to attend to us.

2. *Attend unto me, and hear me.* This also is the language of earnest supplication, as if he was afraid that God would not regard his cry. These varied forms of speech show the intense earnestness of the psalmist, and his deep conviction that he *must* have help from God. ¶ *I mourn.* The word here used—רוּד, *rud*—means properly to wander about; to ramble—especially applied to animals that have broken loose; and then, to inquire after, to seek, as one does "by running up and down;" hence to desire, to wish. Thus in Hosea xi. 12,—"Judah runs wild towards God,"—in our translation, "Judah yet ruleth with God." The word occurs also in Jer. ii. 31, "We are lords" (marg., have dominion); and in Gen. xxvii. 40, "When thou shalt have the dominion." It is not elsewhere found in the Scriptures. The idea here seems not to be to *mourn*, but to *inquire earnestly;* to seek; to look for, as one does who wanders about, or who looks every way for help. David was in deep distress. He looked in every direction. He earnestly desired to find God as a Helper. He was in the condition of one who had lost his way, or who had lost what was most valuable to him; and he directed his eyes most earnestly towards God for help. ¶ *In my complaint.* The word here employed commonly means speech, discourse, meditation. It here occurs in the sense of *complaint*, as in Job vii. 13; ix. 27; xxi. 4; xxiii. 2; Ps. cxlii. 2; 1 Sam. i. 16. It is not used, however, to denote complaint in the sense of fault-finding, but in the sense of deep distress. As the word is now commonly used, we connect with it the idea of fault-finding, complaining, accusing, or the idea that we have been dealt with unjustly. This is not the meaning in this place, or in the Scriptures generally. It is the language of a *troubled*, not of an *injured* spirit. ¶ *And make a noise.* To wit, by prayer; or, by groaning. The psalmist did not hesitate to give vent to his feelings by groans, or sobs, or prayers. Such expressions are not merely indications of deep feeling, but they are among the appointed means of relief. They are the effort which nature makes to throw off the burden, and if they are without murmuring or impatience they are not wrong. See Isa. xxxviii. 14; lix. 11; Heb. v. 7; Matt. xxvii. 46.

3. *Because of the voice of the enemy.* He now states the cause of his troubles.

enemy, because of the oppression
of the wicked: for [h] they cast
iniquity upon me, and in wrath
they hate me.
4 My heart is sore pained
within me; and the terrors [i] of
death are fallen upon me.
5 Fearfulness and trembling
are come upon me, and horror
hath [1] overwhelmed me.

h 2 Sam. xvi. 7, 8.

i Ps. cxvi. 3. [1] *covered.*

He had been, and was, unjustly treated by others. The particular idea in the word "*voice*" here is, that he was suffering from slanderous reproaches; from assaults which had been made on his character. He was charged with evil conduct, and the charge was made in such a manner that he could not meet it. The result was, that a series of calamities had come upon him which was quite overwhelming. ¶ *Because of the oppression of the wicked.* The word here rendered *oppression* occurs nowhere else. The *verb* from which it is derived occurs twice, Amos ii. 13: "Behold, I am *pressed* under you as a cart is *pressed* that is full of sheaves." The idea is that of crushing by a heavy weight; and hence of crushing by affliction. The "wicked" alluded to here, if the supposition referred to in the Introduction about the occasion of the psalm is correct, were Absalom and those who were associated with him in the rebellion, particularly Ahithophel, who had showed himself false to David, and had united with his enemies in their purpose to drive him from his throne. ¶ *For they cast iniquity upon me.* That is, they charge me with sin; they attempt to justify themselves in their treatment of me by accusing me of wrong-doing, or by endeavouring to satisfy themselves that I *deserve* to be treated in this manner. If this refers to the time of the rebellion of Absalom, the allusion would be to the charges, brought by him against his father, of severity and injustice in his administration, 2 Sam. xv. 2–6. ¶ *And in wrath they hate me.* In their indignation, in their excitement, they are full of hatred against me. This was manifested by driving him from his throne and his home.

4. *My heart is sore pained within me.* Heavy and sad; that is, I am deeply afflicted. The word rendered *is sore pained,* means properly to turn round; to twist; to dance in a circle; to be whirled round; and then to twist or writhe with pain, especially applied to a woman in travail, Isa. xiii. 8; xxiii. 4; xxvi. 18. Here the idea is, that he was in deep distress and anguish. It is easy to see that this would be so, if the psalm refers to the revolt of Absalom. The ingratitude and rebellion of a son,—the fact of being driven away from his throne,—the number of his enemies, —the unexpected news that Ahithophel was among them,—and the entire uncertainty as to the result, justified the use of this strong language. ¶ *And the terrors of death are fallen upon me.* The Septuagint, the Vulgate, and Luther, render this *the fear of death,* as if he were afraid for his life, or afraid that the result of all this would be his death. A more natural construction, however, is to suppose that the reference is to the ordinary pains of death, and that he means to say that the pangs which he endured were like the pangs of death. The words "*are fallen*" suggest the idea that this had come suddenly upon him, like a "horror of great darkness" (comp. Gen. xv. 12), or as if the gloomy shadow of death had suddenly crossed his path. Comp. Notes on Ps. xxiii. 4. The calamities had come suddenly upon him; the conspiracy had been suddenly developed; and he had been suddenly driven away.

5. *Fearfulness and trembling.* Fear so great as to produce trembling. Comp. Notes on Job iv. 14. He knew not when these things would end. How far the spirit of rebellion

6 And I said, Oh that I had
wings like a dove! *for then* would
I fly away, and be at rest.
7 Lo, *then* would I wander far

had spread he knew not, and he had no means of ascertaining. It seemed as if he would be wholly overthrown; as if his power was wholly at an end; as if even his life was in the greatest peril. ¶ *And horror hath overwhelmed me.* Marg., as in Heb., *covered me.* That is, it had come upon him so as to cover or envelop him entirely. The shades of horror and despair spread all around and above him, and all things were filled with gloom. The word rendered *horror* occurs only in three other places;—Ezek. vii. 18, rendered (as here) *horror;* Job xxi. 6, rendered *trembling;* and Isa. xxi. 4, rendered *fearfulness.* It refers to that state when we are deeply agitated with fear.

6. *And I said.* That is, when I saw these calamities coming upon me, and knew not what the result was to be. ¶ *Oh that I had wings like a dove!* Literally, "Who will give me wings like a dove?" or, Who will give me the pinion of a dove? The original word—אֵבֶר, *aiber*—means properly, *a wing-feather;* a pinion; the penna major or flag-feather of a bird's wing by which he steers his course,—as of an eagle, Isa. xl. 31, or of a dove, as here. It is distinguished from the wing itself, Ezek. xvii. 3: "A great eagle, with great wings, *long-winged,* full of feathers." The reference here is supposed to be to the turtle-dove—a species of dove common in Palestine. Comp. Notes on Ps. xi. 1. These doves, it is said, are never tamed. "Confined in a cage, they droop, and, like Cowper, sigh for 'A lodge in some vast wilderness—some boundless contiguity of shade;' and no sooner are they set at liberty, than they flee to their mountains." Land and the Book (Dr. Thomson), vol. i., p. 416. The annexed cut will furnish a good illustration of the dove here referred to. ¶ For then *would I fly away, and be at rest.* I would escape from these dangers, and be in a place of safety. How often do we feel this in

times of trouble! How often do we wish that we could get beyond the reach of enemies; of sorrows; of afflictions! How often do we sigh to be in a place where we might be assured that we should be safe from *all* annoyances; from all trouble! There *is* such a place, but not on earth. David might have borne his severest troubles with him if he could have fled,—for those troubles are in the heart, and a mere change of place does not affect them; or he might have found new troubles in the place that *seemed* to him to be a place of peace and of rest. But there is a world which trouble never enters. That world is heaven; to that world we shall soon go, if we are God's children; and there we shall find absolute and eternal rest. Without "the wings of a dove," we *shall* soon fly away and be at rest. None of the troubles of earth will accompany us there; no new troubles will spring up there to disturb our peace.

7. *Lo,* then *would I wander far off.* Literally, "Lo, I would make the distance far by wandering;" I would separate myself far from these troubles. ¶ And *remain in the wilderness.* Literally, I would sojourn; or, I would pass the night; or, I would put up for the night.

off, *and* remain in the wilderness. Selah.

8 I would hasten my escape from the windy storm *and* tempest.

9 Destroy, O Lord, *and* divide their tongues: for I have seen[k] violence and strife in the city.

10 Day and night they go

k Jer. vi. 7.

The idea is taken from a traveller who puts up for the night, or who rests for a night in his weary travels, and seeks repose. Comp. Gen. xix. 2; xxxii. 21; 2 Sam. xii. 16; Judges xix. 13. The word *wilderness* means, in the Scripture, a place not inhabited by man; a place where wild beasts resort; a place uncultivated. It does not denote, as with us, an extensive forest. It might be a place of rocks and sands, but the essential idea is, that it was not inhabited. See Notes on Matt. iv. 1. In such a place, remote from the habitations of men, he felt that he might be at rest.

8. *I would hasten my escape.* I would make haste to secure an escape. I would not delay, but I would flee at once. ¶ *From the windy storm* and *tempest.* From the calamities which have come upon me, and which beat upon me like a violent tempest. If this psalm was composed on occasion of the rebellion of Absalom, it is easy to see with what propriety this language is used. The troubles connected with that unnatural rebellion had burst upon him with the fury of a sudden storm, and threatened to sweep everything away.

9. *Destroy, O Lord.* The word rendered *destroy,* properly means to *swallow up;* to *devour,* with the idea of greediness. Isa. xxviii. 4; Ex. vii. 12; Jonah i. 17; Jer. li. 34. Then it is used in the sense of *destroy,* Job xx. 18; Prov. i. 12. The reference here is to the *persons* who had conspired against David. It is a prayer that they, and their counsels, might be destroyed: such a prayer as men always offer who pray for victory in battle. It is a prayer that *they* may be successful in what they regard as a righteous cause; but this implies a prayer that their enemies may be defeated and overcome. That is, they pray for success in what they have undertaken; and if it is right for them to attempt to *do* the thing, it is not wrong to *pray* that *they may be successful.* ¶ And *divide their tongues.* There is evident allusion here to the confusion of tongues at Babel (Gen. xi. 1–9); and as the language of those who undertook to build that tower was confounded so that they could not understand each other, so the psalmist prays that the counsels of those engaged against him might be confounded, or that they might be divided and distracted in their plans, so that they could not act in harmony. It is very probable that there is an allusion here to the prayer which David offered when he learned that Ahithophel was among the conspirators (2 Sam. xv. 31); "And David said, O Lord, I pray thee, turn the counsel of Ahithophel into foolishness." This would tend to divide and distract the purposes of Absalom, and secure his defeat. ¶ *For I have seen violence and strife in the city.* In Jerusalem. Perhaps he had learned that among the conspirators there was not entire harmony, but that there were elements of "strife" and discord which led him to hope that their counsels would be confounded. There was little homogeneousness of aim and purpose among the followers of Absalom; and perhaps David knew enough of Ahithophel to see that *his* views, though he might be enlisted in the cause of the rebellion, would not be likely to harmonize with the views of the masses of those who were engaged in the revolt.

10. *Day and night they go about it, upon the walls thereof.* That is, continually. The word "*they*" in this place probably refers to the violence

about it, upon the walls thereof; mischief also and sorrow *are* in the midst of it.

11 Wickedness *is* in the midst thereof; deceit and guile depart not from her streets.

12 For *it was* not an enemy *that* reproached me; then I could have borne *it*: neither *was it* he that hated me *that* did magnify

---

and strife mentioned in the preceding verse. They are here personified, and they seem to *surround* the city; to be everywhere moving, even on the very walls. They are like a besieging army. Inside and outside; in the midst of the city and on the walls, there was nothing but violence and strife,—conspiracy, rebellion, and crime. ¶ *Mischief also and sorrow* are *in the midst of it.* Crime abounded, and the result was anguish or sorrow. This language would well describe the scenes when Absalom rebelled; when the city was filled with conspirators and rebels; and when crime and anguish seemed to prevail in every part of it.

11. *Wickedness* is *in the midst thereof.* That is, the wickedness connected with rebellion and revolt. ¶ *Deceit and guile depart not from her streets.* They are everywhere. They are found in every street and alley. They pervade all classes of the people. The word rendered *deceit* means rather *oppression.* This was connected with *guile,* or with *deceit.* That is, wrong would be everywhere committed, and the perpetration of those wrongs would be connected with false representations, and false pretences,—a state of things that might be expected in the unnatural rebellion under Absalom.

12. *For* it was *not an enemy* that *reproached me.* The word *reproached* here refers to slander; calumny; abuse. It is not necessarily implied that it was in his presence, but he was apprized of it. When he says that it is not an enemy that did this, the meaning is that it was not one who had been an avowed and open foe. The severest part of the trial did not arise from the fact that it was done by such an one; for *that* he could have borne. That which overwhelmed him was the fact that the reproach came from one who had been his friend; or, the reproach which he felt most keenly came from one whom he had regarded as a personal confidant. It is not to be supposed that the psalmist means to say that he was *not* reproached by his enemies, for the whole structure of the psalm implies that this was so; but his anguish was made complete and unbearable by the discovery that one especially who had been his friend was found among those who reproached and calumniated him. The connexion leads us to suppose, if the right view (*Introd.*) has been taken of the occasion on which the psalm was composed, that the allusion here is to Ahithophel (2 Sam. xv. 31); and the particular distress here referred to was that which David experienced on learning that *he* was among the conspirators. A case of trouble remarkably resembling this is referred to in Ps. xli. 9. See Notes on that place. ¶ *Then I could have borne* it. The affliction would have been such as I could bear. Reproaches from an enemy, being known to be an enemy, we expect; and we feel them comparatively little. We attribute them to the very fact that such an one is an enemy, and that he feels it necessary to sustain himself by reproaching and calumniating us. We trust also that the world will understand them in that way; and will set them down to the mere fact that he *is* our enemy. In such a case there is only the testimony against us of one who is avowedly our foe, and who has every inducement to utter malicious words against us in order to sustain his own cause. But the case is different when the accuser and slanderer is one who has been our intimate friend. He is supposed

himself against me; then I would have hid myself from him.

13 But *it was* thou, *l* a man [1] mine equal, my guide, *m* and mine acquaintance.

l Ps. xli. 9.

[1] *according to my rank.*
m 2 Sam. xv. 12.

to know all about us. He has been admitted to our counsels. He has known our purposes and plans. He can speak not *slanderously* but *knowingly*. It is supposed that he could have no motive to speak ill of us except his own conviction of truth, and that it could be only the *strongest* conviction of truth—the existence of facts to which not even a friend could close his eyes—that could *induce* him to abandon us, and hold us up to reproach and scorn. So Ahithophel—the confidential counsellor and friend of David—would be supposed to be acquainted with his secret plans and his true character; and hence reproaches from such an one became unendurable. *Neither* was it *he that hated me*. That avowedly and openly hated me. If that had been the case, I should have expected such usage, and it would not injure me. ¶ That *did magnify* himself *against me*. That is, by asserting that I was a bad man, thus exalting himself in character above me, or claiming that he was more pure than I am. Or, it may mean, that exalted himself above me, or sought to reach the eminence of power in my downfall and ruin. ¶ *Then I would have hid myself from him*. I should have been like one pursued by an enemy who could hide himself in a cave, or in a fastness, or in the mountains, so as to be safe from his attacks. The arrows of malice would fly harmlessly by me, and I should be safe. Not so, when one reproached me who had been an intimate friend; who had known all about me; *and whose statements would be believed*.

13. *But* it was *thou, a man mine equal*. Marg., *a man according to my rank*. Septuagint, *ἰσόψυχε*, equal-souled, like-souled, "second self" (Thompson); Vulg., *unanimus*, of the same mind; Luther, *Geselle*, companion. The Hebrew word here used—עֵרֶךְ, *airech*—means properly a row or pile, as of the shew-bread piled one loaf on another, Ex. xl. 23; then it would naturally mean one of the same row or pile; of the same rank or condition. The word also means price, estimation, or value, Job xxviii. 13; Lev. v. 15, 18; vi. 6. Here the expression may mean a man *according to my estimation, value*, or *price;* that is, of the same value as myself (Gesenius, Lex.); or more probably it means a man of my own rank; according to my condition; that is, a man whom I esteemed as my equal, or whom I regarded and treated as a friend. ¶ *My guide*. The word here used properly denotes one who is familiar,—a friend,—from the verb אָלַף, *alaph*—to be associated with; to be familiar; to be accustomed to. The noun is frequently used to denote a military leader,—the head of a tribe,—a chieftain; and is, in this sense, several times employed in Gen. xxxvi. to denote the leaders or princes of the Edomites, where it is rendered *duke*. But here it seems to be used, not in the sense of a leader or a guide, but of a familiar friend. ¶ *And mine acquaintance*. The word here used is derived from the verb *to know*—יָדַע, *yada*,—and the proper idea is that of *one well known* by us; that is, one who keeps no secrets from us, but who permits us to understand him thoroughly. The phrase *mine acquaintance* is a feeble expression, and does not convey the full force of the original, which denotes a more intimate friend than would be suggested by the word *acquaintance*. It is language applied to one whom we thoroughly *know*, and who *knows* us;—and this exists only in the case of very intimate friends. All the expressions used in this verse would probably be applicable to Ahithophel, and to the intimacy between him and David.

14 [1] We took sweet counsel together, *and* walked [n] unto the house of God in company.

[1] *Who sweetened counsel.*
n Ps. xlii. 4.

15 Let death seize upon them, *and* let them go down quick [o] into [1] hell: for wickedness *is* in their dwellings *and* among them.

o Num. xvi. 30—32. [1] Or, *the grave.*

---

14. *We took sweet counsel together.* Marg., *who sweetened counsel.* Literally, "We sweetened counsel together;" that is, We consulted together; we opened our minds and plans to each other; in other words, We found that happiness in each other which those do who freely and confidentially communicate their plans and wishes, —who have that mutual satisfaction which results from the approval of each other's plans. ¶ And *walked unto the house of God in company.* We went up to worship God together. The word rendered "*company*" means properly a noisy crowd, a multitude. The idea here is not that which would seem to be conveyed by our translation,—that they went up to the house of God in company *with each other,*—but that both went with the great company—the crowd—the multitude—that assembled to worship God. They were engaged in the same service, they united in the worship of the same God; associated with those that loved their Maker; belonged to the companionship of those who sought his favour. There is nothing that constitutes a stronger bond of friendship and affection than being united in the worship of God, or belonging to his people. Connexion with a church in acts of worship, *ought* always to constitute a strong bond of love, confidence, esteem, and affection; the consciousness of having been redeemed by the same blood of the atonement *should be* a stronger tie than any tie of natural friendship; and the expectation and hope of spending an eternity together in heaven *should* unite heart to heart in a bond which nothing—not even death —can sever.

15. *Let death seize upon them.* This would be more correctly rendered, "Desolations [are] upon them!" That is, Desolation, or destruction *will* certainly come upon them. There is in the original no necessary expression of a wish or prayer that this might be, but it is rather the language of certain assurance—the expression of a fact—that such base conduct—such wickedness —*would* make their destruction certain; that as God is just, they *must* be overwhelmed with ruin. Injury is sometimes done in the translation of the Scriptures by the insertion of a wish or prayer, where all that is *necessarily* implied in the original is the statement of a fact. This has been caused here by the somewhat uncertain meaning of the word which is used in the original. That word is יַשִּׁימָוֶת, *yashimaveth.* It occurs nowhere else. Our translators understood it (as the LXX., the Vulgate, and Luther do) as made up of two words. More correctly, however, it is to be regarded as one word, meaning *desolations,* or *destructions.* So Gesenius (*Lex.*), Rosenmüller, and Prof. Alexander understand it. ¶ And *let them go down quick into hell. Alive,* or *living,*—for that is the meaning of the word *quick* here—חַיִּים, *hhayyim*—as it commonly is in the Scriptures. Comp. Lev. xiii. 10; Numb. xvi. 30; Acts x. 42; 2 Tim. iv. 1; Heb. iv. 12; 1 Pet. iv. 5. The word *hell* is rendered in the margin *the grave.* The original word is *sheol,* and means here either the grave, or the abode of departed spirits. See Notes on Isa. xiv. 9; Job x. 21, 22. There is a harshness in the translation of the term here which is unnecessary, as the word *hell* with us now uniformly refers to the place of punishment for the wicked beyond death. The meaning here, however, is not that they would be consigned to wrath, but that they would be cut

16 As [p] for me, I will call upon God; and the LORD shall save me.

17 Evening, [q] and morning, and at noon, will I pray, and cry aloud; and he shall hear my voice.

18 He hath delivered my soul in peace from the battle *that was*

p Ps. lxxiii. 28. *q* Dan. vi. 10; Acts iii. 1.

off from the land of the living. The idea is that their destruction might be as sudden as if the earth were to open, and they were to descend *alive* into the chasm. Probably there is an implied allusion here to the manner in which the company of Korah, Dathan, and Abiram was destroyed, Numb. xvi. 31–33. Comp. Ps. cvi. 17. ¶ *For wickedness* is *in their dwellings*, and *among them.* Wickedness abounds in all their transactions. It is in their houses, and in their hearts. This is mentioned as a reason why they should be cut off and consigned to the grave. It *is* the reason why men are cut down at all; it is often a fact that wicked men are most manifestly cut down for their sins. And because it will be better for the community that the wicked should be punished than that they should escape, so there is no evidence that David cherished malice or ill-will in his heart. See General Introduction, § 6 (5).

16. *As for me, I will call upon God.* That is, I have no other refuge in my troubles, yet I can go to him, and pour out all the desires of my heart before him. ¶ *And the* LORD *shall save me.* This expresses strong confidence. On the supposition that the psalm refers to the rebellion of Absalom, David was driven from his home, and his throne, and from the house of God,—a poor exile, forsaken by nearly all. But his faith did not fail. He confided in God, and believed that He was able to effect his deliverance, and that He would do it. Rarely can we be placed in circumstances so trying and discouraging as were those of David; never should we, in any circumstances, fail to believe, as he did, that God can deliver us, and that, if we are his friends, we shall be ultimately safe.

17. *Evening, and morning, and at noon, will I pray.* In another place (Ps. cxix. 164) the psalmist says that he engaged in acts of devotion seven times in a day. Daniel prayed three times a day, Dan. vi. 10. David went, in his troubles, before God evening, morning, and midday, in solemn, earnest prayer. So Paul, in a time of great distress, gave himself on three set occasions to earnest prayer for deliverance. See Notes on 2 Cor. xii. 8. This verse, therefore, does not *prove* that it was a regular habit of David to pray three times a day; but in view of the passage, it may be remarked (*a*) that it is proper to have regular seasons for devotion, of frequent occurrence; and (*b*) that there are favourable and suitable *times* for devotion. The morning and the evening are obviously appropriate; and it is well to *divide* the day also by prayer,—to seek, at midday, the rest from bodily and mental toil which is secured by communion with God, — and to implore that strength which we need for the remaining duties of the day. True religion is cultivated by *frequent* and REGULAR seasons of devotion. ¶ *And cry aloud.* The word here employed properly means to murmur; to make a humming sound; to sigh; to growl; to groan. See Notes on Ps. xlii. 5. Here the language means that he would give utterance to his deep feelings in appropriate tones—whether words, sighs, or groans. To the deep thoughts and sorrows of his soul he would often give suitable expression before God. ¶ *And he shall hear my voice.* The confident language of faith, as in ver. 16.

18. *He hath delivered my soul in peace.* The Hebrew is, "He has *redeemed*;" so also the Septuagint and Vulgate. The meaning is, He has

against [r] me: for there were many with me.

19 God shall hear and afflict them, even he that abideth of old. Selah. [1] Because they have no changes, [s] therefore they fear not God.

[r] Ps. xviii. 17; cxxiv. 1, 2.

[1] Or, *With whom* also there be *no changes, yet they.* [s] Ps. lxxiii. 5, etc.

rescued me, or has saved me from my enemies. Either the psalmist composed the psalm *after* the struggle was over, and in view of it, here speaks of what had actually occurred; or he is so confident of being redeemed and saved that he speaks of it as if it were already done. See ver. 19. There are many instances in the Psalms in which the writer is so *certain* that what he prays for will be accomplished that he speaks of it as if it had already actually occurred. The words "*in peace*" mean that God had given him peace; or that the result of the Divine interposition was that he had calmness of mind. ¶ *From the battle* that was *against me.* The hostile array; the armies prepared for conflict. ¶ *For there were many with me.* This language conveys to *us* the idea that there were many on his side, or many that were associated with him, and that this was the reason why he was delivered. It is doubtful, however, whether this is the meaning of the original. The idea may be that there were many contending with him; that is, that there were many who were arrayed against him. The Hebrew will admit of this construction.

19. *God shall hear and afflict them.* That is, God will hear my prayer, and will afflict them, or bring upon them deserved judgments. As this looks to the future, it would seem to show that when in the previous verse he uses the past tense, and says that God *had* redeemed him, the language there, as suggested above, is that of strong confidence, implying that he had such certain assurance that the thing would be, that he speaks of it as if it were already done. Here he expresses the same confidence in another form,—his firm belief that God *would* hear his prayer, and would bring upon his enemies deserved punishment. ¶ *Even he that abideth of old.* The eternal God; he who is from everlasting. Literally, "He inhabits antiquity;" that is, he sits enthroned in the most distant past; he is eternal and unchanging. The same God who has heard prayer, will hear it now; he who has always shown himself a just God and an avenger, will show himself the same now. The fact that God is from everlasting, and is unchanging, is the only foundation for our security at any time, and the only ground of success in our plans. To a Being who is always the same we may confidently appeal; for we *know* what he will do. But who could have confidence in a changeable God? Who would know what to expect? Who can make any *calculation* on mere chance? ¶ *Because they have no changes,* &c. Marg., *With whom there be no changes, yet they fear not God.* Literally, "To whom there are no changes, and they fear not God." Prof. Alexander supposes this to mean that God will "hear" the reproaches and blasphemies of those who have no changes, and who, therefore, have no fear of God. The meaning of the original is not exactly expressed in our common version. According to that version, the idea would seem to be that the fact that they meet with no changes or reverses in life, or that they are favoured with uniform prosperity, is a *reason* why they do not fear or worship God. This may be true in fact (comp. Notes on Job xxi. 9–14), but it is not the idea here. The meaning is, that the God who is unchanging—who is always true and just—will "afflict," that is, will bring punishment on those who heretofore have had no changes; who have ex-

20 He hath put forth his hands against such as be at peace with him; he hath [1] broken his covenant.

21 *The words* of his mouth

[1] *profaned.*

perienced no adversities; who are confident of success because they have always been prosperous, and who have no fear of God. Their continual success and prosperity *may* be a reason—as it often is—why they do *not* feel their need of religion, and do *not* seek and serve God; but the precise truth taught here is, that the fact of continued prosperity is no argument for impunity and safety in a course of wrong doing. God is unchangeable *in fact*, as they *seem* to be; and an unchangeable God will not suffer the wicked always to prosper. To constitute safety there must be a better ground of assurance than the mere fact that we have been uniformly prospered, and have experienced no reverses hitherto. ¶ *They fear not God.* They do not regard him. They do not dread his interposition as a just God. How many such there are upon the earth, who argue secretly that because they have always been favoured with success, therefore they are safe; who, in the midst of abundant prosperity,—of unchanging "good fortune," as they would term it,—worship no God, feel no need of religion, and are regardless of the changes of life which may soon occur, and even of that one great change which death must soon produce!

20. *He hath put forth his hands against such as be at peace with him.* Against those who were his friends, or who had given him no occasion for war. The Septuagint and Vulgate render this, "He hath put forth his hands *in recompensing;*" that is, in taking vengeance. The Hebrew would bear this construction, but the more correct rendering is that in our common version. The *connexion* here would seem to indicate that this is to be referred to God, as God is mentioned in the previous verse. But evidently the design is to refer to the enemies, or the principal enemy of the psalmist,—the man whom he had particularly in his eye in the composition of the psalm; and the language is that of one who was *full* of the subject,—who was thinking of one thing,—and who did not deem it necessary to specify by name the man who had injured him, and whose conduct had so deeply pained him. He, therefore, begins the verse, "*He* hath put forth his hands," etc.; showing that his mind was fixed on the base conduct of his enemy. The language is such as leads us to suppose that the psalmist had Ahithophel in view, as being eminently the man that had in this cruel and unexpected manner put forth his hands against one who was his friend, and who had always treated him with confidence. ¶ *He hath broken his covenant.* He, Ahithophel. The margin, as the Hebrew, is, "*He hath profaned.*" The idea is, that he had defiled, or polluted it; or he had treated it as a vile thing,—a thing to be regarded with contempt and aversion, as a polluted object is. The "covenant" here referred to, according to the views expressed above, may be supposed to refer to the compact or agreement of Ahithophel with David as an officer of his realm—as an adviser and counsellor—that he would be faithful to the interests of the king and to his cause. All this he had disregarded, and had treated as if it were a worthless thing, by identifying himself with Absalom in his rebellion. See 2 Sam. xv. 12, 31.

21. The words *of his mouth were smoother than butter.* Prof. Alexander renders this, "Smooth are the butterings of his mouth." This is in accordance with the Hebrew, but the general meaning is well expressed in our common version. The idea is, that he was a hypocrite; that his professions of friendship were false; that he only used pleasant words—

were smoother than butter, but war *was* in his heart: his words were softer than oil, yet *were* they drawn swords.

t Matt. vi. 25, 30; 1 Pet. v. 7.

22 Cast *t* thy [1] burden upon the LORD, and he shall sustain thee: he [u] shall never suffer the righteous to be moved.

[1] Or, *gift*. *u* Ps. cxxi. 3.

---

words expressive of friendship and love—to deceive and betray. We have a similar expression when we speak of *honeyed words*, or *honeyed accents*. This would apply to Ahithophel, and it will apply to thousands of similar cases in the world. ¶ *But war* was *in his heart*. He was base, treacherous, false. He was really my enemy, and was ready, when any suitable occasion occurred, to show himself to be such. ¶ *His words were softer than oil*. Smooth, pleasant, gentle. He was full of professions of love and kindness. ¶ *Yet* were *they drawn swords*. As swords drawn from the scabbard, and ready to be used. Comp. Ps. xxviii. 3; lvii. 4.

22. *Cast thy burden upon the* LORD. This may be regarded as an address of the psalmist to himself, or to his own soul,—an exhortation to himself to roll all his care upon the Lord, and to be calm. It is expressed, however, in so general language, that it may be applicable to all persons in similar circumstances. Comp. Matt. xi. 28, 29; Phil. iv. 6, 7; 1 Pet. v. 7. The Margin here is, *gift*. The *literal* rendering would be, "Cast upon Jehovah what he hath given (or laid upon) thee; that is, thy lot." (Gesenius, *Lex.*) The phrase, "he gives thee," here means what he appoints for thee; what he allots to thee as thy portion; what, in the great distribution of things in his world, he has assigned to *thee* to be done or to be borne;—cast it all on him. Receive the allotment as coming from him; as what *he* has, in his infinite wisdom, assigned to thee as thy portion in this life; as what *he* has judged it to be best that thou shouldest do or bear; as *thy* part of toil, or trouble, or sacrifice, in carrying out his great arrangements in the world. All that is to be *borne* or to be *done* in this world he has *divided up* among men, giving or assigning to each one what He thought best fitted to his ability, his circumstances, his position in life,—what *he* could do or bear best,—and what, therefore, would most conduce to the great end in view. That portion thus assigned to *us*, we are directed to "cast upon the Lord;" that is, we are to look to him to enable us to do or to bear it. As it is *his* appointment, we should receive it, and submit to it, without murmuring; as it is *his* appointment, we may feel assured that no more has been laid upon us than is commensurate with our ability, our condition, our usefulness, our salvation. We have not to re-arrange what has been thus appointed, or to adjust it anew, but to do all, and endure all that he has ordained, leaning on his arm. ¶ *And he shall sustain thee*. He will make you sufficient for it. The word literally means *to measure*; then to hold or contain, as a vessel or measure; and then, to hold up or sustain *by* a sufficiency of strength or nourishment, as life is sustained. Gen. xlv. 11; xlvii. 12; l. 21; 1 Kings iv. 7; xvii. 4. Here it means that God would give such a *measure* of strength and grace as would be adapted to the duty or the trial; or such as would be sufficient to bear us up under it. Comp. Notes on 2 Cor. xii. 9. ¶ *He shall never suffer the righteous to be moved*. Literally, *He will not give moving for ever to the righteous*. That is, he will not so appoint, arrange, or permit things to occur, that the righteous shall be *ultimately* and *permanently* removed from their steadfastness and their hope; he will not suffer them to fall away and perish. In all their trials and temptations he will sustain them, and will ultimately bring them off in triumph. The meaning here cannot be that the

23 But thou, O God, shalt bring them down into the pit of destruction: [1] bloody and deceitful men shall not [2] live out half their days; [v] but I will trust in thee.

[1] *men of bloods and deceit.* [2] *halve.* [v] Prov. x. 27.

righteous shall never be "moved" in the sense that their circumstances will not be changed; or that none of their plans will fail; or that they will never be disappointed; or that their minds will never in any sense be discomposed; but that whatever trials may come upon them, they will be *ultimately* safe. Comp. Ps. xxxvii. 24.

23. *But thou, O God, shalt bring them down into the pit of destruction.* The word "*them,*" here evidently refers to the enemies of the psalmist; the wicked men who were arrayed against him, and who sought his life. The "pit of destruction" refers here to the grave, or to death, considered with reference to the fact that they would be *destroyed* or *cut off*, or would not die in the usual course of nature. The meaning is, that God would come forth in his displeasure, and cut them down for their crimes. The word *pit* usually denotes *a well*, or *cavern* (Gen. xiv. 10; xxxvii. 20; Exod. xxi. 34), but is often used to denote the grave (Job xvii. 16; xxxiii. 18, 24; Ps. ix. 15; xxviii. 1; xxx. 3, 9, *et al.*); and the idea here is that they would be cut off for their sins. The word "destruction" is added to denote that this would be by some direct act, or by punishment inflicted by the hand of God. ¶ *Bloody and deceitful men.* Marg., as in Heb., *Men of bloods and deceit.* The allusion is to men of violence; men who live by plunder and rapine; and especially to such men considered as false, unfaithful, and treacherous,—as they commonly are. The special allusion here is to the enemies of David, and particularly to such as Ahithophel,—men who not only sought his life, but who had proved themselves to be treacherous and false to him. ¶ *Shall not live out half their days.* Marg., as in Heb., *shall not halve their days.* So the Septuagint, and the Latin Vulgate. The statement is general, not universal. The meaning is, that they do not live half as long as they might do, and would do, if they were *not* bloody and deceitful. Beyond all question this is true. Such men are either cut off in strife and conflict, in personal affrays in duels, or in battle; or they are arrested for their crimes, and punished by an ignominious death. Thousands and tens of thousands thus die every year, who, *but* for their evil deeds, might have doubled the actual length of their lives; who might have passed onward to old age respected, beloved, happy, useful. There is to all, indeed, an outer limit of life. There is a bound which we cannot pass. That natural limit, however, is one that in numerous cases is much *beyond* what men actually reach, though one to which they *might* have come by a course of temperance, prudence, virtue, and piety. God has fixed a limit beyond which we cannot pass; but, wherever that may be, as arranged in his providence, it is our duty not to cut off our lives *before* that natural limit is reached; or, in other words, it is our duty *to live on the earth just as long as we can.* Whatever makes us come short of this is self-murder, for there is no difference in principle between a man's cutting off his life by the pistol, by poison, or by the halter, and cutting it off by vice, by crime, by dissipation, by the neglect of health, or by those habits of indolence and self-indulgence which undermine the constitution, and bring the body down to the grave. Thousands die each year whose proper record on their graves would be *self-murderers.* Thousands of young men are indulging in habits which, unless arrested, *must* have such a result, and who are destined to an early grave—who will not live out half their days—unless their mode of life is changed, and they be-

come temperate, chaste, and virtuous. One of the ablest lawyers that I have ever known—an example of what often occurs—was cut down in middle life by the use of tobacco. How many thousands perish each year, in a similar manner, by indulgence in intoxicating drinks!

PSALM LVI.

This purports to be a psalm of David, and there is no sufficient reason for doubting the correctness of its being thus attributed to him. De Wette indeed thinks that the contents of the psalm do not well agree with the circumstances of David's life, and especially with that period of his life referred to in the title, and supposes that it was composed by some Hebrew in exile in the time of the Captivity. But this is evidently mere conjecture. There *were* times in the life of David to which all that is said in this psalm would be applicable; and it is not difficult to explain all the allusions in it with reference to the circumstances specified in the title.

On the words "To the chief Musician," see Introd. to Ps. iv. In the expression in the title *upon Jonath-elem-rechokim*, the first word—*Jonath*—means a *dove*, a favourite emblem of suffering innocence; and the second—*elem*—means *silence*, dumbness, sometimes put for uncomplaining submission; and the third—*rechokim* — means *distant* or *remote*, agreeing here with places or persons, probably the latter, in which sense it is applicable to the Philistines, as aliens in blood and religion from the Hebrews. Thus understood, the whole title is an enigmatical description of David as an innocent and uncomplaining sufferer among strangers. See Prof. Alexander. De Wette, however, renders it, "The dove of the far-off terebinth trees." The Septuagint and the Vulgate render it, "for the people who are made remote from their sanctuary." The common rendering of the phrase is, "Upon, or respecting the dove of silence, in remote places," or "far-off from its nest," or "in distant groves." Gesenius (*Lex.*) renders it, "the silent dove among strangers," and applies it to the people of Israel in the time of the exile, as an uncomplaining, unmurmuring people. This explanation of the *words*, "the silent dove among strangers," is probably the true one; but it is applicable here, not to the people of Israel, as Gesenius, the Septuagint, and the Vulgate, render it, but to David, as an exile and a wanderer,—one who was driven away from country and home, as a dove wandering from its nest. Whether it was the title of a "tune" or a piece of music already known, or whether it was music that was composed for this occasion, and with reference to this very psalm, it is not practicable now to determine. It is very *possible* that there was already a piece of music in existence, and in common use, to which this beautiful title of "*A silent dove among strangers*," or "*A patient dove driven from her nest into remote places*," was given,—plaintive, tender, pensive music, and therefore peculiarly appropriate for a psalm composed to describe the feelings of David when driven from home, and compelled to seek a place of safety in a remote region, like a dove driven from its nest. On the meaning of the word *Michtam*, see Notes on the introd. to Psalm xvi. The portion of the title "When the Philistines took him in Gath," evidently refers to the event recorded in 1 Sam. xxi. 10, *et seq.* when David, fleeing from Saul, took refuge in the country of Achish, king of Gath, and when the "servants" of the king of Gath made him known to Achish, whose fears they so aroused as to lead him to drive the stranger away. The words "*took him in Gath*," refer not to their *apprehending* him, or *seizing* him, but to their following him, or overtaking him, to wit, by their calumnies and reproaches, so that he found no safety there. He was persecuted by Saul; he was also persecuted by the Philistines, among whom he sought refuge and safety.

The psalm embraces the following points:—

I. An earnest prayer for the Divine interposition in behalf of the author of the psalm, vers. 1, 2.

II. An expression of his trust in God in times of danger, vers. 3, 4.

III. A description of his enemies:—of their wresting his words; of their evil thoughts against him; of their gathering together; of their watching his steps; of their lying in wait for his life, vers. 5, 6.

IV. His confident belief that they would not escape by their iniquity; that God knew all his wanderings; that God remembered his tears, as if He put them in His bottle; and that his enemies would yet know that God was with him, vers. 7–9.

PSALM LVI.

To the chief Musician upon Jonath-elem-rechokim, [1] Michtam of David, when [w] the Philistines took him in Gath.

BE merciful unto me, O God; for man would swallow [x] me
up: he fighting daily oppresseth me.

2 Mine [2] enemies would daily swallow *me* up: for *they be* many that fight against me, O thou Most High.

3 What time I am afraid, [y] I

[1] Or, *a golden* Psalm *of David*, Ps. xvi. *title*. [w] 1 Sam. xxi. 11; xxix. 4.

[x] Hos. viii. 8. [y] 1 Sam. xxx. 6. [2] *observers*.

V. His entire trust in God, and his firm assurance that he would yet be kept from falling, and would walk before God in the light of the living. vers. 10–13.

The general *subject* of the psalm, therefore, is *confidence or trust in God in the time of danger*.

1. *Be merciful unto me, O God.* See Notes on Ps. li. 1. ¶ *For man would swallow me up.* The word here used means properly to breathe hard; to pant; to blow hard; and then, to pant after, to yawn after with open mouth. The idea is, that men came upon him everywhere with open mouth, as if they would swallow him down whole. He found no friend in man—in any man. Everywhere his life was sought. There was no *man*, wherever he might go, on whom he could rely, or whom he could trust; and his only refuge, therefore, was in God. ¶ *He fighting daily.* Constantly; without intermission. That is, all men seemed to be at war with him, and to pursue him always. ¶ *Oppresseth me.* Presses hard upon me; so presses on me as always to endanger my life, and so that I feel no security anywhere.

2. *Mine enemies.* Marg., *mine observers.* The Hebrew word here used means properly to twist, to twist together; then, to be firm, hard, tough; then, *to press together*, as a rope that is twisted,—and hence the idea of oppressing, or pressing hard on one, as an enemy. See Ps. xxvii. 11; liv. 5. In the former verse the psalmist spoke of *an* enemy, or of *one* that would swallow him up (in the singular number), or of *man* as an enemy to him anywhere. Here he uses the plural number, implying that there were *many* who were enlisted against him. He was surrounded by enemies. He met them wherever he went. He had an enemy in Saul; he had enemies in the followers of Saul; he had enemies among the Philistines, and now when he had fled to Achish, king of Gath, and had hoped to find a refuge and a friend there, he found only bitter foes. ¶ *Would daily swallow me up.* Constantly; their efforts to do it are unceasing. A new day brings no relief to me, but every day I am called to meet some new form of opposition. ¶ *For* they be *many that fight against me.* His own followers and friends were few; his foes were many. Saul had numerous followers, and David encountered foes wherever he went. ¶ *O thou Most High.* The word here used — מָרוֹם, *marom* — means properly height, altitude, elevation; then, a high place, especially heaven, Ps. xviii. 16; Isa. xxiv. 18, 21; then it is applied to anything high or inaccessible, as a fortress, Isa. xxvi. 5. It is supposed by Gesenius (*Lex.*), and some others, to mean here *elation of mind, pride*,—implying that his enemies fought against him with elated minds, or proudly. So the LXX, the Vulgate, and Luther render it; and so De Wette understands it. Yet it seems most probable that our translators have given the correct rendering, and that the passage is a solemn appeal to God as more exalted than his foes, and as one, therefore, in whom he could put entire confidence. Comp. Ps. xcii. 8; xciii. 4; Micah vi. 6.

3. *What time I am afraid.* Literally, *the day I am afraid.* David did not hesitate to admit that there were times when he was afraid. He saw

will trust in thee.

4 In God I will praise his word; in God I have put my trust: [z] I will not fear what flesh can do unto me.

5 Every day they wrest my words: [a] all their thoughts *are* against me for evil.

6 They gather themselves to-

z Luke xii. 4, 5. a Luke xi. 54.

himself to be in danger, and he had apprehensions as to the result. There is a natural fear of danger and of death; a fear implanted in us—(*a*) to make us cautious, and (*b*) to induce us to put our trust in God as a Preserver and Friend. Our very nature—our physical constitution—is full of arrangements most skilfully adjusted, and most wisely planted there, to lead us to God as our Protector. Fear is one of these things, designed to make us feel that we *need* a God, and to lead us to him when we realize that we have no power to save ourselves from impending dangers. ¶ *I will trust in thee.* As one that is able to save, and one that will order all things as they should be ordered. It is only this that can make the mind calm in the midst of danger:—(*a*) the feeling that God *can* protect us and save us from danger, and that he *will* protect us if he sees fit; (*b*) the feeling that whatever may be the result, whether life or death, it will be such as God sees to be best,—if *life*, that we may be useful, and glorify his name yet upon the earth; if *death*, that it will occur not because he had not *power* to interpose and save, but because there were good and sufficient reasons why he should *not* put forth his power on that occasion and rescue us. Of this we may be, however, assured, that God has *power* to deliver us always, and that if not delivered from calamity it is not because he is inattentive, or has not power. And of this higher truth also we may be assured always, that he has power to save us from that which we have most occasion to fear—a dreadful hell. It is a good maxim with which to go into a world of danger; a good maxim to go to sea with; a good maxim in a storm; a good maxim when in danger on the land; a good maxim when we are sick; a good maxim when we think of death and the judgment,—"*What time I am afraid,* I WILL TRUST IN THEE."

4. *In God I will praise his word.* The meaning of this seems to be, "In reference to God—or, in my trust on God—I will especially have respect to his *word*—his gracious promise; I will make that the special object of my praise. In dwelling in my own mind on the Divine perfections; in finding there materials for praise, I will have special respect to his revealed truth—to what he has *spoken* as an encouragement to me. I will be thankful that he *has* spoken, and that he has given me assurances on which I may rely in the times of danger." The idea is, that he would *always* find in God that which was the ground or foundation for praise; and that that which called for *special* praise in meditating on the Divine character, was the *word* or *promise* which God had made to his people. ¶ *I will not fear what flesh can do unto me.* What man can do to me. Comp. Notes on Matt. x. 28; Rom. viii. 31–34; Heb. xiii. 6.

5. *Every day they wrest my words.* The word here rendered *wrest*, means literally to give pain, to grieve, to afflict; and it is here used in the sense of *wresting*, as if force were applied to words; that is, they are *tortured*, twisted, perverted. We have the same use of the word *torture* in our language. This they did by affixing a meaning to his words which he never intended, so as to injure him. ¶ *All their thoughts* are *against me for evil.* All their plans, devices, purposes. They never seek my good, but always seek to do me harm.

6. *They gather themselves together.* That is, they do not attack me singly, but they unite their forces; they com-

gether, they hide themselves, they mark [b] my steps, when they wait for my soul.
7 Shall they escape by iniquity? [c] in *thine* anger cast down the people, O God.
8 Thou tellest my wanderings: put thou my tears into thy bottle; *are they* not in [d] thy book?

b Ps. xxxvii. 32. c Ec. viii. 13. d Mal. iii. 16.

bine against me. ¶ *They hide themselves.* They lurk in ambush. They do not come upon me openly, but they conceal themselves in places where they cannot be seen, that they may spring upon me suddenly. ¶ *They mark my steps.* They watch me whatever I do. They keep a spy upon me, so that I can never be sure that I am not observed. ¶ *When they wait for my soul.* As they watch for my life; or, as they watch for opportunities to take away my life. I am never secure; I know not at what time, or in what manner, they may spring upon me. This would apply to David when he fled to Achish, king of Gath; when he was driven away by him; and when he was watched and pursued by Saul and his followers as he fled into the wilderness. 1 Sam. xxi; xxii.

7. *Shall they escape by iniquity?* This expression in the original is very obscure. There is in the Hebrew no mark of interrogation; and a literal rendering would be, "By iniquity [there is] escape to them;" and, according to this, the sense would be, that they contrived to escape from just punishment by their sins; by the boldness of their crimes; by their wicked arts. The LXX. render it, "As I have suffered this for my life, thou wilt on no account save them." Luther, "What they have done evil, that is already forgiven." De Wette reads it, as in our translation, as a question: "Shall their deliverance be in wickedness?" Probably this is the true idea. The psalmist asks with earnestness and amazement whether, under the Divine administration, men *can* find safety in mere wickedness; whether great crimes constitute an evidence of security; whether his enemies owed their apparent safety to the fact that they were so eminently wicked. He prays, therefore, that God would interfere, and show that this was not, and could not be so. ¶ *In* thine *anger cast down the people, O God.* That is, show by thine own interposition—by the infliction of justice—by preventing the success of their plans—by discomfiting them—that under the Divine administration wickedness does *not* constitute security; in other words, that thou art a just God, and that wickedness is not a passport to thy favour.

8. *Thou tellest my wanderings.* Thou dost *number* or *recount* them; that is, in thy own mind. Thou dost keep an account of them; thou dost notice me as I am driven from one place to another to find safety. "*My wanderings,*"—to Gath, 1 Sam. xxi. 10; to the cave of Adullam, 1 Sam. xxii. 1; to Mizpeh, in Moab, 1 Sam. xxii. 3; to the forest of Hareth, 1 Sam. xxii. 5; to Keilah, 1 Sam. xxiii. 5; to the wilderness of Ziph, 1 Sam. xxiii. 14; to the wilderness of Maon, 1 Sam. xxiii. 25; to En-gedi, 1 Sam. xxiv. 1, 2. ¶ *Put thou my tears into thy bottle.* The tears which I shed in my wanderings. Let them not fall to the ground and be forgotten. Let them be remembered by thee as if they were gathered up and placed in a bottle—*a lachrymatory*—that they may be brought to remembrance hereafter. The word here rendered *bottle* means properly a bottle made of skin, such as was used in the East; but it may be employed to denote a bottle of any kind. It is possible, and, indeed, it seems probable, that there is an allusion here to the custom of collecting tears shed in a time of calamity and sorrow, and preserving them in a small bottle or "*lachrymatory,*" as a memorial of the grief. The Romans had a custom, that in a time of mourning—on a

funeral occasion—a friend went to one in sorrow, and wiped away the tears from the eyes with a piece of

TEAR-BOTTLES.

cloth, and squeezed the tears into a small bottle of glass or earth, which was carefully preserved as a memorial of friendship and sorrow. Many of

LACHRYMATORIES.

these lachrymatories have been found in the ancient Roman tombs. I myself saw a large quantity of them in the *Columbaria* at Rome, and in the Capitol, among the relics and curiosities of the place. The above engraving will illustrate the form of *these* lachrymatories. The annexed remarks of Dr. Thomson (" Land and the Book," vol. i. p. 147), will show that the same custom prevailed in the East, and will describe the forms of the "tear-bottles" that were used *there*:— " These lachrymatories are still found in great numbers on opening ancient tombs. A sepulchre lately discovered in one of the gardens of our city had scores of them in it. They are made of thin glass, or more generally of simple pottery, often not even baked or glazed, with a slender body, a broad bottom, and a funnel-shaped top. They have nothing in them but *dust* at present. If the friends were expected to contribute their share of tears for these bottles, they would very much need cunning women to cause their eyelids to gush out with water. These forms of ostentatious sorrow have ever been offensive to sensible people. Thus Tacitus says, 'At my funeral let no tokens of sorrow be seen, no pompous mockery of woe. Crown me with chaplets, strew flowers on my grave, and let my friends erect no vain memorial to tell where my remains are lodged.' "

¶ Are they *not in thy book?* In thy book of remembrance; are they not numbered and recorded so that they will not be forgotten? This expresses strong confidence that his tears *would* be remembered; that they would not

9 When I cry *unto thee*, then
shall mine enemies turn back:
this I know; for [e] God *is* for me.
10 In God will I praise *his*
word; in the LORD will I praise
his word.
11 In God have I put my trust:

[e] Rom. viii. 31.

be forgotten. All the tears that we shed *are* remembered by God. If *properly* shed—shed in sorrow, without murmuring or complaining, they will be remembered for our good; if *improperly* shed—if with the spirit of complaining, and with a want of submission to the Divine will, they will be remembered against us. But it is not wrong to weep. David wept; the Saviour wept; nature prompts us to weep; and it cannot be wrong to weep if *our eye "poureth out" its tears "unto God"* (Job xvi. 20); that is, if in our sorrow we look to God with submission and with earnest supplication.

9. *When I cry* unto thee. This expresses strong confidence in prayer. The psalmist felt that he had only to cry unto God, to secure the overthrow of his enemies. God had all power, and his power would be put forth in answer to prayer. ¶ *Then shall mine enemies turn back.* Then shall they cease to pursue and persecute me. He did not doubt that this would be the ultimate result,—that this blessing would be conferred, though it might be delayed, and though his faith and patience might be greatly tried. ¶ *For God* is *for me.* He is on my side; and he is with me in my wanderings. Comp. Notes on Rom. viii. 31.

10. *In God will I praise* his *word.* Luther renders this, "I will praise the word of God." The phrase "in God" means probably "in respect to God;" or, "in what pertains to God." That which he would *particularly* praise or celebrate in respect to God,—that which called for the most decided expressions of praise and gratitude, was his "*word,*" his promise, his revealed truth. So in Ps. cxxxviii. 2, "Thou hast magnified thy *word* above all thy name;" that is, above all the other manifestations of thyself. The allusion in the passage here is to what God had *spoken* to David, or the *promise* which he had made,—the declaration of his gracious purposes in regard to him. Amidst all the perfections of Deity, and all which God had done for him, this now seemed to him to have special pre-eminence in his praises. The *word* of God was to him that which impressed his mind most deeply,—that which most tenderly affected his heart. There are times when *we* feel this, and properly feel it; times when, in the contemplation of the Divine perfections and dealings, our minds so rest on his word, on his truth, on what he has revealed, on his gracious promises, on the disclosures of a plan of redemption, on the assurance of a heaven hereafter, on the instructions which he has given us about himself and his plans—about ourselves, our duty, and our prospects, that this absorbs all our thoughts, and we feel that this is *the* great blessing for which we are to be thankful; this, *the* great mercy for which we are to praise him. What would the life of man be without the Bible! What a dark, gloomy, sad course would ours be on earth if we had nothing to guide us to a better world! ¶ *In the* LORD *will I praise* his *word.* In *Jehovah.* That is, whether I contemplate God in the usual name by which he is known—*Elohim* (Heb.)—or by that more sacred name which he has assumed—*Jehovah* (Heb.)—that which seems now to me to lay the foundation of loftiest praise and most hearty thanksgiving, is that he has *spoken* to men, and made known his will in his revealed truth.

11. *In God have I put my trust.* The sentiment in this verse is the same as in ver. 6, except that the word "*man*" is used here instead of "flesh." The meaning, however, is

I will not be afraid what man can do unto me.

12 Thy vows *are* upon me, O God: I will render praises unto thee.

13 For thou hast delivered my soul from death; *wilt* not *thou deliver* my feet from falling, that I may walk before God in the light of the living?

---

the same. The idea is, that he would not be afraid of what *any man*—any human being—could do to him, if God was his friend.

12. *Thy vows* are *upon me, O God.* The word *vow* means something promised; some obligation under which we have voluntarily brought ourselves. It differs from duty, or obligation in general, since that is the result of the Divine command, while this is an obligation arising from the fact that we have *voluntarily* taken it upon ourselves. The extent of *this* obligation, therefore, is measured by the nature of the promise or vow which we have made; and God will hold us responsible for carrying out our vows. Such voluntary obligations or vows were allowable, as an expression of thanksgiving, or as a means of exciting to a more strict religious service, under the Mosaic dispensation (Gen. xxviii. 20; Num. vi. 2; xxx. 2, 3; Deut. xxiii. 21; 1 Sam. i. 11); and they cannot be wrong under any dispensation. They are not of the nature of *merit,* or works of supererogation, but they are (*a*) a *means* of bringing the obligations of religion to bear upon us more decidedly, and (*b*) a proper expression of gratitude. Such vows are those which all persons take upon themselves when they make a profession of religion; and when such a profession of religion is made, it should be a constant reflection on our part, that "the vows of God are upon us," or that we have voluntarily consecrated all that we have to God. David had made such a vow (*a*) in his general purpose to lead a religious life; (*b*) very probably in some specific act or promise that he would devote himself to God if he would deliver him, or as an expression of his gratitude for deliverance. Comp. Notes on Acts xviii. 18; xxi. 23, 24. ¶ *I will render praises unto thee.* Literally, "I will *recompense* praises unto thee;" that is, I will *pay* what I have vowed, or I will faithfully perform my vows.

13. *For thou hast delivered my soul from death.* That is, my *life.* Thou hast kept *me* from death. He was surrounded by enemies. He was pursued by them from place to place. He had been, however, graciously delivered from these dangers, and had been kept alive. Now he gratefully remembers this mercy, and confidently appeals to God to interpose still further, and keep him from stumbling. ¶ Wilt *not* thou deliver *my feet from falling.* This *might* be rendered, "Hast thou not delivered;" thus carrying forward the thought just before expressed. So the Septuagint, the Vulgate, and Luther and De Wette render it. The Hebrew, however, will admit of the translation in our common version, and such a petition would be an appropriate close of the psalm. Thus understood, it would be the recognition of dependence on God; the expression of gratitude for his former mercies; the utterance of a desire to honour him always; the acknowledgment of the fact that God only could keep him; and the manifestation of a wish that he might be enabled to live and act as in His presence. The word here rendered "falling" means usually a *thrusting* or *casting down,* as by violence. The prayer is, that he might be kept amid the dangers of his way; or that God would uphold him so that he might still honour Him. ¶ *That I may walk before God.* As in his presence; enjoying his friendship and favour. ¶ *In the light of the living.* See Notes on Job xxxiii. 30. The grave is represented everywhere in the Scriptures as a region of darkness (see Notes on Job x. 21, 22; comp. Ps. vi. 5; xxx. 9; Isa. xxxviii. 11, 18, 19),

PSALM LVII.

To the chief Musician, [1] Al-taschith, Michtam of David, when *f* he fled from Saul in the cave.

[1] Or, *Destroy not, A golden* Psalm.

BE merciful unto me, O God, be merciful unto me: for my

f Ps. cxlii., *title;* 1 Sam. xxii. 1.

---

and this world as light. The prayer, therefore, is, that he might continue to live, and that he might enjoy the favour of God: a prayer always proper for man, whatever his rank or condition.

PSALM LVII.

This is another psalm which purports to be a psalm of David. The propriety of ascribing it to him cannot be called in question. It is addressed to "the chief Musician" (see Notes to Introd. of Ps. iv.). Though relating to an individual case, and to the particular trials of an individual, yet it had much in it that would be appropriate to the condition of others in similar circumstances, and it contained, moreover, such general sentiments on the subject of religion, that it would be useful to the people of God in all ages. The expression in the title, *Al-taschith*, rendered in the margin, *Destroy not*, and by the Septuagint, μὴ διαφθείρῃς (*destroy not*), and in the same manner in the Latin Vulgate, occurs also in the titles of the two following psalms, and of the seventy-fifth. It is regarded by some as a musical expression,—and by others as the first words of some well-known poem or hymn, in order to show that this psalm was to be set to the music which was employed in using that poem; or, as we should say, that the *tune* appropriate to that was also appropriate to this, so that the words would at once suggest the tune, in the same manner as the Latin designations *De Profundis*, *Miserere*, *Non Nobis Domine*, *Te Deum*, etc., indicate well-known tunes as pieces of music,—the tunes to which the hymns beginning with those words are always sung. The author of the Chaldee Paraphrase regards this psalm as belonging to that period of David's history when he was under a constant necessity of using language of this nature, or of saying "*Destroy not*," and as therefore suited to all similar emergencies. The language seems to be derived from the prayer of Moses, Deut. ix. 26; "I prayed therefore unto the Lord, and said, O Lord God, *destroy not* thy people," etc. This very expression is found in 1 Sam. xxvi. 9, in a command which David addressed to his followers, and it *may* have been a common expression with him.—On the meaning of the word *Michtam* in the title, see Notes on the Introd. to Ps. xvi. It is found in the three following psalms—in the two former of them, in connexion with the phrase *Al-taschith*, showing that probably those psalms had reference to the same period of David's life. ¶ *When he fled from Saul in the cave.* Possibly the cave of Adullam (1 Sam. xxii. 1), or that of En-gedi (1 Sam. xxiv. 1-3). Or, the word may be used in a *general* sense as referring not to any *particular* cave, but to that period of his life when he was compelled to flee from one place to another for safety, and when his home was *often* in caves.

The psalm consists of the following parts:—

I. An earnest prayer of the suffering and persecuted man, with a full expression of confidence that God would hear him, vers. 1-3.

II. A description of his enemies, as men that resembled lions; men, whose souls were inflamed and infuriated; men, whose teeth were like spears and arrows, ver. 4.

III. The expression of a desire that God might be exalted and honoured, or that all these events might result in his honour and glory, ver. 5.

IV. A further description of the purposes of his enemies, as men who had prepared a net to take him, or had digged a pit into which he might fall, but which he felt assured was a pit into which they themselves would fall, ver. 6.

V. A joyful and exulting expression of confidence in God; an assurance that he would interpose for him; a determination to praise and honour him; a desire that God might be exalted above the heaven, and that his glory might fill all the earth,—forgetting his own particular troubles, and pouring out the desire of his heart that *God* might be honoured whatever might occur to *him*.

1. *Be merciful unto me, O God.* The same beginning as the former psalm,—a cry for mercy;—an overwhelming sense of trouble and danger leading him to come at once to the throne of

soul trusteth in thee: yea, in
[g] the shadow of thy wings will I
make my refuge, until *these* calamities be overpast.
2 I will cry unto God most
high; unto God that performeth
all things for me.

3 He shall send from heaven,
and save me [1] *from* the reproach
of him that would swallow me
up. Selah. God shall send forth
his mercy and his truth.
4 My soul *is* among lions; *and*
I lie *even among* them that are

g Ps. lxiii. 7.

[1] Or, *he reproacheth.*

God for help. See Notes on Ps. lvi. 1. ¶ *For my soul trusteth in thee.* See Notes on Ps. lvi. 3. He had nowhere else to go; there was no one on whom he could rely but God. ¶ *Yea, in the shadow of thy wings will I make my refuge.* Under the protection or covering of his wings, — as young birds seek protection under the wings of the parent bird. See Notes on Ps. xvii. 8. Comp. Ps. xxxvi. 7. ¶ *Until* these *calamities be overpast.* Comp. Notes on Job xiv. 13; Ps. xxvii. 13; also on Isa. xxvi. 20. He believed that these calamities *would* pass away, or would cease; that a time would come when he would not thus be driven from place to place. At present he knew that he was in danger, and he desired the Divine protection, for under *that* protection he would be safe.

2. *I will cry unto God most high.* The idea is,—God is exalted above all creatures; all events are *under* him, and he can control them. The appeal was not to man, however exalted; not to an angel, however far he may be above man; it was an appeal made at once to the Supreme Being, the God to whom all worlds and all creatures are subject, and under whose protection, therefore, he must be safe. ¶ *Unto God that performeth* all things *for me.* The word here used, and rendered *performeth* — גָּמַר, *gamar*—means properly to bring to an end; to complete; to perfect. The idea here is, that it is the character of God, that he *completes* or *perfects,* or brings to a happy issue all his plans. The psalmist had had experience of that in the past. God had done this in former trials; he felt assured that God would do it in this; and he, therefore, came to God with a confident belief that all would be safe in his hands.

3. *He shall send from heaven.* That is, from himself; or, he will interpose to save me. The psalmist does not say *how* he expected this interposition,—whether by an angel, by a miracle, by tempest or storm, but he felt that help was to come from God alone, and he was sure that it *would* come. ¶ *And save me* from *the reproach,* etc. This would be more correctly rendered, "He shall save me; he shall reproach him that would swallow me up." So it is rendered in the margin. On the word rendered "would swallow me up," see Notes on Ps. lvi. 1. The idea here is, that God would *rebuke* or *reproach,* to wit, by overthrowing him that sought to devour or destroy him. God had interposed formerly in his behalf (ver. 2), and he felt assured that he would do it again. ¶ *Selah.* This seems here to be a mere musical pause. It has no connexion with the sense. See Notes on Ps. iii. 2. ¶ *God shall send forth his mercy.* In saving me. He will *manifest* his mercy. ¶ *And his truth.* His fidelity to his promise; his faithfulness to those who put their trust in him. He will show himself *true* to all the promises which he has made. Comp. Ps. xl. 11.

4. *My soul* is *among lions.* That is, among men who resemble lions; men, fierce, savage, ferocious. ¶ And *I lie* even among *them that are set on fire.* We have a term of similar import in common use now, when we say that one is *inflamed* with passion, referring to one who is infuriated and enraged. So we speak of *burning*

set on fire, *even* the sons of men, whose teeth *are* spears and arrows, and their tongue [h] a sharp sword.

5 Be thou exalted, O God, above the heavens; *let* thy glory *be* above all the earth.

6 They have prepared a net [i] for my steps; my soul is bowed down: they have digged a pit before me, into the midst whereof they are fallen *themselves*. Selah.

7 My heart is [1] fixed, O God,

h Ps. lii. 2. *i* Mic. vii. 2. [1] Or, *prepared.*

with rage or wrath—an expression derived, perhaps, from the inflamed *appearance* of a man in anger. The idea here is not that he *would* lie down calmly among those persons, as Prof. Alexander suggests, but that he actually *did* thus lie down. When he laid himself down at night, when he sought repose in sleep, he was surrounded by such persons, and seemed to be sleeping in the midst of them. ¶ Even *the sons of men.* Yet they are not wild beasts, but *men* who seem to have the ferocious nature of wild beasts. The phrase, "sons of men," is often used to denote men themselves. ¶ *Whose teeth* are *spears and arrows.* Spears and arrows in their hands are what the teeth of wild beasts are. ¶ *And their tongue a sharp sword.* The mention of the tongue here has reference, probably, to the abuse and slander to which he was exposed, and which was like a sharp sword that pierced even to the seat of life. See Notes on Ps. lv. 21.

5. *Be thou exalted, O God, above the heavens.* Comp. Ps. viii. 1. The language here is that of a man who in trouble lifts his thoughts to God; who feels that God reigns; who is assured in his own soul that all things are under his hand; and who is desirous that God should be magnified whatever may become of himself. His prime and leading wish is not for himself, for his own safety, for his own deliverance from danger; it is that *God* may be honoured,—that the name of God may be glorified,—that God may be regarded as supreme over all things,—that God may be exalted in the highest possible degree—an idea expressed in the prayer that he may be exalted *above the heavens.* ¶ Let *thy glory* be *above all the earth.* The honour of thy name; thy praise. Let it be regarded, and be in fact, *above* all that pertains to this lower world; let everything on earth, or that pertains to earth, be subordinate to thee, or be surrendered for thee. This was the comfort which David found in trouble. And this *is* the only true source of consolation. The welfare of the universe depends on God; and that God should be true, and just, and good, and worthy of confidence and love,—that he should reign,—that his law should be obeyed,—that his plans should be accomplished,—is of more importance to the universe than anything that merely pertains to us; than the success of any of our own plans; than our health, our prosperity, or our life.

6. *They have prepared a net for my steps.* A net for my goings; or, into which I may fall. See Notes on Ps. ix. 15. ¶ *My soul is bowed down.* The Septuagint, the Vulgate, and Luther render this in the plural, and in the active form: "They have bowed down my soul;" that is, they have caused my soul to be bowed down. The Hebrew may be correctly rendered, "he pressed down my soul,"—referring to his enemies, and speaking of them in the singular number. ¶ *They have digged a pit before me,* etc. See Notes on Ps. vii. 15, 16; ix. 15; Job v. 13.

7. *My heart is fixed, O God.* Marg., as in Heb., *prepared.* Comp. Notes on Ps. li. 10. The word *fitted* or *prepared* accurately expresses the sense of the Hebrew, and it is so rendered in the Septuagint (ἑτοίμη); in the Vulgate, *paratum;* and by Luther, *bereit.* The word is used, however, in the sense of *standing*

my heart is fixed: I will sing and give praise.
8 Awake up, my glory; awake,
[k] psaltery and harp; I *myself*
will awake early.
9 I will praise thee, O LORD,
among the people; I will sing
unto thee among the nations.

k Ps. cviii. 1—5.

---

erect, Ps. ix. 7; to *establish* or *strengthen*, Ps. lxxxix. 4; x. 17; and hence, to be erect; to be firm, steady, constant, fixed. This seems to be the meaning here, as it is expressed in our common version. His heart was firm and decided. He did not waver in his purpose, or lean now to one side and then to the other; he was not *swayed* or *moved* by the events that had occurred. He felt conscious of standing firm in the midst of all his troubles. He confided in God. He did not doubt his justice, his goodness, his mercy; and, even in his trials, he was ready to praise him, and was *resolved* to praise him. The repetition of the word *fixed* gives emphasis and intensity to the expression, and is designed to show in the strongest manner that his heart, his purpose, his confidence in God, did not waver in the slightest degree. ¶ *I will sing and give praise.* My heart shall confide in thee; my lips shall utter the language of praise. In all his troubles God was his refuge; in all, he found occasion for praise. So it should be the fixed and settled purpose of our hearts that we will at all times confide in God, and that in every situation in life we will render him praise.

8. *Awake up, my glory.* By the word *glory* here some understand the tongue; others understand the soul itself, as the glory of man. The *word* properly refers to that which is weighty, or important; then, anything valuable, splendid, magnificent. Here it seems to refer to all that David regarded as glorious and honourable in himself,—his noblest powers of soul,—all in him that *could* be employed in the praise of God. The occasion was one on which it was proper to call all his powers into exercise; all that was noble in him as a man. The words *awake up* are equivalent to *arouse;*—a solemn appeal to put forth all the powers of the soul. ¶ *Awake, psaltery and harp.* In regard to these instruments, see Notes on Isa. v. 12. The instrument denoted by the word *psaltery*—נֵבֶל, *nebel*—was a stringed instrument, usually with twelve strings, and played with the fingers. See Notes on Ps. xxxiii. 2. The *harp* or *lyre*—כִּנּוֹר, *kinnor*—was also a stringed instrument, usually consisting of ten strings. Josephus says that it was struck or played with a key. From 1 Sam. xvi. 23; xviii. 10; xix. 9, it appears, however, that it was sometimes played with the fingers. ¶ *I* myself *will awake early.* That is, I will awake early in the morning to praise God; I will arouse myself from slumber to do this; I will devote the first moments—the early morning—to his worship. These words do not imply that this was an evening psalm, and that he would awake on the morrow—the next day—to praise God; but they refer to what he intended should be his general habit,—that he would devote the early morning (arousing himself for that purpose) to the praise of God. No time in the day is more appropriate for worship than the early morning; no object is more worthy to rouse us from our slumbers than a desire to praise God; in no way can the day be more appropriately begun than by prayer and praise; and nothing will conduce more to keep up the flame of piety—the life of religion in the soul—than the habit of devoting the early morning to the worship of God; to prayer; to meditation; to praise.

9. *I will praise thee, O Lord, among the people.* So great a deliverance as he here hoped for, would

10 For thy mercy *is* great unto the heavens, and thy truth unto the clouds.

11 Be thou exalted, O God, above the heavens: *let* thy glory *be* above all the earth.

PSALM LVIII.

To the chief Musician, [1] Al-taschith, Michtam of David.

DO ye indeed speak righteousness, O congregation? do ye

[1] Or, *Destroy not, A golden* Psalm *of David.*

---

make it proper that he should celebrate the praise of God in the most public manner; that he should make his goodness known as far as possible among the nations. See Notes on Ps. xviii. 49.

10. *For thy mercy* is *great unto the heavens,* etc. See this explained in the Notes on Ps. xxxvi. 5.

11. *Be thou exalted, O God, above the heavens.* See Notes on ver. 5. The sentiment here is repeated as being that on which the mind of the psalmist was intensely fixed; that which he most earnestly desired; that which was the crowning aim and desire of his life.

PSALM LVIII.

This psalm is also inscribed as a psalm of David. Both the title and the contents agree in fixing the time of its composition, and the occasion, as being the same as in the two previous psalms. Knapp indeed refers it to the time of Absalom, and De Wette supposes that it was composed in the time of the Babylonish captivity. But there is no reason for departing from the supposition that the title is correct. There is nothing in the psalm inconsistent with the supposition that it was composed by David, and in the time of the persecutions under Saul. On the meaning of the expression in the title, "*To the chief Musician,*" see Notes on the Introd. to Ps. iv. On the phrase "*Al-taschith,*" see Introd. to Ps. lvii. On the word "*Michtam,*" see Introd to Ps. xvi.

The psalm consists of three parts:—

I. A description of the enemies of the psalmist, suggesting a *general* description of the character of the wicked, vers. 1–5. The psalmist, by an emphatic *question* impliedly affirms that those whom he referred to were wicked and false (vers. 1, 2); and this leads him to a general reflection on the character of wicked men; (*a*) as estranged from the womb; (*b*) as going astray as soon as they are born; (*c*) as resembling the serpent injecting deadly poison; and (*d*) as deaf to all appeals of conscience, virtue, and religion—like an adder that will not listen to the voice of the charmer, vers. 3–5.

II. A prayer that God would interpose and deal with them as they deserved, vers. 6–9. This prayer is expressed in different illustrations:—(*a*) by comparing them with lions, and praying that their teeth might be broken out, ver. 6; (*b*) by comparing them with water, and praying that they might disappear as waters flow off, ver. 7; (*c*) by comparing them with a snail, and praying that they might be dissolved, and pass away as a snail appears to do, ver. 8; (*d*) by comparing them with the untimely birth of a woman, that is cast away, ver. 8; (*e*) by comparing them with a pot which is made to feel the heat of thorns on fire, and made to boil quickly,—praying that God would take them away before even that could be done, ver. 9.

III. The exultation of the righteous at such a result, vers. 10–11. (*a*) They would rejoice at the deliverance, ver. 10; (*b*) they would see that God is a righteous God; that he is not a friend of wickedness, but that he regards the cause of truth; that there is in fact a just moral government in the world; that there is a God who is a judge in the earth, ver. 11.

1. *Do ye indeed speak righteousness, O congregation?* Luther renders this, "Are you then dumb, that you will not speak what is right, and judge what is proper, ye children of men?" The meaning of the verse is exceedingly obscure; but probably the whole sense of the psalm turns on it. The word rendered *righteousness,* אֵלֶם, *elem*—occurs only in this place and in the title to Ps. lvi., "Jonath-*elem*-rechokim." See Notes on that title. The word properly means *dumbness, silence.* Gesenius (*Lex.*) renders it here, "Do ye indeed decree dumb justice?" *i.e.,* "Do ye really at

judge uprightly, O ye sons of men?
2 Yea, in heart [l] ye work wickedness: ye weigh the violence of your hands in the earth.

l Ps. xxi. 11.

length decree justice, which so long has seemed dumb?" Professor Alexander renders it, "Are ye indeed dumb when ye should speak righteousness?" The allusion is clearly to some public act of judging; to a judicial sentence; to magistrates and rulers; to men who *should* give a righteous sentence; to those in authority who *ought* to pronounce a just opinion on the conduct of others. The *fact* in the case on which the appeal is made seems to have been that they did *not* do this; that their conduct was wicked and perverse; that no reliance could be placed on their judicial decisions. Rosenmüller renders it, "There is, in fact, silence of justice;" that is, justice is not declared or spoken. Perhaps the meaning of the phrase may be thus expressed: "Is there truly a dumbness or silence of justice when ye speak? do you judge righteously, O ye sons of men?" That is, "You indeed speak; you do declare an opinion; you pronounce a sentence; but *justice* is, in fact, *dumb* or *silent* when you do it. There is no correct or just judgment in the matter. The opinion which is declared is based on error, and has its origin in a wicked heart." There is no expression in the original to answer to the words "O congregation" in our translation, unless it is the word אֵלֶם (*elem*), which never has this signification. It is not so rendered in any of the versions. It is not easy to determine *who* is referred to by this question. It cannot be, as is implied in our common version, that it is to any "*congregation*," any people gathered together for the purpose of pronouncing judgment. Yet it is evidently a reference to some persons, or classes of persons, who were expected to *judge*, or to whom it appertained to pass judgment; and the most natural supposition is that the reference is to the rulers of the nation,—to Saul, and the heads of the government. If the supposition is correct that the psalm was composed, like Ps. lvi., lvii., lix., in the time of the Sauline persecutions, and that it belongs to the same *group* of psalms, then it would have reference to Saul and to those who were associated with him in persecuting David. The subject of the psalm would then be the unjust judgments which they passed on him in treating him as an enemy of the commonwealth; in regarding him as an outlaw, and in driving him from his places of refuge as if hunting him down like a wild beast. The contents of the psalm well accord with this explanation. ¶ *Do ye judge uprightly?* Do you judge right things? are your judgments in accordance with truth and justice? ¶ *O ye sons of men.* Perhaps referring to the fact that in their judgments they showed that they were men—influenced by the common passions of men; in other words, they showed that they could not, in forming their judgments, rise above the corrupt passions and prejudices which usually influence and sway mankind.

2. *Yea, in heart ye work wickedness.* Whatever might be the outward appearances, whatever pretences they might make to just judgment, yet in fact their hearts were set on wickedness, and they were conscious of doing wrong. ¶ *Ye weigh the violence of your hands in the earth.* It is difficult to attach any meaning to this language; the translators evidently felt that they could not express the meaning of the original; and they, therefore, gave what seems to be a literal translation of the Hebrew. The Septuagint renders it, "In heart you work iniquity in the land; your hands weave together iniquity." The Latin Vulgate: "In heart you work iniquity; in the land your hands prepare injustice." Luther: "Yea, willingly do you work iniquity in the

3 The wicked are estranged from the womb; they go astray [1] as soon as they be born, speaking lies.

[1] *from the belly.*

land, and go straight through to work evil with your hands." Professor Alexander: "In the land, the violence of your hands ye weigh." Perhaps the true translation of the whole verse would be, "Yea, in heart ye work iniquity in the land; ye weigh [weigh out] the violence of your hands;" that is, the deeds of violence or wickedness which your hands commit. The idea of *weighing* them, or *weighing them out*, is derived from the administration of justice. In all lands men are accustomed to speak of *weighing out* justice; to symbolize its administration by scales and balances; and to express the doing of it as holding an even balance. Comp. Notes on Job xxxi. 6; Dan. v. 27; Rev. vi. 5. Thus interpreted, this verse refers, as ver. 1, to the act of pronouncing judgment; and the idea is that instead of pronouncing a just judgment—of holding an equal balance—they determined in favour of violence,—of acts of oppression and wrong to be committed by their own hands. That which they weighed out, or dispensed, was not a just sentence, but violence, wrong, injustice, crime.

3. *The wicked are estranged from the womb.* The allusion here undoubtedly is to the persons principally referred to in the psalm—the enemies of David. But their conduct towards him suggests a more general reflection in regard to *all* the wicked as having the same characteristics. The psalmist, therefore, instead of confining his remarks to them, makes his observations general, on the principle that all wicked men have essentially the same character, and especially in respect to the thing here affirmed, that they go astray early; that they are apostate and alienated from God from their very birth. The words, *the wicked*, here do not necessarily refer to the whole human family (though what is thus affirmed is true of all the human race), but to men who in their lives develop a wicked character; and the affirmation in regard to them is that they go astray early in life—from their very infancy. Strictly speaking, therefore, it cannot be shown that the psalmist in this declaration had reference to the whole human race, or that he meant to make a universal declaration in regard to man as being early estranged or alienated from God; and the passage, therefore, cannot directly, and with exact propriety, be adduced to prove the doctrine that "original sin" appertains to all the race,—whatever may be true on that point. If, however, it is demonstrated from *other* passages, and from facts, that all men *are* "wicked" or depraved, then the assertion here becomes a proof that this is from the womb—from their very birth—that they begin life with a propensity to evil—and that all their subsequent acts are but developments of the depravity or corruption with which they are born. It is only, therefore, after it is proved that men *are* depraved or "wicked," that this passage can be cited in favour of the doctrine of original sin. The word rendered *are estranged*—זֹרוּ, *zoru*—means properly, *to go off, to turn aside*, or *away, to depart;* and then it comes to mean *to be strange*, or *a stranger*. The proper idea in the word is that one is a stranger, or a foreigner, and the word would be properly applied to one of another tribe or nation, like the Latin *hostis*, and the Greek ξεῖνος. Exod. xxx. 33; Isa. i. 7; xxv. 2; xxix. 5; Ps. xliv. 20. The meaning of the term as thus explained is, that, from earliest childhood, they are *as if* they belonged to another people than the people of God; they manifest another spirit; they are governed by other principles than those which pertain to the righteous. Comp. Eph. ii. 19. Their first indications of character are not those of the children of God, but are *alien, strange, hostile*

4 Their [m] poison *is* [1] like the poison of a serpent; *they are* like the deaf [2] adder *that* stoppeth her ear;

m Rom. iii. 13.

[1] *according to the likeness of.* [2] Or, *asp.*

to him. The phrase "from the womb," refers, undoubtedly, to their birth; and the idea is, that as soon as they begin to act they act wrong; they show that they are strangers to God. Strictly speaking, this passage does not affirm anything directly of what exists in the heart *before* men begin to act, for it is by their "*speaking* lies" that they show their estrangement; yet it is proper to *infer* that where this is universal, there *is* something lying back of this which makes it certain that they *will* act thus—just as when a tree always bears the same kind of fruit, we infer that there is something *in* the tree, back of the actual *bearing* of the fruit, which makes it certain that it *will* bear such fruit and no other. This *something* in the heart of a child is what is commonly meant by *original sin.* ¶ *They go astray.* The Hebrew word here used means to go astray, to wander, to err. It is used in reference to drunken persons who reel, Isa. xxviii. 7; and to the soul, as erring or wandering from the paths of truth and piety, Ezek. xlviii. 11; Ps. xcv. 10; cxix. 110; Prov. xxi. 16. The *manner* in which the persons here referred to did this, is indicated here by their *speaking lies.* ¶ *As soon as they be born.* Marg., as in Heb., *from the belly.* The meaning is, not that they speak lies *as soon as* they are born, which could not be literally true, but that this is the *first act.* The first thing *done* is not an act of holiness, but an act of sin—showing what is in the heart. ¶ *Speaking lies.* They are false in their statements; false in their promises; false in their general character. This is *one* of the forms of sin, indicating original depravity; and it is undoubtedly selected here because this was particularly manifested by the enemies of David. They were false, perfidious, and could not be trusted. If it be proved, therefore, that all men are wicked, then *this* passage becomes a proper and an important text to demonstrate that this wickedness is not the result of temptation or example, but that it is the expression of the depravity of the heart by nature; that the tendency of man by nature is not to goodness, but to sin; that the first developments of character are sinful; that there is something lying back of sinful acts in men which makes it certain that they will act as they do; and that this always manifests itself in the first acts which they perform.

4. *Their poison.* Their malignity; their bad spirit; that which they utter or throw out of their mouth. The reference here is to what they speak or utter (ver. 3), and the idea is, that it is penetrating and deadly. ¶ *Like the poison of a serpent.* Marg., as in Heb., *according to the likeness.* In this expression no particular class of serpents is referred to except those which are *poisonous.* ¶ *Like the deaf adder.* Marg., *asp.* The word may refer either to the viper, the asp, or the adder. See Notes on Isa. xi. 8. The *particular* idea here is, that the serpent referred to was as it were *deaf;* it could not be tamed or charmed; it seemed to stop its own ears, so that there was no means of rendering it a safe thing to approach it. The supposition is that there *were* serpents which, though deadly in their poison, *might* be charmed or tamed, but that *this* species of serpent could *not.* The sense, as applied to the wicked, is, that there was no way of overcoming their evil propensities,—of preventing them from giving utterance to words that were like poison, or from doing mischief to all with whom they came in contact. They were malignant, and there was no power of checking their malignity. Their poi-

5 Which will not hearken to
the voice of charmers, [1] charming
never so wisely.

[1] Or, *be the charmer never so cunning.*

son was deadly, and there was no possibility of restraining them from doing evil. ¶ That *stoppeth her ear.* Which *seems* to stop her ear; which refuses to hear the words and incantations by which other serpents are subdued and tamed. Others, however, refer this to the man himself, meaning, *like the deaf adder he stops his ear;* that is, he voluntarily makes himself like the adder that does not hear, and that will not be tamed. The former interpretation, however, is to be preferred.

5. *Which will not hearken to the voice of charmers.* The word rendered *charmers* — לְחַשׁ, *lahhash* — means properly *whisperers, mutterers,* and it refers here to those who made use of spells or incantations,—sorcerers or magicians. See Notes on Isa. viii. 19. These incantations were accompanied usually with a low, muttering sound, or with a gentle whisper, as if for the purpose of calming and controlling the object of the incantation. Such charmers of serpents (or pretended charmers) abounded among the ancients, and still abound in India. The art is carried in India to great perfection; and there are multitudes of persons who obtain a livelihood by this pretended or real power over venomous serpents. Their living is obtained either by *exhibiting* their power over serpents which they carry with them in their peregrinations, or by *drawing* them by their incantations from the walls of gardens, houses, and hedges, where they had taken up their abode. Multitudes of facts, referred to by those who have resided in India, seem to confirm the opinion that this power is real. ¶ *Charming never so wisely.* Marg., *Be the charmer never so cunning.* The word rendered here *charming*—חוֹבֵר, *hhobair*—means properly to bind; to bind together. The *literal* meaning of the original Hebrew is, *binding spells that are wise,*—or, that are *cunning;* in other words, making use of the most cunning or skilful of their incantations and charms. The meaning is, that the utmost skill of enchantment will be unsuccessful. They are beyond the reach of any such arts. So with the men referred to by David. They were malignant and venomous; and nothing would disarm them of their malignity, and destroy their venom. What is here affirmed of these men is true in a certain sense of all men. The depravity of the human heart is such that nothing that man can employ will subdue it. No eloquence, no persuasion, no commands, no remonstrances, no influence that man can exert, will subdue it. It cannot be charmed down; it cannot be removed by any skill or power of man, however great. The following remarks from Dr. Thomson, who has spent twenty years in Palestine (Land and the Book, vol. i. pp. 221–223), will illustrate this passage:—"I have seen many serpent-charmers who do really exercise some extraordinary power over these reptiles. They carry enormous snakes, generally black, about them, allow them to crawl all over their persons and into their bosoms; always, however, with certain precautions, either necessary, or pretended to be so. They repeatedly breathe strongly into the face of the serpent, and occasionally blow spittle, or some medicated composition upon them. It is needless to describe the mountebank tricks which they perform. That which I am least able to account for is the power of detecting the presence of serpents in a house, and of enticing or 'charming' them out of it. The thing is far too common to be made a matter of scepticism. The following account, by Mr. Lane, is a fair statement of this matter:—'The charmer professes to discover, without ocular perception

(but perhaps he does so by a peculiar smell), whether there be any serpents in the house, and if there be, to attract them to him, as the fowler, by the fascination of his voice, allures the bird into his net. As the serpent seeks the darkest place in which to hide himself, the charmer has, in most cases, to exercise his skill in an obscure chamber, where he might easily take a serpent from his bosom, bring it to the people without the door, and affirm that he had found it in the apartment, for no one would venture to enter with him, after having been assured of the presence of one of these reptiles within. But he is often required to perform in the full light of day, surrounded by spectators; and incredulous persons have searched him beforehand, and even stripped him naked, yet his success has been complete. He assumes an air of mystery, strikes the walls with a short palm-stick, whistles, makes a clucking noise with his tongue, and spits upon the ground, and generally says, —I adjure you, by God, if ye be above or if ye be below, that ye come forth; I adjure you by the most great name, if ye be obedient, come forth, and if ye be disobedient, die! die! die!' The serpent is generally dislodged by his stick from a fissure in the wall or from the ceiling of the room. I have heard it asserted that a serpent-charmer, before he enters a house in which he is to try his skill, always employs a servant of that house to introduce one or more serpents; but I have known instances in which this could not be the case, and am inclined to believe that the dervishes above mentioned are generally acquainted with some physical means of discovering the presence of ser-

SERPENT-CHARMERS.

6 Break their teeth, O God, in their mouth; break out the great teeth of the young lions, O LORD.
7 Let them melt [n] away as waters *which* run continually: *when* he bendeth *his bow to shoot* his arrows, let them be as cut in pieces.
8 As a snail *which* melteth, let *every one of them* pass away; *like* the untimely birth of a woman, *that* they may not see the sun.

n Exod. xv. 15.

pents without seeing them, and of attracting them from their lurking-places. What these 'physical means' may be is yet a secret, as also the 'means' by which persons can handle live scorpions, and can put them into their bosom without fear or injury. I have seen this done again and again, even by small boys. This has always excited my curiosity and astonishment, for scorpions are the most malignant and irascible of all insects. The Hindoos, and after them the Egyptians, are the most famous snake-charmers, scorpion-eaters, etc., etc., although gipsies, Arabs, and others are occasionally found, who gain a vagabond livelihood by strolling round the country, and confounding the ignorant with these feats."

6. *Break their teeth, O God, in their mouth.* The word here rendered *break* means properly *to tear out.* The allusion is to his enemies, represented as wild beasts; and the prayer is, that God would deprive them of the means of doing harm,—as wild animals are rendered harmless when their teeth are broken out. ¶ *Break out the great teeth of the young lions, O* LORD. The word here used means properly *biters* or *grinders:* Job xxix. 17; Prov. xxx. 14; Joel i. 6. Comp. Notes on Ps. iii. 7. The word rendered *young lions* here does not refer to mere whelps, but to full-grown though young lions in their vigour and strength, as contrasted with old lions, or those which are enfeebled by age. The meaning is, that his enemies were of the most fierce and violent kind.

7. *Let them melt away as waters* which *run continually.* Let them vanish or disappear as waters that flow off, or floods that run by, and are no more seen. *Perhaps* the allusion here may be to the waters of a torrent that is swollen, which flow off and are lost in the sand, so that they wholly disappear. See Notes on Job vi. 15–19. The prayer is, that his enemies might perish, or be cut off, and that he might thus be saved from them. ¶ When *he bendeth* his bow to shoot *his arrows.* Literally, "he treads on his arrows." See Notes on Ps. xi. 2. The meaning here is, When he prepares for an attack,—or, prepares to make war, as one does who bends his bow, and places his arrow on the string. The allusion here is to the enemies of David, as seeking his life. ¶ *Let them be as cut in pieces.* That is, Let his arrows be as if they were cut off or *blunted,* so that they will produce no effect. Let them be such, that they will not penetrate and wound.

8. *As a snail* which *melteth, let* every one of them *pass away.* Or rather, As the snail which melteth as it goes; that is, which leaves a slimy trail as it moves along, and thus melts away the more as it advances, until at length it dies. Gesenius, *Lex.* The allusion is to what *seems* to occur to the snail; it seems to melt or to be dissolved as it moves along; or seems to leave a part of itself in the slime which flows from it. ¶ Like *the untimely birth of a woman.* The Hebrew word means literally *that which falls from a woman;* and hence the word is used to denote an abortion. The prayer is, that they might utterly pass away; that they might become like those who never had real life; that their power might wholly disappear. ¶ That *they may not see the sun.* May not be among the living. Comp. Notes on Job iii. 16.

9 Before your pots can feel the thorns, he shall take them away as [o] with a whirlwind, [1] both living, and in *his* wrath.

o Prov. x. 25.

[1] as *living as wrath.*

9. *Before your pots can feel the thorns.* The word *thorns* here—אָטָד, *atad*—refers to what is called *Christ's thorn*,—the southern buckthorn. *Gesenius.* The fire made of such thorns when dry would be quick and rapid, and water would be soon heated by it. The idea is, that what is here referred to would occur *quickly*—sooner than the most rapid and intense fire could make an impression on a kettle and its contents. The destruction of the wicked would be, as it were, instantaneous. The following quotation from Prof. Hackitt (Illustrations of Scripture, p. 135) will explain this passage: "A species of thorn, now very common near Jerusalem, bears the name of *Spina Christi*, or *Christ's thorn.* The people of the country gather these bushes and plants, and use them as fuel. As it is now, so it was of old. 'As the crackling of thorns under a pot, so is the laughter of the fool,' (Eccles. vii. 6.) 'Before your pots can feel the thorns,' namely, the fire of them, 'he shall sweep them away,' (Ps. lviii. 9.) The figure in this case is taken from travellers in the desert, or from shepherds tenting abroad, who build a fire in the open air, where it is exposed to the wind; a sudden gust arises and sweeps away the fuel almost before it has begun to burn. 'As thorns cut up shall they be burned in the fire' (Isa. xxxiii. 12). The meaning is that the wicked are worthless, —their destruction shall be sudden and complete." ¶ *He shall take them away.* The word rendered *shall take them away* means properly *to shiver, to shudder;* and it is then applied to the commotion and raging of a tempest. They shall be taken away as in a storm that makes everything shiver or tremble; Job xxvii. 21. It would be done *suddenly* and *entirely.* A sudden storm sent by God would beat upon them, and they would be swept away in an instant. ¶ *Both living and in* his *wrath.* Marg., *as living as wrath.* This expression is exceedingly obscure. The LXX. render it, "he shall devour them as it were living,—as it were in wrath." The Latin Vulgate: "He shall devour them as living, so in wrath." Prof. Alexander: "Whether raw or done." He supposes that the idea is, that God would come upon them while forming their plans; and that the illustration is derived from the act of *cooking*, and that the meaning is, that God would come upon them whether those plans were matured or not,—*cooked* or *raw.* This seems to me to be a very forced construction, and one which it is doubtful whether the Hebrew will bear. The word rendered *living*—חַי—means properly *alive, living;* and then, *lively, fresh, vigorous;* and is applicable then to a plant that is living or green. It *may* be here applied to the *thorns* that had been gathered for the fire, still green or alive; and the idea *here* would be, that even while those thorns were alive and green—before they had been kindled by the fire (or while they were trying to kindle them), a sudden tempest would come and sweep them all away. It is not, indeed, an uncommon occurrence in the deserts of the East, that while, in their journeyings, travellers pause to cook their food, and have gathered the fuel,—thorns, or whatever may be at hand,—and have placed their pot over the fire, a sudden tempest comes from the desert, and sweeps everything away. Rosenmüller *in loc.* Such an occurrence *may* be referred to here. The word rendered *wrath*—חָרוֹן, *hharon*—means properly *burning;* and then it is used to denote anything burning. It is applied to wrath or anger, because it seems to *burn.* Num. xxv. 4; xxxii. 14; 1 Sam. xxviii. 18. Here, however, it *may* be taken literally as applicable to thorns when they begin to

10 The righteous shall rejoice [p] when he seeth the vengeance: he [q] shall wash his feet in the blood of the wicked.

p Rev. xi. 17, 18. q Ps. lxviii. 23.

be kindled, though still green. They are seen first as gathered and placed under the pots; then they are seen as still green,—not dried up by the kindling flame; then they are seen as on fire; and, in a moment—before the pots could be affected by them—all is swept away by a sudden gust of wind. The *idea* is that of the sudden and unexpected descent of God on the wicked, frustrating their schemes even when they seemed to be well formed, and to promise complete success. This does not mean, therefore, that God would cut off and punish the wicked while *living*, but it refers to the fact that their schemes would be suddenly defeated even while they supposed that all things were going on well;—defeated before there was, in fact, any progress made towards the accomplishment, as the arrangements for the evening-meal would all be swept away before even the pot had begun to be warm.

10. *The righteous shall rejoice when he seeth the vengeance.* When he sees the just punishment inflicted on the wicked. He will approve of it; he will see that it is right; he will be glad that law is maintained, and that wickedness does not triumph; he will rejoice in the safety of those who do right, and in their deliverance from the assaults and the designs of the wicked. Men everywhere approve of the just administration of law, even though it consigns the transgressors to prison or to death; and it is a matter of gratification to all who love law and order when a righteous government is maintained; when wickedness is checked; when justice is administered in a community. This is the end of government and of law; this is what all magistrates are appointed to secure; this is what all good citizens are aiming to accomplish. There is no evidence that the psalmist had any vindictive or revengeful feeling when he uttered the sentiment in this verse. See Notes on Ps. lii. 6. Comp. Ps. xxxvii. 34; xl. 3. ¶ *He shall wash his feet in the blood of the wicked.* Comp. Ps. lxviii. 23. The image here is taken from a battle-field, where the victor treads in the blood of the slain. It is strong language denoting the entire overthrow of the wicked. There can be no doubt, however, that the allusion is to the *feelings* of satisfaction and triumph with which a victor walks over such a field;—the exultation which he has that his foes are subdued, and that he has triumphed. The *idea* is that the righteous will have emotions, when the wicked are subdued and punished, which in some respects *resemble* the feelings of the victor who walks over a field covered with the blood of the slain. Still it is not *necessary* to suppose that these are, in either case, vindictive feelings; or that either the victor or the righteous have pleasure in the shedding of blood, or in the sufferings of others; or that they would not have preferred that the discomfited and slain should *not* have been wicked, and should *not* have been made to suffer in this manner. All that is *essentially* implied in this is, that there is a feeling of satisfaction and approval when law is vindicated, and when the triumph of wickedness is prevented. It would be difficult to show that the feelings expressed by the psalmist are *less* proper than those which an officer of justice *may* have, and *ought* to have, and *does* have, when he has faithfully discharged his duty, and has secured the arrest and punishment of the violators of law; or that the psalmist has expressed anything more than every man must feel who sees *just* punishment inflicted on the guilty. Assuredly it is a matter of rejoicing that wickedness does *not* triumph; it is a thing to exult in when it *is* arrested.

11 So that a man shall say, Verily *there is* [1] a reward for the righteous: verily he is a God that judgeth [r] in the earth.

[1] *fruit of*, Isa. iii. 10.

r Ps. ix. 16.

11. *So that a man shall say.* That is, every man shall say, or men everywhere shall see this. This expresses the result of a close observation of the Divine dealings among men. The conclusion from those dealings is, (*a*) that there is, on the whole, a reward for the righteous on earth, or that righteousness tends to secure the favour of God and to promote human happiness; and (*b*) that there is a God—a just Being presiding over human affairs. ¶ *A reward for the righteous.* Marg., as in Heb., *fruit for the righteous.* That is, righteousness will produce its appropriate *fruits*, as trees that are cultivated will reward the cultivator. The idea is, that there is a course of things on earth, even with all there is that is mixed and mysterious, which is favourable to virtue; which shows that there is an *advantage* in being righteous; which demonstrates that there is a moral government; which makes it certain that God is the friend of virtue and the enemy of vice; that he is the friend of holiness and an enemy of sin. Comp. Notes on 1 Tim. iv. 8. ¶ *Verily he is a God that judgeth in the earth.* Or, Truly there is a God that judges in the earth. In other words, the course of things demonstrates that the affairs of the world are not left to chance, to fate, or to mere physical laws. There are results of human conduct which show that there is a *Mind* that presides over all; that there is One who has a purpose and plan of his own; that there is One who *administers* government, rewarding the good, and punishing the wicked. The argument is, that there is a course of things which cannot be explained on the supposition that the affairs of earth are left to chance; that they are controlled by fate; that they are regulated by mere physical laws; that they take care of themselves. There is a clear proof of Divine interposition in those affairs, and a clear proof that, on the whole, and in the final result, that interposition is favourable to righteousness and opposed to sin. No man, in other words, can take the *facts* which occur on the earth, and explain them satisfactorily, except on the supposition that there is a God. All other explanations fail; and numerous as it must be admitted are the difficulties that meet us even on this supposition, yet all other suppositions utterly fail in giving any intelligible account of what occurs in our world. See this argument stated in a manner which cannot be confuted, in Bishop Butler's Analogy, part i. chap. iii.

PSALM LIX.

The general title to this psalm is the same as in the two preceding psalms. That it was written by David, as is affirmed in the title, there is every reason to believe. The *occasion* on which it is said to have been composed was "when Saul sent, and they watched the house to kill him." This incident is related in 1 Sam. xix. 11: "Saul also sent messengers unto David's house to watch him, and to slay him in the morning." There is nothing in the psalm inconsistent with this statement in regard to the time and the occasion of its composition, unless it is in the word *heathen*—גּוֹיִם, *Goim*—twice used (vers. 5, 8),—a term, which (De Wette maintains) belongs properly to people of a foreign nation, and a foreign religion. It is true, however, that while the word originally had this meaning, it came to be used to denote any people or persons who had the general character and spirit which was supposed to distinguish nations without the knowledge of the true God; those who were cruel, harsh, unfeeling, oppressive, savage. Ps. ii. 1, 8; ix. 5, 15, 19, 20; x. 16; lxxix. 6, 10; cvi. 47, *et al.* In this sense it might be used here, without impropriety, as applicable to the enemies of David.

At what precise *time* the psalm was composed, it is, of course, impossible now to ascertain. All that is determined by

PSALM LIX.

To the chief Musician, Al-taschith, s Michtam of David; when t Saul sent, and they watched the house to kill him.

DELIVER [u] me from mine enemies, O my God: [1] defend me from them that rise up against me.

2 Deliver me from the workers of iniquity, and save me from bloody [v] men.

3 For, lo, they lie in wait for

s Ps. lvii., *title.* t 1 Sam. xix. 11. etc. u Ps. xviii. 48.

1 *set me on high.* v Ps. cxxxix. 19.

---

the title is that it was on that occasion, or with reference to that event; but whether it was at the very time when those enemies were known to be watching the house, or whether it was in view of that scene as recollected afterwards, recalling the feelings which then passed through his mind, cannot now be determined with certainty. That David was aware that his enemies were thus watching him is apparent from 1 Sam. xix. 11; that such thoughts as are recorded in the psalm passed through his mind in that time of danger is not improbable, but it can hardly be supposed that such an occasion would allow of the leisure necessary to express them in the form in which we now have them in the psalm. The probability, therefore, seems to be, that the psalm is a subsequent composition, recording the thoughts which then actually passed through his mind.

The psalm has no very regular order. The mind passes from one thing to another,—now uttering fervent prayer; now describing the enemy—his character and plans; and now expressing the confident hope of deliverance, and the purpose to praise God. Indeed the very structure of the psalm seems to me to furnish evidence that it describes feelings which *would* pass through the mind on such an occasion. Thus we have in vers. 1, 2, 5, 11-15, *prayer* for deliverance; in vers. 3, 4, 6, 12, intermingled with these prayers, a description of the character and designs of these enemies; and in vers. 8, 9, 16, 17, an expression of confident hope,—a purpose to praise God for deliverance and mercy. All this is indicative of such feelings as *might*, and probably *would*, pass through the mind in such a time of peril as that referred to in the title.

On the different phrases in the title, see Introd. to Psalms iv., lvii., and xvi.

1. *Deliver me from mine enemies, O my God.* See Notes on Ps. xviii. 48. This prayer was offered when the spies sent by Saul surrounded the house of David. They had come to apprehend him, and it is to be presumed that they had come in sufficient numbers, and with sufficient power, to effect their object. Their purpose was not to break in upon him in the night, but to watch their opportunity, when he went forth in the morning, to slay him (1 Sam. xix. 11), and there seemed no way for him to escape. Of their coming, and of their design, Michal, the daughter of Saul, and the wife of David, seems to have been apprised,—perhaps by some one of her father's family. She informed David of the arrangement, and assured him that unless he should escape in the night, he would be put to death in the morning. She, therefore, let him down through a window, and he escaped, 1 Sam. xix. 12. It was in this way that he was in fact delivered; in this way that his prayer was answered. A faithful wife saved him. ¶ *Defend me from them that rise up against me.* Marg., as in Heb., *Set me on high.* The idea is that of placing him, as it were, on a tower, or on an eminence which would be inaccessible. These were common places of refuge or defence. See Notes on Ps. xviii. 2.

2. *Deliver me from the workers of iniquity.* The workers of iniquity here referred to were Saul and those whom he employed to carry out his murderous purpose,—the men that had been sent to slay him. ¶ *And save me from bloody men.* Heb., *Men of bloods;* that is, men whose trade is blood; who seek to shed my blood, or who seek my life. See Notes on Ps. v. 6; xxvi. 9; lv. 23.

3. *For, lo, they lie in wait for my soul.* They lie in wait as wild beasts

my soul; the mighty are gathered against me; not [w] *for* my transgression, nor *for* my sin, O LORD.

4 They run and prepare themselves without *my* fault: awake to [1] help me, and behold.

5 Thou therefore, O LORD God of hosts, the God of Israel, awake to visit all the heathen;

w 1 Sam. xxiv. 11, 17.

1 meet.

---

do for their prey, ready to spring upon it. The word here used is often employed to denote the act of lying in ambush; of watching in secret places to spring upon a victim: Judges ix. 32; xxi. 20; Ps. x. 9. The word *soul* here means *life.* They lie in ambush that they may kill me. ¶ *The mighty are gathered against me.* Strong men; hostile men; cruel men. Saul would employ on this occasion not the weak, the cowardly, the faint-hearted, but men of courage and strength; men who were unscrupulous in their character; men who would not be likely to be moved by entreaty, or turned from their purpose by compassion. It is not mere *strength* that is here referred to, but that kind of strength or courage which can be employed in a desperate enterprise, and which is fitted to accomplish any scheme of wickedness, however daring or difficult. ¶ *Not* for *my transgression, nor* for *my sin.* This is done not on account of my violating the laws of the land, nor because it is alleged that I am a sinner against God. David was conscious that he did not deserve this treatment from the hand of man. He had been guilty of no wrong against Saul that exposed him to just punishment. He carried with him the consciousness of innocence as to any crime that could have made this treatment proper; and he felt that it was all the result of unjust suspicions. It was not improper for him to refer to this in his prayer; for, however he might feel that he was a sinner in the sight of God, yet he felt that a great and grievous wrong was done him by man; and he prayed, therefore, that a righteous God would interpose. See Notes on Ps. vii. 8; xvii. 2; xxxv. 24; xliii. 1.

4. *They run and prepare themselves.* That is, they *hasten* to accomplish this; they are quick to obey the command of Saul requiring them to slay me. The word *prepare* refers to whatever was deemed necessary to enable them to accomplish what they had been commanded to do,—arming themselves, making provision for their journey, etc. ¶ *Without* my *fault.* That is, without anything on my part to deserve this, or to justify Saul and those employed by him in what they attempt to do. David, in all this, was conscious of innocence. In his own feelings towards Saul, and in all his public acts, he knew that he had sought only the king's welfare, and that he had been obedient to the laws. ¶ *Awake to help me.* That is, *arouse,* as one does from sleep. See Notes on Ps. vii. 6. Comp. Ps. xxxv. 23. The word rendered *to help me,* is rendered in the margin, *to meet me.* This is the meaning of the Hebrew. It is a prayer that God would meet him, or come to him, and aid him.

5. *Thou therefore, O* LORD *God of hosts.* God of armies:—commanding all the armies of heaven,—the angels, and the stars and constellations drawn out in the form of armies;—thou, thus endowed with all power, and able to subdue all men though arrayed and combined for purposes of evil,—awake to my help. On the meaning of the phrase *God of hosts,* see Notes on Isa. i. 9. ¶ *The God of Israel.* The God of the Hebrew people—the descendants of Jacob or Israel,—the Protector of thy people,—awake to help *me,* one of those who, being of that covenant people, come under the promise of protection. ¶ *Awake to visit all the heathen.* On the word here rendered *heathen*—גּוֹיִם, *Goim*—

be not merciful to any wicked transgressors. Selah.

6 They return at evening: they make a noise like a dog, and go round about the city.

7 Behold, they belch out with their mouth: swords *x* *are* in their lips; for who, *say they*, doth hear?

x Prov. xii. 18.

see Notes on Ps. ii. 1. It is from the use of this word in this verse and in ver. 8, as remarked in the Introd. to the psalm, that De Wette infers that the psalm could not have been composed on the occasion referred to in the title, and argues, that this term could not be applied by David to Saul and his followers. This objection, however, will lose its force if the word is understood as denoting men who had the usual character of heathens, who were fierce, bloody, savage, cruel. In this sense the word might be employed with reference to those who were engaged in seeking the life of David. David, using the common word *heathen* or *nations*, as denoting those who are wicked, cruel, harsh, prays that God would awake to visit them; that is, to visit them for purposes of punishment, or so to visit them as to prevent their carrying out their designs. ¶ *Be not merciful to any wicked transgressors.* That is, Arrest and punish them *as* transgressors, or *being* transgressors. This prayer is not inconsistent with a desire that such men might be converted, and *thus* obtain mercy; but it is a prayer that God would not suffer them, being wicked men, to go at large and accomplish the work of wickedness which they designed. See General Introd. § 6. (5) (*e*). ¶ *Selah.* A musical pause. See Notes on Ps. iii. 2.

6. *They return at evening.* Many have rendered this in the imperative, as in ver. 14, "*Let* them return at evening," etc. So Luther renders it, and so also De Wette. But the more natural and obvious interpretation is to render it in the indicative, as describing the manner in which his enemies came upon him—like dogs seeking their prey; fierce mastiffs, howling and ready to spring upon him. From the phrase "they return at evening," thus explained, it would seem probable that they watched their opportunity, or lay in wait, to secure their object; that having failed at first, they drew off again until evening, perhaps continuing thus for several days unable to accomplish their object. ¶ *They make a noise like a dog.* So savages, after lurking stealthily all day, raise the war-whoop at night, and come upon their victims. It is possible that an assault of this kind *had* been attempted; or, more probably, it is a description of the manner in which they *would* make their assault, and of the spirit with which it would be done. ¶ *And go round about the city.* The word *city* is used in a large sense in the Scriptures, and is often applied to places that we should now describe as *villages*. Any town within the limits of which David was lodged, would answer to this term.

7. *Behold, they belch out with their mouth.* The word rendered *belch out* means properly to boil forth; to gush out, to flow; and then, to pour forth copiously, or in a running stream, as a fountain does. Hence the word means also to pour out *words*—words that flow freely—words of folly, abuse, or reproach. Prov. xv. 2, "The mouth of fools poureth out (Marg., *belcheth* or *babbleth*) foolishness." Prov. xv. 28, "The mouth of the wicked poureth out evil things;" that is, *gushes over* with wicked things—as a fountain overflows. In this place, the word means that the enemies of David who were in pursuit of his life, poured out reproaches and threatenings like a gushing fountain. ¶ *Swords* are *in their lips.* Their words are as sharp swords. See Notes on Ps. lvii. 4. ¶ *For who,* say they, *doth hear?* That is, no one hears who will be able

8 But thou, O LORD, shalt
laugh [y] at them; thou shalt have
all the heathen in derision.
9 *Because of* his strength will
I wait upon thee: for God *is* my
[z] defence.
10 The God of my mercy shall
prevent [a] me: God shall let me
see *my desire* upon [1] mine enemies.
11 Slay [b] them not, lest my
people forget: scatter them by

y Ps. ii. 4. *z* Prov. xviii. 10. *a* Ps. xxi. 3.

[1] *observers,* Ps. lvi. 2.
b Gen. iv. 12, 15; Rev. ix. 6.

to punish us. They dread no man; and they have no fear of God. Comp. Notes on Ps. x. 11. The words "say they" are, however, supplied here by the translators, and are not in the original; and the language *may* be understood as that of David himself, *as if* no one heard; that is, It is no wonder that they thus pour out words of reproach, for who *is* there to hear and to punish them? The former interpretation, however, is to be preferred. The language expresses the feelings of the enemies of David, who indulged freely in language of abuse and reproach *as if* there were none to hear.

8. *But thou, O* LORD, *shalt laugh at them.* That is, God will hear them, and will have all their efforts in derision, or will treat them with contempt. See Notes on Ps. ii. 4; xxxvii. 13. ¶ *Thou shalt have all the heathen in derision.* All those referred to in this psalm—the enemies of David—who have the character, and who manifest the spirit of the heathen; that is, of those who are not actuated by true religion. See Notes on ver. 5. This verse expresses the strong conviction of David, that all the efforts of his enemies would be vain; that God *would be* his Protector; and that he would save him from their evil designs.

9. Because of *his strength will I wait upon thee.* Literally, "His strength—I will wait upon thee." The reference here is not to the strength or power of God, as if the fact that *He* was powerful was a reason why the psalmist should look to him,—but it is to the strength or power of the enemy,—of Saul and his followers. There is much abruptness in the expression. The psalmist looks at the power of his enemy. "'His strength,' he cries. It is great. It is beyond my power to resist it. It is so great that I have no other refuge but God; and *because* it is so great, I will fix my eyes on him alone." The word rendered *wait upon* means rather to look to; to observe; to fix the eyes upon. ¶ *For God* is *my defence.* Marg., *My high place.* That is, God was to him *as* a high place, or a place of refuge; a place where he would be safe. See Notes on Ps. xviii. 2.

10. *The God of my mercy shall prevent me.* Or rather, "My God—his mercy shall prevent me." This is in accordance with the present reading of the Hebrew text, and is probably correct. The psalmist looks to God as his God, and then the feeling at once springs up that his mercy—his favour—his loving-kindness—*would* "prevent" him. On the word *prevent,* see Notes on Ps. xxi. 3; comp. Ps. xvii. 13; xviii. 5. The meaning here is, that God would *go before him,* or would *anticipate* his necessities. ¶ *God shall let me see* my desire *upon mine enemies.* That is, He will let me see them discomfited, and disappointed in their plans. This is equivalent to saying that God would give him the victory, or would not suffer them to triumph over him. See Notes on Ps. liv. 7.

11. *Slay them not, lest my people forget.* The meaning of this seems to be, Do not destroy them at once, lest, being removed out of the way, the people should forget what was done, or should lose the impression which it is desirable should be produced by their punishment. Let them live, and let them wander about, as exiles under the Divine displeasure, that they may be permanent and

thy power; and bring them down, O Lord our shield.

12 *For* [c] the sin of their mouth, *and* the words of their lips, let them even be taken in their pride; and for cursing and lying *which* they speak.

13 Consume *them* in wrath, consume *them*, that they *may* not *be*; and [d] let them know that God ruleth in Jacob unto the ends of the earth. Selah.

c Prov. xii. 13.

d Ps. xlvi. 10, 11.

enduring proofs of the justice of God; of the evil of sin; of the danger of violating the Divine law. So Cain wandered on the earth (Gen. iv. 12–14), a living proof of that justice which avenges murder; and so the Jews still wander, a lasting illustration of the justice which followed their rejection of the Messiah. The prayer of the psalmist, therefore, is that the fullest expression might be given to the Divine sense of the wrong which his enemies had done, that the salutary lesson might not be soon forgotten, but might be permanent and enduring. ¶ *Scatter them by thy power.* Break up their combinations, and let them go abroad as separate wanderers, proclaiming everywhere, by being thus vagabonds on the earth, the justice of God. ¶ *And bring them down.* Humble them. Show them their weakness. Show them that they have not power to contend against God. ¶ *O Lord our shield.* See Notes, Ps. v. 12; xxxiii. 20. The words "*our*" here, and "*my*" in the former part of the verse, are designed to show that the author of the psalm regarded God as *his* God, and the people of the land as *his*, in the sense that he was identified with them, and felt that his cause was really that of the people.

12. For *the sin of their mouth*, etc. That is, in belching out words of reproach and malice, ver. 7. ¶ *Let them even be taken in their pride.* In the very midst of their schemes, or while confidently relying on the success of their plans. Even while their hearts are elated, and they are sure of success, let them be arrested, and let their plans be foiled. ¶ *And for cursing and lying* which *they speak.* That is, on account of the false charges which they have brought against me, and of their bitter imprecations on me. The allusion is to the accusations brought against David, and which were believed by Saul, and which were the foundation of the efforts made by Saul to take his life.

13. *Consume* them *in wrath.* Or, in thy justice. The idea in the word *consume* here is to finish; to complete; to bring to an end. It does not mean to *burn* them as our word might seem to imply, nor is there any reference to the *mode* or *manner* in which their power was to be brought to an end. It is merely a prayer that all their plans might be frustrated; that there might be an entire completion of their attempts; or that they might be in no sense successful. ¶ *Consume* them. The expression is repeated for the sake of emphasis, implying a desire that the work might be *complete.* ¶ *That they* may *not* be. That things might be as if they were not in the land of the living. ¶ *And let them know.* Those who are now plotting my death. ¶ *That God ruleth in Jacob.* That God rules among his people, protecting them and guarding them from the attacks of their enemies; that he is their friend, and that he is the enemy of all those who seek to injure and destroy them. ¶ *Unto the ends of the earth.* Everywhere. All over the world. Let it be shown that the same principles of government prevail wherever man abides or wanders—that God manifests himself everywhere as the friend of right, and the enemy of wrong. The phrase "*the ends of the earth,*" is in accordance with the prevailing conception that the earth was an extended plane, and that it had limits or boundaries. Comp. Notes on Isa. xl. 22, 28.

14 And at evening let them return, *and* let them make a noise like a dog, and go round about the city.

15 Let them wander up and down [1] for meat, [2] and grudge if they be not satisfied.

16 But I will sing of thy power; yea, I will sing aloud of thy mercy in the [e] morning: for thou hast been my defence and refuge in the day of my trouble.

[1] *to eat*, Isa. lxv. 13.
[2] Or, *if they be not satisfied, then they will stay all night.*

e Ps. xxx. 5.

14. *And at evening let them return.* See Notes on ver. 6. The original here is the same as in ver. 6, with the exception of the word "*and*" at the beginning. This qualifies the sentence, and makes the construction in our version proper. The language is that of confident triumph. They came around the city to take David; they shouted and shrieked as dogs bark and howl when they come upon their prey. David asked God to interpose and save him; and *then*, says he, let them come if they will, and howl around the city; they will find no prey; they will be like hungry dogs from whom their anticipated victim has escaped. Let them come, and howl and rage. They can do no harm. They will meet with disappointment; and such disappointment will be a proper punishment for their sins.

15. *Let them wander up and down for meat.* Let them be like dogs that wander about for food, and find none. The idea is, that they would not find *him*, and would be then as dogs that had sought in vain for food. ¶ *And grudge if they be not satisfied.* Marg., *If they be not satisfied, then they will stay all night.* The marginal reading is most in accordance with the Hebrew. The sentence is obscure, but the idea seems to be that they would not be satisfied,—that is, they would not obtain that which they had sought; and, like hungry and disappointed dogs, they would be compelled to pass the night in this miserable and wretched condition. The word which our translators have rendered *grudge*—from לוּן, *lun*—means properly to pass the night; then, to abide, to remain, to dwell; and then, in Hiphil, to show oneself obstinate and stubborn,—from the idea of remaining or persisting in a bad cause; and hence the word sometimes means to murmur: Num. xiv. 29; Ex. xvii. 3. It has not, however, the signification of *grudging*, though it *might* mean here to murmur or complain because they were disappointed. But the most natural meaning is that which the word properly bears—that of passing the night, as referring to their wandering about, disappointed in their object, and yet still hoping that they might possibly obtain it. The anticipated feeling in the mind of the psalmist is that which *he* would have in the consciousness of his own safety, and in the pleasure of knowing that they must sooner or later find out that their victim had escaped.

16. *But I will sing of thy power.* That is, I will praise thee for the manifestation of thy power in rescuing me from danger. ¶ *Yea, I will sing aloud of thy mercy in the morning.* When the light dawns; when these troubles are over; when the night of calamity shall have passed by. There is an allusion here, probably, to the fact that they encompassed the place of his abode at night (vers. 6, 14); but there is also the implied idea that that night was emblematic of sorrow and distress. The morning would come; morning after such a night of sorrow and trouble; a morning of joy and gladness, when he would feel that he had complete deliverance. Then would he praise God aloud. Comp. Notes on Isa. xxi. 12. ¶ *For thou hast been my defence and refuge in the day of my trouble.* That is, he looked to the time when he would feel this; when

17 Unto *f* thee, O my strength, will I sing: for God *is* my defence, *and* the God of my mercy.

f Ps. xviii. 1.

looking back he could say this; when in view of it he would praise God.

17. *Unto thee, O my strength, will I sing.* The source of strength to me; the real strength by which I have obtained deliverance is in thee. See Notes on Ps. xviii. 1. ¶ *For God* is *my defence.* See Notes on ver. 9. ¶ And *the God of my mercy.* The God who has showed mercy to me; he from whom all these favours have sprung. Whatever means might be used to secure his own safety (comp. 1 Sam. xix. 12, *et seq.*) still he felt that his deliverance was to be traced wholly to God. *He* had interposed and had saved him; and it was proper, therefore, that praise should be ascribed to him. The experience of David in the case referred to in this psalm should be an inducement to all who are in danger to put their trust in God; his anticipated feelings of gratitude, and his purpose to praise God when he should be delivered, should awaken in us the resolution to ascribe to God all the praise when we are delivered from impending troubles, and when our lives are lengthened out where we have been in imminent danger. Whatever may have been the means of our rescue, it is to be traced to the interposition of God.

PSALM LX.

In the title, this psalm is ascribed to David. The occasion on which it is said to have been composed was after he had been engaged in wars in the East—in Aramea—and when he was meditating the completion of his conquests in the subjugation of Idumea. The time of its composition, according to the title, was that referred to in 2 Sam. viii., comp. 1 Chron. xviii. The occasion will be best understood by an explanation of the title.

On the phrase "To the chief Musician," see Notes on the Introd. to Ps. iv.

The phrase "upon Shushan-eduth" means properly *Lily of Testimony.* The word *shushan*—שׁוּשַׁן—means properly *lily.* See Notes on the title to Ps. xlv., where, as in the titles to Ps. lxix. and lxxx., the *plural* form of the word occurs. This is the only instance in which it is found in the singular number, when in the *title* to a psalm. The word *eduth*—עֵדוּת—means properly testimony; law; precept; revelation. It is applied to the law of God, as a *testimony* which God bears to the truth, Ps. xix. 7; 2 Kings xi. 12; and especially to the *ark,* called "the ark of the testimony," as containing the law or the Divine *testimony* to the truth. Ex. xxv. 21, 22 (comp. xvi. 34); xxvi. 33, 34; xxx. 6, 26; xxxi. 7. The word occurs frequently, and is uniformly translated *testimony.* Ex. xxvii. 21; xxx. 36; xxxi. 18, *et sæpe.* See Notes on Ps. xix. 7. *The lily of the law* would properly express the meaning of the phrase here, and it *may* have been the name of a musical instrument having a resemblance to a *lily*—open-mouthed like the lily; perhaps some form of the trumpet. Why the term *eduth—testimony* or *law*—was connected with this, it is not easy to determine. Gesenius (*Lex.*) supposes that the word means *revelation,* and that the term was used in these inscriptions because the authors of the psalms wrote by *revelation.* But if this was the reason, it would not explain why the title was prefixed to these psalms rather than others, since all were composed by revelation. Prof. Alexander, somewhat fancifully, supposes that the name *lily* is used in this title to denote *beauty;* that the reference is to *the beauty of the law,* and that the psalm is designed to celebrate that beauty. But it is sufficient to say in reply to this that there is no particular mention of the *law* in this psalm, and no special commemoration of its beauty. If the title had been prefixed to Ps. xix., or to Ps. cxix., there would then have been some foundation for the remark. On the whole, it seems impossible to determine the *reason* of the use of the term here. It would seem most probable that the allusion is to a musical instrument, or to some classes of musical instruments to which the term had been originally applied with reference to the use of those instruments in the services connected with the "ark of the testimony," or the celebration of the *law* of God; but on what occasion such instruments were first used, or why the term was applied, we cannot hope now to understand.

On the word *Michtam*, see Notes on the Introd. to Ps. xvi. It indicates nothing here in regard to the character of the psalm to which it is prefixed. It may be merely one form of denoting that it was a composition of David.

The word rendered *to teach*, means here that the psalm was adapted to impart instruction, and in this sense it is not unlike the word *Maschil* (Title to Ps. xxxii.), as being a psalm fitted to impart valuable information on the subject referred to, or perhaps to be learned and treasured up in the memory. It is not possible for us, however, to understand why the language was applied to this psalm rather than to others.

The psalm is said to have been composed when David "strove with Aram-naharaim and with Aram-zobah, when Joab returned and smote in the valley of salt twelve thousand." The allusion is to the transactions referred to in 2 Sam. viii. and 1 Chron. xviii. In those chapters we learn that David made extensive conquests in the East, extending his victories over Moab, Syria, and Hamath, and subduing the country as far as the Euphrates. It is to these victories that the psalm refers, see vers. 7, 8. The words rendered *Aram-naharaim* mean properly *Aram* (or Aramea) *of the two rivers*, and the reference is to Syria or Mesopotamia. The compound word occurs elsewhere in the following places, in all of which it is rendered *Mesopotamia*, Gen. xxiv. 10; Deut. xxiii. 4; Judges iii. 8; 1 Chron. xix. 6. The word *Aram* is of frequent occurrence, and properly refers to *Syria*. The name comprehended more than Syria proper, and the term *Aram-naharaim*, or *Aram of the two rivers*, was used to designate that part of the general country of Aramea which was between the Tigris and the Euphrates. The compound term *Aram-zobah* refers also to a part of Aramea or Syria. This kingdom was in the neighbourhood of Damascus, and perhaps comprehended *Hamath*, and probably extended as far as the Euphrates. The king of this country is represented as making war with Saul (1 Sam. xiv. 47), and with David (2 Sam. viii. 3; x. 6). In 2 Sam. viii. 3, David is represented as having smitten "Hadadezer, the son of Rehob, king of Zobah, as he went to recover his border at the river Euphrates." It is to these wars, and to this conquest, that the title of the psalm alludes.

The language in the title "when Joab returned," would seem to imply that these conquests were achieved not by David in person, but by *Joab*,—a circumstance not at all improbable, as he was the leader of the armies of David; 2 Sam. xx. 23, "Now Joab was over all the host of Israel." David had thus subdued Syria, and Moab, and the children of Ammon, and the Philistines, and the Amalekites, and Hadadezer, king of Zobah, and had dedicated to the Lord the silver and the gold which he had taken in these conquests (2 Sam. viii. 11, 12); but it would seem probable that Edom or Idumea still held out, or that at the time of composing the psalm that country had not been subdued. But the subjugation of that land was necessary to complete the conquests of David, and to make his kingdom safe. It was at this time probably, in the interval between 2 Sam. viii. 12 and 2 Sam. viii. 14, that the psalm was composed, or *in view* of the strong desire of David to subdue Edom; see vers. 8, 9 of the psalm, "Over Edom will I cast out my shoe," . . . "Who will lead me into Edom?" It would seem that there were some special difficulties in the conquest of that country; or that there had been some partial discomfiture in attempting it (Ps. lx. 1-3), and David was now fearful that he had in some way incurred the Divine displeasure after all his conquests, and that Edom—a place so strong and so important—was likely to remain unsubdued. And yet the conquest *was* made, for it is said in the title "that Joab smote of Edom in the valley of salt twelve thousand." Comp. 2 Sam. viii. 13.

The phrase "the Valley of Salt" is explained by the fact that not a few valleys are found in Arabia and Syria, which are at certain periods—in the wet seasons—stagnant pools; but which, when they are dried up, leave an incrustation of salt, or a saline deposit on the sand. Travellers make mention of such pools, from which they obtain their supplies of salt. Van Hamelsveld, Bib. Geog., i. p. 402. *What* valley is here referred to is not certain. It would seem most probable that it was the valley in which the Dead Sea is situated, as being eminently the valley of salt, or the valley in which such deposits abounded. Dr. Robinson (Researches in Palestine, vol.

ii. p. 483), supposes that this "valley of salt" is situated at the southern end of the Dead Sea—the Ghor south of the Dead Sea, and adjacent to the *Mountain of Salt*,—"the whole body of the mountain being a solid mass of rock-salt," p. 482. This valley separates the ancient territories of Judah and Edom, and would, therefore, be the place where the battle would naturally be fought.

This victory is said in the title of the psalm to have been achieved by Joab; in 2 Sam. viii. 13, it is attributed to David; in the parallel place in 1 Chron. xviii. 12, it is said to have been achieved by Abishai,—in the margin, Abshai. There is no discrepancy between the account in 2 Sam., where the victory is ascribed to David, and that in the title to the psalm where it is ascribed to Joab, for though the battle may have been fought by Joab, yet it was really one of the victories of David, as Joab acted under him and by his orders,—as we speak of the conquests of Napoleon, attributing to him the conquests which were secured by the armies under his command. There is greater difficulty in reconciling the account in 1 Chronicles with the title to the psalm, where one ascribes the victory to Joab, and the other to Abishai. Some have supposed that either in the title to the psalm or in 1 Chronicles there has been an error in transcribing. But such an error could hardly have occurred. The most probable opinion seems to be that the victory was achieved by the *joint* action of the forces under Joab and his brother Abishai, and that with propriety it may be spoken of as the victory of either of them. We know that on one occasion Joab thus divided his forces, retaining the command of a portion of the army to himself, and assigning the other portion to his brother Abishai (2 Sam. x. 9, 10), and it is possible that there may have been such a division of the army here, and that the victory may have been so connected with the skill and valour of Abishai that it might without impropriety be spoken of as *his* victory, while there was no impropriety also in ascribing it to *Joab*, as entrusted with the general command, or to *David* who had planned and directed the expedition.

There is, also, a discrepancy in the numbers mentioned as slain, in the title to the psalm, and in the account in Samuel and Chronicles. In 2 Sam. viii. 13, and in 1 Chron. xviii. 12, the number is "eighteen thousand;" in the title to the psalm, it is "twelve thousand." Why the statement varies, it is impossible to determine with certainty. We cannot suppose that the author of the psalm was ignorant of the usual estimate of the number, and we have no evidence that there is an error in the transcription. The probability is, that there may have been, as is often the case, in the account of battles, *two* estimates. The common and more moderate estimate may have been that the number was twelve thousand,—and this was adopted by the author of the psalm. The more accurate and well-ascertained estimate may have been that which was placed in the regular history, in the Books of Samuel and the Chronicles. If the actual number was in fact as great as eighteen thousand, then there is no contradiction, —for the greater number includes the less. If eighteen thousand were actually slain, there was no falsehood in the assertion, according to the first estimate, that twelve thousand had fallen in the battle; for that statement was in fact true, though a subsequent and more accurate "return" from the army made the number larger. Both statements were true. In saying that three men were drowned in a flood, or lost at sea in a storm, I do not falsify a declaration which may be made subsequently that not only three perished but six or more.

There is no reference, in the accounts in Samuel and the Chronicles, to the partial discomfiture referred to in the psalm (vers. 1-3); and the impression from those historical narratives would *probably* be that the armies of David had been uniformly successful. Yet it is possible that some things may have been omitted in the rapid survey of the conquests of David in Samuel and the Chronicles. The design of the authors of those books may have been to give a *general summary* of the wars or series of wars by which David obtained a final victory over his enemies, and brought into subjection all that he regarded as properly his territory, or all that had been included in the general promise to Abraham and his posterity, without noticing the reverses or disasters that *may* have occurred in securing those triumphs. Perhaps the most probable supposition in the case is, that during the absence of the armies in the east the Edomites had taken occasion to invade the land of Palestine from the south, and that in endeavouring to

PSALM LX.

To the chief Musician upon *g* Shushan-eduth, [1] Michtam of David, to teach; when *h* he strove with Aram-naharaim and with Aram-zobah, when Joab returned, and smote of Edom in the valley of salt twelve thousand.

g Ps. lxxx., *title*. [1] Or, *a golden* Psalm.
h 2 Sam. viii. 3—13.

O GOD, thou *i* hast cast us off, thou hast [2] scattered us, thou hast been displeased; O turn *k* thyself to us again.
2 Thou hast made the earth to

i Ps. xliv. 9. [2] *broken.*
k Lam. iii. 31, 32; Zech. x. 6.

repel them, there had been some defeats and losses in the comparatively small forces which David was then able to employ. He now summoned his armies on their return, and made a vigorous and decided effort to expel the Edomites from the land, to carry the warfare into their own country, and to add their territory to that which he had already brought under subjection. In this he was entirely successful. 2 Sam. viii. 14; 1 Chron. xviii. 13.

The contents of the psalm are as follows:—

I. A statement of the disaster which had occurred, as if God had cast his people off, and as if, after all, they might be given up into the hands of their enemies, vers. 1-3.

II. A statement of the object for which God now summoned his people to war,—that of carrying forth the banner of truth, or of bringing nations into subjection to the true religion, vers. 4, 5.

III. A reference to the conquests already made, or to the dominion which David had set up over Shechem, Succoth, Gilead, Manasseh, Ephraim, Judah, Moab, and Philistia, vers. 6-8.

IV. The expression of a strong desire to complete the series of conquests by subduing Edom or Idumea, vers. 8, 9. That alone remained. That offered formidable resistance to the armies of David. The conquest of that seemed difficult, if not hopeless, and the psalmist, therefore, asks with deep solicitude who would aid him in this war; who would bring him successfully into the strong city—the strong fortifications of Edom, ver. 9.

V. An appeal to God to do it; to that God who had cast them off; to him who had left their armies to go forth alone. David now calls on him to return to those forces, and to render aid,—expressing the confident assurance that he *would* thus return, and that the victory would be secured, vers. 10-12.

1. *O God, thou hast cast us off.* The word here used means properly to be foul, rancid, offensive; and then, to treat anything *as if* it were foul or rancid;—to repel, to spurn, to cast away. See Notes on Ps. xliii. 2. It is strong language, meaning that God had seemed to treat them as if they were loathsome or offensive to him. The allusion, according to the view taken in the Introd. to the psalm, is to some defeat or disaster which had occurred after the conquests in the East, or during the absence of the armies of David in the East (2 Sam. viii.; 1 Chron. xviii.);—probably to the fact that the Edomites had taken occasion to invade the southern part of Palestine, and that the forces employed to expel them had been unsuccessful. ¶ *Thou hast scattered us.* Marg., *broken.* So the Hebrew. The word is applied to the forces of war which are *broken* and *scattered* by defeat, 2 Sam. v. 20. ¶ *Thou hast been displeased.* The word here used means to breathe; to breathe hard; and then, to be angry. See Notes on Ps. ii. 12. God had treated them *as if* he was displeased or angry. He had suffered them to be defeated. ¶ *O turn thyself to us again.* Return to our armies, and give us success. This might be rendered, "Thou *wilt* turn to us;" that is, thou wilt favour us, — expressing a confident belief that God would do this, as in ver. 12. It is more in accordance, however, with the usual structure of the Psalms to regard this as a prayer. Many of the psalms begin with a prayer, and end with the expression of a confident assurance that the prayer has been, or would certainly be heard.

2. *Thou hast made the earth to tremble.* This refers, doubtless, to some calamity that might be compared with an earthquake,—some disaster, discomfiture, or defeat that had

tremble; thou hast broken it:
heal [l] the breaches thereof: for
it shaketh.
3 Thou hast showed thy people
[m] hard things; thou hast made us
to [n] drink the wine of astonishment.
4 Thou hast given a banner
[o] to them that fear thee, that
it may be displayed because of
the truth. Selah.

l 2 Chron. vii. 14; Jer. xxx. 17. *m* Ps. lxxi. 20. *n* Isa. li. 17, 22. *o* Isa. xi. 10.

shaken their hopes, as a city is shaken by an earthquake. Such comparisons are common in the Scriptures. ¶ *Thou hast broken it.* As if it were broken up, or convulsed. ¶ *Heal the breaches thereof.* That is, Appear for thy people, and repair their disasters, *as if* after an earthquake thou shouldst appear and fill up the rents which it had made. The prayer is that he would place things in their former condition of prosperity and success. ¶ *For it shaketh.* It is convulsed or agitated. That is, there is still commotion. Things are unsettled and disturbed. The prayer is, that there might be stability or continued success.

3. *Thou hast showed thy people hard things.* Thou hast caused them to see reverses, disappointments, and trials. This refers, according to the supposition in the Introd. to the psalm, to some calamitous events which had occurred. The probability seems to be that the Edomites may have spread desolation over the land. ¶ *Thou hast made us to drink the wine of astonishment.* The word rendered *astonishment* — תַּרְעֵלָה, *tarailah*—occurs only here and in Isa. li. 17, 22,—in both of which verses in Isaiah it is rendered *trembling.* It means properly *reeling, drunkenness;* and the idea here is, that it was as if he had given them a cup—that is, an intoxicating drink—which had caused them to reel as a drunken man; or, in other words, their efforts had been unsuccessful. Comp. Notes on Ps. xi. 6; Isa. li. 17.

4. *Thou hast given a banner to them that fear thee.* The word rendered *banner* — נֵס, *nais*—means properly anything elevated or lifted up, and hence a standard, a flag, a sign, or a signal. It may refer to a standard reared on lofty mountains or high places during an invasion of a country, to point out to the people a place of rendezvous or a rallying place (Isa. v. 26; xi. 12; xviii. 3); or it may refer to a standard or ensign borne by an army; or it may refer to the flag of a ship, Ezek. xxvii. 7; Isa. xxxiii. 23. Here it doubtless refers to the flag, the banner, the standard of an army; and the idea is that *God* had committed such a standard to his people that they might go forth as soldiers in his cause. They were enlisted in his service, and were fighting his battles. ¶ *That it may be displayed because of the truth.* In the cause of truth; or, in the defence of justice and right. It was not to be displayed for vain parade or ostentation; it was not to be unfolded in an unrighteous or unjust cause; it was not to be waved for the mere purpose of carrying desolation, or of securing victory; it was that a righteous cause might be vindicated, and that the honour of God might be promoted. This was the *reason* which the psalmist now urges why God should interpose and repair their disasters,—that it was *his* cause, and that they were appointed to maintain and defend it. What was true then of the people of God, is true of the church now. God has given to his church a banner or a standard that it may wage a war of justice, righteousness, and truth; that it may be employed in resisting and overcoming his enemies; that it may carry the weapons of truth and right against all injustice, falsehood, error, oppression, and wrong; that it may ever be found on the side of humanity and benevolence,—of virtue, temperance, liberty, and equality;

5 That [p] thy beloved may be delivered, save *with* thy right hand, and hear me.

p Ps. cviii. 6, etc.

6 God hath spoken in his holiness: I will rejoice; I will divide Shechem, and mete out the valley of Succoth.

and that it may bear the great principles of the true religion to every territory of the enemy, until the whole world shall be subdued to God.

5. *That thy beloved may be delivered.* The word *beloved* is in the plural number, and might be rendered *beloved ones.* It refers not merely to David as his servant and friend, but to those associated with him. The reference is to the calamities and dangers then existing, to which allusion has been made above. The prayer is, that the enemy might be driven back, and the land delivered from their invasion. ¶ *Save* with *thy right hand.* The right hand is that by which the sword is handled, the spear hurled, the arrow drawn on the bow. The prayer is, that God would put forth his power and deliver his people. ¶ *And hear me.* Literally, *Answer* me. The answer which he desired was that God would lead his armies successfully into Edom, vers. 8, 9.

6. *God hath spoken in his holiness.* That is, as a holy God; a God who is true; a God whose promises are always fulfilled. The idea is, that the holiness of God was the public pledge or assurance that what he had promised he would certainly perform. God had made promises in regard to the land of Canaan or Palestine, as a country to be put into the possession of Abraham and his posterity. Gen. xii. 7; xiii. 15; xvii. 8; Ps. cv. 8–11. The original promise of the gift of that land, made to Abraham under the general name of *Canaan* (Gen. xii. 7), embraced the whole territory from the river (that divided the land from Egypt) to the Euphrates: "Unto thy seed [addressed to Abraham] have I given this land, from the river of Egypt unto the great river, the river Euphrates," Gen. xv. 18. This would embrace the country of *Edom*, as well as the other countries which are specified in the psalm. The natural and proper boundary of the land on the east, therefore, according to the promise, was the river Euphrates; on the west, Egypt and the Mediterranean sea; on the south, the outer limit of Edom. It was the object of David to carry out what was implied in this promise, and to secure the possession of all that had been thus granted to the Hebrews as the descendants of Abraham. Hence he had been engaged in carrying his conquests to the east, with a view to make the Euphrates the eastern border or boundary of the land: "David smote also Hadarezer, the son of Rehob, king of Zobah, *as he went to recover his border at the river Euphrates,*" 2 Sam. viii. 3. Comp. 1 Chron. xviii. 3. In the prosecution of the same purpose he was anxious also to subdue *Edom*, that the entire territory thus promised to Abraham might be put in possession of the Hebrews, and that he might transmit the kingdom in the fulness of the original grant to his posterity. It is to this *promise* made to Abraham that he doubtless refers in the passage before us. ¶ *I will rejoice.* I, David, will exult or rejoice in the prospect of success. I will find my happiness, or my confidence in what I now undertake, in the promise which God has made. The meaning is, that since God had made this promise, he would certainly triumph. ¶ *I will divide Shechem.* That is, I will divide up the whole land according to the promise. The *language* here is taken from that which was employed when the country of Canaan was conquered by Joshua, and when it was *divided* among the tribes: "Be strong and of a good courage: for unto this people shalt thou *divide* for an inherit-

ance the land which I sware unto their fathers to give them," Josh. i. 6. Comp. Josh. xiii. 6, 7; xiv. 5; xviii. 10; xix. 51; xxiii. 4; Ps. lxxviii. 55; Acts xiii. 19. David here applies the same language to *Shechem,* and *the valley of Succoth,* as portions of the land, meaning that he would accomplish the original purpose in regard to the land by placing it in possession of the people of God. *Shechem* or *Sichem* was a city within the limits of the tribe of Ephraim, between Mount Ebal and Mount Gerizim, called by the Romans Neapolis, and now Nablûs. It is about two hours, or eight miles, south of Samaria. It seems to be mentioned here as being the spot where the law of Moses was read to the people of Israel, and especially the blessings and curses recorded in Deut. xxvii. and xxviii., which Moses commanded to be read to the different tribes on the above-named mountains, Deut. xxvii. 11–13. This was actually done, Josh. viii. 33. *Shechem,* therefore, as lying between these mountains, and as being the place where the great mass of the people were assembled to hear what was read, became a central place, a representative spot of the whole land, and to say that *that* was conquered or subdued, was to speak of that which implied a victory over the land. David speaks of having secured this, as significant of the fact that the central point of influence and power had been brought under subjection, and as in fact implying that the land was subdued. The importance of that place, and the allusion to it here, will justify a more extended reference to it, which I copy from "The Land and the Book," by Dr. Thomson, vol. ii. p. 203, 204.

"Nablûs is a queer old place. The streets are narrow, and vaulted over; and in the winter time it is difficult to pass along many of them on account of brooks which rush over the pavement with deafening roar. In this respect, I know no city with which to compare it except Brusa; and, like that city, it has mulberry, orange, pomegranate, and other trees, mingled in with the houses, whose odoriferous flowers load the air with delicious perfume during the months of April and May. Here the bilbûl delights to sit and sing, and thousands of other birds unite to swell the chorus. The inhabitants maintain that theirs is the most *musical* vale in Palestine, and my experience does not enable me to contradict them.

"Imagine that the lofty range of mountains running north and south was cleft open to its base by some tremendous convulsion of nature, at right angles to its own line of extension, and the broad fissure thus made is the vale of Nablûs, as it appears to one coming up the plain of Mukhna from Jerusalem. Mount Ebal is on the north, Gerizim on the south, and the city between. Near the eastern end, the vale is not more than sixty rods wide; and just there, I suppose, the tribes assembled to hear the 'blessings and the curses' read by the Levites. We have them *in extenso* in the 27th and 28th chapters of Deuteronomy; and in Joshua viii. we are informed that it was actually done, and how:—Simeon, and Levi, and Judah, and Issachar, and Joseph, and Benjamin, stood on Gerizim; and Reuben, Gad, Asher, Zebulon, Dan, and Naphtali, on Ebal; while all Israel, and their elders, and officers, and their judges, stood on this side of the ark and on that side before the priests which bare the ark of the covenant of the Lord; the whole nation of Israel, with the women and little ones, were there. And Joshua read all the words of the law, the blessings and the cursings; there was not a word of all that Moses commanded which Joshua read not before all the congregation of Israel. This was, beyond question or comparison, the most august assembly the sun has ever shone upon; and I never stand in the narrow plain, with Ebal and Gerizim rising on either hand to the sky, without involuntarily recalling and reproducing the scene. I have shouted to hear the echo, and

ENTRANCE TO NABLÛS.

7 Gilead *is* mine, and Manasseh *is* mine; Ephraim also *is* the strength of mine head; Judah *is* my lawgiver;

then fancied how it must have been when the loud-voiced Levites proclaimed from the naked cliffs of Ebal, 'Cursed be the man that maketh any graven image, an abomination unto Jehovah.' And then the tremendous AMEN! tenfold louder, from the mighty congregation, rising, and swelling, and re-echoing from Ebal to Gerizim, and from Gerizim to Ebal. AMEN! even so let him be accursed. No, there never was an assembly to compare with this."

The preceding cut, taken also from "The Land and the Book," will illustrate these references to the places. ¶ *And mete out the valley of Succoth.* Measure out; that is, measure or *survey* for the purpose of "dividing" it, or assigning it to the conquerors, to the people of God, according to the promise. There is the same allusion here, as in the former clause, to the dividing of the land in the time of Joshua. Succoth, in the division of the land by Joshua, fell to the tribe of Gad; Josh. xiii. 27. It was on the east side of the river Jordan, and is now called *Sakut.* It is first mentioned in Gen. xxxiii. 17, in the account of the journey which Jacob took on returning from the East to the land of Canaan. At this place he paused in his journey, and made *booths* for his cattle; and hence the name *Succoth,* or *booths. Why* this place is referred to here by David, as representing his conquests, cannot now be ascertained. It seems most probable that it was because it was a place *east* of the Jordan, as Shechem was *west* of the Jordan, and that the *two* might, therefore, represent the conquest of the whole country. Succoth, too, though not more prominent than many other places, and though in itself of no special importance, was well known as *among* the places mentioned in history. It is *possible,* also, though no such fact is mentioned, that there may have been some transaction of special importance there in connexion with David's conquests in the East, which was well understood at the time, and which justified this special reference to it.

7. *Gilead* is *mine, and Manasseh* is *mine.* That is, My dominion or authority is extended over these regions—Gilead, Manasseh, Ephraim, and Judah. The *idea* here is substantially the same as in the former verse, that his dominion extended over the country on both sides of the Jordan; or that in the direction of east and west it embraced *all* that had been promised,—"from the great sea to the river Euphrates." In verse 6, this idea is expressed by selecting two *spots* or *towns* as representatives of the whole country—Shechem on the west, and Succoth on the east; in this verse, the same idea is expressed by a reference to the two *regions* so situated,—Gilead and Manasseh on the east, and Ephraim and Judah on the west. Gilead was on the east of the river Jordan, properly embracing the mountainous region south of the river Jabbok, Gen. xxxi. 21—48; Cant. iv. 1. The word has sometimes, however, a wider signification, including the whole mountainous tract between the rivers Arnon and Bashan, and thus including the region occupied by the tribes of Gad, Reuben, and Manasseh, Num. xxxii. 26, 29, 39. Hence, in this place, it is put for the region occupied by the tribes of Reuben and Gad. "Manasseh" refers to the district or region occupied by the half tribe of Manasseh, on the east of the Jordan. These two portions — Gilead and Manasseh — or, Reuben, Gad, and Manasseh—would, therefore, embrace the whole of the land of promise, north and south, on the east of the Jordan. The limits of these regions to the *east* were properly the banks of the Euphrates; that is, the original promise would embrace this. David had gone to

8 Moab *is* my wash-pot; over Edom will I cast out my shoe: Philistia, triumph thou [1] because of me.

[1] Or, *over me:* (by an irony.)

carry the boundaries of his country to those assigned limits (2 Sam. viii. 3), and he now says that he had completed that undertaking. ¶ *Ephraim also.* Ephraim and Judah were the principal tribes on the west of the Jordan, and they would well *represent* that part of Canaan. The idea is, that the *whole* of the promised land, east and west, was now under his control. There needed only the territory of *Edom,* on the south, to complete the conquest, and place the *whole* of the promised land under his dominion, vers. 8, 9. ¶ Is *the strength of my head.* This means that Ephraim constituted his chief strength, or was that on which he mainly relied. It was that which protected him, as the helmet does the head; that on which his very life in battle depended. This honour is given to the tribe of Ephraim because it was one of the largest tribes, and because it was situated in the very centre of the land. ¶ *Judah* is *my lawgiver.* This means that the tribe of Judah, by its position, its numbers, and the prominence given to it in the prophecies (Gen. xlix. 8–12), actually gave law to the nation. Its influence was felt in all the institutions of the land. The controlling influence went out from that tribe in the time of David; and its authority in this respect was recognized, perhaps partly in anticipation of what it had been said *would be* its importance in future times:—"The sceptre shall not depart from Judah, nor a lawgiver from between his feet until Shiloh come." Gen. xlix. 10.

8. *Moab* is *my washpot.* Moab was a region of country on the east of the Dead Sea, extending as far north as the river Arnon. See Notes on Isa. xv. The words rendered *wash-pot* mean properly a pot or basin for washing, a wash-basin; and the expression is used here as one of contempt, as if he would use it as the meanest vessel is used. It implies that Moab was already subdued, and that the author of the psalm could make any use of it he pleased. It also implies that Moab was not regarded as adding much to his strength, or to the value of his dominions; but that, compared with other portions of his kingdom, it was of as little value as a wash-basin compared with the more valuable vessels in a house. ¶ *Over Edom will I cast out my shoe.* Edom or Idumea was the country which still remained unsubdued. This David was anxious to possess, though the conquest had been delayed and prevented by the adverse circumstances to which allusion has already been made in the Notes on the psalm. On the situation of Idumea, see Notes on Isa. xxxiv. It was a region whose possession was necessary to complete the acquisition of territory that properly pertained to the Promised Land; and David was now intent on acquiring it. He here expresses the utmost confidence that he would succeed in this, notwithstanding the adverse events which had occurred. It is supposed that there is allusion in the expression "I will cast out my shoe," to the custom, when transferring a possession, of *throwing down a shoe* on the ground as a symbol of occupancy. Comp. Ruth iv. 7. In the middle ages this was expressed by throwing down a glove; in the time of Columbus, by solemnly taking possession and setting up a cross; in other times, by erecting a standard, or by building a fort. Comp. Rosenmüller, Das alte und neue Morgenland, No. 483. The idea is, that he would take possession of it, or would make it his own. ¶ *Philistia, triumph thou because of me.* On the situation of Philistia, see Notes on Isa. xi. 14. In the margin this is, "*triumph thou over me,* by an irony." It *may* be regarded as irony, or as a taunt, meaning that

9 Who will bring me *into* the [1] strong city? who will lead me into Edom.

10 *Wilt* not thou, O God, *which* hadst cast us off? and *thou,* O God, *which* didst not go out with our armies?

11 Give us help from trouble; for vain *is* the [2] help of man.

12 Through God we shall do valiantly: for he *it is that* shall tread down our enemies.

[1] *city of strength.*

[2] *salvation.*

Philistia was no longer now in a situation to triumph over him; or it *may* be understood as referring to the exultation and shouting which would ensue on the reception of its sovereign. The former seems to be the most probable interpretation, as the language is undoubtedly intended to denote absolute *subjection,* and not the *voluntary* reception of a king. The language in the entire passage is that of triumph over foes.

9. *Who will bring me* into *the strong city?* The strong city—the fenced, the fortified city—referred to here is doubtless the capital of Idumea. This was the celebrated city *Petra,* situated in the rocks, and so difficult to be taken by an enemy. For a description of it, see Notes on Isa. xvi. 1. It was this city, as the capital of the land of Edom, which David was now so anxious to secure; and he asks, therefore, with interest, who among his captains, his mighty men, would undertake the task of conducting his armies there. ¶ *Who will lead me into Edom?* Into the capital, and thence into the whole land to subdue it. This was done under the combined command of Joab and Abishai his brother. See Notes on the title to the psalm.

10. Wilt *not thou, O God,* which *hadst cast us off?* See Notes on ver. 1. The meaning is, that although God had seemed to reject and forsake them, they had no other resource, and the appeal might be still made to him. The psalmist hoped that he would again be favourable to his people, and would not forsake them altogether. It is still true that although God may *seem* to forsake us, that although he may leave us for a time to discouragement and darkness, yet we have no other resource but himself; it is still true that we *may* hope in his mercy, and plead for his return. ¶ *And* thou, *O God,* which *didst not go out with our armies?* Who didst suffer us to be defeated. See Notes on vers. 2, 3.

11. *Give us help from trouble.* From the troubles which have now come upon us and overwhelmed us. ¶ *For vain* is *the help of man.* Marg., *salvation.* The idea is, that they would look in vain to man to assist them in their present difficulties. They must depend on God alone. What is here said of temporal troubles is true as absolutely in the matter of salvation. When we are burdened with the consciousness of guilt, and trembling under the apprehension of the wrath to come, it is not man that can aid us. Our help is in God alone. Man can neither guide, comfort, pardon, nor save; and in vain should we look to any man, or to all men, for aid. We *must* look to God alone:—to God as the only one who can remove guilt from the soul; who can give peace to the troubled heart; who can deliver us from condemnation and ruin.

12. *Through God.* By the help of God. ¶ *We shall do valiantly.* Literally, *we shall make strength.* That is, we shall gain or gather strength; we shall go forth with spirit and with courage to the war. This expresses the confident assurance that they would secure the aid of God, and that under him they would achieve the victory. ¶ *For he* it is that *shall tread down our enemies.* He will himself tread or trample them down; that is, he will enable us to do it. The psalm, therefore, though begun in despondency and sadness, closes, as the Psalms often

PSALM LXI.

To the chief Musician upon Neginah.
A Psalm of David.

HEAR my cry, O God; attend unto my prayer.

2 From the end of the earth will I cry unto thee, when my heart is overwhelmed: [q] lead me to the rock *that* is higher than I.

q Isa. xxvi. 4 (*marg.*)

do, with confident hope; with the assurance of the favour of God; and with the firm belief that the object sought in the psalm would be obtained. The history shows that the prayer was answered; that the armies of David were successful; that Edom was subdued; and that thus the territories of the Hebrew people had, in fact, in the time of David, the boundaries promised to Abraham.

PSALM LXI.

This psalm (*title*) is inscribed "To the chief Musician upon Neginah." On the meaning of the expression, "To the chief Musician," see Notes on the title to Ps. iv., where also we have the following word in another form,—"*on Neginoth*" —the plural, instead of the singular. The word means a stringed instrument; and the idea is, that the psalm was committed to the leader of those who played on stringed instruments in the sanctuary.

The psalm is ascribed to David, but the occasion on which it was composed is not specified. From the psalm itself it is evident that it was composed by one who was in exile (ver. 2), and by one who was a king (ver. 6). The supposition which best agrees with all the circumstances alluded to in the psalm is, that it was composed by David when he was driven into exile on the rebellion of Absalom, and that it was composed when he was still beyond the Jordan (2 Sam. xvii. 22), and when his life was yet in danger. The xlii. and xliii. psalms refer to the same period, and have the same general characteristics.

The psalm consists of the following parts:

I. A prayer for the Divine interposition, vers. 1, 2. The psalmist was far away from his home—in exile—and his heart was overwhelmed.

II. A reference to former mercies, and to the Divine interposition in other days, as a ground of hope and of pleading now, vers. 3–5.

III. An expression of confident assurance that his prayer would be heard; that his life would be preserved; that his days would be lengthened out, and that he would be delivered from danger, vers. 6, 7.

IV. The result of this deliverance; or, as an expression of gratitude for it, a purpose to devote himself to God, in a life spent in the daily performance of his vows, ver. 8.

1. *Hear my cry, O God.* See Notes on Ps. v. 2. The word rendered *cry* in this place sometimes denotes a joyful shout—a shout of triumph; but the connexion makes it certain that it here refers to the voice of prayer. It is implied that it was *audible* prayer, or that the psalmist gave utterance to his desires in words. It is language such as would be produced by deep distress; when a sad and burdened heart gives vent to its feelings in a loud cry for mercy. ¶ *Attend unto my prayer.* Give ear; incline the ear to me, Ps. v. 1; xvii. 1, 6; xxxix. 12; lxxi. 2.

2. *From the end of the earth will I cry unto thee.* This language is derived from the idea that the earth is one extended plain, and that it has limits or boundaries. Such language is common in the Scriptures, and indeed is in constant use now, even although we *know* that the earth is globular, and that there *are* no parts which can properly be called "the *ends* of the earth." The meaning is plain. The psalmist was far from the place where he was accustomed to live; or, in other words, he was in exile or in banishment. The language agrees well with the supposition that the psalm was composed when David was driven from his home and his throne by Absalom, and was in exile beyond the Jordan, 2 Sam. xvii. 22. Comp. Ps. xlii. ¶ *When my heart is overwhelmed.* The word here used—עָטַף, *ataph*—means properly to cover, as with a garment,

3 For thou hast been a shelter for me, *and* a strong [r] tower from the enemy.

4 I will abide in thy tabernacle for ever; I will [1] trust in the covert of thy wings. Selah.

5 For thou, O God, hast heard my vows: thou hast given *me* the heritage of those that fear thy name.

r Prov. xviii. 10.

1 Or, *make my refuge.*

Ps. lxxiii. 6; then, with corn—as a field, Ps. lxv. 14; then, with darkness or calamity, Ps. cii. title; Isa. lvii. 16. The meaning here is, that darkness or calamity seemed to have covered or enveloped his soul. He saw no light, he had no comfort. Comp. Ps. xlii. 3, 6, 7. ¶ *Lead me to the rock* that *is higher than I.* To *a* rock; to some place of refuge; to some stronghold where I may be safe. The allusion is to God *as* such a rock or place of refuge. See Notes on Ps. xviii. 2. The idea is, that he had no strength in himself; that if he depended on himself, he could not be safe. He was, as it were, in a low vale, exposed to every enemy. He wished to be put in a place of safety. To such a place of safety—to Himself—he prayed that God would lead him. We need one much higher than we are to save us. A Saviour—a Redeemer—on the same level with ourselves could not help us. We must have one that is supreme over all things; one that is Divine.

3. *For thou hast been a shelter for me.* A place of refuge; a place where I have found safety. He refers here to what had occurred in former times. God had protected him when in danger, and he pleads that fact as a reason why God should now interpose and deliver him. That reason seems to be founded on two considerations: (*a*) God had thus shown that he had *power* to deliver him; and (*b*) it might be expected that God who is unchangeable, and who had interposed, *would* manifest the same traits of character still, and would not leave him now. Both of these are proper grounds for prayer. ¶ And *a strong tower from the enemy.* See Notes on Ps. xviii. 2.

4. *I will abide in thy tabernacle for ever.* This expresses the confident assurance that he would be restored to his home, and to the privileges of public worship. The word *for ever* here means *perpetually;* that is, his permanent home would be there, or he would dwell with God who dwelt in the tabernacle. The word "tabernacle" refers to the sacred tent which was erected for the worship of God, within which were the ark, the tables of the law, the table of shew-bread, etc. In the innermost part of that tent—the Holy of Holies—the symbol of the Divine presence rested on the mercy-seat or cover of the ark of the covenant. David regarded it as a great privilege to abide near that sacred tent; near to the place of public worship; near to the place where God was supposed to dwell. See Notes on Ps. xxiii. 6; xxvi. 8; xxvii. 4. It is possible that his mind looked beyond the tabernacle on earth to an eternal residence in the very presence of God; to his being admitted into his own sacred abode in heaven. ¶ *I will trust in the covert of thy wings.* Marg., *Make my refuge.* See Notes on Ps. xvii. 8. Comp. Ps. xxxvi. 7; lvii. 1. The idea is, that he would seek and find protection in God,—as young birds do under the outstretched wings of the parent bird.

5. *For thou, O God, hast heard my vows.* That is, my prayers accompanied with solemn pledges or promises that I will devote myself to thy service. In some way David had the assurance that those vows and prayers had been heard; that God would answer his supplications,—that he would restore him to his home, and to the privilege of uniting with others in the sacred services of the sanctuary. In what way he had this assurance we are not informed, but the state-

6 Thou[1] wilt prolong the king's life; *and* his years as [2] many generations.

7 He shall abide before God for ever: O prepare mercy and truth, [s] *which* may preserve him.

[1] *shall add days to the days of the king.*

[2] *generation and generation.* [s] Ps. xliii. 3.

---

ment here accords with what we often find in the Psalms. His troubled mind became calm, for he looked upon the blessing as already granted. He entertained no doubt that what he had asked would be bestowed. The mind of a true believer often feels this assurance now. *Somehow* he feels an undoubting persuasion that the prayer which he has offered has been heard; that God will be merciful; that the blessing which has been sought will assuredly be conferred. That there may be danger of illusion here, no one can doubt,—for we are not, as David was, inspired; but no one can prove that God *may* not impart such a gracious assurance to the soul; no one can show that it is *wrong* for a believer to allow peace to flow into his soul, in the confident hope that the blessing which he had sought will be his. ¶ *Thou hast given* me *the heritage of those that fear thy name.* The *heirship* which pertains to such; the *privileges* of those who are the true children of God. One of these privileges is that of prayer; another is the peace which results from adoption into the family of God; of feeling that we are his heirs. Comp. Notes on Rom. viii. 16, 17.

6. *Thou wilt prolong the king's life.* Literally, "Days upon the days of the king thou wilt add;" that is, Thou wilt add days to those which thou hast already permitted him to live. The language does not necessarily mean that he would have a *long* life, but that he would still be permitted to live. He had apprehended death. He knew that his life was sought by those who were engaged with Absalom in the rebellion. At first it was uncertain what the issue would be. He had fled for his life. But now, in answer to prayer, he felt assured that his life would be preserved; that he would be permitted to return to his home and his throne; and that *as* king—as the sovereign of his people—he would be permitted to honour God. ¶ And *his years as many generations.* Marg., as in Heb., *generation and generation.* This probably means that he would be permitted to live longer than the ordinary time of a generation; that he would live *as if* one generation—or as if one ordinary lifetime—were added to another, so that he would live *through* successive generations of men. The average life of a generation is about thirty years. David is supposed to have lived from 1085 before the Christian era to 1016—or sixty-nine years—which would reach a *third* generation. This is a more natural interpretation of the passage than to suppose that he refers to an "*ideal*" king, or that his *dynasty* would continue for many generations.

7. *He shall abide before God for ever.* That is, perpetually; without danger of change, or of being driven into exile. This *may* allude, however, to the hope which David had that he would *always* live with God in a higher world—a world where there would be no danger of change or banishment. His restoration to his home, to his throne, and to the privileges of the sanctuary, he may have regarded as an emblem of his ultimate reception into a peaceful heaven, and his mind may have glanced rapidly from the one to the other. On earth, after his restoration, he would have no fear that he would be banished again; in heaven, of which such a restoration might be regarded as an emblem, there could be no change, no exile. ¶ *O prepare mercy and truth.* Literally, *divide,* or *divide out;* then, *allot* or *appoint;* and then, *make ready* or *prepare.* The prayer is, that God would mea-

8 So will I sing praise unto thy name for ever, that I may daily perform my vows.

---

sure out to him, or impart to him, such favour that this desire of his heart would be realized. On the phrase *mercy and truth,* see Notes on Ps. xxv. 10; lvii. 3, 10. ¶ *Which may preserve him.* They will preserve him. That is, the manifestation of such mercy and truth would make his permanent occupancy of his throne on earth, and his ultimate reception into heaven, secure.

8. *So will I sing praise unto thy name for ever.* As the result of this gracious interposition. Comp. Notes on Isa. xxxviii. 20. The meaning is, that he would do this constantly. It would be the regular business of his life. ¶ *That I may daily perform my vows.* The solemn promises which I have made in my exile; the purposes which I have expressed to devote myself to thee. Or, the language may have been used in a more general sense, denoting that, as a religious man, the vows of God were constantly on him, or that he had pledged himself to serve God faithfully and always, and that he could better perform this duty at the tabernacle—in the place consecrated to public worship—than he could in exile. He desired, therefore, to be restored to the sanctuary, that he might keep up the performance of the daily duties of religion without interruption or hindrance. The whole psalm indicates a fervent desire to be engaged in the worship and service of God; a desire to be with Him and to enjoy His favour on earth; a confident hope that he would be permitted to enjoy His presence for ever.

PSALM LXII.

On the phrase in the title to this psalm, "To the chief Musician," see Notes on the title to Ps. iv. On the expression "To Jeduthun," see Notes on the title to Ps. xxxix. Jeduthun was one of those who were appointed by David to preside over the music of the tabernacle (1 Chron. xxv. 1-3), but it is impossible now to determine why *this* psalm, and the others where his name is found in the title (xxxix. and lxxvii.), were dedicated to him, or committed to his special care. The psalm is, in the title, ascribed to David as the author, but we have no certain knowledge on what occasion it was composed. Its contents agree well with the common supposition that it is to be referred to the time of Absalom, and to the troubles which David experienced in his rebellion.

The psalm, apparently for musical purposes only, is divided into three parts, the divisions being indicated by the word *Selah,* vers. 4, 8. Another division is indicated in the original by the recurrence of the word אַךְ—*truly*—at the beginning of vers. 1, 4, 5, 6, 9, as if the mind of the author had been greatly impressed with the importance of the particular sentiment introduced by that word.

The general purpose of the psalm is to lead men to trust in God. The contents are as follows:

I. A statement of the humble trust of the author in God—trust in him as his only hope,—as his rock and his refuge, vers. 1, 2.

II. A description of his enemies and of their designs. They devised mischief; they sought to cast down others from their high places; they delighted in falsehood; they made great pretensions of friendship, but they were false in heart, vers. 3, 4.

III. A renewed expression of the confidence of the psalmist in God,—repeating what he had said in vers. 1, 2,—and reaffirming his entire trust in the Divine protection, vers. 5-7.

IV. An exhortation to others to trust in God, and not in men; whether men of high or low condition; to trust in nothing else than God:—not in power—the power of oppression; not in the robbery of others, or that which was obtained from others by violence; not in riches, in whatever way they might have been acquired, vers. 8-10.

V. Reasons for trusting in God, vers. 11, 12.

(*a*) All power belongs to him, ver. 11.
(*b*) He is merciful or kind, ver. 12.
(*c*) He is just or equitable, ver. 12.

PSALM LXII.

To the chief Musician, to *t* Jeduthun.
A Psalm of David.

TRULY [1] my soul [2] waiteth upon God; from him *cometh* my salvation.

2 He only *is* my rock and my salvation; *he is* my [3] defence: I shall not be *u* greatly moved.

3 How long will ye imagine

t 1 Chron. xxv. 1, 3. [1] Or, *Only*.

[2] *is silent*, Ps. lxv. 1. [3] *high place*.
u Ps. xxxvii. 24; Mic. vii. 8.

1. *Truly.* Indeed; really. The state of mind indicated by this particle is that of one who had been seriously contemplating a subject; who had looked round on his own actual condition; who had taken an estimate of all his resources, and of all his means of reliance, and who had carefully examined his own state of mind to see what was his real trust, and what were his real feelings towards God. Having done all this, he, at last, breaks out with the expression,—"My soul does sincerely confide in God; I have no other resource; I have no power to meet my foes, and I am sure—my inmost soul testifies—that my real trust is, where it ought to be, in God; I see nothing in myself on which to rely; I see so much crime, falsehood, treachery in men, that I cannot confide in them; I have had so much painful experience of their insincerity and baseness that I cannot rely on them; but I do see that in God which leads me to trust in him, and I am sure that my heart truly does rely on him." ¶ *My soul waiteth upon God.* Marg., *is silent.* Sept., "Is not my soul subject to God?" So the Latin Vulgate. Luther, "My soul is still [calm] in God." The Hebrew word—דּוּמִיָּה, *dumiyah*—means *silence, quiet, rest;* and then, a silent expectation or hope. The idea here is, "Truly towards God is the silent waiting of my soul;" that is, "In him alone do I trust; there *is* calmness of mind; I have no apprehension as to what can happen. My mind is at peace, for I feel that all is in the hands of God, and that he is worthy of entire trust and confidence." The feeling is that which exists when we have entrusted all to God; when, having entire confidence in his power, his goodness, his wisdom, his mercy, we commit the whole case to him as if it were no longer our own. Such is the calmness—the peace—the quiet—the *silence* of the soul—when all is left with God. See Notes on Isa. xxvi. 3, and Phil. iv. 6, 7. ¶ *From him* cometh *my salvation.* That is, My safety is from him; my security is with him. It is true, also, that all that is ever implied in this word *salvation,* whether pertaining to this life or the life to come, is derived from God.

2. *He only* is *my rock,* etc. See Notes on Ps. xviii. 2. ¶ *I shall not be greatly moved.* The word *greatly* here, or *much,*—"I shall not be much moved,"—implies that he did not anticipate perfect security from danger or calamity; he did not suppose that he would escape all disaster or trouble, but he felt that no *great* evil would befal him, that his most important interests were safe, and that he would be ultimately secure. He would be restored to his home and his throne, and would be favoured with future peace and tranquillity. None of us can hope wholly to escape calamity in this life. It is enough if we can be assured that our *great* interests will be ultimately secured; that we shall be safe at last in the heavenly world. Having that confidence the soul may be, and should be, calm; and we need little apprehend what will occur in this world.

3. *How long will ye imagine mischief against a man?* The original word here rendered "imagine mischief,"—from הָתַת, *hathath*—occurs only in this place. It means, according to Gesenius (*Lex.*), to break in upon; to set upon; to assail:—"How long will ye break in upon a man?" that is, set upon him. So the Septuagint, and the Latin Vulgate.

mischief against a man? ye shall be slain all of you: as a bowing wall *shall ye be, and as* a tottering fence.

4 They only consult to cast *him* down from his excellency; they delight in lies: they bless with their mouth, but they curse [1] inwardly. Selah.

[1] *in their inward parts.*

It does not refer to their merely forming *purposes* of mischief against a man, but to their making *assaults* upon him; to their endeavouring to take his life or to destroy him. The address here is to the enemies of David, and the language would apply well to the attempts made upon his life by Absalom and his followers. The question here is, "*how long*" they would continue to do this; how long they would show this determined purpose to take his life; whether they would *never* cease thus to persecute him. They had already done it long; they had showed great perseverance in this course of wickedness; and he asks whether it would *never* come to an end? *Who* these persons were he does not intimate; but there can be no great danger of mistake in referring the description to Absalom and his adherents. ¶ *Ye shall be slain all of you.* Prof. Alexander renders this entire passage, "*Will ye murder* (*i.e.* seek to murder him) *all of you* (combined against a single person, who is consequently) *like a wall inclined* (or bent by violence), *a fence* (or hedge) *crushed* (broken down)." So, substantially, De Wette renders it. Those who thus interpret the passage give it an *active* signification, meaning that his enemies pressed upon him, like a wall that was bent by violence, or a fence that was likely to fall on one. The original word rendered "ye shall be slain,"—תְּרָצְּחוּ, *teratzehhu*—is in the *active* form (Piel), and cannot without violence be rendered in the passive, as it is in our translation. But the active form may still be retained, and a consistent meaning be given to the whole passage without the forced meaning put on it in the rendering by Prof. Alexander. It is not natural to speak of enemies as so coming on a man as to make him like a falling wall, or a tottering fence. The evident idea is, that *they themselves* would be as a falling wall; that is, that they would be defeated or disappointed in their purpose, as a wall that has no solid foundation tumbles to the ground. The meaning of the original may be thus expressed: "How long will ye assail a man, that ye may put him to death? All of you shall be as a bowing wall," etc. That is, You will not accomplish your design; you will fail in your enterprise, as a wall without strength falls to the ground. ¶ *As a bowing wall.* A wall that *bows out*, or *swells out;* a wall that may fall at any moment. See Notes on Isa. xxx. 13. ¶ And as *a tottering fence.* A fence that is ready to fall; that has no firmness. So it would be with them. Their purposes would suddenly *give way*, as a fence does when the posts are rotted off, and when there is nothing to support it.

4. *They only consult to cast* him *down from his excellency.* This is the object of all their counsels and plans. They aim at one high in rank,—and their purpose, their sole purpose, is to bring him down. This would apply well to the case of David in the time of the rebellion of Absalom. ¶ *They delight in lies.* In false pretences; in secret plans of evil; in hypocritical assurances. This was eminently true of Absalom, who made use of these arts to seduce the people from allegiance to his father. 2 Sam. xv. 1–6. ¶ *They bless with their mouth, but they curse inwardly.* They profess true attachment and zeal, but they are traitors at heart. See Notes on Ps. xxviii. 3. This, too, would apply well to the conduct of Absalom and those associated with him.

5 My soul, wait thou only upon God; for my expectation *is* from him.

6 He only *is* my rock and my salvation: *he is* my defence: I shall not be moved.

7 In God *is* my salvation, and my glory: the rock of my strength, *and* my refuge, *is* in God.

8 Trust in him at all times; ye people, pour [v] out your heart

v 1 Sam. i. 15.

---

5. *My soul, wait thou only upon God.* See Notes on ver. 1. There is, in the word used here, and rendered *wait*, the same idea of *rest* or *repose* which occurs in verse 1. The meaning is, that he would commit the whole cause to God, and that his soul would thus be calm and without apprehension. ¶ *For my expectation is from him.* In verse 1, this is *salvation.* The idea here is, that all that he expected or hoped for must come from God. He did not rely on his fellow men; he did not rely on himself. God alone could deliver him, and he confidently believed that God would do it. Often are we in such circumstances that we feel that our *only* "expectation"—our only hope—is in God. All our strength fails; all our resources are exhausted; our fellow-men cannot or will not aid us; our own efforts seem to be vain; our plans are frustrated, and we are shut up to the conclusion that God alone can help us. How often is this felt by a Christian parent in regard to the conversion of his children. All his own efforts seem to be vain; all that he says is powerless; his hopes, long-cherished, are disappointed; his very prayers seem not to be heard; and he is *made* to feel that his only hope is in God—a sovereign God,—and that the whole case must be left in His hands. This state of mind, when it is fully reached, is often all that is needful in order that our desires may be granted. It is desirable that this state of mind *should be* produced; and when it *is* produced, the prayer is answered.

6. *He only* is *my rock,* etc. See Notes on ver. 2. The only difference between this verse and verse 2 is, that in this verse the word "greatly" is omitted. The psalmist declares here, in the most absolute manner, that he shall not be "moved" at all. In verse 2, he said that he would not be "*greatly* moved;" his mind would not be much or materially disturbed. The language here indicates more entire confidence—more certain conviction — showing that the slight apprehension or fear which existed in the beginning of the psalm, had been wholly dissipated, and that his mind had become *perfectly* calm.

7. *In God* is *my salvation.* See ver. 1. That is, his salvation, his safety, his anticipated deliverance, was to come only from God. ¶ *And my glory.* That in which I glory or boast; the source of all in me that is glorious or honourable. He gloried that there was such a God; he gloried that He was *his* God. ¶ *The rock of my strength.* The strong rock; the refuge that cannot be successfully assailed; where I shall feel strong and secure. See Notes on Ps. xviii. 2. ¶ *My refuge.* That to which I may flee for safety. See Notes on Ps. xlvi. 1.

8. *Trust in him at all times.* This exhortation, addressed to all persons, in all circumstances, and at all times, is founded on the personal experience of the psalmist, and on the views which he had of the character of God, as worthy of universal confidence. David had found him worthy of such confidence; he now exhorts all others to make the same trial, and to put their trust in God in like manner. What he had found God to be, all others would find him to be. His own experience of God's goodness and mercy—of his gracious interposition in the time of trouble—had been such that he could confidently exhort all others, in similar circumstances, to make the same trial of his love. ¶ *Ye people, pour out your*

before him: God *is* a refuge for us. Selah.
9 Surely men of low degree
are vanity, *and* men of high degree *are* a lie: to be laid in the balance, they *are* [1] altogether *lighter* than vanity.
10 Trust not in oppression,
and become not vain in robbery:

[1] Or, *alike*.

heart before him. All people. On the meaning of the phrase "pour out your heart," see Notes on Ps. xlii. 4. The idea is, that the heart becomes tender and soft, so that its feelings and desires flow out as water, and *all* its emotions, all its wishes, its sorrows, its troubles, are poured out before God. All that *is* in our hearts may be made known to God. There is not a desire which he cannot gratify; not a trouble in which he cannot relieve us; not a danger in which he cannot defend us. And, in like manner there is not a spiritual want in which he will not feel a deep interest, nor a danger to our souls from which he will not be ready to deliver us. Much more freely than to any earthly parent—to a father, *or even to a mother*—may we make mention of all our troubles, little or great, before God. ¶ *God* is *a refuge for us.* For all. For one as well as another. He is the *only* refuge; he is *all* the refuge that we need.

9. *Surely men of low degree* are *vanity.* Literally, "vanity are the sons of Adam," but the word Adam here is used evidently to represent *men*, or the race. The same word is also employed particularly to represent *common men*, or men of the humbler rank, in contradistinction to the word אִישׁ, *ish*—which is the other word used here, and rendered "men of high degree." Compare, for this use of the word, Hos. vi. 7. The same antithesis between the two words is found in Isa. ii. 9; v. 15. The idea here is, that in the great matters which pertain to us, we cannot depend on men, and that our hope—our trust—must be in God. Of men of the humbler or lower classes, it is said that they are "vanity;" that is, they are like a vain, empty, unsubstantial thing. They cannot help us. It is useless to rely on them when we most need aid. ¶ *Men of high degree* are *a lie.* Men of exalted rank, kings, princes, nobles. This does not refer to their personal character, as if they were always false, deceitful, treacherous; but the idea is, that any prospect of protection or aid from men of rank and station—from any power which they wield—is unworthy to be relied on. It is not that which we need; it is not that on which we can depend. ¶ *To be laid in the balance.* Literally, "*In the scales to go up;*" that is, they are seen to go up, or to show how *light* they are. They have no real *weight;* no real value. On the *scales* or *balance,* see Notes on Dan. v. 27. ¶ *They* are *altogether* lighter *than vanity.* They are *all* vain; single or combined, they have no power to save us. The meaning is not that if these two ranks of persons were weighed *against* each other they would both be found to be vanity; but that it is true of each and every rank of men,—high and low—whether single or combined,—that, as weighed against our interests and wants, they are nothing. All the kings of the earth with all their hosts of war, all princes and nobles with all that they can summon from the lower ranks of their people, cannot save one soul from death,—cannot deliver us from the consequences of our transgressions. God, and God alone, can do this.

10. *Trust not in oppression.* The general meaning here is, that we are not to trust in *anything* but God. In the previous verse the psalmist had stated reasons why we should not trust in *men* of any rank. In this verse he enumerates several things on which men are *accustomed* to rely, or in which they place confidence, and he

if riches increase, set not your
heart *upon them.*
11 God hath spoken once;
twice have I heard this, that
[1] power [w] *belongeth* unto God.

12 Also unto thee, O Lord,
belongeth mercy; for [x] thou renderest
to every man according to
his work.

[1] Or, *strength.* w Rev. xix. 1. x 2 Cor. v. 10.

says that we should put *no* confidence in them in respect to the help which we need, or the great objects which are to be accomplished by us. The first thing mentioned is *oppression;* and the idea is, that we must not hope to accomplish our object by oppressing others; extorting their property or their service; making them by force subject to us, and subservient to our wishes. Many do this. Conquerors do it. Tyrants do it. The owners of slaves do it. ¶ *And become not vain in robbery.* That is, Do not resort to theft or robbery, and depend on that for what is needed in life. Many do. The great robbers of the world—conquerors—have done it. Thieves and burglars do it. Men who seek to defraud others of their earnings do it. They who withhold wages from labourers, and they who cheat in trade, do it. ¶ *If riches increase, set not your heart* upon them. If you become rich *without* oppression, or *without* robbery. If your riches seem to grow of themselves—for that is the meaning of the original word (comp. Mark iv. 28)—do not rely on them as being all that you require. Men are prone to do this. The rich man confides in his wealth, and supposes that he has all he needs. The psalmist says that none of these things constitute the true reliance of man. None of them can supply his real wants; none can defend him in the great perils of his existence; none can save his soul. He needs, over and above all these, a God and Saviour; and it is such a God and Saviour only that can meet the real wants of his nature.

11. *God hath spoken once; twice have I heard this.* This repetition, or this declaration that he had heard the thing *repeated,* is designed to give emphasis to what was said, or to call attention to it as particularly worthy of notice. See Notes on Job xxxiii. 14. Comp. Job xl. 5. The sentiment here *is* particularly important, or is deserving of special attention, because, as the psalmist had shown, all other resources fail, and confidence is to be placed in nothing else for that which man so much needs;—neither in men, whether of low degree or high (ver. 9); not in oppressive acts—acts of mere power; not in plunder; not in wealth, however acquired, ver. 10. ¶ *That power* belongeth *unto God.* Marg., *strength.* The idea is, that the strength which man needs—the ability to defend and to save him—is to be found in God. All else may fail, but the power of God will not fail. The result of all, therefore, should be to lead us to put our trust in God alone.

12. *Also unto thee, O Lord,* belongeth *mercy.* Power, indeed, belongs to God (ver. 11); but this is an attribute to be feared, and while, in one respect, it will inspire confidence, or while it gives us the assurance that God is *able* to defend us when all else shall fail, yet, unattended by any other attribute, it might produce only apprehension and alarm. What man, weak and sinful man, *wants* to know is not merely that God has almighty power, but *how* that power will be wielded, or with what other attributes it is combined;—whether it will be put forth to destroy or to save; to kill or to keep alive; to crush or to uphold. Man, therefore, needs the assurance that God is a benevolent Being, as really as that he is a powerful Being; that he is disposed to show mercy; that his power will be put forth in behalf of those who confide in him, and not employed against them. Hence the attribute of *mercy* is so essential to a proper conception

PSALM LXIII.

A Psalm of David, when *y* he was in the wilderness of Judah.

y 2 Sam. xvii. 29.

O GOD, thou *art* my God; early *z* will I seek thee: my soul

z Prov. viii. 17; S. Song iii. 1—3.

of God; and hence the psalm so appropriately closes by a reference to his mercy and compassion. ¶ *For thou renderest to every man according to his work.* As this stands in our version, it would seem that the psalmist regarded what is here referred to as a manifestation of *mercy.* Yet the "rendering to every man according to his work" is an act of *justice* rather than of *mercy.* It is probable, therefore, that the word rendered "for"—כִּי, *ki*—does not refer here to either of the attributes mentioned exclusively—either *power* or *mercy*—but is to be understood with reference to the general course of argument in the psalm, as adapted to lead to confidence in God. The fact that he is a God who will deal impartially with mankind, or who will regard what is right and proper to be done in view of the characters of men, *is* a reason why they should confide in God,—since there could be no just ground of confidence in a Being who is not thus impartial and just. All these combined—power, mercy, equity—constitute a reason why men should confide in God. If either of these were wanting in the Divine character, man could have no confidence in God. If these things *do* exist in God, unlimited confidence may be placed in him as having all needful *power* to save; as being so *merciful* that sinful men may trust in him; and as being so *just* and *equal* in his dealings that all may feel that it is right to repose confidence in a Being by whom all the interests of the universe will be secured. Comp. 1 John i. 9.

PSALM LXIII.

This psalm purports to be a "psalm of David," and there can be no just ground of doubt in regard to the correctness of the title in this respect. De Wette indeed supposes that the way in which mention is made of the "king" in ver. 11, seems to indicate that the psalm was not composed by David himself, but that it was written by some friend of his, who was his companion in the troubles which he experienced; but it is not necessary to resort to this supposition, for it is not very uncommon for an author to refer to himself in the third person, as Cæsar does everywhere. The psalm further purports to have been composed by David "when he was in the wilderness of Judah." The "wilderness of Judah" was that wild and uncultivated tract of country lying on the east side of the territory of the tribe of Judah, commonly called "the wilderness of Judea" (Matt. iii. 1; comp. Notes on Matt. iv. 1), lying along the Jordan. David was repeatedly driven into that wilderness in the time of Saul; and the general structure of the psalm would accord well with any one of those occasions; but the mention of the "king" in ver. 11, as undoubtedly meaning David, makes it necessary to refer the composition of the psalm to a later period in his life, since the title "*king*" was not given to him in the time of Saul. The psalm, therefore, was doubtless composed in the time of Absalom—the period when David was driven away by the rebellion, and compelled to seek a refuge in that wilderness. It belongs, if this view is correct, to the same period in the life of David as Psalms xlii., xliii., lxi., and probably some others.

The psalm consists of the following parts:—

I. An expression of earnest desire to see the power and glory of God again, as he had formerly done in the sanctuary, vers. 1, 2.

II. His sense of the goodness of God, and of the value of the Divine favour, as being greater than that of life; and his purpose to find his happiness in God, and to praise and bless him in all situations, especially in those moments of solemn meditation when he was alone upon his bed, vers. 3-6.

III. His remembrance of former mercies, and his conviction that God still upheld him by his right hand, vers. 7, 8.

IV. His firm belief that all his enemies would be destroyed, vers. 9-11.

1. *O God, thou* art *my God.* The words here rendered *God* are not the

thirsteth *a* for thee, my flesh longeth for thee in a dry and
[1] thirsty land [2] where no water is;
2 To see *b* thy power and thy

a Ps. xlii. 2; John vii. 37.
[1] *weary.*
[2] *without water,* Isa. xli. 17.
b Ps. xxvii. 4.

same in the original. The first one—*Elohim*—is in the plural number, and is the word which is usually employed to designate God (Gen. i. 1); the second—אֵל, *ail*—is a word which is very often applied to God with the idea of *strength,*—a strong, a mighty One; and there is probably this underlying idea here, that God was the source of his strength, or that in speaking of God as *his* God, he was conscious of referring to him as Almighty. It was the Divine attribute of *power* on which his mind mainly rested when he spoke of him as *his* God. He did not appeal to him merely *as* God, with no reference to a particular attribute; but he had particularly in his eye his *power* or his ability to deliver and save him. In Ps. xxii. 1, where, in our version, we have the same expression, "My God, my God," the two words in the original are identical, and are the same which is used here—אֵל, *ail*—as expressive of strength or power. The idea suggested here is, that in appealing to God, while we address him as our God, and refer to his general character as God, it is not improper to have in our minds some *particular* attribute of his character—power, mercy, love, truth, faithfulness, etc.—as the special ground of our appeal. ¶ *Early will I seek thee.* The word here used has reference to the early dawn, or the morning; and the noun which is derived from the verb, means *the aurora, the dawn, the morning.* The proper idea, therefore, would be that of seeking God in the morning, or the early dawn; that is, as the first thing in the day. Comp. Notes on Isa. xxvi. 9. The meaning here is, that he would seek God as the first thing in the day; first in his plans and purposes; first in all things. He would seek God before other things came in to distract and divert his attention; he would seek God when he formed his plans for the day, and before other influences came in, to control and direct him. The favour of God was the supreme desire of his heart, and that desire would be indicated by his making him the earliest—the first—object of his search. His first thoughts,—his best thoughts,—therefore, he resolved should be given to God. A desire to seek God as the *first* object in life—in youth—in each returning day—at the beginning of each year, season, month, week—in all our plans and enterprises—is one of the most certain evidences of true piety; and religion flourishes *most* in the soul, and flourishes *only* in the soul, when we make God the first object of our affections and desires. ¶ *My soul thirsteth for thee.* See Notes on Ps. xlii. 2. ¶ *My flesh longeth for thee.* All my passions and desires—my whole nature. The two words—"soul" and "flesh," are designed to embrace the entire man, and to express the idea that he longed supremely for God; that all his desires, whether springing directly from the soul, or the wants of the body, rose to God as the only source from which they could be gratified. ¶ *In a dry and thirsty land.* That is, As one longs for water in a parched desert, so my soul longs for God. The word *thirsty* is in the margin, as in Heb., *weary.* The idea is that of a land where, from its parched nature—its barrenness—its rocks—its heat—its desolation—one would be faint and weary on a journey. ¶ *Where no water is.* No running streams; no gushing fountains; nothing to allay the thirst.

2. *To see thy power and thy glory.* The reference here is to what was manifested of the presence and the power of God in the services of public worship;—the praises, the prayers, the rejoicings, the evidences of the Divine presence. ¶ *So as I have*

glory, so *as* I have seen thee in
the [c] sanctuary.
3 Because thy loving-kindness
is [d] better than life, my lips shall
praise thee.
4 Thus will I bless thee while
I live; I will lift up my hands in
thy name.
5 My soul shall be satisfied

c Ps. lxxxiv.2; Isa. lx. 13.
d Ps. xxx. 5.

seen thee in the sanctuary. At the tabernacle, amidst the solemn services of Divine worship. There seems to be no reason for supposing that he here refers to the mere *external* pomp and splendour of public worship, but he doubtless includes the power of the Divine presence which he had felt in such services on his own soul. As applied now to a place of *Christian* worship, it may be observed that there are nowhere more striking exhibitions of the *power* of God on earth than those which occur in such a place, especially in a revival of religion. The scene on the day of Pentecost was as striking an exhibition of the *power* of God as that which goes forth in the fury of the storm, in the raging of the ocean, or in the guidance of the heavenly bodies. Nothing can so well express what occurs in such a scene as the words "*power*" and "glory;" nothing shows more certainly the *power* of God than that influence which bows down haughty sinners, and makes them humble; which produces a deep stillness and awe in the assembled multitudes; which extorts the cry, "Men and brethren, what *must* we do to be saved?" which makes hardened men weep, and men long addicted to habits of sin willing to abandon their iniquities, and turn to God:—and nothing shows more clearly the "*glory*" of God than that power, that grace, that mercy, which thus turns multitudes from the ways of sin and death, and directs their feet into the path of peace and salvation. They who have ever witnessed the power of God in a revival of religion, will ever afterwards long to see again "the power and glory" of God, as they "*have* seen" it "in the sanctuary."

3. *Because thy loving-kindness is better than life.* Thy favour; thy mercy. This is of more value than life; more to be desired than life. *Life* is the most valued and valuable thing pertaining to this world which we can possess. See Notes on Job ii. 4. But, above this, David valued the favour and friendship of God. If one or the other was to be sacrificed, he preferred that it should be his life; he would be willing to exchange that for the favour of God. Life was not desirable, life furnished no comforts—no joys—without the Divine favour.

"My life itself, without Thy love,
No taste of pleasure could afford;
'Twould but a tiresome burden prove,
If I were banished from the Lord."

¶ *My lips shall praise thee.* That is either (*a*) because of this loving-kindness;—because I *have* this trust in thy character; or (*b*) because thou *wilt* restore me to the place of public worship, and I shall be *permitted* again to praise thee. Probably the latter is the true idea.

4. *Thus will I bless thee while I live.* In my life; or, as long as life lasts, will I praise thee. The word "*thus*" refers to the sentiment in the previous verse, meaning that as the result of his deep sense of the value of the loving-kindness of God, he would praise him through all the remainder of his life, or would never cease to praise him. A true purpose of serving God embraces the whole of this life, and the whole of eternity. He who loves God, and who has any proper sense of his mercy, does not anticipate a time when he will cease to praise and bless him, or when he will have any desire or wish *not* to be engaged in his service. ¶ *I will lift up my hands in thy name.* In solemn prayer and praise. See Notes on Ps. xxviii. 2.

5. *My soul shall be satisfied.* See Notes on Ps. xxxvi. 8. The idea is, that his soul now longed for the ser-

[e] as *with* [1] marrow and fatness;
and my mouth shall praise *thee*
with joyful lips:
6 When I remember thee upon
my [f] bed, *and* meditate on thee
in the *night*-watches.
7 Because thou hast been my
help, therefore in the shadow of
thy wings will I rejoice.
8 My soul followeth hard after

e Matt. v. 6. [1] *fatness.* *f* S. Song v. 2.

vice of God as one who is hungry longs for food, or as one who is thirsty longs for drink; and that the time would come when this longing desire would be satisfied. He would engage in the service of God as he desired to do; he would be permitted to enjoy that service without interruption. ¶ *As* with *marrow and fatness.* See Notes on Ps. xxxvi. 8. The words here employed denote rich food; and the comparison is between the pleasure of serving God, and the satisfaction derived from food when one is hungry. It is not uncommon to compare the pleasures of religion with a feast or banquet. Comp. Isa. xxv. 6. ¶ *And my mouth shall praise* thee *with joyful lips.* Lips full of joy; or, which give utterance to the joy of the heart.

6. *When I remember thee upon my bed.* See Notes on Ps. xlii. 8. That is, when I lie down at night; when I compose myself to sleep. Nothing can be more proper than that our last thoughts, as we sink into quiet slumber, should be of God;—of his being, his character, his mercy, his loving-kindness; of the dealings of his providence, and the manifestations of his grace towards us, during the day; and nothing is better fitted to compose the mind to rest, and to induce quiet and gentle slumber, than the calmness of soul which arises from the idea of an Infinite God, and from confidence in him. Often when restless on our beds,—when nothing else will lull the body to rest, the thought of God,—the contemplation of his greatness, his mercy, and his love—the sweet sense of an assurance of his favour will soothe us, and cause us to sink into gentle repose. So it may be—so it will be—when we are about to sleep the long sleep of death, for then the most appropriate thoughts—the thoughts that will best prepare us *for* that long sleep—will be thoughts of God. ¶ And *meditate on thee in the* night-*watches.* See Notes on Ps. i. 2. The word *watches* here refers to the ancient divisions of the night for municipal or military purposes,—periods of the night assigned to different persons to keep *watch* around a camp or city. The most common division of the night was into three parts, though the arrangement varied at different times. See Matt. xiv. 25; Luke xii. 38.

7. *Because thou hast been my help.* Because thou hast interposed to defend me in danger. The idea is, that he had experienced the Divine interposition in times of danger, and that this was a reason why he should still confide in God. The argument is, that God's mercy and favour in the past is a reason why we should confide in him in time to come. ¶ *Therefore in the shadow of thy wings will I rejoice.* Under the shadow or protection of thy wings will I feel safe. See Notes on Ps. xvii. 8. Comp. Ps. xxxvi. 7; lvii. 1; lxi. 4.

8. *My soul followeth hard after thee.* The word here used—דָּבַק, *dabak*—means properly to cleave to; to adhere; to be glued to; to stick fast. Then it means to attach oneself to anything; and then, to pursue or follow after. The idea here is that of adhering to, or cleaving to; and the meaning is, that the psalmist adhered firmly to God, as pieces of wood glued together adhere to each other; that he, as it were, *stuck fast* to him; that he would not leave him or be separated from him. The language represents the feelings of true piety in adhering firmly and constantly to

thee: thy *g* right hand upholdeth me.

9 But those *that* seek my soul, to destroy *it*, shall go into the lower parts of the earth.

10 They shall [1] fall by the sword; they shall be a portion for foxes.

11 But the king shall rejoice

g Ps. xviii. 35.

[1] *make him run out* like water *by the hands of the sword.*

God, whatever there may be that tends to separate us from him. The adhesion of bodies by *glue* is a striking but not an adequate representation of the firmness with which the soul adheres to God. Portions of matter held together by glue *may be* separated; the soul of the true believer never *can be* separated from God. ¶ *Thy right hand upholdeth me.* The right hand is that by which we accomplish anything; and, by constant use, is stronger than the left hand. Hence the expression is equivalent to saying that God upheld him with all his strength. The meaning is, that God sustained him in life; defended him in danger; kept him from the power of his enemies.

9. *But those* that *seek my soul to destroy* it. Who seek my *life;* who endeavour to kill me. This language would well describe the purposes of Absalom and his followers. ¶ *Shall go into the lower parts of the earth.* Shall descend into the earth; into the deepest graves. He would live; but they would perish.

10. *They shall fall by the sword.* Marg., *They shall make him run out like water by the hands of the sword.* The word rendered in the text "they shall fall," and in the margin "they shall make him run out"—נָגַר, *nagar*—means properly, to flow, to pour out, as water; and then, to pour out; then, to give up or deliver. The idea here is that of delivering over, as one pours out water from a basin or pitcher: they shall be delivered over to the sword. The original rendered "*sword*" is, as in the margin, "by the hands of the sword;" that is, the sword is represented as accomplishing its purpose *as if* it had hands. The sword shall slay them. ¶ *They shall be a portion for foxes.* The original word—שׁוּעָל, *shual*—means properly and commonly *a fox.* But under this general name *fox,* the Orientals seem to have comprehended other animals also, having some resemblance to a fox, and particularly *jackals.* Thus jackals seem to be meant in Judges xv. 4; since foxes are with great difficulty taken alive; and in this place also it has the same meaning, inasmuch as foxes do not feast on dead bodies, though a favourite repast of the jackal. Gesenius, *Lex.* Comp. Bochart Hieroz. T. ii. p. 190, ed. Lips. Jackals are wild, fierce, savage; they howl around dwellings at night,—producing most hideous music, beginning "in a sort of solo, a low, long-drawn wail, rising and swelling higher and higher until it quite overtops the wind," (Thomson's "Land and the Book," i. 133),—and ready to gather at any moment when there is prey to be devoured. "These sinister, guilty, wo-begone brutes, when pressed with hunger, gather in gangs among the graves, and yell in rage, and fight like fiends over their midnight orgies; but on the battle-field is their great carnival. Oh! let me never even dream that any one dear to me has fallen by the sword, and lies there to be torn, and gnawed at, and dragged about by these hideous howlers." The following engraving, taken from the "Land and the Book," represents them.

11. *But the king shall rejoice in God.* This passage, as was remarked in the Introd. to the psalm, shows that this psalm could not have been composed in the time of Saul, since the title *king* was not then given to David. The use of the term here in the third person does not prove that the psalm could not have been written

in God; every one that sweareth [h] by him shall glory: but the mouth of them [i] that speak lies shall be stopped.

h Isa. lxv. 16.

i Ps. lv. 21, 23.

by David himself, for he may have spoken of himself simply as "*the* king," and all the more forcibly and properly as he was driven unjustly from his throne, and was now an exile, yet was still *a king—the* king. The title was his; the throne belonged to

JACKALS.

him, and not to Absalom who had driven him from it. It was not improper to allude to this fact in the manner in which it is referred to here, and to say that "*the* king"—the true, the real king—himself—should and would rejoice in God. He would find God to be his helper; and by God he would yet be restored to his throne. ¶ *Every one that sweareth by him shall glory.* Every one that sweareth *to* him, or maintains his oath of allegiance to him, shall be honoured. ¶ *But the mouth of them that speak lies.* All who have sworn falsely; all who have professed allegiance and have proved unfaithful; all those who, contrary to their oaths and their obligations, have been found in the rebellion. They shall not be permitted to exult or rejoice, but they shall be confounded and silenced. This expresses, therefore, the fullest confidence in God; the absolute belief of David that he would be again placed on his throne, and again permitted "to see the power and glory of God as" he *had* "seen it in the sanctuary" (ver. 2); the belief that he would be restored to prosperity, and that his enemies would be humbled and destroyed.—So it will be with all who put their trust in

PSALM LXIV.

To the chief Musician. A Psalm of David.

HEAR my voice, O God, in my prayer: preserve my life from fear of the enemy.

2 Hide me from the secret counsel [k] of the wicked: from

k Gen. xlix. 6.

God. There is certain joy and triumph for them, if not in this world, at least in the world to come.

PSALM LXIV.

This psalm is described as a "psalm of David," and it bears internal evidence that it was composed by him, as it contains first, a prayer for deliverance from enemies (vers. 1-6); and second, a confident expectation of deliverance, vers. 7-10; a form of structure found in many of the psalms written by David. It is addressed, or dedicated, as many others are, "To the chief Musician." This fact shows that it was not designed as an expression of mere private feeling, but was intended to be employed in the worship of God. See Notes on the Introd. to Ps. iv.

The occasion on which this psalm was composed is unknown. In its general structure and character, it bears a strong resemblance to Ps. lviii. Indeed, many of the expressions in the two psalms are the same, and it would seem probable that it was composed with reference to the same occasion, or that the circumstances in the two cases were so similar as to make the same expressions in the main appropriate. The occasion may have been, either the times of persecution under Saul, or the rebellion of Absalom. Perhaps we may suppose, without impropriety, that the former psalm (lviii.) was composed in the time of Saul, and this in the time of Absalom, and that the circumstances in the two cases were so similar, that the author found the same phraseology which he had used on the former occasion to be appropriate to his present position, or that his feelings were so identical now with what they were then, that he naturally expressed himself in substantially the same language.

The psalm, as observed above, is composed of two parts:—

I. A prayer for deliverance from his enemies, with a description of their character, vers. 1-6.

II. An expression of confident expectation that his prayer would be answered, and that God would interpose in his behalf, vers. 7-10.

1. *Hear my voice, O God, in my prayer.* The use of the word *voice* here would seem to imply that this was *audible* prayer, or that, though alone, he gave utterance to his petitions aloud. We have this same use of the word often in the Psalms, making it probable that even private prayers were uttered in an audible manner. In most cases, when there is no danger of being overheard, or of its being construed as ostentation or Pharisaism, this is favourable to the spirit of secret devotion. Comp. Notes on Daniel vi. 10. The word here rendered *prayer* means properly speech, discourse; then, complaint; then, meditation. It is most *commonly* rendered *complaint.* See Job vii. 13; ix. 27; x. 1; xxi. 4; Ps. lv. 2 (*Notes*); Ps. cii. (*Title*); Ps. cxlii. 2. It refers here to a state of mind caused by trouble and danger, when the deep *meditation* on his troubles and dangers found expression in audible words—whether those words were complaint or petition. As there are no indications in the psalm that David was disposed to complain in the sense of *blaming* God, the proper interpretation here is that his deep meditations took the form of *prayer.* ¶ *Preserve my life from fear of the enemy.* Either Saul or Absalom. He prayed that his life might be made so secure that he would not have occasion to be afraid of his enemy.

2. *Hide me.* Or, more literally, *thou wilt hide me.* There is both an implied prayer that this might be done, and a confident belief that it would be done. The idea is, Protect me; guard me; make me safe—as one is who is hidden or concealed so that his enemies cannot find him. ¶ *From the secret counsel.* The word here used—סוֹד, *sodh*—means properly *couch, cushion;* and then, a *divan,* a

the insurrection of the workers of iniquity.

3 Who *l* whet their tongue like a sword, *and* bend *their bows* *to shoot* their arrows, *even* bitter words:

4 That they may shoot in secret at the perfect: suddenly do they shoot at him, and fear not.

l Jer. ix. 3.

circle of friends sitting together on couches for familiar conversation, or for counsel. See Notes on Ps. xxv. 14; lv. 14; comp. Job xv. 8; xxix. 4. Here the reference is to the consultations of his enemies for the purpose of doing him wrong. Of course, as they took this counsel together, he could not know it, and the word *secret* is not improperly applied to it. The idea here is, that although *he* did not know what that counsel or purpose was, or what was the result of their consultations, yet *God* knew, and he could guard him against it. ¶ *Of the wicked.* Not the wicked in general, but his particular foes who were endeavouring to destroy him. Luther renders this, "from the *assembling* of the wicked." ¶ *From the insurrection.* The word here used — רִגְשָׁה, *rigsha* — means properly a *noisy crowd, a multitude.* The allusion is to such a crowd, such a disorderly and violent rabble, as constituted a *mob.* He was in danger not only from the secret purposes of the more calm and thoughtful of his enemies who were *plotting* against him, but from the excited passions of the multitude, and thus his life was in double danger. If he escaped the one, he had no security that he would escape the other. So the Redeemer was exposed to a double danger. There was the danger arising from the secret plottings of the Scribes and Pharisees assembled in council, and there was also the danger arising from the infuriated passions of the multitude. The former calmly laid the plan for putting him to death by a judicial trial; the others took up stones to stone him, or cried, "Crucify him, crucify him!"—The word *insurrection* here does not well express the idea. The word *tumult* would better represent the meaning of the original. ¶ *Of the workers of iniquity.* That is, of those who were arrayed against him.

3. *Who whet their tongue like a sword.* Who sharpen their tongue; that is, they utter words that will *cut deep,* or *penetrate* the soul. The idea is that of slander or reproach—the same idea which we have in Shakespeare (Cymbeline),—

> "'Tis slander;
> Whose edge is sharper than the sword."

This comparison is a favourite one with David. Comp. Ps. lii. 2; lvii. 4; lix. 7. ¶ And *bend* their bows, etc. That is, they *prepare* for this,—as they make ready to shoot who bend their bows, and fix their arrows on the string. The idea here is, that this was *deliberate,* or was the result of counsel and purpose. It was not an outbreak of mere passion and excitement; it was by fixed design and careful preparation. See Notes on Ps. xi. 2; lviii. 7. ¶ Even *bitter words.* We apply the same term *bitter* now to words of malice and reproach.

4. *That they may shoot in secret.* From an unobserved quarter; from a place where they are so concealed that it cannot be known where the arrows come from. There was a purpose to ruin him, and at the same time to conceal themselves, or not to let him know from what source the ruin came. It was not an open and manly fight, where he could see his enemy, but it was a warfare with a concealed foe. ¶ *At the perfect.* At the upright; at one who is *perfect* so far as his treatment of *them* is concerned. Comp. Notes on Ps. xviii. 20, 23. ¶ *Suddenly do they shoot at him.* At an unexpected time, and from an unlooked-for quarter. They accomplish what they intended; they carry out their design. ¶ *And fear not.* They feel confident that they are not

5 They [m] encourage themselves *in* an evil [1] matter: they commune [2] of laying snares privily; they say, Who shall see them?

6 They search out iniquities; [3] they accomplish [4] a diligent search: both the inward *thought* of every one *of them*, and the heart, *is* deep.

7 But God shall shoot at them

m Prov. i. 11—13. [1] Or, *speech*. [2] *To hide*.

[3] Or, *we are consumed by that which they have throughly searched*.
[4] *a search searched*.

known, and that they will not be detected. They have no fear of God or man. Comp. Ps. lv. 19.

5. *They encourage themselves.* Literally, *they strengthen themselves*, or make themselves strong. That is, they take counsel; they encourage each other; they urge one another forward; they suggest to each other methods by which what they purpose may be done, and by which difficulties may be overcome. This was a part of their "secret counsel" or their consultation, ver. 2. ¶ In *an evil matter*. Marg., as in Heb., *speech*. The reference is to their purpose or plan. They strengthen themselves for doing what they know to be a wrong or wicked thing. ¶ *They commune.* Literally, *they tell* or *speak*. That is, they tell each other how it may be done, or suggest different methods by which it may be successfully accomplished. They compare views, that they may select that which will be most likely to be successful. All this indicates plan, consultation, design. ¶ *Of laying snares privily.* Marg., as in Heb., *to hide snares*. This is a figure derived from the method of taking wild beasts. See Notes on Ps. vii. 15; xxxviii. 12. The reference here is to some *secret* plan by which they intended that the author of the psalm should be *entrapped* and ruined. It was not a plan of open and manly warfare, but a purpose to destroy him when he would have no opportunity of defence. ¶ *They say, Who shall see them?* That is, Who will see the *snares* or *pit-falls?* Who will be aware of their existence? They sought to make the plan so secret that no one could discover it, or even suspect it; to keep it so concealed that he for whom it was intended could not be put on his guard. Comp. Ps. x. 8, 9.

6. *They search out iniquities.* They search deep; they examine plans; they rack their invention to accomplish it. The original word—חָפַשׂ, *hhaphas*—is a word which is used to denote the act of *exploring*—as when one searches for treasure, or for anything that is hidden or lost—implying a deep and close attention of the mind to the subject. So here they examined every plan, or every way which was suggested to them, by which they could hope to accomplish their purpose. ¶ *They accomplish.* This would be better translated by rendering it, "We have perfected it!" That is, We have found it out; it is complete;—meaning that they had found a plan to their liking. It is the language of self-congratulation. ¶ *A diligent search.* Or rather, "The search is a deep search." In other words, "The plan is a consummate plan; it is just to our mind; it is exactly what we have sought to find." This, too, is language of self-congratulation and satisfaction at the plan which they had thought of, and which was so *exactly* to their mind. ¶ *Both the inward* thought. Literally, *the inside;* that is, the hidden design. ¶ *And the heart.* The plan formed in the heart; the secret purpose. ¶ Is *deep.* A deep-laid scheme; a plan that indicates profound thought; a purpose that is the result of consummate sagacity. This is the language of the author of the psalm. He admitted that there had been great talent and skill in the formation of the plan. Hence it was that he cried so earnestly to God.

7. *But God shall shoot at them* with *an arrow.* That is, Instead of

with an arrow; suddenly [1] shall they be wounded.

8 So they shall make their own tongue to fall upon themselves: all that see them shall flee away.

9 And all men shall fear, and shall declare the work of God:

[1] *their wound shall be.*

---

their being able to carry out their purposes of shooting the arrows which they had prepared against others, *God* will shoot his arrows against *them.* The tables will be turned. They themselves will experience what they had intended to inflict on others. God will deal with them as they intended to deal with others. The sentiment here is substantially the same as in Ps. vii. 15; see Notes on that passage. It is also in accordance with what we often find in the writings of David, when in the close of a psalm he expresses a confident expectation that the prayer which he had offered in the beginning *would* be heard, or rejoices in the assurance that he *had* been heard.—The idea, also, is involved in this part of the psalm that God will deal with men as they purpose to deal with others; that is, according to their true character. Comp. Notes on Ps. xviii. 25, 26. ¶ *Suddenly shall they be wounded.* Marg., *their wound shall be.* The Hebrew is, "Suddenly shall be their wounds." The idea is, that the wounds in the case would be *theirs;* and would be inflicted suddenly. The blows which they thought to give to others would come on themselves, and this would occur at an unexpected moment.

8. *So they shall make their own tongue to fall upon themselves.* In verse 3, their tongue is represented as a *sword;* and here, keeping up the figure, the tongue, as a sword, is represented as falling on *them,* or as inflicting the wound on themselves which they had intended to inflict on others. This *might* be rendered, "And they have cast him down; upon them is their own tongue;" or, "Upon them their own tongue has come." That is, some one would cast them down, and they would fall as if smitten by their own tongue like a sword. It is not said *who* would do this, but the most natural interpretation is that it would be done by God. The idea is, that the instrument which they had employed to injure others would be the means of their own ruin. ¶ *All that see them shall flee away.* Comp. Ps. xxxi. 11. That is, they shall flee in consternation from those who are so fearfully overthrown. They shall see that God is just, and that He will punish the wicked; and they will desire to escape from a ruin so dreadful as that which comes upon the ungodly. The idea is, that when God punishes sinners, the effect on others is, and should be, to lead them to wish *not* to be associated with such men, but to escape from a doom so fearful.

9. *And all men shall fear.* That is, a deep impression would be made, not only on the associates and companions of the wicked, but on all that should hear of what was done. Men, in view of the just punishment of the wicked, would learn to reverence God, and to stand in awe of One so powerful and so just. Judgments, punishment, wrath, are adapted and designed to make a deep impression on mankind. On this principle, the final punishment of the wicked will make a deep and salutary impression on the universe FOR EVER. ¶ *And shall declare the work of God.* Shall make it known to others. It will become a subject of conversation, or they will *talk* about it, as illustrating the Divine perfections and character. Such *should always be* the effect of the judgments of God, for they illustrate his true character; they make known his attributes; they convey to the world lessons of the utmost importance. Nothing is more proper than to *talk about* the judgments of God, and to endeavour to derive from

for they shall wisely consider of his doing.

10 The righteous shall be glad in the LORD, and shall trust in him; and all the upright in heart shall glory.

---

them the instructions which they are *adapted* to convey about the Divine nature, and the principles of the administration under which the universe is placed. Wars, pestilences, famines, earthquakes, conflagrations, inundations, diseases, *all* teach important lessons about God; and each one bears its own peculiar message to mankind. ¶ *For they shall wisely consider of his doing.* They shall attentively and carefully consider it; they shall endeavour to derive such lessons from his dealings as they are fitted to convey. In other words, an attentive consideration of his doings will contribute to maintain a just knowledge of him in the world, and to keep the world in subjection to him. God is thus *always* speaking to men; and nothing is more proper for men than to give their minds to a careful consideration of what is really intended to be *taught* us by the events which are occurring in his providential dealings.

10. *The righteous shall be glad in the* LORD, *and shall trust in him.* That is, As the result of his gracious intervention, or as the effect of his judgments on the wicked, the righteous will rejoice on account of their own security, and put their trust in One who has thus shown himself to be the friend of holiness, and the enemy of sin. Whatever tends to reveal the Divine character, or to make a proper exhibition of that character, will also lead good men to confide in God, and to feel that they are safe. ¶ *And all the upright in heart shall glory.* Shall rejoice; shall feel that they have cause for trust and triumph. The good—the pure—the righteous—the godly—will always rejoice in everything which tends to show that God is just, and true, and holy;—for all their own hope of security and salvation rests upon the fact that the God in whom they trust is a righteous God.

PSALM LXV.

This also purports to be a psalm of David. It is dedicated to "the chief Musician," or committed to him to be set to appropriate music for the public worship of God. See Notes on the Introd. to Ps. iv. It is described as both "*a psalm*," and "*a song*." It is not easy to account for this double appellation, or to distinguish between the meaning of these words, though *probably* the real distinction is that the former word—*psalm*—refers to that to which it is applied, considered merely as a *poem* or *composition*; the latter—*song*—is applied with reference to its being *sung* in public worship. See Introd. to Ps. xlviii.

Though the psalm is ascribed to David, and though there is nothing in its general character which is inconsistent with this supposition, yet it has been maintained by De Wette and some others that the expressions in ver. 4 demonstrate that the psalm was composed *after* the temple was erected. The ground of this supposition is, that the words "*courts*," "*house*," and "*holy temple*," occurring in that verse, are applicable only to the temple. This, however, is not decisive, for all these words *may* have been used in reference to the tabernacle, or to the tent which David erected on Mount Zion (2 Chron. i. 4), and where he was accustomed to worship. Comp. Notes on ver. 4. If this is so, then there is nothing to forbid the supposition that the psalm was composed by David. Comp. also Notes on ver. 1.

The occasion on which it was written is not indicated in the title, and it is impossible now to determine it. It would seem from the psalm itself to have been composed after a copious and much-needed *rain*, perhaps after a long drought, when the earth was again refreshed by showers from heaven. The language, however, is of so general character that it *may* have had no particular reference to any recent event in the time of the psalmist, but may have been suggested, like Ps. civ., by a general contemplation of the power and the beneficence of God as manifested in his providential dealings. Possibly it may have been a song composed for some

PSALM LXV.

To the chief Musician. A Psalm *and* Song of David.

PRAISE [1] waiteth for thee, O God, in Sion; and unto thee shall the vow be performed.

2 O thou that hearest prayer,

[1] *is silent*, Ps. lxii. 1.

annual occasion, recounting the acts of God in the revolving seasons of the year—the *general* reasons which his people had to praise him. It evidently refers to some public solemnity—some acts of praise to be rendered to God in his house (ver. 1, 4), and would be eminently appropriate when his people approached him in an annual *thanksgiving*.

The contents of the psalm are as follows:—

I. The blessedness of praising God, or of coming before him, in his house, with the language of prayer and praise, vers. 1-4. (*a*) Praise "waits" for God; (*b*) he is the hearer of prayer; (*c*) he alone can cleanse the soul from sin; (*d*) it is a blessed privilege to be permitted to come before him, and to dwell in his courts.

II. The things for which he is to be praised, vers. 5-13.

(1) He is to be praised for the exhibitions of his *power*, or as the Almighty God; as one who answers the prayers of his people by heavy judgments; as one who shows that all may have confidence in him, on the earth and on the sea; as one who makes the mountains firm, who stills the noise of the waves, who calms the tumults of the people, who displays the tokens of his power everywhere, and makes the outgoings of the morning and evening to rejoice, vers. 5-8.

(2) For his *beneficence*, especially in sending down refreshing rains upon the earth, and causing the corn to spring up, the grass to grow, and the hills to rejoice on every side, vers. 9-13.

1. *Praise waiteth for thee, O God, in Sion.* That is, all the arrangements are made; the people are assembled; their hearts are prepared to praise thee. The fact that *Zion* is here mentioned as the seat of praise would seem to imply that this psalm was composed *before* the building of the temple, contrary to the opinion of De Wette and others, as noticed in the Introd. to the psalm; for after the building of the temple the seat of worship was transferred from Mount *Zion*, where David had placed the ark and prepared a tent for it (1 Chron. xv. 1; xvi. 1; 2 Chron. i. 4), to Mount Moriah. It is true that the general name *Zion* was given familiarly to Jerusalem as a city, but it is also true that the particular place for the worship of God in the time of David was Mount Zion strictly so called. See Notes on Ps. ii. 6. The margin in this place is, "Praise *is silent*." The Hebrew is, "To thee is silence-praise,"—a kind of compound phrase, not meaning "*silent praise*," but referring to a condition where everything is ready; where the preparations have been entirely made; where the *noise* usually attendant on preparation has ceased, and all is in readiness *as if waiting* for that for which the arrangements had been carried forward. The noise of building—of preparation—was now hushed, and all was calm. The *language* here would also denote the state of feeling in an individual or an assembly, when the heart was *prepared* for praise; when it was filled with a deep sense of the majesty and goodness of God; when all feelings of anxiety were calmed down, or were in a state of *rest;* when the soul was ready to burst forth in expressions of thanksgiving, and nothing would meet its wants *but* praise. ¶ *And unto thee shall the vow be performed.* See Notes on Ps. xxii. 25; l. 14; lvi. 12. The reference here is to the vows or promises which the people had made in view of the manifested judgments of God and the proofs of his goodness. Those vows they were now ready to carry out in expressions of praise.

2. *O thou that hearest prayer.* Who hast revealed thyself as a God hearing prayer,—one of the leading characteristics of whose nature it is that thou *dost* hear prayer. Literally, "Hearer of prayer, to thee shall all flesh come." Nothing as applied even to God is

unto thee shall all flesh come.
3 [1] Iniquities prevail against
me: *as for* our transgressions,
thou shalt [n] purge them away.

[1] *Words,* or, *matters of iniquities.*

n 1 John i. 7, 9.

more sublime and beautiful than the appellative "Hearer of prayer." Nothing in his attributes is of more interest and importance to man. Nothing more indicates his condescension and goodness; nothing so much encourages us in the endeavour to overcome our sins, to do good, to save our souls, and to save the souls of others. Dark and dismal would this world be, if God did *not* hear prayer; gloomy, inexpressibly gloomy, would be the prospects of man, if he had not the assurance that God is a prayer-hearing God,—if he might not come to God at all times with the assurance that it is his *very nature* to hear prayer, and that his ear is ever open to the cries of the guilty, the suffering, the sad, the troubled, the dying. ¶ *Unto thee shall all flesh come.* That is, *all men*—for the word is here used evidently to denote mankind. The idea is, that there is no other resource for man, no other help, no other refuge, but the God that hears prayer. No other being can meet his actual wants; and those wants are to be met only in connexion with prayer. All men are *permitted* to come thus to God; all have *need* of his favour; all must perish unless, in answer to prayer, he interposes and saves the soul. It is also true that the period will arrive on earth when all flesh—all men—*will* come to God and worship him; when, instead of the scattered few who now approach him, all nations, all the dwellers on continents and islands, will worship him; will look to him in trouble; will acknowledge him as God; will supplicate his favour.

3. *Iniquities prevail against me.* Marg., as in Heb., *Words,* or *matters of iniquities.* The literal meaning is *words;* and the idea may be that *words* spoken in iniquity, or slanderous words spoken by others, prevailed against him. The phrase, however, is susceptible of the interpretation which refers it to iniquity itself;—meaning the *matter* of iniquity—the thing—iniquity itself—as if that overcame him, or got the mastery of him. The psalmist here, in his own name, seems to represent the *people* who thus approached God, for the psalm refers to the worship of an assembly or a congregation. The idea is, that when they thus came before God; when they had prepared all things for his praise (ver. 1); when they approached him in an attitude of prayer, they were so bowed down under a load of transgression — a weight of sin—as to hinder their easy access to his throne. They were so conscious of unworthiness; their sin had such an effect on their minds; it rendered them so dull, cold, and stupid, that they could not find access to the throne of God. How often do the people of God find this to be the case! ¶ As for *our transgressions, thou shalt purge them away.* That is, In reference to these very transgressions or iniquities that now press us down, thou wilt remove them. The language expresses the rising confidence and hope of the worshippers that God would not allow those transgressions so to prevail as to prevent their worshipping God acceptably. Heavy as was the burden of sin, and much as the consciousness of guilt tended to impede their worship, yet they felt assured that God would so remove their transgressions that they might have access to his mercy-seat. The word rendered *purge away* —כָּפַר, *kaphar*—is the word which is commonly rendered *to atone for,* or which is used to represent the idea of *atonement.* See Notes on Isa. xliii. 3. The word has here the sense of *cleansing* or *purifying,* but it always carries with it, in the Scriptures, a reference to that through which the heart is cleansed—the atonement, or

4 Blessed *is the man whom* thou choosest, and causest to approach *unto thee, that* he may dwell in thy courts: we [o] shall be satisfied with the goodness of thy house, *even* of thy holy temple.

o Ps. lxiii. 5.

the expiatory offering made for sin. The language here expresses the feeling which all *may* have, and *should* have, and which very many *do* have, when they approach God, that, although they are deeply conscious of sin, God *will* so graciously remove the guilt of sin, and lift off the burden, cleansing the soul by his grace, as to make it *not improper* that we should approach him, and that he will enable us to do it with peace, and joy, and hope. Comp. Notes on Ps. li. 2.

4. *Blessed* is the man whom *thou choosest.* That is, Happy is the man; or, "*Oh, the happiness of the man* whom thou dost thus permit to approach thee." The construction here in the Hebrew is the same as in Ps. i. 1. See Notes on that passage. The word *choosest* refers to the fact that true piety regards all such blessings as the result of the Divine favour; the fruit of his electing grace and love. Comp. Notes on Eph. i. 3, 4; 1 Pet. i. 2, 3. We approach God with confidence, with the spirit of true worshippers, with the spirit of his children, *only* as he inclines us to him, and calls us to partake of his favour. Comp. John vi. 44. ¶ *And causest to approach* unto thee. That is, that he may worship thee. The idea is here recognised in the word *causest,* that it is only by a Divine influence that men are led to worship God. The *cause*—the efficient reason—why any man worships his Maker at all, is to be found in God himself. This idea is fairly implied in the form of the word as it is used in the Hebrew. ¶ That *he may dwell in thy courts.* That is, either temporarily for the purpose of worship; or permanently, that he may serve thee in the sanctuary. See Notes on Ps. xxiii. 6; xxvii. 4. Comp. Ps. xv. 1. The word *courts* refers properly to the *area* around the tabernacle or the temple, and not to the tabernacle or temple itself. The worship of the people was offered in those courts, and not *in* the tabernacle or temple. See Notes on Matt. xxi. 12. ¶ *We shall be satisfied with the goodness of thy house.* Our souls will find thus what they need; what they long for. See Notes on Ps. xxxvi. 8. It is the nature of religion to *satisfy* the mind; that is, the soul finds in religion what meets its wants, for religion leaves no necessity of its nature unsupplied. It may be added that nothing else will do this *but* religion.—The word *house* here denotes a place where God *dwells,* and it might be applied to the temple, as it often is in the Scriptures (comp. Isa. ii. 3; lvi. 7; Matt. xxi. 13; Mark xi. 17; Luke xix. 46; John ii. 16; *et al.*); or to the tabernacle, before the temple was reared. Ps. xlii. 4; Matt. xii. 4; Judges xviii. 31; xx. 18, 26, 31. The reference here is to the tabernacle or tent which David reared on Mount Zion, and where the worship of God was celebrated before the temple was built. ¶ Even *of thy holy temple.* The word *temple* is most commonly applied in the Scriptures to the structure which Solomon built for the worship of God; and it is on the ground that the word is usually so applied, that De Wette and others have argued that this psalm could not have been written by David, but that it was composed after the temple was reared. But the word rendered *temple*—הֵיכָל, *haichal*—is a word of so general a character that it may be applied to *any* house erected for the worship of God. It is not unfrequently applied to the tabernacle. See Notes on Ps. v. 7. This psalm, therefore, may have been composed while the tabernacle was standing, and before the temple was built, and hence may have been composed by David, as the title intimates.

5 *By* terrible[p] things in righteousness wilt thou answer us, O God of our salvation; *who art* the confidence of all the ends of the earth, and of them that are afar off *upon* the sea:

6 Which by his strength setteth fast the mountains; *being* girded with power:

7 Which[q] stilleth the noise of

p Ps. xlv. 4.

q Matt. viii. 26.

5. By *terrible things in righteousness wilt thou answer us.* That is, By things fitted to inspire us and all men with *awe*, or with a deep sense of thy majesty, thy power, and thy glory. The answer to their prayers would be in such a manner as deeply to impress their minds and hearts. God's judgments on his foes, and the manner of his manifesting his favour to his people, would be such as to impress the mind with a deep sense of his own greatness. Yet all this would be *in righteousness;* in the infliction of a just sentence on the wicked; in direct interposition in favour of the righteous. The judgments of God on guilty men have been always such as to keep the world in awe; such as were adapted deeply to impress mankind with a sense of his own majesty and glory. ¶ *O God of our salvation.* The God on whom our salvation, or our safety depends. ¶ Who art *the confidence of all the ends of the earth.* Of all parts of the earth, the word *ends* being used on the supposition that the earth is a *plain* having appropriate limits. This allusion is often found in the Scriptures, the sacred writers speaking, as all men do, as things *appear* to be. Thus all philosophers, as well as other men, speak of the sun as *rising* and *setting*, which is, in itself, no more strictly accurate than it is to speak of the earth as if it had limits or boundaries. The word *confidence* as used here means that God is the source of trust, or, that all proper reliance, by all men, in all parts of the earth and on the sea, must be in him; that is, that there is no other on whom men *can* properly rely. It does not mean that all men actually *repose* such confidence in him, which would not be true,—but that he is the only true source of confidence. ¶ *And of them that are afar off* upon *the sea.* That is, of all men on sea and land. The seaman has no other source of security amidst the dangers of the deep than God. Comp. Ps. cvii. 23-30. The language does not mean that all mariners actually *do* put their trust in God, but that they cannot confide in the winds and the waves,—in the strength of their vessel, — or their own power or skill in managing it,—but that the true and only ground of trust is God.

6. *Which by his strength setteth fast the mountains.* Fixing them firm on their foundations. This is an exhibition of vast *strength* or *power* on the part of God, as if he fixed them so firm that they could not be moved,—as if he handled with ease those vast masses of matter, with all their rocks and forests, — and caused them to repose steadily and calmly on their foundations. We have few more exalted conceptions of the power of God than to suppose him lifting with ease a vast mountain; letting it down where he pleases, and settling it so firmly that it cannot be moved. ¶ Being *girded with power.* That is, they seemed to be surrounded or encompassed with *power*, as a man girds himself up when he wishes to put forth a great effort of strength.

7. *Which stilleth the noise of the seas.* He calms the seas when they have been agitated by the storm. He causes the mighty waves to settle down, and the whole surface of the ocean becomes calm and smooth. The storm subsides at his command, and the sea is still. It was the manifestation of this power which demonstrated so clearly the divinity of the Lord Jesus, when he said to the troubled waves, "Peace, be still; and the wind ceased, and

the seas, the noise of their waves,
and the tumult of the people.
8 They also that dwell in the
uttermost parts are afraid at thy
tokens: thou makest the outgoings of the morning and evening to [1] rejoice.
9 Thou visitest the earth, and
[2] waterest it: thou greatly enrichest it with the river of God,

[1] Or, *sing*.

[2] Or, *after thou hadst made it to desire* rain.

there was a great calm." Mark iv. 39. Comp. Ps. cvii. 29. ¶ *The noise of their waves.* The loud roar of the waters, so that they are still. ¶ *And the tumult of the people.* The raging; the fury; the excitement of assembled multitudes, resembling the raging waves of the ocean. This comparison is very common. See Isa. xvii. 12, 13. Comp. Notes on Rev. xix. 6. This is perhaps a more striking and wonderful exhibition of the power of God than that of calming down the waves of the ocean. In the one case, it is the exertion of mere power on nature, acting through its established laws, and where there is no resistance of *will;* in the other, it is power exerted over the will; power over agents conscious that they are free, and where the worst passions meet and mingle and rage.

8. *They also that dwell in the uttermost parts.* That is, Those who dwell in the remotest regions; far from civilised lands; far from those places where men are instructed as to the causes of the events which occur, and as to the being and character of the great God who performs these wonders. The idea is, that even they see enough of the evidences of the Divine presence and power to fill their minds with awe. In other words, there are in all lands evidences of the Divine existence and might. There is enough to fill the minds of men with awe, and to make them solemn. ¶ *Are afraid.* Thus the thunder, the storm, the tempest, the earthquake, the eclipse of the sun or the moon, fill the minds of barbarous nations with terror. ¶ *At thy tokens.* Or *signs.* That is, the signs which really indicate the existence, the presence, and the power of God. ¶ *Thou makest the outgoings.* The word rendered *outgoings* means properly *a going forth,* as of the rising of the sun (Ps. xix. 7); and then, *a place of going forth,* or from which anything goes forth, as a gate or door (Ezek. xlii. 11), or fountains from which water issues (Isa. xli. 18); and hence, the east, where the sun seems to come forth from his hiding-place. The representation here is that the morning *seems* to come forth, or that the rays of light stream out from the east; and, in like manner, that the fading light of the evening—the twilight—*seems* to come from the west. ¶ *Of the morning and evening to rejoice.* The allusion is to the east and the west. The sun in his rising and his setting *seems* to rejoice; that is, he appears happy, bright, cheerful. The margin is *to sing*—a poetic expression indicating exultation and joy.

9. *Thou visitest the earth.* God seems to come down that he may attend to the wants of the earth; survey the condition of things; arrange for the welfare of the world which he has made; and supply the wants of those whom he has created to dwell upon it. See Notes on Ps. viii. 4. ¶ *And waterest it.* Marg., *After thou hadst made it to desire* rain. This difference between the translations in the text and in the margin can be accounted for by the various meanings of the original word. The Hebrew term—שׁוּק, *shuk*—means properly (*a*) to run; (*b*) to run after anything, to desire, to look for; (*c*) *to run over,* to overflow; and then, (*d*) to cause to overflow. The meaning here evidently is, *he drenched the earth,* or caused the water to run abundantly. The reference is to a copious rain after a drought. ¶ *Thou greatly enrichest it.* That is, Thou givest to it *abundance;* thou pourest

which is full of water: thou preparest them corn, when thou hast so provided for it.

10 Thou waterest the ridges thereof abundantly; thou [1] settlest the furrows thereof; thou [2] makest it soft with showers: thou blessest the springing thereof.

11 Thou crownest the year [3] with thy goodness; and thy paths drop fatness.

[1] Or, *causest* rain *to descend* into.
[2] *dissolvest it.* [3] *of.*

---

water upon it in such quantities, and in such a manner, as to make it *rich* in its productions. ¶ *With the river of God.* A river so abundant and full that it seems to come from God; it is such as we should expect to flow from a Being infinite in resources and in benevolence. Anything *great* is in the Scriptures often described as belonging to God, or his name is added to it to denote its greatness. Thus, *hills of God* mean lofty hills; *cedars of God*, lofty cedars, etc. ¶ Which *is full of water.* The waters are so abundant that it seems as if they *must* come from God. ¶ *Thou preparest them corn.* Grain. Thou givest to those who cultivate the earth an abundant harvest. ¶ *When thou hast so provided for it.* Or rather, When thou hast thus prepared the earth, to wit, by sending down abundant rains upon it. God prepares the earth to bear an abundant harvest, and then *he* gives that harvest. The *preparation* of the earth *for* the harvest, and then the *giving of* the harvest, are alike from him. The harvest could not be without the previous rain, and neither the rain nor the harvest could be without God. He does not create a harvest by miracle, but follows the order which he has himself ordained, and has respect to his own laws.

10. *Thou waterest the ridges thereof abundantly.* Or rather, its *furrows;* for so the Hebrew word properly means. Job xxxi. 38; xxxix. 10. The allusion is to the furrows made by the plough, which are filled with water by the rains. ¶ *Thou settlest the furrows thereof.* Or rather, *thou beatest down the ridges thereof.* Literally, *thou makest them to descend.* That is, The rain—falling on them—beats them down, so that the ground becomes level. ¶ *Thou makest it soft with showers.* Marg., *thou dissolvest it.* The idea is, to soften, to loosen, to make the soil light and open. All farmers know that this is necessary, and that it cannot be done without water. ¶ *Thou blessest the springing thereof.* Or, what springs from it; the vegetation. Thou dost bless it by causing it to grow luxuriantly, thus producing an abundant harvest.

11. *Thou crownest the year with thy goodness.* Marg., *the year of thy goodness.* The Hebrew is literally *the year of thy goodness,*—meaning a year remarkable for the manifestation of kindness; or a year of abundant productions. But the Hebrew will admit of the other construction, meaning that God crowns or adorns the year, as it revolves, with his goodness; or that the harvests, the fruits, the flowers of the year are, as it were, a crown set on the head of the year. The Septuagint renders it, "Thou wilt bless the crown of the year of thy goodness." De Wette renders it, "Thou crownest the year with thy blessing." Luther, "Thou crownest the year with good." On the whole, the most probable meaning is that expressed in our common version, referring to the beauty and the abundant productions of the year as if they were a crown on its head. The seasons are often personified, and the year is here represented as a beautiful female, perhaps, walking forward with a diadem on her brow. ¶ *And thy paths drop fatness.* That is, *fertility;* or, Fertility attends thy goings. The word rendered "drop," means properly *to distil;* to let fall gently, as the rain or the dew falls to the earth; and the idea is, that wherever God goes, marching through the

12 They drop *upon* the pastures of the wilderness; and the little hills [1] rejoice on every side.
13 The pastures are clothed

[1] *are girded with joy.*

earth, fertility, beauty, abundance seems to distil or to fall gently along his path. God, in the advancing seasons, passes along through the earth, and rich abundance springs up wherever he goes.

12. *They drop* upon *the pastures of the wilderness.* The waste places, or the waste parts of the land; the uncultivated places, the places of rocks and sands. The word *wilderness* in the Scriptures does not mean, as with us, a tract of country covered with *trees,* but a place of barren rocks or sands—an uncultivated or thinly inhabited region. See Notes on Matt. iii. 1; Isa. xxxv. 1. *In* those wastes, however, there would be valleys, or places watered by springs and streams that would afford pastures for flocks and herds. Such are the "pastures of the wilderness" referred to here. God's passing along those valleys would seem to "drop," or distil, fertility and beauty, causing grass and flowers to spring up in abundance, and clothing them with luxuriance. ¶ *And the little hills rejoice on every side.* Marg., as in Heb., *are girded with joy.* That is, Joyful, happy scenes surround them; or, they seem to be full of joy and happiness. The valleys and the hills alike seem to be made glad. The following remarks of Professor Hackett ("Illustrations of Scripture," p. 30), will explain this passage. "Another peculiarity of the desert is that, though the soil is sandy, it rarely consists, for successive days together, of mere sand; it is interspersed, at frequent intervals, with clumps of coarse grass and low shrubs, affording very good pasturage, not only for camels, the proper tenants of the desert, but for sheep and goats. The people of the villages on the borders of the desert are accustomed to lead forth their flocks to the pastures found there. We frequently passed on our way shepherds so employed; and it was interesting to observe as a verification of what is implied in the Saviour's statement (Matt. xxv. 33), that the sheep and goats were not kept distinct, but intermixed with one another. The shepherds not only frequent the parts of the desert near their places of abode, but go often to a considerable distance from them; they remain absent for weeks and months, only changing their station from time to time, as their wants in respect to water and herbage may require. The incident related of Moses shows that the pastoral habits of the people were the same in his day: 'Now Moses kept the flock of Jethro, his father-in-law, the priest of Midian; and he led the flock *to the further part of the desert,* even to Horeb,' Exod. iii. 1. It is of the desert in this sense, as supplying to some extent the means of pasturage, that the prophet Joel speaks in i. 19, and ii. 22. The psalmist also says (lxv. 12, 13), with the same reference:

'Thou crownest the year with thy goodness,
And thy paths drop fatness;
They drop fatness on the pastures of the wilderness.'"

13. *The pastures are clothed with flocks.* The flocks stand so thick together, and are spread so far, that they seem to be a clothing for the pasture; or, the fields are entirely covered with them. ¶ *The valleys also are covered over with corn.* With grain. That is, the parts of the land—the fertile valleys—which are devoted to tillage. They are covered over, or clothed with waving grain, as the pasture-fields are with flocks. ¶ *They shout for joy, they also sing.* They seem to be full of joy and happiness. What a beautiful image is this! How well does it express the loveliness of nature; how appropriately does it describe the goodness of God! Everything seems to be happy; to be full of song; and all this is to be traced to the goodness

with flocks; the valleys also are covered over with corn: they [r] shout for joy, they also sing.

r Isa. lv. 12.

of God, as it all serves to express that goodness. Strange that there should be an atheist in such a world as this;—strange that there should be an unhappy man;—strange that amidst such beauties, while all nature joins in rejoicing and praise—pastures, cultivated fields, valleys, hills—there can be found a human being who, instead of uniting in the language of joy, makes himself miserable by attempting to cherish the feeling that God is *not* good!

PSALM LXVI.

The name of the author of this psalm is unknown. There is no certain evidence that it was composed by David, yet there is nothing in the psalm itself which is inconsistent with the supposition that he was the author. Perhaps the most natural and obvious interpretation of vers. 13-15, would be that there is reference there to the temple; and if so, of course, the psalm must have been written by some one else. But it is not absolutely necessary to suppose that the temple is there referred to, for the language *might* be applied to the tabernacle as the "house" or the place of the worship of God. There is, however, no positive evidence that it was composed by David, and it is impossible now to determine its authorship.

As little can the occasion on which the psalm was composed be determined. It is evident only that it was after there had been some calamity of a private nature, or after the nation had been subjected to oppression by some powerful enemies, and when there had been deliverance from that calamity, vers. 11, 12. The calamity was *similar* to those which had been endured by the nation in the time of the Egyptian oppressions, and naturally brought to mind the sufferings endured by the people of God at that time, while their own deliverance suggested a recollection of the deliverance of their fathers from that bondage, ver. 6. On the whole, the supposition of Rosenmüller that it was composed after the Babylonish captivity, and in view of the return of the people to their native land,—perhaps to be sung on their journey from the land of exile, seems to me to be the most probable of any. Venema supposes that it refers to the time of Hezekiah, and the overthrow of Sennacherib; others regard it as referring to the persecutions of David by Saul; others, to the rebellion of Absalom; others, to the famine which is mentioned in 2 Sam. xxi., or the pestilence, 2 Sam. xxiv. Paulus supposes that it had reference to the times of the Maccabees. The psalm relates to "vows" or promises which had been made in a time of trouble; and its composition and use are designed as the fulfilment of those vows, vers. 13-15. Such a psalm of praise would be a proper fulfilment of "vows" which it might be supposed the Hebrews *would* make in the time of their exile; to wit, that if they were ever permitted to return to their native land, they would go to the house of God, and sacrifice again on his altars.

On the phrase in the title, "To the chief Musician," see Introd. to Ps. iv. On the words, "A Song *or* Psalm," see Notes on the titles to Ps. xxx. and lxv.

The psalm contains,—

I. An exhortation, addressed to all the earth, to praise God, as a matter pertaining to all lands, vers. 1, 2.

II. A reference to the mighty acts of God, as a reason for worshipping him, vers. 3-7.

III. A reference to his gracious interposition in time of national danger and trouble, and to the fact that he had rescued the nation in a marvellous manner, vers. 8-12.

IV. A reference to the vows which had been made in that time of trouble, and the purpose now to execute those vows, by going to the house of God, and sacrificing on his altars, vers. 13-15.

V. A call on all people to hear what God had done for the worshippers: viz., That he had heard prayer; that he had interposed for their deliverance; that he had attended to the voice of supplication; that he had not turned away his mercy, vers. 16-20.

PSALM LXVI.

To the chief Musician. A Song *or* Psalm.

MAKE a joyful noise unto God, all [1] ye lands.

2 Sing forth the honour of his name; make his praise glorious.

3 Say unto God, How terrible *art thou in* thy works! through the greatness of thy power shall thine enemies[2] submit themselves unto thee.

4 All the earth shall worship

[1] *the earth.*

[2] *lie,* or, *yield feigned obedience,* Ps. lxxxi. 15.

1. *Make a joyful noise unto God.* Literally, *Shout.* It is a call for exultation and praise. ¶ *All ye lands.* Marg., as in Heb., *all the earth.* The occasion was one that made universal exultation and praise proper. They who had been so deeply affected by the gracious interposition of God, could not but call on all the nations of the earth to unite with them in the expression of joy. The deliverance was so great that they wished all to rejoice with them (comp. Luke xv. 6, 9); and the intervention of God in the case of his people, furnished lessons about his character which gave occasion to all men to rejoice.

2. *Sing forth the honour of his name.* That is, Celebrate in appropriate praise the honour due to his name. Make that honour known in connexion with songs. ¶ *Make his praise glorious.* Literally, "Place honour, his praise;" that is, Give him honour; give him praise. The meaning is, Set forth his praise with songs—with music—with shouts;—*that* will be the appropriate expression of the praise which is due to him.

3. *Say unto God.* In your songs of praise. Let your songs be directly addressed to him, setting forth the grounds of that praise, or the reasons why it is due to him. ¶ *How terrible art thou in thy works!* How fearful! how much to be reverenced! The meaning is, that the manifestations of his power and greatness, in the events which occur under his government, are fitted to impress the mind with awe and reverence. ¶ *Through the greatness of thy power.* By the putting forth of thy power. Or, Thou hast such power over thine enemies as to be able to compel them to submit to thee. ¶ *Shall thine enemies submit themselves unto thee.* Margin, *Lie,* or *yield feigned obedience.* The Hebrew word means to lie, to speak lies; then, to feign, to flatter, to play the hypocrite. It is thus applied to the vanquished, who make a hollow profession of submission and love to their victors. See the word explained in the Notes on Ps. xviii. 44; comp. Ps. lxxxi. 15; Deut. xxxiii. 29; Job xxxi. 28. The meaning here is, that he had power to subdue them, and to compel them to acknowledge his right to reign. It is the putting forth of mere *power* which is here referred to; and all that such *power* can do, is to secure outward and feigned submission. It cannot of itself secure the submission of the heart, the will, and the affections. That is to be secured by *love,* not by *power;* and the difference between the submission of the true people of God and that of all others is that the former are subdued by *love,* the latter by *power;* the submission of the former is genuine, that of the latter is forced. The inhabitants of heaven will be submissive to God because they love him; the dwellers in hell will be restrained by power, because they cannot deliver themselves. So now, the submission of a true child of God is that of love, or is a willing submission; the submission of a hypocrite is that of fear, when he feigns obedience because he cannot help it, or because he simply dreads the wrath of God. The *object* here is to celebrate the *power* of God, and it was sufficient, in order to set that forth, to say that it *awed,* and *outwardly subdued* the enemies of God.

4. *All the earth shall worship thee.* That is, all the inhabitants of the world will bow down before thee, or

thee, and shall sing unto thee; they shall sing *to* thy name. Selah.

5 Come and see the works of God: *he is* terrible *in his* doing toward the children of men.

6 He *s* turned the sea into dry *land*: they went through the flood on foot: there did we rejoice in him.

7 He ruleth by his power for ever; his eyes behold the nations: let not the rebellious exalt themselves. Selah.

8 O bless our God, ye people,

s Ex. xiv. 21.

render thee homage. The time will come when thy right to reign will be universally acknowledged, or when thou wilt everywhere be adored as the true God. This is in accordance with all the statements in the Bible. See Notes on Ps. xxii. 27; Comp. Notes on Isa. xlv. 23; Rom. xiv. 11. ¶ *And shall sing unto thee.* Shall celebrate thy praises. ¶ To *thy name.* To thee.

5. *Come and see the works of God.* See Notes on Ps. xlvi. 8, where substantially the same expression occurs. The idea is, "Come and see what God has done and is doing; come and learn from this what he is; and let your hearts in view of all this, be excited to gratitude and praise." The *particular* reference here is to what God had done in delivering his people from their former bondage in Egypt (ver. 6); but there is, connected with this, the idea that he actually rules among the nations, and that in his providence he has shown his power to govern and subdue them. ¶ He is *terrible* in his *doing,* etc. That is, His acts are fitted to inspire awe and veneration. See Notes on ver. 3.

6. *He turned the sea into dry* land. The Red Sea, when he brought his people out of Egypt, Exod. xiv. 21. This was an illustration of his power, and of his ability to defend and deliver his people. The *terror* in that case, or that which was "*terrible,*" was the overthrow of their enemies—the destruction of the Egyptians in the Red Sea—thus showing that he had power to destroy all the enemies of his people. ¶ *They went through the flood on foot.* Literally, *through the river.* It is probable that the reference here is to the passage of the river Jordan, when the Israelites were about to pass into the promised land (Joshua iii. 14–17);—thus combining the two great acts of Divine interposition in favour of his people, and showing his power over streams and floods. ¶ *There did we rejoice in him.* We, as a nation—our fathers—thus rejoiced in God. See Exod. xv.

7. *He ruleth by his power for ever.* Literally, "Ruling by his power for ever." The idea is, that he does this constantly; in each age and generation. He never has ceased to rule; he never will. His dominion extends from age to age, and will stretch forward for ever. The power which he evinced in delivering his people he retains now, and will retain for ever. In that unchanging power, his people may confide; that unchanging power, the wicked should fear. ¶ *His eyes behold the nations.* All nations; all people. He sees all their conduct. They can conceal nothing from him. They should, therefore, stand in awe. The wicked have much to fear from One who *sees* all that they do, and who has *power* to crush and destroy them. Comp. Notes on Ps. xi. 4. ¶ *Let not the rebellious exalt themselves.* Be lifted up with pride, or feel secure. They cannot overcome an Almighty God; they cannot escape from his power. The word *rebellious* here has reference to those who are impatient under the restraints of the law of God, and who are disposed to cast off his authority. The admonition is one that may be addressed to all who thus rebel against God, whether they are nations or individuals. Alike they must feel the vengeance of his arm, and fall beneath his power.

8. *O bless our God, ye people.* That is, particularly the people of the

and make the voice of his praise
to be heard.
9 Which [1] holdeth our soul in
life, and suffereth not our feet to
be moved.
10 For thou, O God, hast
proved us: thou hast tried us,
as silver [t] is tried.
11 Thou broughtest us into
the [u] net; thou laidst affliction
upon our loins.
12 Thou hast caused men to ride
over our heads: we went through

[1] *putteth.* [t] Isa. xlviii. 10; 1 Pet. i. 7. [u] Hos. vii. 12.

---

nation; the Hebrew people. The call here to praise or bless God is on account of some special benefit which had been conferred on them, and which is referred to more particularly in the following verses. It was his gracious interposition in the time of danger, by which they were delivered from their foes, vers. 11, 12. ¶ *And make the voice of his praise to be heard.* Let it be sounded out afar, that it may be heard abroad.

9. *Which holdeth our soul in life.* Marg., as in Heb., *putteth.* That is, He has put (or placed) us in a state of safety. The word rendered "in life" means literally *among the living.* The word *soul* here is equivalent to *us,—ourselves;* and the idea is, that he keeps *us among the living.* What is here said of this special deliverance is true of all men at all times, that they owe the fact that they are among the living to the care of God; or, it is because he *puts* them among the living, or *keeps* them alive. ¶ *And suffereth not our feet to be moved.* That is, from their firm position of safety. The idea is taken from one who is walking, and who is kept from slipping or falling.

10. *For thou, O God, hast proved us.* That is, Thou hast tried us; thou hast tested the reality of our attachment to thee, as silver is tried by the application of fire. God had proved or tried them by bringing calamity upon them to test the reality of their allegiance to him. The nature of the *proof* or *trial* is referred to in the following verses. ¶ *Thou hast tried us, as silver is tried.* That is, by being subjected to appropriate tests to ascertain its real nature, and to remove from it imperfections. Comp. Notes on 1 Pet. i. 7; Isa. i. 25; xlviii. 10; see also Zech. xiii. 9; Mal. iii. 3.

11. *Thou broughtest us into the net.* That is, Thou hast suffered or permitted us to be brought into the net; thou hast suffered us to be taken captive, as beasts are caught in a snare. See Notes on Ps. ix. 15. The allusion here is to the efforts made by their enemies to take them, as hunters lay gins, or spread nets, to capture wild beasts. The idea here is, that those enemies had been successful; God had suffered them to fall into their hands. If we suppose this psalm to have been composed on the return from the Babylonish captivity, the propriety of this language will be apparent, for it well describes the fact that the nation had been subdued by the Babylonians, and had been led captive into a distant land. Comp. Lam. i. 13. ¶ *Thou laidst affliction upon our loins.* The loins are mentioned as the seat of strength (comp. Deut. xxxiii. 11; 1 Kings xii. 10; Job xl. 16); and the idea here is, that he *had put their strength to the test;* he had tried them to see how much they could bear; he had made the test effectual by applying it to the part which was able to bear most. The idea is, that he had called them to endure as much as they were able to endure. He had tried them to the utmost.

12. *Thou hast caused men to ride over our heads.* This refers evidently to some national subjection or conquest—most probably to their having been subdued by the Babylonians. Professor Alexander renders this, "Thou hast caused men to ride *at* our head," as if leading them forth as captives in war. The most probable meaning, however, is that they had

fire and through water; but thou
broughtest us out into a [1] wealthy
place.
13 I will go into thy house
with burnt-offerings; I will pay
thee my vows,
14 Which my lips have [2] uttered, and my mouth hath spoken, when I was in trouble.

[1] *moist.*

[2] *opened.*

been subdued, as if on a field of battle, and as if their conquerors had ridden over them when prostrate on the ground. Comp. Notes on Ps. xliv. 5, and Isa. li. 23. ¶ *We went through fire and through water.* This is designed to represent the nature of their trials. It was *as if* they had been made to pass through burning flames and raging floods. Comp. Notes on Isa. xliii. 2. Instead of passing through the seas and rivers when the waters had been turned back, and when a dry and safe path was made for them, as was the case with their fathers (ver. 6), they had been compelled to breast the flood itself; and yet, notwithstanding this, God had brought them into a place of safety. In either way, by *parting* the floods, or by conducting his people *through* them, as shall seem best pleasing to him, God can conduct his people safely, and deliver them from danger. The power, the protecting care, the love, and the faithfulness of God are shown with equal clearness *whether* he divides the flood and causes his people to march through as on dry land, or *whether* he suffers the flood to rage and heave around them while he conducts his chosen people safely through. ¶ *But thou broughtest us out into a wealthy* place. Marg., *moist.* Professor Alexander, *overflow, abundance.* Vulgate, *into a place of refreshment*—refrigerium. The LXX., *εἰς ἀναψυχήν.* Luther, *Thou hast led us forth and quickened us.* De Wette, *zum Ueberflusse—to overflowing*, or *abundance.* The Hebrew word—רְוָיָה, *revayah*—means properly *abundant drink, abundance.* It occurs only here and in Ps. xxiii. 5, where it is rendered *runneth over.* See Notes on that place. The proper idea here is, that he had brought them into a land where there was plenty of water—as emblematic of abundance in general. He had led them to a place where there were ample rivers, springs, and streams, producing fertility and abundance. This would be the language of the people *after* their return from exile, and when they were permitted again to re-visit their native land—a land always characterized as a land of plenty. See Deut. viii. 7; comp. Exod. iii. 8; Lev. xx. 24; Num. xiii. 27.

13. *I will go into thy house with burnt-offerings.* To thy temple—the place of worship. This is language designed to represent the feelings and the purpose of the *people.* If the psalm was composed on occasion of the return from the Babylonish captivity, it means that, as their first act, the people would go to the house of God, and acknowledge his goodness to them, and render him praise. On the word *burnt-offerings*, see Notes on Isa. i. 11. ¶ *I will pay thee my vows.* I will keep the solemn promises which I had made; that is, the promises which the people had made in the long period of their captivity. On the word *vows*, see Notes on Ps. xxii. 25.

14. *Which my lips have uttered*, etc. Marg., *opened.* The Hebrew word, however,—פָּצָה, *patzah*—means properly to tear apart; to rend; and then, to open wide, as the mouth, for example,—or the throat,—as wild beasts do, Ps. xxii. 13. Then it means to open the mouth in scorn (Lam. ii. 16; iii. 46); and then, to utter hasty words, Job xxxv. 16. The idea would be expressed by us by the phrases *to bolt* or *blurt out;* to utter hastily; or, to utter from a heart full and overflowing; to utter with very

15 I will offer unto thee burnt-sacrifices of [1] fatlings, with the incense of rams: I will offer bullocks with goats. Selah.

16 Come [v] *and* hear, all ye that fear God, and I will declare what he hath done for my soul.

[1] *marrow.* *v* Ps. xxxiv. 2.

little care as to the language employed. It is the fulness of the *heart* which would be suggested by the word, and not a nice choice of expressions. The *idea* is, that the heart was *full;* and that the vows were made under the influence of deep emotion, when the heart was so full that it could not *but* speak, and when there was very little attention to the language. It was not a calm and studied selection of words. Such vows are not less acceptable to God than those which are made in the best-selected language. Not a little of the most popular sacred poetry in all tongues is of this nature; and when refined down to the nicest rules of art it ceases to be popular, or to meet the wants of the soul, and is laid aside. The psalmist here means to say, that though these vows were the result of deep feeling—of warm, gushing emotion—rather than of calm and thoughtful reflection, yet there was no disposition to *disown* or *repudiate* them now. They were made in the depth of feeling—in real sincerity—and there was a purpose fairly to carry them out. ¶ *When I was in trouble.* When the people were in captivity, languishing in a foreign land. Vows made in trouble—in sickness, in bereavement, in times of public calamity—should be faithfully performed when health and prosperity visit us again; but, alas, how often are they forgotten!

15. *I will offer unto thee burnt-sacrifices of fatlings.* Marg., *marrow.* On the word rendered *burnt-offerings* see Notes on Isa. i. 11. The word rendered *fatlings* is rendered in Isa. v. 17, *lambs.* It may be applied to any animal considered as *fat*—a qualification required in sacrifices to be made on the altar, Isa. i. 11. ¶ *With the incense of rams.* The word here rendered *incense* is commonly applied to aromatics which were burned in the tabernacle or temple, producing a grateful odour (see Notes on Isa. i. 13); but it seems here to be used with reference to the smoke ascending from burning rams offered in sacrifice—ascending as the smoke of incense did. The smoke thus ascending would be as grateful and acceptable as incense. ¶ *I will offer bullocks with goats.* Bullocks *and* goats. That is, I will present sacrifices in *all* the forms *required* in worship; in all the forms that will express gratitude to God, or that will be an acknowledgment of dependence and guilt; in all that would properly express homage to the Deity. Bullocks and goats were both required in the ancient worship.

16. *Come* and *hear, all ye that fear God.* All who are true worshippers of God,—the idea of *fear* or *reverence* being put for worship in general. The call is on all who truly loved God to hear what he had done, in order that he might be suitably honoured, and that due praise might be given him. ¶ *And I will declare what he hath done for my soul.* This is probably the personification of an individual to represent the people, considered as delivered from oppression and bondage. The words "*for my soul*" are equivalent to *for me.* Literally, *for my life.* The phrase would embrace *all* that God had done by his gracious intervention in delivering the people from bondage. The *language* here is such as may be used by any one who is converted to God, in reference (*a*) to all that God has done to redeem the soul; (*b*) to all that he has done to pardon its guilt; (*c*) to all that he has done to give it peace and joy; (*d*) to all that he has done to enable it to overcome sin; (*e*) to all that he has done to give it comfort in the prospect of death; (*f*) to all that he has done to impart the hope of heaven.

17 I cried unto him with my mouth, and he was extolled with my tongue.

18 If [w] I regard iniquity in my heart, the Lord will not hear *me*;

w Prov. xxviii. 9.

The *principle* here is one which it is right to apply to all such cases. It is right and proper for a converted sinner to call on others to hear what God has done for him; (*a*) because it is due to God thus to honour him; (*b*) because the converted heart naturally gives utterance to expressions of gratitude and praise, or wishes to make known the joy derived from pardoned sin; (*c*) because there is in such a soul a strong desire that others may partake of the same blessedness, and find the same satisfaction and peace in the service of God. It is the *duty* of those who are pardoned and converted thus to call on others to hear what God has done for them;—(*a*) because others have the same *need* of religion which they have; (*b*) because the *same* salvation is provided for them which has been provided for those who have found peace; (*c*) because all are under obligation to make known as far as possible the fact that God *has* provided salvation for sinners, and that all *may* be saved. He who has no such sense of the mercy of God, manifested towards himself, as to desire that others may be saved,—who sees no such value in the religion which he professes as to have an earnest wish that others may partake of it also,—can have no real evidence that his own heart has ever been converted to God. Comp. Notes on Rom. ix. 1–3; x. 1.

17. *I cried unto him with my mouth.* That is, in my trouble; when distress came upon me. This, according to the explanation of the design of the psalm given above, is one individual speaking on behalf of the nation, or uttering the sentiment of the people. At the same time, however, all this is language appropriate to an individual when recording his own experience. ¶ *And he was extolled with my tongue.* I praised him; I acknowledged his supremacy. I recognised my dependence on him, and looked to him as that God who had all things under his control, and who could grant me the deliverance which I desired.

18. *If I regard iniquity in my heart.* Literally, "*If I have seen* iniquity in my heart." That is, If I have indulged in a purpose of iniquity; if I have had a wicked end in view; if I have not been willing to forsake all sin; if I have cherished a purpose of pollution or wrong. The meaning is not literally, If I have "*seen*" any iniquity in my heart—for no one can look into his own heart, and not see that it is defiled by sin; but, If I have *cherished* it in my soul; if I have gloated over past sins; if I am purposing to commit sin again; if I am not willing to abandon all sin, and to be holy. ¶ *The Lord will not hear* me. That is, He will not regard and answer my prayer. The idea is, that in order that prayer may be heard, there must be a purpose to forsake all forms of sin. This is a great and most important principle in regard to prayer. The same principle is affirmed or implied in Ps. xviii. 41; xxxiv. 15; Prov. i. 28; xv. 29; xxviii. 9; Isa. i. 15; Jer. xi. 11; xiv. 12; Zech. vii. 13; John ix. 31. It is also *especially* stated in Isa. lviii. 3–7. The principle is applicable (*a*) to secret *purposes* of sin; to sinful desires, corrupt passions, and evil propensities; (*b*) to *acts* of sin in individuals, as when a man is pursuing a business founded on fraud, dishonesty, oppression, and wrong; (*c*) to public acts of sin, as when a people fast and pray (Isa. lviii.), and yet hold their fellow-men in bondage; or enact and maintain unjust and unrighteous laws; or uphold the acts of wicked rulers; or countenance and support by law that which is contrary to the law of God; and (*d*) to the feelings of an awakened and trembling

19 *But* verily God hath heard *me*; he hath attended to the voice of my prayer.

20 Blessed *be* God, which hath not turned away my prayer, nor his mercy from me.

sinner when he is professedly seeking salvation. If there is still the love of evil in his heart; if he has some cherished purpose of iniquity which he is not willing to abandon; if there is any *one* sin, however small or unimportant it may seem to be, which he is not willing to forsake, he cannot hope that God will hear his prayer; he may be assured that he will not. *All prayer, to be acceptable to God,* MUST *be connected with a purpose to forsake all sin.*

19. But *verily God hath heard* me, etc. That is, He has given me evidence that he has heard my prayer; and, in doing this, he has thus given me the assurance also that I do *not* regard iniquity in my heart. The evidence that he has heard me is at the same time proof to my mind that I do *not* love sin. As it is a settled and universal principle that God does *not* hear prayer when there is in the heart a cherished love and purpose of iniquity, so it follows that, if there is evidence that he *has* heard our prayers, it is proof that he has seen that our hearts are sincere, and that we truly desire to forsake all forms of sin.

20. *Blessed* be *God, which hath not turned away my prayer.* That is, It is fit that I should praise and adore God for the fact that he *has* graciously condescended to listen to the voice of my supplications. ¶ *Nor his mercy from me.* There is no more proper ground of praise than the fact that God hears prayer—the prayer of poor, ignorant, sinful, dying men. When we consider how great is his condescension in doing this;—when we think of his greatness and immensity;—when we reflect that the whole universe is dependent on him, and that the farthest worlds need his care and attention;—when we bear in mind that we are creatures of a day and "know nothing;" — and especially when we remember how we have violated his laws, how sensual, corrupt, and vile our lives have been, how low and grovelling have been our aims and purposes, how we have provoked him by our unbelief, our ingratitude, and our hardness of heart —we can never express, in appropriate words, the extent of his goodness in hearing our prayers, nor can we find language which will properly give utterance to the praises due to his name for having condescended to listen to our cries for mercy.

PSALM LXVII.

On the phrases in the title, "To the chief Musician" and "on Neginoth," see Notes on the Introd. to Ps. iv. On the words "psalm" and "song," see Notes on the title to Ps. xlviii.

Four of the psalms (iv., vi., liv., lv.), where the phrase "on Neginoth" occurs, are ascribed to David; one (Ps. lxxvii.) is ascribed to Asaph; but there is no intimation in the title of this psalm (or in the psalm itself), which would enable us to determine by whom it was composed. It cannot be demonstrated that it was *not* written by David, but there is no certain evidence that it *was.* Nor is it possible to ascertain the occasion on which it was composed. Venema supposes that it was written in the time of Hezekiah, after the land was delivered from the Assyrian invasion, and was at peace; and, especially, in reference to the prediction in Isa. xxxvii. 30, "Ye shall eat this year such as groweth of itself; and the second year such as groweth of the same: and in the third year sow ye, and reap, and plant vineyards, and eat the fruit thereof." This was to be a "sign" to the people of Israel that the land would not be subjugated to the foreigners (see my Notes on that passage); and the psalm, according to this supposition, was written in view of the fact that God had, at the time of its composition, mercifully interposed in the destruction of the Assyrian army. The psalm contains, according to this idea, an expression of praise for the merciful interposition

PSALM LXVII.

To the chief Musician on Neginoth. A Psalm *or* Song.

GOD [x] be merciful unto us, and bless us; *and* cause [y] his face to shine [1] upon us; Selah.

2 That thy way may be known

x Num. vi. 25. *y* Ps. iv. 6. [1] *with.*

---

which God had thus vouchsafed, and a prayer that the promise might be *fully* accomplished; that the land might be free from any future invasion; and that, according to the prediction, it might produce abundantly, or that it might be cultivated in peace, and with no fear of foreign conquest. Thus, (ver. 6): "Then shall the earth yield her increase; and God, even our own God, shall bless us." There is much plausibility in this supposition, though it is not possible with certainty to determine its correctness.

Thus understood, the psalm is designed to express the feelings—the desires—the hopes of the Hebrew people in those circumstances. It contains,

I. A prayer that God would still be merciful to them and bless them, as if there were still some danger to be apprehended, ver. 1.

II. A desire that his ways—the principles of his administration—might be made known to all people, ver. 2.

III. A call on the people to praise God for what he had done, with the expression of a wish that all nations might be glad and rejoice; that they might put their trust in God as a righteous God; that they might understand the great principles on which he governs the world, vers. 3-5.

IV. A statement of the fact that *then* —in connexion with this universal recognition of God—the prophecy would be fulfilled in its most complete sense; that the earth would yield her increase as it was made to do; that there would be universal prosperity: in other words, that the proper acknowledgment of God, and the prevalence of true religion, would be an incalculable benefit to man's temporal interests; or, that under such a state of things, the true fertility and productiveness of the earth would be developed, vers. 6, 7. The psalm thus illustrates *the influence of true religion in securing the proper cultivation of the earth* (*accomplishing so far the purpose for which man was made*, Gen. i. 28; ii. 15), *and consequently in promoting the happiness of mankind.*

1. *God be merciful unto us, and bless us.* There is, perhaps (as Prof. Alexander suggests), an allusion, in the language used here, to the sacerdotal benediction in Numb. vi. 24–26: "The Lord bless thee, and keep thee; the Lord make his face shine upon thee, and be gracious unto thee: the Lord lift up his countenance upon thee, and give thee peace." The prayer is that God would bestow upon his people the blessing implied in the form of benediction which he had directed the ministers of his religion to use. The first cry is, of course, for mercy or favour. The beginning of all blessings to mankind is the favour or mercy of God. There is no higher blessing than his *favour;* there is none that comes from him which should not be regarded as *mercy.* ¶ And *cause his face to shine upon us.* Marg., *With us.* That is, among us. It is an invocation of his presence and favour. On the phrase "cause his face to shine," see Notes on Ps. iv. 6.

2. *That thy way may be known upon earth.* The law of God; the principles and methods of the Divine administration; the way in which God rules mankind, and in which he bestows his blessings on men. The prayer is, that all the earth might be made acquainted with the methods in which God deals with his people, or confers favours on men. The happiness of man depends on a knowledge of the principles on which God bestows his favours; for all men are, in all things, dependent on him. The success of a farmer depends on his understanding, and complying with, the laws and principles on which God bestows a harvest; the preservation of health, the restoration of health when we are sick, depends on a knowledge of the great laws which God has ordained for the continuance of the healthy functions of our bodies,

upon earth, thy saving health among all [z] nations.

3 Let the people praise thee, O God; let all the people praise thee.

4 O let the nations be glad, and sing for joy; for thou shalt judge the people righteously, and [1] govern the nations upon earth. Selah.

5 Let the people praise thee, O God; let all the people praise thee.

z Matt. xxviii. 19. 1 *lead.*

---

and on the use of the means which he has provided for restoring health when those functions are disordered; and, in like manner, the salvation of the soul depends on the right understanding of the method which God has appointed to secure his favour. In neither of these cases—in no case—is it the business of men to *originate* laws of their own;—laws for the cultivation of the earth, or for the preservation of health, or for the saving of the soul. The business of man is to *find out* the rules in accordance with which God bestows his favours, and then to act in obedience to them. The psalmist here supposes that there *are* certain rules or principles, in accordance with which God bestows blessings on mankind; and he prays that those rules and principles may be everywhere made known upon the earth. ¶ *Thy saving health among all nations.* The original word here rendered *saving health,* is *salvation.* It is with great uniformity so rendered. It is indeed translated *welfare,* in Job xxx. 15; *help,* in Ps. iii. 2; xlii. 5; *deliverance,* in Ps. xviii. 50; xliv. 4; Isa. xxvi. 18; *helping,* Ps. xxii. 1; and *health,* in Ps. xlii. 11; but elsewhere it is in all cases rendered *salvation.* The words *saving health* were adopted from an older version, but no argument should be founded on them. The word *salvation* expresses all that there is in the original; and the prayer is, that the method by which God confers salvation on men may be made known throughout all lands. Assuredly no more appropriate prayer could be offered than that all the race may be made acquainted with the way in which God saves sinners.

3. *Let the people praise thee, O God.* Do thou incline them to praise thee:—a prayer that all people might so understand the character and ways of God, and might have such a sense of his claims upon them, as to lead them to praise him. ¶ *Let all the people praise thee.* The people of all lands. See Notes on Ps. xxii. 27. Comp. Ps. lxvi. 4.

4. *O let the nations be glad, and sing for joy.* All the nations of the earth. Let them all be made acquainted with thee; with thy character; with the principles of thy government; with the methods by which thou dost bestow thy favours, that they all *may* be made glad. These things pertain to them all. The knowledge of these things would convey inestimable blessings to them all, and fill all their hearts with joy. Nothing would, in fact, diffuse so much happiness over a miserable and guilty world—nothing would furnish such an occasion for universal joy, gratitude, and praise—as the possession of the knowledge of the great principles on which God rules the world, and on which he blesses men. ¶ *For thou shalt judge the people righteously.* That is, The great principles of thy administration are *right,* or *righteous,* and the nations will have occasion to rejoice in them. ¶ *And govern the nations upon earth.* Marg., *lead.* So the Hebrew. That is, God would instruct them what to do; he would guide them in paths of prosperity, happiness, salvation. Individuals and nations, as they follow the counsels of God, are safe and happy; and in no other way.

5. *Let the people praise thee,* etc. See ver. 5. The repetition shows that this was the principal thought in the mind of the author of the psalm. It

6 *Then* [a] shall the earth yield her increase; *and* God, *even* our own God, shall bless us.

a Lev. xxvi. 4; Ezek. xxxiv. 27. Hos. ii. 21, 22.

expresses an earnest—an intense—desire, that all nations should acknowledge God as the true God, and praise him for his mercies.

6. Then *shall the earth yield her increase.* The word rendered *increase*—יְבוּל, *yebul*—means properly *produce*, or that which the earth produces when properly cultivated. It is rendered *increase*, as here, in Lev. xxvi. 4, 20; Deut. xxxii. 22; Judges vi. 4; Job xx. 28; Ps. lxxviii. 46; lxxxv. 12; Ezek. xxxiv. 27; Zech. viii. 12; and *fruit*, in Deut. xi. 17; Hab. iii. 17; Hag. i. 10. It does not elsewhere occur. The Hebrew verb here is in the past tense—"*has yielded* her increase," but the connexion seems to demand that it shall be rendered in the future, as the entire psalm pertains to the future,—to the diffusion of the knowledge of the way of God, ver. 2; to the desire that the nations might praise him, vers. 3–5; and to the fact that God would bless the people, vers. 6, 7. Thus understood, the idea is, that the prevalence of true religion in the world would be connected with prosperity, or that it would tend greatly to increase the productions of the earth. This it would do, (*a*) as such an acknowledgment of God would tend to secure the Divine favour and blessing on those who cultivate the earth, preventing the necessity, by way of judgment, of cutting off its harvests by blight, and drought, and mildew, by frost, and storm, and destructive insects, caterpillars, and locusts; (*b*) as it would lead to a much more extensive and general cultivation of the soil, bringing into the field multitudes, as labourers, to occupy its waste places, who are now idle, or intemperate, or who are cut down by vice and consigned to an early grave. If all who are now idle were made industrious—as they would be by the influence of true religion; if all who by intemperance are rendered worthless, improvident, and wasteful, were made sober and working men; if all who are withdrawn from cultivating the earth by wars — who are kept in standing armies, consumers and not producers,—or who are cut down in battle, should be occupied in tilling the soil, or should become producers in any way; and if all who are now *slaves*, and whose labour is not worth half as much as that of freemen, should be restored to their equal rights,—the productions of the earth would at once be increased many times beyond the present amount. The prevalence of true religion in the world, arresting the cause of idleness and improvidence, and keeping alive those who are now cut off by vice, by crime, and by the ravages of war, would soon make the whole world assume a different aspect, and would accomplish the prediction of the prophet (Isa. xxxv. 1) that the "wilderness and the solitary place shall be glad, and that the desert shall rejoice and blossom as the rose." The earth has never yet been half cultivated. Vast tracts of land are still wholly unsubdued and uninhabited. No part of the earth has yet been made to produce all that it could be made to yield; and no one can estimate *what* the teeming earth might be *made* to produce if it were brought under the influence of proper cultivation. As far as the true religion spreads, it *will* be cultivated; and in the days of the millenium, when the true religion shall be diffused over all continents and islands, the earth will be a vast fruitful field, and much of the beauty and the fertility of Eden be reproduced in every land. ¶ And *God*, even *our own God, shall bless us.* The true God; the God whom we adore. That is, He will bless us with this abundant fertility; he will bless us with every needed favour.

7 God shall bless us; and all [b] the ends of the earth shall fear him.

b Ps. xxii. 27.

7. *God shall bless us.* That is, with prosperity, peace, salvation. The making of his name known abroad will be the means of blessing the world; will be the highest favour that can be conferred on mankind. ¶ *And all the ends of the earth shall fear him.* All parts of the earth. See Notes on Ps. xxii. 27. The time, therefore, looked for is that when the knowledge of the Lord shall pervade all lands;—the time to which the ancient prophets were constantly looking forward as the sum of all their wishes, and the burden of all their communications;—that time, for the coming of which all who love their fellow-men, and who earnestly desire the welfare of the world, should most earnestly pray. The hope that this may occur, is the only bright thing in the future respecting this world; and he lives most in accordance with the high ends for which man was made who most earnestly desires this, and who, by his prayers and efforts, contributes most to this glorious consummation.

PSALM LXVIII.

This psalm purports to be a psalm of David. It is dedicated to "the chief Musician." See Notes on the Introd. to Ps. iv. There is no reason to doubt the correctness of the title, as there is nothing *in* the psalm which conflicts with the supposition that David was the author, and as it accords so much, in its scope and language, with his undoubted compositions. On the phrase in the title "*A Psalm* or *Song*," see Notes on the title to Ps. lxv.

It is not certainly known on what occasion the song was composed. It is evidently, like the eighteenth psalm, a triumphal song designed to celebrate victories which had been achieved; but whether composed to celebrate some particular victory, or in view of all that had been done in subduing the enemies of the people of God, it is impossible now to determine. Prof. Alexander supposes that it was in reference to the victory recorded in 2 Sam. xii. 26-31, the last important victory of David's reign. Venema supposes that it was composed on the occasion of removing the ark to Mount Zion, to the place which David had prepared for it. This also is the opinion of Rosenmüller. De Wette inclines to the opinion that it was written in view of the victory over the Ammonites and others, as recorded in 2 Sam. viii.-xii. There are some things, however, in regard to the time and occasion on which the psalm was composed, which can be determined from the psalm itself.

(1) It is clear that it was not composed *before* the time of David, because before his time Jerusalem or Zion was not the seat of the royal authority, nor the place of Divine worship, which it is evidently supposed to be in the psalm, ver. 29.

(2) It was composed when the Hebrew nation was one, or before the separation of the ten tribes and the formation of the kingdom of Israel under Jeroboam; for Benjamin, Judah, *Zebulon* and *Naphtali* are especially mentioned as taking part in the solemnities referred to in the psalm, ver. 27.

(3) It was consequently before the Babylonish captivity.

(4) It was composed on some occasion of bringing up the ark, and putting it in the place which had been prepared for it, vers. 16, 24, 25. These verses can be best explained on the supposition that the psalm was written on that occasion. Indeed they cannot well be explained on any other supposition.

(5) It was in view of *past* triumphs; of victories secured in former times; of what God had then done for his people, and *especially* of what he had done when the ark of the covenant had been placed at the head of the armies of Israel, ver. 14. Comp. vers. 7, 8, 12, 17, 18.

(6) It was in anticipation of future triumphs--the triumphs of the true religion; under the feeling and belief that *Jerusalem* would be the centre from which wholesome influences would go out over the world; and that through the influences which would go out from Jerusalem *the world* would be subdued to God, vers 20-23; 29-31. Comp. Isa. ii. 3.

PSALM LXVIII.

To the chief Musician. A Psalm *or* Song of David.

LET [c] God arise, let his enemies be scattered: let them also that hate him flee [1] before him.

2 As [d] smoke is driven away, *so* drive *them* away: as wax

c Num. x. 35; Isa. xxxiii. 3.

[1] *from his face.* d Hos. xiii. 3.

The psalm was composed, therefore, I apprehend, when the ark was brought up from the house of Obed-edom, and placed in the city of David, in the tent or tabernacle which he had erected for it there: 2 Sam. vi. 12; 1 Chron. xv. It is not improbable that other psalms, also, were composed for this occasion, as it was one of great solemnity.

The contents of the psalm accord entirely with this supposition. They are as follows:—

I. A prayer that God would arise and scatter all his enemies, vers. 1, 2.

II. A call on the people to praise God, with reference to his greatness, and to his paternal character, vers. 3-6.

III. A reference to what he had done in former times for his people in conducting them from bondage to the promised land, vers. 7-14.

IV. A particular reference to the ark, vers. 15-18. After it had been lying neglected, God had gone forth with it, and Zion had become distinguished above the hills; the chariots of God had been poured forth; victory had attended its movements; and God had gone up leading captivity captive.

V. The anticipation of future triumphs,—the confident expectation of future interposition,—as derived from the history of the past, vers. 19-23.

VI. A description of the procession on the removing of the ark, vers. 24-27.

VII. The anticipation of future triumphs expressed in another form, not that of subjugation by mere *power*, but of a *voluntary* submission of kings and nations to God, vers. 28-31. Kings would come with presents (ver. 29); nations—Egypt and Ethiopia—would stretch out their hands to God, ver. 31.

VIII. A call on all the nations, in view of these things, to ascribe praise to God, vers. 32-35.

1. *Let God arise.* See Notes on Ps. iii. 7. There is an obvious reference here to the words used by Moses on the removal of the ark in Num. x. 35. The same language was also employed by Solomon when the ark was removed to the temple, and deposited in the most holy place (2 Chron. vi. 41): "Now therefore arise, O Lord God, into thy resting place, thou, and the ark of thy strength." It would seem probable, therefore, that this psalm was composed on some such occasion. ¶ *Let his enemies be scattered.* So in Num. x. 35: "Rise up, Lord, and let thine enemies be scattered; and let them that hate thee flee before thee." The ark was the symbol of the Divine presence, and the idea is, that wherever that was, the enemies of God would be subdued, or that it was only by the power of Him who was supposed to reside there that his enemies could be overcome. ¶ *Let them also that hate him flee before him.* Almost the exact language used by Moses in Num. x. 35. It is *possible* that this may have been used on some occasion when the Hebrews were going out to war; but the more probable supposition is that it is general language designed to illustrate the power of God, or to state that his rising up, at any time, would be followed by the discomfiture of his enemies. The placing of the ark where it was designed to remain permanently would be a proper occasion for suggesting this general truth, that all the enemies of God must be scattered when he rose up in his majesty and power.

2. *As smoke is driven away.* To wit, by the wind. Smoke—vapour—easily disturbed and moved by the slightest breath of air—represents an object of no stability, or having no power of resistance, and would thus represent the real weakness of the most mighty armies of men as opposed to God. ¶ So *drive* them *away.* With the same ease with which smoke is driven by the slightest breeze, so

[e] melteth before the fire, *so* let the wicked perish at the presence of God.

3 But let the righteous be glad: let them rejoice [f] before God; yea, let them [1] exceedingly rejoice.

4 Sing unto God, sing praises to his name: extol him that rideth upon the heavens by his name JAH, and rejoice before him.

e Micah i. 4. f 1 Thess. v. 16.

1 *rejoice with gladness.*

do the enemies of God disappear before his power. Comp. Notes on Ps. i. 4. ¶ *As wax melteth before the fire.* Comp. Ps. xxii. 14. The meaning here is plain. As wax is melted down by fire—losing all its hardness, its firmness, its power of resistance, so must the most mighty armies melt away before God. ¶ So *let the wicked perish at the presence of God.* That is, those who rise up against him; his enemies. It will be as easy for God to destroy wicked men as it is for fire to melt down wax.

3. *But let the righteous be glad.* That is, Let them be prosperous and happy; let them be under thy protecting care, and partake of thy favour. While the wicked are driven away like smoke, let the righteous live, and flourish, and be safe. Comp. Ps. xxxii. 11. ¶ *Let them rejoice before God.* In the presence of God; or as admitted to his presence. The wicked will be driven far off; the righteous will be admitted to his presence, and will rejoice before him. ¶ *Yea, let them exceedingly rejoice.* Marg., as in Heb., *rejoice with gladness.* The expression is designed to express great joy; joy that is multiplied and prolonged. It is joy of heart accompanied with all the outward expressions of joy.

4. *Sing unto God, sing praises to his name.* That is, *to him;* the name being often put for the person himself. The repetition denotes intensity of desire; a wish that God might be praised with the highest praises. ¶ *Extol him.* The word here rendered *extol*—סָלַל, *salal*—means to lift up, to raise, to raise up, as into a heap or mound; and especially to cast up and prepare a way, or to make a way level before an army by casting up earth; that is, to prepare a way for an army. See Notes on Isa. xl. 3. Comp. also Isa. lvii. 14; lxii. 10; Job xix. 12; xxx. 12; Prov. xv. 19 (*marg.*); Jer. xviii. 15. This is evidently the idea here. It is not to "*extol*" God in the sense of praising him; it is to prepare the way before him, as of one marching at the head of his armies, or as a leader of his hosts. The allusion is to God as passing before his people in the march to the promised land; and the call is to make ready the way before him,—that is, to remove all obstructions out of his path, and to make the road smooth and level. ¶ *That rideth.* Rather, "that *marcheth.*" There is, indeed, the idea of *riding*, yet it is not that of "riding *upon the heavens,*" which is the meaning, but of riding at the head of his hosts on their march. ¶ *Upon the heavens.* The word here used—עֲרָבָה, *arabah*—never means either heaven, or the clouds. It properly denotes an arid tract, a sterile region, a desert; and then, a plain. It is rendered *desert* in Isa. xxxv. 1, 6; xl. 3; xli. 19; li. 3; Jer. ii. 6; xvii. 6; l. 12; Ezek. xlvii. 8; and should have been so rendered here. So it is translated by De Wette, Prof. Alexander, and others. The LXX. render it, "Make way for him who is riding westward." So the Latin Vulgate. The Chaldee renders it, "Extol him who is seated upon the throne of his glory in the north heaven." The reference, doubtless, is to the passage through the desert over which the Hebrews wandered for forty years. The Hebrew word which is employed here is still applied by the Arabs to that region. The idea is that of Jehovah marching over those deserts at the head of his armies, and the call is to

5 A father of the fatherless, [g] and a judge of the widows, *is* God in his holy habitation.

g Jer. xlix. 11.

prepare a way for him on his march, comp. vers. 7, 8. ¶ *By his name JAH.* This refers to his riding or marching at the head of his forces through the desert, *in the character described by that name*—or, *as Jah;* that is, Jehovah. *Jah* is an abbreviation of the word *Jehovah,* which was assumed by God as his peculiar name, Ex. vi. 3. The word *Jehovah* is usually rendered, in our version, LORD, printed in small capitals to denote that the original is *Jehovah;* the word itself is retained, however, in Ex. vi. 3; Ps. lxxxiii. 18; Isa. xii. 2 (see Notes); and Isa. xxvi. 4. The word *Jah* occurs in this place only, in our translation. It is found in combination, or in certain formulas—as in the phrase *Hallelujah,* Ps. civ. 35; cv. 45; cvi. 1. The meaning here is, that God went thus before his people in the *character* of the true God, or *as* Jehovah. ¶ *And rejoice before him.* Or, in his presence. Let there be joy when he thus manifests himself as the true God. The presence of God is fitted to give joy to all the worlds that he has made, or wherever he manifests himself to his creatures.

5. *A father of the fatherless.* Or, of orphans. Comp. Ps. x. 14, 18. That is, God takes the place of the parent. See Jer. xlix. 11: "Leave thy fatherless children, I will preserve them alive; and let thy widows trust in me." This is one of the most tender appellations that could be given to God, and conveys one of the most striking descriptions that can be given of his character. We see his greatness, his majesty, his power, in the worlds that he has made,—in the storm, the tempest, the rolling ocean; but it is in such expressions as this that we learn, what we most desire to know, and what we cannot elsewhere learn, that he is *a Father;* that he is to be *loved* as well as *feared.* Nothing suggests more strikingly a state of helplessness and dependence than the condition of orphan children and widows; nothing, therefore, conveys a more affecting description of the character of God—of his condescension and kindness—than to say that he will take the place of the parent in the one case, and be a protector in the other. ¶ *And a judge of the widows.* That is, He will see justice done them; he will save them from oppression and wrong. No persons are more liable to be oppressed and wronged than widows. They are regarded as incapable of defending or vindicating their own rights, and are likely to be deceived and betrayed by those to whom their property and rights may be entrusted. Hence the care which *God* manifests for them; hence his solemn charges, so often made to those who are in authority, and who are entrusted with power, to respect their rights; hence his frequent and solemn rebukes to those who violate their rights. See Notes on Isa. i. 17. Comp. Deut. x. 18; xiv. 29; xxiv. 17; Ex. xxii. 22; Job xxiv. 3, 21; Jer. vii. 6; Mal. iii. 5; James i. 27. ¶ Is *God in his holy habitation.* Where he dwells; to wit, in heaven. The design of the psalmist seems to be to take us at once up to God; to let us see what he is in his holy home; to conduct us into his very presence, that we may see him as he is. What a man is we see in his own home,—when we get near to him; when we look upon him, not on great or state occasions, when he is abroad, and assumes appearances befitting his rank and office, but in his own house; as he is constantly. This is the idea here, that if we approach God most nearly, if we look upon him, not merely in the splendour and magnificence in which he appears in governing the worlds, in his judgments, in storm and tempest, riding on the clouds and controlling the ocean, but, as it were, in his own dwelling, his quiet heavens,—if we look most

6 God setteth the solitary in [1]families: he [h]bringeth out those which are bound with chains; but the rebellious dwell in a dry *land*.

7 O God, when thou wentest forth before thy people, when

[1] *a house.* [h] Ps. cvii. 10, 14.

---

closely at his character, we shall find that character best represented by the kind and benignant traits of a father,—in his care for widows and orphans. In other words, the more we see of God,—the more we become intimately acquainted with his real nature,—the more evidence we shall find that he is benevolent and kind.

6. *God setteth the solitary in families.* Marg., as in Heb., *in a house.* The word rendered *solitary* means properly one alone, as an only child; Gen. xxii. 2, 12, 16; and then it means *alone*, solitary, wretched, forsaken. See Notes on Ps. xxii. 20. The word rendered *families* would be more literally and better translated as in the margin, *houses.* The idea then is, not that he constitutes families of those who were solitary and alone, but that to those who are alone in the world—who seem to have no friends—who are destitute, wretched, forsaken, he gives comfortable dwellings. Thus the idea is carried out which is expressed in the previous verse. God is the friend of the orphan and the widow; and, in like manner, he is the friend of the cast out—the wandering—the homeless;—he provides for them *a home.* The meaning is, that he is benevolent and kind, and that they who have no other friend may find a friend in God. At the same time it is true, however, that the family organization *is* to be traced to God. It is his original appointment; and all that there is in the family that contributes to the happiness of mankind—all that there is of comfort in the world that depends on the family organization—is to be traced to the goodness of God. Nothing more clearly marks the benignity and the wisdom of God than the arrangement by which men, instead of being solitary wanderers on the face of the earth, with nothing to bind them in sympathy, in love, and in interest to each other, are grouped together in families. ¶ *He bringeth out those which are bound with chains.* He releases the prisoners. That is, He delivers those who are unjustly confined in prison, and held in bondage. The principles of his administration are opposed to oppression and wrong, and in favour of the rights of man. The meaning is not that he always does this by his direct power, but that his law, his government, his requirements are all against oppression and wrong, and in favour of liberty. So Ps. cxlvi. 7, "The Lord looseth the prisoners." Comp. Notes on Isa. lxi. 1. ¶ *But the rebellious dwell in a dry* land. The rebels; all who rebel against him. The word rendered *dry land* means a dry or arid place; a desert. The idea is, that the condition of the rebellious as contrasted with that of those whom God has under his protection would be as a fertile and well-watered field compared with a desert. For the one class he would provide a comfortable home; the other, the wicked, would be left as if to dwell in deserts and solitudes. In other words, the difference in condition between those who are the objects of his favour, and those who are found in proud rebellion against him, would be as great as that between such as have comfortable abodes in a land producing abundance, and such as are wretched and homeless wanderers in regions of arid sand. While God befriends the poor and the needy, while he cares for the widow and the orphan, he leaves the rebel to misery and want. The *allusion* here probably is to his conducting his people through the desert to the land of promise and of plenty; but still the passage contains a general truth in regard to the principles of his administration.

thou didst march through the wilderness; Selah:
8 The earth [i] shook, the heavens also dropped at the presence of God: *even* Sinai [k] itself *was moved* at the presence of God, the God of Israel.
9 Thou, O God, didst [1] send a plentiful rain, [l] whereby thou didst confirm [2] thine inheritance, when it was weary.
10 Thy congregation hath

i Hab. iii. 13. *k* Ex. xix. 16—18.

[1] *shake out.* *l* Deut. xi. 11—14. [2] *it.*

7. *O God, when thou wentest forth before thy people,* etc. That is, in conducting them through the desert to the promised land. The statement in regard to the paternal character of God in the previous verses is here illustrated by his guiding his own people, when fleeing from a land of oppression, through the barren desert,—and his interpositions there in their behalf. All that had been said of him in the previous verses is here confirmed by the provision which he made for their wants in their perilous journey through the wilderness.

8. *The earth shook.* See Ex. xix. 16–18. ¶ *The heavens also dropped at the presence of God.* That is, dropped down rain and food. The idea is that the very heavens seemed to be shaken or convulsed, so that rain and food were *shaken down,*—as ripe fruit falls from a tree that is shaken. Comp. Notes on Isa. xxxiv. 4. So also, Isa. lxiv. 1–3. The meaning is not that the heavens themselves dropped down, but that they dropped or distilled rain and food. ¶ Even *Sinai itself* was moved. This was true; but this does not seem to be the idea intended here, for the words "even" and "was moved" are not in the original. The Hebrew is, literally, "This Sinai;" meaning probably "this was at Sinai,"—or, "this took place at Sinai." The correct translation perhaps would be, "The heavens distilled rain at the presence of God, this at Sinai, at the presence of God." ¶ *At the presence of God, the God of Israel.* The whole region seemed to be moved and awed at the presence of God, or when he came down to visit his people. The earth and the heavens, all seemed to be in commotion.

9. *Thou, O God, didst send a plentiful rain.* Marg., *shake out.* Prof. Alexander, "a rain of free gifts." The Septuagint and the Vulgate render it, "a voluntary or willing rain." The Syriac, "the rain of a vow." The Hebrew word translated "plentiful" means free, voluntary, of its own accord—נְדָבָה, *nedabah*—(See Notes on Ps. li. 12, where it is rendered *free*); then it means that which is given freely; and hence, abundantly. It means, therefore, in this place, plentiful, abundant. The reference, however, is to the manna, with which the people were supplied from day to day, and which seemed to be *showered* upon them in abundance. The word rendered "didst send" means properly *to shake out,* as if God shook the clouds or the heavens, and the abundant supplies for their wants were thus *shaken out.* ¶ *Whereby thou didst confirm thine inheritance, when it was weary.* Thou didst *strengthen* thy people when they were exhausted, or were in danger of fainting. In other words, God sent a supply of food—manna, quails, etc.—when they were in the pathless wilderness, and when they were ready to perish.

10. *Thy congregation hath dwelt therein.* In the land of promise; for the connexion requires us to understand it in this manner. The idea of the writer all along pertains to that land, and to the mercy which God had shown to it. After showing by an historical reference what God had done for the people in the wilderness, he returns here, though without expressly mentioning it, to the land of promise, and to what God had done *there* for his people. The word ren-

dwelt therein: thou, O God, hast prepared of thy goodness for the [m] poor.

11 The Lord gave the word; great *was* the [1] company of those that published *it*.

12 Kings of armies [2] did flee apace; and she that tarried at home divided the spoil.

m Matt. xi. 5. [1] *army.* [2] *did flee, did flee.*

dered *congregation*—חַיָּה, *hhaiyah*—means properly a beast, an animal, Gen. i. 30; ii. 19; viii. 19; xxxvii. 20. Then it comes to be used as a collective noun, meaning a *herd* or *flock;* thus, a *troop* of men, an army or host, 2 Sam. xxiii. 11, 13; and it is applied here to the *people*, under the idea so common in the Scriptures that God is a Shepherd. ¶ *Thou, O God, hast prepared of thy goodness for the poor.* For thy flock considered as poor or wretched. That is, Thou hast provided for them when they had no resources of their own,—when they were a poor, oppressed, and afflicted people,—wanderers wholly dependent on thee.

11. *The Lord gave the word.* The command, or the order. It is not certain to what the psalmist here refers; whether to some particular occasion then fresh in the recollection of the people, when a great victory had been gained, which it was the design of the psalm to celebrate; or whether it is a *general* statement in regard to the doings of God, having reference to *all* his victories and triumphs, and meaning that in *all* cases the command came from him. The subsequent verses make it evident that there is an allusion here to the ark of the covenant, and to the victories which had been achieved under that as a guide or protector. The entire psalm refers to the ark, and its triumphs; and the idea here seems to be, that in all the victories which had been achieved the "word" or the command came from God, and that its promulgation was immediately made by a "great company" who stood ready to communicate it or to "publish" it. ¶ *Great* was *the company of those that published* it. Marg., *army.* More literally, "The women publishing it were a great host." The word used is in the feminine gender, and refers to the Oriental custom whereby females celebrated victories in songs and dances. See Ex. xv. 20, 21; Judges xi. 34; xxi. 21; 1 Sam. xviii. 6, 7. The idea here is, that when there was a proclamation of war,—when God commanded his people to go out to battle, and to take with them the ark, the females of the land—the singers—were ready to make known the proclamation; to celebrate the will of the Lord by songs and dances; to cheer and encourage their husbands, brothers, and fathers, as they went out to the conflict. The result is stated in the following verse.

12. *Kings of armies did flee apace.* Marg., as in Heb., *did flee, did flee.* This is the Hebrew mode of expressing that which is emphatic or superlative. It is by simply repeating the word. The idea is, that they fled speedily; they fled at once, and in alarm. The 12th and 13th verses are marked by De Wette as a quotation, and the language is supposed by him to be the substance of the song that was sung by the women as referred to in ver. 11. This supposition is not improbable. The reference is, undoubtedly, to the former victories achieved by the people of God when they went out to war; and the idea is, that when the command came, when God gave the word (ver. 11), their foes fled in consternation. ¶ *And she that tarried at home divided the spoil.* The women remaining in their homes, while the men went out to war. On them devolved the office of dividing the plunder, and of giving the proper portions to each of the victors. They would take an interest in the battle, and receive the booty, and assign the

13 Though ye have lien among the pots, *n* *yet shall ye be as* the wings of a dove covered with silver, and her feathers with yellow gold.

n Ps. lxxxi. 6.

portion due to each of the brave soldiers,—the more acceptable as given to them by female hands. Possibly, however, the meaning *may* be, that the victors would bring the plunder home, and lay it at the feet of their wives and daughters to be divided among the women themselves. The dividing of the spoils of battle after a victory was always an important act. Comp. Judges v. 30; Josh. vii. 21; 1 Chron. xxvi. 27; Heb. vii. 4.

13. *Though ye have lien among the pots.* There are few passages in the Bible more difficult of interpretation than this verse and the following. Our translators seem to have supposed that the whole refers to the ark, considered as having been neglected, or as having been suffered to remain among the common vessels of the tabernacle, until it became *like* those vessels in appearance,—that is, until its brilliancy had become tarnished by neglect, or by want of being cleaned and furbished,—yet that it would be again like the wings of a dove covered with silver, as it had been formerly, and pure like the whitest snow. But it is not certain, if it is probable, that this is the meaning. Prof. Alexander renders it, "When ye lie down between the borders (ye shall be like) the wings of a dove covered with silver;" that is, "when the land had rest," or was restored to a state of tranquillity. De Wette renders it, "When ye rest between the cattle-stalls:" expressing the same idea, that of quiet repose as among the herds of cattle lying calmly down to rest. The Septuagint renders it, "Though you may have slept in kitchens." The words rendered "Though ye have lien" mean literally, "If you have lain," alluding to some act or state of lying down quietly or calmly. The verb is in the plural number, but it is not quite clear what it refers to. There is *apparently* much confusion of number in the passage. The word rendered "*pots*"—שְׁפַתַּיִם, *shephattaim*—in the *dual* form, occurs only in this place and in Ezek. xl. 43, where it is translated *hooks* (marg., *end-irons*, or *the two hearth-stones*). Gesenius renders it here *stalls*, that is, folds for cattle, and supposes that in Ezekiel it denotes places in the temple-court, where the victims for sacrifice were fastened. Tholuck renders it, "When you shall again rest within your stone-borders [that is, within the limits of your own country, or within your own borders], ye shall be like the wings of a dove." For other interpretations of the passage, see Rosenmüller *in loc.* I confess that none of these explanations of the passage seem to me to be satisfactory, and that I cannot understand it. The wonder is not, however, that, in a book so large as the Bible, and written in a remote age, and in a language which has long ceased to be a spoken language, there should be here and there a passage which cannot now be made clear, but that there should be so few of that description. There is no ancient book that has not more difficulties of this kind than the Hebrew Scriptures. ¶ Yet shall ye be as *the wings of a dove covered with silver*, etc. The phrase "yet shall ye be" is not in the original. The image here is simply one of *beauty*. The allusion is to the changeable colours of the plumage of a dove, now seeming to be bright silver, and then, as the rays of light fall on it in another direction, to be yellow as gold. If the allusion is to the ark, considered as having been laid aside among the ordinary vessels of the tabernacle, and having become dark and dingy by neglect, then the meaning would be, that, when restored to its proper place, and with the proper degree of attention and care bestowed upon it,

14 When *o* the Almighty scattered kings [1] in it, it was *white* as snow in Salmon.

o Jos. xii. 1, etc. [1] Or, *for her, she was.*

it would become a most beautiful object. *If* the allusion is to the people of the land considered *either* as lying down in dishonour, *as if* among filth, *or* as lying down calmly and quietly as the beasts do in their stalls, *or* as peacefully reposing within their natural limits or borders, *then* the meaning would be, that the spectacle would be most beautiful. The varied tints of loveliness in the land—the gardens, the farms, the flowers, the fruits, the vineyards, the orchards, the villages, the towns, the cheerful homes—would be like the dove—the emblem of calmness—so beautiful in the variety and the changeableness of its plumage. The comparison of a beautiful and variegated country with *a dove* is not a *very* obvious one, and yet, in this view, it would not be wholly unnatural. It is not easy always to vindicate philosophically the images used in poetry; nor is it always easy for a Western mind to see the reasons of the images employed by an Oriental poet. It seems probable that the comparison of the *land* (considered as thus variegated in its beauty) with the changing beauties of the plumage of the dove is the idea *intended* to be conveyed by this verse; but it is not easy to make it out on strictly exegetical or philological principles.

14. *When the Almighty scattered kings in it.* The Hebrew here is, "In the scattering of [*i.e.* by] the Almighty of kings." The reference is to the act of God in causing kings to abandon their purposes of invasion, or to flee when their own countries were invaded. Comp. Ps. xlviii. 5, 6. The language here is so general that it might be applied to *any* such acts in the history of the Hebrew people; to *any* wars of defence or offence which they waged. It *may* have reference to the scattering of kings and people when Joshua invaded the land of Canaan, and when he discomfited the numerous forces, led by different kings, as the Israelites took possession of the country. The close connexion of the passage with the reference to the journey through the wilderness (vers. 7–9) would make it probable that this is the allusion. The phrase "*in it*," (marg., *for her*), refers doubtless to the land of Canaan, and to the victories achieved there. ¶ *It was* white *as snow in Salmon.* Marg., *She was.* The allusion is to the land of Canaan. But about the meaning of the phrase "white as snow in Salmon," there has been great diversity of opinion. The word rendered "was white as snow" is correctly rendered. It means to be snowy; then, to be white *like* snow. The *verb* occurs nowhere else. The *noun* is of frequent occurrence, and is always rendered *snow.* Ex. iv. 6; Num. xii. 10; 2 Sam. xxiii. 20; 2 Kings v. 27; *et al.* The word *Salmon* properly means *shady,* and was applied to the mountain here referred to, probably on account of the dark forests which covered it. That mountain was in Samaria, near Shechem. Judges ix. 48. It is not known why the snow of *that* mountain is particularly alluded to here, as if there was any *special* whiteness or purity in it. It is probably specified by name only to give more vivacity to the description. There is much difference of opinion as to what is the meaning of the expression, or in what respects the land was thus *white.* The most common opinion has been that it was from the bones of the slain which were left to bleach unburied, and which covered the land so that it seemed to be white. Comp. Virg. Æn. v. 865; xii. 36. Ovid uses similar language, Fast. i: "Humanis ossibus albet humus." So also Horace, Serm. 1, 8: "Albis informem spectabant ossibus agrum." This interpretation of the passage is adopted by Rosenmüller, Gesenius, and De Wette.

15 The hill of God *is as* the hill of Bashan; an high hill, *as* the hill of Bashan.

Others suppose it to mean that the land was like the dazzling whiteness of snow in the midst of blackness or darkness. This was the opinion of Kimchi, and this interpretation is adopted by Prof. Alexander. Tholuck supposes it to mean that, when war was waged on the kings and people, they fell as fast as snow-flakes on Mount Salmon; and that the idea is not so much the *whiteness* of the land, as the fact that they fell in great numbers, covering the land as the snow-flakes do. It is perhaps not possible to determine which of these explanations is correct. Either of them would accord with the meaning of the words and the general sense of the psalm. That of Tholuck is the most poetical, but it is less obvious from the Hebrew words used.

15. *The hill of God.* The phrase "the hill of God," or the mountain of God, is elsewhere applied in the Scriptures only to Mount Horeb or Sinai (Ex. iii. 1; xviii. 5; xxiv. 13; 1 Kings xix. 8), and to Mount Zion, Ps. xxiv. 3; Isa. xxx. 29. There is no reason for supposing that there is a reference here to Mount Horeb or Sinai, as the psalm does not particularly relate to that mountain, and as there is nothing in the psalm to bring that mountain into comparison with other mountains. The allusion is, I think, clearly to Mount Zion; and the idea is, that that mountain, though it was not distinguished for its elevation or grandeur,—though it had nothing in itself to claim attention, or to excite wonder,—yet, from the fact that it had been selected as the place where God was to be worshipped, had an honour not less than that of the loftiest mountain, or than those which showed forth the Divine perfections by their loftiness and sublimity. There is connected with this, also, the idea that, although it might be less defensible by its natural position, yet, because God resided there, it was defended by his presence more certainly than loftier mountains were by their natural strength. It should be remarked, however, that many other interpretations have been given of the passage, but this seems to me to be its natural meaning. ¶ *Is as the hill of Bashan.* Luther renders this, "The mount of God is a fruit-bearing hill; a great and fruitbearing mountain." On the word *Bashan*, see Notes on Isa. ii. 13; xxxiii. 9; Ps. xxii. 12. Bashan was properly the region beyond Jordan, bounded on the north by Mount Hermon or the Anti-Libanus, and extending south as far as the stream Jabbok, and the mountains of Gilead. The "hill" of Bashan, or the "mountain of Bashan," was properly Mount Hermon —the principal mountain pertaining to Bashan. The name Bashan was properly given to the country, and not to the mountain. The mountain referred to—Hermon—is that lofty range which lies on the east of the Jordan, and in the northern part of the country—a range some twelve thousand feet in height. See Notes on Ps. xlii. 6. It is the most lofty and distinguished mountain in Palestine, and the idea here, as above expressed, is, that Mount Zion, though not so lofty, or not having so much in itself to attract attention, was not less honoured, and not less safe, as being the peculiar dwelling-place of God. ¶ *An high hill*, etc. Or rather, a mount of peaks or ridges as Bashan. Mount Hermon was not a single hill, or a detached mountain, but a chain of mountains,—a range of lofty peaks or summits. So of Zion. It was by the presence and protection of God what Bashan was by its natural strength and grandeur. Comparatively low and unimportant as Zion was, it had in fact *more* in it to show what God is, and to constitute safety, than there was in the loftiness and grandeur of Bashan. The latter,

16 Why leap ye, ye high hills? *this* [p] *is* the hill *which* God desireth to dwell in; yea, the LORD will dwell *in it* for ever.

17 The chariots of God *are* twenty thousand, *even* [1] thousands [q] of angels: the Lord *is* among them *as in* Sinai, in the holy *place*.

p 1 Kings ix. 3.

1 Or, *many thousands*.
q Deut. xxxiii. 2.

though thus lofty and grand, had no *advantage* over Zion, but Zion might in every way be compared with that lofty range of hills which, by their natural position, their strength, and their grandeur, showed forth so much the greatness and glory of God. The teaching would be, as applied to Zion, or the Church, that there is *as much* there to show the Divine perfections, to illustrate the greatness and the power of God, as there is in the most sublime works of nature; or that they who look upon the works of God in nature to learn his perfections, have no advantage over those who seek to learn what he is in his church.

16. *Why leap ye, ye high hills?* That is, with exultation; with pride; with conscious superiority. Why do you seem to regard yourselves as so superior to Mount Zion, in strength, in beauty, in grandeur? The Hebrew, however,—רָצַד, *ratzad*—rather means, "Why do ye watch insidiously? why do ye look askance at?" The word occurs only in this place. In Arabic it means to watch closely; to lie in wait for. This is the idea here. The mountains around Palestine—the mountains of the heathen world—the lofty hills—as if conscious of their grandeur, are represented as looking *askance*, in their pride, at Mount Zion; as eyeing it with silent contempt, as if it were not worthy of notice; as if it were so insignificant that it had no claim to attention. The idea is not that of "*leaping*," as in our English Bible, or of "*hopping*," as in the version of the Episcopal Prayer Book, but that of a look of silent disdain, as if, by their side, Zion, so insignificant, was not worthy of regard. *Perhaps*, by the high hills here, however, are disguisedly also represented the mighty powers of the heathen world, as if looking with contempt on the people of the land where Zion was the place of worship. ¶ This is *the hill* which *God desireth to dwell in*. The hill which *he* has selected as his abode, and which *he* has honoured above all the mountains of the earth, by his permanent residence there. As such, Zion has an honour above the loftiest hills and ranges of mountains in the earth. ¶ *Yea, the* LORD *will dwell* in it *for ever*. Permanently; he will make it his fixed habitation on earth. Notwithstanding the envy or the contempt of surrounding hills, he will make this his settled abode. He has chosen it; he delights in it; he will not forsake it for the mountains and hills that are in themselves more grand and lofty.

17. *The chariots of God*. The meaning of this verse is, that God is abundantly able to maintain his position on Mount Zion; to defend the place which he had selected as his abode. Though it has less natural strength than many other places have,—though other hills and mountains, on account of their natural grandeur, may be represented as looking on this with contempt, as incapable of defence, yet he who has selected it is fully able to defend it. He is himself encompassed with armies and chariots of war; thousands of angels guard the place which he has chosen as the place of his abode. *Chariots*, usually two-wheeled vehicles, often armed with scythes attached to their axles, were among the most powerful means of attack or defence in ancient warfare. See Notes on Ps. xx. 7; xlvi. 9; Isa. xxxi. 1; xxxvii. 24; Comp. Ex. xiv. 7; Josh. xvii. 16; Judges iv. 15. ¶ Are *twenty thousand*. A closer

18 Thou [r] hast ascended on high, thou hast led captivity captive: thou [s] hast received gifts [1] for men; yea, *for* the rebellious [t] also, that the LORD God might [u] dwell *among them.*

r Acts i. 2, 9; Eph. iv. 8. *s* Acts ii. 4, 33. [1] *in the man.*

t 1 Cor. vi. 9—11; 1 Tim. i. 13, 15. *u* Rev. xxi. 3.

version is *two myriads*, or twice ten thousand. The original word is in the dual form. The language is designed to denote a very great number. A myriad was a great number; the idea here is that even *that* great number was doubled. ¶ Even *thousands of angels.* Marg., *many thousands.* The Hebrew is, *thousands repeated*, or *multiplied.* There is in the Hebrew no mention of angels. The Septuagint and the Vulgate render it, "thousands of the rejoicing;" that is, thousands of happy attendants. The original, however, would most naturally refer to the chariots, as being multiplied by thousands. ¶ *The Lord* is *among them.* The real strength, after all, is not in Zion itself, or in the chariots of the Lord surrounding it, but in the Lord himself. *He* is there as the Head of the host; He, as the Protector of his chosen dwelling-place. ¶ As in *Sinai, in the holy* place. Literally, "The Lord is among them; Sinai, in the sanctuary." The idea seems to be, that even Sinai with all its splendour and glory—the Lord himself with all the attending hosts that came down on Sinai—seemed to be in the sanctuary, the holy place on Mount Zion. All that there was of pomp and grandeur on Mount Sinai when God came down with the attending thousands of angels, was really around Mount Zion for its protection and defence.

18. *Thou hast ascended on high.* That is, Thou hast gone up to the high place; to thy throne; to thine abode. The idea is, that God had descended or come down from his dwelling-place in the case referred to in the psalm, and that having now secured a victory by vanquishing his foes, and having given deliverance to his people, he had now returned, or reascended to his seat. This may either mean his throne on earth, or his abode in heaven. It would seem most probable that the latter is the idea. ¶ *Thou hast led captivity captive.* "Thou hast made captivity captive," or "Thou hast captured a captivity." The main idea is, that he had achieved a complete victory; he had led all his foes captive. The language *would* also express the idea that he had made captives for himself of those who were captives to others, or who were in subjection to another. As applied in the Christian sense, this would refer to those who were captives to Satan, and who were held in bondage by him, but who had been rescued by the Redeemer, and brought under another captivity—the yielding of voluntary service to himself. Those once captives to sin were now led by him, captives in a higher sense. See Notes on Eph. iv. 8. ¶ *Thou hast received gifts for men.* Marg., *in the man.* That is, *Among men*, or while among them as a conqueror. The idea here most naturally conveyed would be, that he had obtained "gifts," privileges, advantages, *in* man; that is, that men, considered as captives, constituted the victory which he had achieved—the advantage which he had acquired. It was not so much *for* them as *in* them, and *by* them, to wit, by possessing them as captives or subjects to him. With this victory achieved, he had now ascended on high. ¶ *Yea, for the rebellious also.* Or, more properly, *even the rebellious.* That is, Those who had been in a state of rebellion he had subdued to himself, and had thus led captivity captive. It was a triumph by which they had become subdued to him. ¶ *That the* LORD *God might dwell* among them.

19 Blessed *be* the Lord, *who* daily loadeth us *with benefits, even* the God of our salvation. Selah.
20 *He that is* our God *is* the God of salvation; and [v] unto GOD the Lord *belong* the issues from death.

v Deut. xxxii. 39; Rev. i. 18.

Literally, *For the dwelling of Jah, God.* The idea is, that he had achieved such a triumph; he had so brought the rebellious under subjection to himself, that he could take up his abode with them, or dwell with them as his people. His rule could be extended over them, and they would acknowledge him as their sovereign. This would be applicable to a people in ancient times that had been subdued by the people of God. It might now be properly applied, also, to sinners who by the power of truth have been so subdued as to submit to God. It is applicable to all who have been conquered by the Gospel—whose enmity has been slain —who have been changed from enemies to friends—so that the Lord may dwell in their hearts, or rule over them. This passage is applied by the apostle Paul (Eph. iv. 8) to the Messiah, not as having original reference to him, but as suggesting language which would appropriately express the nature of his work, and the glory of his triumph. See Notes on that place.

19. *Blessed* be *the Lord,* who *daily loadeth us* with benefits, etc. Literally, *day, day;* that is, day by day; or, constantly. The words "with benefits" are not in the original, and they do not convey the true idea of the passage. The word rendered *loadeth* means to take up; to lift, as a stone, Zech. xii. 3; to bear, to carry, Isa. xlvi. 3. Then it means "to take up and place upon a beast of burden;" to load, Isa. xlvi. 1; Gen. xliv. 13. Hence it means to impose or lay a burden or a load on one; and the idea here is, "Blessed be the Lord God *even if* he lays a burden on us, and if he does this *daily;* for he is the God of our salvation." He enables us to bear it; he gives us strength; and finally he delivers us from it. *Though,* therefore, he constantly lays on us a burden, he as constantly aids us to bear it. He does not leave us. He enables us to triumph in him, and through him; and we have occasion constantly to honour and to praise his name. This accords with the experience of all his people, that however heavy may be the burden laid on them, and however constant their trials, they find him as constant a helper, and they daily have occasion to praise and bless him.

20. He that is *our God* is *the God of salvation.* Literally, "God is for us a God of salvation." That is, The God whom we worship is the God from whom salvation comes, and who brings salvation to us. It is not a vain thing that we serve him, for he is the only being who can save us, and he will save us. ¶ *And unto* GOD *the Lord* belong *the issues from death.* The *outgoings* or *escapes* from death. That is, He only can save from death. The Hebrew word means, properly, a going forth, a deliverance; then, a place of going forth, as a gate, Ezek. xlviii. 30; a fountain, Prov. iv. 23. Probably the only idea intended here by the psalmist was, that safety or deliverance from death proceeds solely from God. The sentiment, however, is true in a larger sense. All that pertains to deliverance from death, all that prepares for it, all that makes it easy to be borne, all that constitutes a rescue from its pains and horrors, all that follows death in a higher and more blessed world, all that makes death *final,* and places us in a condition where death is no more to be dreaded,—all this belongs to God. All this is under his control. He only can enable us to bear death; he only can conduct us from a bed of death to a world where we shall never die.

21 But God shall wound[w] the head of his enemies, *and* the hairy scalp of such an one as goeth on still in his trespasses.
22 The Lord said, I will bring again [x] from Bashan; I will bring *my people* [y] again from the depths of the sea:
23 That thy foot may be [1] dipped in the blood [z] of *thine* enemies, *and* the tongue of thy dogs in the same.
24 They have seen thy goings,

w Hab. iii. 13. x Num. xxi. 33. y Ex. xiv. 22.

1 *red.* z Isa. lxiii. 1—6.

21. *But God shall wound the head of his enemies.* More properly, "God shall *crush* the head," etc. The idea is that of complete destruction,—as, if the head is crushed, life becomes extinct. See Gen. iii. 15; comp. Ps. cx. 6. ¶ And *the hairy scalp.* More literally, *the top of the hair.* The Hebrew word used here for *scalp* means the vertex, the top, the crown, as of the head, where the hair *divides itself;* and the idea is properly, *the dividing of the hair.* Gesenius, *Lex.* The allusion is to the top of the head; that is, the blow would descend on the top of the head, producing death. ¶ *Of such an one as goeth on still in his trespasses.* Of the man who perseveres in a course of wickedness. If he repents, God will be merciful to him; if he persists in sin, he will be punished. The literal rendering would be, "the hairy scalp *going on,* or going [sc. *about*] in his trespasses." The reference is to a wicked man *continuing* in his transgressions.

22. *The Lord said, I will bring again from Bashan.* On the situation of Bashan, see Notes on ver. 15. There may be an allusion here to the victory achieved over Og, king of Bashan, in the time of Moses, Num. xxi. 33-35. The idea may be that as, at that time, a victory was achieved over a formidable enemy, so in times of similar peril, God would deliver his people, and save them from danger. Or, as Bashan was the remote frontier of the Holy Land, the meaning may be, that God would bring his people from the remotest borders where they should be scattered. Another meaning is suggested by Professor Alexander, viz., that as the subject referred to in the subsequent verses is the *enemy* of God, the meaning may be that God would bring back his enemies for punishment, even from the remotest borders, when they were endeavouring to escape, and even when they supposed they were safe. The first of these opinions is probably the true one. God would rescue his people, as he had done from the attacks of the mighty king of Bashan; he would deliver them, as he had brought their fathers from the depths of the sea. ¶ *I will bring* my people *again from the depths of the sea.* The words *my people* are not in the Hebrew, but they seem to be not improperly supplied by the translators. If so, the allusion is to the interposition of God in conducting his people through the Red Sea (Exod. xiv. 22); and the idea is, that God would at all times interpose in their behalf, and deliver them from similar dangers.

23. *That thy foot may be dipped in the blood of* thine *enemies,* etc. Marg., *red.* A more literal rendering would be, "That thou mayest crush—thy foot in blood—the tongue of thy dogs from the enemies, from him." The idea of *dipping* the foot in blood is not in the passage directly; but the leading thought is that of *crushing* the enemy. It is then *added* that the foot would be in blood. So of the tongue of the dogs. The *meaning* is, that the tongues of dogs would be employed in licking up the blood of the enemies, though that is not *expressed* in so many words. The sense of the whole is, that the foes of the people would be slain.

24. *They have seen thy goings, O God.* That is, the lookers on in the solemn procession referred to in ver. 25; or, in other words, Thy goings

O God; *even* the goings of my
God, my King, in the sanctuary.
25 The singers [a] went before,
the players on instruments *fol-*
lowed after; among *them were* the
damsels playing with timbrels.
26 Bless ye God in the congregations; *even* the Lord, [1] from
the fountain of Israel.

a 1 Chron. xv. 27.

[1] Or, ye that are *of.*

have been attended by pomp and magnificence, and have been witnessed by multitudes. The word "goings" here refers to the solemn triumphal processions which celebrated the victories achieved by God. ¶ Even *the goings of my God, my King.* The psalmist here speaks of God as *his* God and *his* King. The idea seems to have suddenly crossed his mind that this great God, so glorious, is *his* God. He exults and rejoices that He whom he adores is such a God; that a God so great and glorious is *his.* So the believer now, when he looks upon the works of God, when he contemplates their vastness, their beauty, and their grandeur, is permitted to feel that the God who made them is *his* God; to find consolation in the thought that his "Father made them all."

"He looks abroad into the varied field
Of Nature, and, though poor, perhaps, compared
With those whose mansions glitter in his sight,
Calls the delightful scenery all his own.
His are the mountains, and the valleys his,
And the resplendent rivers;—his to enjoy
With a propriety that none can feel
But who, with filial confidence inspired,
Can lift to heaven an unpresumptuous eye,
And smiling say, 'My Father made them all!'
Are they not his by a peculiar right,
And by an emphasis of interest his,
Whose eye they fill with tears of holy joy,
Whose heart with praise, and whose exalted mind
With worthy thoughts of that unwearied love
That plann'd, and built, and still upholds a world
So clothed with beauty for rebellious man?"

TASK, Book v.

¶ *In the sanctuary.* Or, *to* the sanctuary; in other words, as the ark was borne to the sanctuary, the place appointed for its rest; for, as above remarked, the psalm seems to have been composed on such an occasion.

25. *The singers went before.* That is, in the removal of the ark; in the solemn procession referred to in the previous verse. *In* that procession those who sang preceded those who performed on instruments of music. Comp. 1 Chron. xiii. 8; xv. 16. ¶ *The players on instruments* followed *after.* The different classes of performers would naturally be ranged together. In 1 Chron. xiii. 8, the following instruments of music are mentioned as having been employed on a similar occasion, if not on this very occasion;—harps, psalteries, timbrels, cymbals, and trumpets. ¶ *Among* them were *the damsels playing with timbrels.* The true construction of the passage is, "Behind were the players in the midst of damsels playing." The singers and the players were surrounded by these women playing on timbrels. The word rendered "playing with timbrels"—תָּפַף, *taphaph*—means to strike, to beat; and hence to strike or beat upon a timbrel. A timbrel is a kind of drum, a tabret, or tambourine, usually beaten with the fingers. See a description of it in the Notes on Isa. v. 12, under the word *tabret.* It is an instrument which has been in use from the remotest antiquity.

26. *Bless ye God in the congregations.* In the assemblages of the people; not only as individuals, but in solemn processions; in triumphal marches; when the people are assembled together. In this public manner acknowledge God as the true God, and render him praise. ¶ Even *the Lord, from the fountain of Israel.* Marg., "Ye that are *of;*" that is, *of the fountain of Israel.* The margin has undoubtedly expressed the correct idea. The appeal is to the Hebrew people represented as descending from

27 There *is* little Benjamin *with* their ruler, the princes of Judah [1] *and* their council, the princes of Zebulun, *and* the princes of Naphtali.

28 Thy God hath commanded thy strength: [b] strengthen, O God, that which thou hast wrought for us.

[1] Or, with *their company*. [b] Isa. xxvi. 4, 12.

a common stock or ancestor—Jacob or Israel,—as a stream or river flows from a fountain. Comp. Notes on Isa. xlviii. 1; see also Isa. li. 1; Deut. xxxiii. 28. All the descendants of Jacob or Israel are thus called on to unite in solemnly praising the Lord their God.

27. *There* is *little Benjamin.* In that solemn procession. That is, the tribe of Benjamin is *represented* there; or, there are in the procession those who are connected with that tribe. The name " little " is given to the tribe either because Benjamin was the youngest of the sons of Jacob, or, more probably, because that tribe was among the smallest of the tribes of Israel. In fact, the tribe was so small, as compared with that of Judah, for instance, that, after the revolt of the ten tribes, the name of Benjamin was lost, and the whole nation was called, after the tribe of Judah, *Jews.* ¶ With *their ruler.* The word *with* is not in the original. The Hebrew is literally *ruling them.* This would seem to mean that, on the occasion referred to, Benjamin, or those who were connected with that tribe, had the oversight, or the direction of those who were engaged in this solemn procession. Though small, it had the preeminence on this occasion. To it was committed the important duty of presiding over these solemnities; that is, those who were prominent in the arrangements for the occasion were of the tribe of Benjamin. This seems to me to be a better explanation than to suppose, as Professor Alexander does, that it has reference to the enemies of the people of God, and that Benjamin had *conquered* or *subdued* them. ¶ *The princes of Judah.* The principal men of the tribe of Judah. ¶ And *their council.* Marg., *with their company.* The Hebrew word here—רִגְמָה, *rigmah*—means crowd, throng, band. It never means *council.* The idea is, evidently, that large numbers of the tribe of Judah attended,—that the "princes" or leaders were accompanied by throngs of their own people;—in allusion to the fact that Judah was one of the largest of the tribes of Israel,—and in contrast with Benjamin, which was few in number, and yet thus occupied the most honourable place as having *charge* of the arrangements. ¶ *The princes of Zebulun,* and *the princes of Naphtali.* These were remote or border tribes, and they seem to be mentioned here to show that all the tribes were represented; that is, that this was a national celebration. The fact that these tribes are mentioned as being represented on the occasion, proves that this psalm was composed before the revolt of the ten tribes, and the formation of the kingdom of Israel; that is, as *early* as the time of Solomon. This increases the probability that the psalm was written by David.

28. *Thy God hath commanded thy strength.* Has ordered thy strength to appear, or to be manifested. This is addressed, evidently, to the people of the land; and the idea is, that, on this occasion, God had called forth a full representation of the strength of the nation; or, as we should say, there had been a full "*turn out.*" It was an impressive sight, showing the real strength of the people. ¶ *Strengthen, O God, that which thou hast wrought for us.* Increase the strength thus manifested. Let it be still greater. The scene is now impressive and grand; make it still more so, by adding to the number and the prosperity of thy people. This is an illustration of the desire in the heart of every pious man that, whatever pros-

29 Because of thy temple at Jerusalem shall kings bring presents unto thee.

30 Rebuke [1] the company of spearmen, the multitude of the bulls, with the calves of the people, *till every one* submit himself with pieces of silver: [2] scatter

[1] Or, *the beasts of the reeds*, Jer. li. 32.

[2] Or, *he scattereth*.

perity God may have given to his people, he would give a still larger measure,—that however greatly he may have increased their numbers, he would add to them many more. This desire of the heart of piety will not be satisfied until the whole world shall be converted to God.

29. *Because of thy temple at Jerusalem.* The word rendered *temple* here properly means a palace; then, the abode of God considered as a king, or his residence as a king. It might, therefore, be applied either to the tabernacle or to the temple, erected as the peculiar dwelling-place of God. As the word has so general a meaning, the passage here does not prove that the psalm was composed after Solomon's temple was reared, for it may refer to the tabernacle that David set up for the ark on Mount Zion. See Notes on Ps. v. 7; lxv. 4. ¶ *At Jerusalem.* Literally, *upon*, or *above* Jerusalem. Perhaps the idea is, that as the place of worship was built on Mount Zion, it was *above*, or seemed to *overhang* the city. The city was built mostly in the valleys that lay between the different hills or eminences—Mount Zion, Mount Moriah, Mount Ophel. ¶ *Shall kings bring presents unto thee.* In honour of God and his religion. Comp. Ps. lxxii. 10. See also Notes on Isa. xlix. 7, 23; lx. 5, 16.

30. *Rebuke the company of spearmen.* Marg., *the beasts of the reeds.* This is in the form of a prayer—"*Rebuke;*" but the idea is, that this *would* occur; and the meaning of the whole verse, though there is much difficulty in interpreting the particular expressions, is, that the most formidable enemies of the people of God, represented here by wild beasts, would be subdued, and would be made to show their submission by bringing presents,—by "pieces of silver,"—or, with tribute. Thus the idea corresponds with that in the previous verse, that "kings would bring presents." The rendering in the margin here expresses the meaning of the Hebrew. It *might* perhaps be possible to make out from the Hebrew the sense in our common translation, but it is not the *obvious* meaning, and would not accord so well with the scope of the passage. On the word rendered *company*, which primarily means an animal, see Notes on ver. 10 of this psalm. It is applied to an army as being formidable, or terrible, *like* a wild beast. The word rendered *spearmen*—קָנֶה, *kaneh*—means *a reed* or *cane; calamus.* Comp. Notes on Isa. xlii. 3; xxxvi. 6. This phrase, "the beast of the reeds," would properly denote a wild beast, as living among the reeds or canes that sprang up on the banks of a river, and having his home there. It would thus, perhaps, most naturally suggest the crocodile, but it might also be applicable to a lion or other wild beast that had its dwelling in the jungles or bushes on the banks of a river. Comp. Jer. xlix. 19; l. 44. The comparison here would, therefore, denote any powerful and fierce monarch or people that might be compared with such a fierce beast. There is no particular allusion to Egypt, as being the abode of the crocodile, but the reference is more general, and the language would imply that fierce and savage people—kings who might be compared with wild beasts that had their homes in the deep and inaccessible thickets—would come bending with the tribute money, with pieces of silver, in token of their subjection to God. ¶ *The multitude of the bulls.* Fierce and warlike kings, who might be compared with bulls. See Notes on Ps.

thou the people *that* delight in war.

31 Princes shall come out of *c* Egypt; Ethiopia *d* shall soon stretch out her hands unto God.

c Isa. xix. 18—25. *d* Zep. iii. 10; Acts viii. 27.

xxii. 12. ¶ *With the calves of the people.* That is, the nations that might be compared with the calves of such wild herds,—fierce, savage, powerful. Their leaders might be compared with the bulls; the people —the multitudes—were like the wild and lawless herd of young ones that accompanied them. The general idea is, that the most wild and savage nations would come and acknowledge their subjection to God, and would express that subjection by an appropriate offering. ¶ Till every one *submit himself with pieces of silver.* The word here rendered *submit* means properly to tread with the feet, to trample upon; and then, in the form here used, to let oneself be trampled under feet, to prostrate oneself; to humble oneself. Here it means that they would come and submissively offer silver as a tribute. That is, they would acknowledge the authority of God, and become subject to him. ¶ *Scatter thou the people* that *delight in war.* Marg., *He scattereth.* The margin expresses the sense most accurately. The reference is to God. The psalmist sees the work already accomplished. In anticipation of the victory of God over his foes, he sees them already discomfited and put to flight. The mighty hosts which had been arrayed against the people of God are dissipated and driven asunder; or, in other words, a complete victory is obtained. The people that "delighted in war" were those that had a pleasure in arraying themselves against the people of God,—the enemies that had sought their overthrow.

31. *Princes shall come out of Egypt.* That is, Shall come and acknowledge the true God. Egypt is referred to here as one of the most prominent of the foreign nations then known; and the idea is, that the distinguished men of foreign nations—the rulers and princes of the world—would come and submit themselves to God, and be united to his people. The word rendered *princes* here—חַשְׁמַנִּים, *hhashmannim*—occurs nowhere else in the Scriptures. It means, according to Gesenius (*Lex.*), the fat; then, the rich; the opulent; nobles. It is the word from which the name *Hasmonean* (or Asmonean), which was given by the Jews to the Maccabees, or Jewish princes in the time of the Jewish history between the Old and New Testaments, is supposed to have been derived. The Septuagint, the Vulgate, and the Syriac, render it *legates* or *ambassadors.* Luther renders it *princes.* The reference is undoubtedly to men of station or rank. ¶ *Ethiopia.* Heb., *Cush.* On the meaning of this word in the Scriptures, see Notes on Isa. xi. 11. ¶ *Shall soon stretch out her hands.* Literally, *Shall make its hands to run.* The expression denotes the eagerness or haste with which it would be done. The act is an act of supplication, and the reference is to prayer. ¶ *Unto God.* To the true God. The nation will supplicate the mercy of God, or will worship him. The idea, in accordance with that in the previous verses, is, that the country here referred to would become subject to the true God. It is a view of the future; of the time when the nations would be converted to the true faith, or would acknowledge the true God. Whether this refers to the Cush in Arabia, or to the Cush in Africa (Ethiopia as commonly understood), it is a description of what will yet occur; for all these lands, and all other lands, will be converted to the true religion, and will stretch out their hands in supplication and prayer, and will find acceptance with God. Even Africa—wronged, degraded, oppressed, injured Africa—will do it; and the worship of her children will be as acceptable to the Universal Father as

32 Sing unto God, ye kingdoms of the earth; O sing praises unto the Lord; Selah:

33 To him that rideth upon the heavens of heavens, *which were* of old: lo, he doth [1] send out his voice, *and that* a mighty voice.

34 Ascribe ye strength unto God: his excellency *is* over Israel, and his strength *is* in the [2] clouds.

35 O God, *thou art* terrible [e] out of thy holy places: the God of Israel *is* he [f] that giveth strength and power unto *his* people. Blessed *be* God.

[1] *give.* [2] Or, *heavens.*

e Ex. xv. 11. *f* Isa. xlv. 24.

that of any other of the races of men that dwell on the earth.

32. *Sing unto God, ye kingdoms of the earth.* That is,—that acknowledge the true God,—celebrate his praise. The psalmist sees the conversion of the world to God to be so certain an event that he calls on all nations to join in the song.

33. *To him that rideth upon the heavens of heavens.* The highest heavens. The heaven of heaven would properly mean the heaven above that which is heaven to us; that is, the heaven above the sky. This is represented as the peculiar dwelling-place of God. The Jews were accustomed to speak of three heavens:—(*a*) The aerial heaven, or the region above us, where the birds fly, and the winds blow; (*b*) the starry heavens, or the firmament in which the stars are fixed; and (*c*) the heaven above all, the abode of God and of angels. The word *rideth* here means that he appears there as a conqueror, or that he moves in majesty and glory. See Notes on Ps. xviii. 10. ¶ Which were *of old.* The words "*of old*" refer here to the heavens, and denote their antiquity. He rides upon those ancient heavens. He occupies a position above those ancient works of his power. ¶ *Lo, he doth send out his voice.* Marg., as in Heb., *give.* The reference is to thunder. The design of this is to increase the impression of his majesty and power. ¶ And that *a mighty voice.* See Notes on Ps. xxix. 3, etc.

34. *Ascribe ye strength unto God.* Literally, *give.* That is, Acknowledge him as a God of power. Recognise his omnipotence in your worship. See Notes on Ps. xxix. 1. ¶ *His excellency* is *over Israel.* His majesty; his glory; his protecting care. The idea is, that his glorious character — his majesty — was manifested particularly in his protection of his people. ¶ *And his strength* is *in the clouds.* Marg., *heavens.* The Hebrew word rather means *clouds.* The idea is, that while his character as Protector was evinced particularly in his care of his people, his *power* was particularly seen in the clouds — the storm—the thunder—the lightning. Thus, all the manifestations of his character, alike in nature, and towards his people, are adapted to produce a deep and solemn impression in regard to his majesty and glory, or to lay the just foundation of praise.

35. *O God,* thou art *terrible out of thy holy places.* The places where thou dwellest, and from which thou dost manifest thyself. That is, The manifestations which thou dost make of thyself when thou seemest to come forth from thine abode are *terrible,* or are fitted to fill the mind with awe. Comp. Notes on Ps. xlv. 4; lxv. 5; lxvi. 5. ¶ *The God of Israel.* The God who is adored by Israel, or by his true people; our God. ¶ Is *he that giveth strength and power unto* his *people.* He is not weak and feeble. He is able to protect them. He shows that he can gird them with strength; that he can defend them; that he can sustain them in the trials of life. The God whom they acknowledge as their God is not one whose strength fails, or who is seen to be feeble and powerless when his aid is needed. He is fully equal to all their wants, and they never trust him in vain.

PSALM LXIX.

To the chief Musician upon *g* Shoshannim. *A Psalm* of David.

g Ps. xlv., *title*.

SAVE me, O God; for the waters are come in unto *my* soul.

¶ *Blessed be God.* For all that he is; for all that he has done. This is the language of joy and praise in view of the contemplation of his character as depicted in the psalm. At the close of every right contemplation of his character, his government, his plans, his claims, his law, his gospel, the heart that is right will say, *Blessed be such a God.* To one endowed with *such* attributes, praise—everlasting praise—is due.

PSALM LXIX.

This psalm is said in the title to be a psalm of David, but on what occasion it was composed is not there intimated, nor can it be determined from the psalm itself. There is nothing *in* the psalm which is inconsistent with the supposition that it was composed by David; and, in fact, it has, in many respects, a strong resemblance to not a few of his undoubted compositions, as Psalms vi., xxii., xxv., xxxv., xxxviii. Comp. Ps. xiii. On the expression in the title "To the chief Musician," see Notes in the Introd. to Ps. iv. On the words "upon Shoshannim," see Notes on the Title to Ps. xlv.

On what occasion in the life of David the psalm was written cannot now be determined. There were many occasions in his life to which all that is said in the psalm might be applicable, for his was a life of many trials and perils; but the most natural interpretation would be that which ascribes it to the time of the rebellion of Absalom. Some have supposed that it was written at a later period than the time of David. Thus De Wette maintains that the closing verses (34–36) demonstrate that it must have been written in the time of the exile. Rosenmüller coincides with that opinion in regard to those verses, but supposes that they were added to the psalm (as originally composed) by some later author. It will be found, however, on examination of these verses, that there is nothing in them inconsistent with the supposition that the entire psalm was composed by David. The psalm evidently pertains to an individual sufferer; a man who regarded himself as suffering in the cause of religion, or on account of his zeal for the service of God. It is this fact which is laid at the foundation of the psalmist's prayer for the Divine intervention. The author is a sufferer in the cause of God and of truth, and he beseeches God, in whose cause he suffers, on that account to interpose in his behalf.

There are several passages in the psalm which are applied in the New Testament to the Messiah and his times; ver. 9, comp. John ii. 17, and Rom. xv. 3; ver. 4, comp. John xv. 25; ver. 21, comp. Matt. xxvii. 34, 48 (Mark xv. 23, and John xix. 29); ver. 25, comp. Matt. xxiii. 38, and Acts i. 20. These passages, however, are of so *general* a character that they do not seem to have been designed to refer exclusively to the Messiah, or even to have had *any* original reference to him. The language is such that it *would accurately describe* the events to which it is applied; and the fact that the language is quoted in this manner in the New Testament history does not prove that the psalm had any original reference to the Messiah.

In the psalm, the sufferer first (vers. 1-6) describes his condition; he then (vers. 7-13) represents himself as suffering in the cause of God or of religion; then (vers. 14-18), prays to be delivered from these troubles. In vers. 19-21 he again adverts to his sufferings with a more explicit reference to their cause, the malice of his enemies; and then (vers. 22-28) prays that his enemies may be destroyed. He anticipates that his prayer will be heard, and that this will have a favourable effect on others, leading them to praise God (vers. 29-33); and this leads him to look forward to the general prosperity of Zion—to the fact that Zion will be delivered out of all its troubles—as laying the foundation for universal praise (vers. 34-36).

1. *Save me, O God.* That is, Interpose and deliver me from the dangers which have come upon me. ¶ *For the waters are come in unto* my *soul.* So as to endanger my life. Waters, deep, raging, overwhelming, are images of calamity or danger. See

2 I sink in [1] deep mire, where
there is no standing: I am come
into [2] deep waters, where the
floods overflow me.
3 I am weary of my crying;
my throat is dried: mine eyes
fail while I wait for my God.
4 They [h] that hate me without
a cause are more than the hairs
of mine head: they that would

[1] *the mire of the depth.* [2] *depth of.*

[h] John xv. 25.

Notes on Ps. xxxii. 6. Comp. Ps. xlii. 7.

2. *I sink in deep mire.* Marg., as in Heb., *the mire of the depth.* This would denote either mire which was itself so deep that one could not extricate himself from it; or, mire found in a deep place, as at the bottom of a pit. Comp. Notes on Ps. xl. 2. An illustration of this might be drawn from the case of Joseph, cast by his brethren into a deep pit (Gen. xxxvii. 24); or from the case of Jeremiah, thrown into a deep dungeon: "And they let down Jeremiah with cords; and in the dungeon there was no water, but mire: so Jeremiah sunk in the mire," Jer. xxxviii. 6. ¶ *Where* there is *no standing.* No solid ground; nothing for the foot to rest on. ¶ *I am come into deep waters.* Marg., as in Heb., *depth of waters.* That is, waters where he could not touch the bottom,—an image of some peril that threatened his life. ¶ *Where the floods overflow me.* The waters. They break over my head. My life is *in danger.*

3. *I am weary of my crying.* The word *crying* here does not mean weeping, or shedding tears, but calling upon God for help. He had grown weary; his strength had been exhausted in the act of calling upon God to assist him. See Notes on Ps. vi. 6. This was an instance where one had called so long on God, and prayed so much and so earnestly, that his strength was gone. Comp. Matt. xxvi. 41. ¶ *My throat is dried.* Or, *is parched up.* The Hebrew word denotes to burn; to be enkindled; and then, to be inflamed. Here it means that by the excessive exertion of his voice, his throat had become parched, so that he could not speak. ¶ *Mine eyes fail.* That is, become dim from exhaustion. I have looked so long in that one direction that the power of vision begins to fail, and I see nothing clearly. See Notes on Ps. vi. 7. Comp. Job xvii. 7; Ps. xxxi. 9; xxxviii. 10. ¶ *While I wait for my God.* That is, by continued *looking* to God. The word *wait* is not here used, nor is it generally in the Bible, as it is now with us, in the sense of looking for *future* interposition, or of doing nothing ourselves in expectation of what *may* occur; but it is used in the sense of looking to God alone; of exercising dependence on him; of seeking his aid. This is indeed connected with the ordinary idea of abiding his will, but it is also an *active* state of mind—a state expressive of intense interest and desire. See Notes on Ps. lxii. 5.

4. *They that hate me without a cause.* Without any just reason; without any provocation on my part. There were many such in the case of David, for to those who rose up against him in the time of Saul, and to Absalom also, he had given no real occasion of offence. An expression similar to the one here used occurs in Ps. xxxv. 19. See Notes on that passage. The *language* is applied to the Saviour (John xv. 25), not as having had original reference to him, but as language which received its most perfect fulfilment in the treatment which he received from his enemies. See Notes on John xv. 25. ¶ *Are more than the hairs of mine head.* The number is so great that it cannot be estimated. ¶ *They that would destroy me,* being *mine enemies wrongfully, are mighty.* Literally, "More than the hairs of my head are my haters falsely [those who hate me falsely]; strong are those destroying me; my enemies." The idea is, that

destroy me, *being* mine enemies wrongfully, are mighty: then I restored *that* which I took not away.

5 O God, thou knowest my foolishness; and my [1] sins are not hid from thee.

[1] *guiltiness.*

6 Let not them that wait on thee, O Lord GOD of hosts, be ashamed for my sake; let not those that seek thee be con-

those who were numbered among his foes without any just provocation on his part were so numerous and strong that he could not contend with them. ¶ *Then I restored* that *which I took not away.* Prof. Alexander renders this, "What I did not rob, then must I restore." This seems to have a proverbial cast, and the idea is, that under this pressure of circumstances—borne down by numbers—he was compelled to give up what he had not taken away from others. They regarded and treated him as a bad man,—as if he had been a robber; and they compelled him to give up what he possessed, *as if* he had no right to it, or *as if* he had obtained it by robbery. This does not seem to refer to anything that was *voluntary* on his part—as if, for the sake of peace, he had proposed to give up that to which they had no claim, or to surrender his just rights, but to the act of compulsion by which he was *forced* to surrender what he had, *as if* he had been a public offender. How far it is proper to yield to an unjust claim for the sake of peace, or to act *as if* we had done wrong, rather than to have controversy or strife, is a point which, if this interpretation is correct, is not settled by this passage. It seems here to have been merely a question of *power*.

5. *O God, thou knowest my foolishness.* The errors and follies of my life. Though conscious of innocence in this case,—though he felt that his enemies hated him "without cause," and that they took what belonged to him and not to them, yet he was not insensible to the fact that he was a sinner, and he was not unwilling to confess before God, that, however conscious of uprightness he might be in his dealings towards men, yet towards God, he was a sinful man. From him he deserved all that had come upon him. Indeed the very calamities which had been permitted to come upon him were proof to his own mind that he was a sinner, and served, as they were doubtless designed, to turn his mind to that fact, and to humble him. The effect of calamities coming upon us, as reminding us of the fact that we are sinners, is often referred to in the Psalms. See Ps. xxxviii. 2–4; xl. 12. ¶ *And my sins are not hid from thee.* Marg., *guiltiness.* The word used here has always attached to it the idea of *guilt.* The meaning is, that God knew all his life; and that however unjust the conduct of *men* toward him might be when they treated him as if he had wronged them, yet considered as a part of the dealings of God, or as having been suffered to come upon him from God, all that had occurred was right, for it was a proper expression of the Divine displeasure against his sins. We may feel that we have not wronged our fellow-men; yet even the treatment which we receive from them, however unjust so far as they are concerned, may be regarded as deserved by us at the hand of God, and as proper on his part as an expression of his displeasure for our transgressions against him, and as a proof that we are sinners. Trial never comes to us from any quarter except as founded on the fact that we are sinners; and even where there is entire innocence towards our fellow-men, God may make use of their passions to rebuke and discipline us for our sins towards himself.

6. *Let not them that wait on thee.* Those who worship thee; those who are thy true friends. True piety is often, in the Scriptures, represented

founded for my sake, O God of
Israel.
7 Because for thy sake I have
borne reproach: shame hath covered my face.
8 I [i] am become a stranger
unto my brethren, and an alien
unto my mother's children.
9 For [k] the zeal of thine house
hath eaten me up; and [l] the reproaches of them that reproached
thee are fallen upon me.

i John vii. 5. k John ii. 17. l Rom. xv. 3.

as waiting on the Lord. See Ps. xxv. 3, 5; xxxvii. 9; Isa. xl. 31. ¶ *Be ashamed for my sake.* On account of me; or, in consequence of what I do. Let me not be suffered to do anything that would make them ashamed of me, or ashamed to have it known that I belong to their number. I know that I am a sinner; I know that judgments come justly on me; I know that if left to myself I shall fall into sin, and shall dishonour religion; and I pray, therefore, that I may be kept from acting out the depravity of my heart, and bringing dishonour on the cause that I profess to love. No one who knows the evil of his own heart can fail to see the propriety of this prayer; no one who remembers how often men high in the church, and zealous in their professed piety, fall into sin, and disgrace their profession, can help feeling that what has happened to others *may* happen to him also, and that he has need of special prayer, and special grace, that he may go down into the grave at last without having brought dishonour upon religion. ¶ *Let not those that seek thee.* Another phrase to denote men of true piety—as those who are *seeking* after God; that is, who are desirous of understanding his character, and obtaining his favour. ¶ *Be confounded for my sake.* Let them not feel *disgraced* in me; let them not feel it a dishonour to have it said that I am one of their number, or that I profess to be united to them.

7. *Because for thy sake I have borne reproach.* In thy cause; in defence of thy truth; because I have professed to be a friend of God. The true reason why these calamities have come upon me is that I have been thy professed friend, and have endeavoured to do my duty to thee. The reproach connected with religion in a world of sin, or where true religion is hated, has fallen on me. ¶ *Shame hath covered my face.* The idea here is not that he had himself been ashamed of religion or of the service of God, but that he had suffered shame, derision, reproach among men for his professed attachment to the truth. Comp. Ps. xliv. 15, 16.

8. *I am become a stranger unto my brethren.* That is, They treat me as they would a stranger; as one in whom they have no interest, and whom they regard with no friendship. Comp. Notes on Ps. xxxi. 11. ¶ *And an alien unto my mother's children.* A foreigner; one of another tribe or nation; one to whom they were bound by no tie of relationship. The allusion in the language "unto my *mother's* children" is intended to denote the most intimate relationship. In families where a man had many wives, as was common among the Hebrews, the nearest relationship would be denoted by being of the same *mother* rather than of the same *father*. See Notes on Ps. l. 20. The same thing occurs also where polygamy is not practised, in cases where a man has married more wives than one. The idea of the psalmist here, therefore, is, that his nearest relatives treated him as if he were a stranger and a foreigner. Comp. Job xix. 13–19.

9. *For the zeal of thine house hath eaten me up.* My zeal—my ardour—in the cause of religion (that is, of thy pure worship) has been so great as to consume me. It has been like a devouring fire within me. Zeal is represented under the idea of heat—

10 When [m] I wept, *and chastened* my soul with fasting, that was to my reproach.
11 I made sackcloth also my garment; and I became a proverb to them.
12 They that sit in the gate speak against me: and I *was* the song of the [1] drunkards.
13 But as for me, my prayer

[m] Ps. xxxv. 13, etc.

[1] *drinkers of strong drink.*

as it is in the Greek language; and the characteristics of heat or fire are here applied to it. This passage is quoted in John ii. 17, and applied to the Saviour, not as having had originally a reference to him, but as language which would accurately describe his character. See Notes on that passage. ¶ *And the reproaches of them that reproached thee are fallen upon me.* This, too, is applied, in the same way, to the Saviour, by the Apostle Paul, in Rom. xv. 3. See Notes on that passage.

10. *When I wept,* and chastened *my soul with fasting.* The words *and chastened* are not in the original. The literal translation would be, "And I wept [away] my soul with fasting;" that is, I gave myself so much to fasting accompanied with weeping, that my strength was exhausted. This refers to his acts of devotion; to his endeavours to discipline his soul so as to lead a strictly religious life. ¶ *That was to my reproach.* This may either mean that they accused him of hypocrisy and insincerity; or, that they charged him with folly for being so religious, so strict, so self-sacrificing, so serious,—perhaps they would say, so superstitious, so gloomy, so fanatical. The latter best accords with the connexion, since it was for his *religion* mainly that they reproached him, vers. 7–9.

11. *I made sackcloth also my garment.* I put on sackcloth. This was often done as expressive of grief and sorrow. See Notes on Ps. xxx. 11; xxxv. 13. Comp. Isa. xxii. 12; Dan. ix. 3. In the case here referred to, this was an act of religion; an expression of penitence and humiliation. ¶ *And I became a proverb to them.* A jest; a subject of derision; a byword. They ridiculed me for it. Comp. 1 Kings ix. 7.

12. *They that sit in the gate speak against me.* The gates of cities were places of concourse; places where business was transacted; places where courts were frequently held. See Notes on Job xxix. 7. Comp. Isa. xiv. 31; xxviii. 6; Ps. ix. 14. Calvin supposes that as the gates were the places where the judges sat to administer justice, the meaning here is that magistrates, or those who were high in rank and power, joined in the cry of reproach against him. The more probable interpretation, however, is, that he was subject to the reproach of those who were gathered around these places,—the men of business, and the idlers who were assembled there; or, as we should say, that he was the subject of "town-talk." ¶ *And I* was *the song of the drunkards.* Marg., as in the Heb., *drinkers of strong drink.* They made ballads or low songs about me. They selected me for an example in their drunken songs. David was not alone in this. It has not been uncommon that the songs of revellers and drunkards have been designed to turn piety and the pious into derision. Compare, alas! some of the songs of Burns. See Notes on Job xxx. 9; Ps. xxxv. 15, 16.

13. *But as for me.* In respect to my conduct and my feelings in these circumstances, and under this treatment. ¶ *My prayer* is *unto thee.* I indulge in no reproaches of others, and no recriminations. I do not permit myself to indulge in any revengeful feelings. I give myself to prayer. I look to God alone. I keep up my devotions, I maintain my habits of religion, notwithstanding their reproaches and revilings. I do not

is unto thee, O LORD, *in* an acceptable [n] time: O God, in the multitude of thy mercy hear [o] me, in the truth of thy salvation.

14 Deliver me out of the mire, and let me not sink: let me be delivered from them that hate me, and out of the deep waters.

15 Let [p] not the waterflood overflow me, neither let the deep swallow me up, and let not the pit [q] shut her mouth upon me.

16 Hear me, O LORD; for thy loving-kindness *is* good: turn [r] unto me according to the multitude of thy tender mercies.

17 And hide not thy face from thy servant; for I am in trouble: [1] hear me speedily.

n Isa. xlix. 8; 2 Cor. vi. 2. *o* Heb. v. 7. *p* Isa. xliii. 1, 2.

q Ps. xvi. 10; Acts ii. 24, etc. *r* Ps. lxxxvi. 16; Micah vii. 19. [1] *make haste to hear me.*

allow these things to alter my course of life. Comp. Notes on Dan. vi. 10. ¶ In *an acceptable time.* A time that is well-pleasing to thee; a time when thou wilt hear me. See Isa. xlix. 8; lxi. 2; 2 Cor. vi. 2. This implies (*a*) that he had come to God when he was *disposed* to hear; and (*b*) that he had heard him, and had answered his requests. While others mocked, he continued to pray, and the Lord heard him. No time for prayer can be more "acceptable" to God than when others are reproaching us because we are his friends. ¶ *In the multitude of thy mercy hear me.* In the abundance of thy mercy; or, in thy abounding compassion. This was the substance of his prayer. ¶ *In the truth of thy salvation.* In the exercise of that faithfulness on which salvation depends; or which is manifested in the salvation of men. He prayed that God would show himself faithful to the promises which he had made to those who were seeking salvation.

14. *Deliver me out of the mire.* Out of my troubles and calamities. See vers. 1, 2. ¶ *And let me not sink.* As in mire. Let me not be overwhelmed by my sorrows. ¶ *Let me be delivered from them that hate me.* All my enemies. Let me be saved from their machinations and devices. ¶ *And out of the deep waters.* See vers. 1, 2. From my troubles.

15. *Let not the waterflood overflow me.* The stream; the volume of waters. The idea is that of a flood or stream rolling along, that threatened to drown him. ¶ *Neither let the deep swallow me up.* The abyss; the deep waters. ¶ *And let not the pit shut her mouth upon me.* In his anguish and distress he passes here from the idea of running streams, and deep waters, to that of a well, pit, or cavern—representing himself as *in* that pit, and praying that it might not be closed upon him, leaving him in darkness and in mire, from which he could not then escape. The general idea in all these expressions is the same—that of overwhelming calamities from which he prayed to be delivered.

16. *Hear me, O* LORD; *for thy lovingkindness* is *good.* Thy mercy—thy favour—is *good;* that is, it is ample, abundant, great: it delights in deeds of mercy; in acts of benevolence. This was the only ground of his plea; and this was enough. Comp. Ps. lxiii. 3. ¶ *Turn unto me.* Incline thine ear unto me; turn not away, but be favourable to me. ¶ *According to the multitude of thy tender mercies.* See Notes on Ps. li. 1. He felt that he had occasion for the exercise of *all* the mercy of God; that the case was one which could be reached only by the exercise of the highest kindness and compassion.

17. *And hide not thy face from thy servant.* See Notes on Ps. xxvii. 9. ¶ *For I am in trouble.* In the midst of dangers and sorrows. Literally, "there is trouble upon me." ¶ *Hear me speedily.* Marg., as in Heb., *Make haste to hear me.* That is, Grant me without delay what I ask. The case

18 Draw nigh unto my soul, *and* redeem it: deliver me, because of mine enemies.

19 Thou hast known my [s] reproach, and my shame, and my dishonour: mine adversaries *are* all before thee.

20 Reproach hath broken my heart, and I am full of heaviness: and I [t] looked *for some* to [1] take pity, but *there was* [u] none; and for comforters, but I found none.

s Ps. xxii. 6, 7; Isa. liii. 3; Heb. xii. 2.

t Isa. lxiii. 5. 1 *lament* with me. u Mark xiv. 50.

is one of urgent necessity. I *must* have relief or I shall perish. It is not wrong to ask God to interpose at once in our behalf when we are in trouble, though it is our duty to be patient and resigned if his interposition is delayed, for he may have important ends to accomplish by our continuing to suffer. In our distress on account of sin also, it is right to plead with him to interpose *at once*, and to relieve us by forgiveness. In this respect we are not to be contented with delay; we are to cast ourselves upon his mercy, and to plead for immediate pardon; for as it is our only safety, so it is for the honour of God that we should be forgiven, and that we should not continue in a state of guilt. An afflicted child of God will be safe in the final issue, whether he is relieved at once, or whether he is suddenly cut off by death, or whether he continues to suffer for even many years; but an unpardoned sinner is *not* safe for a moment, and if he should be cut off, unforgiven, even when under the deepest conviction for sin, he would perish. Every consideration, therefore, makes it proper that he should plead for forgiveness at once, and ask that God would not *delay* to show him mercy.

18. *Draw nigh unto my soul.* To me,—for my life is in danger. ¶ And *redeem it.* Ransom it; save it from ruin. See Notes on Isa. xliii. 3; xliv. 22. ¶ *Deliver me, because of mine enemies.* Because they are so numerous, so powerful, and so determined on my destruction. Comp. Ps. xiii. 4.

19. *Thou hast known my reproach.* The reproach that has come upon me; the shame and contempt which I am called to endure. God had seen all this; and the psalmist appeals to him as having seen it, as a reason why he should now interpose and save him. ¶ *And my shame, and my dishonour.* These are different words to express the same idea. They are accumulated here to denote the *greatness* of his distress. In other words, shame and reproach had come upon him in every possible form. ¶ *Mine adversaries* are *all before thee.* All who persecute and oppose me are constantly in thine eye. Thou knowest who they are; thou seest all that they do. Nothing in their conduct is concealed from thee. God, therefore, could take an accurate view of his troubles, and could see all the reasons which existed for interfering in his behalf.

20. *Reproach hath broken my heart.* The reproaches, the calumnies, the aspersions, the slanders of others, have crushed me. I am not able to bear up under them; I fail under the burden. Distress may become so great that life may sink under it, for many die of what is called "a broken heart." Undeserved reproaches will be as likely to produce this result on a sensitive heart as any form of suffering; and there are thousands who are crushed to the earth by such reproaches. ¶ *And I am full of heaviness.* Or, I am sick; I am weak; I am ill at ease. My strength is gone. ¶ *And I looked* for some *to take pity.* Marg., *to lament with me.* The meaning of the Hebrew word is to pity; to commiserate; to show compassion. Job ii. 11; xlii. 11; Isa. li. 19; Jer. xvi. 5. ¶ *But* there was *none.* There was no one whose heart seemed to be touched with compassion in the case; none who sympathized with me. ¶ *And for comforters.* For those

21 They [v] gave me also gall for my meat; and in my thirst they gave me vinegar to drink.

v Matt. xxvii. 34, 48.

---

who would show sympathy for me; who would evince a friendly feeling in my distress. ¶ *But I found none.* He felt that he was utterly forsaken by mankind. There is no feeling of desolation like that.

21. *They gave me also.* My enemies; all persons around me. No one would show me even so much kindness as to give me food when I was hungry, or drink when I was thirsty. They utterly forsook me; they left me to die unpitied. Nay, they did more than this. When I was perishing with hunger, they not only refused to give me wholesome food, but they mocked my sufferings by giving me a bitter and poisonous herb for food, and vinegar for my drink. ¶ *Gall for my meat.* For my food. Or, they gave me this *instead* of wholesome food. The word here rendered *gall*—ראשׁ, *rosh*—is the same *in form* which is commonly rendered *head*, and occurs in this sense very often in the Scriptures. It is also used to denote a *poisonous plant*,—perhaps from the idea that the plant referred to was distinguished for, or remarkable for its *head*—as the poppy; and *then* the name may have been given also to some other similar plants. The word then comes to denote poison; venom; anything poisonous; and then, anything very bad-tasted; *bitter*. It is rendered *gall*, as here, in Deut. xxix. 18; Jer. viii. 14; ix. 15; xxiii. 15; Lam. iii. 5, 19; Amos vi. 12; *venom* in Deut. xxxii. 33; *poison*, in Job xx. 16; and *hemlock*, in Hos. x. 4. In Deut. xxix. 18, it is rendered, in the margin, *rosh*, or *a poisonful herb*. It does not occur elsewhere with any such signification. It may not be possible to determine precisely what is denoted here by the word, but it undoubtedly refers to some poisonous, bitter, deadly, stupefying substance given to a sufferer, *instead* of that which would be wholesome food, or fitted to sustain life. ¶ *And in my thirst they gave me vinegar to drink.* Instead of giving me pure water, they gave me sour wine—vinegar—that which would not slake my thirst, or which would not answer the purpose of drink. The form of trial here referred to is that where one is dying of thirst, and where, instead of giving water to assuage the thirst, one should give, in mockery, that which could not be drunk, or which would answer none of the purposes required. The word translated *vinegar*—חֹמֶץ, *hhometz*—is rendered in the ancient versions *sour grapes*, but the proper signification here seems to be vinegar—the usual meaning of the word. What is here stated to have been done to David was also done to the dying Saviour, though without any intimation that the passage here had an original reference to him,—or that what was done to him was intended to be a fulfilment of what is here said. See Matt. xxvii. 34, 48; Mark xv. 23; John xix. 29. In the case of the Saviour, they first gave him vinegar mingled with myrrh,—a usual custom in reference to those who were crucified,—for the purpose of deadening the pain, or stupefying the sufferer. Matt. xxvii. 34. At a subsequent part of the crucifixion they gave him vinegar, extended to him in a sponge affixed to a reed. Matt. xxvii. 48; John xix. 29. This was for a different purpose. It was to allay his thirst, and it seems (as the former may have been) to have been an act of kindness or compassion on the part of those who were appointed to crucify him. The former he refused to take, because he came to suffer; the latter he just tasted as he died. John xix. 30. The *coincidence* in the cases of David and the Saviour was remarkable; but in the case of the Saviour no further use is made of what occurred to David than to employ the *language* which he employed to describe his own sufferings. The one was not, in any proper

22 Let [w] their table become a snare before them: and *that which should have been* for *their* welfare, *let it become* a trap.

23 Let their eyes be darkened, that they [x] see not; and make their loins continually to shake.

24 Pour out [y] thine indignation upon them, and let thy wrathful anger take hold of them.

25 Let their [1] habitation be

w Rom. xi. 8—10. x 2 Cor. iii. 14. y 1 Thess. ii. 15, 16. 1 *palace.*

sense, a *type* of the other; nor does the language in the psalm refer to the Saviour.

22, 23. *Let their table become a snare before them.* These verses are quoted by Paul (Rom. xi. 9, 10) as descriptive of the character of persons in his time, or as *language* which would express what he desired to say. See the passage explained at length in the Notes on Rom. xi. 9, 10. The whole passage is a prayer that they might receive a proper recompense for what they had done. The word *table* here means the table at which they were accustomed to eat. As they refused food to a hungry man, the prayer is, that they might find the recompense for their conduct *in that very line;* or that, as they refused food to the hungry, they might find *their* food a "snare" to them. That is, Let it be the means of punishing them for their not giving wholesome food to the hungry, or for their offering poisonous herbs to a starving man. The word *snare* here means unexpected danger; danger sprung suddenly upon them,—as a snare is upon a wild beast. ¶ *And* that which should have been *for* their *welfare,* let it become *a trap.* Much of this is supplied by the translators. The literal rendering would be, "And to those at peace [or secure] a trap." The word here rendered *welfare* is the plural form of the word meaning *peace,* and may denote those who feel that they are at peace; that they are secure; that they are in no danger. The ancient versions give it the sense of *requitals,*—that is, a recompence for their transgressions; but the other signification best accords with the connexion. The word *trap* is usually applied to the devices for capturing wild beasts, and the meaning is, "Let the recompence come suddenly upon them, while they think themselves at peace, or when they are surrounded by all the comforts and luxuries of life." This prayer is such as occurs frequently in the Psalms. It cannot be *proved* that it was uttered in a malignant spirit, or that anything more is intended by it than that the psalmist desired that justice might be done to all men,—an object which all magistrates, and all good citizens, should pray for.

23. *Let their eyes be darkened,* etc. See Notes on Rom. xi. 10. ¶ *And make their loins continually to shake.* As under a heavy burden. The apostle (Rom. xi. 10) varies the language, but retains the idea: "and bow down their back alway."

24. *Pour out thine indignation upon them.* That is, Punish them for their sins; or, do justice to them. ¶ *And let thy wrathful anger.* Literally, "the burning of thy wrath;" glow of anger; burning wrath. See Numb. xxv. 4; xxxii. 14; 1 Sam. xxviii. 18. This is undoubtedly a petition that God would visit them with the severity of his indignation; or, it expresses the belief of the psalmist that they *deserved* such tokens of his displeasure. ¶ *Take hold of them.* Seize upon them; overtake them when they expect to escape.

25. *Let their habitation be desolate.* Marg., *their palace.* The Hebrew word means properly a wall; then, a fortress or castle; and then it means also a nomadic encampment, a rustic village, a farm-hamlet. The word conveys the idea of an *enclosure,* with special reference to an encampment, or a collection of tents. The LXX. render it here ἔπαυλις, meaning a

[z] desolate; *and* let [1] none dwell in their tents.
26 For [a] they persecute *him*
whom thou hast smitten; [b] and they talk to the grief of [2] those whom thou hast wounded.
27 Add [3] iniquity unto their

[z] Matt. xxiii. 38. [1] *there not be a dweller.* [a] Zech. i. 15. [b] Isa. liii. 4.
[2] *thy wounded.* [3] Or, *punishment of iniquity.*

place to pass the night in, especially for flocks and herds. The Hebrew word — טִירָה, *tirah* — is rendered *castles* in Gen. xxv. 16; Numb. xxxi. 10; 1 Chron. vi. 54; *palaces* in Cant. viii. 9; Ezek. xxv. 4; *rows* in Ezek. xlvi. 23; and *habitation* in this place. It does not occur elsewhere. Here it means their *home*,—their place of abode,—but with no particular reference to the *kind* of home, whether a palace, a castle, or an encampment. The idea is, that the place which they had occupied, or where they had dwelt, would be made vacant. They would be removed, and the place would be solitary and forsaken. It is equivalent to a prayer that they might be destroyed. ¶ And *let none dwell in their tents.* Marg., as in Heb., *let there not be a dweller.* That is, Let their tents where they had dwelt be wholly forsaken. This passage is quoted in Acts i. 20, as applicable to Judas. See Notes on that passage.

26. *For they persecute* him *whom thou hast smitten.* That is, instead of pitying one who is afflicted of God, or showing compassion for him, they *add* to his sorrows by their own persecutions. The psalmist was suffering as under the hand of God. He needed sympathy from others in his trials. Instead of that, however, he found only reproaches, opposition, persecution, calumny. There was an entire want of sympathy and kindness. There was a disposition to take advantage of the fact that he was suffering at the hand of God, to increase his sorrows in all ways in which they could do it. ¶ *And they talk to the grief of those.* What they say adds to their sorrow. They speak of the character of those who are afflicted; they allege that the affliction is the punishment of some crime which they have committed; they take advantage of any expressions of impatience which they may let fall in their affliction to charge them with being of a rebellious spirit, or regard it as proof that they are destitute of all true piety. See Notes on Ps. xli. 5–8. It was this which added so much to the affliction of Job. His professed friends, instead of sympathizing with him, endeavoured to prove that the fact that he suffered so much at the hand of God demonstrated that he was a hypocrite; and the expressions of impatience which he uttered in his trial, instead of leading them to sympathize with him, only tended to confirm them in this belief. ¶ *Whom thou hast wounded.* Literally, as in the margin, *thy wounded.* That is, of those whom *thou* hast afflicted. The reference is to the psalmist himself as afflicted by God, while, at the same time, he makes the remark general by saying that this was their character; this was what they were accustomed to do.

27. *Add iniquity unto their iniquity.* Marg., *punishment of iniquity.* The literal rendering is, "Give iniquity upon their iniquity." Luther understands this as a prayer that "sin may be made a punishment for sin;" that is, that they may, as a punishment for their former sins, be left to commit still more aggravated crimes, and thus draw on themselves severer punishment. So Rosenmüller renders it, "Suffer them to accumulate sins by rushing from one sin to another, until their crimes are matured, and their destined punishment comes upon them." An idea similar to this occurs in Rom. i. 28, where God is represented as having "given the heathen over to a reprobate mind, to do those things which are not convenient" [fit, or proper] "*because* they

iniquity; and let them not come into thy righteousness.

28 Let them be blotted out of the book of the living, and not be written *c* with the righteous.

c Rev. xiii. 8.

29 But I *am* poor and sorrowful: let thy salvation, O God, set me up on high.

30 I will praise the name of God with a song, and will magnify him with thanksgiving.

---

did not like to retain him in their knowledge." Perhaps this is the most natural interpretation here, though another has been suggested which the original will bear. According to that, there is an allusion here to the double sense of the equivocal term rendered "iniquity" — עָוֹן, *avon*—which properly denotes sin as such, or in itself considered, but which sometimes seems to denote sin in its consequences or effects. This latter is the interpretation adopted by Prof. Alexander. Thus understood, it is a prayer that God would add, or give, to their sin that which sin deserved; or, in other words, that he would punish it *as* it deserved. ¶ *And let them not come into thy righteousness.* Let them not be treated *as* righteous; as those who are regarded by *thee* as righteous. Let them be treated as they deserve. This is the same as praying that a murderer may not be treated as an innocent man; a burglar, as if he were a man of peace; or a dishonest man, as if he were honest. Let men be regarded and treated as they *are in fact;* or, as they deserve to be treated. It seems difficult to see why this prayer may not be offered with propriety, and with a benevolent heart,—for to bring this about is what all officers of justice are endeavouring to accomplish.

28. *Let them be blotted out of the book of the living.* That is, Let them cease to live; let them not be numbered among living men; let them be cut off. This language is taken from the custom of registering the names of persons in a list, roll, or catalogue, Ex. xxxii. 32. See Notes on Phil. iv. 3. Comp. Rev. iii. 5. The language has no reference to the future world; it is *not* a prayer that they should not be saved. ¶ *And not be written with the righteous.* Let them not be registered or numbered with the righteous. As they *are* wicked, so let them be numbered; so regarded. Let them be reckoned and treated as they are. They deserve to be punished; so let them be. All that this *necessarily* means is, that they should not be treated as righteous, when they were in fact *not* righteous. It cannot be shown that the author of the psalm would not have desired that they should *become* righteous, and that they should *then* be regarded and treated as such. All that the language here implies is, a desire that they should be regarded and treated as they were; that is, as they deserved. The language is evidently derived from the idea so common in the Old Testament that length of days would be the reward of a righteous life (see Job v. 26; Prov. iii. 2; ix. 11; x. 27), and that the wicked would be cut off in the midst of their days. See Notes on Ps. lv. 23.

29. *But I* am *poor and sorrowful.* I am afflicted and suffering. The word here rendered *poor* often means *afflicted.* ¶ *Let thy salvation, O God, set me up on high.* Let thy help raise me up from my low condition, and exalt me to a place of safety.

30. *I will praise the name of God with a song.* As the result of my deliverance, I will *compose* a song or a psalm especially adapted to the occasion, and fitted to express and perpetuate my feelings. It was in such circumstances that a large part of the psalms were composed; and since others besides the psalmist are often in such circumstances, the Book of Psalms becomes permanently useful in the church. It is not always necessary now to *compose* a song or hymn to express our feelings in the

31 *This* also shall please the
LORD better than an ox *or* bullock
that hath horns and hoofs.
32 The [1] humble shall see *this*,
and be glad: and your heart shall
live that seek God.
33 For the LORD heareth the
poor, and despiseth not his prisoners.
34 Let the heaven and earth
praise him, the seas, and every
thing that [2] moveth therein.
35 For God will save Zion, and
will build [d] the cities of Judah;

[1] Or, *meek*.

[2] *creepeth*.

[d] Ez. xxxvi. 35, 36.

circumstances in which we are placed in life,—for we may commonly find such sacred songs ready at our hand; yet no one can doubt the propriety of adding to the number of such by those who can do it, or of increasing the compositions for praise in the church in view of the ever-varied experience of the children of God. ¶ *And will magnify him.* Will exalt his name; will endeavour to make it *seem* greater; or, will spread it further abroad. ¶ *With thanksgiving.* I will use expressions of thanks to make his name more widely known.

31. This *also shall please the* LORD. This will be more acceptable to the Lord. ¶ *Better than an ox* or *bullock that hath horns and hoofs.* Better than a burnt sacrifice—horns, and hoofs, and all. The original here is, *horning and hoofing;* that is, an ox whose horns were fully grown, and whose hoofs were compact and solid; —a perfect animal in its kind, offered whole on the altar. The psalmist does not say that such an offering would *not* be acceptable to the Lord, but that the offering of the heart—the sacrifice of praise—would be *more* acceptable than any such offering in itself considered. This sentiment accords with the common language of the Old Testament. See Notes on Ps. xl. 6–8. Comp. Ps. li. 16, 17; 1 Sam. xv. 22.

32. *The humble shall see* this, and *be glad.* Marg., *The meek.* That is, Others who are thus afflicted—the poor, the needy, the oppressed, the sad—shall be made acquainted with what has been done in my behalf, and shall take courage, or be strengthened. They will learn to trust that God will also interpose in *their* troubles, and bring them out of *their* distresses. ¶ *And your heart shall live that seek God.* Shall be revived; shall be encouraged, strengthened, animated.

33. *For the* LORD *heareth the poor.* The needy; the humble; the unprotected. The reference is to those who are in circumstances of want and distress. The truth stated here is in accordance with all that is said in the Scriptures. Comp. Notes on Ps. xxxiv. 6. See also Job v. 15; Ps. x. 14; xii. 5; xxxv. 10; lxviii. 10. ¶ *And despiseth not his prisoners.* He does not overlook them; he does not treat them as if they were worthy of no attention or regard. The word "prisoners" here may refer to those who are, as it were, bound by affliction under his own providential dealings; or to those who are oppressed, or are held as captives, or are thrown into prison, on his account. The particular reference here seems to be to David, and to those associated with him, who were straitened or deprived of their freedom in the cause of God.

34. *Let the heaven and earth praise him.* All things; all above and all below. ¶ *The seas.* The waters—the oceans. This is in accordance with what often occurs in the Scriptures, when all things, animate and inanimate, are called on to praise God. Comp. Ps. cxlviii. ¶ *And every thing that moveth therein.* Marg., as in Heb., *creepeth.* Comp. Notes on Ps. viii. 8. See also Notes on Isa. lv. 12.

35. *For God will save Zion.* See Notes on Ps. li. 18. That is, he will save his people; he will protect and defend them. This expresses the confident assurance of the psalmist

that they may dwell there, and have it in possession.

36 The seed also of his servants shall inherit it: and they [e] that love his name shall dwell therein.

e John xiv. 23; Rev. xxi. 27.

that, whatever might be the existing troubles, God would not forsake his people, but would interpose in their behalf. ¶ *And will build the cities of Judah.* Though they may now lie waste, or be desolate. See Notes on Ps. li. 18. The general idea here is, that God would be favourable to his land; that he would give success and prosperity to his people; that he would manifest his mercy to them. There is no necessity from the language used here to suppose, as De Wette and Rosenmüller do, that there is an allusion to the time of the exile, and to the restoration of the Jews from Babylon, and that consequently either the whole psalm must have been composed at that time,—or (as Rosenmüller supposes) that the last verses of the psalm were added by a later hand, and that thus the whole psalm was adapted to the time of the exile. From ver. 9 it would seem that, when the psalm was composed, the place of public worship was still standing, and the language here, as in Ps. li. 18, is so general that it might have been employed at any time. ¶ *That they may dwell there,* etc. That his people may dwell there according to the ancient promise. The idea is, that he would be the protector of his people, and that all his promises to them would be fulfilled.

36. *The seed also of his servants.* The children or the descendants of his people. ¶ *Shall inherit it.* Shall continue to dwell in it. ¶ *And they that love his name.* They that love him; they that are his true friends. ¶ *Shall dwell therein.* They shall be safe there; they shall find there a home. This indicates the confident belief of the author of the psalm that the favour of God would be shown to the land. Whatever might be the present troubles, his faith was unwavering—his confidence unshaken—in regard to the faithfulness of God. Palestine—the promised land—would still be the inheritance of those who loved God, and the interests of those who dwelt there would be secure. As applied to the church of God now, the idea is, that it is safe; that it will always be under the Divine protection; and that it will be the loved and the secure abode of all that "love the name" of their God and Saviour.

PSALM LXX.

This psalm bears to the closing part of Ps. xl. (vers. 13-17, see Notes in the Introd. to that psalm) a resemblance similar to that between the fourteenth and the fifty-third psalms. The one is not indeed a mere copy of the other, but the one is substantially the same as the other, with some slight variations, apparently introduced to fit it for some new occasion on which it was to be used. We do not know what the occasion in either case was; but it would seem that in this instance, the psalmist found, in the closing verses of the fortieth psalm, language which *very nearly* expressed what he felt on some particular occasion, and which might, by a slight change, be applied to the use for which it was then desired.

We have no further knowledge of the *occasion* on which this was done, than what is implied in the title: *to bring to remembrance.* For the meaning of this, see Notes on the title to Ps. xxxviii. It determines nothing, however, as to the reason why the closing part of Ps. xl. was selected as the subject of a separate psalm, or why the changes were made which here occur. It merely denotes that there were things which it was proper to preserve in the recollection; or principles which it was of importance for the people of God to remember.

It will be necessary, in considering the psalm, only to note, in each verse successively, the alterations which are made from Ps. xl.

PSALM LXX.

To the chief Musician. *A Psalm* of David, to *f* bring to remembrance.

MAKE *g* *haste*, O God, to deliver me; make haste to
[1] help me, O LORD.
2 Let them be ashamed and confounded that seek after my soul: let them be turned backward, and put to confusion, that desire my hurt.
3 Let them be turned back for a reward of their shame that say, Aha, aha!
4 Let all those that seek [h] thee
[i] rejoice and be glad in thee: and let such as love thy salvation say continually, Let God be magnified.
5 But I *am* poor and needy: make haste unto me, O God: thou *art* my help and my deliverer: O LORD, make no tarrying.

f Ps. xxxviii., *title*. *g* Ps. xl. 13—17. [1] *my help*. *h* Lam. iii. 25. *i* Ps. xcvii. 12; Isa. lxi. 10.

1. *Make haste*. These words are supplied by our translators. The first word in Ps. xl. 13, rendered "*be pleased*," is here omitted in the original. The psalm in the Hebrew begins abruptly,—"O God, to deliver me,"—leaving the impression that this is a fragment—a fragment commencing without even the care necessary to make the grammatical construction complete. ¶ *O God*. Heb., *Elohim*. In the corresponding place in Ps. xl. (ver. 13) the word is *Jehovah*. Why the change was made is unknown. The remainder of the verse is the same as in Ps. xl.

2. *Let them be ashamed and confounded that seek after my soul*. The only change here from Ps. xl. 14, is the omission of the word *together* which occurs there, and the omission of the words *to destroy it*. ¶ *Let them be turned backward, and put to confusion, that desire my hurt*. This corresponds in the Hebrew entirely with Ps. xl. 14.

3. *Let them be turned back for a reward of their shame*. The only change which occurs in this verse is the substitution of the milder phrase "Let them be *turned back*," for "Let them be *desolate*." See Notes on Ps. xl. 15.

4. *Let all those that seek thee*, etc. The only change in this verse from Ps. xl. 16, is in the insertion of the word "*and*" in the beginning of the second clause,—"*and* let such as love," etc.

5. *But I* am *poor and needy*. This is the same as in Ps. xl. 17. ¶ *Make haste unto me, O God*. Heb., *Elohim*. In the parallel place in Ps. xl. 17, this is, "*The Lord thinketh upon me*,"—where the Hebrew word is not *Elohim*, but *Adonai* (Lord). The word "make haste" seems to have been introduced here by design,—thus carrying out the main idea in Ps. xl., but turning here to *petition* what is there stated as *a fact*. ¶ *Thou* art *my help and my deliverer*, etc. The close of the psalm is the same as the close of Ps. xl., except that the word LORD (Jehovah) is used here instead of *God* (Elohim). It is not possible to ascertain whether these changes were mere matters of taste, or whether they were designed to adapt the psalm to some new circumstance, or to the peculiar feelings of the psalmist at the time. There is no evidence that they are mere errors of transcribers, and indeed the changes are so made that this cannot be supposed. The change of the names Elohim, Jehovah, and Adonai, for example, is such as must have been by design, and could not have been made by copyists. But what that design was must remain unknown. The alterations do not in any way, as far as we can understand, affect the sense.

PSALM LXXI.

This psalm is without a title, as is the case with the first, second, tenth, and some others. Of course it is impossible to determine on what occasion it was

PSALM LXXI.

IN [k] thee, O LORD, do I put my trust; let me never be put to confusion.

k Ps. xxxi. 1—3.

composed. There is some plausibility in the supposition that Ps. lxx. might have been placed before it, or in connexion with it, as a kind of introduction, or as indicating the character of the psalms among which it is found; but nothing of certainty can be ascertained on that point. It evidently belongs to the *class* of psalms which refer to the trials of the righteous; but it was rather in view of past troubles than of those which were then existing.

There is no certain evidence that the psalm was composed by David. If so, it was when he was advanced in life. There is, indeed, much in the psalm which would be appropriate to David,—much which he might have written; but there is no way now of ascertaining with certainty who was the author. In the Syriac version, the psalm is, indeed, ascribed to David, and this may perhaps express the prevailing idea in regard to the authorship as it had been handed down by tradition. The title in Syriac is, "Composed by David. When Saul warred against the house of David. And a prophecy respecting the passion and resurrection of the Messiah." The Latin Vulgate and the Septuagint also ascribe it to David. The title in both is the same,—"By David. Of the sons of Jonadab, and the first captives." But these titles are of no authority, as they are not in the Hebrew, and they are of little historic value.

All that is known respecting the occasion on which the psalm was composed, whoever was the author, is, that it was composed when old age was drawing near, and in view of the trials and the blessings of life as considered from the contemplation of its approaching close, vers. 5, 9, 17, 18. The life of the author had been one of trials (ver. 20), but also of great mercies (vers. 6, 7, 17). He was then surrounded with difficulties; the infirmities of age were coming upon him, and he was encompassed with enemies (vers. 10, 11, 20); therefore he sought the continued favour and blessing of God in the little that remained to him of life.

It is a psalm of great value as describing the feelings of a good man when he is growing old, and is an illustration of what there has been occasion so often to remark in this exposition of the Book of Psalms, that the Bible is adapted to all the conditions of human life. In a book professing to be a revelation from God, and in a world where *old age*, with its trials, its infirmities, its recollections, and its hopes, must be so prominent in the actual state of things existing, it would have been unaccountable if there had been nothing to illustrate the feelings of those in advancing or advanced years,—nothing to suggest the kind of reflections appropriate to that period of life,—nothing to cheer the heart of the aged man, and to inspire him with hope,—nothing to prompt him to recall the lessons of the past, and to make use of those lessons to prepare him for the future; even as, in a world so full of trial, it would have been strange if there had been nothing to comfort the mind in affliction, and to enable men to derive proper lessons from the experiences of life. This psalm, therefore, is one of the most valuable portions of the Bible to a certain class of mankind, and may be to any of the living, as suggesting the proper reflections of a good man as the infirmities of age draw on, and as he reviews the mercies and the trials of the past.

It is not necessary to make a more particular analysis of its contents. The psalm, in general, embraces these points: (1) A prayer for deliverance from troubles, and from wicked men, vers. 1-4. (2) An acknowledgment of God's goodness in early life; a grateful review of Divine mercies manifested from the earliest years of life, vers. 5-8. (3) A prayer that God would still preserve him as old age came on; a prayer that God would interpose in his behalf, and enable him still to be useful to the world,—to that generation, and to the generations to come, vers. 9-18. (4) The expression of a confident expectation that his prayer would be answered, and that God would be merciful to him, vers. 19-21. (5) The expression of a purpose to offer praise to God as a suitable return for the mercies of the past, and for all that he hoped to receive in time to come, vers. 22-24.

1. *In thee, O* LORD, *do I put my trust.* See Notes on Ps. xxv. 2. Comp. Ps. xxii. 4, 5; xxxi. 1. ¶ *Let*

2 Deliver me in thy righteousness, and cause me to escape: incline thine ear [l] unto me, and save me.

3 Be thou [1] my strong habitation, whereunto [m] I may continually resort: thou hast given commandment to save me; for thou *art* my rock and my fortress.

4 Deliver me, O my God, out of the hand of the wicked, out of the hand of the unrighteous and cruel man.

5 For thou *art* my hope, [n] O Lord GOD: *thou art* my trust from my youth.

l Ps. xxxiv. 15.
[1] *to me for a rock of habitation.*
m Prov. xviii. 10. *n* Jer. xvii. 7, 17.

me never be put to confusion. Let me never be ashamed; that is, Let me not be so disappointed in the trust that I repose in thee as to have occasion to feel ashamed that I have done it.

2. *Deliver me in thy righteousness.* See Notes on Ps. xxxi. 1. The first three verses of this psalm seem in fact to have been taken, with slight variations, from the first three verses of Ps. xxxi. ¶ *And cause me to escape.* That is, from impending dangers; from the power of my enemies. ¶ *Incline thine ear unto me.* In Ps. xxxi. 2, this is, "Bow down thine ear to me." The idea is the same. See Notes on that place. Comp. Notes on Ps. xvii. 6. ¶ *And save me.* In Ps. xxxi. 2, this is, "Deliver me speedily."

3. *Be thou my strong habitation.* Marg., as in Heb., *Be thou to me for a rock of habitation.* That is, a rock where I may safely make my abode, or to which I may resort and feel safe. In Ps. xxxi. 2, this is, "Be thou my strong rock, for an house of defence to save me." The idea is the same. See Notes on that passage, and compare Notes on Ps. xviii. 2. ¶ *Whereunto I may continually resort.* Where I may take refuge at all times, in all circumstances of danger. ¶ *Thou hast given commandment to save me.* There was some command, or some promise, on which the psalmist relied, or which he felt he might plead as the ground of his appeal. This may refer to some *special* promise or command made to the author of the psalm,—and, if the psalm was composed by David, there were many such; or the reference may have been to the general commands or promises made to the people of God as such, which he felt he was at liberty to plead, and which all may plead who are the friends of God. *We* cannot refer, as David could, to any special promise made to *us* as *individuals;* but, in proportion as we have evidence of piety, we can refer to the promises made to all the people of God, or to all who devote themselves to him, as a reason why he should interpose in our behalf. In this respect the promises made in the Scriptures to the children of God, may be pleaded by us *as if* they were made personally to ourselves; for, if we are his, they are made to us,—they are intended for us. ¶ *For thou* art *my rock and my fortress.* See Notes on Ps. xviii. 2.

4. *Deliver me, O my God, out of the hand of the wicked.* It is, of course, not possible now to ascertain who are particularly referred to here. If David was the author of the psalm, they may have been any of the numerous enemies that he had in his life. ¶ *Out of the hand of the unrighteous and cruel man.* Heb., "out of the *palm.*" This means here the same as hand, and refers to the *grasp* which any one makes in taking hold of a thing by the hand.

5. *For thou* art *my hope, O Lord* GOD. The ground of my hope and my expectation is in thee. (1) I have no other help; no other defence;—but (2) I *have* confidence; on thee I *do* rely. ¶ Thou art *my trust from my youth.* From my earliest years.

6 By [o] thee have I been holden up from the womb: thou art he that took me out of my mother's bowels: my [p] praise *shall be* continually of thee.

7 I am as a wonder [q] unto many: but thou *art* my strong refuge.

8 Let my mouth be filled *with* thy praise *and with* thy honour all the day.

9 Cast me not off in the time of old age: forsake me not when my strength faileth.

o Ps. xxii. 9, 10; Isa. xlvi. 3, 4. *p* Ps. cxlv. 1, 2. *q* Zech. iii. 8.

The meaning is, that he had always trusted in God, and had always found him a helper. All that he was, and all that he possessed, he owed to God; and he felt now that God had been his protector from his earliest years. Perhaps it could not be shown certainly from this expression that he meant to say he had *actually trusted* in God from his youth, for the *language* means no more than that God had actually protected him, and holden him up, and had continually interposed to save and keep him. As God had always been his Protector, so he felt that he might come to Him now, and put his trust in Him.

6. *By thee have I been holden up from the womb.* From the beginning of my existence. The *idea* in all this is, that, since God had sustained him from his earliest years,—since he had shown his power in keeping him, and manifested his care for him, there was ground to pray that God would keep him still, and that he would guard him as old age came on. The sentiment in this verse is substantially the same as in Ps. xxii. 9, 10. See Notes on that passage. ¶ *My praise* shall be *continually of thee.* My praise shall ascend to thee constantly. I will not cease to praise thee. Comp. Notes on Ps. xxii. 25.

7. *I am as a wonder unto many.* The word here rendered *wonder*—מוֹפֵת, *mophaith*—means properly a miracle, a prodigy; then things that are fitted to excite wonder or admiration; then, a sign, a token. See Notes on Isa. viii. 18. The meaning here is, that the course of things in regard to him—the Divine dealings towards him—had been such as to excite attention; to strike the mind as something unusual, and out of the common course, in the same way that miracles do. This might be either from the number and the character of the calamities which had come upon him; or from the narrow escapes which he had had from death; or from the frequency of the Divine intervention in his behalf; or from the abundant mercies which had been manifested towards him. The connexion makes it probable that he refers to the unusual number of afflictions which had come upon him, and the frequency of the Divine interpositions in his behalf when there was no other refuge, and no other hope. ¶ *But thou* art *my strong refuge.* See Notes on Ps. xviii. 2. That is, God had been his Protector, his hiding-place.

8. *Let my mouth be filled.* This is an appeal to himself, in view of the goodness of God, to praise him always. See Notes on Ps. xxxv. 28. ¶ With *thy praise.* With the expressions of praise. ¶ And with *thy honour all the day.* With such expressions as shall promote thy glory, and make thy honour known.

9. *Cast me not off in the time of old age.* When old age comes with its infirmities; its weaknesses; its trials. When my strength fails me; when my eyes grow dim; when my knees totter; when my friends have died; when I am no longer able to labour for my support; when the buoyant feelings of earlier years are no more; when my old companions and associates are gone, and I am left alone. Thou who didst watch over me in infancy; who didst guard me in childhood and youth; who hast defended me in manhood; who hast upheld me

10 For mine enemies speak against me; and they that [1] lay wait for my soul take counsel [r] together,
11 Saying, God hath forsaken him: persecute and take him; for *there is* none to deliver *him*.
12 O God, be not far from me: O my God, make haste for my help.
13 Let them be confounded *and* consumed that are adver-

[1] *watch*, or, *observe*.

r 2 Sam. xvii. 1, etc.

in the days of sickness, danger, bereavement, trouble,—do thou not leave me when, in advanced years, I have peculiar need of thy care; when I have reason to apprehend that there may come upon me, in that season of my life, troubles that I have never known before; when I shall not have the strength, the buoyancy, the elasticity, the ardour, the animal spirits of other years, to enable me to meet those troubles; and when I shall have none of the friends to cheer me whom I had in the earlier periods of my course. It is not unnatural or improper for a man who sees old age coming upon him to pray for special grace, and special strength, to enable him to meet what he cannot ward off, and what he cannot but dread;—for who can look upon the infirmities of old age as coming upon himself but with sad and pensive feelings? Who would wish *to be* an old man? Who can look upon a man tottering with years, and broken down with infirmities,—a man whose sight and hearing are gone,—a man who is alone amidst the graves of all the friends that he had in early life,—a man who is a burden to himself and to the world, a man who has reached the "last scene of all, that ends the strange eventful history,"—that scene of

"Second childishness and mere oblivion,
Sans teeth, sans eyes, sans taste, sans everything,"—

that scene when one can say,

"I have lived long enough; my way of life
Is fallen into the sear, the yellow leaf;
And that which should accompany old age,
As honour, love, obedience, troops of friends,
I must not look to have,"—

who can think of all this, and not pray for special grace for himself should he live to see those days of infirmity and weakness? And who, in view of such infirmities, can fail to see the propriety of seeking the favour of God in early years? Comp. Eccles. xii. 1–6. ¶ *Forsake me not when my strength faileth.* As I may expect it to do, when I grow old. A man can lay up nothing better for the infirmities of old age than the favour of God sought, by earnest prayer, in the days of his youth and his maturer years.

10. *For mine enemies speak against me.* That is, they said substantially, as it is stated in ver. 11, that God had forsaken him, and that therefore they would arise and punish him, or treat him as an outcast from God. ¶ *And they that lay wait for my soul.* For my life; or, to take my life. The margin here—as the Hebrew—is, *watch*, or *observe*. The *watchers for my life;* that is, they who watch for an opportunity to take my life, or to destroy me. ¶ *Take counsel together.* About the best means of accomplishing their object.

11. *Saying, God hath forsaken him.* That is, God has given him over; he no longer protects him; he regards him as a wicked man, and we shall therefore not only be *safe* in our attempts upon his life, but we shall be *justified* in those attempts. ¶ *Persecute and take him.* It can be done safely now; it can be done with propriety. ¶ *For* there is *none to deliver* him. He has no one now to whom to look; no one on whom he can rely. Abandoned by God and by man, he will be an easy prey. Comp. Notes on Ps. xli. 7, 8.

12. *O God, be not far from me.* See Notes on Ps. xxii. 11. ¶ *O my God, make haste for my help.* See Notes on Ps. xl. 13.

13. *Let them be confounded* and

saries to my soul; let them be covered *with* reproach and dishonour that seek my hurt.

14 But I will hope continually, and will yet praise thee more and more.

15 My mouth shall show forth thy righteousness *and* thy salvation all the day; for [s] I know not the numbers *thereof*.

16 I will go in the strength of the Lord GOD: I will make mention of thy righteousness, [t] *even* of thine only.

17 O God, thou hast taught me from my youth: and hitherto

s Ps. cxxxix. 17, 18.

t Isa. xlv. 24, 25; Phil. iii. 9.

consumed. See Notes on the similar passage in Ps. xxxv. 4. The sentiment in this verse is the same; the language is slightly varied. See also Ps. xl. 14, where the same sentiment occurs.

14. *But I will hope continually.* I will always cherish hope; I will not give up to despair. I will trust in God whatever may be the number, the power, and the confidence of my enemies. None of these things shall make me despair, for as long as I have a God, I have every ground for hope. No man should despair who has God for his Friend. Comp. Ps. xlii. 5, 11; xliii. 5. ¶ *And will yet praise thee more and more.* Literally, *I will add upon all thy praise.* That is, I will accumulate it; I will increase it. He saw abundant cause in the past for praising God; he had such confidence in him, and he felt such an assurance that he would interpose in his behalf, that he did not doubt that in the future dealings of God with him, he would have every reason to "*add*" to that praise.

15. *My mouth shall show forth thy righteousness,* etc. See Notes on ver. 8. The word *righteousness* here refers to the righteous character of God, particularly as manifested in his behalf; the word *salvation* refers to what God had done to deliver him from his dangers. ¶ *For I know not the numbers* thereof. That is, I cannot estimate the amount of thy favours; they are innumerable. See Notes on Ps. xl. 5.

16. *I will go in the strength of the Lord* GOD. In my future journey through life; in my trials; in my duties; in my conflicts; in my temptations. Admonished in the past of my own weakness, and remembering how often God has interposed, I will hereafter lean only on his arm, and not trust to my own strength. But thus leaning on his arm, I *will* go confidently to meet the duties and the trials of life. If one has the strength of God to lean on, or can use that strength *as if* it were his own, there is no duty which he may not discharge; no trial which he may not bear. The Hebrew here is, "I will come with the mighty deeds [more literally, *strengths*] of the Lord God." The word is used to denote the *mighty acts* of Jehovah, in Deut. iii. 24; Ps. cvi. 2; Job xxvi. 14. De Wette proposes to render this, "I will go in the mighty deeds of Jehovah;" that is, I will sing of his mighty deeds. Rosenmüller explains it, "I will go into the temple to celebrate his praise there;" that is, I will bring the remembrance of his mighty acts there as the foundation of praise. So Professor Alexander explains it. It seems to me, however, that our translation has expressed the true idea, that he would go in the strength of God; that he would rely on no other; that he would make mention of no other. Old age, trials, difficulties, arduous duties, were before him; and in all these he would rely on no other strength but that of the Almighty. ¶ *I will make mention of thy righteousness,* even *of thine only.* Of thy just and holy character. I will allude to nothing else; I will rely on nothing else as the foundation of my hope, and as my encouragement in the duties and trials of life.

17. *O God, thou hast taught me from my youth.* See vers. 5, 6. That

have I declared thy wondrous works.
18 Now also [1] when I am old
[u] and greyheaded, O God, forsake me not, until I have shewed
[2] thy strength unto *this* generation

[1] *unto old age and grey hairs.*

[u] Isa. xlvi. 4. [2] *thine arm.*

is, God had guided and instructed him from his earliest years. He had made known to him his own being and perfections; he had made his duty plain; he had led him along the dangerous path of life. ¶ *And hitherto have I declared.* I have made known. That is, he had done this by public praise; he had done it by his writings; he had done it by maintaining and defending the truth. In all situations of life, up to that time, he had been willing to stand up for God and his cause. ¶ *Thy wondrous works.* See Notes on Ps. ix. 1; xxvi. 7. Doings or acts which were fitted to attract attention; to awe the mind by their greatness; to inspire confidence by their wisdom.

18. *Now also when I am old and grey-headed.* Marg., *unto old age and grey hairs.* This does not necessarily mean that he was then actually old and grey-headed, but it would imply that he was approaching that period, or that he had it in prospect. The time of youth was past, and he was approaching old age. The literal rendering would be, "And also unto old age and grey hairs, do not forsake me." This is the prayer of one who had been favoured in youth, and in all his former course of life, and who now asked that God would continue his mercy, and not forsake him when the infirmities of age drew on. ¶ *Forsake me not.* Still keep me alive. Give me health, and strength, and ability to set forth thy praise, and to make known thy truth. See Notes on ver. 9. ¶ *Until I have showed thy strength.* Marg., as in Heb., *thine arm.* The arm is the instrument by which we execute a purpose, and it thus becomes a symbol of strength. ¶ *Unto* this *generation.* Literally, *to a generation.* The reference is to the generation then living; that is, the generation which had come on the stage since he had reached manhood,—the generation—the new generation—which one who is approaching old age sees engaged in the active scenes of life, cultivating the fields, filling the offices, constructing the bridges and roads, manning the ships, occupying the dwellings, instead of those with whom he was formerly associated, and who are now in their graves. His own generation—the companions of his own early years—had passed away. He had lived to speak to a new generation, and he was desirous that they should start on the journey of life with the advantage of his experience, as of one that had gone before. Each generation *may* thus enter on life with all the accumulated wisdom of the past; that is, as wise as those had become who had themselves had the experience, and treasured up results from the observations, of a long life. Society thus makes progress. One generation becomes wiser and better than the one which went before it, and the experience of all ages thus accumulates as the world advances, enabling a future age to act on the results of all the wisdom of the past. Man thus differs from the inferior creation. The animals, governed by instinct alone, make no progress. Comp. Notes on Ps. xlix. 13. They profit neither by the wisdom, nor the follies of the past. The first robin built its nest of the same materials, and with as much art, as the robin does now; the first stock of bees constructed their cells with as nice and accurate adaptations, with mathematical precision as complete, as a swarm of bees will do now. Neither the bird nor the bee has learned anything by experience, by study, or by observation,—nor lays up, to transmit to future generations of birds or bees, the results of its own

tion, *and* thy power to every one *that* is to come.

19 Thy righteousness also, O God, *is* very high, [v] who hast done great things: O God, who *is* like unto thee!

20 *Thou,* which hast showed me great and sore troubles, shalt [w] quicken me again, and shalt

v Isa. lv. 9. w Hos. vi. 1, 2.

sagacity or observation. Not so with man. The result of the experiences of one generation goes into the general experience of the world, and becomes its capital; a new thought, or a new invention struck out by some splendid genius, becomes the common property of the race; and society, as it rolls on, gathers up all these results, as the Ganges or the Mississippi, rolling on to the ocean, gathers into one mighty volume all the waters that flow in a thousand streams, and all that come from rivulets and fountains, however remote. It is this which makes the life of *a man* so valuable in this world; this which makes it so desirable for a man, even when approaching old age, yet to live a little longer; for, as the fruit of his experience, his observation, his ripe wisdom, his acquired knowledge, he may yet suggest something, by writing or otherwise, which may add to the intelligence of the world; some principle which may be elaborated and perfected by the coming age. ¶ And *thy power.* Thy greatness; majesty; glory. ¶ *To every one* that *is to come.* To all future generations. That I may state truths which may benefit future ages. He who suggests one truth which the world was not in possession of before, is a benefactor to mankind, and will not have lived in vain, for that truth will do something to set the race forward, and to make the world better and happier. It is not a vain thing, then, for a man to live; and every one should endeavour *so* to live that the world may not be the worse—or may not go backward—by his living in it, but that it may be the wiser and the better:—not merely so that it may keep on the same level, but that it may rise to a higher level, and start off on a new career.

19. *Thy righteousness also, O God,* is *very high.* See Notes on Ps. xxxvi. 5. The purpose of the psalmist is to exalt that righteousness as much as possible, and he, therefore, compares it with that which is high—the heavens—the highest thing of all. The literal rendering would be, "even to the high," or the height; that is, to the highest place. The passage is designed to express his confidence in God, in the infirmities and troubles which he must expect to come upon him with advancing years. ¶ *Who hast done great things.* In his work of creation; in his providence; in his manifested mercy towards his people. He had done things so great as to show that he could protect those who put their trust in him. ¶ *O God, who* is *like unto thee!* Who can be compared to thee! See Notes on Ps. xxxv. 10. Comp. Notes on Isa. xl. 18. See also Ps. lxxxix. 8; Ex. xv. 11; 2 Sam. vii. 22.

20. Thou, *which hast showed me great and sore troubles.* Or rather, Who hast caused us to see or experience great trials. The psalmist here, by a change from the singular to the plural, connects himself with his friends and followers, meaning that he had suffered with them and through them. It was not merely a personal affliction, but others connected with him had been identified with him, and his personal sorrows had been increased by the trials which had come upon them also. Our severest trials often are those which affect our friends. ¶ *Shalt quicken me again.* Literally, "Shalt return and make us live." The word *quicken* in the Scriptures has always this sense of *making to live again.* See Notes on John v. 21; comp. Rom. iv. 17; 1 Cor. xv. 36; Eph. ii. 1. The plural form should have been retained here, as in

bring me up again from the depths of the earth.

21 Thou shalt increase my greatness, and comfort me on every side.

22 I will also praise thee with the [1] psaltery, [x] *even* thy truth, O my God: unto thee will I sing with the harp, [y] O thou Holy One of Israel.

23 My lips shall greatly rejoice when I sing unto thee; and my soul, which thou hast redeemed.

[1] *instrument of psaltery.* *x* Ps. cl. 3. *y* Ps. xcii. 3.

the former member of the sentence. The authors of the Masoretic punctuation have pointed this as if it were to be read in the singular, but the plural is undoubtedly the true reading. Alike in his affliction, and in his hope of the returning mercy of God, he connects himself here with those who had suffered with him. The language expresses firm confidence in the goodness of God,—an assurance that these troubles would pass away, and that he would see a brighter day. ¶ *And shalt bring me up again from the depths of the earth.* As if he had been sunk in the waters, or in the mire. See Ps. cxxx. 1. The word here used means commonly *wave, billow, surge;* then, a mass of waters, a *flood,* the deep; then, a gulf, an abyss. The idea here is, that, instead of being on the mountain top, in a place of security, he had sunk down to the lowest point; he had, as it were, sunk *into* the very earth. Yet from that low estate he felt assured that God would raise him up, and place him in a condition of happiness and safety. This is one of the many instances which we have in the Psalms, where the psalmist in great trouble expresses the most entire confidence that God would interpose in his behalf.

21. *Thou shalt increase my greatness.* Thou wilt not merely restore me to my former condition, but wilt enlarge my happiness, and wilt do still greater things for me. ¶ *And comfort me on every side.* Literally, "Thou wilt turn thyself; thou wilt comfort me." The word also means to surround; to encompass (Gen. ii. 11, 13; 1 Kings vii. 24; Ps. xviii. 5); and the idea here may be that God would *go around him,* or encircle him, and would thus comfort him. This idea is expressed in our common version. It was the confident assurance of entire, or complete consolation.

22. *I will also praise thee with the psaltery.* Marg., as in Heb., *with the instrument of psaltery.* The Hebrew word is *nebel.* In Isa. v. 12 it is rendered *viol.* See Notes on that passage. It is rendered *psaltery* in 1 Sam. x. 5; 2 Sam. vi. 5; 1 Kings x. 12; and elsewhere. Comp. Notes on Ps. xxxiii. 2. ¶ Even *thy truth.* I will make mention of thy truth and faithfulness in my songs of praise; or, I will celebrate these in connexion with appropriate music. ¶ *Unto thee will I sing with the harp.* Heb., *kinnor.* See Notes on Isa. v. 12. Comp. Notes on Ps. xxxiii. 2. ¶ *O thou Holy One of Israel.* The God of Israel or the Hebrew people; the God regarded by them as most holy, and worshipped by them as their God. This is the first time that this title occurs in the Psalms, but it is common in the Prophets, particularly in Isaiah. See Isa. i. 4; v. 19, 24; x. 20; xii. 6. It occurs also in Ps. lxxviii. 41; lxxxix. 18.

23. *My lips shall greatly rejoice,* etc. My lips will seem to be happy in the *privilege* of celebrating the praises of God. ¶ *And my soul, which thou hast redeemed.* Comp. Ps. xxxiv. 22. The word *soul* here seems to be employed to denote *the soul* properly, as we understand the word—the immortal part. The usual meaning of the word, in the Psalms, however, is *life,* and it is possible that the psalmist meant merely to say here that the *life* which had been spared should find pleasure in celebrating the praises of

24 My tongue also shall talk of thy righteousness all the day long: for they are confounded, for they are brought unto shame, that seek my hurt.

God; but there is no impropriety in supposing that he has reference to his higher—his immortal—nature.

24. *My tongue also shall talk of thy righteousness.* Thy righteous character; the truthfulness, the goodness, the fidelity which thou hast manifested in delivering me. The word rendered *talk* means properly to meditate; then, to think aloud, to talk to oneself; and the idea may be, that his mind would be so full of the subject that he would give utterance to his thoughts in audible expressions when alone. It denotes fulness of heart, and language naturally flowing out from a full soul. ¶ *All the day long.* Continually. This shall occupy my mind at all times. See Notes on Ps. i. 2. ¶ *For they are confounded,* etc. That is, they are put to confusion; they are disappointed in their hopes; they are defeated in their plans. The psalmist sees this to be so certain that he speaks of it as if it were already done. The Psalms often conclude in this way. They begin in trouble, they end in joy; they begin in darkness, they end in light; they begin with a desponding mind, they end with a triumphant spirit; they begin with prayer, they end in praise. On the *language* used here, see Notes on ver. 13. On such a *close* of the Psalms, see Ps. iii. 7, 8; vi. 9, 10; vii. 17; xvii. 15; xxii. 30, 31; xxvi. 12; xlii. 11; xliii. 5; lii, 8, 9.

PSALM LXXII.

The title of this psalm, in the original, is simply "*For Solomon.*" The words "*a psalm*" are supplied by the translators. In the margin this is "*of;*" to wit, of Solomon,—as if Solomon were the writer. Prof. Alexander renders it, "By Solomon," and supposes, of course, that he was the author. The Septuagint renders it, "For"—εἰς—"Solomon." So the Latin Vulgate: "In Salomonem." The Syriac: "Of David; when he constituted Solomon king." Luther: "Of Solomon." It is true that the Hebrew in the title is the same which is used in other psalms where the author is designated, as in Ps. lxviii., lxix., lxx., and elsewhere, "of David;" in Ps. lxxiii., lxxiv., and elsewhere, "of Asaph," etc.; and it is true that the mode of expression would most *naturally* convey the idea that Solomon was the author; but it is also true that this construction is not necessary, as is shown by the fact that it is understood otherwise by the Septuagint, the Latin Vulgate, the Syriac, and by the author of the Chaldee Paraphrase. No one can doubt that the Hebrew is susceptible of this latter interpretation, (see Gesenius on the letter ל), and that the translation "*for* Solomon" is a fair rendering. The contents of the psalm also demand this construction here. It is wholly improbable that Solomon would pen the predictions in the psalm as referring to himself; but not at all improbable that David would utter these predictions and prayers in reference to his son about to ascend the throne. The language of the psalm is every way appropriate to the supposition that it was composed by David in view of the anticipated glories and the peaceful reign of his son and successor, as an inspired production indicating what that reign would be, and looking onward to the still more glorious and peaceful reign of the Messiah as king. It seems to me, therefore, that the evidence is sufficiently clear that the psalm was composed in reference to Solomon, and not by him; and, if so, the most natural supposition is that it was composed by David. The evidence, indeed, is not positive, but it is such probable evidence as to leave little room for doubt.

It is a question of much importance whether the psalm had original reference to Solomon alone, or whether it had a reference to the Messiah, and is to be reckoned among the Messianic psalms. That it was applicable to the reign of Solomon, as a reign of peace and prosperity, there can be no doubt, and there seems to be as little reason to doubt that it was *intended* to describe his reign, and that the principal images in the psalm are taken from what it was foreseen would characterise his government; but that it also had reference to the Messiah, and to his reign, will be apparent, I think, from the following considerations:—

(1) The testimony of tradition. Thus the ancient Chaldee Paraphrase, which undoubtedly gives the prevailing opinion of the ancient Jews, regards it as referring to the Messiah. The first verse of the psalm is thus rendered in that Paraphrase: "O God, give the knowledge of thy judgments to the king the Messiah — לְמַלְכָּא מְשִׁיחָא — and thy righteousness to the sons of David the king." The older Jewish writers, according to Schöttgen, agreed in applying it to the Messiah.

(2) The fact that it is not applicable, in the fulness of its meaning, to the reign of Solomon. It is true that the psalm describes the general characteristics of that reign as one of peace and prosperity; but it is also true, as will be seen in the progress of the explanation of the psalm, that there are passages in it which cannot be well applied to him, or which have a fulness of meaning — an amplitude of signification— which requires an application to some other state of things than that which occurred under his rule.

(3) The psalm *is* applicable to the Messiah, and accords in its general character, and in the particular expressions, with the other descriptions of the Messiah in the Old Testament. Comp. vers. 2, 4, with Isa. xi. 4;—ver. 3, with Isa. ix. 6;—ver. 5, with Isa. ix. 7. See also vers. 8, 11, 17. It will be shown in the exposition of these verses that they accurately describe the state of things under the Messiah, and that they cannot be literally applied to the reign of Solomon.

(4) It may be added that this interpretation is in accordance with the prevalent style of the Old Testament. No one can doubt, however the fact may be explained, that the writers of the Old Testament *did* look forward to a remarkable personage who was to appear in the future. Whether the reality of the inspiration of the Prophets is admitted or denied, they somehow had conceived *that notion*, and this idea is constantly manifesting itself in their writings. They delight to dwell upon the prospect of his appearing; they dwell with pleasure on his characteristics; they turn to him in times of national trouble; they anticipate final deliverance under him alone. They describe him as clothed with regal magnificence; they exalt him to the highest rank; they represent him as most beautiful in character, and most mighty in power; they apply to him the most exalted names;—priest; prophet; prince; king; warrior; angel; *God.* We are not surprised to find the sacred writers recurring to this idea at any time, whatever may be the subject on which they are writing; and to think of the Old Testament *without a Messiah*, would be much the same as to think of the Iliad without Achilles; or the Æneid without Æneas; or "Hamlet" without Hamlet. It is for those who deny the inspiration of the Prophets to explain *how* this idea sprang up in their minds; they cannot deny the fact that it was there. There is, perhaps, no part of the Old Testament where this is more manifest than in the psalm before us. It bears all the marks of having been composed under the influence of such an idea.

The psalm consists of two parts:—

I. A description of the reign of the "king"—the Messiah, vers. 1–17.

II. A doxology, vers. 18, 19.

I. A description of the reign of the "king" — the Messiah. That reign would be

(1) A reign of righteousness. Justice would be done to all; the poor and down-trodden would be protected; prosperity would attend the righteous; the whole course of the administration would be in favour of virtue and religion, vers. 1–7.

(2) The reign would be universal, vers. 8–11. The king would have dominion from sea to sea; foreign princes would send him presents; all kings would bow down before him; and all nations would serve him.

(3) It would be a reign of benevolence; a reign that would have special regard for the poor, the needy, and the oppressed, vers. 12–14.

(4) It would be perpetual; it would spread afar, and endure for ever, vers. 15–17.

II. The doxology, vers. 18, 19;—a doxology eminently appropriate in view of the prospective glories of the reign of the Messiah. For such a kingdom, for such a reign of glory and beneficence, for such mercy shown to mankind in the prospect of setting up such a dominion, it was meet that the heart should be filled with adoration, and that the

PSALM LXXII.

A Psalm [1] for Solomon.

GIVE [z] the king thy judgments, O God, and thy righteousness unto the king's son.

2 He [a] shall judge thy people with righteousness, and thy poor with judgment.

3 The mountains [b] shall bring peace to the people, and the little hills, by righteousness.

[1] Or, *of*, Ps. cxxvii., *title*.
[z] 1 Kings i. 36, 37.
[a] Isa. xi. 2—5; xxxii. 1. [b] Ps. lxxxv. 11, 12.

---

lips should pour forth blessings on the name of God.

To the psalm a postscript is added, (ver. 20), intimating that this was the close of the collection of psalms ascribed to David. On the meaning of this, see Notes on the verse.

1. *Give the king.* Supposing the psalm to have been composed by David in view of the inauguration of his son and successor, this is a prayer that God would bestow on him the qualifications which would tend to secure a just, a protracted, and a peaceful reign. Though it is to be admitted that the psalm was designed to refer ultimately to the Messiah, and to be descriptive of *his* reign, yet there is no impropriety in supposing that the psalmist believed the reign of Solomon would be, in some proper sense emblematic of that reign, and that it was his desire the reign of the one *might*, as far as possible, resemble that of the other. There is no improbability, therefore, in supposing that the mind of the psalmist might have been directed to both in the composition of the psalm, and that while he used the language of prayer for the one, his eye was mainly directed to the characteristics of the other. ¶ *Thy judgments.* Knowledge; authority; ability to execute thy judgments, or thy laws. That is, he speaks of the king as appointed to administer justice; to maintain the laws of God, and to exercise judicial power. It is one of the primary ideas in the character of a king that he is the fountain of justice; the maker of the laws; the dispenser of right to all his subjects. The officers of the law administer justice *under* him; the last appeal is to him. ¶ *And thy righteousness.* That is, Clothe him, in the administration of justice, with a righteousness like thine own. Let it be seen that he represents *thee;* that his government may be regarded as thine own administration through him. ¶ *Unto the king's son.* Not only to him, but to his successor; that is, let the administration of justice in the government be perpetuated. There is no improbability in supposing that in this the psalmist may have designed also to refer to the last and the greatest of his successors in the line—the Messiah.

2. *He shall judge thy people with righteousness.* On this verse see Notes on Isa. xi. 3, 4. The fact that this so entirely accords with the description in Isa. xi., which undoubtedly refers to the Messiah, has been alluded to above as confirming the opinion that the psalm has a similar reference.

3. *The mountains shall bring peace to the people.* The idea in this verse is that the land would be full of peace and the fruits of peace. All parts of it would be covered with the evidences that it was a land of quietness and security, where men could pursue their callings in safety, and enjoy the fruit of their labours. On the mountains and on all the little hills in the land there would be abundant harvests, the result of peace (so strongly in contrast with the desolations of war)—all showing the advantages of a peaceful reign. It is to be remembered that Judea is a country abounding in hills and mountains, and that a great part of its former fertility resulted from terracing the hills, and cultivating them as far as possible towards the summit. The idea here is, that one who should look upon the land,—who could take in at a glance the whole

4 He shall judge the poor of the people, he shall save the children of the needy, and shall break in pieces the oppressor.[c]
5 They shall fear thee as long as the sun and moon endure, throughout all generations.
6 He shall come down like rain upon [d] the mown grass; as showers *that* water the earth.

c Isa. li. 12, 13; Rev. xii. 10.

d 2 Sam. xxiii. 4; Hos. vi. 3.

country,—would see those mountains and hills cultivated in the most careful manner, and everywhere bringing forth the productions of peace. Comp. Ps. lxv. 11–13. See also Notes on Ps. lxxxv. 11, 12. ¶ *And the little hills, by righteousness.* That is, By the prevalence of righteousness, or under a reign of righteousness, the little hills would furnish illustrations of the influence of a reign of peace. Everywhere there would be the effects of a reign of peace. The whole land would be cultivated, and there would be abundance. Peace always produces these blessings; war always spreads desolation.

4. *He shall judge the poor of the people.* The afflicted; the downtrodden; the needy. He would vindicate their cause against their oppressors; his reign would be one of impartial justice, under which the rights of the poor as well as of the rich would be respected. See Notes on Isa. xi. 4. ¶ *He shall save the children of the needy.* Those in humble life; those most likely to be oppressed by others; those who have no natural protectors. ¶ *And shall break in pieces the oppressor.* Shall subdue, or destroy, those who live to oppress others. See Notes on Ps. xii. 5.

5. *They shall fear thee.* That is, *men* shall fear thee, or thou shalt be feared, or reverenced. The idea is, that his reign would continue, or that he would be obeyed during all the time here mentioned. ¶ *As long as the sun and moon endure.* Literally, "With the sun, and before the moon;" that is, as long as they have the sun with them, or have it to shine upon them, and as long as they are in the presence of the moon, or have its light. In other words, they would continue to the end of time; or to the end of the world. It does not denote *eternity*, for it is not assumed in the Bible that the sun and moon will continue for ever; but the idea is, that as long as the sun shall continue to shine upon the earth—as long as men shall dwell upon the earth—the kingdom would be perpetual. There would be no change of dynasty; no new empire would arise to displace and to supersede this. This would be the dynasty under which the affairs of the world would be wound up; this the kingdom which would be found at the consummation of all things. The reign of the Messiah will be the *final* reign in the earth; that under which the affairs of earth will close. ¶ *Throughout all generations.* While the generations of men dwell on the earth.

6. *He shall come down.* That is, The influence of his reign will be like fertilising showers. The word "*he*" in this place might have been "*it*," referring to his reign, or to the influence of his government. ¶ *Like rain upon the mown grass.* The word rendered *mown grass*—גֵּז, *gaiz*—means properly *a shearing*, and is applied in Deut. xviii. 4, and Job xxxi. 20, to a fleece of wool. So it is understood here by the Septuagint, by the Latin Vulgate, by the Syriac, and by Luther; and, in accordance with this, it has been supposed by some that there is an allusion to the dew that descended on the fleece spread out by Gideon, Judges vi. 37. The Chaldee Paraphrase renders it, "As the grass that has been eaten off by locusts;" where the idea would be that after locusts have passed over a field, devouring everything, when the rain descends the fields revive, and nature again puts on the appearance of life. This idea is adopted by

7 In his days shall the righteous flourish; and abundance of peace[1] so long as the moon endureth.

[1] *till* there be *no moon.*

8 He *e* shall have dominion also from sea to sea, and from the river unto the ends of the earth.

e 1 Kings iv. 20—24; Ps. lxxxix. 25; Zech. ix. 10.

Rosenmüller. The common interpretation, however, which refers the word to a *mowing,* that is, a *mown meadow,* is probably the correct one; and thus understood, the image is very beautiful. The reign of the Messiah would resemble the gently-descending shower, under which the grass which has been mown springs up again with freshness and beauty. ¶ *As showers* that *water the earth.* Literally, "like showers, the watering of the earth." The original word rendered "that water" suggests the idea of distilling, or *gently* flowing.

7. *In his days shall the righteous flourish.* It will be a period when just and upright men will be protected, or when they shall receive the countenance of him who reigns. The administration of the kingdom that is to be set up will be in favour of righteousness or justice. The word *flourish* here is derived from the growth of plants—as plants sprout, or spring up—an emblem of prosperity. ¶ *And abundance of peace.* Literally, "*multitude* of peace;" that is, The things which produce peace, or which indicate peace, will not be few, but numerous; they will abound everywhere. They will be found in towns and villages, and private dwellings; in the calm and just administration of the affairs of the State; in abundant harvests; in intelligence, in education, and in undisturbed industry; in the protection extended to the rights of all. ¶ *So long as the moon endureth.* Marg., as in Heb., *till there be no moon.* That is, till the moon shall cease to shine upon the earth. See ver. 5.

8. *He shall have dominion also from sea to sea.* There is probably an allusion here to the promise in Ex. xxiii. 31: "And I will set thy bounds from the Red Sea even unto the sea of the Philistines, and from the desert unto the river." This was the original promise in regard to the bounds of the promised land. A promise similar to this occurs also in Gen. xv. 18: "In the same day the Lord made a covenant with Abram, saying, Unto thy seed have I given this land, from the river of Egypt unto the great river, the river Euphrates." The meaning here is, that what was implied in these ancient promises would be carried out under the reign of the king referred to in the psalm. The *immediate* allusion, therefore, in the phrase "from sea to sea," may have been from the Red Sea on the East to the Mediterranean on the West; but still the language is susceptible of a more enlarged application, and may mean from one sea to another; that is, embracing all the lands or countries lying between seas and oceans; or, in other words, that the dominion would be universal. Comp. Notes on Ps. ii. 8. ¶ *And from the river,* etc. The Euphrates. This was emphatically "*the* river" to the Hebrews—the great river—the greatest river known to them; and this river would be naturally understood as intended by the expression, unless there was something to limit it. Besides, this was expressly designated in the original covenant as the boundary of the promised land. See, as above, Gen. xv. 18. The meaning here is, that, taking that river as one of the boundaries, or as a starting point, the dominion would extend from that to the utmost limits of the earth. It would have no other boundary but the limits of the world. The promise, therefore, is, that the dominion would be universal, or would pervade the earth;—at once a kingdom of peace, and yet spreading itself all over the

9 They that dwell in the wilderness shall bow before him: and [f] his enemies shall lick the dust.

10 The [g] kings of Tarshish and of the isles shall bring presents: the kings of Sheba and Seba shall offer gifts.

11 Yea, all kings shall fall down [h] before him; all nations shall serve him.

12 For he shall deliver [i] the needy when he crieth; the poor also, and *him* that hath no helper.

f Micah vii. 17

g 2 Chron. ix. 21; Matt. ii. 11.
h Isa. xlix. 7. i Isa. xli. 17; Heb. vii. 25.

world. It is hardly necessary to say that this did not occur under Solomon, and that it could not have been expected that it would occur under him, and especially as it was expected that his reign would be one of peace and not of conquest. It would find its complete fulfilment only under the Messiah.

9. *They that dwell in the wilderness shall bow before him.* The word rendered "they that dwell in the wilderness"—צִיִּים, *tziyyim* — means properly those who abide in deserts, dry places, solitudes; and it might be applied either to animals or to men. It is applied to the former in Isa. xiii. 21 (see Notes on that place); xxiii. 13; xxxiv. 14; Jer. l. 39. In all these, except Isa. xxiii. 13, it is rendered *wild beasts of the desert,* denoting jackals, ostriches, etc.; but here, and in Ps. lxxiv. 14, it is evidently applied to men, as denoting shepherds, — nomadic tribes, — men who have no permanent home, but who wander from place to place. The idea is, that these wild, wandering, unsettled hordes would become subject to him, or would bow down and acknowledge his authority. This can be fulfilled only under the Messiah. ¶ *And his enemies shall lick the dust.* This is expressive of the most thorough submission and abject humiliation. It is language derived from what seems actually to occur in Oriental countries, where men prostrate themselves on their faces, and place their mouths on the ground, in token of reverence or submission. Rosenmüller (Morgenland, vol. ii., pp. 82, 83) quotes a passage from Hugh Boyd's Account of his embassage to Candy in Ceylon, where he says that when he himself came to show respect to the king, it was by kneeling before him. But this, says he, was not the case with other ambassadors. "They almost literally *licked the dust.* They cast themselves on their faces on the stony ground, and stretched out their arms and legs; then they raised themselves upon their knees, and uttered certain forms of good wishes in the loudest tones,—May the head of the king of kings reach above the sun; may he reign a thousand years." Comp. Notes on Isa. xlix. 23.

10. *The kings of Tarshish.* On the situation of Tarshish, see Notes on Isa. ii. 16. Comp. Ps. xlviii. 7. The word seems to be used here to denote any distant region abounding with riches. ¶ *And of the isles,* etc. Representing also distant lands; or lands beyond the seas. The word *islands* among the Hebrews commonly denoted distant sea-coasts, particularly those of the Mediterranean. See Notes on Isa. xli. 1. ¶ *The kings of Sheba and Seba.* Places in Arabia. On the word *Sheba,* see Notes on Isa. lx. 6. On the word *Seba,* see Notes on Isa. xliii. 3. ¶ *Shall offer gifts.* See Notes on Ps. xlv. 12. Comp. Isa. lx. 5–7, 13–17.

11. *Yea, all kings shall fall down,* etc. That is, his reign will be universal. The kings and people mentioned in the previous verses are only *specimens* of what will occur. *All* kings—*all* nations—will do what these are represented as doing. They will submit to the Messiah; they will own him as their Lord. See Notes on Ps. ii. 8. Comp. Isa. xlix. 23.

13 He shall spare the poor and needy, and shall save the souls of the needy.

14 He shall redeem their soul from deceit and violence: and precious shall their blood be in his sight.

15 And he shall live, [k] and to him [1] shall be given of the gold of Sheba: [l] prayer also shall be made for him continually; *and* daily shall he be praised.[m]

k Rev. i. 18. 1 one *shall give.*
l 2 Chron. ix. 1. m Jude, ver. 25.

12. *For he shall deliver the needy when he crieth.* The sufferer; the down-trodden; the oppressed. See Notes on ver. 4. Comp. Notes on Isa. lxi. 1. ¶ *The poor also,* etc. All who have no protector; all who are exposed to injustice and wrong from others. This is everywhere declared to be the characteristic of the reign of the Messiah. See Notes on Isa. xi. 4.

13. *He shall spare the poor and needy.* He will have pity on; he will show mercy or favour to them. ¶ *And shall save the souls of the needy.* Will guard and defend them; will be their protector and friend. His administration will have special respect to those who are commonly overlooked, and who are exposed to oppression and wrong.

14. *He shall redeem their soul from deceit and violence.* He will rescue their lives; that is, he will deliver them from the hands of men who practise deceit, or who are dishonest and unjust,—and from the hands of those who oppress. This is stating in another form the idea that his reign would be one of equity, protecting the rights of the poor, and delivering the oppressed. ¶ *And precious shall their blood be in his sight.* That is, so precious that he will not permit it to be shed unjustly, but will come to their rescue when their life is in danger; or, that—being shed—he will regard it as so valuable that he will not permit it to go unavenged. He will never be indifferent to their safety, or their reputation.

15. *And he shall live.* So far as the *language* here is concerned, this may either refer to the king—the Messiah,—or to the poor and the oppressed man. If the former, then it means that the life of the Messiah would be perpetual; that he would not be cut off as other sovereigns are; that there would be no change of dynasty; that he would be, as a king, the same—unchanging and unchanged—in all the generations of men, and in all the revolutions which occur on the earth. This would accord with the truth, and with what is elsewhere said of the Messiah; but, perhaps, the more correct interpretation is the latter,—that it refers to the poor and the oppressed man,—meaning that he would live to bring an offering to the Messiah, and to pray for the extension of his kingdom upon the earth. ¶ *And to him shall be given.* Marg., *one shall give.* Literally, *he shall give to him;* that is, the man who has enjoyed his protection, and who has been saved by him, will do this. As a token of his gratitude, and as an expression of his submission, he will bring to him a costly offering, the gold of Sheba. ¶ *Of the gold of Sheba.* One of the gifts referred to in ver. 10, as coming from Sheba. Comp. Isa. xliii. 3; xlv. 14. The meaning is, that those who are redeemed by him,—who owe so much to him for protecting and saving them—will bring the most valued things of the earth, or will consecrate to him all that they are, and all that they possess. Comp. Isa. lx. 5–7, 13–17. ¶ *Prayer also shall be made for him continually.* Not for him personally, but for the success of his reign; for the extension of his kingdom. Prayer made for *that* is made for *him,* for he is identified with that. ¶ And *daily shall he be praised.* Every day; constantly. It will not be only at stated and distant intervals—at set seasons, and on

16 There shall be an handful of corn in the earth upon the top of the mountains; the fruit thereof shall shake like Lebanon:

special occasions,—but those who love him will do it every day. It is not necessary to say that this accords with the truth in reference to those who are the friends and followers of the Messiah—the Lord Jesus. Their lives are lives of praise and gratitude. From their dwellings daily praise ascends to him; from their hearts praise is constant;—praise uttered in the closet and in the family; praise breathed forth from the heart, whether on the farm, in the workshop, on a journey, or in the busy marts of commerce. The time will come when this shall be universal; when he who can take in at a glance the condition of the world, will see it to be a world of praise; when he who looks on all hearts at the same moment will see a world full of thankfulness.

16. *There shall be an handful of corn.* Of *grain,*—for so the word means in the Scriptures. The *general* idea in this verse is plain. It is, that, in the time of the Messiah, there would be an ample supply of the fruits of the earth; or that his reign would tend to the promotion of prosperity, industry, abundance. It would be as if fields of grain waved everywhere, even on the tops of mountains, or as if the hills were cultivated to the very summit, so that the whole land would be covered over with waving, smiling harvests. There is a difference of opinion, however, and consequently of interpretation, as to the meaning of the word rendered *handful.* This word—פִּסָּה, *pissah*—occurs nowhere else, and it is impossible, therefore, to determine its exact meaning. By some it is rendered *handful;* by others, *abundance.* The former interpretation is adopted by Prof. Alexander, and is found in the older interpreters generally; the latter is the opinion of Gesenius, De Wette, and most modern expositors. It is also the interpretation in the Syriac. The Vulgate and the LXX. render it *strength*—meaning something *firm* or *secure,*—*firmamentum,* στήριγμα. According to the explanation which regards the word as meaning *handful,* the idea is, that there would be a great contrast between the small beginnings of the Messiah's reign and its ultimate triumph—as if a mere handful of grain were sown on the top of a mountain,—on a place little likely to produce anything—a place usually barren and unproductive, — which would grow into an abundant harvest, so that it would wave everywhere like the cedar trees of Lebanon. According to the other interpretation, the idea is simply that there would be an *abundance* in the land. The whole land would be cultivated, even to the tops of the hills, and the evidences of plenty would be seen everywhere. It is impossible to determine which of these is the correct idea; but both agree in that which is essential — that the reign of the Messiah would be one of peace and plenty. The former interpretation is the most poetic, and the most beautiful. It accords, also, with other representations — as in the parable of the grain of mustard-seed, and the parable of the leaven; and it accords, also, with the fact that the beginning of the Gospel was small in comparison with what would be the ultimate result. This would seem to render that interpretation the most probable. ¶ *In the earth.* In the land; the land of Canaan; the place where the kingdom of the Messiah would be set up. ¶ *Upon the top of the mountains.* In places *like* the tops of mountains. The mountains and hills were seldom cultivated to the tops. Yet here the idea is, that the state of things under the Messiah would be *as if* a handful of grain were sown in the place most unlikely to produce a harvest, or which no one thought of cultivating. No one needs to be told how well this would represent the cold and barren human heart in

and [n] *they* of the city shall flourish like grass of the earth.
17 His name shall [1] endure for
ever; his name shall be [2] continued as long as the sun; and
men shall be blessed [o] in him:
all nations shall call him blessed.
18 Blessed *be* the LORD God,
the God of Israel, who only
[p] doeth wondrous things.
19 And blessed [q] *be* his glorious
name for ever: and let the whole

n Hos. xiv. 5—7. [1] *be.*
[2] *as a son to continue his father's name for ever.*
o Eph. i. 3. *p* Ex. xv. 11.
q Rev. v. 13.

general; or the state of the Jewish world in respect to true religion, at the time when the Saviour appeared. ¶ *The fruit thereof.* That which would spring up from the mere handful of grain thus sown. ¶ *Shall shake like Lebanon.* Like the cedar-trees of Lebanon. The harvest will wave as those tall and stately trees do. This is an image designed to show that the growth would be strong and abundant, far beyond what could have been anticipated from the small quantity of the seed sown, and the barrenness of the soil. The word rendered *shake* means more than is implied in our word *shake* or *wave.* It conveys also the idea of a rushing sound, such as that which whistles among cedar or pine trees. "The origin of the Hebrew verb," says Gesenius, "and its primary idea lies in the *noise* and *crashing* which is made by concussion." Hence it is used to denote the *rustling* motion of grain waving in the wind, and the sound of the wind whistling through trees when they are agitated by it. ¶ *And* they *of the city.* Most interpreters suppose that this refers to Jerusalem, as the centre of the Messiah's kingdom. It seems more probable, however, that it is not designed to refer to Jerusalem, or to any particular city, but to stand in contrast with the top of the mountain. Cities and hills would alike flourish; there would be prosperity everywhere—in barren and unpopulated wastes, and in places where men had been congregated together. The *figure* is changed, as is not uncommon, but the *idea* is retained. The indications of prosperity would be apparent everywhere. ¶ *Shall flourish like grass of the earth.* As grass springs out of the ground, producing the idea of beauty and plenty. See Notes on Isa. xliv. 3, 4.

17. *His name shall endure for ever.* Marg., as in Heb., *Shall be for ever;* that is, *He* shall endure for ever. ¶ *His name shall be continued as long as the sun.* As long as that continues to shine—an expression designed to express perpetuity. See Notes on ver. 5. The margin here is, *shall be as a son to continue his father's name for ever.* The Hebrew word—נוּן, *nun*—means *to sprout, to put forth;* and hence, to *flourish.* The idea is that of a tree which continues always to sprout, or put forth leaves, branches, blossoms;—or, which never dies. ¶ *And* men *shall be blessed in him.* See Gen. xii. 3; xxii. 18. He will be a source of blessing to them, in the pardon of sin; in happiness; in peace; in salvation. ¶ *All nations shall call him blessed.* Shall praise him; shall speak of him as the source of their highest comforts, joys, and hopes. See Luke xix. 38; Matt. xxi. 9; xxiii. 39. The time will come when all the nations of the earth will honour and praise him.

18. *Blessed* be *the* LORD *God, the God of Israel.* The God who rules over Israel; the God who is worshipped by the Hebrew people, and who is recognised as their God. They adore him as the true God; and he *is* their God, their Protector, their Friend. ¶ *Who only doeth wondrous things.* Things that can properly be regarded as *wonders;* things fitted to excite admiration by their vastness and power. Comp. Ex. xv. 11.

19. *And blessed* be *his glorious name for ever.* The name by which

earth be filled [r] *with* his glory. Amen, and amen.

20 The prayers of David the son of Jesse are ended.

r Num. xiv. 21; Hab. ii. 14.

he is known,—referring perhaps particularly to his name *Jehovah.* Still the prayer would be, that all the names by which he is known, all by which he has revealed himself, might be regarded with veneration always and everywhere. ¶ *And let the whole earth be filled* with *his glory.* With the knowledge of himself; with the manifestations of his presence; with the influences of his religion. Comp. Num. xiv. 21. This prayer was peculiarly appropriate at the close of a psalm designed to celebrate the glorious reign of the Messiah. Under that reign the earth will be, in fact, filled with the glory of God; the world will be a world of glory. Assuredly all who love God, and who love mankind, all who desire that God may be honoured, and that the world may be blessed and happy, will unite in this fervent prayer, and re-echo the hearty "Amen and amen" of the psalmist. ¶ *Amen, and amen.* So be it. Let this occur. Let this time come. The expression is doubled to denote intensity of feeling. It is the going out of a heart full of desire that this might be so.

20. *The prayers of David the son of Jesse are ended.* This is not found in the Syriac. The following is added in that version at the close of the psalm:—"The end of the Second Book." In regard to this twentieth verse, it is quite clear that it is no part of the psalm; and it is every way probable that it was not placed here by the author of the psalm, and also that it has no special and exclusive reference to *this* psalm, for the psalm could in no special sense be called "a prayer of David." The words bear all the marks of having been placed at the close of a collection of psalms, or a division of the Book of Psalms, to which might be given as an appropriate designation, the title "The Prayers of David, the son of Jesse;" meaning that that book, or that division of the book, was made up of the compositions of David, and might be thus distinguished from other portions of the general collection. This would not imply that in this part of the collection there were literally no other psalms than those which had been composed by David, or that none of the psalms of David might be found in other parts of the general collection, but that this division was more entirely made up of his psalms, and that the name might therefore be given to this as *his collection.* It may be fairly inferred from this, that there *was* such a collection, or that there *were,* in the Book of Psalms, divisions which were early recognised. See the General Introduction. Bishop Horsley supposes, however, that this declaration, "The prayers of David the son of Jesse are ended," pertains to this psalm alone, as if David had nothing more to pray for or to wish than what was expressed in these glowing representations of the kingdom of the Messiah, and of the happy times which would be enjoyed under his rule.

PSALM LXXIII.

This psalm (with the ten succeeding psalms, together with Psalm l.,—twelve in all) is ascribed to Asaph, unless the reading in the margin, "*for* Asaph" be correct. The most natural sense of the expression in the title, however, is that they are psalms *of* Asaph; that is, that they were composed by him. See Introd. to Ps. l. It has been maintained that a part of these psalms, particularly Ps. lxxiv., lxxix., and lxxx., could not be his, for it is alleged that they refer to events long subsequent to his age. There seems to be no objection, however, to the supposition that *this* psalm was composed by him, as it has no particular reference to any particular age or country, but is made up of general reflections, which might have arisen in any age, or in any land.

Respecting the particular occasion on which the psalm was composed we have no information. It was in view of the prosperity of the wicked, and suggests the reflections which troubled the writer in regard to the Divine administration in view of that prosperity. The thoughts which are recorded are such as might occur to any mind, and do often occur, arising from the fact that wicked men are so successful and so happy in the world, living in prosperity, and dying apparently without pain or alarm, while so many of the good are poor and sorrowful in their lives, and their whole course on earth is one of so much grief and sorrow. Such thoughts as are expressed in this psalm *will* often cross the mind, and the question *will* arise why God permits this; whether there is any advantage in being good; and whether that God who sees this, and permits this, *can* be just and benevolent, —the friend of the righteous, and the enemy of the wicked,—or whether there *is* any God. The psalm describes these feelings, and shows how the difficulties were solved in the case of its author, suggesting as the solution, that this is not the world of retribution; that there is a future state where exact justice will be done, and where all the inequalities of the present system will be adjusted. *In* that future world—*in eternity*—there will be ample time and room to make such an adjustment; to do exact justice to all. The *idea* in the psalm is, that these things cannot be explained except on the supposition that there is a future state; and the psalm, therefore, is an argument *for* a future state of existence. The affairs of earth cannot be explained, and the character of God cannot be vindicated, except on that supposition.

The psalm in its general structure and design bears a strong resemblance to Ps. xxxvii., though there is no evidence that the author of this psalm had that before him, or in his eye. The *expressions* are not the same, nor does one appear to have been copied from the other. They contain independent reflections on the same general subject, suggesting the same perplexities, and finding a solution of the difficulties in the same way,—in looking to the future, to a just retribution in the end. In this case — Ps. lxxiii. — the psalmist says that he learned the solution of the problem by the instructions of the sanctuary (ver. 17); in the former case — Ps. xxxvii.,—the solution was found by an observation of the comparative effects of a wicked and a religious life, Ps. xxxvii. 10, 11, 20, 23-25, 35-37. The idea in both is, that the ultimate effect of goodness or piety must be happiness; the ultimate effect of sin must be misery. The author of one of these psalms finds this solution in the present life; the author of the other, in the life to come. In either case, the character of God is vindicated, and the troubled feelings of the soul calmed down.

The general *idea* in the psalm is stated in the first verse, that "God is good to Israel, to such as are of a clean heart;" that is, that he is the true friend of the righteous, or that his administration is in favour of virtue, or in favour of those who are righteous. The psalm states the process by which the writer came to this conclusion; the mental conflicts through which he passed before this result was reached; his own agitation of mind, and the difficulties he saw in the subject, in view of the facts which exist in this world. His mind had been greatly perplexed when he had meditated on the subject, and the mental conflict had gone so far with him as almost to lead him to abandon the idea that there was a God, or that there was anything in religion, and to conclude that it was all a delusion.

The psalm, therefore, consists of the following parts:—

I. The statement of the general proposition that the Divine administration *is* favourable to virtue, or that there *is* a God who presides in the affairs of men, ver. 1.

II. The facts which the psalmist had observed, out of which his doubts had sprung, or which had given him so much perplexity and trouble, vers. 2-14. Those facts were, that the wicked seemed to be prosperous and happy; that they lived without trouble, and died without any tokens of the Divine disapproval; that their eyes stood out with fatness, and that they had more than heart could desire; that they set their mouths against the heavens, and were proud blasphemers, while God took no notice of them, or manifested no disapprobation; that they contemned God, and yet were prospered in the world, while, on the other hand, he himself—the psalmist—was chastened, and afflicted, and plagued,—suggesting the idea that there could be no advantage in piety, and that all his anxiety to have pure hands and a pure heart was in vain.

III. The statement of his purpose to conceal his feelings on the subject, lest

PSALM LXXIII.

A Psalm [1] of Asaph.

TRULY [2] God *is* good to Israel, *even* to such as are [3] of a clean heart.

2 But as for me, my feet were almost gone: my steps had well nigh slipped.

[1] Or, *for*. [2] Or, *Yet*. [3] *clean of heart*.

he should do injury to those who had *not* these troublesome thoughts, but who endeavoured in humility to serve God, ver. 15. He had thoughts which he did not consider it proper to make known to others, — thoughts which would only pain them, or unsettle their faith in God, without doing any good.

IV. The means by which his mind had been made calm on the subject, and his difficulties solved, vers. 17–20. He had gone to the sanctuary; he had looked at the end of these things; he had seen what was to be the result; he had been instructed to look forward to a time when all these inequalities would be adjusted, and when, in the punishment of the wicked, it would be seen that there is a God, and that he is just.

V. He now condemns his own former folly, and sees that his conduct had been wholly irrational; that his views had been short-sighted; that he had been stupid, like a beast, in the low conceptions which he had taken of God, vers. 21, 22.

VI. In view of all, the psalmist now commits himself to God. He sees that there is reason to trust in him. He resolves to murmur or complain no more. He finds his portion in God. He believes that God will guide him by his counsel, and ultimately receive him to glory. He says that there is none in heaven or on earth that he desires beside him. He is cheered with the thought that when his strength and heart should fail, God would be the strength of his heart, and his portion for ever. He would, therefore, henceforth, confide in the Lord God, vers. 23–28.

1. *Truly God* is *good to Israel.* That is, to his people; to the righteous; to those who serve him. That is, God is the *real* friend of the righteous. He has not forgotten them. He does not abandon them. He is not indifferent to them. He is *not* the friend of wicked men; and the administration of his government is *not* in favour of wickedness. After all that *seems* to indicate this, after all that troubles the mind in regard to his dealings, it is a truth that God *is* the friend of righteousness, and not of wickedness, and that there *is* advantage in his service. To see the force of what is said here by the psalmist we must realize that the train of thought in the psalm *had* passed through his mind, and that his perplexities had been relieved in the manner specified in the psalm. The margin here is "*yet;*"—*yet God is good to Israel.* This word *yet* would, in this place, be a happy translation. The psalmist then would be represented as having been engaged in meditating on the subject and in looking at all its perplexities, and then he says, "*Yet* God *is* good; notwithstanding all the difficulties in the case, it is nevertheless true that he *is* the friend of his people—the friend of righteousness." ¶ Even *to such as are of a clean heart.* Marg., as in Heb., *clean of heart.* See ver. 13. The reference is to those who are truly righteous, for all true righteousness has its seat in the heart. See Ps. li. 10.

2. *But as for me.* Literally, *And I.* The meaning is, "And I, who so confidently now trust in God, and believe that he is good, was formerly in a far different state of mind; I was so hesitating, so troubled, and so doubtful, that I had almost entirely lost confidence in him as a wise and just moral governor." ¶ *My feet were almost gone.* I was just ready to fall. Of course, this refers to his state of mind. In regard to his faith or confidence in God, he was like a man standing in a slippery place, and scarcely able to remain upright. ¶ *My steps had well nigh slipped.* The expression rendered *well nigh* means

3 For I was envious [s] at the foolish, *when* I saw the prosperity of the wicked.

4 For *there are* no bands in their death; but their strength *is* [1] firm.

5 They *are* not in [2] trouble *as other* men; neither are they plagued [3] like *other* men.

6 Therefore pride compasseth them about as a chain; violence covereth them *as* a garment.[t]

s Ps. xxxvii. 1; James iv. 5. [1] *fat.* [2] *the trouble of.* [3] *with.* *t* Ps. cix. 18.

like nothing, or *as nothing;* that is, in reference to firmness it was as if there was *nothing* left. There was nothing which would keep him from slipping. The word rendered *slipped* means *poured out.* That is, in his going he was like water poured out, instead of being like something solid and firm. The idea is, that his faith seemed to be all gone. He was like a falling man; a man who had no strength to walk.

3. *For I was envious at the foolish.* The word *foolish* here refers to sinners. It may either refer to them *as* foolish, or as proud, insolent, vain,—for so the word is elsewhere used. See Ps. xiv. 1. ¶ When *I saw the prosperity of the wicked.* More literally, "the *peace* of the wicked." The reference is not so much to their *prosperity* in general as to their *peace;* their conscious safety; their freedom from trouble; and especially their calmness, and their freedom from suffering, in death. From all this he was led for the moment to doubt whether there was any advantage in religion; whether God was just; and whether he befriended the righteous any more than he did the wicked.

4. *For* there are *no bands in their death.* The word rendered *bands* here means properly *cords tightly drawn,* Isa. lviii. 6; then, pains, pangs, torments—*as if* one were twisted or tortured with pain, as a cord is closely twisted. The word occurs only in Isa. lviii. 6, and in this place. The fact which is here referred to by the psalmist, and which gave him so much uneasiness, was that which so often occurs, that when the wicked die, they do not seem to suffer in proportion to their wickedness; or there seem to be no especial marks of the Divine displeasure as they are about to leave the world. They have lived in prosperity, and they die in peace. There is no uncommon agony in death; there is no special alarm about the future world. They have enjoyed this world, and a sinful life seems now to be followed by a peaceful death. They do not even suffer as much in death as good men often do;—what then is the advantage of piety? And how can we believe that God is just; or that he is the friend of the righteous; or even that there *is* a God? Of the *fact* here adverted to by the psalmist, that the wicked do thus live and die, there can be no doubt, and that fact has given perplexity to good men in all ages of the world. ¶ *But their strength* is *firm.* Marg., as in Heb., *fat.* That is, They are not emaciated and weakened by disease, but they go down to death apparently from good health, and without wasting disease. See Notes on Job xxi. 23–26.

5. *They* are *not in trouble* as other *men.* Marg., *In the trouble of other men.* Literally, "In the labour of man they are not;" that is, they are exempt from the common burdens and troubles of humanity, or those which pertain to man as man. There seems to be some special interposition in their favour to save them from the common calamities which come upon the race. ¶ *Neither are they plagued like* other *men.* Marg., *with.* Literally, "And with mankind they are not afflicted," or smitten. The calamities which come so thickly and heavily on the race do not seem to come upon them. They are favoured, prospered, happy, while others are afflicted.

6. *Therefore pride compasseth them about as a chain.* Therefore they are

7 Their eyes stand out with
fatness: they [1] have more than
heart could wish.
8 They are corrupt, and speak
wickedly *concerning* oppression:
they speak [u] loftily.
9 They set their mouth against
the heavens; and their tongue
walketh through the earth.
10 Therefore his people return

[1] *pass the thoughts of the heart.*

[u] Jude, ver. 16.

proud, haughty, imperious. They put on the ornaments and trappings of pride; their clothing and their adorning all are indicative of a proud heart. They seem to imagine that they are better than others, and that they are treated in this manner *because* they are better than others. In the original it is a single word which is rendered "compasseth about as a chain." The word means *to adorn with a necklace or collar;* and the idea is, that pride surrounds them as with a neck-chain, or a collar for the neck. They wear it as an ornament. They make it conspicuous. It is apparent on a haughty neck,—in an erect and stiff demeanour. Comp. Notes on Isa. iii. 16: "The daughters of Zion walk with stretched forth necks." ¶ *Violence covereth them as a garment.* Injustice or cruelty seems to be their very clothing. It is manifest in their whole gait and demeanour that they are men of haughtiness and pride; that they are destitute of tenderness, sympathy, sensibility.

7. *Their eyes stand out with fatness.* As the fruit of their high living. They are not weakened and emaciated by toil and want, as other men often are. Comp. Notes on Ps. xvii. 10. ¶ *They have more than heart could wish.* Marg., *they pass the thoughts of the heart.* Literally, "the imaginations [or thoughts] of the heart pass;" pass along; pass forth. The meaning seems to be, not that they have more than heart could desire, as in our translation,—for that would not probably be true; nor, that the thoughts of the heart are *disclosed,* as Prof. Alexander supposes,—for that idea does not seem to be in the language; but that their thoughts, their plans, their purposes, *pass freely along* without any obstruction; their wishes are all gratified; their purposes are accomplished; they have all that they wish. Whatever comes into the mind as an object of desire is obtained without hindrance or trouble. They seem only to *wish* for a thing, or to *think* of a thing, and they have it.

8. *They are corrupt.* Literally, *they mock.* The word rendered "they are corrupt" never has this signification. It is the very word—מוּק, *muk*—from which our word *mock* is derived, and means the same thing. The idea is that they deride religion, or *mock* at all that pertains to God, and to the retributions of the future world. ¶ *And speak wickedly* concerning *oppression,* etc. Literally, "they speak in wickedness; oppression they speak from on high." That is, they use arrogant language; they speak in a proud manner, as if they were *above* others; they use harsh and violent language, not regarding the feelings or the rights of others.

9. *They set their mouth against the heavens.* Comp. Rev. xiii. 6. Literally, "They set their mouth *in* heaven," or in the heavens. The idea is, they speak as if they were *in* the heavens; as if they were clothed with all authority; as if they were superior beings, and had a right to command the universe. ¶ *And their tongue walketh through the earth.* It has no limit; it is *as if* it roamed over all the earth. They speak without any restraint of law, or propriety; without any regard to the command of God, or to what is due to men. In other words, they seem to set themselves above all law, and to act as if there were no one in heaven or in earth to control them.

10. *Therefore his people.* Those

hither: and waters of a full *cup* are wrung out to them.

11 And they say, How [v] doth God know? and is there knowledge in the Most High?

12 Behold, these *are* the un-

v Job xxii. 13; Ps. xciv. 7.

that truly love God; the pious in the earth. ¶ *Return hither.* Return to this subject. In their musings—their meditations on Divine things—they come back to this inquiry. The subject occupies their minds, and they recur to it as a subject which perplexes them; as a thing that is incomprehensible. They think it over again and again, and are more and more perplexed and embarrassed. The difficulties which these facts suggest about God and his government are such that they cannot solve them. ¶ *And waters of a full* cup *are wrung out to them.* Literally, *waters of fulness;* or, full waters. The Chaldee renders this, *Many tears flow from them.* The LXX., and the Latin Vulgate, "And full days shall be found by them." The word rendered *are wrung out*—from מָצָה, *matzah*—means properly to *suck;* then, to suck out; to drink greedily. See Isa. li. 17. It is applied to one who drinks greedily of an intoxicating cup; and then, to one who drinks a cup of poison to the dregs. Ps. lxxv. 8. The meaning here is, that the facts in the case, and the questions which arose in regard to those facts, and which so perplexed them, were like a bitter cup; a cup of poison, or an intoxicating cup which overpowered their faculties,—and that they, in their perplexities, *exhausted* the cup. They drank it all, even to the dregs. They did not merely *taste it;* but they *drank* it. It was a subject *full* of perplexity; a subject that *wholly* overpowered all their faculties, and *exhausted* all their powers.

11. *And they say.* His people say. The connexion demands this interpretation. The meaning is, that his people, as they return again and again to this subject (ver. 10), are constrained to put this question. They are compelled by these facts to start such painful inquiries about God; and distressing as the inquiries are, and as are the doubts which they involve, these thoughts *will* pass through their mind, even though to avoid giving needless pain to those who have no such perplexities and difficulties they keep these thoughts to themselves, ver. 15. ¶ *How doth God know?* That is, How can these facts be reconciled with God's omniscience? How *can* it be that he sees all this, and yet suffers it to occur, or that he does not interpose to prevent it? Is it not a fair inference from these facts that God does *not* see them, and that he is *not* an Omniscient Being? Can it be explained, can it be believed, that God sees all this, and that he calmly looks on, and does nothing to prevent it? If he sees it, why does he not interpose and put an end to it? These perplexities were not confined to the psalmist. They are such as have been felt by good men in all ages; and no one yet has been able to furnish a solution of them that is wholly free from difficulty. ¶ *And is there knowledge in the Most High? Can* there be in God a knowledge of these facts? Are we not driven to the conclusion that he *must* be ignorant of them? for, if he knew them, would he not interpose to prevent them? How *can* it be consistent with the idea that he *knows* them, and *sees* them, that he does *not* interpose, and that he suffers these things to take place without any attempt to check such evils? Who, even now, can answer these questions?

12. *Behold, these* are *the ungodly, who prosper in the world.* This is also to be understood as the language of the good man perplexed and embarrassed by the fact that the wicked are prosperous and happy. The meaning is, "Lo, these are wicked men—men of undoubted depravity;

godly, who prosper in the world; they increase *in* riches.

13 Verily [w] I have cleansed my heart *in* vain, and washed my hands in innocency.

14 For all the day long have I been plagued, and [1] chastened every morning.

15 If I say, I will speak thus;

w Job ix. 27—31. [1] *my chastisement* was.

---

they are men who live regardless of God; and yet they are peaceful, tranquil, happy, prospered." This was one of the facts which so much embarrassed the psalmist. If there had been any doubt about the *character* of those men, the case would have been different. But there was none. They were men whose character for wickedness was well known, and yet they were permitted to live in peace and prosperity, *as if* they were the favourites of heaven. The literal meaning of the words rendered "who prosper in the world" is, "tranquil [or secure] for the age;" that is, for ever, or constantly. They know no changes; they see no reverses; they are the same through life. They are always tranquil, calm, happy, successful. ¶ *They increase* in *riches*. Literally, "They become great in substance." They make constant accumulations in wealth, until they become great.

13. *Verily I have cleansed my heart* in *vain*. That is, There is no advantage in all my efforts to become pure and holy. It does not assist me in obtaining the favour of God; and it would be just as well to live a sinful life,—to indulge in the pleasures of sense,—to make the world my portion. Nothing is to be gained by all my painful efforts at self-discipline; by all my endeavours to become righteous. It would have been as well for me—or better—if I had lived a life of sin like other men. The righteous obtain from God fewer blessings than the wicked; they have less happiness and less prosperity in this world; they are subjected to more trouble and sorrow;—and to all else there must be added the struggles, the conflict, the warfare, the painful effort *to be* pure, and to lead a holy life, all of which is now seen to be of no advantage whatever. Such thoughts as these were not confined to the psalmist. They are thoughts which *will* start up in the mind, and which it is not easy to calm down. ¶ *And washed my hands in innocency*. That is, It has been of no use that I have washed my hands in innocency. The word *innocency* here means *purity*. He had washed his hands in that which was pure; as, pure water. To wash the hands is emblematic of innocence or purity. See Notes on Ps. xxvi. 6.

14. *For all the day long*. Continually. All my life. ¶ *Have I been plagued*. Smitten; afflicted; troubled. My life has been a life of trial. I have not known prosperity. ¶ *And chastened every morning*. Marg., as in Heb., *My chastisement was*. That is, my sufferings—my trials—have been repeated with every returning morning. Each new day has brought some new form of affliction, designed to rebuke and punish me. I never have found exemption from trial even for a single day. So different is my lot from the lot of wicked men, who know nothing of this, and who are always prospered and happy. See Notes on Job vii. 18.

15. *If I say, I will speak thus*. If I should resolve to give expression to my feelings. If I should utter all that is passing in my mind and my heart. It is implied here that he had *not* given utterance to these thoughts, but had confined them to his own bosom. He knew how they might be regarded by others; how others might be led to feel as if no confidence was to be placed in God; how this might suggest thoughts to them which would not otherwise occur to them, and which would only tend to fill their minds with distress; how such thoughts might unsettle the foundations of their faith, their peace, their hope,

behold, I should offend *against* the generation of thy children.
16 When I thought to know this, it *was* [1] too painful for me;
17 Until I went into the sanc-

[1] *labour in mine eyes.*

and their joy. ¶ *I should offend* against *the generation of thy children.* The word rendered "I should offend," means to treat perfidiously, or in a faithless or treacherous manner. Then it means, *to deal falsely with.* And this is the meaning here;—"I should not be *true* to them; I should not be *faithful* to their real interests; I should do that which would be equivalent to dealing with them in a false and perfidious manner." The idea is, that he *ought* not to say or do anything which would tend to lessen their confidence in God, or which would suggest to their minds grounds of distrust in God, or which would disturb their peace and hope. This was alike an act of justice and benevolence on his part. Whatever might be his own troubles and doubts, he had no *right* to fill their minds with doubts and distrust of God; and he felt that, as it was desirable that the minds of others should not be harassed as his own had been, it could not be *kind* to suggest such thoughts. This, however, should not forbid any one from mentioning such difficulties to another for the purpose of having them removed. *If* they occur to the mind, as they may to the minds of any, however sincere and pious they may be, nothing can make it improper that they should be laid before one of greater age, or longer experience, or wider opportunities of knowledge, in order that the difficulties may be solved. Nothing can make it improper for a child to have recourse thus to a parent,—or a member of a church, to a pastor. If, however, these doubts can be calmed down otherwise, it is better that they should be mentioned to no one. Some little additional strength may be given them even by dwelling on them long enough to mention them to another, and by putting them in such a form that they would be understood by another; and the true way is to go to God with them by prayer, and to spread them out before the mercy seat. Prayer, and a careful study of the word of God *may* calm them down without their being suggested to any human being. At any rate, they *should not* be suggested at all to the young, or to those with fewer advantages of education, or of less experience than we have had, on whom the only effect would be to fill their minds with doubts which they could not solve,—and with thoughts tending only to perplexity and unbelief,—such as would never have occurred to themselves.

16. *When I thought to know this.* When I endeavoured to comprehend this, or to explain it to myself. The idea is that he *thought* on the subject, or *meditated* on it with a view to be able to understand it. He did not express his opinions and feelings to others, but he dwelt on them in his own mind;—not to find additional difficulties, not to confirm himself in opposition to God, and not to find new occasions for distrusting the Divine government, but to understand exactly *how this was.* It was his object to seek and understand *the truth.* ¶ *It* was *too painful for me.* Marg., *It was labour in mine eyes.* The Hebrew word rendered *painful,* means properly labour, toil, a burden; and the idea is, that the question was a burden—was too weighty for his weak powers.

17. *Until I went into the sanctuary of God.* The word *sanctuary* we now apply to a place of public worship; and, thus understood, the passage here would mean that he learned the truth on the subject only by the statements and disclosures made there in regard to the Divine plans and dealings, and the results of human conduct. This interpretation makes good sense, and is in itself true, but it is not the idea

tuary of God; *then* understood I their end.[x]

18 Surely thou didst set them in slippery places: thou castedst them down into destruction.

19 How are they *brought* into desolation, as in a moment! they are utterly consumed with terrors.

x Ps. xxxvii. 38.

in the original. The word *sanctuary* in the Old Testament, in the singular number, is applied to the tabernacle, or the temple, or, more especially to the most holy place *in* the tabernacle or the temple; the place of the peculiar dwelling of God. Thus understood, the idea would be that he learned the solution of the mystery *there.* But these were not places of *instruction,* and it cannot be supposed that the reference is to either of them. The word in the original is in the plural number—*sanctuaries,*—things that God regarded as holy; and the meaning seems to be, that the only solution of the case was to be learned from those things which pertained to God's most holy and secret places; or in those places which were nearest to him, and where he most clearly manifested himself. The difficulty was not to be solved by any mere human reasoning—by the powers of man, away from God; it was to be learned in the presence of God himself, and in the disclosures which He made about his Divine plans and purposes. The psalmist had tried his own powers of reason, and the subject was above his reach. The only solution of the difficulty was to be obtained by a near approach to God himself. There the mystery *could* be solved, and there it *was* solved. The "end" of all this, as disclosed by God, would determine *why* it was permitted, and would remove the perplexity of the mind. ¶ Then *understood I their end.* Literally, *their after things;* that is, the things which will occur to them hereafter. That solves all the difficulty. There will be a judgment hereafter, and dark as things may now appear, it will be seen in the end, or in the result, that exact and equal justice will be done to all.

18. *Surely thou didst set them in slippery places.* Not in a solid and permanent position; not where their foothold would be secure, but as on smooth and slippery rocks, where they would be liable any moment to fall into the foaming billows. However prosperous their condition may seem to be now, yet it is a condition of uncertainty and danger, from which they must soon fall into ruin. In their prosperity there is nothing of permanence or stability; and this fact will explain the difficulty. ¶ *Thou castedst them down into destruction.* They are placed, not in a permanent condition, but in a condition from which they will be cast down to destruction. Ruin is before them; and the end will demonstrate the justice of God. Nothing can be determined from their present condition as to the question which caused so much perplexity, but in order to a proper solution we must wait to see the end. As an illustration of this, see the interesting account of the interview between Solon of Athens, and Crœsus, the rich king of Lydia, as given in Herodotus, book i., 30–33.

19. *How are they* brought *into desolation, as in a moment!* How suddenly and unexpectedly does destruction come upon them! Nothing can be argued from their apparent prosperity, for there is no ground of security in *that,* —no basis for an argument that it will continue. The *end* must be seen in order to form a correct estimate on the subject, and that end may soon come. Comp. Notes on Job xv. 20, 21. ¶ *They are utterly consumed with terrors.* Literally, "they perish; they are destroyed by terrors;" that is, by *terrible things,* or by things fitted to produce terror in the mind. The idea is not that they are destroyed by their own fears, but that things come

20 As a dream *y* when *one* awaketh; *so*, O Lord, when thou awakest, thou shalt despise their image.

21 Thus my heart was grieved, and I was pricked in my reins.

22 So foolish *was* I, and [1] ignorant; I was *as* a beast [2] before thee.

y Isa. xxix. 7, 8. [1] *I knew not.* [2] *with.*

upon them which are fitted to overwhelm the soul, and that by those things they are utterly destroyed. It is by this *result* that we are to determine in regard to the equity of the Divine administration, and not by their prosperity and their apparent safety.

20. *As a dream when* one *awaketh.* Their prosperity is like the visions of a dream; the reality is seen when one awakes. A man in a dream may imagine that he is a king; that he dwells in a palace; that he is surrounded by flatterers and courtiers; that he walks in pleasant groves, listens to the sounds of sweet music, sits down at a table loaded with the luxuries of all climes, and lies upon a bed of down. He may awake only to find that he is encompassed with poverty, or that he is on a bed of languishing, or that he is the miserable tenant of a hovel or a dungeon. The reality is when he awakes. So it is in regard to our present condition on earth. The reality is seen when the dream—the gorgeous dream—of life is over. ¶ So, *O Lord, when thou awakest.* The Hebrew expression here—בְּעִיר—*bâ-ir*—occurs in more than fifty other places in the Scriptures, and is in all these places translated *in the city.* This interpretation, however, would be quite unmeaning here, and the probability is that the expression is a form of the verb עוּר, *ur, to awake, to arouse;* and the idea is not, as in our version, that of *God's* awaking as if *he* had been asleep, but it refers to the dreamer when *he* shall awake. It is, literally, *in the awaking;* that is, when the dream is over. ¶ *Thou shalt despise their image.* The image that floated before their imaginations in the dream of life. Thou wilt pay no attention to it; there is no reality in it; it will at once vanish. In the future world, God will pay no regard to the dreams of human life, to the outward show, to the appearance; but the affairs of eternity will be regulated by what is real—by that which constitutes the character of the man. By that, and not by the vain dreams of the world, will the destiny of men be determined. We are to look at *that* in determining the question about the government of God, and not at what *appears* in the brief dream of life.

21. *Thus my heart was grieved.* Literally, and more expressively, *was soured.* The meaning is, that his heart was grieved, pained, dissatisfied. His mind was embittered, and he was rendered unhappy, by the views which he cherished about God, as doubting the wisdom and justice of his dealings with men—and about men, as being envious at their prosperity. ¶ *And I was pricked in my reins.* The reins are often in the Scriptures represented as the seat of the thoughts or affections. See Notes on Ps. vii. 9. The word rendered *pricked* means to sharpen, as a sword; and then, to pierce and penetrate as a sword does. The idea is, that these thoughts, so distressing and painful, seemed to be like a sharp sword penetrating to the seat of life.

22. *So foolish* was *I, and ignorant.* Such low and imperfect views did I take of the subject. The margin is, *I knew not.* So the Hebrew: "And I am brutish, and know not;" that is, I did not understand the case; I had no correct views in regard to it. ¶ *I was* as *a beast before thee.* Marg., as in Heb., *with thee.* That is, in thy very presence; or, I was guilty of such foolishness in the very presence of my Maker. If it had been when I was alone, or when no one saw me, the folly would not have been so aggra-

23 Nevertheless, I *am* continually with thee; thou hast holden *me* by my right hand.

24 Thou [z] shalt guide me with thy counsel, and afterward receive me *to* glory.

25 Whom have I in heaven *but thee*? and *there is* none upon earth *that* I desire beside thee.

26 My flesh and my heart faileth: *but* God *is* the [1] strength of

z Ps. xlviii. 14. [1] *rock.*

vated, and so much to be regretted, but it was when the very eye of God was upon me. Comp. Isa. i. 7; Jer. vii. 30; xviii. 10; Ps. li. 4. When he says that he was as a beast, he means that he was stupid and senseless; he had no proper understanding of the case; he did not take any just views of it.

23. *Nevertheless, I* am *continually with thee.* I am kept by thee in the land of the living; I am permitted to abide in thy presence; I am allowed to hope in thy mercy. Notwithstanding my low and unworthy views, notwithstanding my doubts about the justice of the Divine administration, notwithstanding my envy at the prosperity of the wicked, and my spirit of complaining against God, I am not driven away from God; I am not banished from his presence, or cut off from his favour. Well may we marvel when we reflect on our thoughts about God, that He has not risen in his anger, and banished us from his presence for ever and ever. ¶ *Thou hast holden* me *by my right hand.* Thou hast not left me. Thou hast stretched out thy hand to keep me. Thou hast been to me as a Protector and Friend. Thou hast not been angry at my unkind and ungrateful thoughts; thou hast not banished me eternally from thy presence.

24. *Thou shalt guide me with thy counsel.* With thy advice; with thy teaching. This implies two things: (*a*) his belief that God *would* do this, notwithstanding his folly; and (*b*) his purpose that God *should* be his guide now. He would no longer murmur or complain, but would entrust all to God, and allow himself to be led as God should be pleased to direct him. ¶ *And afterward receive me* to *glory*. After thou hast led me along the path of the present life in the way in which thou wouldst have me to go, thou wilt then receive me to thyself in heaven—to a world where all shall be clear; where I shall never have any doubts in regard to thy being, to the justice of thy dispensations, or to the principles of thy government.

25. *Whom have I in heaven* but thee? Literally, "Who is to me in the heavens?" That is, There is no one there that in my love for him can be compared with thee; no one who can do for me what thou canst do; no one who can meet and satisfy the wants of my soul as thou canst; no one who can be to me what God *is*—what a God *must be.* After all my complaining and my doubts there is no one, not even in the heavens, who can supply the place of *God,* or be to me what God is; and the warm affections of my soul, therefore, are *really* towards him. I feel my need of him; and I must and do find my supreme happiness in him. What would even heaven be to me without God? who there, even of the angels of light, could supply the place of God? ¶ *And* there is *none upon earth* that *I desire beside thee.* That is, Thou art all-sufficient; thou dost meet and satisfy the wants of my nature. All my happiness is in thee; no one on earth could be substituted in thy place, or be to me what thou art as God.

26. *My flesh and my heart faileth.* Flesh and heart here seem to refer to the whole man, body and soul; and the idea is, that his powers of body and mind failed; were spent; were exhausted. This seems to have been said in an *ideal* sense, or by anticipation. He does not mean to say that his strength then had actually failed,

my heart, and my portion [a] for ever.

27 For, lo, they that are far from thee shall perish; thou hast destroyed all them that go a whoring from thee.

28 But *it is* good for me to draw near to God: I have put my trust in the Lord GOD, that I may declare all thy works.

a Lam. iii. 24.

---

but he seems to have placed himself by imagination in the situation where his strength *would* be all gone—in sickness, in weakness, in sorrow, on the bed of death. He asks himself now what would be his strength then,—what would be the object of chief interest and love,—on what he would rely; and he answers without hesitation, and with entire confidence, that he could rely on God, and that He would be his portion for ever. Even then, when heart and flesh should fail, when all the powers of mind and body should be exhausted, the love of God would survive, and he would find strength and joy in Him. ¶ But *God* is *the strength of my heart.* Marg., as in Hebrew, *rock;*—the rock on which my heart relies; that is, my refuge, my defence. See Notes on Ps. xviii. 2. Comp. Ps. lxi. 2. ¶ *And my portion for ever.* The source of my happiness. Not wealth, then; not honour; not earthly friends; not fame,—will be my reliance and the ground of my hope; but that which I shall regard as most valuable—my supreme joy and rejoicing—will be the fact that God is my friend and portion. With all the doubts which I have had in regard to the rectitude of his government, I am sure that when I come to die, I shall cling to him as my hope, my joy, my all. My last refuge—my sufficient refuge—is God. When men come to die, they *have* no *other* refuge but God. Nothing that they can accumulate of this world's goods will meet their wants then, for God only can give strength and comfort on the bed of death. Of each and all, however vigorous they may now be, it will be true that "flesh and heart" *will* "*fail;*" of each and all it is true that when this shall occur, none but God can be the portion and the strength of the soul.

27. *For, lo, they that are far from thee shall perish.* All that are estranged from thee; all who are not thy friends. They will certainly be destroyed. For them there can be no hope. This is the fact which solved the difficulty of the psalmist in regard to the Divine dealings with men, vers. 3–7. The fact that there will be a righteous judgment, in which God will deal with men according to their deserts, made all plain. Comp. vers. 16–20. ¶ *Thou hast destroyed.* That is, Thou wilt certainly destroy. The psalmist places himself in the future, and speaks of this as if it were already done. It will be so certainly done that he could speak of it as if it were already accomplished. ¶ *All them that go a whoring from thee.* The relation of God to his people is often compared in the Scriptures with the marriage relation (comp. Ps. xlv.); and a departure from Him is compared with a want of fidelity to the marriage contract. See Matt. xii. 39; xvi. 4; Jer. iii. 8, 9; v. 7; xiii. 27; Ezek. xxiii. 37; Rev. ii. 22.

28. *But* it is *good for me to draw near to God.* That is, It is pleasant; it is profitable; it is *the chief good.* For myself, happiness is to be found in that alone; there I find what my nature pants for and desires. Others find, or attempt to find, happiness in other things; my happiness is found in God alone. This is the result to which the psalmist came after all his perplexity. With all his doubts and difficulties, his *real* desire was to be near to God; his supreme happiness was found there. ¶ *I have put my trust in the Lord* GOD. I have truly confided in him; he is my portion and the sole ground of my reliance. The

doubts which he had had were not, after all, real doubts about the claim of God to confidence. There was an underlying trust in God in the midst of all this. He had not desired to cherish such doubts; he did, on the most calm reflection, still trust in God. ¶ *That I may declare all thy works.* That I might make known thy doings towards the children of men. I have desired rightly to understand thee and thy government, that I might vindicate thy name, and assert thy claim to the love and confidence of mankind. His doubts and perplexities had not really been because he was an enemy of God, or because he *desired* to cherish doubts in regard to him, but because, when appearances were against the equity of the Divine government, he wished to see how the things which occurred *could* be explained consistently with a proper belief in the goodness and justice of God, in order that he might go and explain the matter to his fellow-men. Such perplexities and doubts, therefore, are not really inconsistent with true love for God and genuine confidence in him; and it is well when such doubts are made the means of enabling us more clearly to explain the Divine dealings,—it is well when, under all such doubts and difficulties, we can still find evidence that we truly love God.

PSALM LXXIV.

This psalm is entitled "Maschil of Asaph." On the word *Maschil*—meaning *didactic*, or adapted *to give instruction*—see Notes on the title to Psalm xxxii. On the phrase "of Asaph," see Notes on the title to Psalm lxxiii. It may mean either *for* Asaph, or *of* Asaph; that is, it may either mean that it was composed *by* him, or that it was composed *for* him, to be used by him as the leader of music in public worship. The former is the most common, and the most probable opinion. The title, however, *may* mean that the psalm was dedicated or composed for one of the descendants of this Musician, among whom the office of their ancestor Asaph was hereditary. Thus understood, it might denote simply that the psalm belonged to that class of psalms which were composed for the one who, at the time, presided over the music.

If this is the meaning, there would be no impropriety in supposing that this psalm was composed near the time of the captivity, and had reference to the destruction of the temple by the Chaldeans, to which the language seems *naturally* to refer. Yet the occasion on which it was composed is not certainly known, and cannot be ascertained *from* the psalm. All that is manifest is, that it was at a time when the land was invaded; when great ravages were committed; and when a work of desolation was perpetrated on the edifices upon Mount Zion, and particularly on the temple. The *language* could be applied either to the destruction of the temple in the time of the Babylonish invasion; or to the times of the Maccabees, and to the desolations brought upon the land by Antiochus Epiphanes; or to some former desolation before the temple was built. Rosenmüller, Venema, De Wette, and some others, suppose that the reference is to the time of the Maccabees. The reason alleged for this opinion is founded on what is said in vers. 4, 9, particularly ver. 9, where it is asserted that "there is no more any prophet;" that is, no one to instruct the people, or to declare what the result or the issue will be. It is alleged by them that at the time of the invasion by the Chaldeans there were prophets in the land, and particularly that Jeremiah was then living, who distinctly predicted what the result of it would be. But this is not a conclusive objection to the idea that the reference is to the destruction of the city and the temple by the Chaldees. The meaning of verse 9 may be that there was no Divine teacher who could *save* the people, or who could *prevent* those desolations; the matter had gone so far that all Divine interference and protection appeared to be withdrawn, and the nation seemed to be abandoned to its fate. Still there can now be no certainty as to the time or the occasion when the psalm was composed; though the most *probable* reference of the psalm is to the destruction of Jerusalem by the Babylonians.

The psalm consists essentially of two parts: a prayer; and the reasons why the prayer is urged, and should be answered.

I. The prayer, vers. 1-3. It is a prayer that God would remember Mount

PSALM LXXIV.

Maschil of [1] Asaph.

O GOD, why hast thou cast *us* off for ever? *why* doth thine anger smoke against the sheep of thy pasture?

2 Remember thy congregation, *which* thou hast purchased of old; the [2] rod of thine inheritance, *which* thou hast redeemed; this mount Zion, wherein thou hast dwelt.

[1] Or, A Psalm *for Asaph to give instruction.*

[2] Or, *tribe.*

Zion, now made desolate, or in ruins.

II. The reasons why the prayer is urged, vers. 4–23.

(1) The desolations which had come upon the city and upon the edifices devoted to religion, vers. 4–8.

(2) The fact that there was among the people, in those times of calamity, no prophet—no messenger of God—no one to show them how long this would continue, or to give them assurance that these desolations would cease, vers. 9–11.

(3) A reference to what God had done for his people in former times when he interposed to save them from their enemies, vers. 12–15.

(4) The fact that God rules over the earth, and has control of all things; that day and night, light and darkness, summer and winter, are all under him, and are directed and controlled *by* him, vers. 16, 17.

(5) A prayer that God would not forget his own cause; that he would remember that these reproaches were reproaches of his own name; that he would call to mind his own solemn covenant; and that he would pity and relieve the people that loved him, now poor and oppressed,—the people that desired to serve and praise him, vers. 18–23.

1. *O God, why hast thou cast* us *off for ever?* Thou *seemest* to have cast us off for ever, or finally. Comp. Notes on Ps. xliv. 9; xiii. 1. ¶ Why *doth thine anger smoke.* See Deut. xxix. 20. The presence of smoke indicates *fire,* and the language here is such as often occurs in the Scriptures, when anger or wrath is compared with fire. See Deut. xxxii. 22; Jer. xv. 14. ¶ *Against the sheep of thy pasture.* Thy people, represented as a flock. See Ps. lxxix. 13; xcv. 7. This increases the tenderness of the appeal. The wrath of God seemed to be enkindled against his own people, helpless and defenceless, who needed his care, and who might naturally look for it—as a flock needs the care of a shepherd, and as the care of the shepherd might be expected. He seemed to be angry with his people, and to have cast them off, when they had every reason to anticipate his protection.

2. *Remember thy congregation.* The word rendered *congregation* means properly an *assembly,* a *community,* and it is frequently applied to the Israelites, or the Jewish people, considered as a body or a community associated for the service of God. Ex. xii. 3; xvi. 1, 2, 9; Lev. iv. 15; Num. xxvii. 17. The word used by the Septuagint is *συναγωγή—synagogue*—but refers here to the whole Jewish people, not to a particular synagogue or congregation. ¶ Which *thou hast purchased of old.* In ancient times; in a former age. That is, Thou hast "purchased" them to thyself, or as thine own, by redeeming them from bondage, thus securing to thyself the right to them, as one does who redeems or purchases a thing. See Notes on Isa. xliii. 3. ¶ *The rod of thine inheritance.* Marg., as in Heb., *tribe.* The Hebrew word—שֵׁבֶט, *shebet*—means properly a *staff,* stick, rod; then, a shepherd's staff, a crook; then, a sceptre; and then it is used to denote a *tribe,* so called from the staff or sceptre which the chief of the tribe carried as the symbol of authority. Ex. xxviii. 21; Judges xx. 2. The word *inheritance* is frequently applied to the children of Israel considered as belonging to God, as property inherited belongs to him who owns it,—perhaps suggesting the idea that the right to them had come down, as inherited property does, from age to age. It was a right over them ac-

3 Lift up thy feet unto the
perpetual desolations; *even* all
that the enemy hath done wickedly in the sanctuary.
4 Thine *b* enemies roar in the
midst of thy congregations; they
set up their ensigns *for* signs.
5 *A man* was famous according as he had lifted up axes upon the thick trees.

b Lam. ii. 7, etc.

quired long before, in the days of the Patriarchs. ¶ Which *thou hast redeemed.* By delivering them out of Egyptian bondage. So the church is now redeemed, and, as such, it belongs to God. ¶ *This mount Zion.* Jerusalem—the seat of government, and of public worship—the capital of the nation. ¶ *Wherein thou hast dwelt.* By the visible symbol of thy presence and power.—On all these considerations the psalmist prays that God would not forget Jerusalem in the present time of desolation and trouble.

3. *Lift up thy feet.* That is, Advance, or draw near. Come and look directly and personally on the desolations which now exist in the holy city. ¶ *Unto the perpetual desolations.* Heb., "the ruins of perpetuity," or eternity; that is, such as have been long continued, and threaten to continue for ever. The ruin had not suddenly come, and it did not seem likely soon to pass away, but appeared to be entire and permanent. The destruction of the city seemed to be complete and final. ¶ Even *all* that *the enemy hath done wickedly.* That is, with wicked intent and purpose. The reference seems to be to the Chaldeans, and to the ruin which they had brought upon the temple and city. ¶ *In the sanctuary.* That is, either Jerusalem, considered as a holy place; or the temple, the place of the public worship of God.

4. *Thine enemies roar.* This refers to the shout and tumult of war. They raised up the war-cry even in the very place where the congregations had been assembled; where God had been worshipped. The word rendered *roar* properly has reference to wild beasts; and the meaning is, that their war-cry resembled the howling of beasts of prey. ¶ *In the midst of thy congregations.* Literally, *in the midst of thine assembly.* This is a different word from that which is rendered *congregation* in ver. 2. This word—מוֹעֵד, *moaid*—means a meeting together by mutual appointment, and is often applied to the meeting of God with his people at the tabernacle, which was therefore called "the tent of the congregation,"—or, more properly, "the tent of meeting,"—as the place where God *met* with his people, Ex. xxix. 10, 44; xxxiii. 7; Lev. iii. 8, 13; x. 7, 9; *et sæpe.* The meaning here is, that they roared like wild beasts in the very place which God had appointed as the place where he would meet with his people. ¶ *They set up their ensigns* for *signs.* That is, they set up *their* banners or standards, as *the* standards of the place; as that which indicated sovereignty over the place. They proclaimed thus that it was a conquered place, and they set up their own standards as denoting their title to it, or as declaring that they ruled there. It was no longer a place sacred to God; it was publicly seen to belong to a foreign power.

5. A man *was famous.* Literally, "He is known;" or, shall be known. That is, he was or shall be celebrated. ¶ *According as he had lifted up axes.* Literally, "As one raising on high axes;" *i. e.* as one lifts up his axe high in the air in order to strike an effectual stroke. ¶ *Upon the thick trees.* The clumps of trees; the trees standing thick together. That is, As he showed skill and ability in cutting these down, and laying them low. His celebrity was founded on the rapidity with which the strokes of the axe fell on the trees, and his success in laying low the pride of the forest. According to our common

6 But now they break down the carved work thereof at once with axes and hammers.

7 They have[1] cast fire into thy sanctuary; they have defiled *by casting down* the dwelling-place of thy name to the ground.

8 They said in their hearts, Let us[2] destroy them together:

[1] *sent thy sanctuary into the fire.* [2] *break.*

translation the meaning is, that *formerly* a man derived his fame from his skill and success in wielding his axe so as to lay the forest low, but that *now* his fame was to be derived from another source, viz., the skill and power with which he cut down the elaborately-carved work of the sanctuary, despoiled the columns of their ornaments, and demolished the columns themselves. But another interpretation *may* be given to this, as has been suggested by Prof. Alexander. It is, that "the ruthless enemy is known or recognized as dealing with the sanctuary no more tenderly than a woodman with the forest which he fells." The former, however, is the more natural, as well as the more common interpretation. Luther renders it, "One sees the axe glitter on high, as one cuts wood in the forest." The Vulgate, and the Septuagint, "The signs pointing to the entrance above that they did not know." What idea was attached to this rendering, it is impossible to determine.

6. *But now they break down the carved work thereof*, etc. Literally, "But now the carvings of it together [at once] with sledge and hammers they beat down." The carved work refers evidently to the ornaments of the temple. The word used here—פִּתּוּחַ, *pittuahh*—is rendered *engraving, carved work,* or *carving;* Ex. xxviii. 11, 21, 36; xxxix. 6, 14, 30; Zech. iii. 9; 2 Chron. ii. 14. It is the very word which in 1 Kings vi. 29 is applied to the ornaments around the walls of the temple—the "carved figures of cherubim, and palm trees, and open flowers,"—and there can be no doubt that the allusion here is to those ornaments. These were rudely cut down, or knocked off, with axes and hammers, as a man lays low the trees of the wood. The phrase "at once" means that they drove forward the work with all despatch. They spared none of them. They treated them all alike as an axeman does the trees of a forest when his object is to clear the land.

7. *They have cast fire into thy sanctuary.* Into the temple to destroy it. Literally, "They have cast thy sanctuary into the fire." The meaning is, that they had burned it down. This was actually done by the Chaldeans, 2 Kings xxv. 9; 2 Chron. xxxvi. 19. ¶ *They have defiled* by casting down *the dwelling-place of thy name to the ground.* The place where thy name dwelt or was recorded (Ex. xx. 24); that is, the place where God's name was known, or where he was worshipped. The literal meaning is, "To the earth they have defiled the dwelling of thy name." The idea is, that they had defiled or polluted the temple by throwing it to the ground; by making it a heap of ruins; by making it undistinguishable from common earth.

8. *They said in their hearts.* They purposed; they designed it. ¶ *Let us destroy them together.* Let us destroy all these buildings, temples, towers, and walls at the same time; let us make an entire destruction of them all. ¶ *They have burned up all the synagogues of God in the land.* The phrase "they have burned up" must refer to the places or edifices where assemblies for public worship were held, since it cannot be supposed that the idea is that they had burned up the assemblies of worshippers themselves. The word rendered *synagogues* is the same in the Hebrew that is used in ver. 4, and is there rendered *congregations.* It means *assemblies*, persons collected together for public worship. See

they have burned up all the synagogues of God in the land.
9 We see not our signs: *there is* no more any prophet: neither *is there* among us any that knoweth how long.

Notes on that verse. It is not used in the Bible to denote *places* for the meetings of such assemblies, nor is it elsewhere rendered *synagogues*. It is translated by the word *seasons*, Gen. i. 14; Ex. xiii. 10, *et al.*;—*set time*, Gen. xvii. 21; Ex. ix. 5, *et al.*; *time appointed*, Ex. xxiii. 15; 2 Sam. xxiv. 15, *et al.*;—*congregation*, Lev. i. 1, 3, 5; iii. 2, 8, 13, *and very often*;—*feasts*, Lev. xxiii. 2, 4, 37, *et al.*;—*solemnity*, Deut. xxxi. 10; Isa. xxxiii. 20;—and so also, set feasts, solemn feasts, appointed feasts, etc. But in no instance does it *necessarily* refer to an *edifice*, unless it is in the place before us. There is no reason, however, for doubting that, from the necessity of the case, in the course of events, there would be other places for assembling for the worship of God than the temple, and that in different cities, villages, towns, and neighbourhoods, persons would be collected together for some form of social religious service. Buildings or tents would be necessary for the accommodation of such assemblages; and this, in time, might be developed into a system, till in this way the whole arrangement for *synagogues* might have grown up in the land. The exact origin of synagogues is not indeed known. Jahn ('Biblical Archæology,' § 344) supposes that they sprang up during the Babylonish captivity, and that they had their origin in the fact that the people, when deprived of their customary religious privileges, would collect around some prophet, or other pious man, who would teach them and their children the duties of religion, exhort them to good conduct, and read to them out of the sacred books. Comp. Ezek. xiv. 1; xx. 1; Dan. vi. 11; Neh. viii. 18. There seems, however, no good reason for doubting that synagogues may have existed before the time of the captivity, and may have sprung up in the manner suggested above from the necessities of the people, probably at first without any fixed rule or law on the subject, but as convenience suggested, and that they may at last, by custom and law, have grown into the regular form which they assumed as a part of the national worship. Comp. Kitto's Encyc. Art. '*Synagogue*.' I see no improbability, therefore, in supposing that the word here *may* refer to such edifices at the time when this psalm was composed. These, if they existed, would naturally be destroyed by the Chaldeans, as well as the temple itself.

9. *We see not our signs.* The emblems of worship, or the national emblems or banners, which we have been accustomed to see. There are no signals or tokens of our nationality in the land. All have been removed by the invaders, and we see everywhere evidences of the presence of a foreign power. The marks of our own independency are gone. The nation is subdued and conquered. ¶ There is *no more any prophet*. No one is raised up as the special messenger of God to assure us of his favour, or to take the lead in the national troubles. In times of danger God had been accustomed to send to them some special teacher who would declare his will, direct the nation what to do, and give encouraging assurances that the national troubles would cease, and that deliverance would come. They saw no such messengers of God now. This is not inconsistent with the supposition that this psalm was written before the captivity, and in the time of the Chaldean invasion, or with the supposition that Jeremiah was then alive; for the meaning may be, not that literally there was *no* prophet in the land, but that there was no one who had come from God as a special messenger of comfort and deliverance. Ruin had come upon them, and there were no indications

10 O God, how long shall the adversary reproach? shall the enemy blaspheme thy name for ever?

11 Why withdrawest thou thy hand, even thy right hand? pluck *it* out of thy bosom.

12 For God *is* my King [c] of old, working salvation in the midst of the earth.

13 Thou [d] didst [1] divide the sea by thy strength: thou brakest [e] the heads of the [2] dragons in the waters.

c Ps. xliv. 4. d Ex. xiv. 21. 1 *break.* e Isa. li. 9, 10; Ez. xxix. 3. 2 Or, *whales.*

of Divine interposition in their behalf. ¶ *Neither* is there *among us any that knoweth how long.* How long these calamities are to continue. No one can tell when they are to end. The prophetic office seemed to have ceased among them. It was renewed, however, after the captivity, in the case of Daniel, Ezra, Nehemiah, Haggai, and Malachi.

10. *O God, how long shall the adversary reproach?* etc. How long shall this state of things be allowed to continue? Is there to be no end to it? Are these desolations never to be repaired,—these ruins never to be rebuilt? It *seemed* so; and hence this earnest appeal. So to us it often appears as if our trials were never to come to an end. One calamity succeeds another; and there comes no relief. Yet there *is* relief. Deliverance *may* come, and soon come, in the present life;—or if not in the present life, yet to all those who are the children of God it *will* soon come by their removal to a world where trial will be for ever unknown.

11. *Why withdrawest thou thy hand, even thy right hand?* Why dost thou not stretch forth thy hand for our deliverance? The hand, especially the right hand, is the instrument by which we wield a sword, or strike a blow; and the expression here is equivalent to asking why God did not interfere and save them. ¶ *Pluck* it *out of thy bosom.* As if God had hidden his hand beneath the folds of his garment, or had wrapped his robe tightly around him. It *seemed* as if he had done this, as if he looked calmly on, and saw the temple fired, the synagogues burned up, the land laid waste, and the people slaughtered, without an attempt to interpose. How often are we constrained to use similar language,—to ask a similar question,—when iniquity abounds, when crime prevails, when sinners are perishing, when the church mourns,—for God *seems* to have withdrawn his hand, and to be looking on with unconcern! No one can tell *why* this is so; and, without irreverence, or a spirit of murmuring, but deeply affected with the mystery of the fact, we *may* ask "Why" this is so.

12. *For God* is *my King of old.* That is, the king, or ruler of his people. The people had acknowledged him as their king and ruler, and he had showed himself to be such. This is given as a reason why he should now interpose in their behalf. It is an argument, proper always to be urged, drawn from the faithfulness and unchangeableness of God. ¶ *Working salvation in the midst of the earth.* Salvation for his people. The reference here particularly is to what he had done for his people in delivering them from bondage in Egypt, and conducting them to the promised land, as is stated in the following verses.

13. *Thou didst divide the sea by thy strength.* Marg., as in Heb., *break.* That is, he had by his power *broken up* the strength of the sea so that it offered no resistance to their passing through it. The allusion is evidently to the passage through the Red Sea, Ex. xiv. 21. ¶ *Thou brakest the heads of the dragons.* Marg., *whales.* On the meaning of the word used here—*Tannin*—see Notes on Isa. xiii. 22; Job xxx. 29. It refers here, undoubtedly, to croco-

14 Thou brakest the heads of leviathan in pieces, *and* gavest him *to be* meat to the people inhabiting the wilderness.
15 Thou didst cleave [f] the fountain and the flood: thou driedst up [1] mighty rivers.
16 The day [g] *is* thine, the night also *is* thine: thou hast prepared the light [h] and the sun.
17 Thou hast set all the bor-

f Jos. iii. 13, etc.
1 *rivers of strength.*
g Ps. lxv. 8. h Ps. cxxxvi. 7—9.

diles or sea-monsters. The language here is used to denote the absolute power of God as manifested over the sea when the people of Israel passed through it. It was *as if* by slaying all the mighty monsters of the deep that would have resisted their passage, he had made their transit entirely safe. ¶ *In the waters.* That reside in the waters of the sea.

14. *Thou brakest the heads of leviathan in pieces.* On the meaning of the word *leviathan*, see Notes on Job xli. 1. The word is used here as descriptive of sea-monsters. ¶ And *gavest him* to be *meat.* Gavest him for *food.* ¶ *To the people inhabiting the wilderness.* That is, the sea-monsters were killed, and, being thrown on shore, were gathered for food. The "inhabitants of the wilderness" or the desert, *may* refer either to the wild and savage tribes of men that lived on the shores of the sea, and that subsisted mainly on fish, or it *may* refer to the wild animals of the desert that consumed such sea-monsters as they were cast up on the shore. There is no allusion to the Israelites considered as passing through the desert, as if *they* had fed on these sea-monsters. The essential *idea* is, that these monsters were put to death, or were so removed out of the way as to offer no obstruction to the passage of the Israelites through the sea. It was *as if* they had been killed. The image is entirely poetic, and there is no necessity for supposing that such a thing literally occurred.

15. *Thou didst cleave the fountain and the flood.* That is, the source of the streams and the streams themselves. The main allusion is probably to the Jordan, and the idea is, that God had, as it were, divided *all* the waters, or prevented any obstruction to his people from the river in any respect;—as if the waters in the very springs and fountains, and the waters in the channel of the river flowing from those springs and fountains, had been so restrained and *divided* that there was a safe passage through them. Josh. iii. 14–17. ¶ *Thou driedst up mighty rivers.* Marg., *rivers of strength.* The Hebrew—אֵיתָן, *aithan*—(comp. Deut. xxi. 4; Amos v. 24; 1 Kings viii. 2)—means rather perennial, constant, ever-flowing. The allusion is to rivers or streams that flow constantly, or that do not dry up. It was this which made the miracle so apparent. It could not be pretended that they had gone over the bed of a stream which was *accustomed* to be dry at certain seasons of the year. They passed over rivers that *never* dried up; and, therefore, it could have been only by miracle. The main allusion is undoubtedly to the passage of the Jordan.

16. *The day* is *thine, the night also* is *thine.* Thou hast universal dominion. All things are under thy control. Thou hast power, therefore, to grant what we desire of thee. ¶ *Thou hast prepared the light and the sun.* He who has made the sun—that greatest and noblest object of creation to the view of man—must have almighty power, and must be able to give what we need.

17. *Thou hast set all the borders of the earth.* Thou hast established all the boundaries of the world;—that is, the boundaries of the earth itself;—or the natural boundaries of nations and people, made by seas, mountains, rivers, and deserts. The language in regard to the first of

ders of the earth : thou hast made [l] summer and winter.

18 Remember this, *that* the enemy hath reproached, O LORD, and *that* the [i] foolish people have blasphemed thy name.

19 O deliver not the soul of thy turtle-dove unto the multitude *of the wicked*: forget not the congregation of thy [k] poor for ever.

[l] *them.* *i* Ps. xciv. 7, 8. *k* Ps. lxviii. 10.

these—the earth itself—would be derived from the prevalent mode of speaking, as if the earth were a plane, and had limits—a common mode of expression in the Scriptures, as it is in all ancient writings, and in the common language of men, even of philosophers. In regard to the latter idea, the language would imply that God had fixed, by his own power and will, all the natural boundaries of nations, or that his dominion is over all the earth. There *are* natural boundaries, or arrangements in nature, which tend to break up the one great family of man into separate nations, and which seem to have been designed for that. Comp. Acts xvii. 26. Over all these God presides, and he has his own great plans to accomplish by the arrangement. ¶ *Thou hast made summer and winter.* Literally, as in the margin, *Summer and winter, thou hast made them.* That is, he has so made the earth that these various seasons will occur. The fact that there are different seasons of the year, or that the year is divided into seasons, is to be traced to the agency of God. He has so made the world that these changes will take place. Nothing is the result of chance; all things in the arrangements of nature are by his design.

18. *Remember this*, that *the enemy hath reproached.* Has used opprobrious and abusive words in regard to thee, and to thy people. The idea is, that *religion*—the true religion—had been reproached by the foe. They had treated that religion as if it were false; they had reproached God as if he were a false God, and as if he were unable to defend his people. Comp. Isa. xxxvi. 4–10, 13–20; xxxvii. 10–13, 23. The prayer here is, that God would remember that these words of reproach were against *himself*, and that he would regard them *as such.* ¶ *And* that *the foolish people have blasphemed thy name.* Have blasphemed *thee*—the *name* often being put for the person himself. The word *foolish* here may refer to them as *wicked* as well as foolish. *Wickedness* and *folly* are so connected,—they are so commonly combined, that the word may be used to describe the enemies of God in either sense—characterising their conduct as *either* the one or the other. Comp. Notes on Ps. xiv. 1.

19. *O deliver not the soul of thy turtle-dove.* The *life* of thy turtle-dove; or, thy turtle-dove itself. The turtle-dove is a name of endearment for one beloved, in Cant. ii. 12, and is thus applied here to the people of Israel. The leading idea in such an application of the word is that of innocence, harmlessness, timidity, gentleness. The thought here is that of a people dear to God, now timid and alarmed. It is the prayer of a people beloved by God that he would not deliver them to their enemies. The prayer may be regarded as one which was *used* on the occasion referred to in the psalm; or, as a *general* prayer for the people of God, considered as exposed to ravening enemies. ¶ *Unto the multitude* of the wicked. The words *of the wicked* are not in the original. The word rendered *multitude*—חַיָּה, *hhayyah*—(comp. Notes on Ps. lxviii. 10)—is the same which in the other member of the sentence is rendered *congregation.* It may be applied to a *herd* of cattle, tame or wild; and then to a *people*—a band, a troop, a host—whether of orderly and civilized, or of wild and savage people. It seems to be used in this double sense in the verse before us; in the first member of the verse, "deliver not thy

20 Have respect unto the [l] covenant: for the dark places of the earth are full of the habitations of cruelty.

21 O let not the oppressed return ashamed: let the poor and needy praise thy name.

22 Arise, O God, plead thine

l Gen. xvii. 7, 8; Lev xxvi. 45; 2 Sam. xxiii. 5; Ps. cvi. 45; Jer. xxxiv. 13; Heb. viii. 8—13.

turtle-dove *to the multitude*—to the wild beast, or to the savage hosts; in the latter, "forget not *the congregation* of thy poor"—thy flock—thy people—considered as timid or alarmed. Save the timid and trembling flock from beasts of prey.

20. *Have respect unto the covenant.* The covenant which thou hast made with thy people, promising, on thy part, to protect them, and to be their God. Comp. Deut. iv. 13; v. 2; xxvi. 18, 19. The prayer here is, that God would remember, in the day of national calamity, the solemn promise implied in that covenant, and that he would interpose to save his people. Comp. Gen. ix. 15; Lev. xxvi. 42; Ezek. xvi. 60; Luke i. 72. This may be regarded as the language which the people *did* use when these calamities were about to come upon them. ¶ *For the dark places of the earth.* The allusion here is to the lands from whence came the armies that had invaded Judea, and that threatened desolation. They were dark regions of heathenism and idolatry. ¶ *Are full of the habitations of cruelty.* The abodes of violence, or of violent and cruel men. They had sent forth their armies from such places for purposes of conquest and rapine, and no compassion could be expected from them. Their numbers were so great, and their character was so fierce and warlike, that the people of Israel could find defence and security only in God; and they, therefore, plead with him that he would interpose in their behalf. The prayer in this passage may with propriety be used by the people of God now. It is still true that "the dark parts of the earth are full of the habitations of cruelty;" and in view of this fact, and of the utter hopelessness of the renovation of the world by any human means, or by any progress which society can make of itself, it is proper to seek God's interposition. And it is proper in such prayers to him now, as in ancient times, to make the ground of our appeal to him his own gracious covenant; his promises made to his church; his solemn assurances that this state of things shall not always continue, but that the time will arrive when the earth shall be filled with the knowledge of the Lord.

21. *O let not the oppressed return ashamed.* Ashamed by being disappointed, as if they had trusted in that which had no claims to confidence. Comp. Notes on Job vi. 20. The word rendered *oppressed*, means *trodden down, crushed, broken, afflicted.* It refers to the people as attacked by foreign armies, or as crushed by those who had gained power over them. The word *return* refers to their coming back from God—from the throne of mercy. Let them not come back from thee with no assurance of thy favour; with no evidence that their prayers have been heard; let them not come back, subject to the reproach that they had made their appeal to thee in vain. ¶ *Let the poor and needy praise thy name.* The people who are oppressed and helpless. Let them have occasion to praise thee because their prayer has been heard, and because thou dost save them.

22. *Arise, O God.* As if God were now insensible to the wrongs and sufferings of his people; as if he were inattentive and indisposed to come to their help. See Notes on Ps. iii. 7. ¶ *Plead thine own cause.* Literally, "Contend thine own contention." That is, Maintain a cause which is really thine own. Thine own honour is concerned; thine own law and au-

own cause: remember how the foolish man reproacheth thee daily.

23 Forget not the voice of thine enemies: the tumult of those that rise up against thee [1] increaseth continually.

[1] *ascendeth*, Jonah i. 2.

thority are assailed; the war is really made on *thee*. This is always the true idea in the prayers which are offered for the conversion of sinners, for the establishment of truth, and for the spread of the Gospel in the world. It is not originally the cause of the church; it is the cause of God. Everything in regard to truth, to justice, to humanity, to temperance, to liberty, to religion, is the cause of God. All the assaults made on these, are assaults made on God. ¶ *Remember how the foolish man reproacheth thee daily.* Constantly. He does not cease. The word *foolish* refers to the wicked. The idea is, that the wicked constantly reproach God—either by their language or their conduct; and this is a reason for calling on him to interpose. No better reason for asking his interposition can be given, than that such conduct *is* a real reproach to God, and reflects on his honour in the world.

23. *Forget not the voice of thine enemies.* The voice of thine enemies clamouring for the destruction of thy people. Comp. Ps. cxxxvii. 7. The prayer is, that God would bring deserved chastisement upon them for their purposes and their aims against his people. It is not necessarily a prayer for vengeance; it is a prayer for just retribution. ¶ *The tumult of those that rise up against thee.* Of those that make war on thee, and on thy people. The word *tumult* here means clamour or shout—as the shout of battle. The reference is to the movement of a host pressing on to conquest, encouraging and exciting each other, and endeavouring to intimidate their enemies by the loud clamour of the war-cry. It is a description of what had occurred among the main events referred to in the psalm, when the enemy came in to lay waste the capital, and to spread desolation throughout the land. ¶ *Increaseth continually.* Marg., as in Heb., *Ascendeth.* That is, it seems to go up; it is the swelling clamour of a great multitude of warriors intent on conquest. A cry or clamour thus seems to swell or rise on the air, and (as it were) to ascend to God. The prayer here is, that God would regard that cry, not in the sense that he would grant them the fulfilment of their wishes, but in the sense that he would recompense them as they deserved. It is in this sense that the clamours of the wicked ascend to heaven,—in this sense that God will regard them, *as if* they were a prayer for just retribution.

PSALM LXXV.

This psalm, like the two previous psalms, is ascribed to Asaph (see Introd. to Ps. lxxiii.), and there is no reason to doubt that it is correctly attributed to him. On the phrase in the title, "To the chief Musician," see Introd. to Ps. iv. On the phrase "Al-taschith," see Notes on the title to Ps. lvii. The phrase "A Psalm or Song" (in Heb., *a psalm—a song*), occurs also in the title to other psalms, as Ps. xxx., lxv., etc.

It is not possible now to determine the occasion on which this psalm was composed, as it is not indicated in the title, and there are no historical references in the psalm itself which would enable us to ascertain it. The general purpose is indicated in ver. 1, which is to ascribe praise to God for some particular manifestation of his favour. So far as can be conjectured from the psalm, there are two things which may have been referred to. (I.) The first is, that it was composed by some one—or for some one, in his name, as expressing his feelings—who was about to enter on the administration of the affairs of the nation, apparently a young prince soon to ascend the throne. See ver. 2, "When I shall receive the congregation," etc. (II.) The second is, that it would seem to have been a time

PSALM LXXV.

To the chief Musician, [1] Al-taschith. *m* A Psalm *or* Song [2] of Asaph.

UNTO thee, O God, do we give thanks, *unto thee* do we give thanks: for *that* thy name is near, thy wondrous works declare.

2 [3] When I shall receive the

[1] Or, *Destroy not.* *m* Ps. lvii., *title.*

[2] Or, *for.* [3] Or, *Shall I take a set time.*

---

of national danger; a time when there may have been other aspirants for the throne; a time when wicked and powerful men had combined for the purpose of usurping the authority, and setting aside the legitimate claimant to power, or when there seemed to have been a universal dissolution of authority, or general anarchy. See ver. 3, "The earth and all the inhabitants thereof are dissolved." Comp. vers. 4, 5. In these circumstances, in this general rebellion, in this time of resistance to lawful authority, and of combination and conspiracy against right, the speaker in the psalm expresses confidence in God as the source of all authority (ver. 6); as the "Judge" (ver. 7); as a God in whose hand is a cup of punishment which he will administer to all wicked men, ver. 8. *The psalm, therefore, expresses confidence in God in the endeavour to assert the claims of legitimate authority.*

Another, and a more common view, however, has been taken of the psalm, which is, that it refers to God as the Ruler among the nations, and as asserting that he will in due time take vengeance on those who are in rebellion against him. This is the view of De Wette, Prof. Alexander, Luther, and others. It was also the view taken by the translators of the Septuagint, and the Latin Vulgate. Comp., however, Notes on ver. 2.

The contents of the psalm are as follows:—(1) A purpose of the author of the psalm to praise God for the manifestation of his wondrous works, ver. 1. (2) His purpose when he should "receive the congregation," or should be invested with authority, to judge uprightly, or to discharge his duties with fidelity, ver. 2. (3) A statement of the existing disorder and confusion, as if the very structure of society was broken up, ver. 3. (4) Advice addressed to the authors of the prevailing disorder not to pursue their plans of evil (vers. 4–8), for two reasons:—(*a*) Promotion or success must come from God, or from his counsels, and not by chance, or by any laws of nature (vers. 6, 7); and (*b*) because God is a righteous Judge, and the wicked can expect nothing but punishment at his hand, ver. 8. (5) A purpose to praise God, in view of the fact that all the power of the wicked would be broken, but the power of the righteous would be maintained and exalted, vers. 9, 10.

1. *Unto thee, O God, do we give thanks.* We, the people; language which would be appropriate to public thanksgiving,—showing that the psalm was designed for public use. The *reasons* for this public thanksgiving are stated in the subsequent part of the psalm. ¶ *Do we give thanks.* The repetition is emphatic. The idea is, that the occasion was one for *special* thanksgiving. ¶ *For* that *thy name is near.* Literally, "and near is thy name." The word *name* is often used to designate the person himself; and the idea here is, that *God* was near; that he had manifested himself to them in some special manner, and that for this there was occasion of praise. Comp. Jer. xxiii. 23. ¶ *Thy wondrous works declare.* Or, "They declare thy wondrous works." The Septuagint renders it, "I will declare all thy wondrous works." The Latin Vulgate, "We will declare thy wonders." Luther, "We will declare thy wonders, that thy name is so near." Prof. Alexander, "They recount thy wonders." The meaning seems to be, "They," that is, the people, "declare thy wondrous works." Thy marvellous doings constitute the foundation for praise—for the praise now offered.

2. *When I shall receive the congregation.* The marginal rendering is, *Take a set time.* The phrase is thus rendered in most of the versions. So the Septuagint, "When I take the time"—ὅταν λάβω καιρὸν. So the

congregation, I will judge [n] uprightly.

3 The earth and all the inhabitants thereof are dissolved: I bear up the pillars of it. Selah.
4 I said unto the fools, Deal

n 2 Sam. xxiii. 3, 4.

Vulgate, "When I accept the time." So Luther, "When in its own time." So De Wette, "When I take the time." According to this interpretation, this is the language of God, as if implying that, although "the earth" was then "dissolved," or although disorders were allowed to exist, yet he would take a set time, or take the appointed time for judgment, and would pronounce a sentence on the conduct of men, and deal with them in a righteous manner, punishing the rebellious, and vindicating his own cause. The proper interpretation of the passage turns on the meaning of the Hebrew word rendered in the text *congregation*—מוֹעֵד *moaid.* See the word explained in the Notes on Ps. lxxiv. 8. It may mean a set time, an appointed season, 1 Sam. xiii. 8, 11; or a coming together, an assembly, Job xxx. 23; or a place of assemblage, as the tabernacle, etc.; Ex. xxvii. 21; xl. 22; Ps. lxxiv. 8. It *may*, therefore, be applied to the congregation of the Jewish people—the nation considered *as* an assemblage for the worship of God; and the idea of *taking* this, or *receiving* this, may be applied to the act of assuming authority or sovereignty over the people, and hence the language may be used to denote the entrance on the discharge of the duties of such sovereignty. The language would be applicable to one who had the right of such an elevation to power—a prince—an heir apparent,—in a time when his right was disputed; when there was an organized opposition to him; or when the nation was in a state of anarchy and confusion. It seems to me that this supposition best accords with the proper meaning of the language, and with the scope of the psalm. ¶ *I will judge uprightly.* I will put down all this opposition to law. I will deal with exact justice between man and man. I will restore order, and the supremacy of law, to the state. The language, therefore, according to this interpretation, is not the language of God, but that of a prince having a right to the throne, and about to ascend it in a time of great misrule and disorder.

3. *The earth and all the inhabitants thereof are dissolved.* The word rendered *dissolved* means properly to melt, to flow down; then, to melt away, to pine away, to perish. Isa. lxiv. 7; Job xxx. 22; Nahum i. 5; Ps. cvii. 26. Here it means that there was, as it were, a general breaking up of things; or that none of the institutions of the land seemed to have any stability. There seemed to be no government, but universal anarchy and confusion. ¶ *I bear up the pillars of it.* Of the earth; of society. The earth here is compared with an edifice supported by pillars. Comp. Judges xvi. 26; 1 Sam. ii. 8; 1 Tim. iii. 15. As applied to a prince or ruler, this means that the permanent structure of the state, the welfare of society, depended on his administration. If, according to the view of others, it is applied to God, the meaning is, that as he upholds the world, there cannot be permanent misrule; that amidst all the commotions of earth, and all that seemed to threaten ruin, his hand sustained all, and he would not allow things to proceed to permanent disorder. In the former case, the assertion *would* be true if a prince felt that he had power to support the government, and to restore order; in the latter case, it *must* be true, for God sustains the earth, and as he can check disorder when he shall judge it best to interpose, so he will not permit it ultimately to prevail. ¶ *Selah.* A musical pause. See Notes on Ps. iii. 2.

4. *I said unto the fools.* To the wicked men in rebellion. Folly and wickedness in the Bible are synonymous terms, as they are identical in

not foolishly; and to the wicked,
Lift not up the [o] horn:
5 Lift not up your horn on
high: speak *not with* a stiff neck.

6 For promotion *cometh* neither from the east, nor from the
west, nor from the [1] south:

o Zech. i. 21. 1 *desert.*

fact. See Notes on Ps. xiv. 1. ¶ *Deal not foolishly.* Act not foolishly; carry not out your wicked plans. Do not pursue your schemes of wickedness and folly, for they cannot be successful, and they will only tend to involve you in ruin. ¶ *And to the wicked.* The wicked men engaged in rebellion—either against a lawful human government, or against God. ¶ *Lift not up the horn.* The horn is a symbol of strength. Comp. Job xvi. 15; Dan. vii. 7, 8, 11, 21; viii. 5, 8, 9, 21. This is to be understood as the language of the person represented as speaking in the psalm—whether a prince, or whether God himself. It is counsel addressed to the wicked, that they should not attempt to put forth their strength in the accomplishment of their evil purposes. The reason given for this is stated in ver. 6, viz. that success does not depend on chance, or on human power, but must come from God.

5. *Lift not up your horn on high.* In a proud, self-confident, arrogant manner. ¶ *Speak* not with *a stiff neck.* With arrogance and pride; in a haughty, imperious manner. The word rendered *stiff* (literally *a neck of stiffness*)—עָתָק, *athak*—means properly bold, impudent, wicked; and the idea is that of speaking as those do who are impudent, shameless, bold, licentious,—indicating confidence in themselves, and a reckless disregard of truth and of the rights of others. The Septuagint and the Vulgate render it, "And speak not unrighteousness against God."

6. *For promotion.* The word here used in the original, and rendered *promotion*—הָרִים, *harim*—is susceptible of two quite different significations. According to one—that which is adopted by our translators—it is the infinitive (Hiphil) of רוּם, *rum, to raise*—the word used in vers. 5, 6, and there rendered *lift up.* Thus it would mean, that *to lift up* is not the work of men, or is not originated by the earth—does not originate from any part of it, east, west, or south, but must come from God alone. According to the other view, this word is the plural of הַר, *har, mountain,* and would mean that *something*—(something understood—as *judgment*)—comes not "from the east, nor the west, nor *from the desert of mountains,*" the mountainous regions of the south, but must come from God. The Septuagint, the Latin Vulgate, and the ancient versions generally, adopt the latter interpretation. De Wette renders it as our translators have done. This interpretation—rendering it *promotion*—seems to be the true one, for in the two previous verses this was the prominent idea—a caution against attempting *to lift themselves up,* or to exalt themselves, and in this and the following verse a reason is given for this caution, to wit, that the whole question about success or prosperity depends not on anything here below; not on any natural advantages of situation, or on any human skill or power; but on God alone. It was in vain, in regard to such an object, to form human alliances, or to depend on natural advantages; and therefore men should not depend on these things, but only on God. ¶ *Neither from the east.* Literally, *from the outgoing; i. e.* of the sun. The meaning may either be that success would not depend on any natural advantages of country furnished in the East; or that the persons referred to were seeking to form alliances with an Eastern people, and then the statement would be that no such alliances would of themselves secure success. ¶ *Nor from the west.* The *setting;* that is, the place where the sun goes down. This also may

7 But God *is* the judge; he
[p] putteth down one, and setteth
up another.
8 For in the hand of the LORD
there is a cup, [q] and the wine is
red; it is full of mixture, and he
poureth out of the same: but
the dregs thereof, all the wicked
of the earth shall wring *them* out,
and drink *them*.

p 1 Sam. ii. 7, 8.

q Rev. xiv. 9, 10.

refer either to the natural advantages of a Western country, or to some alliance which it was intended to form with the people there. ¶ *Nor from the south.* Marg., as in Heb., *desert.* The reference is to the rocky and barren regions south of Palestine, and the allusion here also may be either to some natural advantages of those regions, or to some alliance which it was proposed to form.

7. *But God* is *the judge.* All depends on him, not on the natural advantages of a country; not on human strength, human skill, or human prowess. Whatever may be the natural resources of a country; whatever may be the enterprise, the numbers, or the valour of its inhabitants; whatever alliances of peace or war they may form with other nations, yet success depends on God. He presides over all; he can give success when it is least expected; and he also can humble men when they have made the most ample preparations for success, and anticipate it in the most confident manner. ¶ *He putteth down one, and setteth up another.* Literally, "This one he humbles, and this he exalts." This is true alike of an individual or a nation. The word rendered *setteth up* is the same which is used in vers. 4, 5, 6, rendered "Lift up," and "promotion." The idea is, that in the matter of "lifting up," or "promotion," all depends on God. He is a sovereign, and he confers exaltation, whether of an individual or a nation, as he pleases.

8. *For in the hand of the* LORD, etc. The general idea in this verse is, that God holds in his hand a cup for men to drink; a cup whose contents will tend to prolong life, or to cause death. See the idea in this passage fully explained in the Notes on Job xxi. 20; Ps. lx. 3; Isa. li. 17; Rev. xiv. 10. ¶ *And the wine is red.* The word here used—חָמַר, *hhamar*—may mean either to boil up, or to be red—from the idea of boiling, or becoming heated. The Septuagint and the Vulgate render it, "And he pours it out from this into that;" that is, he draws it off, as is done with wine. The true idea in the expression is probably that it *ferments;* and the meaning may be that the wrath of God seems to boil like fermenting liquor. ¶ *It is full of mixture.* Mixed with spices, in order to increase its strength; or, as we should say, *drugged.* This was frequently done in order to increase the intoxicating quality of wine. The idea is, that the wrath of God was *like* wine whose native strength, or power of producing intoxication, was thus increased by drugs. ¶ *And he poureth out of the same.* He pours it out in order that his enemies may drink it; in other words, they reel and stagger under the expressions of his wrath, as men reel and stagger under the influence of spiced or drugged wine. ¶ *But the dregs thereof.* The *lees*—the settlings—what remains after the wine is racked off. See Notes on Isa. xxv. 6. This would contain the strongest part of the mixture; and the idea is, that they would drink the wrath of God to the utmost. ¶ *All the wicked of the earth.* Wicked men everywhere. The expression of the wrath of God would not be confined to one nation, or one people; but wherever wicked men are found, he will punish them. He will be just in his dealings with all men. ¶ *Shall wring* them *out.* Wine was kept in skins; and the idea here is, that they would wring out these skins so as to get out *all* that there was in them, and leave nothing remaining. The

9 But I will declare for ever; I will sing praises to the God of Jacob.
10 All [r] the horns of the wicked also will I cut off; *but* the horns of the righteous shall be exalted.

r Ps. ci. 8.

wrath of God would be exhausted in the punishment of wicked men, *as if* it were all *wrung out.* ¶ And *drink* them. Not merely the wine; but the dregs; all that there was. Wicked men will suffer *all* that there is in the justice of God.

9. *But I will declare for ever.* I,—the author of the psalm. I will make known at all times the character of God, and will declare the truth respecting his works and ways. The particular *mode* as referred to here, was *praise.* ¶ *I will sing praises to the God of Jacob.* The God whom Jacob worshipped; the God who proved himself to be his Friend, thus showing that he is the Friend of all that trust in him. See Notes on Ps. xxiv. 6.

10. *All the horns of the wicked,* etc. See Notes on ver. 4. The meaning is, I will destroy all their power. This, too, may refer to the author of the psalm, supposed to be a prince or ruler about to ascend the throne, and to assert his rightful authority. This indicates his purpose in regard to his administration (comp. ver. 2); the principles on which he would administer his government. It would be an administration under which the wicked would be punished, and where the righteous would be protected. In this manner it would be an emblem of the administration of God. All just human governments are founded on the same principles as the government of God. Men have only to apply to the affairs of civil society the principles on which God governs the universe, to constitute the most perfect human administration. Those which come nearest to that, most nearly approximate perfection; and civil governments will reach their end, and accomplish their design, only when those principles shall be universally applied among men.

PSALM LXXVI.

This psalm is one of those which in the title are ascribed to Asaph (see Introduction to Psalm lxxiii.), and there is no reason to call in question that statement. On the phrase "To the chief Musician on Neginoth," see Introd. to Ps. iv.

The occasion on which the psalm was composed is not stated, and cannot now be ascertained. The Septuagint regards it as having had reference to the Assyrians—ᾠδὴ προς τὸν Ἀσσύριον—"An ode to the Assyrian." So the Latin Vulgate; Canticum ad Assyrios. This is the opinion adopted also by Jarchi. The title in the Syriac version is, "When Rabbah of the Ammonites was laid waste; and farther it describes the judgment of the Messiah against the wicked." Grotius supposes that it was intended to describe the victory over the Ammonites. Rüdinger ascribes its composition to the time of the Maccabees. De Wette supposes that it refers to some late period of the Jewish history, but that the particular time is unknown. It would be vain to attempt to ascertain with any certainty the particular occasion on which the psalm was composed. It was evidently on some occasion when an attack had been made on "Salem," that is, on Jerusalem (vers. 2, 3), and when that attack had been repelled, and the enemy had been driven back. Many of the circumstances in the psalm would agree well with the account of the invasion of the Assyrians under Sennacherib, but there were many other occasions in the Jewish history to which it would, in like manner, be applicable.

The psalm is a song of praise for deliverance from an enemy. The contents are as follows:—I. The fact that God had made himself known *in Judah,* or to the Jewish people,—or, that he had manifested himself to them in a remarkable manner, ver. 1. II. The fact that he had showed this in a special manner in "Salem," the capital of the nation,—referring to some particular time in which this was done, ver. 2. III. The manner in which he had done this,—by breaking the arrows of the bow, and the shield; by showing that his power was

PSALM LXXVI.

To the chief Musician on Neginoth. A Psalm *or* Song [1] of Asaph.

IN [s] Judah [t] *is* God known; his name *is* great in Israel.

2 In [u] Salem also is his tabernacle, and his dwelling-place in Zion.

3 There [v] brake he the arrows of the bow, the shield, and the sword, and the battle. Selah.

4 Thou *art* more glorious *and*

[1] Or, *for*. [s] Ps. xlviii. 1, etc. [t] Deut. iv. 7, 8. [u] Ps. cxxxii. 13.

[v] Ps. xlvi. 9.

superior to all the defences which men had set up; and by overcoming entirely the invading foe, vers. 3-6. IV. The fact that, on this account, God was to be feared and reverenced, vers. 7-9. V. The statement of a great truth, and a most important principle, which had been particularly illustrated by the occurrence; to wit, that the wrath of man would be made to praise God, and that the remainder of wrath he would restrain, ver. 10. VI. A call on all men to acknowledge God in a suitable manner, by bringing presents, and by standing in awe of him, vers. 11, 12.

1. *In Judah* is *God known.* That is, he has made himself known there in a special manner; he has evinced his watchful care over the city so as to demand a proper acknowledgment; he has manifested himself there as he has not elsewhere. It is true that God is known, or makes himself known everywhere; but it is also true that he does this in some places, and at some times, in a more marked and striking manner than he does in other places and at other times. The most clear and impressive displays of his character are among his own people,—in the church. ¶ *His name* is *great in Israel.* Among the people of Israel; or, among his own people. The meaning here is, that, by some act referred to in the psalm, he had so displayed his power and his mercy in favour of that people, as to make it proper that his name should be exalted or praised.

2. *In Salem also.* This was the ancient name for Jerusalem, and is evidently so used here. It continued to be given to the town until the time of David, when it was called *Jerusalem.* See Notes on Isa. i. 1. The word properly means *peace,* and is so rendered here by the Septuagint,—*ἐν εἰρήνῃ ὁ τόπος αὐτοῦ—his place is in peace.* There *may* have been an allusion here to that ancient signification of the name, as being more poetical, and as suggesting the fact that God had restored peace to the city and nation when invaded. ¶ *Is his tabernacle.* The *tent,* or sacred place where he is worshipped. Salem or Jerusalem was made the place of public worship, and the ark removed there by David, 2 Sam. vi. 17. ¶ *And his dwelling-place in Zion.* That is, on Mount Zion,—the portion of Jerusalem in which David built his own palace, and which he made the place of public worship. This remained so until the temple was built on Mount Moriah; see Notes on Ps. ii. 6; comp. Ps. ix. 11; xlviii. 12; lxv. 1.

3. *There brake he the arrows of the bow.* That is, in Salem, or near Salem. The language is such as would be used in reference to invaders, or to armies that came up to storm the city. The occasion is unknown; but the meaning is, that God drove the invading army back, and showed his power in defending the city. The phrase "the arrows of the bow," is literally, *the lightnings of the bow,*—the word rendered *arrows* meaning properly *flame;* and then, *lightning.* The idea is, that the arrows sped from the bow with the rapidity of lightning. ¶ *The shield.* Used for defence in war. See Ps. v. 12; xxxiii. 20; comp. Notes on Eph. vi. 16. ¶ *And the sword.* That is, he disarmed his enemies, or made them as powerless *as if* their swords were broken. ¶ *And the battle.* He broke the force of the battle; the strength of the armies drawn up for conflict.

4. *Thou* art *more glorious* and *excellent.* The word rendered *glorious*

excellent than the mountains of
prey.
5 The stout-hearted [w] are spoiled, they have slept [x] their sleep;
and none of the men of might
have found their hands.
6 At thy rebuke, O God of
Jacob, both the chariot and
horse [y] are cast into a dead
sleep.
7 Thou, [z] *even* thou, *art* to be
feared; and who [a] may stand in
thy sight when once thou art
angry?

w Isa. xlvi. 12. *x* Jer. li. 39. *y* Zec. xii. 4.

z Jer. x. 7. *a* Nahum i. 6.

—נָאוֹר, *naor*—is from the verb which means *to shine*, to give light, and the word would properly refer to a luminous or *shining* object—as the sun, the source of light. Hence it means *shining*, splendid, glorious; and it is thus applied to the Divine Being with reference to his perfections, being like light. Comp. 1 John i. 5. The word rendered *excellent*, means exalted, noble, great. These words are applied here to God from the manifestation of his perfections in the case referred to. ¶ *Than the mountains of prey.* The word *prey* as employed here—טֶרֶף, *tereph*—means that which is obtained by hunting; and then, plunder. It is usually applied to the food of wild beasts, *beasts of prey*. Here it refers to the "mountains" considered as the abode or stronghold of robbers and banditti, from whence they sally forth in search of plunder. These mountains, in their heights, their rocks, their fastnesses, furnished safe places of retreat for robbers, and hence they became emblems of power. It is not improbable that the hordes referred to in the psalm had their abodes in such mountains, and hence the psalmist says that God who made those mountains and hills was superior to them in strength and power.

5. *The stout-hearted are spoiled.* The valiant men, the men who came so confidently to the invasion. The word *spoiled* here, as elsewhere in the Scriptures, means *plundered*, not (as the word is now used) *corrupted.* See Notes on Col. ii. 8. ¶ *They have slept their sleep.* They are dead; they have slept their last sleep. Death, in the Scriptures, as in all other writings, is often compared with sleep. ¶ *And none of the men of might.* The men who came forth for purposes of war and conquest. ¶ *Have found their hands.* The Septuagint renders this, "Have found nothing in their hands;" that is, they have obtained no plunder. Luther renders it, "And all warriors must suffer their hands to fall." De Wette, "Have lost their hands." The idea seems to be, that they had lost the use of their hands; that is, that they had no use for them, or did not find them of any use. They could not employ them for the purpose for which they were intended, but were suddenly stricken down.

6. *At thy rebuke, O God of Jacob.* At thy word; thy bidding; or, when God rebuked them for their attempt to attack the city. The idea is, that they were discomfited by a *word* spoken by God. ¶ *Both the chariot and horse*, etc. The Septuagint renders this, "They who are mounted on horses." The word rendered *chariot* here—רֶכֶב *recheb*—may mean *riders, cavalry*, as well as chariot. See Notes on Isa. xxi. 7. Hence there would be less incongruity in the Hebrew than in our translation, where it is said that the *chariots* have fallen into a deep sleep. The idea may be either that horsemen and horses had fallen into a deep slumber, or that the rumbling of the chariot-wheels had ceased, and that there was a profound silence, *like* a deep sleep.

7. *Thou*, even *thou*, art *to be feared.* To be had in reverence or veneration. The repetition of the word "*thou*" is emphatic, as if the mind paused at the mention of God, and remained in a state of reverence, repeating the thought. The particular *reason* suggested here why God should be had

8 Thou [b] didst cause judgment to be heard from heaven; the earth feared, and was still,
9 When God arose to judgment, to save all the meek of the earth. Selah.
10 Surely the wrath of man [c] shall praise thee: the remainder [d] of wrath shalt thou restrain.

b Ex. xix. 10, etc. c Dan. iii. 19, 28. d Ps. lxv. 7.

in reverence, was the display of his power in overthrowing by a word the mighty hosts that had come against the holy city. ¶ *And who may stand in thy sight.* Who can stand before thee?—implying that no one had the power to do it. ¶ *When once thou art angry.* If such armies have been overcome suddenly by thy might, then what power is there which could successfully resist thee?

8. *Thou didst cause judgment to be heard from heaven.* It seemed to come from heaven; it was manifestly from thee. The overthrow of these enemies of thy people was a manifest judgment from thee, and should be so regarded. ¶ *The earth feared.* The world itself seemed to hear the voice of God, and to stand in awe. ¶ *And was still.* It seemed to be profoundly attentive to what God said, and as if it reverently listened to his voice. It is not uncommon in the Scriptures to represent the earth,—the hills, the mountains, the streams, the rivers, the plains,—as conscious of the presence of God; as either rejoicing or trembling at his voice. Comp. Ps. lxv. 12, 13; cxiv. 3–7; Hab. iii. 8–11.

9. *When God arose to judgment.* That is, when he came to overthrow and destroy the enemies of his people, as referred to in the former part of the psalm. ¶ *To save all the meek of the earth.* Of the land,—to wit, the land of Judea; or, to save his people when in affliction. The word *meek*, which with us usually means those who are forbearing under injuries, means here the humble, the afflicted, the crushed, the oppressed.

10. *Surely the wrath of man shall praise thee.* It shall be the *occasion* of praise; or, honour shall accrue to thee from it, *as if* it were employed in thy praise, and *as if* it were voluntarily engaged in promoting thy glory. The deliverance of the people by the direct interposition of God in the case referred to in the psalm, the sudden and entire overthrow of the invading forces by his power, led to this reflection. The overruling power of God was displayed. The "wrath" of the invading host had given *occasion* for this manifestation of the Divine perfections; or, in other words, his character would *not* have been displayed in this manner if it had not been for these wicked purposes of men. It is not that there was anything *in* the wrath itself, or *in* their plans or intentions, that was in itself *adapted* to honour God; but that it was overruled by him, so that he took *occasion* from it to display his own character. The wicked conduct of a child is an *occasion* for the display of the just character and the wise administration of a parent; the act of a pirate, a rebel, a murderer, furnishes an *occasion* for the display of the just principles of law, and the stability and power of a government. In like manner, the sins of the wicked are made an *occasion* for the display of the Divine perfections in maintaining law; in the administering of justice; in preserving order. But there is another sense, also, in which the wrath of man is made the occasion for glorifying God. It is, that since there *is* such wrath, or since there *are* such wicked purposes, God makes *use* of that wrath, or of those wicked purposes, as he does of the powers of nature—of pestilence, disease, and storms, as instruments to accomplish his own designs, or to bring about great results. Thus he made use of the treasonable purpose of Judas, and the mad passions and the angry feelings of the Jews, in bringing about the work of redemption by the death

of his Son; thus he made use of the purposes of Sennacherib in order to punish his own people (see Notes on Isa. x. 5-7); thus he employed Cyrus to "execute his counsel" (Isa. xlvi. 10); and thus he made use of the wrath evinced in persecuting the church to secure its permanent establishment in the world. Whether these things could be accomplished *without* that wrath, is a question which is too high for man to determine. It is certain, also, that the fact that God overrules the wrath of men does not justify that wrath. The purposes of men are, like the pestilence and the storm, what they are in themselves;—and the nature of their conduct is not affected by any use that God may make of it. Men must be judged according to their own deeds, not for what God does through their wickedness. ¶ *The remainder of wrath.* The word *remainder* here—שְׁאֵרִית, *sheairith*—means properly *part;* what remains, especially after a defeat or slaughter,—the *survivors* of a battle, Jer. xi. 23; xliv. 14; Mic. vii. 18; Zeph. ii. 7. Gesenius renders it here (*Lex.*) "extreme wrath,"—retained even in extremity. The Septuagint, ἐγκατάλειμμα—*the things which are left.* So the Vulgate, *reliquiæ.* Luther, "When men rage against thee, thou turnest it to honour; and when they rage yet more, thou art yet prepared." Venema supposes that the meaning is *the whole wrath.* As in Arabic the word used here means *wholeness,* or the whole of anything; and according to this, the idea would be that it was not merely wrath *in general,* or *in a general sense,* that would be made use of, but *all that there was in wrath;* it would *all* be made use of in advancing the Divine purposes. The allusion seems to be to something that had been laid up in a magazine—as provision or arms, when the soldier went forth to war—which he would make use of if necessary, so that *all* might be ultimately consumed or employed. The control of God was over *this* as well as over that which was actually employed; he could overrule that which was employed. He could restrain men from at all using this that was kept in reserve. The idea seems to be that all the "wrath" which is *manifested* among men would be made to praise God, or would be overruled for his glory,—and *all* which would *not* contribute to this end he would keep back, he would check; he would prevent its being put forth,—so that *all* should be under his control, and *all* disposed of as he should will. There was nothing in the heart or the purposes of man that was beyond *his* jurisdiction or control; man could do nothing in his wrathful plans that God could not dispose of in his own way, and for his own honour. ¶ *Shalt thou restrain.* The word here used—חָגַר, *hhagar*—means literally to bind around; to gird; to gird up, as of a garment or sword that is girded on, 1 Sam. xvii. 39; xxv. 13; Ps. xlv. 3; or sackcloth, Isa. xv. 3; Jer. xlix. 3. The Septuagint renders this, "and the remainder of wrath *shall make a feast to thee,*"—ἑορτάσει σοι—that is, it shall praise or honour thee as in a festival. So the Vulgate. Prof. Alexander renders it, "Shalt thou gird about thee;" that is, God would gird it on as a sword, and would make use of it as a weapon for executing his own purposes. So De Wette, "And with the last wrath thou shalt gird thyself." Others render it, "Thou restrainest the remainder of *thy* wrath"—that is, punishment—"when the wrath of man will not promote the knowledge of thyself." It seems to me, however, that our translators have expressed the exact idea in the psalm; and the meaning is, that the *whole* of the wrath of man is under the control of God, and that whatever there is, or would be, in the manifestation of that wrath, or in carrying out the purposes of the heart, which could *not,* in the circumstances, be made to promote his glory, or which would do injury, he

11 Vow, and pay unto the LORD your God: let all that be round about him bring presents [1] unto him that ought to be feared.

12 He [e] shall cut off the spirit of princes: *he is* terrible to the kings of the earth.

[1] *to fear.*

e Ps. ii. 5, 10.

would check and restrain. He would suffer it to proceed no further than he chose, and would make it certain that there should be *no* exhibition of wrathful feelings on the part of man which would not, in some way, be made to promote his honour, and to advance his own great purposes. He has absolute control over the passions of men, as he has over the pestilence, over earthquakes, and over storms, and can make all tributary to his glory, and executioners of his will.

11. *Vow, and pay unto the* LORD *your God.* That is, Pay your vows, or sacredly observe them. On the word *vow,* see Notes on Ps. xxii. 25. Comp. Ps. l. 14; lvi. 12; lxvi. 13. The word refers to a voluntary promise made to God. ¶ *Let all that be round about him.* All that worship him, or that profess to honour him. ¶ *Bring presents.* Bring gifts or offerings; things expressive of gratitude and homage. See Notes on Ps. xlv. 12. Comp. Notes on Isa. xvi. 1; xviii. 7; lx. 5; *et seq.* ¶ *Unto him that ought to be feared.* Marg., *to fear.* The meaning would be well expressed by the word *dread;*—"to the Dread One." It was not to inspire fear that the presents were to be brought; but they were to be brought to One who had shown that he was the proper object of dread or reverence.

12. *He shall cut off the spirit of princes.* That is, He will cut down their pride; he will break them down. Luther renders it, "He shall take away the wrath of princes." The allusion is to what he had done as celebrated in this psalm. He had shown that he could rebuke the pride and self-confidence of kings, and could bring them low at his feet. ¶ He is *terrible to the kings of the earth.* When they are arrayed against him. (1) They are wholly under his control. (2) He can defeat their plans. (3) He can check them when he pleases. (4) He can, and will, make their plans—even their wrath—the means of promoting or carrying out his own purposes. (5) He will allow them to proceed no further in their plans of evil than he can make subservient to the furtherance of his own. (6) He can cut down the most mighty of them at his pleasure, and destroy them for ever.

PSALM LXXVII.

For the meaning of the title to this psalm, see Notes on the title to Ps. xxxix. It purports, like the preceding ones, to be a psalm of Asaph. See Notes in the title to Ps. lxxiii. Nothing is known, or can now be ascertained, of the occasion on which the psalm was composed. It is not absolutely certain whether it refers to some public calamity, and is designed to express the feelings of a pious Hebrew, as of the psalmist himself (Rosenmüller), or some other Jew (De Wette), in view of such a public calamity; or whether it is designed to represent the "complaint of the church in view of her calamity and desertion" (Prof. Alexander); or whether it is the statement of the private and personal experience of the author of the psalm. To me it seems that the latter is the most probable supposition, and that, in this respect, it accords with the purport and design of Ps. lxxiii., which is by the same author. It is an interesting statement of what passed through the mind of the author, and of what may, therefore, pass through the mind of any pious person, in regard to the Divine dealings. The psalm was evidently composed in a time of affliction, and the thoughts which gave the author so much trouble, and which he endeavoured to calm down, were such as were suggested *by* affliction;—by the fact that God *seemed* to have forsaken him, and that he had forgotten to be gracious.

PSALM LXXVII.

To the chief Musician, to *f* Jeduthun. A Psalm of [1] Asaph.

I CRIED unto God with my voice, *even* unto God with my voice; and he gave ear unto me.

2 In the day of my trouble I sought the Lord: my [2] sore ran

f Ps. lxii., *title*. [1] Or, *for*. [2] *hand.*

The contents of the psalm are as follows:—

I. A general statement of the author that he had cried to God, and that he had been heard, ver. 1. This, although it is in the beginning of the psalm, is clearly designed to be a general expression of his experience in the case *as recorded in the psalm*, or as the result of the conflict through which he had passed.

II. A statement of his affliction, and of the exercises of his mind *in* his affliction, vers. 2-9.

(1) The statement of the affliction, ver. 2.

(2) In that affliction he was troubled in mind, or he had painful ideas in regard to God. He could not reconcile his sufferings with such views as he desired to cherish of God, ver. 3.

(3) His meditations, and perhaps the pain of disease, kept him awake, and he was unable to rest. The ordinary time of repose furnished no relief, ver. 4.

(4) He recalled the past; he looked over the dealings of God with men in former times; he summoned up his own reflections in times past, and especially the time when he *could* praise God in trouble, recalling his "*song in the night*"—but in vain, vers. 5, 6.

(5) The result was that he had most painful thoughts in regard to God, *as if* he had forgotten to be gracious, and had cast him off for ever, and would be favourable no more, vers. 7-9.

III. His self-reproach; his recalling himself to a proper state of feeling; his purpose to think of the dealings of God with his people, and to examine them more closely, vers. 10-12. He saw that the course of thought which he had indulged in was wrong, and was satisfied that it was an "infirmity,"—that it was to be traced to his own weakness,—and that he ought to take different views of God.

IV. The result of all;—the things which comforted him in his troubles, and which enabled him at last to put his calm trust in God, vers. 13-20.

He refers

(1) To the fact that God is great, and that he could not hope to be able to comprehend him, vers. 13, 14.

(2) To the fact that God had redeemed his people by surprising manifestations of power, showing that he was faithful, and that he was able to deliver from the deepest distresses, vers. 15-18.

(3) To the fact that the way of God was in the sea, or in great waters, and that we cannot expect to be able to comprehend him, ver. 19.

(4) To the fact that God *had* led his flock in ancient times amid scenes of danger and of trial, ver. 20.

By all this his mind was comforted, and his soul was made calm. God heard his prayer, and gave him peace.

1. *I cried unto God with my voice.* That is, he cried or prayed audibly. It was not mere mental prayer. See Notes on Ps. iii. 4. ¶ Even *unto God with my voice.* The repetition here is emphatic. The idea is that it was an earnest or fervent cry. Comp. Notes on 2 Cor. xii. 8. ¶ *And he gave ear unto me.* See Notes on Ps. v. 1; xvii. 6.

2. *In the day of my trouble I sought the Lord.* Comp. Notes on Ps. l. 15. This trouble *may* have been either mental or bodily; that is, it may have arisen from some form of disease, or it may have been that which sprang from difficulties in regard to the Divine character, government, and dealings. That it *assumed* the latter form, even if it had its beginning in the former, is apparent from the following verses. Whether it was connected with any form of bodily disease must be determined by the proper interpretation of the next

in the night, and ceased not: my soul refused to be comforted.

3 I remembered God, and was troubled: I complained, and my spirit *g* was overwhelmed. Selah.

g Ps. cxliii. 4, 5; Lam. iii. 17, etc.

clause in this verse. ¶ *My sore ran in the night.* Marg., *My hand.* It is evident that our translators supposed that there was some bodily disease—some running sore—which was the cause of his trouble. Hence they so rendered the Hebrew word. But it is now generally agreed that this is without authority. The Hebrew word is *hand*—יָד, *yad*—a word which is never used in the sense of sore or wound. The Septuagint renders it, "my hands are before him." The Vulgate renders it in the same manner. Luther, "My hand is stretched out at night." De Wette, "My hand is stretched out at night unwearied." The word which is rendered in our version *ran*—נִגַּר, *nagar*—means *to flow;* and, in Niphil, to be poured out, and then, *to be stretched out;* which is evidently its meaning here. The idea is, that his hand was stretched out in earnest supplication, and that this continued in the night when these troubles came most upon him. See vers. 4, 6. In his painful meditations in the night-watches,—in thinking on God and his ways, as he lay upon his bed, he stretched out his hand in fervent prayer to God. ¶ *And ceased not.* The word here used—פּוּג, *pug*—means properly to be cold; then, to be torpid, sluggish, slack. Here it means that the hand did not become weary; it did not fall from exhaustion; or, in other words, that he did not give over praying through weariness or exhaustion. ¶ *My soul refused to be comforted.* I resisted all the suggestions that came to my own mind, that *might* have comforted me. My heart was so melancholy and downcast; my spirits were so crushed; my mind was so dark; I had become so *morbid,* that I loved to cherish these thoughts. I chose to dwell on them. They had obtained possession of me, and I could not let them go. There was nothing that my own mind could suggest, there was nothing that occurred to me, that would relieve the difficulty or restore peace to my soul. These sad and gloomy thoughts filled all my soul, and left no room for thoughts of consolation and peace. A truly pious man *may,* therefore, get into a state of mind—a sad, dispirited, melancholy, morbid state—in which nothing that can be said to him, nothing that will occur to himself, will give him comfort and peace. Comp. Jer. xxxi. 15.

3. *I remembered God.* That is, I thought on God; I thought on his character, his government, and his dealings; I thought on the mysteries — the incomprehensible things—the apparently unequal, unjust, and partial doings—of his administration. It is evident from the whole tenour of the psalm that these were the things which occupied his attention. He dwelt on them till his whole soul became sad; till his spirit became so overwhelmed that he could not find words in which to utter his thoughts. ¶ *And was troubled.* The Septuagint renders this, εὐφράνθην—*I was rejoiced* or *delighted.* So the Vulgate. Luther renders it, "When I am troubled, then I think on God." Our translation, however, has probably given the true idea; and *in* that has expressed (*a*) what often occurs in the case of even a good man,—that by dwelling on the dark and incomprehensible things of the Divine administration, the soul becomes sad and troubled to an extent bordering on murmuring, complaint, and rebellion; and may also serve to illustrate (*b*) what often happens in the mind of a sinner,—that he delights to dwell on these things in the Divine administration: (1) as most in accordance with what he *desires* to think about God, or with the views which he *wishes* to cherish of him;

4 Thou holdest mine eyes waking: I am so troubled that I cannot speak.

5 I have considered [h] the days of old, the years of ancient times.

h Deut. xxxii. 7; Isa. lxiii. 11.

---

and (2) as justifying himself in his rebellion against God, and his refusal to submit to him,—for if God *is* unjust, partial, and severe, the sinner is right; such a Being would be unworthy of trust and confidence; he *ought* to be opposed, and his claims *ought* to be resisted. ¶ *I complained.* Or rather, *I mused* or *meditated.* The word here used does not necessarily mean to complain. It is sometimes used in that sense, but its proper and common signification is to meditate. See Ps. cxix. 15, 23, 27, 48, 78, 148. ¶ *And my spirit was overwhelmed.* With the result of my own reflections. That is, *I* was amazed or confounded by the thoughts that came in upon me.

4. *Thou holdest mine eyes waking.* Literally, "Thou holdest the watchings of my eyes." Gesenius (*Lex.*) translates the Hebrew word rendered *waking,* "eyelids." Probably that is the true idea. The eyelids are the watchers or guardians of the eyes. In danger, and in sleep, they close. Here the idea is, that God *held* them so that they did not close. He overcame the natural tendency of the eye to shut. In other words, the psalmist was kept awake; he could not sleep. This he traces to God. The idea is, that God so kept himself before his mind — that such ideas occurred to him in regard to God—that he could not sleep. ¶ *I am so troubled.* With sad and dark views of God;—so troubled in endeavouring to understand his character and doings; in explaining his acts; in painful ideas that suggest themselves in regard to his justice, his goodness, his mercy. ¶ *That I cannot speak.* I am struck dumb. I know not what to say. I cannot find *anything* to say. He must have a heart singularly and happily free by nature from scepticism, or must have reflected little on the Divine administration, who has not had thoughts pass through his mind like these. As the psalmist was a good man, a pious man, it is of importance to remark, in view of his experience, that such reflections occur not only to the minds of *bad* men—of the profane—of sceptics—of infidel philosophers, but they come unbidden into the minds of good men, and often in a form which they cannot calm down. He who has never had such thoughts, happy as he may and should deem himself that he has *not* had them, has never known some of the deepest stirrings and workings of the human soul on the subject of religion, and is little qualified to sympathize with a spirit torn, crushed, agitated, as was that of the psalmist on these questions, or as Augustine and thousands of others have been in after-times. But let not a man conclude, *because* he has these thoughts, that therefore he cannot be a friend of God — a converted man. The wicked man invites them, cherishes them, and rejoices that he *can* find what seem to him to be reasons for indulging in such thoughts against God; the good man is pained; struggles against them; endeavours to banish them from his soul.

5. *I have considered the days of old.* Rather, "I *do* consider;" that is, "I think upon." This refers to his resolution in his perplexity and trouble; the method to which he resorted in examining the subject, and in endeavouring to allay his troubles. He resolved to look at the past. He asked what was the evidence which was furnished on the subject by the former dealings of God with himself and with mankind; what could be learned from those dealings in regard to the great and difficult questions which now so perplexed his mind. ¶ *The years of ancient times.* The records and remembrances of past ages. What is the testimony which the his-

6 I call to remembrance my
song [i] in the night: I commune
[k] with mine own heart, and my
spirit made diligent [l] search.
7 Will the Lord cast off for
[m] ever? and will he be favourable
no more?

i Ps. xlii. 8. *k* Ps. iv. 4. *l* Lam. iii. 40.

8 Is his mercy clean gone for
ever? doth *his* promise fail [1] for
evermore?
9 Hath God forgotten [n] to be
gracious? hath he in anger shut
up his tender mercies? Selah.

m Ps. lxxiv. 1; Lam. iii. 31, 32.
[1] *to generation and generation.* *n* Isa. xlix. 15.

tory of the world bears on this subject? Does it prove that God is worthy of confidence or not? Does it or does it not authorize and justify these painful thoughts which pass through the mind?

6. *I call to remembrance my song in the night.* Comp. Notes on Job xxxv. 10; Ps. xlii. 8. The word here rendered *song* — נְגִינָה, *Neginah* — means properly the music of stringed instruments, Lam. v. 14; Isa. xxxviii. 20; then, a stringed instrument. It is the word which we have so often in the titles to the psalms (Ps. iv.; vi.; liv.; lv.; lxvii.; lxxvi.); and it is here used in the sense of song or psalm. The idea is, that there had been times in his life when, even in darkness and sorrow, he could sing; when he could find things for which to praise God; when he could find something that would cheer him; when he could take some bright views of God adapted to calm down his feelings, and to give peace to his soul. He recalls those times and scenes to his remembrance, with a desire to have those cheerful impressions renewed; and he asks himself what it *was* which then comforted and sustained him. He endeavours to bring those things back again; for if he found comfort *then*, he thinks that he might find comfort from the same considerations now. ¶ *I commune with mine own heart.* I think over the matter. See Notes on Ps. iv. 4. ¶ *And my spirit made diligent search.* In reference (*a*) to the grounds of my former support and comfort; and (*b*) in reference to the whole matter as it lies before me now.

7. *Will the Lord cast off for ever?* This was the subject, and the substance, of his inquiry:—whether it was a fair and just conclusion that God would show no mercy; would never be gracious again. Evidently the thought passed through his mind that this seemed to be the character of God; that things *looked* as if this were so; that it was difficult, if not impossible, to understand the Divine dealings otherwise;—and he asks whether this *was* a fair conclusion;—whether he *must* be constrained to believe that this was so. ¶ *And will he be favourable no more?* Will he no more show favour to men? Will he pardon and save no more of the race of mankind?

8. *Is his mercy clean gone for ever?* The word rendered *clean gone* means to fail; to fail utterly. The idea is, Can it be that the compassion of God has become exhausted,—that no more mercy is to be shown to mankind,—that henceforth all is to be left to stern and severe justice? What would the world be if this were so! What must be the condition of mankind if mercy were no more to be shown to the race! ¶ *Doth* his *promise fail for evermore?* Marg., as in Heb., *to generation and generation.* The original Hebrew rendered *promise* means *word;* and the question is, whether it can be that what God has *spoken* is to be found false. Can we no longer rely on what he has *said?* All the hopes of mankind depend on that, and if that should fail, all prospect of salvation in regard to our race must be at an end.

9. *Hath God forgotten to be gracious?* Has he *passed over* mercy in administering his government? Has he ceased to remember that man needs mercy? Has he forgotten that

10 And I said, This [o] *is* my infirmity: *but I will remember* the years of the right hand of the Most High.

o Ps. xxxi. 22.

this is an attribute of his own nature? ¶ *Hath he in anger shut up his tender mercies?* The original word here rendered *tender mercies* refers to the *bowels*, as the seat of compassion or mercy, in accordance with a usage common in Hebrew. See Notes on Ps. xxv. 6; Isa. xvi. 11; lxiii. 15. Comp. Luke i. 78 (in Greek); Phil. i. 8; ii. 1; 1 John iii. 17. We speak of the *heart* as the seat of affection and kindness. The Hebrews included the heart, but they used a more general word. The word rendered *shut up* means *closed;* and the question is whether his mercy was *closed*, or had *ceased* for ever. The psalmist concludes that if this were done, it must be as the result of *anger*—anger in view of the sins of men.

10. *And I said, This* is *my infirmity.* The meaning of this phrase is not, as would appear from our translation, that his reflections on the subject were to be traced to his weakness, or were a proof of weakness of mind, but that the subject overpowered him. This verse has been very variously rendered. The Septuagint and the Vulgate translate it, "And I said, now I begin; this is a change of the right hand of the Most High,"—with what meaning it is difficult to see. Luther renders it, "But yet I said, I must suffer this; the right hand of the Most High can change all;"—a beautiful sentiment, but probably not the idea in the original. The Hebrew means, "This makes me sick;" that is, "This distresses me; it afflicts me; it overwhelms me. Such reflections prostrate me, and I cannot bear up under them. I *must* seek relief. I *must* find it somewhere. I *must* take some view of this matter which will save me from these dreadful thoughts that overpower and crush the soul." Any deep mental emotion may have this effect, and it is not strange that such a result should be produced by the momentous thoughts suggested by religion, as it sometimes attends even the manifestation of the Divine mercy to the soul. Comp. Notes on Dan. x. 8, 9. The course of thought which the psalmist pursued, and in which he found relief, is stated in the following verses. It consisted of an attempt to obtain, from the remembrance of the Divine administration in past times, views of God which would lead to confidence in him. The views thus obtained, as will be seen, were two-fold: (*a*) That, as far as his dealings could be understood, God was worthy of confidence; and (*b*) That in the ways of God there are, and must be, many things which man cannot comprehend. ¶ But I will remember *the years of the right hand of the Most High.* That is, the years when God displayed his power; when he reached out his right hand; when he manifested his true character; when there was a proper exhibition to the world of what he is, and of the true principles of his administration. The words "*But I will remember*" are not in the original, though, as they occur in the following verse, they are not improperly supplied by the translators. The original, however, is more striking and emphatic:—"This makes me sick!—The years of the right hand of the Most High!" The history of those years occurred to his mind. They rose to his view suddenly in his sorrow. They came before him in such a form and manner that he felt they should be inquired into. Their history should be examined. In that history—in those remembered years—relief *might* be found. It was natural to look there *for* relief. He instinctively turned, therefore, to examine the records of those years, and to inquire what testimony they bore in regard to God; what there might be in them that would give relief to a troubled heart.

11 I will remember the works
p of the LORD; surely I will remember thy wonders of old.
12 I will meditate also of all thy work, and talk of thy doings.
13 Thy way, O God, *is* q in the sanctuary: who r *is so* great a God as *our* God!

p Ps. cxi. 4. q Ps. lxviii. 24. r Ex. xv. 11, etc.

11. *I will remember the works of the* LORD. That is, I will call them to remembrance, or I will reflect on them. I will look to what God has *done*, that I may learn his true character, or that I may see what is the proper interpretation to be put on his doings in respect to the question whether he is righteous or not; whether it is proper to put confidence in him or not. Or, in other words, I will examine those doings to see if I cannot find in them something to calm down my feelings; to remove my despondency; and to give me cheerful views of God. ¶ *Surely I will remember thy wonders of old.* Thy wonderful dealings with mankind; those acts which thou hast performed which are fitted to excite amazement and wonder.

12. *I will meditate also of all thy work.* That is, with a view to learn thy real character; to see whether I am to be constrained by painful facts to cherish the thoughts which have given me such trouble, or whether I may not find reasons for cherishing more cheerful views of God. ¶ *And talk of thy doings.* Or rather, "I will *muse* on thy doings"—for so the Hebrew word signifies. It is not conversation with others to which he refers; it is meditation—musing—calm contemplation — thoughtful meditation. He designed to reflect on the doings of God, and to ask what was the proper interpretation to be put on them in regard to his character. Thus we must, and may, judge of God, as we judge of our fellow-men. We may, we must, inquire what is the proper interpretation to be put on the events which occur under his administration, and form our opinions accordingly. The result of the psalmist's reflections is stated in the following verses.

13. *Thy way, O God,* is *in the sanctuary.* Luther renders this, "O God, thy way is holy." Prof. Alexander, "O God, in holiness is thy way." De Wette, "O God, holy is thy way." The word rendered *sanctuary*—קֹדֶשׁ, *kodesh*—means properly *holiness.* It is not the same word which in Ps. lxxiii. 17 is rendered *sanctuary*—מִקְדָּשׁ, *mikdosh.* The word here employed, however, *may* mean a holy place, a sanctuary, as the tabernacle (Ex. xxviii. 43; xxix. 30), or the temple (1 Kings viii. 8; 2 Chron. xxix. 7). In this passage the word is ambiguous. It means either that the way of God is holy, or in holiness; or, that it is in the sanctuary, or holy place. If the former, it is a statement of the result to which the psalmist came in regard to the Divine character, from a contemplation of his doings. If the latter, it means that the way of God—the true principles of the Divine administration—are to be learned in the place where he is worshipped, and from the principles which are there set forth. Comp. Notes on Ps. lxxiii. 17. It seems to me that the former is the correct interpretation, as it accords better with the scope of the passage. ¶ *Who* is so *great a God as* our *God!* In greatness no one can be compared with him. He is supreme over all. This is the first reflection of the psalmist in regard to God,—that he is great; that he is superior to all other beings; that no one can be compared with him. The evident *inference* from this in the mind of the psalmist, as bearing on the subject of his inquiry, is, that *it is to be expected* that there will be things in his administration which man cannot hope to understand; that a rash and sudden judgment should not be formed in regard to him from

14 Thou *art* the God that doest wonders: thou hast declared thy strength among the people.
15 Thou hast with *thine* arm redeemed thy people, the sons of Jacob and Joseph. Selah.
16 The waters [s] saw thee, O God, the waters saw thee: they were afraid; the depths also were troubled.
17 The clouds [1] poured out water; the skies sent out a sound: thine arrows also went abroad.

s Hab. iii. 8, etc.

1 *were poured forth with water.*

his doings; that men should wait for the developments of his plans; that he should not be condemned because there are things which we cannot comprehend, or which *seem* to be inconsistent with goodness. This is a consideration which ought always to influence us in our views of God and his government.

14. *Thou* art *the God that doest wonders.* It is, it must be, the characteristic of God, the true God, to do *wonderful things;* things which are fitted to produce amazement, and which we can little hope to be able to understand. Our judgment of God, therefore, should not be hasty and rash, but calm and deliberate. ¶ *Thou hast declared thy strength among the people.* Thou hast manifested thy greatness in thy dealings with the people. The word *people* here refers not peculiarly to the Hebrew people, but to the *nations*—the people of the world at large. On a wide scale, and among all nations, God had done that which was fitted to excite wonder, and which men were little qualified as yet to comprehend. No one can judge aright of what another has done unless he can take in the whole subject, and see it as he does who performs the act,—unless he understands all the causes, the motives, the results near and remote,—unless he sees the necessity of the act,—unless he sees what would have been the consequences if it had *not* been done; for in that which is *unknown* to us, and which lies beyond the range of our vision, there *may be* full and sufficient reasons for what has been done, and an explanation *may be* found there which would remove all the difficulty.

15. *Thou hast with* thine *arm.* That is, with strength or power, the arm being a symbol of strength. Ex. vi. 6; xv. 16; Ps. x. 15. ¶ *Redeemed thy people.* Thou didst rescue or deliver them from Egyptian bondage. See Notes on Isa. xliii. 3. ¶ *The sons of Jacob and Joseph.* The descendants of Jacob and Joseph. Jacob is mentioned because he was the ancestor of the twelve tribes; Joseph, because he was conspicuous or eminent among the sons of Jacob, and particularly because he acted so important a part in the affairs of Egypt, from whose dominion they were redeemed.

16. *The waters saw thee,* etc. The waters of the Red Sea and the Jordan. There is great sublimity in this expression; in representing the waters as conscious of the presence of God, and as fleeing in consternation at his presence. Comp. Rev. xx. 11; Hab. iii. 10, 11. ¶ *They were afraid.* On the word here used—חוּל, *hhul*—see Notes on Ps. x. 5; lv. 4. It may mean here to tremble or quake, as in pain (Deut. ii. 25; Joel ii. 6). Alarm, distress, anguish, came over the waters at the presence of God; and they trembled, and fled. ¶ *The depths also were troubled.* The deep waters, or the waters *in* the depths. It was not a ripple on the surface; but the very depths—the usually calm and undisturbed waters that lie below the surface—were heaved into commotion at the Divine presence.

17. *The clouds poured out water.* Marg., *The clouds were poured forth with water.* The translation in the text is the more correct. This is a description of a storm; but to what particular storm in history does not appear. It was evidently some ex-

18 The voice [t] of thy thunder *was* in the heaven: the lightnings lightened the world: the earth trembled and shook.

19 Thy way *is* in the sea, and thy path in the great waters, and thy footsteps are not known.

t 2 Sam. xxii. 14.

hibition of the Divine greatness and power in delivering the children of Israel, and may have referred to the extraordinary manifestation of God at Mount Sinai, amidst lightnings, and thunders, and tempests. Exod. xix. 16. For a general description of a storm, as illustrating this passage, see Notes on Job xxxvi. 26–33; xxxvii. 1–5; and Ps. xxix. ¶ *The skies sent out a sound.* The voice of thunder, which seems to come from the sky. ¶ *Thine arrows also.* The lightnings,—compared with burning or ignited arrows. Such arrows were anciently used in war. They were bound round with rags, and dipped in some combustible substance—as turpentine—and shot into houses, corn-fields, haystacks, or towns, for the purpose of setting them on fire. It was not unnatural to compare the rapid lightnings with such blazing arrows. ¶ *Went abroad.* They moved rapidly in all directions.

18. *The voice of thy thunder* was *in the heaven.* Comp. Notes on Ps. xxix. The word rendered *heaven* here —גַּלְגַּל, *galgal*—means properly *a wheel*, as of a chariot, Isa. v. 28; Ezek. x. 2, 6; xxiii. 24; xxvi. 10. Then it means a *whirlwind*, as that which rolls along, Ezek. x. 13. Then it is used to denote chaff or stubble, as driven along before a whirlwind, Ps. lxxxiii. 13; Isa. xvii. 13. It is never used to denote heaven. It means here, undoubtedly, the whirlwind; and the idea is, that in the ragings of the storm, or of the whirlwind, the voice of God was heard,—the deep bellowing thunder,—as if God spake to men. ¶ *The lightnings lightened the world.* The whole earth seemed to be in a blaze. ¶ *The earth trembled and shook.* See Notes on Ps. xxix.

19. *Thy way* is *in the sea.* Probably the literal meaning here is, that God had shown his power and faithfulness in the sea (that is, the Red Sea), in delivering his people; it was there that his true character was seen, as possessing almighty power, and as being able to deliver his people. But this seems to have *suggested*, also, another idea,—that the ways of God, in his providential dealings, were *like* walking through the sea, where no permanent track would be made, where the waves would close on the path, and where it would be impossible by any footprints to ascertain the way which he had taken. So in regard to his doings and his plans. There is nothing by which man can determine in regard to them. There are no traces by which he can follow out the Divine designs,— as none can follow one whose path is through the trackless waters. The subject is beyond man's reach, and there should be no rash or harsh judgment of the Almighty. ¶ *And thy path in the great waters.* The *additional* idea here may be, that the ways or plans of God are *vast*—like the ocean. Even in shallow waters, when one wades through them, the path closes at once, and the way cannot be traced; but God's goings are like those of one who should move through the great ocean—over a boundless sea — where none could hope to follow him. ¶ *And thy footsteps are not known.* The word rendered *footsteps* means properly the print made by the *heel*, and the print made by the foot. The idea here is, that there are no traces in regard to many of the dealings of God, which appear most incomprehensible to us, and which trouble us most, as there can be no footprints left in the waters. We should not venture, therefore, to sit in judgment on the doings of God, or presume that we can understand them.

20 Thou [u] leddest thy people like a flock by the hand of Moses and Aaron.

u Isa. lxiii. 11.

20. *Thou leddest thy people like a flock by the hand of Moses and Aaron.* This satisfied and comforted the mind of the psalmist. God had never forsaken his people. He had shown himself faithful in his dealings with them. He had acted the part of a good shepherd. In all the dangers of their way; in their perilous journey through the wilderness; amidst foes, privations, and troubles,—rocks, sands, storms, tempests,—when surrounded by enemies, and when their camp was infested with poisonous serpents,—God had shown himself able to protect his people, and had been faithful to all his promises and covenant-engagements. Looking back to this period of their history, the psalmist saw that there *was* abundant reason for confiding in God, and that the mind *should* repose on him calmly amid all that was dark and mysterious in his dealings. In view of the past, the mind ought to be calm; encouraged by the past, however incomprehensible may be God's doings, men may come to him, and entrust all their interests to him with the confident assurance that their salvation will be secure, and that all which seems dark and mysterious in the dealings of God will yet be made clear.

PSALM LXXVIII.

This is one of the psalms ascribed to Asaph. See Introd. to Psalm lxxiii. If, as is likely, it was composed at a later period than the time of David, the word *Asaph* must be taken as a general term denoting the successor in the family of Asaph, who presided over the music of the sanctuary. On the word *Maschil* in the title, see Notes on the title to Ps. xxxii.

The *time* when the psalm was composed cannot now be ascertained with any certainty. It was evidently written, however, *after* the revolt of the ten tribes, and the establishment of the sovereignty in the tribe of Judah; that is, after the time of David and Solomon. This is apparent from verse 9, and verse 67, where "Ephraim," the chief of the ten tribes, is referred to in distinction from "Judah."

The *design* of the psalm is, evidently, to vindicate the fact that Ephraim had been rejected, and that Judah had been chosen to be the head of the nation. The *reason* of this was found in the conduct of Ephraim, or the ten tribes, in revolting from God, and in forgetting the Divine mercy and compassion shown to the Hebrew people in former days. See vers. 9-11, 67, 68.

The *argument* in the psalm is the following:—

I. A call on all the people, addressed to them by the king or the ruler, to attend to the instructions of former times,—the lessons which it was of importance to transmit to future generations, vers. 1-4.

II. God had established a general law which he had designed for *all* the people, or which he intended should be the law of the nation as such,—that *all* the people might set their hope in God, or be worshippers of Him as the only true God, and that they might all be *one* people, vers. 5-8.

III. Ephraim—the most powerful of the ten tribes, and their head and representative—had been guilty of disregarding that law, and had refused to come to the common defence of the nation, vers. 9-11.

IV. The wickedness of this rebellion is shown by the great favours which, in its former history, God had shown to the nation as such, including these very tribes, vers. 12-66.

V. The reason is stated, founded on their apostasy, why God had rejected Ephraim, and why he had chosen Judah, and made Zion the capital of the nation, instead of selecting a place within the limits of the tribe of Ephraim for that purpose, vers. 67, 68.

VI. The fact is declared that David had been chosen to rule over the people; that he had been taken from humble life, and made the ruler of the nation, and that the line of the sovereignty had been settled in him, vers. 69-72.

PSALM LXXVIII.

Maschil *v* of Asaph.

GIVE *w* ear, O my people, *to* my law: incline your ears to the words of my mouth.

2 I will open my mouth in a *x* parable; I will utter dark sayings of old;

3 Which we have heard and known, and our fathers have told us.

4 We *y* will not hide *them* from their children, shewing to the generation to come the praises of the LORD, and his strength, and his wonderful works that he hath done.

v Ps. lxxiv., *title.* *w* Isa. li. 4. *x* Matt. xiii. 13, 35. *y* Ex. xiii. 8, 14.

1. *Give ear, O my people.* This is not an address of God, but an address of the king or ruler of the people, calling their attention to an important subject; to wit, his right to rule over them, or showing why the power had been vested in him. ¶ To *my law.* The word *law* here seems to mean *what he would say*, as if what *he* should choose to say would have the force and authority of *law.* What follows is not exactly *law* in the sense that it was a rule to be obeyed; but it is something that is *authoritatively said*, and should have the force of law. ¶ *Incline your ears,* etc. Be attentive. What is to be said is worthy of your particular regard. Comp. Notes on Ps. v. 1.

2. *I will open my mouth in a parable.* See Notes on Ps. xlix. 4. The word *parable* here means a statement by analogy or comparison; that is, he would bring out what he had to say by a course of reasoning founded on an analogy drawn from the ancient history of the people. ¶ *I will utter dark sayings of old.* Of ancient times; that is, maxims, or sententious thoughts, which had come down from past times, and which embodied the results of ancient observation and reflection. Comp. Ps. xlix. 4, where the word rendered *dark sayings* is explained. He would bring out, and apply, to the present case, the maxims of ancient wisdom.

3. *Which we have heard and known.* Which have been communicated to us as certain truth. ¶ *And our fathers have told us.* That is, we have heard and known them *by* their telling us; or, this is the means by which we have known them. They have come down to us by tradition from ancient times.

4. *We will not hide* them *from their children.* From their descendants, however remote. We of this generation will be faithful in handing down these truths to future times. We stand between past generations and the generations to come. We are entrusted by those who have gone before us with great and important truths; truths to be preserved and transmitted in their purity to future ages. That trust committed to us we will faithfully discharge. These truths shall not suffer in passing from us to them. They shall not be stayed in their progress; they shall not be corrupted or impaired. This is the duty of each successive generation in the world, receiving, as a trust, from past generations, the result of their thoughts, their experience, their wisdom, their inventions, their arts, their sciences, and the records of their doings, to hand these down unimpaired to future ages, combined with all that they may themselves invent or discover which may be of use or advantage to the generations following. ¶ *Shewing to the generation to come the praises of the* LORD. The *reasons* why he should be praised, as resulting from his past doings,—and the *ways* in which it should be done. We will keep up, and transmit to future times, the pure institutions of religion. ¶ *And his strength.* The records of his power. ¶ *And his wonderful works that he hath done.* In the history of his people, and in his many and varied interpositions in their behalf.

5 For he established a testimony in Jacob, and appointed a law [z] in Israel, which he commanded our fathers, that they should make them known to their children;

6 That [a] the generation to come might know *them, even* the children *which* should be born, *who* should arise and declare *them* to their children:

7 That they might set their hope in God, and not forget the works of God, but keep his commandments:

8 And [b] might not be as their

z Deut. vi. 7; xi. 19. a Ps. cii. 18. b Ez. xx. 18.

5. *For he established a testimony in Jacob.* He ordained or appointed that which would be for a *witness* for him; that which would bear testimony to his character and perfections; that which would serve to remind them of what he was, and of his authority over them. Any law or ordinance of God is thus a standing and permanent *witness* in regard to his character as showing what he is. ¶ *And appointed a law in Israel.* That is, He gave law to Israel, or to the Hebrew people. Their laws were not human enactments, but were the appointments of God. ¶ *Which he commanded our fathers,* etc. He made it a law of the land that these testimonies should be preserved and faithfully transmitted to future times. See Deut. iv. 9; vi. 7; xi. 19. They were not given for themselves only, but for the benefit of distant generations also.

6. *That the generation to come might know* them, etc. That men in future times might enjoy the benefit of them as their fathers had done, and that they should then send them forward to those who were to succeed them. ¶ Who *should arise and declare* them *to their children.* Who, as they appeared on the stage of life, should receive the trust, and send it onward to future ages. Thus the world makes progress; thus one age starts where the previous one left off; thus it enters on its own career with the advantage of all the toils, the sacrifices, the happy thoughts, the inventions of all past times. It is designed that the world *shall* thus grow wiser and better as it advances; and that future generations shall be enriched with all that was worth preserving in the experience of the past. See Notes on Ps. lxxi. 18.

7. *That they might set their hope in God.* That they might place confidence in God; that they might maintain their allegiance to him. The object was to give such exhibitions of his character and government as to inspire just *confidence* in him, or to lead men to trust in him; and not to trust in idols and false gods. All the laws which God has ordained are such as are fitted to inspire confidence in him as a just and righteous ruler; and all his dealings with mankind, when they are properly—that is, *really*—understood, will be found to be adapted to the same end. ¶ *And not forget the works of God.* His doings. The word here does not refer to his "works" considered as the works of creation, or the material universe, but to his *acts*—to what he has *done* in administering his government over mankind. ¶ *But keep his commandments.* That by contemplating his doings, by understanding the design of his administration, they might be led to keep his commandments. The purpose was that they might *see* such wisdom, justice, equity, and goodness in his administration, that they would be *led* to keep laws so fitted to promote the welfare of mankind. If men saw all the reasons of the Divine dealings, or fully understood them, nothing more would be necessary to secure universal confidence in God and in his government.

8. *And might not be as their fathers.* Their ancestors, particularly in the wilderness, as they passed

fathers, a stubborn and rebellious
[c] generation; a generation *that*
[1] set not their heart aright, and
whose spirit was not stedfast
with God.
9 The children of Ephraim

c Ez. ii. 3—8.
[1] *prepared not their heart,* 2 Chron. xx. 33.

being armed, *and* [2] carrying bows,
turned [d] back in the day of battle.
10 They [e] kept not the covenant of God, and refused to walk
in his law;
11 And forgat [f] his works, and

[2] *throwing forth.* *d* Hos. vii. 11.
e Hos. vi. 4, 7. *f* Ps. cvi. 13.

---

through it to the promised land. See Ex. xxxii. 7–9; xxxiii. 3; xxxiv. 9; Acts vii. 51–53. ¶ *A stubborn and rebellious generation.* Stiff-necked, ungovernable; inclined to revolt. Nothing was more remarkable in their early history than this. ¶ *A generation* that *set not their heart aright.* Marg., as in Heb., *prepared not their heart.* That is, they *took no pains* to keep their heart aright, or to cherish right feelings towards God. They yielded to any sudden impulse of passion, even when it led them to revolt against God. This is as true of sinners now as it was of them, that they *take no pains* to have their hearts right with God. If they did, there would be no difficulty in doing it. It is not with them *an object of desire* to have their hearts right with God, and hence nothing is more easy or natural than that they should rebel and go astray. ¶ *And whose spirit was not stedfast with God.* That is, they themselves did not maintain a firm *trust* in God. They yielded readily to every impulse, and every passion, even when it tended to draw them away wholly from him. There was no such *strength* of attachment to him as would lead them to resist temptation, and they easily fell into the sin of idolatry.

9. *The children of Ephraim.* The sons of Ephraim; that is, the descendants of Ephraim; the tribe of Ephraim. Ephraim was one of the *largest* of the tribes of Israel, and was the *chief* tribe in the rebellion, and hence the term is often used to denote the *ten* tribes, or the kingdom of Israel, in contradistinction from that of Judah. See Isa. vii. 2, 5, 8, 9, 17; xi. 13; xxviii. 1. The word is evidently used in this sense here, not as denoting that one tribe only, but that tribe as the head of the revolted kingdom; or, in other words, the name is used as representing the kingdom of that name after the revolt. See 1 Kings xii. This verse evidently contains the *gist* or the main idea of the psalm,—to wit, that *Ephraim,* or the *ten tribes,* had turned away from the worship of the true God, and that, in consequence of that apostasy, the government had been transferred to another tribe—the tribe of Judah. See vers. 67, 68. ¶ Being *armed.* The idea in this phrase is, that they had abundant means for maintaining their independence in connexion with the other tribes, or as a part of the nation, but that they refused to cooperate with their brethren. ¶ And *carrying bows.* Marg., *throwing forth.* Literally, *lifting up.* The idea is, that they were armed with bows; or, that they were fully armed. ¶ *Turned back in the day of battle.* That is, they did not stand by their brethren, or assist them in defending their country. There is probably no reference here to any particular battle, but the idea is, that in the wars of the nation—in those wars which were waged for national purposes—they refused to join with the tribes of Judah and Benjamin in defence of the lawful government.

10. *They kept not the covenant of God.* The covenant which God had made with the entire Hebrew people. They did not maintain their allegiance to Jehovah. Comp. Deut. iv. 13, 23; xvii. 2. ¶ *And refused to walk in his law.* Refused to *obey* his law. They rebelled against him.

11. *And forgat his works.* The

his wonders that he had shewed
them.
12 Marvellous things *g* did he
in the sight of their fathers, in the
land of Egypt, *in* the field of
h Zoan.
13 He divided *i* the sea, and
caused them to pass through;
and he made *k* the waters to
stand as an heap.
14 In *l* the day-time also he
led them with a cloud, and all
the night with a light of fire.
15 He clave *m* the rocks in the
wilderness, and gave *them* drink
as *out of* the great depths.
16 He *n* brought streams also

g Ex. vii.—xii. *h* Isa. xix. 11, 13. *i* Ex. xiv. 21. *k* Ex. xv. 8.

l Ex. xiii. 21. *m* Ex. xvii. 6; Num. xx. 11; 1 Cor. x. 4. *n* Ps. cv. 41.

---

works which he had performed in behalf of the nation. These works are referred to in the verses following. ¶ *And his wonders that he had shewed them.* The wonderful works in Egypt, at the Red Sea, and in the wilderness;—the miracles which he had wrought in behalf of the nation.

12. *Marvellous things did he in the sight of their fathers.* Things fitted to excite wonder and astonishment. Such were all the miracles that he wrought, in effecting the deliverance of his people. ¶ *In the land of Egypt.* In delivering them from Pharaoh. ¶ In *the field of Zoan.* The Septuagint render this ἐν πεδίῳ Τάνεως—*in the plain of Tanis.* So the Latin Vulgate. Zoan or Tanis was an ancient city of Lower Egypt, situated on the eastern side of the Tanitic arm of the Nile. The name given to it in the Egyptian language signified *low region.* See Notes on Isa. xix. 11. The Hebrews seem to have been located in this region, and it was in this part of Egypt—that is, in the country lying round about Zoan—that the wonders of God were principally manifested in behalf of his people.

13. *He divided the sea,* etc. The Red Sea. Ex. xiv. 21, 22. ¶ *And he made the waters to stand as an heap.* The word rendered *heap* means anything piled up, or a mound; and the idea is, that the waters were piled up on each side of them as a *mound.* See Notes on Ps. xxxiii. 7. Comp. Josh. iii. 13, 16; Ex. xv. 8.

14. *In the day-time also he led them with a cloud.* That is, the cloud was the visible symbol of his presence, and its movements determined the way in which they were to go. It was *God* who led them, and who adopted this manner of doing it, so that they had *always* with them, by day and by night, a *visible* proof of his presence. There was that with them which could not be ascribed to any natural causes, and which, therefore, *demonstrated* that God was with them, and that as long as they followed the cloud and the pillar of fire they could not err. See Ex. xiii. 21; xiv. 24. They had the less excuse, therefore, for rebelling against him. ¶ *And all the night with a light of fire.* A column—a pillar—which stood over the camp, and which was a symbol of the Divine presence and guidance. The cloud would not be visible by night, nor would the fire be a good guide by day; and hence the *form* of the symbol was changed. The same thing, however, was intended by both, and together they were standing proofs of the presence of God.

15. *He clave the rocks in the wilderness.* There were two occasions on which the rock was smitten for water; one (Ex. xvii. 6) at Mount Horeb, shortly after they came out of Egypt; and the other (Num. xx. 11), when they had nearly ceased their wanderings in the wilderness. Hence the plural term (*rocks*) is used here. ¶ *And gave* them *drink as* out of *the great depths.* As if he had formed a lake or an ocean, furnishing an inexhaustible supply.

16. *He brought streams also out of the rock,* etc. Literally, *flowings.* The

out of the rock, and caused waters to run down like rivers.

17 And they sinned yet more against him, by provoking [o] the Most High in the wilderness.

18 And [p] they tempted God in their heart, by asking meat for their lust.

19 Yea, they spake against God; they said, Can God [1] furnish a table in the wilderness?

20 Behold, he smote the rock, that the waters gushed out, and

o De. ix. 22; He. iii. 16—19. p Ex. xvi. 2. 1 *order.*

waters were poured out in an overflowing stream. Those streams continued to flow, thus constituting a continued proof of the presence of God. See this fully explained in the Notes on 1 Cor. x. 4.

17. *And they sinned yet more against him.* Literally, "They *added* to sin against him." The idea is, that his mercies, and the proofs of his presence were only made the occasion of greater sin on their part. This may have been in two ways;—(1) their sin was thus more aggravated, as being committed against greater light; and (2) they evinced more and more their depravity, in proportion as he bestowed mercies on them,—not an uncommon thing with men. ¶ *By provoking the Most High.* Literally, *embittering.* They rebelled against him. They refused to submit to him. They forgot his mercies. Comp. Deut. ix. 22. ¶ *In the wilderness.* Literally, *in the dry place;* in the desert. In the very place where they were most manifestly dependent on him—where there were no natural streams of water,—where their wants were met by a miraculous supply,—even there did they provoke him, and rebel against him. If he had simply stopped that miraculous supply of water they must have perished. But sinners forget how dependent they are on God, when they sin against him. On what can they rely, if he withdraws from them, and leaves them to themselves?

18. *And they tempted God in their heart.* Ex. xvi. 2. The *heart* was the source of the evil. They were not satisfied with what he gave them. They asked for that which would be more agreeable to them, and they did it with a complaining and a murmuring spirit. It is not wrong in itself to ask of God that which will be *better* than what we now possess, for that is the object of all our prayers; but this may be done from a wrong motive,—for mere self-gratification, as was the case here; or it may be with a murmuring and dissatisfied spirit, such as was evinced on this occasion. In such a case we cannot expect the prayer to be answered *except as a punishment.* ¶ *By asking meat for their lust.* Food. The word *meat* here does not necessarily denote animal food, as it does with us. They asked another kind of food than manna; and they did it, not because this was *necessary* to sustain life, but in order to gratify their appetites. The original word here, however, is not *lusts,* but *souls;* that is, *they asked food for themselves.*

19. *Yea, they spake against God.* That is, in the manner which is immediately specified — by calling in question his power, or his ability to provide for them in the wilderness. See Num. xi. 4. ¶ *They said, Can God furnish a table in the wilderness?* In the desert. The word rendered *furnish* is in the margin "*order.*" It means to arrange; to set in order; and here to arrange and provide for, as at a feast. The precise words used by the murmuring Hebrews are not quoted here, but the substance of what they said is retained. The idea is, that what they spake was *equivalent* to saying that God could not prepare a table for them; that is, provide for them, in the desert.

20. *Behold, he smote the rock,* etc. See Notes on ver. 15. The smiting of the rock the first time occurred *before* the murmuring about the food.

the streams overflowed; can he
give bread also? can he provide
flesh for his people.
21 Therefore the LORD heard
this, and was [q] wroth: so a fire
was kindled against Jacob, and
anger also came up against
Israel;
22 Because they believed not
in God, and trusted not in his
salvation;
23 Though he had commanded
the clouds from above, and opened the doors [r] of heaven,
24 And had rained down manna upon them to eat, and had
given them of the corn of heaven.
25 [1] Man did eat angels' food:
he sent them meat to the full.

q Num. xi. 1, etc. r Mal. iii. 10.

1 Or, *Every one did eat the bread of the mighty*, Ps. ciii. 20.

The fact that the rock had been smitten could not be doubted. They had thus had abundant evidence that God was able to do that, and to furnish *water* for them in the desert. It was unreasonable, therefore, to doubt whether he could provide *food* for them,—for this in itself was no more difficult than to furnish water. Yet they are represented as affirming that this was far more difficult, and that, although it was admitted that God had provided *water*, yet that to provide *food* was wholly beyond his power. Their special sin, therefore, was, that they doubted the power of God in one case, when, in another, equally difficult, they had had abundant proof of it. The spirit of murmuring had not been put down by one surprising and undoubted miracle wrought in their behalf,—a miracle which proved that God had all the power needful to meet their wants. ¶ *Can he give bread also?* Does the ability to cause water to flow from a rock prove that there is also ability to produce bread when necessary? They doubted it, and thus murmured against God. ¶ *Can he provide flesh for his people?* They supposed that this required greater power than the providing of water, or even of bread, and that if it were admitted that God could furnish the two former, it would by no means follow that he could provide the latter. It was this, as the next verse shows, which was the immediate occasion of the special anger of the Lord.

21. *Therefore the Lord heard* this, *and was wroth.* See Num. xi. 1, 10. ¶ *So a fire was kindled against Jacob,* etc. Fire may be used here, as in Num. xi. 1, as an emblem of wrath; a fire may have been literally sent down to consume them.

22. *Because they believed not in God.* They did not believe in his power, or in his promises. ¶ *And trusted not in his salvation.* In his power and his willingness to save. They had had abundant evidence of that power, but they still doubted his ability to save them, notwithstanding all that he had done for them.

23. *Though he had commanded the clouds from above.* Though he had showed that he had absolute control over the clouds, and had only to command them and they would furnish rain in abundance. Comp. Notes on Isa. v. 6. ¶ *And opened the doors of heaven.* As he had done at the deluge, Gen. vii. 11. The idea is, that he had rained down manna upon them in such abundance that it might be compared with the waters that had been sent down at the deluge.

24. *And had rained down manna upon them to eat.* Ex. xvi. 4, 5, 14; Num. xi. 7–9. Comp. Notes on John vi. 31. ¶ *And had given them of the corn of heaven.* Food that seemed to come down from heaven. The reference here is to the *manna*, and it is called *corn* in the sense that it was *food*, or that it supplied the place of grain. It may also have been called *corn* from its resemblance to grain. See Ex. xvi. 31.

25. *Man did eat angels' food.* Food that came from heaven; food so directly and manifestly from heaven

26 He caused an east wind to [1] blow in the heaven; and by his power he brought in the south wind.
27 He [s] rained flesh also upon them as dust, and [2] feathered fowls like as the sand of the sea;
28 And he let *it* fall in the midst of their camp, round about their habitations.
29 So they did eat, and were well filled: for [t] he gave them their own desire;
30 They were not estranged from their lust: but while their meat *was* yet in their mouths,

[1] *go.* [s] Num. xi. 18, 31. [2] *fowl of wing.* [t] Ps. cvi. 15.

that it might be *supposed* to be the same kind that was eaten there, and that had now been sent down by a special miracle for man;—food so delicate and so free from the ordinary coarse properties of food, that it might be supposed to be such as angels feed on. The word rendered *angels*—אַבִּיר, *abbir*—means properly *strong, mighty,* and may be applied to men in general, Judges v. 22; Lam. i. 15; Jer. xlvi. 15; to animals, Ps. xxii. 13 ("bulls of Bashan"); to princes, Ps. lxviii. 31; or to nobles, Job xxiv. 22. It *might* be rendered here *food of nobles,* or *princes;* that is, food of richer quality, or of a more delicate nature, than common food; such as nobles or princes have on their tables. The immediate connexion, however, would rather seem to demand the rendering in our version, as the food is said to have come down from heaven. It is rendered *food of angels* in the Septuagint, in the Latin Vulgate, in the ancient versions generally, and also by Luther. De Wette renders it, "Each one ate the food of princes;" that is, they all lived like princes. ¶ *He sent them meat to the full.* Food to satisfy; or, as much as they wanted.

26. *He caused an east wind to blow in the heaven.* See Num. xi. 31. In the history, the quarter from which the wind came is not mentioned, except as it might be indicated by the statement that the "quails were brought from the sea;"—that is, evidently, the Red Sea. This wind would have come from the south-east. The phrase "in the heaven" means in the air, or from above. ¶ *And by his power,* etc. By his direct agency. It was a wind which he caused to blow for the purpose; a miracle.

27. *He rained flesh also upon them as dust.* The flesh of quails, Num. xi. 31. The word *rained* means that they seemed to come upon them *like* a copious shower. The word *dust* denotes their great abundance. ¶ *And feathered fowls.* Marg., as in Heb., *fowl of wing.* This is a poetic expression, designed to give beauty to the description by the image of their fluttering wings. ¶ *Like as the sand of the sea.* An expression also designed to denote their great numbers, Gen. xxii. 17; xxxii. 12; xli. 49; Josh. xi. 4; 1 Sam. xiii. 5; Rev. xx. 8.

28. *And he let* it *fall in the midst of their camp,* etc. It was brought to their very doors; they had not to go and seek it abroad.

29. *So they did eat, and were well filled.* The word rendered *well* here is intensive. It means that they were abundantly satisfied; that there was no lack; that they had the most ample supply. ¶ *For he gave them their own desire.* He gave them exactly what they asked. He gave them flesh to eat as they had demanded; and he gave it to them in such quantities that no one could say that he had not enough.

30. *They were not estranged from their lust.* Literally, *They were not made strangers to;* that is, in regard to their lusts or desires they were not in the condition of *foreigners* or aliens; they were not separated from them. The word *lusts* here means *desires, wishes.* It is not used here in the restricted sense in which it is now with us. The reference is to their

31 The wrath of God came upon them, and slew the fattest of them, and [1] smote down the [2] chosen *men* of Israel,
32 For all this they sinned still, and believed not for his wondrous works.

[1] *made to bow.* [2] Or, *young*, Isa. xl. 30, 31.

33 Therefore their days did he consume in vanity, and their years in trouble.
34 When [u] he slew them, then they sought him; and they returned and enquired early after God:

u Isa. xxvi. 16; Hosea v. 15.

desire for food different from manna,—for *flesh;* and the idea is, that they did not restrain their intense desire even when it should have been fully satisfied. They indulged to excess, and the consequence was that many of them perished. ¶ *But while their meat* was *yet in their mouths.* Even while they were eating, and were indulging in this unrestrained manner.

31. *The wrath of God came upon them.* See Num. xi. 33. ¶ *And slew the fattest of them.* Literally, *slew among their fat ones.* That is, The most vigorous among them were cut down; the men most eminent for rank, for influence, for strength, for valour. How far this was the natural effect of indulgence in eating, and how far it was a direct miracle, cannot now be ascertained. In either case it would equally show the Divine displeasure. ¶ *And smote down.* Marg., as in Heb., *made to bow.* That is, they were made to bow in death. ¶ *The chosen* men *of Israel.* Marg., *Young men.* The idea is that of select men; men that would be chosen from among the others; men distinguished for vigour or influence. Not the aged or the feeble particularly, not those who might be naturally expected to fall, but men of strength who might be supposed to be capable of resisting the ordinary attacks of disease. God showed in this way that the judgment came directly from his hand.

32. *For all this they sinned still.* Even this did not reclaim them, and prevent their sinning. Heavy judgments do not always restrain men from sin. Not unfrequently they take occasion *from* such judgments to sin the more. ¶ *And believed not for his wondrous works.* They did not trust in his wondrous works; or, those works did not have the effect of producing faith. See vers. 22, 23. The same thing occurred in the life of the Saviour. John xii. 37.

33. *Therefore their days did he consume in vanity.* He suffered them to spend their days—the days of that entire generation—in vain and fruitless wanderings in the desert. Instead of leading them at once to the promised land, they were kept there to wear out their life in tedious monotony, accomplishing nothing,—wandering from place to place,—until all the generation that had come out of Egypt had died. ¶ *And their years in trouble.* Literally, *in terror.* Amidst the troubles, the alarms, the terrors of a vast and frightful desert. Sin—rebellion against God—leads to a course of life, and a death, of which these gloomy, sad, and cheerless wanderings in the desert were a striking emblem.

34. *When he slew them.* When he came forth in his wrath and cut them down by the plague, by fiery serpents, or by their enemies. ¶ *Then they sought him.* Their calamities had the effect of producing temporary reformation. They became professedly penitent; they manifested a wish to know God, and expressed a purpose to serve him. It was, however, a temporary and hollow, not a deep and real reformation. This often occurs. In times of affliction, in sickness, in bereavement, in the loss of property, men become serious, and express a purpose to repent and turn to God. A deep impression seems to be produced on their minds, to last, alas! only as long as the hand of God rests upon them. Resolutions of re-

35 And they remembered that
God *was* their rock, [v] and the
high God their redeemer.
36 Nevertheless they did flatter [w] him with their mouth, and
they lied unto him with their
tongues:
37 For their heart was not
right with him, neither were
they stedfast in his covenant.
38 But he, *being* full of compassion, forgave [x] *their* iniquity,
and destroyed *them* not: yea,
many a time turned he his anger
away, and [y] did not stir up all
his wrath:

v Deut. xxxii. 4, 15. *w* Deut. v. 28, 29.

x Num. xiv. 18, 20. *y* Isa. xlviii. 9.

---

pentance are formed only to be forgotten when the affliction is removed, and when the days of prosperity again return. ¶ *And they returned and enquired early after God.* The word rendered "*enquired early*" has reference to the first rays of the morning—the aurora—the dawn. Then it comes to denote the beginning of anything; or, the first thing. Thus employed, it may refer to the act of seeking God as the first thing; in youth; in the morning; at the commencement of any enterprise or undertaking. See Prov. viii. 17; i. 28. Here it means that, in their affliction, they did not delay to seek God, but expressed an early intention of serving him. They evinced a prompt purpose to break off their sins, and to return to him.

35. *And they remembered that God* was *their Rock.* See Deut. xxxii. 4, 15, 31. Comp. Notes on Ps. xviii. 2. That is, they were brought to reflect that their only security and defence was God. They were made to feel that they could not rely on themselves, or on any human power, and that their only trust was in God. ¶ *And the high God their Redeemer.* The God who is exalted over all; the true and living God. The truth was brought to their recollection that it was He who had delivered them from bondage in Egypt, and who had brought them out into freedom. On the word *Redeemer,* see Notes on Isa. xli. 14. Comp. Isa. xliii. 14; xliv. 6, 24; xlvii. 4; lix. 20; Ps. xxv. 22; Job v. 20.

36. *Nevertheless they did flatter him with their mouth.* The word rendered *flatter* means properly *to open;* and hence *to be open; to be ingenuous* or *frank;* and then, to be easily persuaded, to be deluded, to be beguiled; and hence, also, in an active form, to persuade, to entice, to seduce, to beguile, to delude. The meaning here is, that they attempted to deceive by their professions, or that their professions were false and hollow. Those professions were the *mere* result of affliction. They were based on no principle; there was no true love or confidence at the foundation. Such professions or promises are often made in affliction. Under the pressure of heavy judgments, the loss of property, the loss of friends, or the failure of health, men become serious, and resolve to give attention to religion. It is rarely that such purposes are founded in sincerity, and that the conversions apparently resulting from them are true conversions. The Septuagint and the Latin Vulgate render the phrase here, "They *loved* with their mouth." ¶ *And they lied unto him with their tongues.* They made promises which they did not keep.

37. *For their heart was not right with him.* Luther renders this, *Not fast with him.* The Hebrew word means *to fit, to prepare;* and the idea is, that the heart was not *adjusted* to such a profession, or did not *accord* with such a promise or pledge. It was a mere profession made by the lips, while the heart remained unaffected. See Notes on ver. 8. ¶ *Neither were they stedfast in his covenant.* In maintaining his covenant, or in adhering to it. Comp. Ps. xxv. 14; xliv. 17. See also ver. 8.

38. *But he,* being *full of compassion.* Literally, *But he, merciful.*

39 For he remembered [z] that they *were but* flesh; a wind [a] that passeth away, and cometh not again.
40 How oft did they [1] provoke
[b] him in the wilderness, *and* grieve him in the desert!
41 Yea, they turned back, and tempted God, and limited [c] the Holy One of Israel.

z Ps. ciii. 14. *a* James iv. 14.
1 Or, *rebel against*.
b Ps. xcv. 8—10. *c* vers. 19, 20.

That is, he was ready to forgive them. ¶ *Forgave* their *iniquity.* Literally, *Atoned for, expiated, covered over their iniquity.* There is connected with the word the idea of expiation or atonement, as the ground of pardon. ¶ *And destroyed* them *not.* Did not cut them off in their repeated acts of rebellion. He bore with them, and spared them. ¶ *Yea, many a time turned he his anger away.* Literally, *He multiplied to turn his anger away.* That is, he did it repeatedly. There were frequent occasions on their journey for doing this, and he did it. ¶ *And did not stir up all his wrath.* Literally, *Did not excite,* or *arouse all his anger.* His anger was stayed or mitigated, and they were suffered still to live.

39. *For he remembered that they* were but *flesh.* That they were human; that they were weak; that they were prone to err; that they were liable to fall into temptation. In his dealings with them he took into view their fallen nature; their training; their temptations; their trials; their weaknesses; and he judged them accordingly. Comp. Ps. ciii. 14. So it was with the Saviour in his treatment of his disciples, "The spirit indeed is willing, but the flesh is weak," Matt. xxvi. 41. God will judge men as they are; he will not in his judgments forget that they *are* men, and that they are weak and feeble. Men often judge their fellow-men with much more harshness, with much less allowance for their infirmities and weaknesses, than God shows in his dealings with mankind. And yet such are the very men who are most ready to blame God for his judgments. If God acted on the principle and in the manner according to which they act, they could hope for no mercy at his hand. It is well for them that there is not one like themselves on the throne of the universe. ¶ *A wind that passeth away, and cometh not again.* Which blows by us, and is gone for ever. What a striking description is this of man! How true of an individual! How true of a generation! How true of the race at large! God remembers this when he thinks of men, and he deals with them accordingly. He is not harsh and severe, but kind and compassionate. To man, a being so feeble,—to the human race, so frail,—to the generations of that race, so transitory, so soon passing off the stage of life,—he is ever willing to show compassion. He does not make use of his great power to crush them; he prefers to manifest his mercy in saving them.

40. *How oft did they provoke him in the wilderness.* Marg., *Or, rebel against him.* The Hebrew word may have the signification in the margin. The idea is, that they were perverse and rebellious; that they excited his displeasure, and gave occasion for his anger. See ver. 17. ¶ And *grieve him in the desert.* The word here rendered *grieve* means (1) *to work, to fashion;* (2) *to suffer pain, to travail, to be afflicted;* and then, (3) to *cause* one to suffer pain, or *to afflict.* The meaning here is that the conduct of the Hebrews was such as was fitted to cause pain,—as the conduct of a disobedient and rebellious child is.

41. *Yea, they turned back, and tempted God.* They turned away from his service; they were disposed to return to Egypt, and to place themselves in the condition in which they were before they were delivered

42 They remembered not his
hand, *nor* the day when he delivered them from the [1] enemy:
43 How he had [2] wrought his
signs in Egypt, and his wonders
[d] in the field of Zoan:
44 And had turned their rivers
into [e] blood; and their floods,
that they could not drink.
45 He [f] sent divers sorts of
flies among them, which devoured them; and frogs, which destroyed them.

[1] Or, *affliction*. [2] *set*. *d* ver. 12. *e* Ex. vii. 20. *f* Ex. viii. 6, 24.

from bondage. ¶ *And limited the Holy One of Israel.* The idea is, that they set a limit to the power of God; they fancied or alleged—(and this is a thing often done practically even by the professed people of God)—that there was a boundary in respect to power which he could not pass, or that there were things to be done which he had not the ability to perform. The original word—תָּוָה, *tavah*—occurs but three times in the Scriptures;—in 1 Sam. xxi. 13, where it is rendered *scrabbled* (in the margin, *made marks*); in Ezek. ix. 4, where it is rendered *set, i.e.*, set a mark (marg., *mark*); and in the place before us. It is rendered here by the Septuagint and the Latin Vulgate, *to provoke to anger.* De Wette translates it *troubled.* Professor Alexander, "On the Holy One of Israel [they] set a mark." The *idea* in the word would seem to be that of making a mark for any purpose; and then it means to delineate; to scrawl; or to set a mark for a limit or boundary. Thus it might be applied to God,—as if, in estimating his character or his power, they set *limits* or *bounds* to it, as one does in marking out a farm or a house-lot in a city or town. There was a limit, in their estimation, to the power of God, beyond which he could not act; or, in other words, his power was *defined* and *bounded,* so that beyond a certain point he could not aid them.

42. *They remembered not his hand.* His gracious interpositions; the manifestations of his power. They forgot that power *had been* exercised which showed that he was omnipotent,—that there *was* no limit to his ability to aid them. ¶ Nor *the day when he delivered them from the enemy.* The time when he rescued them. The power then manifested was sufficient to defend and deliver them in any new dangers that could befall them. The margin is, *from affliction.* The Hebrew will admit of either interpretation. The sense is not materially changed.

43. *How he had wrought his signs in Egypt.* Marg., *set.* The Hebrew word means to set or place. The word *signs* here refers to miracles as signs or indications of God's power and favour. The things which he did were of such a nature as to show that he was almighty, and at the same time to assure them of his disposition to protect them. ¶ *And his wonders in the field of Zoan.* The wonderful things which he did; the things fitted to excite amazement, or astonishment. On the word Zoan, see Notes on ver. 12.

44. *And had turned their rivers into blood.* Ex. vii. 20. There was properly but one *river* in Egypt—the Nile. But there were several branches of that river at the mouth; and there were numerous artificial streams or canals cut from the river, to any one of which the word *river* might be also given. Comp. Notes on Isa. xi. 15. ¶ *And their floods,* etc. Their streams; the canals and branches of the Nile, where they usually obtained a supply of water.

45. *He sent divers sorts of flies,* etc. The account of this plague is found in Ex. viii. 24. The word there used is simply "*swarm,*" without indicating *what* the swarm was composed of. The Rabbins explain the word as denoting a *mixture,* or a *conflux* of noxious insects, as if the word were

46 He *g* gave also their increase unto the caterpillar, and their labour unto the locust.

47 He [1] destroyed their vines with *h* hail, and their sycamore-trees with [2] frost.

48 He [3] gave up their cattle also to the hail, and their flocks to [4] hot thunderbolts.

g Ex. x. 13. [1] *killed.* *h* Ex. ix. 23—25.

[2] Or, *great hailstones.* [3] *shut up.* [4] Or, *lightnings.*

derived from עָרַב—*arab—to mix.* The Septuagint renders it κυνόμυια—*dog-fly*—which Philo describes as so named from its impudence. The common explanation of the word now is that it denotes a species of fly—the gad-fly—exceedingly troublesome to man and beast, and that it derives its name—עָרֹב, *arob*—from the verb עָרַב, *arab*, in one of its significations *to suck*, and hence the allusion to *sucking* the blood of animals. The word occurs only in the following places, Exod. viii. 21, 22, 24, 29, 31, where it is rendered *swarm*, or *swarms*, and Ps. cv. 31, where (as here) it is rendered *divers sorts of flies.* ¶ *And frogs which destroyed them.* Ex. viii. 6. The *order* in which the plagues occurred is not preserved in the account in the psalm.

46. *He gave also their increase unto the caterpillar.* The increase or the produce of their fields. Exod. x. 12–14. The word חָסִיל, *hhasil*—is supposed to denote a species of locust rather than the caterpillar. It literally means *the devourer.* In our version, however, it is uniformly rendered *caterpillar* as here; 1 Kings viii. 37; 2 Chron. vi. 28; Isa. xxxiii. 4; Joel i. 4; ii. 25. It occurs nowhere else. ¶ *And their labour unto the locust.* The fruit of their labour; the harvests in their fields.

47. *He destroyed their vines with hail.* Marg., *killed.* See Exod. ix. 22–26. In the account in Exodus the hail is said to have smitten man and beast, the herb, and the tree of the field. In the psalm only one thing is mentioned, perhaps denoting the ruin by what would be particularly felt in Palestine, where the culture of the grape was so common and so important. ¶ *And their sycamore trees with frost.* The sycamore is mentioned particularly as giving poetic beauty to the passage. Of the sycamore tree, Dr. Thomson remarks ("Land and the Book," vol. i. p. 25), "It is a tender tree, flourishes immensely in sandy plains and warm vales, but cannot bear the hard, cold mountain. A sharp frost will kill them; and this agrees with the fact that they were killed by it in Egypt. Among the wonders wrought in the field of Zoan, David says, 'He destroyed their vines with hail, and their sycamores with frost.' Certainly, a frost keen enough to kill the sycamore would be one of the greatest 'wonders' that could happen at the present day in this same field of Zoan." The word rendered *frost*—חֲנָמַל, *hhanamal*—occurs nowhere else. It is parallel with the word *hail* in the other member of the sentence, and denotes something that would be destructive to trees. The Septuagint, the Vulgate, and the Arabic render it *frost.* Gesenius renders it *ants.*

48. *He gave up their cattle also to the hail.* Marg., *he shut up.* Ex. ix. 22–25. ¶ *And their flocks to hot thunderbolts.* Marg., *lightnings.* The original word means flame; then, lightning. There is no allusion in the word to the idea of a *bolt*, or *shaft*, accompanying the lightning or the thunder, by which destruction is produced. The destruction is caused by the lightning, and not by the thunder, and it is hardly necessary to say that there is no *shaft* or *bolt* that accompanies it. Probably this notion was formerly entertained, and found its way into the common language used. The same idea is retained by us in the word *thunderbolt.* But this idea is not in the original; nor is there any foundation for it in fact.

49 He cast upon them the fierceness of his anger, wrath, and indignation, and trouble, by sending evil angels *among them.*

50 He [1] made a way to his anger; he spared not their soul from death, but gave their [2] life over to the pestilence;

51 And smote all the first-born [i] in Egypt; the chief of *their* strength in the tabernacles of Ham:

52 But made his own people to go forth like sheep, and guided them in the wilderness like a flock.

53 And [k] he led them on safely, so that they feared not: but the sea [3] overwhelmed their enemies.

54 And he brought them to

[1] *weighed a path.* [2] Or, *beasts to the murrain,* Ex. ix. 3—6.

i Ex. xii. 29. *k* Ex. xiv., xv. [3] *covered.*

---

49. *He cast upon them the fierceness of his anger,* etc. This verse is designed to describe the last, and the most dreadful of the plagues that came upon the Egyptians, the slaying of their first-born; and hence there is such an *accumulation* of expressions:—anger,—fierce anger,—wrath,—indignation,—trouble. All these expressions are designed to be emphatic; all these things were combined when the first-born were slain. There was no form of affliction that could surpass this; and in this trial all the expressions of the Divine displeasure seemed to be exhausted. It was *meant* that this should be the last of the plagues; it was meant that the nation should be humbled, and should be made willing that the people of Israel should go. ¶ *By sending evil angels among them.* There is reference here undoubtedly to the slaying of the first-born in Egypt. Ex. xi. 4, 5; xii. 29, 30. This work is ascribed to the agency of a *destroyer* (Ex. xii. 23; comp. Heb. xi. 28), and the allusion seems to be to a *destroying angel,* or to an angel employed and commissioned to accomplish such a work. Comp. 2 Sam. xxiv. 16; 2 Kings xix. 35. The idea here is not that the angel himself was *evil* or *wicked,* but that he was the *messenger* of evil or calamity; he was the instrument by which these afflictions were brought upon them.

50. *He made a way to his anger.* Marg., *he weighed a path.* He levelled a path for it; he took away all hindrance to it; he allowed it to have free scope. The idea of *weighing* is not in the original. The allusion is to a preparation made by which one can march along freely, and without any obstruction. See Notes on Isa. xl. 3, 4. ¶ *He spared not their soul from death.* He spared not their *lives.* That is, he gave them over to death. ¶ *But gave their life over to the pestilence.* Marg., *their beasts to the murrain.* The original will admit of either interpretation, but the connexion seems rather to demand the interpretation which is in the text. Both these things, however, occurred.

51. *And smote all the firstborn in Egypt.* See Ex. xi. 4, 5; xii. 29, 30. ¶ *The chief of* their *strength.* Those on whom they relied; their firstborn; their pride; their glory; their heirs. Comp. Gen. xlix. 3. ¶ *In the tabernacles of Ham.* The tents; the dwelling-places of Ham;—that is, of Egypt. Comp. Gen. x. 6; Ps. cv. 23, 27; cvi. 22.

52. *But made his own people to go forth like sheep,* etc. That is, he was a shepherd to them. He defended them; provided for them; led them—as a shepherd does his flock. See Notes on Ps. xxiii. 1, 2.

53. *And he led them on safely, so that they feared not.* In hope; in confidence; so that they had no occasion for alarm. He showed himself able and willing to defend them. ¶ *But the sea overwhelmed their enemies.* Marg., as in Heb., *covered.* See Ex. xiv. 27, 28; xv. 10.

54. *And he brought them to the border of his sanctuary.* The Septuagint and the Latin Vulgate render this, *to the mountain of his holiness;*

the border of his sanctuary, *even to* this mountain, *which* his right hand had purchased.

55 He cast out the heathen also before them, and divided *l* them an inheritance by line, and made the tribes of Israel to dwell in their tents.

56 Yet they tempted and provoked the most high God, and kept not his testimonies;

57 But turned back, and dealt unfaithfully like their fathers: they were turned aside like a deceitful bow.

58 For *m* they provoked him to anger with their high places, and moved him to jealousy with their graven images.

l Josh. xix. 51. *m* Judges ii. 12, 20.

---

that is, his holy mountain. But the reference is rather to the whole land of Canaan. He brought them to the borders of that land—the land of promise—the holy land. They who came out from Egypt did not indeed enter that land, except Caleb and Joshua, but they were conveyed to its borders before all of them fell. It was true also that the people—the Hebrew people—came *to* the promised land, and secured its possession. ¶ Even to *this mountain.* Mount Zion; for the object of the psalm was to show that the worship of God was properly celebrated there. See ver. 68. The meaning is not that the people who came out of Egypt actually inherited that mountain, but that their descendants—the people of God—had been put in possession of it. ¶ Which *his right hand had purchased.* Had procured, or obtained possession of. That is, he had secured it by his power.

55. *He cast out the heathen also before them.* Literally, *the nations.* The idea of their being *heathen,* in the sense which is now attached to that word, is not in the original. The word is one which would be applied to any nation, without reference to its religion. These nations were, indeed, *heathens* according to the present use of that term, but that idea is not necessarily in the Hebrew word. ¶ *And divided them an inheritance by line.* Divided to his people an inheritance by a measurement of the land. That is, the land was partitioned out among the tribes, by a survey, fixing their limits and boundaries. See Joshua xiii. 7; xviii.; xix. ¶ *And made the tribes of Israel to dwell in their tents.* To dwell securely and quietly, no longer roaming from place to place, but having a fixed habitation and a home.

56. *Yet they tempted and provoked,* etc. They tried the patience of God, and provoked him to anger *after* they were peaceably settled in the promised land. See Judges ii. 10–13. The object is to show that it was the character of the people that they were prone to depart from God. Comp. Notes on vers. 10, 11, 17, 40.

57. *But turned back,* etc. See Notes on ver. 41. ¶ *They were turned aside like a deceitful bow.* Literally, *a bow of deceit.* That is, a bow that could not be depended on; a bow, one of whose arms was longer or more elastic than the other, so that the arrow would turn aside from the mark. The marksman would attempt to hit an object, and would fail. So it was with the people of Israel. They could not be depended on. No reliance could be put on their promises, their covenant-engagements, their attachment, their fidelity; for in these things they failed, as the arrow from a deceitful bow would fail to strike the mark. Their whole history shows how just was this charge; alas! the history of many of the professed people of God has shown how applicable the description has been to *them* also.

58. *For they provoked him to anger with their high places.* Places where idols were worshipped; usually on mountains or elevated places. Lev. xxvi. 30; comp. 1 Kings iii. 2; xii. 31, 32; 2 Kings xvii. 32; 2 Chron.

59 When God heard *this*, he was wroth, and greatly abhorred Israel:

60 So that he forsook the tabernacle of Shiloh, the tent *which* he placed among men;

61 And delivered his strength into captivity, and his glory into the enemy's hand.

62 He [n] gave his people over also unto the sword; and was wroth with his inheritance.

n 1 Sam. iv. 10, 11.

xxxiii. 17. ¶ *And moved him to jealousy.* As one is when affections due to himself are bestowed upon another,—as in the married life. ¶ *With their graven images.* Their idols. Graven images are here put for idols in general.

59. *When God heard* this. Literally, "God heard;" that is, he understood this; he was acquainted with it. He heard their prayers addressed to false gods; he heard their praises sung in honour of idols. ¶ *He was wroth.* This is language taken from the common manner of speaking among men, for language derived from human conceptions and usages must be employed when we speak of God, though it may be difficult to say what is its exact meaning. The general sense is that his conduct towards them was *as if* he was angry; or was that which is used by a man who is displeased. ¶ *And greatly abhorred Israel.* The idea in the word rendered *abhorred* is that of *rejecting them with abhorrence;* that is, the reference is not merely to the internal feeling or emotion, but to the *act* which is the proper accompaniment of such an internal feeling. He cast them off; he treated them as not his own. The addition of the word "*greatly*" shows how intense this feeling was; how decided was his aversion to their conduct.

60. *So that he forsook the tabernacle of Shiloh.* The tabernacle or tent which had been erected at Shiloh. He forsook that as a place where he was to be worshipped; that is, he caused his tabernacle, or his place of worship, to be erected in another place, to wit, on Mount Zion. See ver. 68. The name *Shiloh* means properly *a place of rest,* and seems to have been given to this place *as* such a place, or as a place where the ark might abide after its migrations. Shiloh was a city within the limits of the tribe of Ephraim, on a mountain north of Bethel. Here the ark of God remained for many years after it came into the promised land. Josh. xviii. 1; Judges xviii. 31; xxi. 12, 19; 1 Sam. i. 3, 24; ii. 14; iv. 3, 4. The ark, after it was taken by the Philistines, was never returned to Shiloh, but was deposited successively at Nob (1 Sam. xxi. 1–6), and at Gibeon (1 Kings iii. 4), until David pitched a tabernacle for it on Mount Zion (1 Chron. xv. 1). The meaning here is, that in consequence of the sins of the people, the place of worship was finally and for ever removed from the tribe of Ephraim, within whose limits Shiloh was, to the tribe of Judah, and to Mount Zion. ¶ *The tent* which *he placed among men.* It was the place which he selected as his abode on earth.

61. *And delivered his strength into captivity.* That is, the ark, considered as the symbol of his power. This constituted the defence of the people; this was the emblem of the presence of God, which, when with them, was their real protection. The allusion here is to the time when the ark was taken by the Philistines in the days of Eli. See 1 Sam. iv. 3–11. ¶ *And his glory.* That which was emblematic of his glory, to wit, the ark. ¶ *Into the enemy's hand.* The hand or power of the Philistines.

62. *He gave his people over also unto the sword.* When the ark was taken, 1 Sam. iv. 10. Thirty thousand of the children of Israel fell on that occasion. ¶ *And was wroth with his inheritance.* Was angry with his

63 The fire consumed their young men; and their maidens were not [1] given to marriage.

64 Their priests fell by the sword: and their widows made no lamentation.

65 Then the Lord awaked [o] as one out of sleep, *and* like a mighty man, [p] that shouteth by reason of wine.

66 And he smote his enemies in the hinder part; he put them to a perpetual reproach.

67 Moreover, he refused the tabernacle of Joseph, and [q] chose not the tribe of Ephraim;

1 *praised.* *o* Ps. vii. 6. *p* Isa. xlii. 13. *q* Jer. vii. 12—15.

people, considered as his *inheritance;* that is, considered as his own peculiar people, or his possession.

63. *The fire consumed their young men. Fire* here may be regarded as an image of destructive war, as in Num. xxi. 28: "For there is a fire gone out of Heshbon, a flame from the city of Sihon: it hath consumed Ar of Moab," etc. The idea here is, that the young men had been cut off in war. ¶ *And their maidens were not given to marriage.* As the young men who would have entered into this relation were cut off in war. The margin here is *praised;*—"The maidens were not praised." This is in accordance with the Hebrew. The idea is, "Their virgins were not praised in nuptial songs;" that is, there were no marriage celebrations; no songs such as were usually composed on such occasions in praise of those who were brides. The Septuagint and the Latin Vulgate render this much less accurately, and much less beautifully, *were not lamented.*

64. *Their priests fell by the sword.* Comp. 1 Sam. iv. 11. It was considered a special calamity that the ministers of religion were cut down in war. ¶ *And their widows made no lamentation.* That is, the public troubles were so great, the danger was still so imminent, the calamities thickened so fast, that there was no opportunity for public mourning by formal processions of women, and loud lamentations, such as were usual on these occasions. See Notes on Job xxvii. 15. The meaning is not that there was a want of affection or attachment on the part of the friends of the slain, or that there was no real grief, but that there was no opportunity for displaying it in the customary manner.

65. *Then the Lord awaked as one out of sleep.* Literally, *as one sleeping;* that is, as one who is asleep suddenly arouses himself. The Lord *seemed* to have slept, or to have been inattentive to what was occurring. Suddenly he aroused himself to inflict vengeance on the enemies of his people. Comp. Notes on Ps. vii. 6; xliv. 23. ¶ And *like a mighty man.* The allusion is probably to a warrior. ¶ *That shouteth by reason of wine.* The proper idea here is that of singing, or lifting up the voice in exultation and rejoicing;—the idea of a man who sings and shouts as he is excited by wine, and as he presses onward to conflict and to victory. It is not uncommon in the Scriptures to compare God, as he goes forth to accomplish his purposes on his enemies, with a warrior. See Ex. xv. 3; Ps. xxiv. 8.

66. *And he smote his enemies in the hinder part.* From behind; that is, as they fled. There are two ideas here:—one, that they fled at his approach, or turned their backs; the other, that *as* they fled, he smote and destroyed them. ¶ *He put them to a perpetual reproach.* As discomfited; as defeated and scattered; as unable to contend with him. The allusion is, probably, to the victories of David, occurring *after* the events related in the preceding verses.

67. *Moreover, he refused the tabernacle of Joseph.* As a place where his worship should be celebrated. This is the completion of the statement in ver. 60. The design is to

68 But chose the tribe of Judah, [r] the Mount Zion, [s] which he loved.

69 And he built his sanctuary like high *palaces*, like the earth which he hath [1] established for ever.

70 He chose David [t] also his servant, and took him from the sheep-folds:

71 From [2] following the ewes great with young, he brought him to feed [u] Jacob his people, and Israel his inheritance.

r Gen. xlix. 10. *s* Ps. lxxxvii. 2. [1] *founded.* *t* 2 Sam. vii. 8. [2] *after.* *u* 1 Chron. xviii. 7.

show that there had been a *transfer* of the pre-eminence from the tribe of Ephraim to the tribe of Judah, and from Shiloh to Zion. Joseph is here mentioned as the father of Ephraim, from whom one of the tribes—(one of the most influential and numerous)—was named. Jacob had twelve sons, from whom the twelve tribes in general took their name. As the tribe of Levi, however, being devoted to the sacerdotal work, was not reckoned as one of the twelve, the number was made up by giving to the descendants of the two sons of Joseph—Ephraim and Manasseh (Gen. xlviii. 5)—a place among the tribes; and, on this account, the name *Joseph* does not appear as one of the twelve tribes. Yet Joseph is mentioned here, as the ancestor of one of them—that of Ephraim, from whom the priority and supremacy were withdrawn in favour of the tribe of Judah. ¶ *And chose not the tribe of Ephraim.* To be the tribe within whose limits the tabernacle should be permanently set up; or within whose limits the place of public worship was finally to be established.

68. *But chose the tribe of Judah.* He chose David of the tribe of Judah as ruler and king; he chose a place within the limits of Judah, to wit, Mount Zion, or Jerusalem, as the place where his worship was to be celebrated. Thus, the ancient prediction in regard to the supremacy of Judah was accomplished. Gen. xlix. 8–10. ¶ *The Mount Zion, which he loved.* Which he chose; for which he had an affection. Comp. Ps. lxxxvii. 2.

69. *And he built his sanctuary.* His holy place; that is, his tabernacle. The temple was not then built; and, when reared, it was not on Mount Zion, but on Mount Moriah. The name *Zion*, however, was often given to the whole city. ¶ *Like high palaces.* The word *palaces* is not in the original. The Hebrew means simply *high places*, like hills or mountains. The meaning is, that his sanctuary was exalted, *as if* it were placed on a high hill. It was a conspicuous object; it could be seen from afar; it was the most prominent thing in the land. See Notes on Isa. ii. 2. ¶ *Like the earth.* Permanent and established. ¶ *Which he hath established for ever.* Marg., as in Heb., *founded.* The earth is often represented as founded or established on a solid basis, and thus becomes an emblem of stability and perpetuity.

70. *He chose David also his servant.* He chose him that he might set him over his people as their king. The idea is, that David was selected when he had no natural pretensions to the office, as he did not pertain to a royal family, and could have no claim to such a distinction. The account of this choice is contained in 1 Sam. xv. 1–30. ¶ *And took him from the sheep-folds.* From the humble occupation of a shepherd. 1 Sam. xvi. 11; 2 Sam. vii. 8.

71. *From following the ewes great with young.* Marg., as in Heb., *From after.* The meaning is, that he followed after them; that is, he attended them, or watched over them as a shepherd. The single word rendered *the ewes great with young*—עָלוֹת, *aloth*—is a participle from עָלָה (*alah*), *to ascend, to go up*; and then, to bring up, to nourish. The exact idea here is doubtless that of bringing

72 So he fed them according to the integrity [v] of his heart, and guided them by the skilfulness of his hands.

v 1 Kings ix. 4.

PSALM LXXIX.

A Psalm [1] of Asaph.

O GOD, the heathen [w] are come into thine inheritance; thy

1 Or, *for*. w Lam. i. 10.

up, or of *suckling* them, and the word should have been so translated here. It is so rendered by Luther. The idea in our translation has been derived from the Septuagint and the Latin Vulgate. The meaning is, that he brought him from being a *shepherd* to be the *ruler* of his people—expressed still in the language of a shepherd life. ¶ *To feed Jacob his people.* Rather, to be a shepherd to them; to perform towards them the office of a shepherd, including the ideas of governing them, providing for them, and defending them. See Notes on Ps. xxiii. 1, 2.

72. *So he fed them.* He performed towards them the office of a shepherd. ¶ *According to the integrity of his heart.* Literally, "According *to the perfection* of his heart." That is, he was upright and pure in the administration of his government. ¶ *And guided them by the skilfulness of his hands.* Literally, "by the *understanding* of his hands"—as if the *hand* had been endued with intelligence. Comp. Ps. cxliv. 1: "Which teacheth my hands to war, and my fingers to fight." See also Ps. cxxxvii. 5. The idea is, that he administered the government with integrity and uprightness. This is a beautiful tribute to the integrity and purity of the administration of David. It is not the language of flattery; it is a simple statement, flowing from the heart, in favour of a just and upright administration; and it is a *true* statement of what the administration of David was. Save in the matter of Uriah — over which he afterwards wept so bitterly,—his administration was eminently just, pure, impartial, wise, and benignant; probably none among men have been more so. The whole psalm is thus a beautiful *argument* showing why the government had been transferred from Ephraim to Judah, and why it had been placed in the hands of David.

PSALM LXXIX.

This psalm, also, purports to be a psalm of Asaph; that is, it was either composed by him or for him; or it was the composition of one of his descendants who presided over the music in the sanctuary, and to whom was given the general family name, *Asaph.* The psalm pertains to the same general subject as Ps. lxxiv., and was composed evidently in view of the same calamities. Rüdinger, De Wette, and some others, suppose that the reference in the psalm is to the persecutions under Antiochus Epiphanes. To this opinion, also, Rosenmüller inclines. The most common, and the most probable supposition, however, is that it refers to the destruction of the temple by Nebuchadnezzar and the Chaldeans.

The contents of the psalm are as follows:—I. A statement of the calamity which had come upon the nation. The heathen had come into the heritage of God; they had defiled the sanctuary; they had made Jerusalem desolate; they had murdered the inhabitants; and the nation had become a reproach before the world, vers. 1-4. II. A prayer for the Divine interposition, vers. 5, 6. III. Reasons for that prayer, or reasons why God should interpose in the case, vers. 7-13. These reasons are, (*a*) that they had devoured Jacob, ver. 7; (*b*) that the people, on account of their sins, had been brought very low, ver. 8; (*c*) that the Divine glory was at stake, vers. 9, 10; (*d*) that they were in a suffering and pitiable condition, many being held as captives, and many ready to die, ver. 11; (*e*) that justice demanded this, ver. 12; and (*f*) that this interposition would lay the foundation for praise to God, ver. 13.

1. *O God, the heathen are come into thine inheritance.* The nations; a foreign people. See Notes on Ps. ii. 1, 8; lxxviii. 55. The term is one that would be applicable to the

[x] holy temple have they defiled; they [y] have laid Jerusalem on heaps.

2 The dead bodies of thy servants have they given *to be* meat unto the fowls of the heaven, the flesh of thy saints unto the beasts of the earth.

3 Their blood have they shed like water round about Jerusalem; and *there was* none [z] to bury *them*.

4 We are become a reproach [a] to our neighbours, a scorn and derision to them that are round about us.

5 How long, LORD? wilt thou be angry for ever? shall thy jealousy [b] burn like fire?

6 Pour [c] out thy wrath upon the heathen that have not known

x Ps. lxxiv. 2—7. *y* 2 Kings xxv. 9, 10. *z* Jer. xvi. 4; xxxiv. 20. *a* Deut. xxviii. 37. *b* Zeph. i. 18. *c* Jer. x. 25; Rev. xvi. 1.

Chaldeans, or Babylonians, and the probable allusion here is to their invasion of the Holy Land under Nebuchadnezzar. 2 Chron. xxxvi. 17–21. ¶ *Thy holy temple have they defiled.* They have polluted it. By entering it; by removing the sacred furniture; by cutting down the carved work; by making it desolate. See 2 Chron. xxxvi. 17, 18. Comp. Notes on Ps. lxxiv. 5–7. ¶ *They have laid Jerusalem on heaps.* See 2 Chron. xxxvi. 19: "And they burnt the house of God, and brake down the wall of Jerusalem, and burnt all the palaces thereof with fire, and destroyed all the goodly vessels thereof."

2. *The dead bodies of thy servants,* etc. They have slain them, and left them unburied. See 2 Chron. xxxvi. 17. This is a description of wide-spread carnage and slaughter, such as we know occurred at the time when Jerusalem was taken by the Chaldeans. At such a time, it is not probable that the Chaldeans would pause to bury the slain, nor is it probable that they would give opportunity to the captive Hebrews to remain to bury them. That would occur, therefore, which often occurs in war, that the slain would be left on the field to be devoured by wild animals and by the fowls of heaven.

3. *Their blood have they shed like water round about Jerusalem.* They have poured it out in such quantities that it seems to flow like water—not an uncommon occurrence in war. There was no event in the history of the Hebrews to which this description would be more applicable than to the Babylonian invasion. The *language* might indeed be applicable to the desolation of the city by Antiochus Epiphanes, and also to its destruction by the Romans; but, of course, it cannot refer to the latter, and there is no necessity for supposing that it refers to the former. All the conditions of a proper interpretation are fulfilled by supposing that it refers to the time of the Chaldean invasion. ¶ *And* there was *none to bury* them. The Chaldeans would not do it, and they would not suffer the Hebrew people to do it.

4. *We are become a reproach to our neighbours.* See the language in this verse explained in the Notes on Ps. xliv. 13. The words in the Hebrew are the same, and the one seems to have been copied from the other.

5. *How long,* LORD? See Notes on Ps. lxxiv. 1, 10, and Ps. lxxvii. 7–9. This is the language, not of impatience, but of anxiety; not of murmuring, but of wonder. It is language such as the people of God are often constrained to employ under heavy trials,—trials which continue so long that it *seems* as if they would never end. ¶ *Shall thy jealousy burn like fire?* That is, Shall it *continue* to burn like fire? Shall it utterly consume us? On the word *jealousy,* see Notes on Ps. lxxviii. 58.

6. *Pour out thy wrath upon the heathen.* Punish, as they deserve, the nations that have risen up against thy people, and that have brought desolation upon the land. The word

thee, and upon the kingdoms that have not called upon thy name.

7 For they have devoured Jacob, and laid waste his dwelling-place.

8 O [d] remember not against us [1] former iniquities: let thy tender mercies speedily prevent us; for we are brought very [e] low.

9 Help us, O God of our salvation, for the glory of thy name;

[d] Ps. cxxx. 3; Isa. lxiv. 9.

[1] Or, *the iniquities of them that were before us.*
[e] Deut. xxviii. 43.

rendered here *pour out* is used with reference to a cup or vial, as containing a mixture for the people to drink,—of intoxication, or of poison. See Notes on Rev. xvi. 1; Ps. xi. 6; Isa. li. 17; comp. Jer. xxv. 15, 17; Matt. xx. 22; xxvi. 39, 42. ¶ *That have not known thee.* Who are strangers to thee; who are thy enemies. The prayer that the wrath of God might be poured upon them was not *because* they were ignorant of him, but on account of their wicked conduct toward the people of God. The phrase "that have not known thee" is used merely to designate them, or to describe their character. The prayer is not necessarily a prayer for vengeance, or in the spirit of revenge; it is simply a prayer that justice might be done to them, and is such a prayer as any man may offer who is anxious that justice may be done in the world. See remarks on the imprecations in the Psalms. General Introd. § 6. It is not proper, however, to use this as a proof-text that God *will* punish the "heathen," or will consign them to destruction. The passage obviously has no reference to such a doctrine, whether that doctrine be true or false. ¶ *And upon the kingdoms that have not called upon thy name.* The people that do not worship thee; referring here particularly to those who had invaded the land, and made it desolate.

7. *For they have devoured Jacob.* Literally, "They have eaten." That is, they have eaten up what the land produced. ¶ *And laid waste his dwelling-place.* His home; his habitation; the residence of Jacob, or of the people of Israel.

8. *O remember not against us former iniquities.* Marg., *The iniquities of them that were before us.* The Hebrew may mean either *former times,* or *former generations.* The allusion, however, is substantially the same. It is not *their own* iniquities which are particularly referred to, but the iniquity of the nation as committed in former times; and the prayer is, that God would not visit *them* with the results of the sins of former generations, though their own ancestors. The language is derived from the idea so constantly affirmed in the Scripture, and so often illustrated in fact, that the effects of sin pass over from one generation to the next, and involve it in calamity. See Exod. xx. 5; xxxiv. 7; Lev. xx. 5; xxvi. 39, 40; Num. xiv. 18, 33; comp. Notes on Rom. v. 12, *et seq.* ¶ *Let thy tender mercies speedily prevent us.* Literally, "Hasten; let thy tender mercies anticipate us." The word *prevent* here, as elsewhere in the Scriptures, does not mean to *hinder,* as with us, but to go before; to anticipate. See Notes on Job iii. 12; Ps. xvii. 13; xxi. 3; Isa. xxi. 14; Matt. xvii. 25; 1 Thess. iv. 15. The prayer here is, that God, in his tender mercy or compassion, would *anticipate* their ruin; would interpose *before* matters had gone so far as to make their destruction inevitable. ¶ *For we are brought very low.* The idea in the original word is that of being *pendulous,* or *hanging down*—as vines do, or as anything does that is wilted, or withered, or as the hands do when one is weak, faint, or sick. Then it refers to a failure or exhaustion of strength; and the idea here is that their strength as a nation was exhausted.

9. *Help us, O God of our salva-*

and deliver us, and purge away our sins, for thy name's sake.

10 Wherefore should the heathen say, Where *is* their God? let him be known among the heathen in our sight, *by* the [1] revenging of the blood of thy servants *which is* shed.

11 Let *f* the sighing of the prisoner come before thee; according to the greatness of [2] thy power [3] preserve thou those that are appointed to die:

[1] *vengeance.* *f* Ps. cii. 20.

[2] *thine arm.*
[3] *reserve the children of death.*

tion. On whom our salvation depends; who alone can save us. ¶ *For the glory of thy name.* That thy name may be honoured. We are thy professed people; we have been redeemed by thee; and thine honour will be affected by the question whether we are saved or destroyed. It is the *highest* and *purest* ground for prayer, that the glory or honour of God may be promoted. See Notes on Matt. vi. 9, 13; John xii. 28; Dan. ix. 19. ¶ *And deliver us.* From our enemies. ¶ *And purge away our sins.* Forgive our sins, or cleanse us from them. The original word is that which is commonly used to denote an atonement. Comp. in the Hebrew, Dan. ix. 24; Ezek. xlv. 20; Ex. xxx. 15; xxxii. 30; Lev. iv. 20; v. 26; xvi. 6, 11, 24. ¶ *For thy name's sake.* See Notes on Dan. ix. 19.

10. *Wherefore should the heathen say, Where* is *their God?* The *nations.* Why should such a course of forbearance towards them be pursued as to lead them to ask the question whether God is *able* to punish them, or to come to the conclusion that he is *not* the God of those who profess to worship him. See Notes on Ps. xlii. 3, 10. ¶ *Let him be known among the heathen.* Let him so manifest himself among them that they cannot but see that he is God; that he is a just God; that he is the Friend and Protector of his people. ¶ *In our sight.* So that *we* may see it; or, so that it may be seen that he is *our* Friend and Protector. ¶ By *the revenging of the blood of thy servants* which is *shed.* Marg., *vengeance.* The true idea is, "Let the avenging of the blood of thy servants —the blood poured out [or shed] be known among the nations in our sight." The prayer is that God would so interpose that there could be no doubt that it was on account of the blood of his people which had been shed by their enemies. It is a prayer that just punishment might be executed,—a prayer which may be offered at any time.

11. *Let the sighing of the prisoner come before thee.* The sighing of him who is *bound.* The allusion here is, doubtless, to those among the Hebrews who had been taken captives, and who "sighed" not only on account of the sufferings which they endured in their bondage, but because they had been taken from their country and home. The meaning is, "Hear those sighs, and come for the deliverance of those who are thus held in captivity." ¶ *According to the greatness of thy power.* Marg., as in Heb., *thine arm.* The arm is the symbol of power. It is implied here that great power was needful to deliver those who were held in captivity,—power such as God only could exert,—power which could be wielded only by an Omnipotent Being. It was the power of God only which *could* rescue them, as it is only by the power of God that sinners can be saved. ¶ *Preserve thou those that are appointed to die.* Marg., *Reserve the children of death.* The literal meaning is, "Let remain the sons of death;" that is, Preserve those who are in such circumstances that death is impending, and who may be called *the sons of death.* This might apply to those who were condemned to death; or, to those who were sick and in danger of death; or to those who were prisoners and captives, and who were, by their sufferings, exposed to death. The prayer is that such

12 And render unto our neighbours sevenfold into their bosom their reproach, [g] wherewith they have reproached thee, O Lord.

13 So we thy people, and sheep of thy pasture, will give thee thanks for ever; we will shew [h] forth thy praise to [1] all generations.

g Ps. lxxiv. 18.

h Isa. xliii. 21.

1 *generation and generation.*

might be suffered to *remain* on the earth; that is, that they might be kept alive.

12. *And render unto our neighbours.* That is, the *neighbours* who had reproached them; the surrounding people who had seen these calamities come upon them, and who had regarded these calamities as proof that their God was unable to protect them, or that they were suffering under his displeasure. See Notes on ver. 4. ¶ *Sevenfold.* Seven times the amount of reproach which they have heaped upon us. The word *seven* is often used to denote *many,* as seven was one of the perfect numbers. The idea is that of *complete* or *full* vengeance. Comp. Gen. iv. 15, 24; Prov. vi. 31; Isa. xxx. 26; Matt. xviii. 21, 22; Luke xvii. 4. ¶ *Into their bosom,* etc. Perhaps the allusion here is to the custom of carrying things in the bosom of the flowing dress as it was girded around the loins. "Let them be made *to carry with them* seven times the amount of reproach which they have endeavoured to heap on us."

13. *So we thy people, and sheep of thy pasture.* See Notes on Ps. lxxiv. 1. ¶ *Will give thee thanks for ever.* Will praise thee always; will acknowledge thee as our God, and will evermore render thee thanksgiving. ¶ *We will shew forth thy praise to all generations.* Marg., as in Heb., *to generation and generation.* That is, We will make arrangements that the memory of these gracious acts shall be transmitted to future times; to distant generations. This was done by the permanent record, made in the Scriptures, of these gracious interpositions of God, and by their being carefully preserved by each generation to whom they came. No work has been more faithfully done than that by which the records of God's ancient dealings with his people have been preserved from age to age,—that by which the sacred Scriptures have been guarded against error, and handed down from one generation to another.

PSALM LXXX.

This very touching and beautiful psalm purports also to be a psalm of Asaph. Comp. Notes on the title to Psalm lxxiii. On the phrase "upon Shoshannim-eduth" in the title, see Notes on the titles to Ps. xlv. and Ps. lx. The word rendered *eduth,* which means *testimony,* may have been used here with reference to the contents of the psalm *as* a public testimony in regard to the dealings of God with his people. But it is not possible now to determine with certainty the meaning of these titles.

The psalm, in its design, has a strong resemblance to Ps. lxxiv. and Ps. lxxix., and was probably composed on the same occasion. It has been generally supposed to have reference to the time of the Babylonish captivity. Some have referred it, however, to the time of Antiochus Epiphanes; and others regard it as a prayer of the ten tribes which had been carried away to Assyria. Doederlein supposes that it refers to the wars of Jehoshaphat with the Ammonites (2 Chron. xx.); and others suppose that it refers to the troubles caused by the Philistines. It is impossible now to determine with certainty the time or the occasion of its composition. It can be best explained on the supposition that it refers to the desolations caused by the Chaldeans under Nebuchadnezzar.

The psalm is properly divided into *three* parts, each closing with the prayer "Turn us again, O God, and cause thy face to shine; and we shall be saved," vers. 3, 7, 19.

I. The first part is a prayer, addressed to God as a shepherd—as one who had

PSALM LXXX.

To the chief Musician upon Shoshannim-eduth.*i* A Psalm [1] of Asaph.

GIVE ear, O Shepherd of Israel, thou that leadest [k] Joseph like a flock: [l] thou that dwellest *between* the cherubims, shine [m] forth.

2 Before [n] Ephraim, and Benjamin, and Manasseh, stir up thy

i Ps. lx., *title*. [1] Or, *for*. *k* Ps. xxiii. 1; lxxvii. 20. *l* Ex. xxv. 20, 22; 2 Sam. vi. 2. *m* Deut. xxxiii. 2. *n* Num. ii. 18—24.

led his people like a flock—that he would again shine forth on them now that they were in trouble, and that he would stir up his strength, and come and save them, vers. 1-3.

II. The second is a prayer, also,—founded on the troubles of his people; a people fed with their tears; a strife to their neighbours; and an occasion of laughter or mirth to their foes, vers. 4-7.

III. The third is also a prayer,—founded on the former dealings of God with his people, on his care for them in ancient times, and on the fact that they were now desolate;—their state being represented under the image of a vine brought from abroad; planted with care; attentively nurtured until it sent out its branches in every direction, so that it filled the land; and then broken down—torn—rent—trampled on—by a wild boar out of the wood, vers. 8-19. In view of this desolation the psalmist prays that God would interpose, and he pledges the assurance that if this were done for them, the people would no more go back from God.

1. *Give ear.* Incline the ear; as if the ear of God was then turned away, or as if he was inattentive to what was occurring. See Notes on Ps. v. 1. ¶ *O Shepherd of Israel.* See Notes on Ps. xxiii. 1. ¶ *Thou that leadest Joseph like a flock.* Joseph, the father of Ephraim and Manasseh. See Notes on Ps. lxxviii. 67. The name *Joseph* seems here to be used poetically to represent the whole people of Israel, as he was a man so prominent in their history, and *especially* as *Egypt* is mentioned as the country from which the vine had been transplanted,—a country where Joseph had acted so important a part, and in connexion with which his name would be so naturally associated. The meaning is, that God had led the tribes of the Hebrew people as a shepherd leads or conducts his flock. ¶ *Thou that dwellest* between *the cherubims.* See Notes on Ps. xviii. 10. The allusion here is to God as dwelling, by a visible symbol—the Shechinah—on the mercy-seat, between the cherubims. Ex. xxv. 18, 22; xxxvii. 7; 1 Sam. iv. 4; 1 Kings vi. 25. See Notes on Isa. xxxvii. 16; and Heb. ix. 5. ¶ *Shine forth.* Manifest thyself. Let light come from thy presence in the midst of our darkness and calamity.

2. *Before Ephraim, and Benjamin, and Manasseh.* Ephraim and Manasseh were the two sons of Joseph, and their names were given to two of the tribes of Israel. See Notes on Ps. lxxviii. 67. They seem to have been particularly mentioned here, because *Joseph,* their father, had been referred to in the previous verse; and it was natural, in speaking of the people, to mention his sons. Benjamin is mentioned because, in the encampment and march through the wilderness, these three tribes always went together, *as the descendants of the same mother.* Gen. xlvi. 19, 20; Num. ii. 18-24; x. 22-24. It is probable that they were always peculiarly united in the great operations of the Hebrew people, and that when one was mentioned it was customary to mention the others, as being of the same family, or descended from the same mother. There does not appear, from the psalm itself, any particular reason why the prayer is offered that God would manifest himself especially to these *three* tribes; and nothing in regard to the occasion on which the psalm was composed, can be argued from the fact that they are thus mentioned. Hengstenberg indeed supposes that the common idea that the tribe of Benjamin adhered to Judah in the revolt of the

strength, and come [1] *and* save us.

3 Turn [o] us again, O God, and cause thy face [p] to shine; and we shall be saved.

[1] *for salvation to us.*

o ver. 7, 19; Lam. v. 21. *p* Num. vi. 25.

ten tribes is erroneous, and that Benjamin was *one* of the ten tribes which revolted; and that Simeon was not included in the number because he had no separate territory, but only certain towns and places within the limits of the tribe of Judah. Prof. Alexander, embracing this opinion, supposes that the psalm refers to the calamities which came upon the ten tribes at the time of their captivity. But this supposition seems to me to be improbable. The obvious and fair interpretation of the narrative on the subject is, that the tribe of Benjamin adhered to that of Judah at the time of the revolt, for it is said (1 Kings xii. 21) that "when Rehoboam was come to Jerusalem, he assembled all the house of Judah, *with the tribe of Benjamin*, an hundred and fourscore thousand chosen men, which were warriors, to fight against the house of Israel, to bring the kingdom again to Rehoboam, the son of Solomon." Besides, even on the supposition that Benjamin was one of the ten revolted tribes, the fact that these three tribes are particularly mentioned together would not prove that the psalm referred to the carrying away of the ten tribes into Assyria, for still the question would arise why *these* are particularly mentioned rather than any other of the ten. It seems to me, therefore, that the fact that these are specified can be explained on the suppositions above suggested: (*a*) That the main reference in the psalm was to the coming out of Egypt—the bringing the "vine"—that is, the people—from that land (ver. 8); (*b*) That in alluding to that, it was natural to make mention of *Joseph*, who was so distinguished there, and who, after so many trials, was exalted to so great honour that his name might be given to the whole people; (*c*) That when Joseph had been spoken of, it was natural, in the progress of the psalm, to mention particularly the names of his sons, Ephraim and Manasseh; and (*d*) that having mentioned them, it was natural also to refer to one whose name was always associated with that of Joseph as his younger brother by the same mother, and to the tribe of that name which was always associated with Ephraim and Manasseh in the march. I regard the psalm, therefore, as referring to the entire Hebrew people, and the names of these three tribes as representatives of the whole nation. The prayer is, that God would manifest himself in the presence of his people. ¶ *Stir up thy strength.* As if he were indifferent to their condition; as if he put forth no effort to save them. See Notes on Ps. xxxv. 23. ¶ *And come* and *save us.* Marg., as in Heb., *come for salvation to us.* That is, Come and deliver us from our enemies and our dangers.

3. *Turn us again.* This phrase in our translation would seem to mean, "Turn us again from our sins,"—or, "Bring us back to our duty, and to thy love;" and this idea is commonly attached to the phrase probably by the readers of the Bible. But this, though in itself an appropriate prayer, is not the idea here. It is simply, *Bring us back; cause us to return; restore us.* The idea thus suggested would be either (*a*) Restore us to our former state of prosperity; that is, Cause these desolations to cease; or (*b*) Bring us back, as from captivity, to our own land; restore us to our country and our homes, from which we have been driven out. Thus understood, it would be properly the language of those who were in captivity or exile, praying that they might be restored again to their own land. ¶ *And cause thy face to shine.* Be favourable or propitious to us.

4 O LORD God of hosts, how
long wilt thou [1] be angry against
the prayer of thy people?
5 Thou feedest them with the
[q] bread of tears; and givest them
tears to drink in great measure.

[1] *smoke*, Ps. lxxiv. 1.
[q] Ps. xlii. 3; Isa. xxx. 20.

6 Thou [r] makest us a strife
unto our neighbours; and our
enemies laugh among themselves.
7 Turn us again, O God of
hosts, and cause thy face to
shine; and we shall be saved.

[r] Ps. lxxix. 4.

Let the frown on thy countenance disappear. See Notes on Ps. iv. 6. ¶ *And we shall be saved.* Saved from our dangers; saved from our troubles. It is also true that when God causes his face to shine upon *us*, we shall be saved from our sins; saved from ruin. It is only by his smile and favour that we can be saved in any sense, or from any danger.

4. *O* LORD *God of hosts.* Jehovah, God of armies. That is either (*a*) the God who rules among the hosts of heaven—the inhabitants of that holy world; or (*b*) God of the hosts of the sky—the worlds above—the stars, that seem marshalled as hosts or armies, and that are led forth each night with such order and grandeur; or (*c*) God of the hosts on earth—the armies that are mustered for war. The phrase is one which is often applied to God. See Notes on Ps. xxiv. 10; and on Isa. i. 24. ¶ *How long wilt thou be angry.* Marg., as in Heb., *wilt thou smoke.* The allusion is derived from the comparison of anger with fire. See Notes on Ps. lxxiv. 1. ¶ *Against the prayer of thy people.* That is, Thou dost not answer their prayer; thou seemest to be angry against them even when they pray; or in the act of calling upon thee. The earnest inquiry here is, *how long* this was to continue. It *seemed* as if it would never end. Comp. Notes on Ps. lxxvii. 7-9.

5. *Thou feedest them with the bread of tears.* Literally, "Thou causest them to eat the bread of tears," or of weeping. That is, their food was accompanied with tears; even when they ate, they wept. Their tears seemed to moisten their bread, they flowed so copiously. See Notes on Ps. xlii. 3. ¶ *And givest them tears to drink.* So abundant were their tears that they might constitute their very drink. ¶ *In great measure.* Or rather *by measure;* that is, abundantly. The word here rendered *great measure*—שָׁלִישׁ, *shalish*—means properly *a third*, and is usually applied to a measure for grain—a *third part* of another measure—as, the third part of an ephah. See Notes on Isa. xl. 12. Then the word is used for *any* measure, perhaps because this was the most common measure in use. The idea seems to be, not so much that God gave tears to them in *great* measure, but that he *measured* them out to them, as one measures drink to others; that is, the cup, or cask, or bottle in which their drink was served to them was as if filled with tears only.

6. *Thou makest us a strife.* An occasion of strife or wrangling; that is, of strife among themselves, to see who will get the most of our spoils; or of contention, to see which could do most to aggravate their sufferings, and to bring disgrace and contempt upon them. They were emulous with each other in the work of desolation and ruin. ¶ *Unto our neighbours.* The surrounding nations. See Ps. lxxix. 4. ¶ *And our enemies laugh among themselves.* Over our calamities. They exult; they glory; they triumph in our ruin.

7. *Turn us again, O God of hosts,* etc. This verse is the same as ver. 3, except that here the appeal is to the "God of hosts;" there, it is simply to "God." This indicates greater earnestness; a deeper sense of the need of the interposition of God, indicated by the reference to his attri-

8 Thou hast brought a vine
[s] out of Egypt; thou hast cast
out the heathen, and planted it.
9 Thou preparedst *room* before
it, and didst cause it to take deep
root, and it filled the land.
10 The hills were covered with
the shadow of it, and the boughs
thereof *were like* the [1] goodly
cedars.
11 She sent out her boughs
unto the sea, and her branches
unto the river.
12 Why hast thou *then* broken
down her hedges, so that [t] all they
which pass by the way do pluck
her?

s Isa. v. 1—7; Jer. ii. 21.

1 *cedars of God.* t Nahum ii. 2.

bute as the leader of hosts or armies, and therefore able to save them.

8. *Thou hast brought a vine out of Egypt.* Referring to his people, under the image (which often occurs in the Scriptures) of a vine or vineyard. See Notes on Isa. v. 1–7. Comp. Jer. ii. 21; Ezek. xv. 6; Matt. xx. 1; xxi. 28, 33; Luke xiii. 6. ¶ *Thou hast cast out the heathen.* The nations; to wit, the nations that occupied the land of Canaan before the children of Israel dwelt there. See Notes on Ps. ii. 1, 8; lxxvii. 55. ¶ *And planted it.* Thou hast established thy people there as one plants a vine in a field. See Ps. xliv. 2.

9. *Thou preparedst* room *before it.* The Hebrew word here used means properly to turn; to turn the back; then, to turn in order to look at anything; to look upon; to see; then, in Piel, to cause to turn away; to remove. Then it comes to mean to remove, or to clear from impediments so as to prepare a way (Isa. xl. 3; lvii. 14; lxii. 10; Mal. iii. 1), and hence to remove the impediments to planting a vine, etc.; to wit, by clearing away the trees, brush, stones, etc. Comp. Isa. v. 2. Here it means that the hindrances in planting the vine were taken out of the way; that is, God removed the heathen so that there was room then to establish his own people. ¶ *And didst cause it to take deep root.* Heb., "And didst cause it to root roots;" that is, Its roots struck deep into the soil, and the plant became firm. ¶ *And it filled the land.* Its branches ran everywhere, so as to fill the whole land. See Notes on Isa. xvi. 8.

10. *The hills were covered with the shadow of it.* That is, It made a shade, by its luxuriant foliage, on the hills in every part of the land; it seemed to cover all the hills. ¶ *And the boughs thereof* were like *the goodly cedars.* Marg., as in Heb., *cedars of God;* that is, lofty, majestic cedars. See Notes on Ps. lxv. 9. The reference here is to the cedars of Lebanon, among the most majestic objects known to the Hebrews.

11. *She sent out her boughs unto the sea.* To the Mediterranean Sea on the one side. ¶ *And her branches.* Her *sucklings.* The word is usually applied to little children, and means here the little branches that are nourished by the parent vine. ¶ *Unto the river.* The Euphrates, for so *the river* usually means in the Scriptures. The Euphrates on the one side, and the Mediterranean Sea on the other, were the natural and proper boundaries of the country as promised to Abraham. See Ps. lxxii. 8; 1 Kings iv. 21. Comp. Notes on Ps. lx.

12. *Why hast thou* then *broken down her hedges?* Why hast thou dealt with thy people as one would with a vineyard who should break down all its enclosures, and leave it open to wild beasts? The word rendered *hedges* means wall or enclosure. Comp. Notes on Isa. v. 2. ¶ *So that all they which pass by the way.* All travellers; or, wild beasts. So that there is nothing to prevent their coming up to the vine and plucking the grapes. ¶ *Do pluck her.* Pluck, or pick off the grapes; or, if the phrase "all which pass by the way" denotes wild beasts, then the meaning is, that they

13 The boar out of the wood
doth waste it, and the wild beast
of the field doth devour it.
14 Return, we beseech thee,
O God of hosts: look [u] down
from heaven, and behold, and
visit this vine;

[u] Isa. lxiii. 15.

15 And the vineyard which
thy right hand hath planted,
and the [v] branch *that* thou
madest strong for thyself.
16 *It is* burned with fire; *it is*
cut down: they perish [w] at the
rebuke of thy countenance.

[v] Isa. xi. 1, etc.; Zec. iii. 8. [w] Ps. lxxvi. 7.

---

eat off the leaves and branches of the vine.

13. *The boar out of the wood.* Men come in and ravage the land, whose character may be compared with the wild boar. The word rendered *boar* means simply *swine.* The addition of the phrase "out of the wood" determines its meaning here, and shows that the reference is to wild or untamed swine; swine that roam the woods,—an animal always extremely fierce and savage. ¶ *Doth waste it.* The word here used occurs nowhere else. It means to cut down or cut off; to devour; to lay waste. ¶ *And the wild beast of the field.* Of the uninclosed field; or, that roams at large,—such as lions, panthers, tigers, wolves. The word here used—זִיז *ziz*—occurs besides only in Ps. l. 11; and Isa. lxvi. 11. In Isa. lxvi. 11, it is rendered *abundance.* ¶ *Doth devour it.* So the people from abroad consumed all that the land produced, or thus they laid it waste.

14. *Return, we beseech thee, O God of hosts.* Again come and visit thy people; come back again to thy forsaken land. This is language founded on the idea that God had withdrawn from the land, or had forsaken it; that he had left his people without a protector, and had left them exposed to the ravages of fierce foreign enemies. It is language which will describe what *seems* often to occur when the church is apparently forsaken; when there are no cheering tokens of the Divine presence; and when the people of God, discouraged, *seem* themselves to be forsaken by him. Comp. Jer. xiv. 8. ¶ *Look down from heaven.* The habitation of God. As if he did not now *see* his desolate vineyard, or regard it. The idea is, that if he would look upon it, he *would* pity it, and would come to its relief. ¶ *And behold, and visit this vine.* It is a visitation of mercy and not of wrath that is asked; the coming of one who is able to save, and without whose coming there could be no deliverance.

15. *And the vineyard,* etc. Gesenius renders this as a verb: "*Protect;*" that is, "Protect or defend what thy right hand hath planted." So the Septuagint renders it κατάρτισαι—and the Vulgate, *perfice,*—fit, prepare, order. Prof. Alexander renders it *sustain.* De Wette, "*Guard* what thy right hand hath planted." This is doubtless the true idea. It is a prayer that God would guard, sustain, defend what he had planted; to wit, the vine which he had brought out of Egypt, ver. 8. ¶ *And the branch.* Literally, *the son;* that is, the offspring or shoots of the vine. Not merely the original plant—the parent stock—but all the branches which had sprung from it, and which had spread themselves over the land. ¶ That *thou madest strong for thyself.* Thou didst cause it to grow so vigorously for thine own use or honour. On that account, we now call on thee to defend what is thine own.

16. It is *burned with fire.* That is, the vineyard. This is a description of the desolations that had come upon the nation, such as *would* come upon a vineyard if it were consumed by fire. ¶ It is *cut down.* It has been made desolate by fire and by the axe. ¶ *They perish at the rebuke of thy countenance.* At the frown on thy face,—as if God has only to *look* upon men in anger, and they perish.

17 Let thy hand *x* be upon the man of thy right hand, upon the son of man *whom* thou madest strong for thyself.

18 So will not we go back from thee: quicken *y* us, and we will call upon thy name.

19 Turn us again, O LORD God of hosts, cause thy face to shine, and we shall be saved.

x 1 Chron. iv. 10. *y* Eph. ii. 1, 5.

The word *they* refers to those who were represented by the vine which had been brought out of Egypt—the people of the land.

17. *Let thy hand be upon the man of thy right hand.* Luther renders this, "Let thy hand guard the folks of thy right hand, and the people whom thou hast powerfully chosen." The right hand is the place of honour; and the phrase "the man of thy right hand" means one who occupies such a position of honour. The phrase "Let thy hand be upon" is ambiguous. It may denote either favour or wrath;—let it be upon him either to protect him, or to punish him. The connexion, however, evidently demands the former interpretation, for it is in reference to the "man whom God had made strong for himself." The allusion is either (*a*) to some individual man whom God had raised up to honour, as a prince or ruler of the people; or (*b*) to the people as such,—as Luther understands it. Most probably the former is the correct interpretation; and the prayer is, that God would interpose in behalf of the ruler of the people—the king of the nation—whom he had exalted to so high honour, and whom he had placed in such a position of responsibility; that he would now endow him properly for his work; that he would give him wisdom in counsel, and valour in battle, in order that the nation might be delivered from its foes. It is, therefore, a prayer for the civil and military ruler of the land, that God would give him grace, firmness, and wisdom, in a time of great emergency. Prof. Alexander strangely supposes that this refers to the Messiah. ¶ *Upon the son of man.* This means simply *man,* the language being varied for the sake of poetry. Comp. Notes on Ps. viii. 4. It is true that the appellation "the Son of man" was a favourite designation which the Lord Jesus applied to himself to denote that he was truly a man, and to indicate his connexion with human nature; but the phrase is often used merely to denote a man. Here it refers to the king or civil ruler. ¶ *Whom thou madest strong for thyself.* The man whom thou hast raised up to that exalted station, and whom thou hast endowed to do a work for thee *in* that station. A magistrate is a servant and a representative of God, appointed to do a work for *him*—not for *himself.* See Rom. xiii. 1–6.

18. *So will not we go back from thee.* That is, if thou wilt thus interpose; if thou wilt deliver the nation; if thou wilt help him whom thou hast placed over it, giving him wisdom and valour, we will hereafter be obedient to thy law; we will not apostatize from thee. It is a solemn promise or pledge of future obedience made by the psalmist as expressing the purpose of the people if God would be merciful and would withdraw his judgments; a pledge proper in itself, and often made by the Hebrew people only to be disregarded; a pledge proper for all who are in affliction, and often made in such circumstances, but, as in the case of the Hebrews, often made only to be forgotten. ¶ *Quicken us.* Literally, *Give us life.* See Notes on Eph. ii. 1. Restore life to us as a people; save us from ruin, and reanimate us with thy presence. ¶ *And we will call upon thy name.* We will worship thee; we will be faithful in serving thee.

19. *Turn us again, O LORD God of hosts,* etc. See Notes on vers. 3, 7, 14. This is the sum and the burden

of the psalm. The repetition of the prayer shows the earnestness of the people, and their conviction that their only *hope* in their troubles was that *God* would interpose and bring them back again; that he would be favourable to them, and lift upon them the light of his countenance. So with all. In our backslidings, our afflictions, and our troubles, our only hope is that *God* will bring us back to himself; our proper place is at the throne of mercy; our pleadings should be urgent, earnest, and constant, that he will interpose and have mercy on us; our solemn purpose—our expressed and recorded pledge—should be that *if* we are restored to God, we will wander no more. But, alas! how much easier it is to *say* this than to *do* it; how much easier to promise than to perform; how much easier to pledge ourselves when we are in affliction that *if* the troubles are removed we will be faithful, than it is to carry out such a purpose when the days of prosperity return, and we are again surrounded by the blessings of health and of peace. If all men—even good men—*kept* the vows which they make, the world would be comparatively a pure and happy world; if the church itself would only carry out its own solemn pledges, it would indeed arise and shine, and the world would soon be filled with light and salvation.

PSALM LXXXI.

This psalm purports also to be a psalm of Asaph. See Introd. to Ps. lxxiii. In the absence of any evidence to the contrary, it may be assumed to have been composed *by* or *for* the Asaph who was the contemporary of David, and who was appointed by him to preside over the music of the sanctuary. Venema, indeed, supposes that the psalm was composed in the time of Josiah, at the observance of the great Passover celebrated by him (2 Chron. xxxv.); but there is no positive evidence of this, though there is nothing in the psalm that is inconsistent with such a supposition. On the phrase in the title, *upon Gittith*, see Notes on the title to Ps. viii.

The occasion on which the psalm was composed seems to have been a festal occasion, and the circumstances in the psalm will probably best accord with the supposition that it was the Feast of the Passover. Rosenmüller has indeed endeavoured to show (see his Notes on ver. 4) that it was composed on occasion of the Feast of Trumpets (Lev. xxiii. 24, *et seq.*); but there is nothing in the psalm which would necessarily restrict it to that, and, as we shall see, all the circumstances in the psalm harmonize with the supposition that it was at the Feast of the Passover, the principal and the most important festival of the Hebrews. It is well remarked by De Wette (Introd. to the psalm), that as the Hebrews were required to make known to their children the design of the ordinance of the Passover (see Ex. xii. 26, 27), nothing would be more natural than that the sacred poets should take occasion from the return of that festival to enforce the truths pertaining to it in songs composed for the celebration. Such seems to have been the design of this psalm,—reminding the people of the goodness of God in the past, and recalling them from their sins by a remembrance of his mercies, and by a view of what would be the consequences of fully obeying his law.

It would seem from the psalm not improbable that it was composed in a time of national declension in religion, and when there was a tendency to idolatry, and that the object of the author was to rouse the nation from that state, and to endeavour by a reference to the past to bring them back to a more entire devotedness to God.

The contents of the psalm are as follows:—

I. The duty of praise, particularly on such occasions as that on which the psalm was composed;—a duty enjoined even in Egypt, in the time of Joseph, when God delivered his people out of that strange land, vers. 1-7.

II. The main command which was then ordained to be the guide of the people—the fixed law of the nation—the fundamental idea in their polity,—that there was to be no strange god among them, but that they were to worship the true God, and him alone, vers. 8-10.

III. The fact that the nation had refused to hear; that there had been such a proneness to worship other gods, and to fall into the habits of idolaters,

PSALM LXXXI.

To the chief Musician upon Gittith. z *A Psalm* [1] of Asaph.

SING aloud unto God our strength: make a joyful noise unto the God of Jacob.

2 Take a psalm, and bring hither the timbrel, the pleasant harp with the psaltery.

3 Blow up the trumpet in the new moon, in the time appointed, on our solemn feast day:

z Ps. viii., *title*. [1] Or, *for*.

---

that God had given them up to their own desires, and suffered them to walk in their own ways, vers. 11, 12.

IV. A statement of what God would have done for them if they had been obedient; of what would have been the effect on their national prosperity if they had hearkened to the commands of God; and consequently of what would still be the result if the people should be obedient, and submit themselves wholly to the law of God, vers. 13-16. Particularly—

(1) Their enemies would have been subdued, ver. 14.

(2) Those who hated the Lord would have yielded themselves to him, ver. 15.

(3) God would have given them abundant prosperity; he would have fed them with the finest of the wheat, and would have satisfied them with honey out of the rock, ver. 16.

The psalm is of special importance to the church now, as reminding it of its obligation from the past mercies of God, and as showing what *would be* the consequences if it should be wholly devoted to the service of God.

1. *Sing aloud unto God our strength.* The strength and support of the nation; he from whom the nation has derived all its power. The word rendered *sing aloud* means to rejoice; and then, to make or cause to rejoice. It would be appropriate to a high festal occasion, where music constituted an important part of the public service. And it would be a proper word to employ in reference to any of the great feasts of the Hebrews. ¶ *Make a joyful noise.* A noise indicating joy, as distinguished from a noise of mourning or lamentation. ¶ *Unto the God of Jacob.* Not here particularly the God of the patriarch himself, but of the people who bore his name,—his descendants.

2. *Take a psalm.* Literally, "Lift up a psalm; perhaps, as we should say, "*Raise the tune.*" Or, it may mean, Take an ode, a hymn, a psalm, composed for the occasion, and accompany it with the instruments of music which are specified. ¶ *And bring hither the timbrel.* For the purpose of praise. On the meaning of this word rendered timbrel—*toph*—see Notes on Isa. v. 12. ¶ *The pleasant harp.* On the word here rendered *harp*—*kinnor*,—see also Notes on Isa. v. 12. The word translated *pleasant*—נָעִים, *naim*—means properly *pleasant, agreeable, sweet*, Ps. cxxxiii. 1; cxlvii. 1. It is connected here with the word *harp*, as meaning that that instrument was distinguished particularly for a sweet or pleasant sound. ¶ *With the psaltery.* On the meaning of the word here used—*nebel*—see Notes on Isa. v. 12. These were the common instruments of music among the Hebrews. They were employed alike on sacred occasions, and in scenes of revelry. See Isa. v. 12.

3. *Blow up the trumpet.* The word rendered *blow* means to make a clangour or noise as on a trumpet. The trumpet was, like the timbrel, the harp, and the psaltery, a common instrument of music, and was employed on all their festive occasions. It was at first made of horn, and then was made similar in shape to a horn. Comp. Josh. vi. 5; Lev. xxv. 9; Job xxxix. 25. ¶ *In the new moon.* On the festival held at the time of the new moon. There was a high festival on the appearance of the new moon in the month of Tisri, or October, which was the beginning of their civil year, and it is not improbable that the return of each new moon was celebrated with special services. See Notes on Isa. i. 13; comp. 2 Kings

4 For this *a* was a statute for Israel, *and* a law of the God of Jacob.
5 This he ordained in Joseph *for* a testimony, when he went

a Lev. xxiii. 23, 24.

iv. 23; Amos viii. 5; 1 Chron. xxiii. 31; 2 Chron. ii. 4. It is not certain, however, that the word here used means *new moon.* Prof. Alexander renders it *in the month;* that is, in *the* month, by way of eminence, in which the passover was celebrated. The word used—חֹדֶשׁ, *hhodesh*—means, indeed, commonly *the new moon;* the day of the new moon; the first day of the lunar month (Num. xxix. 6; 1 Sam. xx. 5, 18, 24); but it also means *a month;* that is, a lunar month, beginning at the new moon, Gen. viii. 5; Ex. xiii. 4; *et al.* The corresponding or parallel word, as we shall see, which is rendered in our version, *in the time appointed,* means *full moon;* and the probability is, as Professor Alexander suggests, that in the beginning of the verse the *month* is mentioned in general, and the particular time of the month—the full moon—in the other part of the verse. Thus the language is applicable to the passover. On the other supposition—the supposition that the *new moon* and the *full moon* are both mentioned—there would be manifest confusion as to the time. ¶ *In the time appointed.* The word here used—כֶּסֶה, *keseh*—means properly the full moon; the time of the full moon. In Syriac the word means either "the first day of the full moon," or "the whole time of the full moon." (Isa Bar Ali, as quoted by Gesenius, *Lex.*) Thus the word means, not as in our translation, *in the time appointed,* but *at the full moon,* and would refer to the time of the Passover, which was celebrated on the fourteenth day of the lunar month; that is, when the moon was at the full. Ex. xii. 6. ¶ *On our solemn feast day.* Heb., *In the day of our feast.* The word *solemn* is not necessarily in the original, though the day *was* one of great solemnity. The Passover is doubtless referred to.

4. *For this* was *a statute for Israel,* etc. See Ex. xii. 3. That is, it was a law for the whole Jewish people; for all who had the name *Israel;* for all the descendants of Jacob. The word *was* is not in the original, as if this had been an old commandment which might now be obsolete, but the idea is one of *perpetuity:*—it *is* a perpetual law for the Hebrew people. ¶ *A law of the God of Jacob.* Heb., *a judgment;* or, *right.* The idea is, that it was what was due to God; what was his right. It was a solemn *claim* that he should be thus acknowledged. It was not a matter of conventional arrangement, or a matter of convenience to them; nor was it to be observed merely because it was found to be expedient and conducive to the welfare of the nation. It was a matter of *right* and of *claim* on the part of God, and was so to be regarded by the nation. The same is true now of the Sabbath, and of all the appointments which God has made for keeping up religion in the world. All these arrangements are indeed expedient and proper; they conduce to the public welfare and to the happiness of man; but there is a higher reason for their observance than this. It is that *God demands* their observance; that he *claims* as his own the time so appropriated. Thus he claims the Sabbath, the entire Sabbath, *as his own;* he requires that it shall be employed in his service, that it shall be regarded as *his* day; that it shall be made instrumental in keeping up the knowledge of himself in the world, and in promoting his glory. Ex. xx. 10. Men, therefore, "rob God" (comp. Mal. iii. 8) when they take this time for needless secular purposes, or devote it to other ends and uses. Nor can this be sinless. The highest guilt which man can commit is to "rob" his Maker of what belongs to Him, and of what He claims.

5. *This he ordained in Joseph* for

out [1] through the land of Egypt; *where* I heard a language [b] *that* I understood not.

[1] Or, *against*. [b] Ps. cxiv. 1.

6 I removed his shoulder from the burden: his hands [2] were delivered from the pots. [c]

[2] *passed away*. [c] Ex. i. 14.

a testimony. Literally, *he placed this;* that is, he appointed it. The word *Joseph* here stands for the whole Hebrew people, as in Ps. lxxx. 1. See Notes on that verse. The meaning is, that the ordinance for observing this festival—the Passover—was to be traced back to the time when they were in Egypt. The obligation to observe it was thus enhanced by the very antiquity of the observance, and by the fact that it was one of the direct appointments of God in that strange and foreign land. ¶ *When he went out through the land of Egypt.* Marg., *against*. Or rather, *In his going out of the land of Egypt.* Literally, *In going upon the land of Egypt.* The allusion is, undoubtedly, to the time when the Hebrews went out of the land of Egypt—to the *Exodus;* and the exact idea is, that, in doing this, they passed *over* a considerable portion of the land of Egypt; or, that they passed *over* the land. The idea in the margin, of its being *against* the land of Egypt, is not necessarily in the original. ¶ Where *I heard a language* that *I understood not.* Literally, "The lip [that is, the language] of one that I did not know, I heard." This refers, undoubtedly, not to God, but to the people. The author of this psalm identifies himself here with the people—the whole nation,—and speaks as if he were one of them, and as if he now *recollected* the circumstances at the time—the strange language—the foreign customs—the oppressions and burdens borne by the people. Throwing himself back, as it were, to that time (comp. Notes on 1 Thess. iv. 17),—he seems to himself to be in the midst of a people speaking a strange tongue—a language unintelligible to him—the language of a foreign nation. The Jews, in all their long captivity in Egypt—a period of four hundred years (see Notes on Acts vii. 6),—preserved their own language apparently incorrupt. So far as appears, they spoke the same language, without change, when they came out of Egypt, that Abraham, Isaac, and Jacob had used. The Egyptian was entirely a foreign language to them, and had no affinity with the Hebrew.

6. *I removed his shoulder from the burden.* The burden which the people of Israel were called to bear in Egypt. The reference is undoubtedly to their burdens in making bricks, and conveying them to the place where they were to be used; and perhaps also to the fact that they were required to carry stone in building houses and towns for the Egyptians. Comp. Ex. i. 11–14; v. 4–17. The meaning is, that he had saved them from these burdens, to wit, by delivering them from their hard bondage. The speaker here evidently is God. In the previous verse it is the people. Such a change of person is not uncommon in the Scriptures. ¶ *His hands were delivered from the pots.* Marg., as in Heb., *passed away*. That is, they were *separated* from them, or made free. The word rendered *pots* usually has that signification. Job xli. 20; 1 Sam. ii. 14; 2 Chron. xxxv. 13; but it may also mean *a basket.* Jer. xxiv. 2; 2 Kings x. 7. The latter is probably the meaning here. The allusion is to *baskets* which might have been used in carrying clay, or conveying the bricks after they were made:—perhaps a kind of hamper that was swung over the shoulders, with clay or bricks in each,—somewhat like the instrument used now by the Chinese in carrying tea,—or like the neck-yoke which is employed in carrying sap where maple sugar is manufactured, or milk on dairy farms. There are many representations on Egyptian sculptures which would illustrate this. The idea is that of a

7 Thou calledst in trouble, and
I delivered thee: I answered thee
in the secret place of thunder; I
proved [d] thee at the waters of
[1] Meribah. Selah.
8 Hear, O my people, and I
will testify unto thee: O Israel,
if thou wilt hearken unto me;
9 There shall no strange god
be in thee; neither shalt thou
worship any strange god.
10 I [e] *am* the LORD thy God,
which brought thee out of the

[d] Ex. xvii. 2—7. [1] Or, *strife*. [e] Ex. xx. 2.

burden, or task, and the allusion is to the deliverance that was accomplished by removing them to another land.

7. *Thou calledst in trouble.* The people of Israel. Ex. ii. 23; iii. 9; xiv. 10. ¶ *And I delivered thee.* I brought the people out of Egypt. ¶ *I answered thee in the secret place of thunder.* That is, in the lonely, retired, solemn place where the thunder rolled; the solitudes where there was no voice but the voice of thunder, and where that seemed to come from the deep recesses of the mountain gorges. The allusion is doubtless to Sinai. Comp. Ex. xix. 17-19. The meaning is, that he gave a response—a real reply—to their prayer—amid the solemn scenes of Sinai, when he gave them his law; when he recognized them as his people; when he entered into covenant with them. ¶ *I proved thee.* I tried you; I tested your fidelity. ¶ *At the waters of Meribah.* Marg., as in Heb., *strife.* This was at Mount Horeb. Ex. xvii. 5-7. The *trial*—the *proof*—consisted in his bringing water from the rock, showing that he was God—that he was *their* God.

8. *Hear, O my people, and I will testify unto thee,* etc. See Notes on the similar passage in Ps. l. 7. God calls their attention to what he required of them; to what his law demanded; to what was the condition of their being his people and of securing his favour. What he demanded was, that they should acknowledge him; obey him; serve him; that there should be no strange god among them, and that they should worship no false god, ver. 9.

9. *There shall no strange god be in thee.* Worshipped by thee; or recognised and regarded as a god. This was a condition of his favour and friendship. Comp. Deut. xxxii. 12; Isa. xliii. 12. The word here rendered *strange*—זָר, *zar*—has reference to one of a foreign nation; and the meaning is, that they were not to worship or adore the gods that were worshipped by foreigners. This was a fundamental law of the Hebrew commonwealth. ¶ *Neither shalt thou worship any strange god.* The Hebrew word here is different—נֵכָר, *naikar*—but means substantially the same thing. The allusion is to gods worshipped by foreign nations.

10. *I am the* LORD *thy God,* etc. See Ex. xx. 2. The meaning is, "I am Jehovah, *thy* God; the God to be worshipped and honoured by thee; I *only* am thy God, and no other god is to be recognised or acknowledged by thee." The foundation of the claim to exclusive service and devotion is here laid in the fact that he had brought them out of the land of Egypt. Literally, had caused them to *ascend,* or *go up* from that land. The claim thus asserted seems to be twofold: (*a*) That in doing this, he had shown that he *was* God, or that he had performed a work which none but God could perform, and had thus shown his existence and power; and (*b*) that by this he had brought them under peculiar obligations to himself, inasmuch as they owed all that they had—their national existence and liberty—entirely to him. ¶ *Open thy mouth wide, and I will fill it. Possibly* an allusion to young birds, when fed by the parent-bird. The meaning here is, "I can amply supply all your wants. You need not go to other gods—the gods of other lands—as if there were any deficiency in

land of Egypt: open [f] thy mouth
wide, and I will fill it.
11 But [g] my people would not
hearken to my voice: and Israel
would none of me.
12 So [h] I gave them up [1] unto
their own hearts' lust; *and* they
walked in their own counsels.
13 Oh [i] that my people had
hearkened unto me, *and* Israel
had walked in my ways!

f John xv. 7. g Deut. xxxii. 15, 18. h Acts vii. 42.

[1] Or, *to the hardness of their own hearts*, or, *imaginations*.
i Isa. xlviii. 18; Deut. xxxii. 29.

my power or resources; as if *I* were not able to meet your necessities. *All* your wants I can meet. Ask what you need—what you will; come to me and make *any* request with reference to yourselves as individuals or as a nation—to this life or the life to come—and you will find in me an abundant supply for all your wants, and a willingness to bless you commensurate with my resources." What is here said of the Hebrews may be said of the people of God at all times. There is not a want of our nature—of our bodies or our souls; a want pertaining to this life or the life to come—to ourselves, to our families, to our friends, to the church, or to our country—which God is not *able* to meet; and there is not a *real* necessity in any of these respects which he is not *willing* to meet. Why, then, should his people ever turn for happiness to the "weak and beggarly elements of the world" (comp. Notes on Gal. iv. 9), *as if* God could not satisfy them? Why should they seek for happiness in vain amusements, or in sensual pleasures, *as if* God *could* not, or *would* not, supply the real wants of their souls?

11. *But my people*, etc. See Ps. lxxviii. 10, 11, 17–19. ¶ *And Israel would none of me.* Literally, "Did not *will* me;" that is, "did not incline to me; were not attached to me; were not disposed to worship me, and to find happiness in me." Comp. Isa. i. 19; Job xxxix. 9; Prov. i. 25. They refused or rejected him. See Ex. xxxii. 1; Deut. xxxii. 15, 18.

12. *So I gave them up unto their own hearts' lust.* Marg., as in Heb., *to the hardness of their own hearts.* Literally, "I sent them, or I dismissed them, to the hardness of their hearts." I suffered them to have what, in the hardness of their hearts they desired, or what their hard and rebellious hearts prompted them to desire. I indulged them in their wishes. I gave them what they asked, and left them to themselves to work out the problem about success and happiness in their own way,—to let them *see* what must be the result of forsaking the true God. The world—and the church too—has been often suffered to make this experiment. ¶ And *they walked in their own counsels.* As they thought wise and best. Comp. Acts vii. 42; xiv. 16; Rom. i. 24; Ps. lxxviii. 26–37.

13. *Oh that my people had hearkened unto me.* This passage is designed *mainly* to show what would have been the consequences if the Hebrew people had been obedient to the commands of God, vers. 14–16. At the same time, however, it expresses what was the earnest desire—the wish—the *preference* of God, viz., that they *had* been obedient, and *had* enjoyed his favour. This is in accordance with all the statements, all the commands, all the invitations, all the warnings, in the Bible. In the entire volume of inspiration there is not one command addressed to men to walk in the ways of sin; there is not one statement that God desires they should do it; there is not one intimation that he wishes the death of the sinner. The contrary is implied in all the declarations which God has made,—in all his commands, warnings, and invitations,—in all his arrangements for the salvation of men. See Deut. v. 29; xxxii. 29, 30; Isa. xlviii. 18; Ezek. xviii. 23, 32; xxxiii. 11; 2 Pet. iii. 9; Luke xix. 42. ¶ And *Israel had walked in my*

14 I should soon have subdued their enemies, and turned my hand against their adversaries.

15 The haters of the LORD should have [1] submitted themselves unto him: but their time should have endured for ever.

16 He should have fed them

[1] *lied*, or, *yielded feigned obedience*, Ps. lxvi. 3.

---

ways! Had kept my commandments; had been obedient to my laws. When men, therefore, do *not* walk in the ways of God it is impossible that they should take refuge, as an excuse for it, in the plea that God desires this, *or* that he commands it, *or* that he is pleased with it, *or* that he approves it. There is no possible sense in which this can be true; in every sense, and on every account, he prefers that men should be obedient, and not disobedient; good, and not bad; happy, and not miserable; saved, and not lost. Every doctrine of theology should be held and interpreted in *consistency* with this as a fundamental truth. That there are things which are difficult to be explained on the supposition that this is true, must be admitted; but what truth is there in reference to which there are not difficulties to be explained? And is there anything in this, or in any of the truths of the Bible, which *more* demands explanation than the *facts* which are actually occurring under the government of God:—the *fact* that sin and misery have been allowed to come into the universe; the *fact* that multitudes constantly suffer whom God could at once relieve?

14. *I should soon have subdued their enemies.* This is one of the consequences which, it is said, would have followed if they had been obedient to the laws of God. The phrase rendered *soon* means literally *like a little;* that is, as we might say, *in a little,* to wit, in a little time. The word rendered *subdued* means to bow down; to be curved or bent; and the idea is, that he would have caused them to bow down, to wit, by submission before them. Comp. Deut. xxxii. 29, 30. ¶ *And turned my hand against their adversaries.* Against those who oppressed and wronged them. The act of turning the hand *against* one is significant of putting him away—repelling him—disowning him—as when we would thrust one away from us with aversion.

15. *The haters of the* LORD. The enemies of the Lord, often represented as those who *hate* him,—hatred being always in fact or in form connected with an unwillingness to submit to God. It is hatred of his law; hatred of his government; hatred of his plans; hatred of his character. See Rom. i. 30; John vii. 7; xv. 18; 23–25. Comp. Ex. xx. 5. ¶ *Should have submitted themselves unto him.* Marg., *yielded feigned obedience.* Heb., *lied.* See the phrase explained in the Notes on Ps. xviii. 44. The meaning is, that they would have been so subdued as to *acknowledge* his authority or supremacy, while it is, at the same time, implied that this would have been *forced* and not *cordial.* No external power, though it may so conquer as to make men outwardly obedient, can affect the *will,* or subdue *that.* The grace of God *alone* can do that, and it is the peculiar triumph of grace that it *can* do it. ¶ *But their time.* The time of his people. They would have continued to be a happy and a flourishing nation. ¶ *Should have endured for ever.* Perpetually,—*as long as they continued to be obedient.* If a nation were obedient to the will of God; if it wholly obeyed his laws; if it countenanced by statute no form of sin; if it protected no iniquity; if it were temperate, just, virtuous, honest, there is no reason why its institutions should not be perpetual, or why it should ever be overthrown. Sin is, in all cases, the cause of the ruin of nations, as it is of individuals.

16. *He should have fed them also.* He would have given them prosperity,

also with the [1] finest of the wheat: and with honey [k] out of the rock should I have satisfied thee.

[1] *fat.*

[k] Deut. xxxii. 13.

and their land would have produced abundantly of the necessities—even of the luxuries—of life. This is in accordance with the usual promises of the Scriptures, that obedience to God will be followed by national temporal prosperity. See Deut. xxxii. 13, 14; 1 Tim. iv. 8; Ps. xxxvii. 11. Comp. Notes on Matt. v. 5. ¶ *With the finest of the wheat.* Marg., as in Heb., *with the fat of wheat.* The meaning is, the best of the wheat,—as the words *fat* and *fatness* are often used to denote excellence and abundance. Gen. xxvii. 28, 39; Job xxxvi. 16; Ps. xxxvi. 8; lxiii. 5; lxv. 11. ¶ *And with honey out of the rock should I have satisfied thee.* Palestine abounded with bees, and honey was a favourite article of food. Gen. xliii. 11; Deut. viii. 8; xxxii. 13; 1 Sam. xiv. 25, 26; Isa. vii. 15; Ezek. xvi. 13; Matt. iii. 4. Much of that which was obtained was wild honey, deposited by the bees in the hollows of trees, and as it would seem in the caverns of the rocks. Much of it was gathered also from rocky regions, and this was regarded as the most delicate and valuable. I do not know the cause of this, nor why honey in high and rocky countries should be more pure and white than that obtained from other places; but the whitest and the most pure and delicate honey that I have ever seen I found at Chamouni in Switzerland. Dr. Thomson (Land and the Book, vol. ii. p. 362) says of the rocky region in the vicinity of Timnath, that "bees were so abundant in a wood at no great distance from this spot that the honey dropped down from the trees on the ground;" and that "he explored densely-wooded gorges in Hermon and in Southern Lebanon where wild bees are still found, both in trees and in the clefts of the rocks." The meaning here is plain, that, if Israel had been obedient to God, he would have blessed them with abundance—with the richest and most coveted productions of the field. Pure religion—obedience to God—morality — temperance, purity, honesty, and industry, such as religion requires—are always eminently favourable to individual and national prosperity; and if a man or a nation desired to be most prospered, most successful in the lawful and proper objects of individual or national existence, and most happy, nothing would tend more to conduce to it than those virtues which piety enjoins and cultivates. Individuals and nations, even in respect to temporal prosperity, are most unwise, as well as most wicked, when they disregard the laws of God, and turn away from the precepts and the spirit of religion. It is true of nations, as it is of individuals, that "Godliness is profitable unto all things, having promise of the life that now is," 1 Tim. iv. 8.

PSALM LXXXII.

This, too, is a "Psalm of Asaph." See Introd. to Psalm lxxiii. There is nothing, however, in its contents to determine the time or the occasion of its being composed, although there is no difficulty in ascertaining the *design* for which it was written, or the use to be made of it. It is intended to state the duties and the responsibilities of magistrates or civil rulers. Though the *language* is such as was adapted peculiarly to the Hebrew magistracy, and to the duties of magistrates as specified in the Jewish law, yet the *principles* are such as should guide magistrates at all times and in all countries; and the *truths* suggested are such as are eminently worthy the attention of all who are entrusted with authority.

The psalm was evidently composed at a time when there was much that was unjust and oppressive in the administration of justice; when the magistrates were corrupt; when they could be bribed; when they were forgetful of their obligation to defend the poor and the fatherless — the afflicted and the

PSALM LXXXII.

A Psalm of [1] Asaph.

GOD standeth in the congregation of the mighty: he *l* judgeth among the gods.

[1] Or, *for*.

l 2 Chron. xix. 6, 7.

needy; when manifest consequences of the evil administration of justice prevailed in the land, and "all the foundations of the earth" seemed to be "out of course;" and when those in power were haughty and arrogant, *as if* they were not men, and were not to die. De Wette supposes that the psalm was composed in the time of the Babylonish exile, and had reference to the conduct of the oppressive rulers in that land; but it is not necessary to suppose this. There were doubtless many occasions in the history of the Hebrew people when all that is here said of the conduct of their rulers and judges was applicable to *them*. Comp. Isa. i. 17, 23, 26.

The contents of the psalm are as follows:—

I. A reference to God as the Supreme Ruler;—the Ruler of those that rule;—the God to whom all magistrates, however exalted in rank, are responsible, ver. 1.

II. A reference to the *character* of the magistrates at the time when the psalm was written, as those who judged unjustly; who were partial in the administration of justice; and who favoured men of rank and position, ver. 2.

III. A statement of the *duties* of magistrates, in reference particularly to the poor, the fatherless, the needy, and the afflicted, vers. 3, 4.

IV. A further statement in regard to the character of the magistrates at the time when the psalm was written, particularly as ignorant, and as walking in darkness, ver. 5.

V. A solemn appeal to them as mortal men—as subject to death like others,—though they had a rank which entitled them to the appellation of "*gods*," and were the representatives of the Most High on earth, vers. 6, 7.

VI. A call on God to arise and to execute judgment in the earth, for he was the Supreme Ruler, and the nations, with all their interests, pertained to him, ver. 8.

1. *God standeth in the congregation of the mighty.* In the assembly of the rulers and judges; among those of most exalted rank and station. He is there to observe them; to give them law; to direct their decisions; to judge *them*. He is supreme over them; and he holds them responsible to himself. The word rendered *congregation* is that which is commonly applied to the *assembly* of the people of Israel, considered as an organized body, or as a body politic. It here, however, refers to magistrates considered as a *body* or *class* of men; as those who have assemblages or meetings, with special reference to their duties *as* magistrates. The word rendered *mighty*—אֵל, *ēl*—is in the singular number, and is one of the names which are given to God; hence the literal rendering is, "God standeth in the assembly of God." The Septuagint renders it, *In the synagogue of the gods*. So also the Latin Vulgate. The reference, however, is undoubtedly to magistrates, and the idea is, that they were to be regarded as representatives of God; as acting in his name; and as those, therefore, to whom, in a subordinate sense, the name *gods* might be given. Comp. ver. 6. In Ex. xxi. 6; xxii. 8, 9, 28, also, the same word in the plural is applied to magistrates, and is properly translated *judges* in our common version. Comp. Notes on John x. 34, 35. The idea is, that they were the representatives of the Divine sovereignty in the administration of justice. Comp. Rom. xiii. 1, 2, 6. They were, in a sense, *gods* to other men; but they were not to forget that God stood among them as *their* God; that if they were exalted to a high rank in respect to their fellow-men, they were, nevertheless, subject to One to whom the name of God belonged in the highest sense. ¶ *He judgeth among the gods.* As they to whom the name *gods* is thus given as the representatives of the Divine sovereignty judged among men, so

2 How long will ye judge unjustly, and accept the persons of the wicked? Selah.

3 [1] Defend the poor and fatherless: do justice [m] to the afflicted and needy.

4 Deliver the poor and needy: rid *them* out of the hand of the wicked.

5 They know not, neither will they understand: they walk on in [n] darkness: all the [o] founda-

[1] *Judge.* *m* Jer. xxii. 3. *n* John xii. 35. *o* Ps. lxxv. 3; 2 Tim. ii. 19.

God would judge among them. If they were, in some sense (in consequence of their representing the Divine majesty, and deriving their power and appointment from God), independent of men, they were in no sense independent of God himself.

2. *How long will ye judge unjustly.* Literally, *Judge evil.* This is designed, evidently, to denote the prevailing character of the magistrates at the time when the psalm was written. Unhappily such occasions occur very often in the course of human affairs. ¶ *And accept the persons of the wicked?* Literally, *Lift up* [or *bear*] *the faces of the wicked.* The meaning is, that they showed favour or partiality to wicked men; they did not decide cases according to truth, but were influenced by a regard for particular persons on account of their rank, their position, their wealth, or their relation to themselves. This is a common phrase in the Scriptures to denote favouritism or partiality. Job xxxiv. 19; Acts x. 34; Rom. ii. 11; 1 Pet. i. 17; Lev. xix. 15; Deut. i. 17.

3. *Defend the poor and fatherless.* Literally, *judge;* that is, Pronounce just judgment; see that right is done to them. This is required everywhere in the Scriptures. The meaning is not that judgment is to be pronounced in their favour *because* they are poor, or *because* they are orphans, for this would be to do what they had just been charged with as in itself wrong, *accepting* of *persons;* that is, showing favour on account of condition or rank, rather than on account of a just claim. The idea is, that the poor and the fatherless, having no natural protectors, were likely to be wronged or oppressed; that they had none to defend their claims; and that magistrates, therefore, as if *they* were their natural protectors, should see that their rights were maintained. See Notes on Isa. i. 17. ¶ *Do justice to the afflicted and needy.* See that justice is done them; that they are not wronged by persons of wealth, of power, and of rank. Such care does religion take of those who have no natural guardians. The poor and the needy—the widow and the fatherless—owe to the religion of the Bible a debt which no language can express.

4. *Deliver the poor and needy.* That is, Deliver them from the power and the arts of those who would oppress and wrong them. This would not be showing them partiality; it would be simply doing them justice. ¶ *Rid* them *out of the hand of the wicked.* Deliver, or Rescue them from their hands; that is, from their attempts to oppress and wrong them.

5. *They know not, neither will they understand.* This is designed still further to characterise the magistrates at the time referred to in the psalm. They not merely judged unjustly, and were not merely partial in the administration of justice (ver. 2), but they did not desire to understand their duty, and the true principles on which justice should be administered. They were at no pains to inform themselves, either in regard to those principles, or in regard to the facts in particular cases. All just judgment must be based (*a*) on a true knowledge of what the law is, or what is right; and (*b*) on a knowledge of the facts in a particular case. Where there is no such knowledge, of course there must be a mal-administration of justice. One of the first requisites, therefore, in a magistrate is, that he

tions of the earth [1] are out of course.
6 I have said, Ye *are* gods;
[p] and all of you *are* children of the Most High:
7 But ye shall die like men, and fall like one of the princes.

[1] *moved.* [p] John x. 34, 35.

shall have a proper knowledge of the law; his duty is to ascertain the exact *facts* in each individual case that comes before him, and then impartially to apply the law to that case. ¶ *They walk on in darkness.* In ignorance of the law and of the facts in the case. ¶ *All the foundations of the earth.* See Notes on Ps. xi. 3; lxxv. 3. All settled principles; all the things on which the welfare of society rests; all on which the prosperity of the world depends. The manner in which justice is administered is as if the very foundations of the earth should be disturbed, and the world should move without order. ¶ *Are out of course.* Marg., as in Heb., *moved.* That is, they are moved from their proper place; the earth no longer rests firmly and safely on its foundation. This language is taken from the idea so often occurring in the Scriptures, and in the language of men generally, that the earth rests on solid foundations—as a building does. The idea is derived from the stability and fixedness of the earth, and from the fact that when a building is fixed and stable we infer that it has a solid foundation. The thought here is, that a proper administration of justice is essential to the stability and prosperity of a state,—*as* essential as a solid foundation is to the stability of the edifice which is reared on it. The effect of a mal-administration of justice in any community may be well compared with what the result would be if the foundations of the earth should be removed, or if the laws which now keep it in its place should cease to operate.

6. *I have said, Ye* are *gods.* See Notes on ver. 1. I have given you this title; I have conferred on you an appellation which indicates a greater *nearness* to God than any other which is bestowed on men,—an appellation which implies that you are God's representatives on earth, and that your decision is, in an important sense, to be regarded as his. ¶ *And all of you* are *children of the Most High.* Sons of God. That is, You occupy a rank which makes it proper that you should be regarded as his sons.

7. *But ye shall die like men.* You are mortal, like other men. This fact you have forgotten. You have been lifted up with pride, as if you were in fact more exalted than other men; as if you were not subject to the law which consigns all men to the grave. An ancient monarch directed his servant to address him each morning in this language: "Remember, sire, that thou art mortal." No more salutary truth can be impressed on the minds of the rich and the great than that they are, in this respect, like other men—like the poorest, the meanest of the race:—that they will die under similar forms of disease; that they will experience the same pain; that all which is fearful in death will be their portion as well as that of the most obscure; and that in the grave, with whatever pomp and splendour they descend to it, or however magnificent the monument which may be reared over the spot where they lie, there will be the same offensive and repulsive process of decay which occurs in the most humble grave in the country churchyard. Why, then—oh, why—should man be proud? ¶ *And fall like one of the princes.* And *die* as one of the princes. The idea in the word *fall* may be, perhaps, that they would die by the hand of violence,—or be cut down, as princes often are, *e. g.* in battle. The use of the word *princes* here denotes that they would die as other persons of exalted rank do; that is, that they were mortal as all

8 Arise, O God, judge the earth: for thou *q* shalt inherit all nations.

q Rev. xi. 15.

men, high and low, are—as common men are, and as princes are. Though they had names—*El*, and *Elohim*—that suggested the idea of divinity, yet such appellations did not make any real change in their condition as men, and as subject to the ordinary laws under which men live. Whatever name they bore, it did not afford any security against death.

8. *Arise, O God, judge the earth.* That is, Since there is such a failure in the administration of justice by those to whom it appertains, and who are appointed to do it in thy stead, do thou, O God, come forth thyself, and see that justice is executed among men. Do thou take the matter into thine own hands, and see that impartial justice is done everywhere among men. It pertains to thee as the great Proprietor of the earth to exercise justice; and we have nowhere else to look when men fail to do their duty. ¶ *For thou shalt inherit all nations.* Or rather, All nations belong to thee as thine inheritance; that is, as thine own. The word *inherit* is used here, as it often is, merely to denote possession or proprietorship, without reference to the question *how* the possession is obtained. The word strictly refers to what has been received from parents, or what men are heirs to; and, in this sense, it is commonly applied to the land of Palestine, either as what was derived by the Jewish people from their ancestors the patriarchs, or as what they had received from God as a Father. Ex. xxxii. 13; Deut. i. 38; xii. 10. It is here used simply in the sense of *possessing* it. That is, the whole earth belonged to God, and the administration of its affairs pertained to him. As those had failed who had been appointed under him to the office of judges,—as they had not been faithful to their trust,—as no confidence could be reposed in them,—the psalmist calls upon God to interfere, either by appointing other magistrates; or by leading those who were *in* office to just views of their duty; or by his own direct judgments, punishing the wicked, and rewarding the righteous, by the interpositions of his providence. We may hence learn (1) That there are times on earth when wickedness is so prevalent, and when there is such a want of faithfulness in civil rulers, that we have no other resource but to call upon God to interpose. (2) That it is right to call upon Him to see that justice should be done in the earth even in the punishment of the guilty, since all the interests of society depend on the proper administration of justice. (3) For the same reason it is right to pray that God would judge the world, and that justice may be done on the human race. It is desirable and proper that justice should be done; hence there is no malignity in desiring that there may be a universal judgment, and that the affairs of the universe should be placed on an equal and righteous foundation. It is *possible* that there may be a just and holy joy at the idea that justice *is* done, and that God shows himself the friend of truth, of order, and of law. Comp. Notes on Ps. lviii. 10; Rev. xix. 1–3.

PSALM LXXXIII.

This is another of the psalms of Asaph, the last of the group or collection that is found under his name. Comp. the Introd. to Psalm lxxiii. The occasion on which this was composed is not certainly known, and cannot now be ascertained. Grotius supposes that it relates to the time of David, and especially to the first war with the Syrians referred to in 2 Sam. viii., or to the second war with the Syrians referred to in 2 Sam. x., and 1 Chron. xix. Kimchi, De Wette, and others, suppose that it relates to the time of Jehoshaphat, and to the war with the Ammonites and Moabites, referred to in 2 Chron. xx. Hengstenberg and Prof. Alexander concur in this opinion, and suppose that it was written on the same occasion as Ps. xlvii. and xlviii.;—the first, composed and sung on

PSALM LXXXIII.

A Song *or* Psalm [1] of Asaph.

KEEP not thou silence, O God:
hold not thy peace, and be
not still, O God.
2 For, lo, thine enemies make
a [r] tumult: and they that hate
thee have lifted up the head.
3 They have taken crafty counsel against thy people, and consulted against thy hidden [s] ones.

[1] Or, *for*. *r* Isa. xxxvii. 29. *s* Ps. xxxi. 20.

the field of battle; the second, on the triumphant return to Jerusalem; the third—the one before us—in confident anticipation of victory. This is, perhaps, rather fanciful, and it certainly cannot be demonstrated that this is the correct opinion. It would seem, at least, to be hardly probable that a psalm would be composed and sung in a battle-field.

All that is certain in regard to the psalm is, that it was written in view of a threatened invasion by combined armies, and the prayer is, that God would give help, as he had done when the nation had been threatened on other occasions. The nations which were combined, or which had formed an alliance for this purpose, are specified in vers. 6-8;—Edom; Ishmael; Moab; the Hagarenes; Gebal; Ammon; Amalek; the Philistines; the Tyrians, Assur, and the children of Lot.

The contents of the psalm are as follows:—

I. A prayer that God would no longer keep still, or be silent, ver. 1.

II. A statement of the occasion for the prayer, to wit, the conspiracy or combination formed against his people, vers. 2-5.

III. An enumeration of the nations thus combined, vers. 6-8.

IV. A prayer that God would interpose as he had done in former times, in critical periods of the Jewish history,—as in the case of the Midianites; as in the time of Sisera, and Jabin; and as in the wars waged with Oreb and Zeeb, Zebah and Zalmunna, vers. 9-12.

V. A prayer that these enemies might be utterly overthrown and confounded; that God would promote his own glory; and that his people might be secure and happy, vers. 13-18.

1. *Keep not thou silence, O God.* See Notes on Ps. xxviii. 1. The prayer here is that in the existing emergency God would not seem to be indifferent to the wants and dangers of his people, and to the purposes of their enemies, but that he would *speak* with a voice of command, and break up their designs. ¶ *Hold not thy peace.* That is, *Speak.* Give command. Disperse them by thine own authority. ¶ *And be not still, O God.* Awake; arouse; be not indifferent to the wants and dangers of thy people. All this is the language of *petition;* not of *command.* Its rapidity, its repetition, its tone, all denote that the danger was imminent, and that the necessity for the Divine interposition was urgent.

2. *For, lo, thine enemies make a tumult.* Are excited; are aroused; are moving in a wild, furious, tumultuous manner, rushing on to the accomplishment of their designs. They come like rolling waves of the sea. See the word here used explained in the Notes on Ps. ii. 1, where it is rendered, in the text, *rage;* in the margin, *tumultuously assemble.* ¶ *And they that hate thee.* Thine enemies; the enemies of thy cause, and of thy people. Who they were is specified in vers. 6-8. ¶ *Have lifted up the head.* Have become proud; bold; confident of success,—all of which is indicated by the phrase *lifted up the head.* The head is bowed down in penitence and trouble; pride lifts it up; boldness, confidence, and wickedness, are indicated by its being thus lifted up.

3. *They have taken crafty counsel.* The one word translated *have taken crafty*—עָרַם, *aram*—means properly to make naked; and then, to be crafty, cunning, malignant, 1 Sam. xxiii. 22. It is well rendered here, *they have taken crafty* counsel. The meaning is, they have *made* their counsel or their consultations crafty, cunning, artful, malignant. Instead of pursuing a course in their deliberations that would be just, true, honourable,

4 They have said, [t] Come, and let us cut them off from *being* a nation; that the name of Israel may be no more in remembrance.

[t] Esther iii. 6, 9.

they have followed the reverse. On the word rendered *counsel*—סוֹד, *sodh*—which means a *couch* or *cushion*, and hence a *divan*—see Notes on Job xv. 8; Ps. xxv. 14; lxiv. 2. The idea here is, that the persons referred to in the subsequent part of the psalm (vers. 6–8) had been assembled in a *divan*, or for consultation, and that they had there formed a malignant plan,—against God and his people,—which they were now proceeding to execute. ¶ *Against thy people.* For the purpose of destroying them. ¶ *And consulted against thy hidden ones.* The word rendered *hidden ones*—from the verb צָפַן, *tzaphan*, to hide, to conceal—properly denotes that which is secret, private, inaccessible (Ezek. vii. 22); and then, anything *protected* or hidden so as to be secure. Comp. Notes on Ps. xxvii. 5. It would seem here to refer to those who were so *protected* by Jehovah—so inaccessible to others by reason of his guardian care—that they would be safe.

4. *They have said, Come, and let us cut them off*, etc. Let us utterly destroy them, and root them out from among the nations. Let us combine against them, and overpower them; let us divide their land among ourselves, attaching it to our own. The nations referred to (vers. 6–8) were those which surrounded the land of Israel; and the proposal seems to have been to partition the land of the Hebrews among themselves, as has been done in modern times in regard to Poland. On what principles, and in what proportions, they proposed thus to divide the land is not intimated, nor is it said that the project had gone so far that they had agreed on the terms of such a division. The formation of such a purpose, however, was in itself by no means improbable. The Hebrew people were offensive to all the surrounding nations by their religion, their prosperity, and the constant rebuke of tyranny and idolatry by their religious and their social institutions. There had been enough, also, in their past history—in the remembrance of the successful wars of the Hebrews with those very nations—to keep up a constant irritation on their part. We are not to be surprised, therefore, that there was a deeply-cherished desire to blot out the name and the nation altogether. ¶ *That the name of Israel may be no more in remembrance.* That the nation as such may be utterly extinct and forgotten; that the former triumphs of that nation over us may be avenged; that we may no longer have in our very midst this painful memorial of the existence of one God, and of the demands of his law; that we may pursue our own plans without the silent or the open admonition derived from a religion so pure and holy. For the same reason the world has often endeavoured to destroy the church; to cause it to be extinct; to blot out its name; to make the very names *Christ* and *Christian* forgotten among men. Hence the fiery persecutions under the Roman government in the time of the Emperors; and hence, in every age, and in every land, the church has been exposed to persecution—originated with a purpose to destroy it as long as there was any hope of accomplishing that end. That purpose has been abandoned by Satan and his friends only because the result has shown that the persecution of the church served but to spread its principles and doctrines, and to fix it more firmly in the affections and confidence of mankind, so that the tendency of persecution is rather to overthrow the persecutor than the persecuted. Whether it can be destroyed by prosperity and corruption,—by science,—by error,—seems now to be the great problem before the mind of Satan.

5 For they have consulted [u] together with one [1] consent: they are confederate against thee.
6 The [v] tabernacles of Edom, and the Ishmaelites; of Moab, and the Hagarenes;
7 Gebal, and Ammon, and Amalek: the Philistines, with the inhabitants of Tyre;

u Ps. ii. 2. 1 *heart.* v 2 Chron. xx. 10.

---

5. *For they have consulted together with one consent.* Marg., as in Heb., *heart.* There is no division in their counsels on this subject. They have one *desire*—one *purpose*—in regard to the matter. Pilate and Herod were made friends together against Christ (Luke xxiii. 12); and the world, divided and hostile on other matters, has been habitually united in its opposition to Christ and to a pure and spiritual religion. ¶ *They are confederate against thee.* Literally, "They cut a covenant against thee;" that is, they *ratify* such a covenant, compact, league,—referring to the manner in which bargains and agreements were ratified by *cutting in pieces* a victim sacrificed on such occasions; that is, by giving to such a transaction the solemnity of a religious sanction. Gen. xv. 10; Jer. xxxiv. 18, 19. See Bochart, Hieroz. i. 35. The meaning here is, that they had entered into this agreement in the most solemn manner, under the sanctions of religion.

6. *The tabernacles of Edom.* The *tents* of Edom; meaning here, the dwellers in those tents, that is, the Edomites. The word *tabernacles* or *tents* does not necessarily imply that the nation then led a wandering life, for the word came to signify in process of time a dwelling-place, or a habitation. The Edomites were not, in fact, a roving and wandering people, but a people of fixed boundaries. In early periods, however, like most ancient people, they doubtless dwelt in tents. Edom, or Idumea, was south of Palestine. See Notes on Isa. xi. 14. ¶ *And the Ishmaelites.* The descendants of Ishmael. They dwelt in Arabia Deserta. ¶ *Of Moab.* On the situation of Moab, see Notes on Isa. xv. It was on the south-east of Palestine. ¶ *And the Hagarenes.* The Hagarenes were properly Arabs, so called from Hagar, the handmaid of Abraham, the mother of Ishmael. Gen. xvi. 1; xxv. 12. As connected with the Ishmaelites they would naturally join in this alliance.

7. *Gebal.* The Gebal here referred to was probably the same as Gebalene, the mountainous tract inhabited by the Edomites, extending from the Dead Sea southwards towards Petra, and still called by the Arabs *Djebal.* (Gesenius, *Lex.*) The word means *mountain.* Those who are here referred to were a part of the people of Edom. ¶ *And Ammon.* The word Ammon means *son of my people.* Ammon was the son of Lot by his youngest daughter, Gen. xix. 38. The Ammonites, descended from him, dwelt beyond the Jordan in the tract of country between the streams of Jabbok and Arnon. These also would be naturally associated in such a confederacy. 1 Sam. xi. 1–11. ¶ *And Amalek.* The Amalekites were a very ancient people. In the traditions of the Arabians they are reckoned among the aboriginal inhabitants of that country. They inhabited the regions on the south of Palestine, between Idumea and Egypt. Comp. Ex. xvii. 8–16; Num. xiii. 29; 1 Sam. xv. 7. They also extended eastward of the Dead Sea and Mount Seir (Num. xxiv. 20; Judges iii. 13; vi. 3, 33); and they appear also to have settled down in Palestine itself, whence the name the *Mount of the Amalekites,* in the territory of Ephraim, Judges xii. 15. ¶ *The Philistines.* Often mentioned in the Scriptures. They were the ancient inhabitants of Palestine, whence the *name* Philistia or Palestine. The word is supposed to mean the land of sojourners or stran-

8 Assur also is joined with them: they have[1] holpen the children of Lot. Selah.

[1] *been an arm to.*

9 Do unto them as *unto* the [w] Midianites; as *to* Sisera, [x] as *to* Jabin, at the brook of Kison;

w Num. xxxi. 1—12. *x* Judges iv. 15—24.

gers; hence in the Septuagint they are uniformly called ἀλλόφυλοι, those of *another tribe, strangers*, and their country is called γῆ ἀλλοφύλων. They were constant enemies of the Hebrews, and it was natural that *they* should be engaged in such an alliance as this. ¶ *With the inhabitants of Tyre.* On the situation of Tyre, see the Introd. to Isa. xxiii. Why *Tyre* should unite in this confederacy is not known. The purpose seems to have been to combine as many nations as possible against the Hebrew people, and—as far as it could be done—*all* those that were adjacent to it, so that it might be *surrounded* by enemies, and so that its destruction might be certain. It would not probably be difficult to find some pretext for inducing *any* of the kings of the surrounding nations to unite in such an unholy alliance. Kings, in general, have not been unwilling to form alliances against liberty.

8. *Assur also is joined with them.* Assyria. Assyria was on the north-east of Palestine. The conspirators had secured, it seems, the aid of this powerful kingdom, and they felt confident of success. ¶ *They have holpen the children of Lot.* The sons, or the descendants of Lot. The margin is, as the Hebrew, *been an arm to.* That is, they were an aid, or help; in other words, the sons of Lot were permitted, as it were, to make use of the *arm* of these powerful nations in accomplishing their purposes. The sons of Lot were Moab and Ammon, the ancestors of the Moabites and the Ammonites, Gen. xix. 37, 38. It would appear from this, that the purpose of destroying the Hebrew people had been originated by the Moabites and Ammonites, and that they had called in the aid of the surrounding nations to enable them to carry out their plan. The enumeration of those who had joined in the alliance shows that *all* the nations adjacent to Palestine, on every side, had entered into the agreement, so that the land was completely encompassed, or hemmed in, by enemies. In these circumstances, the conspirators felt secure; in these circumstances, the Hebrew people had no resource but to call upon God. Thus it often occurs that the people of God are so *surrounded* by enemies, or are so *hemmed in* by troubles and trials, that they have no other resource than this:—they are shut up to the necessity of prayer. Often God so orders, or permits things to occur, as to cut off his people from every other dependence, and to make them feel that there *is* no help for them but in Him.

9. *Do unto them as* unto *the Midianites.* That is, Let them be overthrown and destroyed as the Midianites were. The reference here is to the complete overthrow of the Midianites, as related in Numbers xxxi. ¶ *As* to *Sisera.* The captain or commander of the army of Jabin, king of Canaan. He was conquered by the Hebrew armies under the direction of the prophetess Deborah, by the instrumentality of Barak (Judges iv. 4, 6, 14, 15), and was slain by Jael, the wife of Heber the Kenite, Judges iv. 17–21. ¶ *As* to *Jabin.* The king of Canaan, in whose service Sisera was. ¶ *At the brook of Kison.* Judges iv. 13. This is a stream which rises near Mount Tabor, and empties itself into the Bay of Ptolemais. In Judges v. 21, in the song of Deborah on occasion of this victory, it is mentioned as "that ancient river, the river Kishon;" that is, it was a stream which was well known; which had been referred to in ancient tales and poetry;—not a newly discovered river, but a river

10 *Which* perished at En-dor: they became *as* dung for the earth.

11 Make their nobles like Oreb [y] and like Zeeb; yea, all their princes as Zebah, [z] and as Zalmunna:

12 Who said, Let us take to ourselves the houses of God in possession.

13 O my God, make them like a wheel; as [a] the stubble before the wind.

14 As the fire burneth a wood,

y Judges vii. 25. *z* Judges viii. 12—21. *a* Isa. xvii. 13, 14; Matt. iii. 12.

whose name and locality were familiar to all.

10. Which *perished at En-dor.* Endor is not particularly mentioned in the history of the transaction in the book of Judges, but it is known that Endor was in the vicinity of Mount Tabor, and there is no improbability in the tradition which has fixed the site of the battle at or near Endor. The word or name *En-dor* means properly *fount of the dwelling* (or, *habitation*), and was probably given at first to a spring or fountain near to which some distinguished or well-known person dwelt. It is mentioned in Josh. xvii. 11; 1 Sam. xxviii. 7. ¶ *They became* as *dung for the earth.* The land was enriched or made fertile by their flesh, their blood, and their bones, as the field of Waterloo was by that of the slain, or as fields of battle commonly are.

11. *Make their nobles like Oreb and like Zeeb.* These were princes or rulers of the Midianites, slain by Gideon, the one on the rock Oreb, and the other at the wine-press of Zeeb. Judges vii. 25. The prayer here is, that the enemies who had conspired against the land of Israel might be utterly destroyed. ¶ *Yea, all their princes as Zebah, and as Zalmunna.* The word here rendered *princes* means properly *anointed*, and was given to princes, kings, prophets, and priests, as anointed, or as set apart by anointing to their office. Zebah and Zalmunna were kings of Midian, slain also by Gideon. See Judges viii. 5, 21.

12. *Who said, Let us take to ourselves the houses of God in possession.* The *houses* of God here mean the habitations of God, or the places where he dwelt among the people. As there was but one ark, one tabernacle, and one temple, or one place of constituted public worship, this must refer to other places where God was worshipped, or where he might be supposed to reside;—either to synagogues (see Notes on Ps. lxxiv. 8), or to the private dwellings of the people regarded as a holy people, or as a people among whom God dwelt. This may, therefore, imply that their dwellings — their private abodes— were also dwelling-places of God, as now the house of a religious family— a place where God is regularly worshipped—may be regarded as an abode of God on the earth. The language here is not to be understood as that of Oreb and Zeeb, of Zebah and Zalmunna, but of the enemies referred to in the psalm, who had entered into the conspiracy to destroy the Hebrew nation. *They* had said, "Let us *inherit* the houses of God;" that is, Let us take to ourselves, and for our possession, the dwellings of the land where God is supposed to reside.

13. *O my God, make them like a wheel*, etc. Or rather, like *a rolling thing*—something that the wind rolls along. The word גַּלְגַּל — *galgal* — means properly a wheel, as of a chariot, Ezek. x. 2, 6; or a wheel for drawing water from a well, Eccl. xii. 6; then, a whirlwind, Ps. lxxvii. 19; and then, anything driven before a whirlwind, as chaff, or stubble, Isa. xvii. 13. Comp. Notes on Isa. xxii. 18. The prayer here is, that they might be utterly destroyed, or driven away.

14. *As the fire burneth a wood*, etc. The same idea is here presented under another form. No image of desola-

and as the flame setteth the mountains on fire;

15 So persecute them with thy tempest, and make them afraid with thy storm.

16 Fill their faces with shame; that they may seek thy name, O LORD.

17 Let them be confounded and troubled for ever; yea, let them be put to shame, and perish:

tion is more fearful than that of fire raging in a forest; or of fire on the mountains. As trees and shrubs and grass fall before such a flame, so the prayer is, that they who had combined against the people of God might be swept away by his just displeasure.

15. *So persecute them.* So pursue them; so follow them up. The word *persecute* is now used in a somewhat different sense, as denoting pain or suffering inflicted on account of religious opinion. It means here simply *to pursue.* ¶ *With thy tempest.* With the expressions of thy displeasure; with punishment which may be compared with the fury of a storm. ¶ *And make them afraid with thy storm.* Or, Make them afraid, terrify them, so that they will flee away. As all that is here sought by prayer is what men endeavour to *do* when an enemy invades their country,—as they *make arrangements* for repelling those enemies, and overthrowing them, and as they feel that it is *right* to do so,—there is no impropriety in making this the subject of prayer to God. What it is right for men to *attempt*, it is right to pray for; what it would be right for them to *do* if they had the power, it is right to ask God to accomplish; what is free from malignity in the act, and in the design, may be free from malignity in the desire and the prayer; and if men can carry with them the idea that what they are endeavouring *to do* is right, whether as magistrates, judges, rulers, defenders of their country, or as private men, they will have very little difficulty in regard to the so-called *imprecatory psalms.* See this subject treated in the General Introd.

16. *Fill their faces with shame.* As those who are disappointed and foiled in their plans,—such disappointment and confusion commonly manifesting itself in the face. The prayer here is, that their enemies might be so baffled in their designs,—that they might be made so to feel how vain and hopeless were all their plans,—that there might be such a manifest interposition of God in the case, as that they should be led to see that Jehovah reigned; that it was in vain to contend with him, and that his people were under his protection. ¶ *That they may seek thy name, O* LORD. That they may be led to seek *thee.* This explains the drift and design of the whole prayer in the psalm. It is not a malignant prayer for the destruction of their enemies; it is not a wish that they might be made to suffer; but it is a prayer that the Divine dealing might be such as to lead them to the acknowledgment of the true God. It is a benevolent thing to desire that men may be brought to the knowledge of the true God, though it be through the discomfiture of their own plans, by defeat, or by suffering. Anything that leads men to an acquaintance with God, and results in securing his friendship and favour, is a gain, and will be cause of thankfulness in the end.

17. *Let them be confounded.* Let them be ashamed. That is, Let them have that kind of shame and confusion which results from the fact that their plans have not been successful, or that they have been foiled and baffled in their schemes. ¶ *And troubled.* Disturbed; put to confusion. Let them be troubled as men are who are unsuccessful in their projects. ¶ *For ever.* As a people; as confederated nations; as united in such an unholy alliance. Let them *never* again be able thus to combine,

18 That *men* may know that thou whose name [b] alone *is* JEHOVAH, *art* the Most High over all the earth.

b Isa. xlii. 8.

or to form a compact for the destruction of thy people. This does not refer to them as *individuals,* but as *nations.* It is a prayer that they may be so discomfited now that they may see the wickedness and folly of all such efforts, and that they may *never* again form such a combination. ¶ *Yea, let them be put to shame.* By utter failure in their schemes. ¶ *And perish.* Not individually, but as combined—as an alliance. Let there be a complete *end* to such a confederacy, so that it shall never be seen again.

18. *That* men *may know.* That all men may be impressed with the belief that thou art the true and only God. This was the design and aim of the prayer in the psalm. It was that there might be such a manifestation of the power of God; that it might be so evident that the events which had occurred could be traced to no other source than God himself, that all men might be led to honour him. ¶ *That thou whose name alone* is *JEHOVAH.* To whom alone this name belongs; to whom alone it can be properly ascribed. This was the *peculiar* name by which God chose to be known. Ex. vi. 3. Comp. Notes on Isa. xlii. 8. On the word *Jehovah*—יְהוָה—see Notes on Ps. lxviii. 4. It is found in combination, in Gen. xxii. 14; Ex. xvii. 15; Judges vi. 24; Ezek. xlviii. 35; Jer. xxiii. 6; xxxiii. 16. ¶ Art *the Most High over all the earth.* Thou art the Supreme God, ruling over all people. Thy dominion is so absolute over nations, even when combined together, and thy power is so complete in foiling their plans, and disconcerting their purposes, that it is clear that thou dost reign over them. He that could break up *such* a combination—he that could rescue his people from *such* an allied force—*must* have all power over the nations—*must* be the true God.

PSALM LXXXIV.

On the meaning of the phrase in the title, "*upon Gittith,*" see Notes on the title to Psalm viii. On the meaning of the phrase "*for* (marg. *to*) *the sons of Korah,*" see Notes on the title to Psalm xlii. The *author* of the psalm is unknown, though it bears a strong resemblance to the forty-second, and *may* have been composed by David himself. If so, it was dedicated, or devoted, as that was, to "the sons of Korah," to be adapted by them to music, and to be employed in public worship, and it *may* also have been composed on the same occasion. It is to be observed, however, that there were not only numerous occasions in the life of David, but also in the lives of other pious Hebrews, to which the sentiments in this psalm would be appropriate; and we cannot, therefore, affirm with certainty that it was composed by David. If it had been, moreover, it is difficult to account for the fact that his *name* is not prefixed to it. See, however, Notes on ver. 9.

The *occasion* on which the psalm was composed is apparent from the psalm itself. It was evidently when the writer was deprived, for some cause now unknown, of the privileges of the sanctuary. That cause may have been exile, or sickness, or distance, or imprisonment;—but whatever it was, the psalmist expresses his own deep feelings on the subject; the sense which he has of the blessedness of an attendance on the sanctuary, and of the happiness of those who were permitted to attend—regarding it as such a privilege that even the sparrow and the swallow might be supposed to be happy in being permitted to dwell near the altar of God. He describes, also, the joy and rejoicing of those who went up in companies, or in solemn procession, to the place of public worship—a happy, triumphant group on their way to the house of God.

It is not possible, however, to ascertain the *exact* time, or the *particular* occasion, when the psalm was written. The *language* is such as might have been used when the public worship was conducted either in the tabernacle, or in the temple—for the words employed are such as were adapted to either. It

PSALM LXXXIV.

To the chief Musician upon *c* Gittith. A Psalm [1] for the sons of Korah.

HOW amiable *are* thy tabernacles, O LORD of hosts!

2 My *d* soul longeth, yea, even fainteth, for the courts of the LORD; my heart and my flesh crieth out for the living God.

c Ps. viii., *title*. [1] Or, *of*. *d* Ps. xxvii. 4.

must have been, however, before the temple was destroyed, for it is clear that the usual place of public worship was still standing, and consequently it was before the captivity. The psalm is not one indicating *public* calamity; it is one of *private* love and sorrow.

The *contents* of the psalm are as follows:—

I. The psalmist expresses his own sense of the loveliness of the place where God is worshipped, and his earnest longing for the courts of the Lord, vers. 1, 2.

II. He illustrates this feeling by a beautiful image drawn from the sparrow and the swallow,—building their nests unobstructed and unalarmed near the very altar of God—as if they *must* be happy to be so near to God, and to dwell peaceably there, vers. 3, 4.

III. He describes the happiness of those who are *on the way* to the place of public worship: their joy; their progress in strength of purpose as they approached the place; their happiness in appearing before God, vers. 5-7.

IV. He pours forth his earnest prayer that *he* might be permitted thus to approach God; that he might be allowed to abide in the courts of God; that he might find a home there; that he might even spend a day there,—for a day there was better than a thousand elsewhere, vers. 8-12.

The whole psalm is a beautiful expression of love to the sanctuary, as felt by all who truly worship God.

1. *How amiable.* How much to be loved; how lovely. The word *amiable* is now used to denote a quality of mind or disposition—as gentle, affectionate, kind. The word here used, however in the original, means rather *dear, beloved*—as a token of endearment. Comp. Notes on the title to Ps. xlv. The idea here is, that the place of public worship is dear to the heart, as a beloved friend—a child—a wife—is. There is a strong and tender love for it. ¶ Are *thy tabernacles.* Thy dwelling-places. This word might be applied either to the tabernacle or the temple, or to any place where God was supposed to reside, or where his worship was celebrated. The *plural* form is here used probably because the tabernacle and the temple were divided into two parts or rooms, and each might be regarded as in a proper sense the dwelling-place of God. See Notes on Matt. xxi. 12, *et seq.* ¶ *O* LORD *of hosts!* Jehovah of hosts; Jehovah, controlling—ruling—guiding—marshalling—all the armies of heaven and earth:—comp. Notes on Isa. i. 9; Ps. xxiv. 10.

2. *My soul longeth.* The word here used means properly to be pale; then, to be faint or weak; and then, to pine after, to long for, to desire earnestly. It would properly denote such a longing or desire as to *make* one faint or exhausted; that is, it indicates intense desire. In Ps. xvii. 12, it is applied to a hungry lion; "Like a lion that is *greedy* of its prey." In Gen. xxxi. 30, it conveys the idea of intense desire: "Because thou *sore longedst* after thy father's house." For an illustration of the sentiment here expressed, see Notes on Ps. xlii. 1, 2. ¶ *Yea, even fainteth.* Is exhausted; fails of its strength. The word means properly to be completed, finished; then to be consumed, to be spent, to waste or pine away. Gen. xxi. 15; Jer. xvi. 4; Lam. ii. 11; Job xix. 27. ¶ *For the courts of the* LORD. The word here used refers to the different *areas* around the tabernacle or temple, within which many of the services of public worship were conducted, and which were frequented by different classes of persons. See Notes on Matt. xxi. 12. ¶ *My heart and my flesh.* My whole nature; my body and my soul;—all my desires and aspirations—all the longings of my heart are there. The body—the flesh—cries out for *rest*;—the heart—the soul—for *communion with God.* Our whole

3 Yea, the sparrow hath found an house, and the swallow a nest for herself, where she may lay her young, *even* thine altars, O LORD of hosts, my King and my God.

---

nature demands the benefits which spring from the worship of God. Body and soul were made for his service, and the necessities of neither can be *satisfied* without religion. ¶ *Crieth out.* The word here used—רָנַן, *ranan*—means properly to give forth a tremulous sound; then, to give forth the voice in vibrations, or in a tremulous manner; and thence it may mean either to utter cries of joy, (Lev. ix. 24; Job xxxviii. 7; Isa. xii. 6), or to utter a loud wail (Lam. ii. 19). Its common application is to joy (Ps. xcviii. 4; cxxxii. 16; lxv. 8); and it might be rendered here, "*Sing* unto the Lord," or "*Rejoice* unto the Lord." The connexion, however, seems to demand that it be understood as the cry of earnest longing or desire. ¶ *For the living God.* God, the true God, considered as *living*, in contradistinction from idols, always spoken of as dead. Comp. Ps. lxiii. 1.

3. *Yea, the sparrow hath found an house.* A home; a place where she may abide, and build her nest, and rear her young. The word here used —צִפּוֹר, *tzippor*—is a name given to a bird from its chirping or twittering. It is rendered *sparrow* in Lev. xiv. 4 (marg.); Ps. cii. 7; and is often rendered *bird* (Gen. vii. 14; xv. 10, *et al.*), and *fowl*, Deut. iv. 17; Neh. v. 18; *et al.* It may denote a bird of any kind, but is properly applied here to a sparrow, a species of bird very common and abundant in Palestine; a bird that finds its home especially about houses, barns, etc. That sparrows would be *likely* to gather around the tabernacle and even the altar, will appear not improbable from their well-known habits. "The sparrows which flutter and twitter about dilapidated buildings at Jerusalem, and crevices of the city walls, are very numerous. In some of the more lonely streets they are so noisy as almost to overpower every other sound. Their chirping is almost an articulate utterance of the Hebrew term (*tsippor*), which was employed to designate that class of birds. It may be taken for granted that the sparrows are not less numerous in other places where they have similar means for obtaining shelter and building their nests. The sparrows, in their resort to houses and other such places, appear to be a privileged bird. Encouraged by such indulgence, they are not timid—they frequent boldly the haunts of men. The sight of this familiarity reminded me again and again of the passage in the Psalms (lxxxiv. 3), where the pious Israelite, debarred from the privileges of the sanctuary, felt as if he could envy the lot of the birds, so much more favoured than himself."—Professor Hackett, "Illustrations of Scripture," pp. 94, 95. ¶ *And the swallow a nest for herself.* A place where it may make its nest. The word here used—דְּרוֹר, *derōr*—denotes properly, *swift flight, a wheeling* or *gyration;* and it is applied to birds which fly in circles or gyrations, and the name is thus appropriately given to the swallow. It occurs in this sense only here and in Prov. xxvi. 2. ¶ *Where she may lay her young.* Where she may *place* her young. The word *lay* here is not used in the sense in which we now apply it when we speak of "laying" eggs. It means to *place* them; to make a home for them; to dispose and arrange them. ¶ Even *thine altars*, etc. The altars where thou art worshipped. The idea here is, that the sparrows and the swallows seemed to have a happy lot; to be in a condition to be *envied.* Even they might come freely to the place where God was worshipped—to the very altars,—and make their home there undisturbed. How strongly in contrast with this was the condition of the wandering—the exiled—author of the psalm!

4 Blessed [e] *are* they that dwell in thy house: they will be still praising thee. Selah.

5 Blessed *is* the man whose strength *is* in thee: in whose heart *are* the ways *of them*:

6 *Who* passing through the

e Ps. lxv. 4.

---

4. *Blessed* are *they that dwell in thy house.* Who are constantly there; whose permanent abode is there. The reference is to the priests and Levites —the ministers of religion—who had their permanent abode near the tabernacle and the temple, and who were wholly devoted to the sacred duties of religion. Their lot is here spoken of as a *blessed*, or as a happy lot, in contradistinction from those who had only the opportunity of occasionally going up to worship. Comp. Notes on Ps. lxv. 4. ¶ *They will be still praising thee.* They will do it constantly, as their daily employment. It will not be worship begun and ended, but worship continued—the regular business from day to day. Such will heaven be; and this will constitute its glory. There will be (*a*) a permanent residence there:—"Him that overcometh will I make a pillar in the temple of my God, and he shall go no more out," (Rev. iii. 12;) and (*b*) there will be the constant service of God; such a service that it may be described as perpetual praise. The Septuagint and the Latin Vulgate render this, "They will praise thee *for ages of ages;*" that is, for ever.

5. *Blessed* is *the man whose strength* is *in thee.* Not merely are they blessed who dwell there permanently, but the man also whose heart is there; who feels that his strength is in God alone; who loves to go there when opportunity is afforded him, treading his way to Zion. The *idea* is, that all strength must come from God; that this strength is to be obtained by waiting on him (comp. Notes on Isa. xl. 31), and that, therefore, it is a privilege thus to wait on God. Comp. ver. 7. ¶ *In whose heart* are *the ways* of them. Literally, "The ways in their heart." De Wette renders this, "Who thinketh on the ways [or paths] to Jerusalem." The word "ways" may refer either to the ways or paths that lead to the place of worship, or the ways to God and to heaven. As the allusion, however, is evidently to those who were accustomed to go up to the place of public worship, the meaning is, that the man is blessed or happy whose heart is on those ways; who thinks on them; who makes preparation for going up; who purposes thus to go up to worship. The sense is enfeebled in our translation by the insertion of the words "*of them.*" The literal translation is better: "The ways [that is, the paths—the going up—the journey —to the place of public worship]—are in their heart." Their affections; their thoughts are there. The word rendered *ways*, means commonly *a raised way, a highway*, but it may refer to any public path. It would be applicable to what we call a *turnpike* (road), as a way *thrown up* for public use. The allusion is to the ways or paths by which the people commonly went up to the place of public worship; and the idea may be well expressed in the language of Watts,—

"I love her gates, I love the road."

The sentiment thus expressed finds a response in thousands of hearts:—in the happiness—the peace—the joy— with which true worshippers go to the house of God. In the mind of the writer of the psalm this would have an additional beauty and attractiveness as being associated with the thought of the multitudes thronging that path—the groups—the companies—the families—that crowded the way to the place of public worship on their great festal occasions.

6. Who *passing through the valley of Baca.* This is one of the most difficult verses in the Book of Psalms, and has been, of course, very variously interpreted. The Septuagint and the Latin Vulgate, Luther, and Professor Alexander, render it *a valley of tears.*

valley of [1] Baca, make it a well: the rain also [2] filleth the pools.

[1] Or, *mulberry trees make him a well*, 2 Sam. v. 23.

[2] *covereth.*

The word *Baca* (בָּכָא) means properly weeping, lamentation; and then it is given to a certain tree—not probably a mulberry tree, but some species of balsam,—from its *weeping;* that is, because it seemed to distil *tears*, or drops of balsam resembling tears in size and appearance. It is translated *mulberry trees* in 2 Sam. v. 23, 24; 1 Chron. xiv. 14, 15; and so in the margin here, "mulberry trees make him a well." There is no reason, however, to think that it has that meaning here. The true rendering is, "valley of lamentation," or weeping; and it may have reference to some lonely valley in Palestine,—where there was no water—a gloomy way—through which those commonly passed who went up to the place of worship. It would be vain, however, to attempt now to determine the locality of the valley referred to, as the name, if ever given to it, seems long since to have passed away. It may, however, be used as emblematic of human life—"a vale of tears;" and the passage may be employed as an *illustration* of the effect of religion in diffusing happiness and comfort where there was trouble and sorrow, —*as if* fountains should be made to flow in a sterile and desolate valley. ¶ *Make it a well.* Or, a fountain. That is, It becomes to the pilgrims as a sacred fountain. They "*make*" such a gloomy valley *like* a fountain, or like a road where fountains—full, free, refreshing—break forth everywhere to invigorate the traveller. Religious worship—the going up to the house of God—turns that in the journey of life which would otherwise be gloomy and sad into joy; makes a world of tears a world of comfort; has an effect *like* that of changing a gloomy path into one of pleasantness and beauty. The *idea* here is the same which occurs in Isa. xxxv. 7, "And the parched ground shall become a pool" (see Notes on that passage);—and in Job xxxv. 10, "Who giveth songs in the night" (see Notes on that passage);—an idea which was so beautifully illustrated in the case of Paul and Silas in the jail at Philippi, when, at midnight they "sang praises to God" (Acts xvi. 25), and which is so often illustrated in the midst of affliction and trouble. By the power of religion, by the presence of the Saviour, by the influence of the Holy Ghost, the Comforter, such times become seasons of purest joy—times remembered ever afterwards with most fervent gratitude, as among the happiest periods of life. For religion can diffuse smiles over faces darkened by care; can light up the eye sunk in despondency; can change tears of sorrow into tears of joy; can impart peace in scenes of deepest sorrow; and make the most gloomy vales of life like green pastures illuminated by the brightness of noonday. ¶ *The rain also filleth the pools.* Marg., *covereth.* This is a still more difficult expression than the former. The Septuagint and the Vulgate render it, "The teacher—the lawgiver—ὁ νομοθετῶν—*legislator*—gives blessings." Luther, "The teachers shall be adorned with many blessings." Gesenius, "Yea, with blessings the autumnal rain doth cover it." De Wette, "And with blessing the harvest-rain covers it," which he explains as meaning, "Where they come, though it would be sorrow and tears, yet they are attended with prosperity and blessing." Professor Alexander, "Also with blessings is the teacher clothed." The word rendered *rain*—מוֹרֶה, *moreh*—is from יָרָה, *yarah*, to throw, to cast, to place, to sprinkle, and may denote (1) an archer; (2) the early rain; (3) teaching, Isa. ix. 15; 2 Kings xvii. 28; or a teacher, Isa. xxx. 20; Job xxxvi. 22. It is rendered *rain*, in the place before us; and *former rain* twice in Joel ii. 23 (marg., *a teacher*). The

7 They [f] go from [1] strength to strength; *every one of them* in Zion appeareth [g] before God.

[f] Job xvii. 9; Prov. iv. 18.
[1] Or, *company to company.*
[g] Jude 24.

word rendered *filleth* means properly to cover, and would be fitly so translated here. Comp. Lev. xiii. 45; Ezek. xxiv. 17, 22. The word has not naturally the idea of *filling*. The word rendered *pools*—בְּרָכוֹת, *berachoth*—if pointed in one manner—בְּרֵכָה, *beraichah* (in the singular)—denotes a *pond, pool,* or basin of water; if pointed in another manner—בְּרָכָה, *berâchah*—it means *blessing, benediction,* and is often so used in the Scriptures, Gen. xxvii. 12; xxviii. 4; xxxiii. 11; Prov. xi. 11, etc. The rendering of Gesenius, as above, "Yea, with blessings the autumnal rain doth cover it," (that is, the valley so desolate in the heat of summer—the valley of weeping), would perhaps be the most natural, though it is not easy to see the *connexion* according to this interpretation, or according to any other proposed. Least of all is it easy to see the connexion according to the translation of the Septuagint, the Vulgate, Luther, and Prof. Alexander. *Perhaps* the connexion in the mind of the author of the psalm may have been this. He sees the sterile and desolate valley through which the pilgrims are passing made joyous by the cheerfulness — the happiness — the songs—of those who are on their way to the house of God. This fact—this image—*suggests* to him the idea that this is *similar* to the effect which is produced in that valley when copious rains descend upon it, and when, though commonly desolate, it is covered with grass and flowers, or is "*blessed*" by the rain. This latter image is to his mind an *illustration* of the happy scene now before him in the cheerful and exulting movements of the pilgrims on their way to the house of God. The one suggests the other; and the psalmist has a *combined* image before his mind, the one illustrating the other, and *both* showing how a vale naturally desolate and sterile *may* be made cheerful and joyous.

7. *They go from strength to strength,* etc. Marg., *company to company.* The Septuagint and Vulgate, "They go from strength to strength; the God of gods is seen in Zion." Luther, "They obtain one victory after another, that one must see that there is a righteous God in Zion." De Wette, "Going they increase in strength, until they appear before God in Zion." This last is doubtless the true idea. As they pass along, as they come nearer and nearer to the end of their journey, their strength, their ardour, their firmness of purpose increases. By their conversation; by their songs; by encouraging one another; by seeing one difficulty overcome after another; by the fact kept before their minds, and increasingly apparent, that they are constantly approaching the end of their journey,—that the distance to be travelled is constantly diminishing,—that the difficulties become less and less, and that they will soon see the towers and walls of the desired city,—they are invigorated, cheered, comforted. What a beautiful illustration of the life of Christian pilgrims—of the bands of the redeemed—as they journey on towards the end of their course,—the Mount Zion above! By prayer and praise and mutual counsel, by their songs, by the fact that difficulties are surmounted, leaving fewer to be overcome, and that the journey to be travelled is diminishing constantly,—by the feeling that they are ever drawing nearer to the Zion of their home, until the light is seen to glitter and play on its towers and walls,—they increase in strength, they become more confirmed in their purposes, they bear trials better, they overcome difficulties more easily,

8 O LORD God of hosts, hear
my prayer: give ear, O God of
Jacob. Selah.
9 Behold, O God our shield,
and look [h] upon the face of thine
anointed.
10 For a day in thy courts *is*

h Ps. cxix. 132.

they walk more firmly, they tread their way more cheerfully and triumphantly. ¶ Every one of them *in Zion appeareth before God.* Literally, "He shall appear to God in Zion." The meaning evidently is, that they who are referred to in the previous verses as going up to Zion will be seen there, or will come before God, in the place of worship. There is a change of number here, from the plural to the singular,—as, in verse 5, there is a change from the singular to the plural. Such changes are frequent in the Scriptures as in other writings, and the one here can be accounted for on the supposition that the author of the psalm, in looking upon the moving procession, at one moment may be supposed to have looked upon them *as* a procession,—a moving mass,—and then that he looked upon them as individuals, and spake of them as such. The idea here is, that they would not falter and fall by the way; that the cheerful, joyous procession would come to the desired place; that their wishes would be gratified, and that their joy would be full when they came to the end of their journey—to Zion. So it is of all Christian pilgrims. Every true believer—every one that truly loves God—will appear before him in the upper Zion—in heaven. There their joy will be complete; there the long-cherished desires of their hearts will be fully gratified; there all that they ever hoped for, and more, will be realized.

8. O LORD *God of hosts.* See Notes on ver. 1. God is appealed to here as a God of power; as a God who is able to accomplish all his purposes, and to impart every needed blessing. ¶ *Hear my prayer.* A prayer of the psalmist that *he* might also have a place among the servants of God in their worship, ver. 2. To this earnestness of prayer he is excited by the view which he had of the blessedness of those who went with songs up to Zion. His soul longs to be among them; from the sight of them his prayer is the more fervent that he may partake of their blessedness and joy. ¶ *Give ear, O God of Jacob.* With whom Jacob wrestled in prayer, and prevailed. Gen. xxxii. 24–30. On the phrase, *give ear*, see Notes on Ps. v. 1.

9. *Behold, O God our shield.* Our defence, as a shield is a defence in the day of battle. Comp. Notes on Ps. v. 12; xviii. 2; xxxiii. 20. It is an appeal to God *as* a protector. The psalmist was an exile—a wanderer—and he looked to God as his defence. ¶ *And look upon the face of thine anointed.* Look favourably upon; look with benignity and kindness. The word *anointed* here is the word *Messiah* — מָשִׁיחַ (Greek, χριστός, *Christ*; see Notes on Matt. i. 1). Comp. Notes on Ps. ii. 2. It here refers, however, evidently to the author of the psalm; and the word used is evidence that the author was David, as the anointed of the Lord, or some one set apart to the kingly office. It is true that this word was applicable to other kings, and also to priests and prophets, but the circumstances in the case concur best on the supposition that David is referred to. The allusion here is not to Christ; and the language does not suggest or justify the use which is often made of it when prayer is offered, that "God would look upon us in the face of his anointed"—whatever may, or may not be, the propriety of that prayer on other grounds.

10. *For a day in thy courts* is *better than a thousand.* Better—happier—more profitable—more to be desired—than a thousand days spent else-

better than a thousand. [1]I had rather be a doorkeeper in the house of my God, than to dwell in the tents of wickedness.

11 For the LORD God *is* a sun
i and shield: the LORD will give grace and glory: no good *k* *thing* will he withhold from them that walk uprightly.

[1] *I would choose rather to sit at the threshold.*

i Isa. lx. 19. *k* Phil. iv. 19.

where. That is, I should find more happiness—more true joy—in one day spent in the house of God, in his worship, in the exercises of true religion,—more that will be satisfactory to the soul, and that will be dwelt on with pleasure in the memory when life is coming to a close—than I could in a thousand days spent in any other manner. This was much for a man like David—or a man who had been encompassed with all the splendour of royalty—to say; it is much for any man to say. And yet it could be said with truth by him; it can be said with equal truth by others; and when we come to the end of life—to the time when we shall review the past, and ask where we have found *most* true happiness, most that was satisfactory to the soul, most that we shall delight then to dwell on and to remember, most that we should be glad to have repeated and perpetuated, most that would be free from the remembrance of disappointment, chagrin, and care,—it will not be the banqueting hall—the scenes of gaiety—the honours, the praises, the flatteries of men—or even the delights of literature and of the social circle,—but it will be the happy times which we shall have spent in communion with God,—the times when in the closet we poured out our hearts to Him,—when we bowed before him at the family altar, when we approached him in the sanctuary. The sweetest remembrances of life will be the sabbath and the exercises of religion. ¶ *I had rather be a doorkeeper in the house of my God.* Marg., *I would choose rather to sit at the threshold.* The verb here used is derived from a noun signifying *sill* or *threshold*, and it would seem to mean here to stand on the threshold; to be at the door or the entrance, even without the privilege of entering the house: I would prefer that humble place to a residence *within* the abodes of the wicked. The verb here used occurs nowhere else in the Scriptures. The exact idea is not, as would seem from our translation, to *keep* the door, as in the capacity of a sexton or servant, but that of occupying the *sill*—the threshold,—the privilege of standing there, and looking in, even if he was not permitted to enter. It would be an honour and a privilege to be anywhere about the place of public worship, rather than to be the occupant of a dwelling-place of sin. ¶ *Than to dwell in the tents of wickedness.* The word *tents* here is equivalent to *dwellings.* It is used because it was so common in early periods to dwell in tents; and hence the word was employed to denote a dwelling in general. The emphasis here is very much on the word "*in*:"—he would prefer standing at the door of the house of worship to dwelling *within* the abodes of the wicked,—that is, to being admitted to intimacy with those who occupy such dwellings,—however splendid, rich, and gorgeous, those abodes might be.

11. *For the* LORD *God* is *a sun.* The Septuagint and the Latin Vulgate render this, "For the Lord loveth mercy and truth." Our translation, however, is the correct one. The sun gives light, warmth, beauty, to the creation; so God is the source of light, joy, happiness, to the soul. Comp. Isa. lx. 19; Rev. xxi. 23; xxii. 5. ¶ *And shield.* See ver. 9. ¶ *The* LORD *will give grace and glory.* Grace, or favour, here; glory, or honour, in the world to come. He

12 O Lord of hosts, blessed *is* the man that trusteth in thee.

will bestow all needful favour on his people in this life; he will admit them to glory in the world to come. Grace and glory are connected. The bestowment of the one will be followed by the other. Rom. viii. 29, 30. He that partakes of the *grace* of God on earth will partake of *glory* in heaven. Grace comes before glory; glory always follows where grace is given. ¶ *No good* thing *will he withhold*, etc. Nothing really good; nothing that man really needs; nothing pertaining to this life, nothing necessary to prepare for the life to come. Comp. 1 Tim. iv. 8; Phil. iv. 19.

12. *O* Lord *of hosts, blessed* is *the man that trusteth in thee.* Blessed in every respect. His lot is a happy one; — happy in thy friendship; happy in being permitted to worship thee; happy in the blessings which religion scatters along his path here; happy in thy sustaining grace in times of trial; happy in the support given in the hour of death; happy in the eternity to which he is going. Oh that all men would try it, and experience in their own souls the happiness—the real, genuine, deep, permanent joy—*of trusting in God;*—of believing that there *is* a God; of confiding in his character; of leaning on him in every situation in life; of relying on his mercy, his grace, and his faithfulness, in the hour of death!

PSALM LXXXV.

On the phrase in the title, "To the chief Musician," see Notes on the title to Psalm iv. On the expression, "for the sons of Korah," see Notes on the title to Psalm xlii. Neither of these expressions determines anything in regard to the authorship of the psalm, or the occasion on which it was composed, and conjecture on these points would be useless. There were in the Jewish history, as there have been in the Christian church, numerous occasions to which the sentiments of the psalm would be appropriate. It was evidently composed in view of the fact that God *had*, on some former occasion, interposed when his people were in trouble, but that now for similar causes he was again angry with them, and they were suffering similar calamities. The psalm contains a fervent prayer that God would again appear for them, and it implies a confident expectation that he would do this, so that the calamities which had come upon them would be removed—even as by a miraculous interposition. There is nothing to make it absolutely certain that it pertains to the Babylonish captivity, as De Wette supposes, but the language is so general that it might refer to *any* captivity.

The psalm consists essentially of three parts:—

I. An allusion to God's gracious interposition in former times, as the ground of the present appeal to him, vers. 1-3. In those times, when his people had been conquered, he *had* restored to them the possession of their own land; he *had* forgiven their iniquity; he *had* turned himself from the fierceness of his anger. These acts of mercy were now remembered; and this was the ground of confident hope in the present trouble.

II. A description of the state of the people at the time when the psalm was composed, as demanding help from God, vers. 4-7. It is clear that the nation was suffering from some calamity; that the anger of God seemed to be upon them; that it appeared as if his wrath would *never* be turned away; and that unless he should interpose the nation must perish.

III. The expression of a confident hope that God *would* deliver his people, vers. 8-13. (*a*) The psalmist represents himself as willing to hear what God would say, with the hope that he would speak peace to his people; (ver. 8); (*b*) he declares his belief that God is near to them who fear him (ver. 9), and that in the present case—in the manner in which he would meet the present emergency—there would be a mingling of mercy and truth—of righteousness and peace:—that *each* of these, in proper proportions, and without collision, would meet and mingle in the Divine dealings; that is, it would be seen, in his dealings with his people, that God was merciful *and* just,—righteous *and* disposed to peace (ver. 10); (*c*) he expresses his assurance that, dark as things now ap-

PSALM LXXXV.

To the chief Musician. A Psalm [1] for the sons of Korah.

LORD, thou hast been [2] favourable unto thy land: thou hast
brought back the captivity of
Jacob.

[1] Or, *of*, Ps. xlii., *title*.
[2] Or, *well pleased with*, Ps. lxxvii. 7.

2 Thou hast forgiven *l* the
iniquity of thy people; thou hast
covered all their sin. Selah.
3 Thou hast taken away all
thy wrath: thou hast turned
[3] *thyself* from the fierceness of
thine anger.

l Col. ii. 13.
[3] Or, *thine anger from waxing hot*, Deut. xiii. 17.

---

peared, there would be a Divine interposition *as if* truth (or, a just solution of these difficulties) should spring out of the very earth—*as if* it would come from some unknown quarter and in some unexpected manner, as mysterious, and as incomprehensible, and as far removed from human agency *as if* it came up suddenly from the ground,—or *as if* the heavens opened themselves, and it looked down from the sky (ver. 11); and (*d*) he, in conclusion, expresses his confident belief that the Lord would give that which was truly good; that the land would again yield its increase; that righteousness would attend his march through the land, going as it were before him, and causing all the people to walk in his steps, vers. 12, 13.

There does not appear to have been in this psalm any *original* reference to the Messiah, or to his work:—that is, all that there is in the psalm can be explained on the supposition that it has no such reference. But it must be obvious to every one that the *language* is such as is fitted most beautifully and appropriately to describe many things in the plan of redemption, and especially to express the fact that *in* that work the attributes of God, some of which seem not easy to be reconciled, have been most perfectly and beautifully manifested and blended.

1. LORD, *thou hast been favourable unto thy land.* Marg., *well pleased with.* The idea is that he had been kind or propitious to the nation; to wit, on some former occasion. So Luther, (*vormals*) "formerly." The reference is to some previous period in their history, when he had exercised his power in their behalf. ¶ *Thou hast brought back the captivity of Jacob.* That is, at the time referred to. It is not necessary to suppose that the allusion is to the period immediately preceding the time when the psalm was composed, but it may have been any period in their history. Nor is it necessary to suppose that the people had been removed from their land at the time; for all that would be necessary to suppose in interpreting the language would be that the land had been invaded, even though the inhabitants still remained in it.

2. *Thou hast forgiven the iniquity of thy people.* That is, These calamities came upon them in consequence of their sins, and thou hast dealt with them as if those sins were forgiven. The fact that the tokens of his anger had passed away, and that his judgments were withdrawn, seemed to prove that their sins had been forgiven. The same form of expression here used—with the same words in Hebrew—occurs in Ps. xxxii. 5. See Notes on that passage. The language suggests the *idea* of an atonement. Literally, "Thou hast lifted up—or borne—the iniquity of thy people." ¶ *Thou hast covered all their sin.* So that it is hidden; and therefore thou dost treat them *as if* they were righteous, or *as if* there *were* no sin. The idea of *covering* is that expressed in the Hebrew word, which is commonly rendered *atonement*—כָּפַר, *kaphar*—to cover; to cover over; then, to cover over sin; to forgive. The idea suggested in this verse is, that when God withdraws the tokens of his displeasure, we may hope that he has pardoned the sin which was the cause of his anger.

3. *Thou hast taken away all thy wrath.* That is, formerly; on the

4 Turn us, O God of our salvation, and cause thine anger
toward us to cease.
5 Wilt thou be angry with us
for ever? wilt thou draw out
thine anger to all generations?
6 Wilt thou not revive us
again, that thy people may rejoice in thee?

---

occasion referred to. Thou didst so deal with thy people as to make it evident that thou didst cherish no anger or displeasure against them. ¶ *Thou hast turned* thyself, etc. Marg., *thine anger from waxing hot.* Literally, *Thou didst turn from the heat of thine anger.* His indignation was withdrawn, and he was again at peace with them. It is this fact, drawn from the former history of the people, which constitutes the basis of the appeal which follows.

4. *Turn us, O God of our salvation.* The God from whom salvation must come, and on whom we are dependent for it. The prayer here is, "turn *us;*" turn us from our sins; bring us to repentance; make us willing to forsake every evil way; and enable us to do it. This is the proper spirit always in prayer. The first thing is not that he would take away his wrath, but that he would dispose us to forsake our sins, and to turn to himself; that we may be led to abandon that which has brought his displeasure upon us, and *then* that he will cause his anger towards us to cease. We have no authority for asking God to turn away his judgments unless we are willing to forsake our sins; and in all cases we can hope for the Divine interposition and mercy, when the judgments of God are upon us, *only* as we are willing to turn from our iniquities. ¶ *And cause thine anger toward us to cease.* The word here used, and rendered *cause to cease*—פָּרַר, *parar*—means properly *to break;* then, *to violate;* and then, *to annul,* or to bring to an end. The idea here is, that if they were turned from sin, the cause of his anger would be removed, and would cease of course. Comp. Ps. lxxx. 3.

5. *Wilt thou be angry with us for ever?* Thine anger is so long continued that it seems as if it would never cease. ¶ *Wilt thou draw out thine anger.* Wilt thou protract or prolong it? The idea is that of a determined *purpose,* in retaining his anger, as if his wrath would cease of necessity unless there were such a direct exercise of will. ¶ *To all generations.* Literally, "from generation to generation." That is,—so that not merely the generation which has sinned, and which has brought down these tokens of displeasure, shall suffer, but the next, and the next, and the next, for ever. The plea is that the judgment might terminate, and not reach coming generations.

6. *Wilt thou not revive us again.* Literally, "Wilt thou not turn [or return], cause us to live;" that is, *and* cause us to live. The expression is equivalent to "*again*" as in our translation. The Septuagint and Vulgate render it, "Returning, wilt thou not give us life?" The word rendered *revive* means to live; to cause to live; and the idea is that of recovering them from their condition as a state of death; that is, restoring them *as if* they were dead. The *image* is that of returning spring after the death of winter, or the young grass when the rain descends after a long drought, and when everything seemed to be dead. So of the people referred to in the psalm; everything among them was *like* such a winter, when there is neither leaf, nor flower, nor grass, nor fruit; or *like* such a drought, when desolation is seen everywhere; or *like* the grave, where the dead repose. The image of spring, after a long and dreary winter, is one also which will properly describe the condition of the church when the influences of the

7 Shew us thy mercy, O LORD, and grant us thy salvation.
8 I will hear what God the LORD will speak: for he will speak peace unto his people, and to his saints: but [m] let them not turn again to folly.

m Ps. cxxx. 4.

Spirit have been long withheld, and when, under the visitations of grace, religion seems to live again among the people of God. ¶ *That thy people may rejoice in thee.* In thy favour; in thy presence; in *thee* as their God. (*a*) There is always *joy* in a revival of religion. Nothing is so much fitted to make a people happy; nothing diffuses so much joy. Comp. Acts viii. 8. (*b*) This is particularly joy *in God.* It is because he comes near; because he manifests his mercy; because he shows his power and his grace.

7. *Shew us thy mercy, O* LORD. That is, Manifest thy mercy in returning to us; in forgiving our sins; in taking from us the tokens of thy displeasure. ¶ *And grant us thy salvation.* Salvation or deliverance from our present trouble and calamities.

8. *I will hear what God the* LORD *will speak.* I, the psalmist; I, representing the people as looking to God. The state of mind here is that of patient listening; of a willingness to hear God, whatever God should say; of confidence in him that what he would say would be favourable to his people,—would be words of mercy and of peace. Whatever God should command, the speaker was willing to yield to it; whatever God should say, he would believe; whatever God should enjoin, he would do; whatever God should ask him to surrender, he would resign. There was no other resource but God, and there was entire confidence in him that whatever he should say, require, or do, would be right. ¶ *For he will speak peace unto his people.* Whatever he shall say will tend to their peace, their blessedness, their prosperity. He loves his people, and there may be a confident assurance that all he will say will tend to promote their welfare. ¶ *And to his saints.* His holy ones; his people. ¶ *But let them not turn again to folly.* The Septuagint and the Vulgate render this, "To his saints and to those who turn the heart unto him." Our common version, however, has expressed the sense of the Hebrew; and it contains very important truths and admonitions. (*a*) The way which they had formerly pursued was *folly.* It was not mere *sin*, but there was in it the element of *foolishness* as well as *wickedness.* All sin may be contemplated in this twofold aspect:—*as* wickedness, and *as* foolishness. Comp. Ps. xiv. 1; lxxiii. 3. (*b*) There was great danger that they *would* turn again to their former course; that they would forget alike the punishment which had come upon them; their own resolutions; and their promises made to God. Comp. Ps. lxxviii. 10, 11, 17, 18, 31, 32. Nothing is more common than for a people who have been afflicted with heavy judgments to forget all that they promised to do *if* those judgments should be withdrawn; or for an individual who has been raised up from a bed of sickness—from the borders of the grave—to forget the solemn resolutions which he formed on what seemed to be a dying bed,—perhaps becoming more thoughtless and wicked than he was before, as if to make reprisals for the wrong done him by his Maker, or as if to recover the time that was lost by sickness. (*c*) This passage, therefore, is a solemn admonition to all who have been afflicted, and who have been restored, that they return not to their former course of life. To this they should feel themselves exhorted (1) by their obligations to their benefactor; (2) by the remembrance of their own solemn vows

9 Surely his salvation *is* nigh them that fear him; that glory may dwell in our land.

10 Mercy and truth are met together; righteousness *n* and peace have kissed *each other*.

n Isa. xxxii. 17.

made in a time of sincerity and honesty, and when they saw things as they really are; and (3) by the assurance that *if* they do return to their sin and folly, heavier judgments will come upon them; that the patience of God will be exhausted; and that he will bear with them no longer. Comp. John v. 14, "Sin no more, lest a worse thing come unto thee."

9. *Surely his salvation.* His help; his aid. The word here does not mean *salvation* in the restricted use of the term as applied to the future life, but it means deliverance of *all* kinds—rescue from trouble, danger, calamity. ¶ Is *nigh them that fear him.* All who truly reverence him, and look to him in a proper manner. They may expect his aid; they may be sure that he will *soon* come to help them. This expresses the confident assurance of the author of the psalm that God *would* interpose in the troubles of the nation, and would deliver them. ¶ *That glory may dwell in our land.* (*a*) The glory or honour of having such a God to dwell among them;—and (*b*) the peace, the prosperity, the happiness, which will be the consequence—of his interposition. The idea is, that this would be a *permanent* thing; that this honour or glory would then make the land its dwelling-place.

10. *Mercy and truth are met together.* That is, in the Divine dealings referred to in the psalm. There has been a blending of mercy and truth in those dealings; or, both have been manifested;—truth, in the Divine statements, threatenings, and promises; and mercy, in forgiving sin, and in sparing the people. There is no *necessary* contradiction between truth and mercy; that is, the one does not *necessarily* conflict with the other, though the one *seems* to conflict with the other when punishment is threatened for crime, and yet mercy is shown to the offender,—that is, where the punishment is not inflicted, and the offender is treated *as if* he had not sinned. In this respect, the great difficulty in all human governments has been to maintain both; to be true to the threatening of the law, and at the same time to pardon the guilty. Human governments have never been able to reconcile the two. If punishment is inflicted up to the full measure of the threatening, there is no manifestation of mercy; if mercy is shown, there is a departure from justice, or a declaration that the threatenings of the law are not, in all cases, to be inflicted:—that is, there is, to that extent, an abandonment of justice. Human governments have always felt the need, in their practical operations, of some device like *an atonement*, by which the two might be blended, and both secured. Such a method of reconciliation or of securing both objects—truth, in the fulfilment of the threat, and mercy towards the offender—has never been (and could not be) acted on in a human administration. It is only in the Divine government that this has been accomplished, where a true and perfect regard has been paid to *truth* in the threatening, and to *mercy* toward the guilty by an atonement. It is true, indeed, that this passage does not refer to the atonement made by the Redeemer, but there can scarcely be found a better illustration of that work than occurs in the language here used. Comp. Notes on Rom. iii. 26. See also my work on the "Atonement," chapters ii., iii.* ¶ *Righteousness.* In the maintenance of law, or the manifestation of justice. That is, in this case, God had shown his justice in bringing

* And "Way of Salvation," chap. xvii.

11 Truth shall spring out of the earth; and righteousness shall look down from heaven.

12 Yea, the LORD shall give *that which is* good; [o] and our land shall yield her increase.

13 Righteousness [p] shall go before him, and [q] shall set *us* in the way of his steps.

o Ps. lxxxiv. 11. *p* Ps. lxxxix. 14. *q* Ps. cxix. 35.

these calamities on the people for their sins. In the work of the Redeemer this was done by his being "wounded for our transgressions, and bruised for our iniquities;" by the fact that "the chastisement of our peace was upon him," and that "the Lord laid on him the iniquity of us all." Isa. liii. 5, 6. ¶ *And peace.* Pardon; mercy; restoration to favour. In the case of the Hebrew people this was done by his removing the calamities which their sins had brought upon them, and by his returning favour. In the work of redemption, it was done by the pardon of sin, and by reconciliation to God. ¶ *Have kissed* each other. As friends and lovers do; as they do who have been long separated; as they do who, after having been alienated and estranged, are made friends again. In like manner, there seemed to be an alienation—an estrangement—a state of hostility—between righteousness and mercy, between justice and pardon, but they have been now united as separated and alienated friends are, and have embraced each other as such friends do; that is, they blend together in beautiful harmony.

11. *Truth shall spring out of the earth.* As plants do—for this is the meaning of the word. The blessings of truth and righteousness would be like the grass, the shrubs, the flowers, which spring up from the ground,—and like the rain and the sunbeams which come from heaven. Truth would spring up everywhere, and abound in all lands, as plants, and shrubs, and grass spring up all over the earth. There is not an intended *contrast* between the two clauses of this verse, as if truth came from *the earth,* and righteousness *from heaven;* but the idea is that they would come in a manner that might be compared with the way in which God's other abundant blessings are bestowed, as springing, on the one hand, from the fertility of the earth, and on the other, from the rain, the dew, and the sunbeam. ¶ *And righteousness shall look down from heaven.* Shall descend from heaven; or shall come from above,—*as if* the rain, and the sun looked down from heaven, and *saw* the wants of man. The original word here rendered *look down*—שָׁקַף, *shakaph*—means to *lay upon,* or over; then, to project, *lie over,* look forward; then, to *overhang;* and the idea here is that it *bent over,* or *leaned forward* to look at the necessities of man—as one does who is desirous of gazing at an object. There was an *anxiety,* so to speak, to come *to* the earth—to meet the human need. As the rain and the sunbeams seem *anxious* to bestow their blessings on man, so God *seems* anxious to bestow on man the blessings of salvation.

12. *Yea, the* LORD *shall give* that which is *good.* All that is truly good:—all needful temporal blessings; all blessings connected with salvation. ¶ *And our land shall yield her increase.* There shall be fruitful seasons, and the earth shall produce abundance. Comp. Notes on Ps. lxvii. 6.

13. *Righteousness shall go before him.* Shall anticipate his coming, and prepare his way. The *idea* seems to be, that in order to his appearing, there would be a proclamation of righteousness, and a preparation for his advent by the diffusion of righteousness among the people; in other words, the nation, in the prospect of his coming, would turn from sin, and would seek to be prepared for his appearing. Thus John proclaimed the coming of the Redeemer, "*Repent ye,* for the kingdom of heaven is at hand."

PSALM LXXXVI.

A Prayer [1] of David.

BOW down thine ear, O LORD, hear me: for I *am* poor and needy.

2 Preserve my soul, for I *am*

[1] Or, being a Psalm *of*.

Matt. iii. 2. So also "The voice of one crying in the wilderness, Prepare ye the way of the Lord, make his paths straight." Matt. iii. 3. ¶ *And shall set us in the way of his steps.* This might be rendered, "and set its steps for a way;" that is, the steps which would be taken by him would indicate the way in which his people should walk. Perhaps, however, the common interpretation best expresses the sense of the passage. According to that, the idea is, that the effect of his coming would be to dispose men to walk in the way of the steps which he took; to be his imitators and followers. The general thought is, that his coming would have the effect of turning the people to the paths of righteousness and truth. This is the designed effect of all the visitations of God to our world.

PSALM LXXXVI.

This psalm purports to be a psalm of David; and there is nothing in the psalm that is contrary to this supposition. Why it has its place among the psalms which are designated as the compositions of "the sons of Korah," and had not its place among those which are ascribed to David (Ps. i.-lxx.) we have no means of ascertaining. It is not said, however, that those were the *only* psalms of David, and there is no improbability in supposing that he may have composed others. It is not improperly named "*a prayer*," since it is made up mostly of petitions, though this is true of others which are *called* "psalms," and though it is true that this one has so much of *praise* in it that it might also (as it is in the margin) be designated *a psalm*. The occasion on which it was composed is unknown, but it has been commonly supposed that it was written in the time of the persecutions under Saul. De Wette regards it as a national song composed in a time of national trouble.

This psalm does not admit of any minute subdivision. It is made up of earnest prayers, with reasons why those prayers should be answered; and perhaps the leading practical suggestion which would properly follow from the psalm is, that it is proper for us, in our prayers, to urge reasons why they should be answered: the reasons why we pray at all. We cannot, indeed, suppose that we can suggest anything which would not occur to the Divine mind, but in all our prayers there *is* some reason why we pray; there *are* reasons why we ask the particular things which are the burden of our supplications, and it cannot be improper, in order that our own minds at least may be suitably impressed, to mention those reasons when we come before God.

1. *Bow down thine ear, O* LORD, *hear me.* See Notes on Ps. v. 1. ¶ *For I* am *poor and needy.* This is the *reason* here assigned why God should hear him. It is not a plea of merit. It is not that there was any claim on God in the fact that he was a poor and needy man,—a sinner helpless and dependent, or that it would be any injustice if God should *not* hear, for a sinner has no *claim* to favour; but it is that this was a condition in which the aid of God was *needed*, and in which it was proper or *appropriate* for God to hear prayer, and to render help. We may always make our helplessness, our weakness, our poverty, our need, a ground of appeal to God;—not as a claim of justice, but as a case in which he will glorify himself by a gracious interposition. It is also to be remarked that it is a matter of unspeakable thankfulness that the "poor and needy" *may* call upon God; that they will be *as* welcome as any class of men; that there is no condition of poverty and want so low that we are debarred from the privilege of approaching One who has infinite resources, and who is as *willing* to help as he is *able*.

2. *Preserve my soul.* Preserve, or

[1]holy: O thou my God, save thy
servant that trusteth [r] in thee.
3 Be merciful unto me, O
Lord: for I cry unto thee [2]daily.
4 Rejoice the soul of thy servant: for unto thee, O Lord, do
I lift up my soul.
5 For [s]thou, Lord, *art* good,
and ready to forgive; and plenteous in mercy unto all them that
call upon thee.

[1] Or, *one whom thou favourest.*
r Isa. xxvi. 3.

[2] Or, *all the day.*
s Joel ii. 13.

keep, my life;—for so the word rendered *soul* means in this place, as it does commonly in the Scriptures. ¶ *For I* am *holy.* Marg., *One whom thou favourest.* The Hebrew word—חָסִיד, *hhasid*—means properly, benevolent, kind; then, good, merciful, gracious; and then pious, godly. Ps. xxx. 4; xxxi. 23; xxxvii. 28. The *ground* of the plea here is, that he was a friend of God; and that it was proper on that account to look to him for protection. He does not say that he was holy in such a sense that he had a *claim* on that account to the favour of God, or that his personal holiness was a ground of salvation; but the idea is, that he had devoted himself to God, and that it was, therefore, proper to look to him for his protection in the time of danger. A child looks to a parent for protection, because he *is* a child; a citizen looks to the protection of the laws, because he *is* a citizen; and so the people of God may look to him for protection, because they *are* his people. In all this there is no plea of merit, but there is the recognition of what is proper in the case, and what may be expected and hoped for. ¶ *Save thy servant.* Save him from threatening danger and from death. ¶ *That trusteth in thee. Because* I trust or confide in thee. I go nowhere else for protection; I rely on no one else. I look to thee alone, and I do this with entire confidence. A man who does this has a *right* to look to God for protection, and to expect that God will interpose in his behalf.

3. *Be merciful unto me, O Lord.* It was *mercy* after all that he relied on, and not *justice.* It was not because he had any *claim* on the ground that he was "holy," but all that he had and hoped for was to be traced to the *mercy* of God. ¶ *For I cry unto thee daily.* Marg., as in Heb., *All the day.* The meaning is, that he did this constantly, or without intermission.

4. *Rejoice the soul of thy servant.* Cause *me* to rejoice; to wit, by thy gracious interposition, and by delivering me from danger and death. ¶ *For unto thee, O Lord, do I lift up my soul.* Comp. Notes on Ps. xxiv. 4. The idea is that of *arousing* himself, or *exerting* himself, as one does who makes strenuous efforts to obtain an object. He was not languid, or indifferent; he did not put forth merely weak and fitful efforts to find God, but he *bent his whole powers* to that end; he arouses himself thoroughly to seek the Divine help. Languid and feeble efforts in seeking after God will be attended with no success. In so great a matter,—when so much depends on the Divine favour,—when such great interests are at stake,—the whole soul should be roused to one great and strenuous effort;—not that we can obtain his favour by force or power, and not that any strength of ours will prevail of itself, but (*a*) because nothing less will indicate the proper intensity of desire; and (*b*) because such is his appointment in regard to the manner in which we are to seek his favour. Comp. Matt. vii. 7, 8; Luke xiii. 24; xvi. 16.

5. *For thou, Lord,* art *good,* etc. This is another reason why God should hear his prayer; and it is a reason which may be properly urged at all times, and by all classes of persons. It is founded on the benevolence of God; on the fulness of his

6 Give ear, O LORD, unto my prayer; and attend to the voice of my supplications.

7 In the day of my trouble I will [t] call upon thee: for thou wilt answer me.

8 Among the gods *there is* none [u] like unto thee, O Lord; neither [v] *are there any works* like unto thy works.

9 All [w] nations whom thou hast made shall come and wor-

t Ps. l. 15. *u* Isa. xl. 18, 25. *v* Deut. iii. 24. *w* Rev. xv. 4.

mercy to all that invoke his name. We should call in vain on a God who was *not* merciful and ready to forgive; but in the Divine character there is the most ample foundation for such an appeal. In his benevolence; in his readiness to forgive; in the plenitude of his mercy, God is all that a penitent sinner could wish him to be. For if such a sinner should endeavour to describe what he would *desire* to find in God as a ground of appeal in his prayers, he could not express his feelings in language more full and free than God has himself employed about his own readiness to pardon and save. The language of the Bible on this subject would express, better than any language which he could himself employ, what in those circumstances he would *wish* to find God to be.

6. *Give ear, O* LORD, *unto my prayer*, etc. See Notes on Ps. v. 1.

7. *In the day of my trouble I will call upon thee.* That is, I do it now; I have done it; I will do it. The language implies a *habit*, or a steady purpose of mind, that in all times of trouble he would make God his refuge. It was this fixed purpose—this regular habit—which was now the ground of his confidence. A man who *always* makes God his refuge, who has no other ground of reliance, may feel assured that God will interpose and save him. ¶ *For thou wilt answer me.* This also implies a fixed and steady assurance of mind, applicable not only to this case, but to all similar cases. He had firm confidence in God at all times; an unwavering belief that God is a hearer of prayer. This is a just foundation of hope when we approach God. Comp. James i. 6, 7.

8. *Among the gods* there is *none like unto thee, O Lord.* Among all those which are worshipped as gods there is no one that can hear and save. The psalmist, in respect to prayer, and to help to be obtained by prayer, compares his own condition with that of those who worshipped false gods. He had a God who could hear; they had none. A true child of God now in trouble may properly compare his condition in this respect with that of those who make no profession of religion; who do not profess to worship God, or to have a God. To him there is a throne of grace which is always accessible; to them there is none. There is One to whom he may always pray; they profess to have no one on whom they can call. ¶ *Neither* are there any works *like unto thy works.* That is, as wrought by those "gods." There is nothing they have done which can be a ground of confidence that can be compared with what thou hast done. The allusion is to the power, the wisdom, and the skill evinced in the works of creation, and in the merciful interpositions of Providence. From these the psalmist derives a proof that God is able to save. There is no such argument to which the worshippers of false gods can appeal in the time of trouble.

9. *All nations whom thou hast made shall come*, etc. In this verse the psalmist expresses his belief that the conviction which he entertained about the ability of God to save—about his being the only true God—would yet pervade all the nations of the earth; that they all would yet be convinced that *he* was the true God, and would come and worship him alone. So clear to him seemed

ship before thee, O Lord; and shall glorify thy name.

10 For thou *art* great, and doest wondrous things: thou [x] *art* God alone.

x Deut. xxxii. 39; 1 Cor. viii. 4.

11 Teach [y] me thy way, O LORD; I will walk in thy truth: unite [z] my heart to fear thy name.

y Ps. cxix. 33.
z Jer. xxiv. 7; Phil. iii. 13.

---

to be the evidence of the existence and perfections of God that he did not doubt that all men would come yet to see it also, and to acknowledge him. Comp. Isa. ii. 2, 3; lx. 3–14; Ps. ii. 8; lxxii. 17. ¶ *And shall glorify thy name.* Shall honour thee as the true God. They will renounce their idols; they will come and worship thee. This belief—this hope—is held out through the entire volume of revealed truth. It cheered and encouraged the hearts of the saints of the Old Testament and the New; and it may and should cheer and encourage our hearts. It is not less certain because it seems to be long delayed. To the view of man this is *all that is certain* in the future. No man can predict what will occur in regard to any of the existing political institutions on the earth—either the monarchies of the old world, or the republics of the new.* No man can tell in reference to the arts; to the sciences; to social life; to manners; to the cities and towns which now exist on the earth, what they *will be* in the far distant future. Only one thing is certain in that future—that the kingdom of God will be set up, and that the Redeemer's throne will be established over all the earth; that the time is to come when "all nations shall come and worship before God, and shall glorify his name."

* This I wrote some six years ago. Now, on revising it for publication (Oct. 13, 1864), how soon—how strangely—how fearfully—has the course of things in our country illustrated it. Who, six years since, could have foretold what has actually occurred during that time in our then happy Republic? It *seemed* to be permanent and enduring; and we made our boast to the other nations of the earth that it *would* be so. Alas! how have we been rebuked for our boastings; how have we been taught that no human sagacity can predict what will occur to any nation or to any government!

10. *For thou* art *great, and doest wondrous things.* Things fitted to excite wonder or admiration; things which lie beyond the power of any creature, and which could be performed by no one but a being of almighty power. A God who could do these things could also do that which the psalmist asked of him, for what God actually *does* proves that there is nothing within the limits of possibility which he cannot perform. The greatness and the power of God are reasons why we should appeal to him in our weakness, and in our times of trouble. ¶ *Thou* art *God alone.* Thou only canst do what a God can do, or what belongs to God. In those things, therefore, which require the interposition of Divine power our appeal must be to thee alone. So in the matter of salvation.

11. *Teach me thy way, O* LORD. That is, in the present emergency. Show me what thou wouldst have me to do that I may obtain thy favour, and thy gracious help. ¶ *I will walk in thy truth.* I will live and act in accordance with what thou dost declare to be true. Whatever that may be, I will pursue it, having no will of my own. ¶ *Unite my heart to fear thy name.* That is, to worship, obey, and honour thee. (*a*) The *end* which he desired to secure was that he might truly fear God, or properly reverence and honour him; (*b*) the *means* which he saw to be necessary for this was that his "heart" might be "*united*" in this one great object; that is, that his heart might be single in its views and purposes; that there might be no distracting purposes; that one great aim might be always before him. The *word* rendered unite—יַחֵד, *yâhhad*—occurs as a verb only in three

12 I [a] will praise thee, O Lord my God, with all my heart; and I will glorify thy name for evermore.

13 For great [b] *is* thy mercy toward me; and thou hast delivered [c] my soul from the lowest [1] hell.

14 O God, the proud are risen against me, and the assemblies

a Ps. cxlv. 1, 2. *b* Ps. ciii. 11. *c* 1 Thess. i. 10. [1] Or, *grave.*

places. In Gen. xlix. 6, it is rendered *united:* "Unto their assembly, mine honour, be not thou *united.*" In Isa. xiv. 20, it is translated *joined:* "Thou shalt not be *joined* with them." The *adverb*—יַחַד, *ya-hhad,* —occurs often, and is rendered *together,* Gen. xiii. 6; xxii. 6, 8, 19; xxxvi. 7; *et sæpe.* The *idea* is that of union, or conjunction; of being together; of constituting *one;* and this is accomplished in the heart when there is one great ruling object before the mind which nothing is allowed to interfere with. It may be added, that there is no more appropriate prayer which a man can offer than that his heart *may* have such a unity of purpose, and that nothing may be allowed to interfere with that one supreme purpose.

12. *I will praise thee, O Lord my God, with all my heart.* This is but carrying out the idea in the previous verse. He would give his *whole* heart to God. He would allow nothing to divide or distract his affections. He would withhold nothing from God. ¶ *And I will glorify thy name for evermore.* Not merely in the present emergency; but I will do it ever onward—even to eternity. The meaning is, that he would in all cases, and at all times—in this world and in the world to come—honour God. He would acknowledge no God *but* him, and he *would* honour him as God.

13. *For great* is *thy mercy toward me.* In respect to me; or, Thou hast manifested great mercy to me; to wit, in past times. He makes use of this now as an argument or reason why God should interpose again. (*a*) He had shown on former occasions that he had *power* to save; (*b*) the fact that he *had* thus treated him as his friend was a reason why he should now befriend him. ¶ *And thou hast delivered my soul.* My life. The meaning is, that he had kept him alive in times of imminent danger. At the same time David could say, as every child of God can say, that God had delivered his *soul* in the strict and proper sense of the term—from sin, and death, and *hell* itself. ¶ *From the lowest hell.* Marg., *grave;* Hebrew, *sheol*—שְׁאוֹל; Greek, ᾄδης. See the word explained in the Notes on Isa. xiv. 9. Comp. Notes on Job x. 21, 22. The word rendered *lowest* means simply *under,* or *beneath:—the grave or hades beneath.* The idea of *lowest,* or the superlative degree, is not necessarily implied in the word. The idea of the grave *as* deep, or *as* under us, however, *is* implied, and the psalmist means to say that he had been saved from that deep dwelling-place—from the abode of departed spirits, to which the dead descend under ground. The meaning is, that he had been kept alive; but the greatness of the mercy is designed to be set forth by having before the mind a vivid idea of the darkness, the horror, and the gloom of the world to which the dead descend, and where they dwell.

14. *O God, the proud are risen against me.* Men who are self-confident, ambitious, haughty; who do not regard the welfare or the rights of others; who are disposed to trample down all others in order that they may accomplish their own purposes; these are the men who have opposed me and sought my life. This would apply either to the time of Saul or of Absalom. In both these cases there were men who would correspond to this description. ¶ *And the assemblies of violent* men. Marg., *terrible.*

of [1] violent *men* have sought after my soul, and have not set thee [d] before them.

15 But [e] thou, O Lord, *art* a God full of compassion, and gracious; long-suffering, and plenteous in mercy [f] and truth.

16 O turn unto me, and have mercy upon me; give thy strength [g] unto thy servant, and save the son of thine handmaid.

[1] *terrible.* *d* Ps. x. 4. *e* Neh. ix. 17. *f* Ps. lxxxv. 10. *g* Isa. xlv. 24.

The Septuagint and the Vulgate render this, "the synagogue of the wicked." The word rendered *violent* means properly terrible, inspiring terror; then, violent, fierce, lawless, tyrants. The idea here is that they pursued their object by violence and not by right; they did it in a fierce and savage manner, or in such a way as to inspire terror. The word *assembly* here means merely that they were banded together; what was done was the result of a conspiracy or combination. ¶ *Have sought after my soul.* After my life. ¶ *And have not set thee before them.* They do not fear thee; they do not act as if in thy presence; they have no regard for thee; for thy law; for thy favour; for thy threatenings.

15. *But thou, O Lord,* art *a God full of compassion,* etc. See Notes on ver. 5. The words rendered "long-suffering" mean that there was and would be *delay* in his anger; that it was not soon excited; that he did not act from passion or sudden resentment; that he endured the conduct of sinners long without rising up to punish them; that he was not quick to take vengeance, but bore with them patiently. On this account the psalmist, though conscious that he was a sinner, hoped and pleaded that God would save him. ¶ *Plenteous in . . . truth.* That is, in faithfulness. When thou hast made a promise, thou wilt faithfully keep it.

16. *O turn unto me, and have mercy upon me.* Look upon me;—as if God were now turned away, and were unmindful of his danger, his wants, and his pleading. The expression is equivalent to those in which he prays that God would *incline his ear* to him. See vers. 1, 6, and Notes on Ps. v. 1. ¶ *Give thy strength unto thy servant.* Give such strength as proceeds from thee, and such as will accomplish what thou alone canst effect. Enable me to act *as if* clothed with Divine power. The ground of the plea here is, that he was the "*servant*" of God, and he might, therefore, hope for God's interposition. ¶ *And save the son of thine handmaid.* This is, as far as I know, the only separate allusion which David ever makes to his mother individually, unless the passage in Ps. xxxv. 14—"I bowed down heavily as one that mourneth for his mother"—be supposed to refer to his *own* mother. But we have elsewhere no such mention of his mother as can give us any idea of her character, and indeed it is not easy to determine who she was. The language here, however, would seem to imply that she was a pious woman, for the words "thy handmaid," as employed in the Scriptures, would most naturally suggest that idea. If so, then the ground of the plea here is that his mother was a child of God; that she had lived for his service; and that she had trained up her children for him. David now prays that, as he had been devoted to God by her, and had thus been trained up, God would remember all this, and would interfere in his behalf. Can it be wrong to urge before God, as a reason for his interposition, that we have been devoted to him by parental faithfulness and prayer; that we have been consecrated to him by baptism; that we have been trained up for his service; that in reference to us high hopes were cherished that we might carry out the purposes of pious parents, and live to accomplish what was so dear to their hearts? He who has had a pious mother has

17 Shew me a token [h] for good; that they which hate me may see *it*, and be ashamed; because thou, LORD, hast holpen me, and comforted me.

PSALM LXXXVII.

A Psalm *or* Song [1] for the sons of Korah.

HIS foundation *is* in the holy [i] mountains

h 2 Cor. v. 5. [1] Or, *of*. *i* Ps. xlviii. 1.

entered on life under great advantages; he has been placed under solemn responsibilities; he is permitted to hope that a mother's prayers will not be forgotten, but that her example, her teachings, and her piety will shed a hallowed influence on all the paths of life till he joins her in heaven.

17. *Shew me a token for good*, etc. Hebrew, "Make me a sign for good;" that is, Do that for me in my trouble which will be an evidence that thou dost favour me, and wilt save me. Let there be such a manifest interposition in my behalf that others may see it, and may be convinced that thou art God, and that thou art the Protector and Friend of those who put their trust in thee. We need not suppose that the psalmist refers here to a *miracle* in his behalf. Any interposition which would save him from the hands of his enemies,—which would defeat their purposes,—which would rescue him when there seemed to be no help, would be such an evidence that they could not doubt that he was the friend of God. Thus they would be made "*ashamed*" of their purposes; that is, they would be disappointed and confounded; and there would be furnished a new proof that God was the protector of all who put their trust in him.

PSALM LXXXVII.

This psalm, like some others, is entitled "*a psalm* or *song;*" that is, it so far combined the properties of *both* a "psalm" *and* a "song" that it might be called by either name. See Notes on the title to Ps. lxv. The phrase "for the sons of Korah" may mean, as in the margin, "*of* the sons of Korah." See Notes on the title to Ps. xlii.

The *occasion* on which the psalm was composed is unknown. The *design* of the psalm is obvious. It is to exalt Zion as a place to dwell in, and to state the privileges or advantages of having been born there; the honour of such a birth, and the benefit which would be connected with it, from having been brought early under the influence of the true religion, and from having been trained up amidst its institutions. The practical truth which is suggested by the psalm is the honour and benefit of having been born in a land where the true religion prevails; of having been born in connexion with the church; of having been early devoted to God; and of having had the benefits of a religious training. The foundation of what is said in the psalm is the honour which we naturally associate with the idea of *birth;*—birth as connected with a family of distinguished worth, wealth, or rank; birth as connected with a particular country, city, or town.

1. *His foundation.* This is an abrupt commencement of the psalm. The adjective "*his*" has been supposed by some to refer to the psalm itself, and this expression has been considered to be a part of the title to the psalm, meaning that the foundation of the psalm is the holy mountain where the praises of God were celebrated; that is Zion. This, however, is a forced and unnatural interpretation. The most obvious explanation is to refer it to God, and the meaning is, that his "foundation," or that which he had founded and established, to wit, the place for his worship, or for the institutions of religion, was in the holy mountains of Jerusalem. It would seem that the psalmist was contemplating the city,—looking on its walls, and its palaces, and especially on the place which had been reared for the worship of God, and that he breaks out in this abrupt manner, by saying that this was what God had *founded;* that here he had established his home; that here was the place where he was worshipped, and where

2 The [k] LORD loveth the gates of Zion more than all the dwellings of Jacob.
3 Glorious things [l] are spoken of thee, O city of God. Selah.
4 I will make mention of Rahab [m] and Babylon to them that

k Ps. lxxviii. 67, 68.

l Isa. liv. 2, etc.; Rev. xxi. 2, etc.
m Isa. li. 9.

he dwelt; that this was the place which he loved more than all the other places where the descendants of Jacob dwelt. ¶ Is *in the holy mountains.* The mountains of Jerusalem. Jerusalem is surrounded by hills, and within the city itself there were the hills of Zion, Moriah, Acra, and Bezethah; See Notes on Matt. ii. 1. These sacred hills God had selected as the place of his solemn worship—of his own abode. Comp. Notes on Ps. xlviii. 1, 2.

2. *The* LORD *loveth the gates of Zion.* Comp. Ps. lxxviii. 68. The gates of a city were the places of concourse; where business was transacted; where courts were held. The particular allusion here seems to be to the thronging multitudes pressing into the city for public worship—the numbers that gathered together at the great feasts and festivals of the nation; and the meaning is, that he looked with more pleasure on such multitudes as they thronged the gates, pressing in that they might worship him, than on any other scene in the land. ¶ *More than all the dwellings of Jacob.* Than any of the places where the descendants of Jacob, or where his people dwell. Much as he might be pleased with their quiet abodes, with their peace, prosperity, and order, and with the fact that his worship was daily celebrated in those happy families, yet he had superior pleasure in the multitudes that crowded the ways to the place where they would publicly acknowledge him as their God.

3. *Glorious things are spoken of thee, O city of God.* Jerusalem, called the "city of God" as being the place of his peculiar abode on earth. The word rendered "are spoken" may mean either "*have been* spoken," or "*are to be* spoken;" that is, either, such things *have been* said, or they *may* be said. They have been placed on record; or, they may now be put on record concerning thee. Probably the former is the true meaning; and the language would embrace such points as these: (1) Those things which had been spoken as to its beauty of situation; its magnificence and splendour. Comp. Notes on Ps. xlviii. 2, 3, 12, 13. (2) Such things as had been spoken or recorded in regard to its future prosperity, its triumphs, and its influence in the world;—the promises which had been made in reference to the prosperity of Zion, and the spread of the true religion from that point as a centre. Comp. Notes on Isa. ii. 3. The Old Testament abounds with promises concerning the future glory of Zion—the "glorious things" that are spoken respecting the final triumph of religion in the world. Of this the statement here is to be mainly understood, where *Zion* is referred to as the seat of the true religion, and as therefore the representative of the true church on earth. It is that of which the real record has been made, and not merely of Jerusalem or Zion as a city. *That* might pass away; the church, of which that was the representative, will endure for ever. Comp. Isa. liv. 1–3; lx.; Rev. xxi. 2–4.

4. *I will make mention of Rahab and Babylon,* etc. The word *Rahab* here refers to Egypt. See Isa. li. 9. It is also applied to Egypt in Ps. lxxxix. 10. The reason why the name was given to Egypt is not certainly known. The Hebrew word properly means *fierceness, insolence, pride;* and it *may* have been given to Egypt by the Hebrews on account of its haughtiness, pride, and insolence. It has been supposed by some (Jablonski, Opusc. i. 228) that the name is of Egyptian origin, but this has not

know me: behold Philistia, and
Tyre, with Ethiopia: this *man*
was born there.
5 And of Zion [n] it shall be said,
[o] This and that man was born in
her; and the [p] Highest himself
shall establish her.

n Gal. iv. 26, 27.

o Isa. xlviii. 21—23; lx. 1—9.
p Ps. xlviii. 8.

been clearly made out. (Gesenius, *Lex.*) Egypt, Babylon, Philistia, Tyre, and Ethiopia, are here mentioned as among the best known nations and cities of the world; as places where it would commonly be regarded as an honour to have been born. The meaning is, "I will refer to these as places well-known and distinguished; I will refer to the honour of having been born *there;* but great as is such an honour, the honour of having been born in Zion is far above that; it conveys the idea of a much higher distinction; it should be more sacredly cherished as among those things on which men value themselves." The word "*I*" here seems to have reference to the psalmist, and not to God. The psalmist is mentioning what to *him* would seem to have a claim to the highest honour. ¶ *Philistia.* The western portion of Palestine, from which the whole country was afterwards named. See Notes on Ps. lx. 8; comp. Ps. cviii. 9; Isa. xiv. 29, 31. ¶ *And Tyre.* See Notes on Ps. xlv. 12; Isa. xxiii. 1. ¶ *With Ethiopia.* Hebrew, *Cush.* The reference here is probably to the southern portion of Arabia. See Notes on Ps. lxviii. 31; Isa. xviii. 1. ¶ *This* man *was born there.* That is, It would be said of individuals that they were born in one of those places, and it would be regarded as an honour thus to have been born. Men would pride themselves on the fact that they were born there, and the world would hold them in esteem on that account. This refers to a very natural, and a very common feeling among men. We can, of course, claim no credit, and deserve no real honour, on account of the place where we happen to have been born; but the fact that one *has* been born in a place distinguished for its advantages and its fame,—in a place where liberty, religion, and the arts have flourished,—in a place renowned for its public spirit, and for producing illustrious men,—may be properly accounted as an occasion for gratitude, and as a stimulus to high and honourable efforts, and may thus *be made* an important auxiliary to virtue, patriotism, and piety.

5. *And of Zion it shall be said.* In respect to Zion; or, in honour of Zion. Men shall regard it as a privilege to have been born in Zion. They shall speak of such a birth as a marked and honoured distinction. ¶ *This and that man,* etc. Designating them, or pointing them out, as having been born there. Those in a crowd, those passing along, those brought in any way to notice, will be spoken of in reference to their birth in Zion, and will be treated with a degree of favour and esteem, arising from their birth there corresponding to what those receive who are born in Egypt, Babylon, or Tyre. They will not be shunned and avoided on account of their birth as if it were ignoble, but they will be honoured for it. ¶ *And the Highest himself shall establish her.* Will establish Zion, or will give it prosperity and perpetuity. This, too, is what would be "*said*" respecting Zion by such as should speak of those born there; and it indicates (*a*) their *conviction* that it *would* be permanent; and (*b*) their *desire* that it *might* be:—that a place so honoured and distinguished might be perpetuated. The practical truths suggested by this verse, as applied to the church, are (1) That it is a privilege to have been born in connexion with the Christian church; to have had a Christian parentage, and to have been early dedicated to God; (2) that the time will come when this will be a ground of commendation, or when it

6 The LORD shall count, when
he writeth [q] up the people, *that*
this *man* was born there. Selah.
7 As well the singers as the
players on instruments [r] *shall be*
there: all my springs [s] *are* in
thee.

q Ez. xiii. 9. r 1 Chron. xxiii. 5. s Ps. xlvi. 4.

---

will be *spoken of* as an honour, or when it will be regarded as presumptive evidence of a claim to esteem in the eyes of the world, that one was born in the church, was early devoted to God, and was trained up under the influences of religion; (3) that the character of those who are thus born, and who are thus trained up, will constitute, in the view of the world, evidence of the stability of the church, and proof that God regards it with favour. It has not *always* been deemed an honour, or a passport to favour, to have been born in the church, but the time *will* come when this will be universally so; and, even now, no child can fully appreciate the honour and the real advantage of having been born in a family where God is served, and of having been early consecrated to God by parental purpose, by prayer, and by Christian baptism.

6. *The* LORD *shall count.* That is, God himself will honour those who are so born. In the previous verse, the effect of such a birth was described as securing honour from men. Here a higher honour is adverted to,—that which will be derived from God himself. ¶ *When he writeth up the people,* etc. The word rendered *people* here is in the plural number. At the time of making an enrolment of the people, or taking an account or a *census* of the nations, he would mark, or cause to be marked, with peculiar honour the man that had his birth in Zion. Out of such would his own people be taken, and those thus born would have an honour which no one else would receive from him. He would not mark with any peculiar approbation those who had been born in Egypt, in Babylon, or in Tyre, but he would mark with special interest those who had been born in Zion. The practical truth suggested here is, that God will in the main take his people from among those who have been born in the church. As a matter of fact, while it is true that others are converted and added to the church, the great mass of church-members consist of those who have been born of Christian parents; who have been early dedicated to God; and who have been trained up for his service. See Notes on Isa. xliv. 3–5.

7. *As well the singers as the players on instruments* shall be there. Literally, "The singers as the players on instruments." The image is that of a musical procession, where the singers go before, followed by those who play on various instruments of music. The idea seems to be that when the number of the true friends of God shall be made up, or shall all be enrolled, there will be a triumphal procession; or, they are seen by the psalmist, moving before God *as* in a triumphal procession. Comp. Notes on Isa. xxxv. 10. Perhaps the reference is to heaven,—the true Zion; to the assembling of all who shall have been born in Zion, and who shall have become citizens of the true Zion, the Jerusalem above. ¶ *All my springs* are *in thee.* The word rendered *springs* means properly a place of fountains (see Notes on Ps. lxxxiv. 6), and also a fountain, Gen. vii. 11; viii. 2. It thus becomes an emblem of happiness; of delight; of pleasure; and the idea here is that the highest happiness of the psalmist was found in what is here referred to by the word *thee.* That word may refer either to God or to Zion; but as the subject of the psalm is *Zion,* it is most natural to suppose that the reference is to that. Thus it accords with the sentiment so often found in the Psalms, where the writer expresses his love for Zion; his pleasure in its solemnities; his

desire to abide there as his permanent home. Comp. Ps. xxiii. 6; lxxxiv. 2–4, 10. The idea has been beautifully expressed by Dr. Dwight, in his version of Ps. cxxxvii. 6:—

> "I love thy church, O God;
> Her walls before thee stand,
> Dear as the apple of thine eye,
> And graven on thy hand.
>
> "If e'er my heart forget
> Her welfare or her woe,
> Let every joy this heart forsake,
> And every grief o'erflow.
>
> "Beyond my highest joy
> I prize her heavenly ways,
> Her sweet communion, solemn vows,
> Her hymns of love and praise."

PSALM LXXXVIII.

This psalm is altogether of a mournful and desponding character. The author is a sufferer; he is expecting to die; he fears to die; he longs to live; his mind is overwhelmed with gloom which does not seem to be irradiated by one ray of hope or consolation. It is, in this respect, unlike most of the psalms which relate to sickness, to sorrow, to suffering; for in those psalms generally there springs up, in answer to prayer, a gleam of hope,—some cheerful view,—some sustaining prospect;—so that, though a psalm *begins* in despondency and gloom, it *ends* with joy and triumph. Comp., among others, Ps. vi. 9, 10; vii. 17; xiii. 6; xlii. 8, 11; lvi. 11–13; lix. 16; lxix. 34, 36. But in this psalm there is *no* relief; there is *no* comfort. As the Book of Psalms was designed to be useful in all ages, and to all classes of people, and as such a state of mind as that described in this psalm might occur again and often—it was proper that such a condition of utter despondency, even in a good man, should be described, in order that others might see that such feelings are not necessarily inconsistent with true religion, and do not prove that even such a sufferer is not a child of God. It is probable that this psalm was designed to illustrate what *may* occur when disease is such as to produce deep mental darkness and sorrow. And the Book of Psalms would have been incomplete for the use of the church, if there had not been at least *one* such psalm in the collection.

The psalm is said, in the title, to be "A Psalm or Song for (marg., *of*) the sons of Korah"—combining, in some way unknown to us, as several of the other psalms do, the properties of both a psalm and a song. The phrase, "for the sons of Korah," means here, probably, that it was composed for their use, and not *by* them, unless "Heman the Ezrahite" was one of their number. On the phrase, "To the chief Musician," see Notes on the title to Psalm iv. The words, "upon Mahalath Leannoth," are of very uncertain signification. They are rendered by the Septuagint and the Vulgate "for Maeleth, to answer;" by Luther, "to sing, of the weakness of the miserable;" by Prof. Alexander, "concerning afflictive sickness." The word *Mahalath* seems here to be a form of מַחֲלָה, *mahaleh*, which means properly, *sickness, disease*. It is rendered, with a slight variation in the pointing, *disease* in 2 Chron. xxi. 15; Ex. xv. 26; *infirmity*, in Prov. xviii. 14; and *sickness* in Ex. xxiii. 25; 1 Kings viii. 37; 2 Chron. vi. 28. It does not occur elsewhere, and would be properly rendered here, therefore, *disease*, *sickness*, or *infirmity*. The Hebrew which is rendered *Leannoth*, לְעַנּוֹת, is made up of a preposition (לְ) and a verb. The verb—עָנָה, *Anah*—means (1) to chant or sing; (2) to lift up the voice in any way—to begin to speak; (3) to answer; (4) to mean to say, to imply. The verb also has another class of significations; (*a*) to bestow labour upon, (*b*) to suffer, to be afflicted, and might here refer to such affliction or trouble. According to the former signification, which is probably the true one here, the allusion would be to something which was *said* or sung *in respect to the sickness referred to*; as, for example, a mournful melody composed for the occasion; and the purpose would be to express the feelings experienced in sickness. According to the other signification it would refer to affliction, and would be little more than a repetition of the idea implied in the word *Mahalath*. It seems to me, therefore, that there is a reference in the word "Leannoth" to something which was said or sung on that occasion; or to something which *might* be properly said or sung in reference to sickness. It is difficult to translate the phrase, but it might be somewhat literally rendered, "concerning sickness,—to be said or sung;" that is, in reference to it. The word *Maschil* (see Notes on the title to Psalm xxxii.) conveys the idea that it is a *didactic* or *instructive* psalm,—suggesting appropriate thoughts for such a season. The psalm is ascribed to "Heman the Ezra-

PSALM LXXXVIII.

A Song *or* Psalm [1] for the sons of Korah. To the chief Musician upon Mahalath Leannoth, [2] Maschil of Heman *t* the Ezrahite.

O LORD God of my salvation, I *u* have cried day *and* night before thee.

2 Let my prayer come before thee: incline thine ear unto my cry;

3 For my soul is full of troubles, and my life draweth nigh unto the grave.

[1] Or, *of*.

[2] Or, A Psalm *of Heman the Ezrahite, giving instruction.*

t 1 Kings iv. 31. *u* Luke xviii. 7.

hite." The name Heman occurs in 1 Kings iv. 31; 1 Chron. ii. 6; vi. 33; xv. 17, 19; xvi. 42; xxv. 1, 4-6; 2 Chron. v. 12; xxix. 14; xxxv. 15,—usually in connexion with Ethan, as among those whom David placed over the music in the services of the sanctuary.

Nothing is known of the *occasion* on which the psalm was composed, except, as is probably indicated in the title, that it was in a time of sickness; and from the psalm itself we find that it was when the mind was enveloped in impenetrable darkness, with no comfort.

The psalm consists of two parts:—

I. A description of the sick man's suffering, vers. 1-9. His soul was full of troubles, and he drew near to the grave, ver. 3; he was, as it were, already dead, and like those laid in the deep grave, whom God had forgotten, vers. 4-6; the wrath of God lay heavily on him, and all his waves went over him, ver. 7; God had put away all his friends from him, and had left him to suffer alone, ver. 8; his eye mourned by reason of his affliction, and he cried daily to God, ver. 9.

II. His prayer for mercy and deliverance, vers. 10-18. The reasons for the earnestness of the prayer, or the grounds of petition are, (*a*) that the dead could not praise God, or see the wonders of his hand, vers. 10-12; (*b*) that the faithfulness and loving-kindness of God could not be shown in the grave, ver. 11; (*c*) that his troubles were deep and overwhelming, for God had cast off his soul, and had hid his face from him; he had been long afflicted; he was distracted with the terrors of God; the fierce wrath of God went over him; lover and friend and acquaintance had been put far from him, vers. 13-18.

1. *O* LORD *God of my salvation.* On whom I depend for salvation; who alone canst save me. Luther renders this, "O God, my Saviour." ¶ *I have cried day* and *night before thee.* Literally, "By day I cried; by night before thee;" that is, my prayer is constantly before thee. The meaning is, that there was no intermission to his prayers; he prayed all the while. This does not refer to the general habit of his life, but to the time of his sickness. He had prayed most earnestly and constantly that he might be delivered from sickness and from the dangers of death. He had, as yet, obtained no answer, and he now pours out, and records, a more earnest petition to God.

2. *Let my prayer come before thee.* As if there were something which hindered it, or which had obstructed the way to the throne of grace; as if God repelled it from him, and turned away his ear, and would not hear. ¶ *Incline thine ear unto my cry.* See Notes on Ps. v. 1.

3. *For my soul is full of troubles. I* am full of trouble. The word rendered *is full* means properly *to satiate* as with food; that is, when as much had been taken as could be. So he says here, that this trouble was as great as he could bear; he could sustain no more. He had reached the utmost point of endurance; he had no power to bear any more. ¶ *And my life draweth nigh unto the grave.* Heb., *to Sheol.* Comp. Notes on Isa. xiv. 9; Job x. 21, 22. It may mean here either the grave, or the abode of the dead. He was about to die. Unless he found relief he must go down to the abodes of the dead. The Hebrew word rendered *life* is in the plural number, as in Gen. ii. 7; iii. 14, 17; vi. 17; vii. 15; *et al. Why* the plural was used as applicable to life cannot now be known with certainty. It *may* have been to accord with the fact

4 I am counted with them that go down into the pit: I am as a man *that hath* no strength;
5 Free among the dead, like the slain that lie in the grave, whom thou rememberest no more: and they are cut off [1] from thy hand.

[1] Or, *by*.

that man has *two* kinds of life;—the animal life,—or life in common with the inferior creation; and intellectual, or higher life,—the life of the *soul*. Comp. Notes on 1 Thess. v. 23. The meaning here is, that he was about to die; or that his *life* or *lives* approached that state when the grave closes over us; the extinction of the mere animal life; and the separation of the soul—the immortal part—from the body.

4. *I am counted with them that go down into the pit.* I am so near to death that I may be reckoned already as among the dead. It is so manifest to others that I must die,—that my disease is mortal,—that they already speak of me as dead. The word *pit* here means the grave,—the same as *Sheol* in the previous verse. It means properly (1) a pit, (2) a cistern, Gen. xxxvii. 20, (3) a prison or dungeon, Isa. xxiv. 22, (4) the grave, Ps. xxviii. 1; xxx. 4; Isa. xxxviii. 18. ¶ *I am as a man* that hath *no strength.* Who has no power to resist disease, no vigour of constitution remaining;—who must die.

5. *Free among the dead.* Luther renders this, "I lie forgotten among the dead." De Wette renders it, "Pertaining to the dead,—(den Todten angehörend)—stricken down, like the slain, I lie in the grave," and explains it as meaning, "I am as good as dead." The word rendered *free*—חָפְשִׁי, *hhophshi*—means properly, according to Gesenius (*Lex.*), (1) prostrate, weak, feeble; (2) free, as opposed to a slave or a captive; (3) free from public taxes or burdens. The word is translated *free* in Ex. xxi. 2, 5, 26, 27; Deut. xv. 12, 13, 18; 1 Sam. xvii. 25; Job iii. 19; xxxix. 5; Isa. lviii. 6; Jer. xxxiv. 9, 10, 11, 14; and *at liberty* in Jer. xxxiv. 16. It occurs nowhere else except in this verse. In all these places (except in 1 Sam. xvii. 25, where it refers to a *house* or *family* made free, and Job xxxix. 5, where it refers to the freedom of the wild ass), it denotes the freedom of one who had been a servant or slave. In Job iii. 19, it has reference to the grave, and to the fact that the grave delivers a slave or servant from obligation to his master:—"And the servant is *free* from his master." This is the idea, I apprehend, here. It is not, as DeWette supposes, that he was weak and feeble, as the spirits of the departed are represented to be (comp. Notes on Isa. xiv. 9–11), but that the dead are made *free* from the burdens, the toils, the calamities, the *servitudes* of life; that they are like those who are emancipated from bondage (comp. Job vii. 1, 2; xiv. 6); that death comes to discharge them, or to set them at liberty. So the psalmist applies the expression here to himself, as if he had already reached that point; as if it were so certain that he must die that he could speak of it as if it had occurred; as if he were actually in the condition of the dead. The *idea* is that he was to all appearance near the grave, and that there was no hope of his recovery. It is not here, however, the idea of *release* or *emancipation* which was mainly before his mind, or any idea of consolation as from that, but it is the idea of *death*—of hopeless disease that must end in *death.* This he expresses in the usual language; but it is evident that he did not admit any *comfort* into his mind from the idea of *freedom* in the grave. ¶ *Like the slain that lie in the grave.* When slain in battle. They are *free* from the perils and the toils of life; they are emancipated from its cares and dangers. Death *is* freedom; and it is *possible* to derive solace from that idea of death, as Job did (ch. iii. 19);—but the psalmist

6 Thou hast laid me in the lowest pit, in darkness, in the deeps.
7 Thy wrath [v] lieth hard upon me, and thou hast afflicted *me* with all thy waves. Selah.
8 Thou [w] hast put away mine acquaintance far from me: thou hast made me an abomination

v Ps. xxxviii. 2. *w* Job xix. 13, etc.

here, as remarked above, did *not* so admit that idea into his mind as to be comforted by it. ¶ *Whom thou rememberest no more.* As if they were forgotten by thee; as if they were no longer the object of thy care. They are suffered to lie and waste away, with no care on thy part to restore them to life, or to preserve them from offensiveness and decay. So the great, the beautiful, and the good lie neglected in the grave. ¶ *And they are cut off from thy hand.* Marg., *by.* The Hebrew is literally "*from* thy hand," but still the idea is that it was by the agency of God. They had been cut down, and were forgotten,—as if God regarded them no more. So we shall all moulder in the grave—in that deep, dark, cold, silent, repulsive abode, *as if* even God had forgotten us.

6. *Thou hast laid me in the lowest pit.* That is, I am as if I were thus laid; the deep grave seems now to lie so certainly before me, that it may be spoken of as if it were already my abode. The words rendered *lowest pit* mean literally *the pit under*, or *beneath.* The reference is to the sepulchre, as in ver. 4. ¶ *In darkness.* The dark grave; the realms of the dead. See Notes on Job x. 21, 22. ¶ *In the deeps.* The caverns; the deep places of the earth or the sea. All these expressions are designed to convey the idea that he was near the grave; that there was no hope for him; that he must die. Perhaps also there is connected with this the idea of trouble, of anguish, of sorrow;—of that mental darkness of which the grave was an image, and into which he was plunged by the prospect of death. The whole scene was a sad one, and he was overwhelmed with grief, and saw only the prospect of continued sorrow and gloom. Even a good man *may* be made afraid—*may* have his mind made sad and sorrowful—by the prospect of dying. See Isa. xxxviii. Death is naturally gloomy; and when the light of religion does not shine upon the soul, and its comforts do not fill the heart, it is but natural that the mind *should be* full of gloom.

7. *Thy wrath lieth hard upon me.* Presses me down; burdens me. The meaning is, that that which was the proper and usual expression of wrath or displeasure—to wit, bodily and mental suffering—pressed hard on him, and crushed him to the earth. These bodily sufferings he interpreted, in the sad and gloomy state of mind in which he was, as evidences of the Divine displeasure against himself. ¶ *And thou hast afflicted* me. Thou hast oppressed me, or broken me down. ¶ *With all thy waves.* Literally, "*thy breakers;*" that is, with expressions of wrath like the waves of the sea, which foam and break on the shore. Nothing could be a more striking image of wrath. Those "breakers" *seem* to be so furious and angry, they rush along with so much impetuosity, they are so mighty, they dash with such fury on the shore, that it seems as if nothing could stand before them. Yet they find a barrier such as we should little expect. The low and humble beach made of shifting sand, where there *seems* to be no stability, is an effectual barrier against all their rage;—as the humble piety of the child of God, apparently without strength to resist calamity, bears all the beatings of affliction, and maintains its place as the heavy waves of sorrow roll upon it. On the meaning of the word used here, and on the idea expressed, see Notes on Ps. xlii. 7.

8. *Thou hast put away mine acquaintance far from me.* The same

unto them: *I am* [x] shut up, and I cannot come forth.

9 Mine eye mourneth by reason of affliction: LORD, I have called daily upon thee, I have stretched out my hands unto thee.

10 Wilt [y] thou show wonders to the dead? shall the dead arise *and* praise thee? Selah.

11 Shall thy loving-kindness be declared in the grave? *or* thy faithfulness in destruction?

x Job xii. 14. *y* Isa. xxxviii. 18.

ground of complaint, or expression of the depth of affliction, occurs elsewhere, Ps. xxxi. 11; xxxviii. 11; lxix. 8. See also Job xix. 13–17. ¶ *Thou hast made me an abomination unto them.* As something which they would avoid, or from which they would revolt and turn away—as we turn away from the body of a dead man, or from an offensive object. The word means properly an object to be detested or abominated, as things unclean, Gen. xliii. 32; or as idolatry, 1 Kings xiv. 24; 2 Kings xvi. 3; xxiii. 13. ¶ I am *shut up.* As in prison; to wit, by disease, as when one is confined to his house. ¶ *And I cannot come forth.* I cannot leave my couch, my room, my house. Comp. Job xii. 14.

9. *Mine eye mourneth by reason of affliction.* I weep; my eye pours out tears. Literally, My eye pines away, or decays. Comp. Notes on Job xvi. 20; Isa. xxxviii. 3; Ps. vi. 6. ¶ LORD, *I have called daily upon thee.* That is, I have prayed earnestly and long, but I have received no answer. ¶ *I have stretched out my hands unto thee.* I have *spread out* my hands in the attitude of prayer. The idea is that of earnest supplication.

10. *Wilt thou show wonders to the dead?* The wonders—or the things fitted to excite admiration—which the living behold. Shall the dead see those things which here tend to excite reverence for thee, and which lead men to worship thee? The idea is that the dead will be cut off from all the privileges which attend the living on earth; or, that those in the grave cannot contemplate the character and the greatness of God. He urges this as a reason why he should be rescued. The sentiment here is substantially the same as in Ps. vi. 5. See Notes on that passage. Comp. Isa. xxxviii. 18. ¶ *Shall the dead arise* and *praise thee?* The original word, here rendered *the dead,* is *Rephaim*—רְפָאִים. On its meaning, see Notes on Isa. xiv. 9. It means, properly, *relaxed, languid, feeble, weak;* and is then applied to the dead — the *shades* — the *Manes* — dwelling in the under-world in Sheol, or Hades, and supposed to be as shades or shadows, weak and feeble. The question here is not whether they would rise to live again, or appear in this world, but whether *in* Sheol they would rise up from their resting-places, and praise God as men in vigour and in health can on the earth. The question has no reference to the future resurrection. It relates to the supposed dark, dismal, gloomy, inactive state of the dead.

11. *Shall thy loving-kindness be declared in the grave?* Thy goodness; thy mercy. Shall any one make it known there? shall it there be celebrated? ¶ Or *thy faithfulness in destruction?* In the place where destruction seems to reign; where human hopes perish; where the body moulders back to dust. Shall any one there dwell on the fidelity—the truthfulness—of God, in such a way as to honour him? It is *implied* here that, according to the views *then* entertained of the state of the dead, those things would not occur. According to what is *now* made known to us of the unseen world it *is true* that the mercy of God will not be made known to the dead; that the Gospel will *not* be preached to them; that no messenger from God will convey to them the offers of salvation. Comp. Luke xvi. 28–31.

12 Shall thy wonders be known in the dark? and thy righteousness in the land of forgetfulness?
13 But unto thee have I cried, O LORD; and in the morning shall my prayer prevent thee.
14 LORD, why castest thou off my soul? *why* hidest thou thy face from me?
15 I *am* afflicted and ready to die from *my* youth up: *while* [z]

z Job vi. 4.

---

12. *Shall thy wonders be known in the dark?* In the dark world; in "the land of darkness and the shadow of death; a land of darkness, as darkness itself, and where the light is as darkness." Job x. 21, 22. ¶ *And thy righteousness.* The justice of thy character; or, the ways in which thou dost maintain and manifest thy righteous character. ¶ *In the land of forgetfulness.* Of oblivion; where the memory has decayed, and where the remembrance of former things is blotted out. This is a part of the general description, illustrating the ideas then entertained of the state of the dead;—that they would be weak and feeble; that they could see nothing; that even the memory would fail, and the recollection of former things pass from the mind. All these are images of the grave as it *appears* to man when he has not the clear and full light of revelation;—and the grave *is* all this—a dark and cheerless abode—an abode of fearfulness and gloom—when the light of the great truths of the Gospel is not suffered to fall upon it. That the psalmist dreaded this is clear, for he had not yet the full light of revealed truth in regard to the grave, and it seemed to him to be a gloomy abode. That men without the Gospel *ought* to dread it, is clear; for when the grave is not illuminated with Christian truth and hope, it *is* a place from which man by nature shrinks back, and it is not wonderful that a wicked man dreads to die.

13. *But unto thee have I cried, O* LORD. I have earnestly prayed; I have sought thy gracious interposition. ¶ *And in the morning.* That is, each morning; every day. My first business in the morning shall be prayer. ¶ *Shall my prayer prevent thee.* Anticipate thee; go before thee:—that is, it shall be early;—so to speak even before thou dost awake to the employments of the day. The language is that which would be applicable to a case where one made an appeal to another for aid before he had arisen from his bed, or who came to him even while he was asleep—and who thus, with an earnest petition, anticipated his rising. Comp. Notes on Job iii. 12; comp. Ps. xxi. 3; lix. 10; lxxix. 8; cxix. 148; Matt. xvii. 25; 1 Thess. iv. 15.

14. LORD, *why castest thou off my soul?* Why dost thou forsake or abandon me? Why is it that thou dost not interpose, since thou hast all power, and since thou art a God of mercy? Why dost thou not deliver me from my troubles? How often are good men constrained to ask this question! How often does this language express exactly what is passing in their minds! How difficult, too, it is to answer the question, and to see *why* that God who has all power, and who is infinitely benevolent, does *not* interpose to deliver his people in affliction! The answer to this question cannot be fully given in this world; there will be an answer furnished doubtless in the future life. ¶ Why *hidest thou thy face from me?* Why dost thou not lift up the light of thy countenance upon me, and show me thy favour? God seemed to turn away from him. He seemed unwilling even to *look* upon the sufferer. He permitted him to bear his sorrows, unpitied and alone.

15. *I* am *afflicted and ready to die.* I am so afflicted—so crushed with

I suffer thy terrors I am distracted.

16 Thy fierce wrath [a] goeth over me; thy terrors have cut me off.

17 They came round about me [1] daily like water; they compassed me about together.

18 Lover and friend hast thou put far from me, *and* mine acquaintance into darkness.

a Rev. vi. 17. [1] Or, *all the day*.

---

sorrow and trouble—that my strength is nearly gone, and I can endure it but a little longer. ¶ *From* my *youth up*. That is, for a long time;—so long, that the remembrance of it seems to go back to my very childhood. My whole life has been a life of trouble and sorrow, and I have not strength to bear it longer. It may have been literally true that the author of the psalm had been a man always afflicted; or, this may be the language of strong emotion, meaning that his sufferings had been of so long continuance that they seemed to him to have begun in his very boyhood. ¶ While *I suffer thy terrors*. I bear those things which produce terror; or, which fill my mind with alarm; to wit, the fear of death, and the dread of the future world. ¶ *I am distracted*. I cannot compose and control my mind; I cannot pursue any settled course of thought; I cannot confine my attention to any one subject; I cannot reason calmly on the subject of affliction, on the Divine government, on the ways of God. I am distracted with contending feelings,—with my pain, and my doubts, and my fears,—and I cannot think clearly of anything. Such is *often* the case in sickness; and consequently what we need, to prepare us for sickness, is a strong faith, built on a solid foundation while we are in health; such an intelligent and firm faith that when the hour of sickness shall come we shall have nothing else to do *but* to believe, and to take the comfort of believing. The bed of sickness is not the proper place to examine the evidences of religion; it is not the place to make preparation for death; not the proper place to *become* religious. Religion demands the best vigour of the intellect and the calmest state of the heart; and this great subject should be SETTLED in our minds *before we are sick—before we are laid on the bed of death*.

16. *Thy fierce wrath goeth over me*. Like waters. See ver. 7. ¶ *Thy terrors have cut me off*. That is, I am as one already dead; I am so near to death that I may be spoken of *as* dead.

17. *They came round about me daily like water*. Marg., as in Heb., *all the day*. That is, his troubles seemed to be like the waves of the sea constantly breaking on the shore. See Ps. xlii. 7. ¶ *They compassed me about together*. My troubles did not come singly, so that I could meet them one at a time, but they seemed to have banded themselves together; they all came upon me at once.

18. *Lover and friend hast thou put far from me*. That is, Thou hast so afflicted me that they have forsaken me. Those who professed to love me, and whom I loved,—those whom I regarded as my friends, and who seemed *to be* my friends,—are now wholly turned away from me, and I am left to suffer alone. See Notes on ver. 8. ¶ And *mine acquaintance into darkness*. The Septuagint and the Latin Vulgate render this, "my acquaintance *from my misery*." Luther, "Thou hast caused my friends and neighbours, and my kindred, to separate themselves far from me, *on account of such misery*." The literal rendering would be, *my acquaintances are darkness*. This may mean either that they had so turned away that he could not see them, *as if* they were in the dark; or, that his familiars now—his companions—were dark and dismal objects,—gloomy thoughts,—sad forebodings. *Perhaps* the whole

might be translated, "Far away from me hast thou put lover and friend,—my acquaintances!—all is darkness!" That is, When I think of any of them, all is darkness, sadness. My friends are not to be seen. They have vanished. I see no friends; I see only darkness and gloom. All have gone, leaving me alone in this condition of unpitied sorrow! This completes the picture of the suffering man; a man to whom all was dark, and who could find no consolation anywhere—in God; in his friends; in the grave; in the prospect of the future. There *are* such cases; and it was well that there was one such description in the sacred Scriptures of a good man thus suffering,—to show us that when *we* thus feel, it should not be regarded as proof that we have no piety. *Beneath* all this, there may be true love to God; *beyond* all this, there may be a bright world to which the sufferer will come, and where he will for ever dwell.

PSALM LXXXIX.

This psalm is entitled "Maschil of Ethan the Ezrahite." In the margin this is rendered, "A Psalm for Ethan the Ezrahite to give instruction." On the word *Maschil*, see Notes on the title to Psalm xlii. As both Heman (Ps. lxxxviii. *title*) and Ethan, in the title before us, are mentioned as *Ezrahites*, it would seem that they were of the same family, and were probably brethren. Ethan and Heman, in connexion with Zimri, and Calcol, and Dara, five of them in all, are mentioned as "the sons of Zerah,"—grandsons of Judah, 1 Chron. ii. 6. If these were the persons referred to, and if they were the authors of these two psalms, then the period of the composition of these psalms was laid far back in the history of the Hebrew people, far anterior to the time of David. Comp. 1 Chron. ii. 6-12. It is hardly probable, however, that they were composed at so early a period in the Jewish history; and there are some things in *this* psalm, which cannot be reconciled with such a supposition (comp. vers. 3, 20, 35, 39, 49), and which make it certain that it was either composed by David, or after the time of David. The probability, therefore, seems to be that these names, "Heman" and "Ethan," were either the names of some persons subsequent to the time referred to in 1 Chron. ii. 6, (see General Introd., § 2 [5]); or that these their names were given to classes of "the sons of Korah" who had charge of the music, and that the psalms were composed by some persons of those classes. As thus composed, they might be spoken of as the psalms of Heman and Ethan.

There are no certain methods of ascertaining *when* the psalm before us was composed, or what was the *occasion* of its composition. De Wette supposes that it must have been written *about* the time of the exile, as the family of David is represented in the psalm as dishonoured and dethroned,—and yet *before* the exile, as there is no mention of the destruction of the city and temple. He accords, therefore, with the opinion of Venema that it was not far from the time of the death of Josiah, 2 Chron. xxxv. 20-24. The author he supposes to be either a successor of David,—an humbled monarch,—or, some one who personates the king, and who represents the calamity of the king as his own. Hengstenberg also supposes that it was composed between the time of the death of Josiah and the Babylonish exile. There is a strong probability in the psalm itself that it was composed at such a period, but it is impossible to determine the exact time, or the precise occasion. The *burden* of the psalm is, that most precious promises had been made to David of the perpetuity of his throne, but that now these promises *seemed* to fail; that reverses and calamities had come which threatened to overturn his throne, and to bring his kingdom to an end. His "crown" had been "profaned" and "cast to the ground." See vers. 38-44.

The psalm consists properly of three parts:—

I. The promise made to David in respect to the perpetuity of his throne, vers. 1-37. The illustration of this occupies a considerable part of the psalm.

II. The fact that this promise *seemed* to be disregarded; that the "covenant" had been "made void;" that the "crown" had been "profaned," and "cast to the ground," vers. 38-45.

III. An earnest plea for the Divine interposition in the fulfilment of the promise, and the restoration of the Divine favour and mercy, vers. 46-52.

PSALM LXXXIX.

[1] Maschil of Ethan *b* the Ezrahite.

I WILL sing of the mercies of the LORD for ever: with my mouth will I make known thy faithfulness to [2] all generations.

2 For I have said, Mercy shall be built up for ever: thy faithfulness shalt thou establish in the very heavens.

3 I have made a covenant with

[1] Or, A Psalm *for Ethan the Ezrahite to give instruction.*
b 1 Chron. ii. 6.

[2] *generation and generation*; so ver. 4; Ps. cxix. 90.

1. *I will sing of the mercies of the* LORD *for ever.* Particularly how the "mercy" was manifested in the *promise* made to David; the solemn covenant made with him in respect to the perpetuity of his throne. The appointment of David to the throne was an act of mere mercy or favour, since he was not in the royal line, and had no claim to the crown. It will be seen, also, that if it be supposed that the covenant with David, and the promise therein made to him, was intended to include the Messiah as descending from him, there was a still higher reason for celebrating the "*mercies*" of God, inasmuch as all mercy to our world comes through him. ¶ *With my mouth.* Not merely in my heart, but with words. The meaning here is that he would make a record which might be used evermore as the language of praise. ¶ *Will I make known thy faithfulness.* In the fulfilment of these promises. He felt assured that they would be fulfilled. Whatever appearances there might be to the contrary, the psalmist had no doubt that God would prove himself to be faithful and true. See Notes on Isa. lv. 3, on the expression, "the sure mercies of David." ¶ *To all generations.* Marg., as in Heb., *generation and generation.* He would make a record which would carry down the remembrance of this faithfulness to all future ages.

2. *For I have said.* The Septuagint and the Latin Vulgate render this, "Thou hast said," which is more in accordance with what the connexion seems to demand; but the Hebrew will not admit of this construction. The true meaning seems to be, that the *psalmist* had said; that is, he had said in his *mind;* he had firmly believed; he had so received it as a truth that it might be spoken of as firmly settled, or as an indisputable reality. It was in his mind one of the things whose truthfulness did not admit of a doubt. ¶ *Mercy shall be built up for ever.* The mercy referred to; the mercy manifested in the promise made to David. The idea is, that the promise would be fully carried out or verified. It would not be like the foundation of a building, which, after being laid, was abandoned; it would be as if the building, for which the foundation was designed, were carried up and completed. It would not be a forsaken, half-finished edifice, but an edifice fully erected. ¶ *Thy faithfulness shalt thou establish.* In the matter referred to—the promise made to David. ¶ *In the very heavens.* Literally, "The heavens—thou wilt establish thy faithfulness in them." That is, the heavens—the heavenly bodies—so regular, so fixed, so enduring, are looked upon as the emblem of stability. The psalmist brings them thus before his mind, and he says that God had, as it were, made his promise a part of the very heavens; he had given to his faithfulness a place among the most secure, and fixed, and settled objects in nature. The sun in its regular rising; the stars in their certain course; the constellations, the same from age to age, were an emblem of the stability and security of the promises of God. Comp. Jer. xxxiii. 20, 21.

3. *I have made a covenant with my chosen.* With my chosen one; that is, with David. The original is in

my chosen, I have sworn [c] unto David my servant.

4 Thy seed will I establish for ever, and build up thy throne to all generations. Selah.

5 And the heavens [d] shall praise thy wonders, O LORD; thy faithfulness also in the congregation of the saints.

6 For who in the heaven can be compared unto the LORD? *who* among the sons of the mighty can be likened unto the LORD?

c 2 Sam. vii. 11, etc.

d Ps. xix. 1.

the singular number, though by the Septuagint, and the Vulgate, and by Luther, it is rendered in the plural —chosen ones—elect. This is undoubtedly the language of God himself, though it is not expressly ascribed to him. The design is to describe the solemn promise which God had made to David and to his posterity. Comp. Ps. lxxviii. 70, 71. See also, on the use of the phrase "*made a covenant*," Notes on Ps. l. 5; lxxxiii. 5. ¶ *I have sworn unto David my servant.* I have taken a solemn oath in regard to him. The substance of the oath is stated in the next verse. The promise referred to is found in 2 Sam. vii. 11–16.

4. *Thy seed will I establish for ever.* Thy children; thy posterity. The reference is to his successors on the throne. The promise was that there should not fail to be one on his throne; that is, that his dynasty should never become extinct. See 2 Sam. vii. 16: "And thy house and thy kingdom shall be established for ever before thee: thy throne shall be established for ever." Comp. also 1 Kings ii. 4. The word rendered *establish* means properly *to fit;* then, to make firm; to put on a solid basis. ¶ *And build up thy throne.* It shall be kept up; it shall be like a building that is constantly progressing towards completion. The meaning is, that it would not fail. He would not begin the work, and then abandon it. The dynasty, the kingdom, the throne, would be complete and perpetual. ¶ *To all generations.* As long as the world should stand. This can have been accomplished only by the Messiah occupying in a spiritual sense the throne of "his father David." Comp. Luke i. 32, 33.

5. *And the heavens shall praise thy wonders,* O LORD. That is, the inhabitants of heaven shall find new occasion for praise in the faithfulness evinced in carrying out the promise to David, and in the marvellous things which will occur under that promise, and in its accomplishment. If we suppose that this promise embraced the Messiah and his reign, then we shall see what new occasions the angels would find for praise,—in the incarnation of the Redeemer, and in all that would be accomplished by him. ¶ *Thy faithfulness also in the congregation of the saints.* In the assembly of the holy ones; that is, the angels. In their songs of praise, this will be among the things which will fill them with joy. The *idea* is, that the inhabitants of the heavens —the holy angels—would take a deep interest in the fulfilment of this promise, as it would furnish new manifestations of the character of God. Comp. Rev. v. 11–14; 1 Pet. i. 12.

6. *For who in the heaven,* etc. Literally, In the cloud; that is, in the sky. The idea is that none in the regions above—the upper world —can be compared with God. There is no other god,—there is no one among the angels, great and glorious as they are, that can be likened to him. ¶ *Who among the sons of the mighty,* etc. The angels—regarded as mighty. The "sons of the mighty" on earth are spoken of as mighty men,—as men of power,—as men of exalted rank. So here, the idea is, that none of the angels, though of exalted rank ("principalities," or "powers," comp. Rom. viii. 38; Eph. i. 21), could be put in comparison with God. See Notes on Isa. xl. 25.

7 God is greatly to be feared in the assembly of the saints, and to be had in reverence of all *them that are* about him.

8 O LORD God of hosts, who [e] *is* a strong LORD like unto thee? or to thy faithfulness round about thee?

9 Thou [f] rulest the raging of the sea: when the waves thereof arise, thou stillest them.

e 1 Sam. ii. 2. *f* Job xxxviii. 11; Mar. iv. 39, 41.

7. *God is greatly to be feared.* There is that in him which is fitted to fill the mind with solemn feelings, and this is a proper state of mind with which to come before him. Nature teaches us that God should be approached with awe; and all the teachings of revelation confirm this. His power is to be feared; his justice is to be feared; his holiness is to be feared; and there is much also in his goodness, his benevolence, his mercy, to fill the mind with solemn emotions. ¶ *In the assembly of the saints.* The assembly of the holy; the assembly that is convened for his worship. The reference here may be either to worshippers on earth or in heaven. *Wherever*, and *whenever*, in this world or in other worlds, creatures are engaged in the worship of God, there should be deep solemnity and reverence. On the word rendered *assembly* here—סוֹד, *sodh*—a council, or assemblage for counsel, see Notes on Ps. xxv. 14; lxiv. 2; comp. Job xv. 8. The *idea* here is founded on what is said in the previous verse, that none can be compared with God. ¶ *And to be had in reverence.* In fear; in awe. ¶ *Of all* them that are *about him.* That approach him; that are in his presence. The conscious presence of God should fill the mind with awe. When we feel that his eye is upon us, when we know that he sees us, how *can* we trifle and be thoughtless? How *can* we then be sinful?

8. *O* LORD *God of hosts.* See Notes on Isa. i. 9; Ps. xxiv. 10. God, commanding the armies of heaven; leading forth the stars; controlling all forces—all powers. ¶ *Who* is *a strong* LORD *like unto thee?* The original word here rendered *Lord* is יָהּ, *Yah*, or *Jah*. This is one of the few places where that word occurs, except in the compounding of words. It is an abbreviation of the name *Jehovah*, and has the same signification. See Notes on Ps. lxviii. 4. The meaning is, that there was no one who in respect to *power* could be compared with Jehovah. ¶ *Or to thy faithfulness round about thee?* Rather, "thy faithfulness is round about thee." That is, It attends thee at all times; it is always with thee; it is a part of thy very nature. To all round about thee, thou art faithful; wherever God is—and he is everywhere—there is faithfulness. He never changes; and men and angels may always trust in him. The psalmist then proceeds to illustrate the greatness of his power, and of his faithfulness, in the works of creation. The *design* of these illustrations, doubtless, is to keep before the mind the idea of the Divine *faithfulness* as shown in the works of nature, and then to apply this to the covenant which had been made with David. The idea is, that he who is so faithful in nature will be the same in grace; that he who had shown such unchangeableness in the works of creation might be expected to show the like in respect to the promises which he had made.

9. *Thou rulest the raging of the sea.* The pride; the anger; the lifting up of the sea. That is, when the sea is raging and boisterous; when it seems as if everything would be swept away before it, thou hast absolute control over it. There is, perhaps, no more impressive exhibition of Divine *power* than the control which God has over the raging waves of the ocean:—and yet this was the power which Jesus exercised over the raging sea of Galilee,—showing that he had the power of God. Mark iv. 39–41. ¶ *When the waves thereof*

10 Thou hast broken [1] Rahab
in pieces, as one that is slain:
thou hast scattered thine enemies with [2] thy strong arm.
11 The heavens *are* thine, the
earth also *is* thine: *as for* the
world, and the fulness thereof,
thou hast founded them.
12 The north and the south,
thou hast created them: Tabor
and Hermon *h* shall rejoice in
thy name.

[1] Or, *Egypt.* [2] *the arm of thy strength.*

g Judges iv. 6, 12. *h* Josh. xii. 1.

arise. In the lifting up of the waves; when they seem to raise themselves up in defiance. ¶ *Thou stillest them.* At thy pleasure. They rise no higher than thou dost permit; at thy command they settle down into a calm. So in the troubles of life—the storms—the waves of affliction; they rise as high as God permits, and no higher; when he commands they subside, and leave the mind as calm as the smooth sea when not a breath of wind moves over its surface, or makes a ripple on its placid bosom.

10. *Thou hast broken Rahab in pieces.* Marg., *Egypt.* See Notes on Ps. lxxxvii. 4. The reference is to the exodus of the Hebrew people, when he destroyed the power of Egypt. ¶ *As one that is slain.* Slain on the field of battle; as a man pierced through with a sword or spear. ¶ *Thou hast scattered thine enemies.* At the time referred to, in Egypt; and at other times, when the enemies of God and of his people had been discomfited. ¶ *With thy strong arm.* Marg., as in Heb., *the arm of thy strength.* That is, by his power,—the arm being the symbol of power. See Notes on Ps. lxxvii. 15. Comp. Deut. v. 15; vii. 8, 19, *et al.*

11. *The heavens* are *thine.* Are thy work; and, therefore, thy property,—the highest conception of *property* being that which is derived from creation. It is also implied here that as all things belong to God, he has a right to dispose of them as he pleases. ¶ *The earth also* is *thine.* The earth itself, as made by thee; all that the earth produces, as having sprung out of that which thou hast made. The entire proprietorship is in thee. ¶ As for *the world.* In the use of this word, the earth is spoken of as *inhabitable,* meaning that the earth and all that dwell upon it belong to God. ¶ *And the fulness thereof.* All that it produces; what constitutes its *entireness.* That is, the earth itself considered *as* earth, or as a mass of matter; and all that springs from it;—all that constitutes *the earth,* with all its mountains, seas, rivers, men, animals, minerals, harvests, cities, towns, monuments—the productions of nature, the works of power, and the achievements of art. Comp. Notes on Ps. xxiv. 1. ¶ *Thou hast founded them.* They all have their foundation in thee; that is, thou hast caused them all to exist. They have no independent and separate basis on which to rest.

12. *The north and the south, thou hast created them.* All that there is in the north and in the south—in the northern and the southern sky—the constellations and the stars; and all that there is in the earth—in the regions of cold and of heat—far as they extend in either direction. The word rendered *north* here — צָפוֹן, *tzaphon* — means properly that which is hidden or dark, and was applied to the north, because the ancients regarded it as the seat of gloom and darkness. Hom. Od., ix. 25. The south, on the other hand, was regarded by them as illuminated and made bright by the beams of the sun. The word rendered *south* — יָמִין, *yamin* — means literally *the right hand,* and was applied to the south because the ancient geographers were supposed to face the east, as now they are supposed to face the north. Comp. Notes on Job xxiii. 9. ¶ *Tabor and Hermon.* That is, the west and the east,—the former of these mountains being on the western side of Palestine, the

13 Thou [1] hast a mighty arm: strong is thy hand, *and* high is thy right hand.

14 Justice [i] and judgment *are* the [2] habitation of thy throne: mercy and truth shall go before thy face.

15 Blessed *is* the people that know the joyful sound: [k] they shall walk, O LORD, in the light [l] of thy countenance.

[1] *an arm with might.*
[i] Ps. xcvii. 2.
[2] Or, *establishment,* Isa. xvi. 5.

[k] Lev. xxv. 9; Ps. xcviii. 6; Rom. x. 18.
[l] Num. vi. 26.

---

other on the eastern, and both of them being objects of beauty and grandeur. The idea is, that God had control of all parts of the universe; that the world in every direction, and in every part, declared his power, and made known his greatness. ¶ *Shall rejoice in thy name.* Or, *do* rejoice in thee. That is, They, as it were, exult in thee as their God. They are clothed with beauty, as if full of joy; and they acknowledge that all this comes from thee as the great Creator. Comp. Ps. lxv. 8, 12; xcvi. 11, 12.

13. *Thou hast a mighty arm.* Marg., as in Heb., *an arm with might.* That is, Thou hast great power,—the arm being the instrument by which we accomplish our purposes. ¶ *Strong is thy hand.* The hand, too, is an instrument by which we execute our plans. Hence God is so often represented as having delivered his people with a strong hand. ¶ And *high is thy right hand.* It is by the *right* hand particularly that we carry out our purposes. We lift it high when we are about to strike with force. All this is expressive of the Divine omnipotence.

14. *Justice and judgment* are *the habitation of thy throne.* Marg., *establishment.* The Hebrew word—מָכוֹן, *machon*—means properly a place where one stands; then, a foundation or basis. The idea here is, that the throne of God is founded on justice and right judgment; it is this which *supports* it; his administration is maintained *because* it is right. This supposes that there is such a thing as right or justice in itself considered, or in the nature of things, and independently of the will of God; that the Divine administration will be conformed to that, and will be firm *because* it is thus conformed to it. Even omnipotent power could not maintain permanently a throne founded on injustice and wrong. Such an administration would sooner or later make its own destruction sure. ¶ *Mercy and truth shall go before thy face.* Literally, *anticipate* thy face; that is, thy goings. Wherever thou dost go, wherever thou dost manifest thyself, there will be mercy and faithfulness. Thy march through the world will be attended with kindness and fidelity. So certain is this, that his coming will, as it were, be *anticipated* by truth and goodness.

15. *Blessed* is *the people.* Happy is their condition. See Notes on Ps. i. 1. ¶ *That know the joyful sound.* That hear that sound. De Wette explains this of the call to the festivals and offerings, Lev. xxiii. 24; Num. x. 10; Ps. xxvii. 6. That is, says he, those who honour and worship God. The Hebrew word—תְּרוּעָה, *teruah*—means a loud noise; a tumult; especially, shouts of joy, or rejoicing, Job viii. 21; 1 Sam. iv. 5; the "shout of a king," that is, the joyful acclamations with which a king is welcomed, Num. xxiii. 21; the shout of battle, Jer. iv. 19; xlix. 2. Then it means the sound or clangour of trumpets, Lev. xxv. 9; Num. xxix. 1–6. The word is, therefore, especially applicable to the sounding of the trumpets which attended the celebration of the great festivals among the Hebrews, and there can be little doubt that this is the reference here. The idea is, that they are blessed or happy who are the worshippers of Jehovah, the true God; who are summoned to his

16 In thy name shall they rejoice all the day: and in thy righteousness [m] shall they be exalted.

17 For thou *art* the glory of their strength; and in thy favour our horn shall be exalted.[n]

18 For [1] the LORD *is* our defence; and the Holy One of Israel *is* our king.

19 Then thou spakest in vision to thy holy one, and saidst, I have laid help upon *one that is* mighty; [o] I have exalted *one* chosen out of the people.

m 1 Cor. i. 30.
[1] Or, *our shield* is *of the LORD, and our king* is *of the Holy One of Israel,* Ps. xlvii. 9.

n 1 Sam. ii. 1. *o* Isa. ix. 6.

service; who are convened to the place of his worship. ¶ *They shall walk,* O LORD, *in the light of thy countenance.* They shall live in thy favour, and enjoy thy smiles.

16. *In thy name shall they rejoice.* In *thee* shall they rejoice, or find their happiness. In thy being; thy perfections; thy protection; thy government; thy favour. ¶ *All the day.* That is, continually. It is their privilege, and it is their duty to rejoice always. Thou art always the same, and the happiness which is found in thy being and attributes at one time may be found at all times; thy promises are ever the same, and thy people may find happiness in them always. There is no reason why the people of God should not be constantly happy; they who have such a God, and such hopes as they are permitted to cherish, *should be* so. Comp. Notes on Phil. iii. 1; iv. 4. ¶ *And in thy righteousness.* Under thy righteous government; or, in the knowledge of thy righteous character. ¶ *Shall they be exalted.* See Prov. xiv. 34. The effect of that knowledge shall be to exalt or to elevate them in moral character, in happiness, in the esteem of others, and in true prosperity. Comp. 1 Tim. iv. 8.

17. *For thou* art *the glory of their strength.* The ornament; the beauty; the honour; that is, Their strength derives its beauty and honour, not from anything in themselves, but from the fact that it is derived from thee. The strength thus imparted is an honour or ornament in itself; it is an honour and glory to them that it is imparted to them. ¶ *And in thy favour.* Or, *by* thy favour, or good pleasure. ¶ *Our horn shall be exalted.* The horn is a symbol of power. Comp. Notes on Ps. xxii. 21; lxxv. 4; Dan. vii. 8; Job xvi. 15. The meaning here is, that their power had been derived from God; or that all which contributed to their exaltation and honour in the world, had been derived from him.

18. *For the* LORD is *our defence.* Marg., *Our shield is of the Lord.* The original word rendered *defence,* is *shield.* Comp. Notes on Ps. v. 12; xxxiii. 20; lix. 11. The meaning is, that protection was to be found in God alone. The true construction of this verse is, "For to Jehovah [belongs] our shield, and to the Holy One of Israel our king." That is, All that they had, and all that they relied on as a defence, belonged to God, or was of God; in other words, their very protectors were themselves protected by Jehovah. They had no other defence; nothing else on which they could depend.

19. *Then thou spakest in vision.* Or, by a vision. See this word explained in the Notes on Isa. i. 1. The meaning is, that God had spoken this by means of *visions,* or by communications made to his people by the prophets. This "vision" was especially made known to Nathan, and through him to David. See 2 Sam. vii. 4—17. The substance of what is here said is found in that passage in Samuel. In 2 Sam. vii. 17, it is expressly called a "vision." ¶ *To thy holy one.* The vision was addressed particularly to David, but was made through him to the people of Israel. The ancient versions render this in the plural, as referring to the people of Israel. The

20 I [p] have found David my servant; with my holy oil have I anointed him:

21 With [q] whom my hand shall be established; mine arm also shall strengthen him.

22 The enemy shall not exact upon him; nor the son of wickedness afflict him.

p 1 Sam. xvi. 1, 12. *q* 2 Sam. vii. 8—16.

Hebrew is in the singular number. ¶ *I have laid help upon* one that is *mighty.* I have so endowed him that he shall be the protector and defender of my people. He is qualified for the office entrusted to him, and in his hands the interests of the nation will be safe. This was not expressly said in the vision; but this was the substance of what was said. See 2 Sam. vii. 9. ¶ *I have exalted* one *chosen out of the people.* One not of exalted rank; one not descended from kings and conquerors; but one that had grown up among the people; one called from the ranks of common life; one chosen from among those engaged in humble occupations. In this way it was the *more* apparent that the power really came from God. Comp. 2 Sam. vii. 8; see also Notes on Ps. lxxviii. 70–72.

20. *I have found David my servant.* That is, I found him among the sheepfolds; in humble life. I saw there one who was qualified for the high office of being the ruler of the nation, and I designated, or set him apart, for that office. The idea is, that there was in him a *previous* qualification for this work, and that God had seen this, and, in accordance with this, had summoned him to his service. ¶ *With my holy oil have I anointed him.* By the hand of Samuel. 1 Sam. xvi. 13. Oil was used in setting apart prophets, priests, and kings. It was *poured* upon the person,—emblematic of the *pouring out* upon him of wisdom and grace from on high to qualify him for his office.

21. *With whom my hand shall be established.* Septuagint; "My hand shall aid him." Luther; "My hand shall hold him." De Wette; "With him my hand shall be continually." Professor Alexander; "Shall ever be present." The idea is, that God would always defend or protect him. He would not merely interpose *at times*, or *at intervals*, but he would be his *constant* protector. His hand would be permanently, or constantly, extended for his aid—as if it were a part of David's own person, or were his own hand, to be used as he pleased. So God is the *constant* helper of his people. They may rely on his power; they may avail themselves of it, *as if* it were their own. ¶ *Mine arm also shall strengthen him.* In using his own arm, he will in fact make use of the strength of mine. The people of God are as really defended *as if* the strength of God were theirs; or as if they were themselves almighty. The omnipotence of God is employed in their defence, and it will be as certainly exerted in their favour, and as constantly, *as if* it were their own. It will be no less *surely* employed in their defence in the hand of God than if it were in their own hand. It will be more *wisely* employed by him in their behalf than it would be by themselves.

22. *The enemy shall not exact upon him.* The literal meaning here is derived from the force sometimes used in extorting or *demanding* a debt, where no indulgence is shown, but where it is *exacted* to the last mite, whether the man is able to pay it or not. Comp. Matt. xviii. 25, 28. Then it is used to denote oppression, or subjugation, which is the idea here. The enemy shall not be suffered to act the part of one who rigidly exacts the payment of a debt; that is, he shall not be allowed to oppress him. ¶ *Nor the son of wickedness afflict him.* This is copied almost literally from 2 Sam. vii. 10. The phrase "the son of wickedness" means simply *the wicked.* He shall not fall into the hands, or under the power of wicked men.

23 And I will beat down his foes before his face, and plague them that hate him.

24 But my faithfulness and my mercy *shall be* with him; and in my name shall his horn be exalted.

25 I will set his hand also in the [r] sea, and his right hand in the rivers.

26 He shall cry unto me, Thou *art* my Father, my God, and the rock of my salvation.

27 Also I will make him *my* [s] first-born, higher [t] than the kings of the earth.

28 My mercy [u] will I keep for him for evermore, and my covenant [v] shall stand fast with him.

r Ps. lxxii. 8. *s* Col. i. 15. *t* Rev. xix. 16. *u* Isa. lv. 3. *v* 2 Sam. xxiii. 5.

23. *And I will beat down his foes before his face.* I will crush them, or destroy them:—showing that the power of doing this was not his own, but was the power of God exerted in his behalf. ¶ *And plague them that hate him.* His enemies. I will bring "plagues" upon them:—calamities, judgments, afflictions. The word is commonly used to denote those judgments which come directly from the hand of God,—as famine, pestilence, wasting sickness, the plague, or the "plagues" of Egypt. Ex. xii. 13; xxx. 12; Num. viii. 19; xvii. 11, 12. These are all in the hand of God, and can be employed at his pleasure, as storms and tempests may be, in executing his purposes.

24. *But my faithfulness and my mercy* shall be *with him.* I will at the same time be faithful to him, and merciful. These attributes of my nature shall be always attendant on him, *as if* they were his own. ¶ *And in my name.* By me;—or—He, acting in my name, and in my cause, shall be exalted. ¶ *Shall his horn be exalted.* See Notes on ver. 17.

25. *I will set his hand also in the sea,* etc. His dominion shall extend from the sea on the one hand to the rivers on the other. The *sea* here evidently refers to the Mediterranean; and the *rivers* to the great rivers on the east—the Tigris and Euphrates. These were the promised boundaries of the land. Gen. xv. 18. David secured a conquest over all these territories, and united all under his sceptre, thus securing the accomplishment of the promise made to Abraham. See Notes on Ps. lx.

26. *He shall cry unto me, Thou* art *my Father.* He shall appeal to me, or come to me as a Father, and as his only hope and defence. ¶ *My God.* He shall come to me *as* God, and shall recognise me as *his* God, his only trust and hope. ¶ *And the rock of my salvation.* See Notes on Ps. xviii. 2. The meaning of all this is, that he would at all times recognise him as his only trust and hope, and that he would be faithful on his part to God.

27. *Also I will make him* my *first-born.* He shall be regarded and treated by me as the first-born son is in a family; that is, with distinguished favour and honour. Compare Gen. xxvii. 19; xxix. 26; Ex. iv. 22; xiii. 12; Jer. xxxi. 9. See also Notes on Col. i. 15, 18. ¶ *Higher than the kings of the earth.* Than other kings; the most exalted among kings and rulers. This was entirely fulfilled in David, who occupied a pre-eminence among princes and rulers which no other king did:—a prominence alike in his own personal character and his reign; in his relation to God; and in the fact that he was the ancestor of the Messiah, the "King of kings, and Lord of lords" (Rev. xix. 16); "the prince of the kings of the earth," Rev. i. 5.

28. *My mercy will I keep for him for evermore.* I will not withdraw my favour from him, nor from his posterity, vers. 33–36. In him, and in his Great Descendant, the throne

29 His seed also will I make *to endure* for ever, and his throne as the days of heaven.[w]

30 If his children forsake my law, and walk not in my judgments;

31 If they [1] break my statutes, and keep not my commandments;

32 Then will I visit their transgression with the rod, and their iniquity with stripes.

33 Nevertheless [x] my lovingkindness [2] will I not utterly take

w Jer. xxxiii. 17—21. [1] *profane.* x 1 Kings xi. 36. [2] *I will not make void from.*

shall be established for ever. This dominion will not be like the changing dynasties of this world, but will be perpetual and eternal. ¶ *And my covenant shall stand fast with him.* See 2 Sam. vii. 14–16; xxiii. 5. It shall be firm, or established with him and his family.

29. *His seed also will I make* to endure *for ever.* That is, His posterity shall occupy the throne.—(*a*) This *would* have been true of his descendants, if they had been faithful to God, and had not revolted from him; (*b*) It *is* true of him who is the successor of David in his spiritual kingdom, the Lord Jesus, the Messiah. Comp. Notes on Isa. ix. 6, 7. ¶ *And his throne as the days of heaven.* As long as the heavens endure; that is, to the end of the world. Comp. Notes on Ps. lxxii. 5, 7, 17.

30. *If his children.* His posterity; his successors on the throne. ¶ *Forsake my law.* If they are not regulated by it in the administration of their government, and in their private lives. It is here supposed that they might forsake his law, or fail to observe it; but still there is the assurance that the power would not depart permanently from the successors of David, but that it would be restored ultimately to that line, and be permanent and eternal. ¶ *And walk not in my judgments.* And do not obey my commandments.

31. *If they break my statutes.* Marg., *profane.* The Hebrew word means to pollute or defile; and the idea is, If they practically contemn them; if they regard them as things of nought, or treat them with disdain as a polluted or defiled thing. It *is* in this way that the mass of mankind do regard the commands of God. They treat them with no respect; they practically class them among objects that are polluted, and that are to be avoided as defiled and defiling. ¶ *And keep not my commandments.* If they do not regulate their conduct by my laws.

32. *Then will I visit their transgression with the rod.* They shall be *punished,* though my mercy shall not be wholly taken from them. God has two objects in his dealings with his backsliding and offending people; (*a*) one is to show his displeasure at their conduct, or to punish them; (*b*) the other is to reclaim them. All who have been truly converted, or who are truly his people, will be recovered though they fall into sin; but it may be done, and will be likely to be done, in such a way as to show his own displeasure at their offences. ¶ *And their iniquity with stripes.* The word rendered *stripes* means properly a stroke, a blow; then, judgments or calamities, such as God sends on men as a punishment for their sins. Gen. xii. 17; Ex. xi. 1; Ps. xxxviii. 11.

33. *Nevertheless my loving-kindness.* My mercy; my favour. I will not utterly cast him off. He shall not be in the condition of those who are my enemies, or who are entirely forsaken. ¶ *Will I not utterly take from him.* Marg., *I will not make void from.* The Hebrew word — פָּרַר, *parar*—means to break, to break in pieces; then, to violate, as a covenant; then, to make vain, to bring to nought, to frustrate; then, to annul, to abolish. The idea here is that of making entirely vain; wholly removing from; or taking

from him, nor suffer my faithfulness to [1] fail.
34 My covenant will I not
break, [y] nor alter the thing that
is gone out of my lips.
35 Once have I sworn by my
holiness, [2] that I will not lie unto
David.
36 His seed shall endure for
ever, and his throne as the sun
before me.
37 It shall be established for
ever as the moon, and *as* a faithful witness in heaven. Selah.

[1] *lie.* *y* Ps. cxi. 5, 9. [2] *if I lie.*

completely away. The meaning is, that he would *not* wholly take away his favour; he would *not* entirely abandon him; he would not suffer him to become wholly apostate; he would *not* leave him to ruin. The covenant once made would be accomplished; the promise given would be carried out. ¶ *Nor suffer my faithfulness.* My faithfulness as *pledged* in the covenant or promise. ¶ *To fail.* Marg., *lie.* I will not prove false, or deal falsely in the pledge which I have made. It shall not appear at last that I have made a promise which has not been kept. This passage contains a very important principle in regard to the dealings of God with his people. The principle is, that if men are converted, if they in fact become his people—he will never suffer them wholly to fall away and perish. They *may* be suffered to backslide; they *may* fall into sin, but they will not be allowed to go so far as to apostatize wholly. They will be brought back again. Whatever method may be necessary for this, will be adopted. Commands; warnings; entreaties; remonstrances;—their own experience; the admonitions of others; the influences of the Holy Spirit:—judgments and calamities; sickness; loss of property; bereavement; disappointment; disgrace;—any of these, or all of these, may be resorted to, in order to bring them back; but they *will* be brought back. God, in mercy and in love, will so visit them with sorrow and trouble that they shall be recovered, and that their "spirit shall be saved in the day of the Lord Jesus."

34. *My covenant will I not break.* Literally, I will not pollute, defile, profane. See Notes on ver. 31, where the same word is used. God says that *he* will not do in regard to the covenant as *they* had done. ¶ *Nor alter the thing*, etc. The promise which I have made. I will not make it a *different* thing. I will not modify its conditions, or withdraw it. It shall stand precisely as it was when I uttered it. What God promises will be *exactly* performed.

35. *Once have I sworn by my holiness.* That is, once for all;—a single oath—an oath once taken by me—makes it certain. To swear by his "holiness" is to pledge his own holy nature; to make it as certain as that he is holy; to stake the whole question of his holiness on that. That is, *If* this should not be accomplished,—*if* he should fail in this,—it would prove that he was *not* a holy God. ¶ *That I will not lie unto David.* Marg., as in Heb., *if I lie.* The meaning is, He would be found faithful to the promise. See vers. 3, 4; comp. 2 Sam. vii. 8–16.

36. *His seed shall endure for ever*, etc. His posterity. See Notes on ver. 29. There, the expression is, "his throne as the days of heaven." Here it is, "his throne as the sun before me." The meaning is the same. It would stand through all time. Comp. Notes on Ps. lxxii. 5.

37. *It shall be established for ever as the moon.* As long as the moon shall endure. The heavenly bodies are the most permanent objects that we know of; and they, therefore, became the emblems of stability and perpetuity. Comp. Notes on Ps. lxxii. 7. ¶ *And* as *a faithful witness in heaven.* As the witness in heaven, or

38 But [z] thou hast cast off and abhorred, thou hast been wroth with thine anointed.

39 Thou hast made void the covenant of thy servant; thou hast profaned his crown, *by casting it* to the ground.

40 Thou hast broken down [a] all his hedges; thou hast brought his strong holds to ruin.

41 All that pass by the way spoil him: he is a reproach to his neighbours.

42 Thou hast set up the right hand of his adversaries; thou hast made all his enemies to rejoice.

z 1 Chron. xxviii. 9; Ps. lx. 1, 10; Hosea ix. 17.

a Isa. v. 5, 6.

in the sky, is sure. The reference is to the moon, regarded as a *witness* for God. What is said here of the moon as an index of his faithfulness, might be said also of the sun and the stars; but the beauty of the image is increased by the attention being fixed to a single object. As the moon is fixed, regular, enduring,—so are the promises and purposes of God. Such were the promises made to David; such was the oath which had been taken by God; such the covenant which he had made. The psalmist now proceeds (vers. 38–45) to show that this oath and these promises *seemed* to be disregarded; that there were things occurring which *appeared* as if God had forgotten them; that there was not that manifest prosperity and favour which was implied in the promise; but that a series of calamities had occurred which it was difficult to reconcile with these solemn pledges. On the ground of this he prays (vers. 46–52) that God would return, and would remember his covenant, and would bless David and his people.

38. *But thou hast cast off.* Literally, Thou hast treated as a foul, offensive thing; thou hast treated him to whom these promises were made, as if he were a vile and detestable object—as that which one throws away because it is worthless or offensive. ¶ *And abhorred.* Hast despised; that is, as if it were an object of aversion or contempt. Comp. Ps. lx. 1, 10. ¶ *Thou hast been wroth.* Literally, "Thou hast suffered [thine anger] to overflow," or to pour itself forth. See Ps. lxxviii. 21, 59. ¶ *With thine anointed.* With him who had been anointed as king,—anointed as *thine own*—to administer justice, and to rule for thee. 1 Sam. xvi. 1, 13. This *might* seem to refer to the time of Absalom, when David was driven from his throne and his kingdom; see, however, the Introduction to the Psalm.

39. *Thou hast made void the covenant of thy servant.* Thou hast dealt with him as if there were no such covenant; as if no such promise had been made to him. The word rendered *made void,* means *to abhor,* or *reject.* ¶ *Thou hast profaned his crown,* by casting it *to the ground.* Literally, "Thou hast profaned to the earth his crown;" that is, Thou hast treated it *as* a polluted thing; a thing to be rejected and abhorred; a thing which one casts indignantly upon the ground.

40. *Thou hast broken down all his hedges.* His walls or defences; all that he relied on for safety. ¶ *Thou hast brought his strongholds to ruin.* His towers; fortifications; defences. The enemy has been suffered to destroy them. They are now heaps of ruins.

41. *All that pass by the way spoil him.* The sentiment here is substantially the same as in Ps. lxxx. 12. See Notes on that place. The idea is that of fields or vineyards, where all the fences, the walls, and the hedges are thrown down so that they become like an open common. ¶ *He is a reproach to his neighbours.* An object of ridicule, as if he were forsaken by God; as if cast out and despised.

42. *Thou hast set up the right hand of his adversaries.* Hast given them the victory. Thou hast suffered them to accomplish their purposes. ¶ *Thou*

43 Thou hast also turned the edge of his sword, and hast not made him to stand in the battle.
44 Thou hast made his [1] glory to cease, and cast his throne down to the ground.
45 The days of his youth hast thou shortened: thou hast covered him with shame. Selah.
46 How long, LORD? wilt thou hide [b] thyself for ever? shall thy wrath burn like fire?
47 Remember how short my time is: wherefore hast thou made all men in vain?

[1] brightness.

[b] Ps. lxxxv. 5.

hast made all his enemies to rejoice. They joy or rejoice in the success of their plans; in their triumphs over thy servant and over his people.

43. *Thou hast also turned the edge of his sword.* That is, Thou hast turned it *away,* so that when it is raised to strike, it does not descend on the object aimed at by the blow. The meaning is, that he had not been successful in battle, or had been defeated. ¶ *And hast not made him to stand in the battle.* To stand firm; to hold his ground. He has been driven back; his forces have fled.

44. *Thou hast made his glory to cease.* Marg., *brightness.* Luther, "Thou destroyest his purity." The original word means *brightness, splendour.* The literal translation here would be, "Thou causest to cease from being brightness;" that is, Thou hast taken away from his brightness, so that it is gone. The allusion is to the splendour, the glory, the magnificence connected with his rank as king. This had been destroyed, or had come to nought. ¶ *And cast his throne down to the ground.* See ver. 39.

45. *The days of his youth hast thou shortened.* This does not mean that he had shortened his life, but that he had abbreviated the period of his vigour, his hope, and his prosperity; instead of lengthening out these, and prolonging them into advancing years, he had by calamities, disappointments, reverses, and troubles, as it were, abridged them. No such youthful vigour, no such youthful hope now remained. The feelings of age—the cutting off from the world—had come suddenly upon him, even before he had reached the season when this might be expected to occur. Though at a time of life and in circumstances when he might have hoped for a longer continuance of that youthful vigour, he had suddenly been brought into the sad condition of an old man. ¶ *Thou hast covered him with shame.* Hast clothed him with shame or disgrace. Everything in his circumstances and in his appearance indicates shame and disgrace, and the Divine displeasure.

46. *How long,* LORD? How long is this to continue? Can it be that this is to continue always? Is there to be no change for the better? Are the promises which have been made, never to be fulfilled? Comp. Notes on Ps. xiii. 1; lxxvii. 7–9. ¶ *Wilt thou hide thyself for ever?* Thy favour. Wilt thou never come forth and manifest thyself as the Helper of those who trust in thee? ¶ *Shall thy wrath burn like fire?* Fire which entirely consumes; fire which never ceases as long as there is anything to burn; fire which never puts itself out, but which wholly destroys that on which it preys.

47. *Remember how short my time is.* The word rendered *time*—חֶלֶד *hheled*—means *duration; lifetime.* Ps. xxxix. 5. Then it means life; time; age; the world. Literally here, "Remember;—I;—what duration." The meaning is plain. Bear in remembrance that my time *must* soon come to an end. Life is brief. In a short period the time will come for me to die; and if these promises are fulfilled to me, it must be done soon. Remember that these troubles and sorrows cannot continue for a much longer period without exhaust-

48 What[c] man *is he that* liveth,
and shall not see death? shall he
deliver his soul from the hand of
the grave? Selah.
49 Lord, where *are* thy former
loving-kindnesses, *which* thou
swarest[d] unto David in thy
truth?
50 Remember, Lord, the reproach of thy servants; *how* I
do bear in my bosom *the reproach
of* all the mighty people;

c Heb. ix. 27.

d ver. 35.

ing all my appointed time upon the earth. If God was ever to interpose and bless him, it must be done speedily, for he would soon pass away. The promised bestowment of favour must be conferred soon, or it could not be conferred at all. The psalmist prays that God would remember this. So it is proper for *us* to pray that God would bless us *soon;* that he would not withhold his grace now; that there may be no delay; that he would (we may say it with reverence) bear in remembrance that our life is very brief, and that if grace is to be bestowed in order to save us, or in order to make us useful, it must be bestowed soon. A young man may properly employ this prayer; how much more appropriately one who is rapidly approaching old age, and the end of life! ¶ *Wherefore hast thou made all men in vain?* As thou dost *seem* to have done, since they accomplish so little in the world, and since so many appear wholly to miss the great purpose of life! Nothing, in certain moods of mind, will strike one more forcibly or more painfully than the thought that the mass of men seem to have been made *in vain.* Nothing is accomplished by them worthy of the powers with which they are endowed; nothing worthy of so long living for; nothing worthy of the efforts which they actually put forth. In a large portion of mankind there is an utter failure in securing even the objects which they seek to secure; in numerous cases, when they have secured the object, it is not worth the effort which it has cost; in all cases, the same effort, or an effort made less strenuous, laborious, costly, and continuous, *would have secured an object of real value—worth all their effort—the immortal crown!*

48. *What man* is he that *liveth, and shall not see death?* Shall not die,—to *see* death being an expression often used to denote death itself. Death is represented as a real object, now invisible, but which will make itself visible to us when we die. The meaning here is, "All men are mortal; this universal law must apply to kings as well as to other men; in a short time he to whom these promises pertain will pass away from the earth; and the promises made to him cannot then be fulfilled." ¶ *Shall he deliver his soul from the hand of the grave?* His life. Will he be able to deliver that from the *power* of the grave;—in Hebrew, *Sheol.* Death—the grave—Sheol—asserts a universal dominion over mankind, and no one can be rescued from that stern power.

49. *Lord, where* are *thy former loving-kindnesses.* Thy mercies; thy pledges; thy promises. Where are those promises which thou didst make formerly to David? Are they accomplished? Or are they forgotten and disregarded? They *seem* to be treated as a thing of nought; as if they had *not* been made. He relied on them; but they are not now fulfilled. ¶ Which *thou swarest unto David.* Which thou didst solemnly promise, even with the implied solemnity of an oath. ¶ *In thy truth.* Pledging thy veracity.

50. *Remember, Lord, the reproach of thy servants.* Remember this, so as to cause it to pass away; be not forgetful or unmindful of this. Comp. ver. 47. The psalmist desired that all this might be before the mind of God as a reason why he should help him. These promises had been made

51 Wherewith thine enemies have reproached, O LORD; wherewith they have reproached the footsteps of thine anointed.

52 Blessed [e] *be* the LORD for evermore. Amen, and Amen.

e Hab. iii. 17—19.

to David and his people. They had relied on them, and they were now reproached as having trusted to promises which had never been made. This reproach was consequent on what seemed to be the failure to fulfil those promises; and as this reproach came upon God, and was a reflection on his fidelity, the psalmist prays that he would allow it to come before him. ¶ How *I do bear in my bosom* the reproach of *all the mighty people.* Literally, "I bear in my bosom all the many people." That is, everything that pertained to them came upon him. All their troubles; all their reverses; all their complaints; all their murmurings, seemed to come upon him. He was held responsible for everything pertaining to them; all this pressed upon his heart. Comp. the bitter complaint of Moses in Numb. xi. 11–15. The phrase "to bear in the bosom" here, is equivalent to bearing it on the heart. Trouble, anxiety, care, sorrow, seem to press *on the heart,* or fill the bosom with distressing emotions, and lay on it a heavy burden. The allusion here is not merely to *reproach,* but the meaning is that everything pertaining to the people came on him, and it crushed him down. The burdens of his own people, as well as the reproaches of all around him, came upon him; and he felt that he was not able to bear it.

51. *Wherewith thine enemies have reproached, O* LORD. Have reproached thee and me. Wherewith they reproach thy character and cause, and reproach me for having trusted to promises which seem not to be fulfilled. As the representative of thy cause, I am compelled to bear all this, and it breaks my heart. ¶ *Wherewith they have reproached the footsteps of thine anointed.* Of myself, as the anointed king. They have reproached *my footsteps;* that is, they have *followed* me with reproaches—treading along behind me. Wherever I go, wherever I put my foot down in my wanderings, I meet this reproach.

52. *Blessed* be *the* LORD *for evermore.* Praise to God always. So Chrysostom was accustomed to say, even when driven out as an exile and a wanderer, "Blessed be God for everything." The passage here denotes entire acquiescence in God; perfect confidence in him; a belief that he was right, and faithful, and true. It is an instance of the faith which those who are truly pious have in God, in all circumstances, and at all times; of their belief that he is worthy of entire confidence, and ought always to be praised. Comp. Job i. 21. At the close of all kinds of trouble—and in the midst of all kinds of trouble—true piety will enable us to say, "BLESSED BE GOD."

APPENDIX.

PSALM XLII.

For the sons of Korah. Twelve psalms are, in the titles, ascribed to the SONS OF KORAH. The persons so designated were a Levitical family of the line of Kohath, and derived their name from their ancestor Korah—the same whose name is commemorated with infamy in the history of the wanderings. Both by the original Mosaic ordinance, and by the ordinance of "David and Samuel the seer," "the oversight of the gates of the house of the Lord" was committed to them, 1 Ch. ix. 23—a circumstance that sheds new interest on the sentiment expressed by them in the eighty-fourth psalm: "I had rather be a door-keeper in the house of my God than to dwell in the tents of wickedness." When it became known that the Lord had rejected Saul, and anointed David to the kingdom by the hand of their kinsman Samuel, certain Korahites were among the first to cast in their lot with the youthful hope of Israel, 1 Ch. xii. 6. In the person of Heman, the grandson of Samuel, the family furnished David with one of his three prophet-psalmists; and of the twenty-four courses of singers, fourteen were presided over by Heman's sons. "All these were under the hands of their father for song in the house of the LORD, with cymbals, psalteries, and harps, for the service of the house of God," 1 Ch. xxv. 6. As singers, the Korahites are mentioned as late as the reign of Jehoshaphat, 2 Ch. xx. 19; as porters, they are mentioned as serving in the second temple, Neh. xi. 19. None of the psalms bearing their name bears any mark of having been written after the captivity—a circumstance worth noting, as a corroboration of the accuracy of the superscriptions. It may be safely assumed that at least four of the twelve Korahite psalms were written by David's contemporaries. Of these Ps. xliv. appears to have been written in the crisis of David's Syrian and Edomite wars, when destruction seemed impending over the kingdom. Ps. xlii. and xliii. (which go together) must have been written by some of the Korahites who accompanied David in his flight beyond the Jordan during Absalom's rebellion.—*Binnie.*

[*Current of thought in the psalm.*] God is of a twofold sort. At times he is a concealed and hidden God; as, when the conscience in temptation feels sin, feels other injuries, whether bodily or spiritual, it clings to these with heart and thought, and cannot find consolation in the grace and goodness of God. Those who judge of God after such a concealed form, fall, without remedy, into despair and ruin. But there is still another and manifested form of God, or a disclosed and not concealed God, viz. the real form of the good, gracious, compassionate, reconciled God. As also the sun is of two sorts, though there is in reality but one sun, just as there is but one God; for it may be named another sun when it appears dark and covered with clouds, compared with what it is when shining bright and clear from the heavens. And if one were to judge when the sun is dark and veiled in clouds, he would conclude that there would never more be clear day, but only eternal night. Now, however, is this an art, and in truth a golden art, to be able to hold, that though the sun, when covered with clouds and fog, cannot give a clear light, yet it will break forth through the clouds and fog, and again beam upon the world with a bright lustre. So does the prophet act here, when under temptation, comforting himself, and desiring to see the sun when it should break forth through the clouds. He thinks in his heart upon another image than he at present sees before his eyes. And though his conscience is affrighted, though all evil threatens, and he is ready to sink amid doubts, he yet elevates himself in faith, holds fast by hope, and consoles himself that God will help him, and again appoint him to see the service of God in the only place which God had chosen for it on the surface of the earth.—*Luther*.

2. *My soul thirsteth for God.* David earnestly desired restoration to the sanctuary. He loved the place and its privileges. But what he longed chiefly for was the living God himself. Truly pious men, it has been said, were never satisfied with the ordinances of God without the God of ordinances.

6. *Therefore will I remember thee.* He recalls his seasons of choice communion by the river and among the hills, and especially that dearest hour upon the little hill, where love spake her sweetest language and revealed her nearest fellowship. It is great wisdom to store up in memory our choice occasions of converse with Heaven; we may want them another day, when the Lord is slow in bringing back his banished ones, and our soul is aching with fear. "His love in times past" has been a precious cordial to many a fainting one; like soft breath it has fanned the smoking flax into a flame, and bound up the bruised reed. Oh, never-to-be-forgotten valley of Achor, thou art a door of hope. Fair days, now gone, ye have left a light behind you which cheers our present gloom. Or does David mean that even where he was he would bethink him of his God; does he declare that, forgetful of time and place, he would count Jordan as sacred as Siloa, Hermon as holy as Zion, and even Mizar, that insignificant rising ground, as glorious as the mountains which are round about Jerusalem! Oh! it is a heavenly heart which can sing—

"To me remains nor place nor time;
My country is in every clime;
I can be calm and free from care
On any shore, since God is there.

"Could I be cast where thou art not,
That were indeed a dreadful lot;
But regions none remote I call,
Secure of finding God in all."

—*Spurgeon.*

7. *Deep calleth unto deep.* This language is descriptive of a great temptation. For just as on the sea, when there is storm or tempest, wind and sea roar, and the waves and billows mount the ship, now high aloft, now into a great deep, so that one sees on all sides nothing but one abyss calling, in a manner, to another, and one thinks the abyss will swallow all up, and the mighty waves will fall upon the ship and cover her; so happens it invariably with the heart in heavy trials. But God has the floods in his hand and power, can soon alter and assuage them, and by his word still them, as the Lord Christ commands the wind and sea and it becomes a great calm.—*John Arnd.*

Waterspouts. The great home of waterspouts is Cape Horn and the adjacent waters; but Shaw saw them at three points on the coast of Syria. They at times visit all tropical and temperate latitudes. *Anderson:* "A waterspout is a large tube or cylinder formed of clouds by means of the electric fluid, the base being uppermost, and the point being let down perpendicularly from the clouds. It has a particular kind of *circular motion* at the point; and being hollow within, attracts vast quantities of water, which it frequently pours down in torrents on the earth or the sea." It is a great terror to seamen. If one empties itself on a ship, she is gone.—*Plumer.*

PSALM XLIII.

5. *For I shall yet praise thee.* Times of complaint will soon end, and seasons of praise will begin. Come, my heart, look out of the window, borrow the telescopic glass, forecast a little, and sweeten thy chamber with sprigs of the sweet herb of hope.

Who is the health of my countenance and my God. My God will clear the furrows from my brow and the tear-marks from my cheek; therefore will I lift up my head and smile in the face of the storm. The psalm has a blessed ending, such as we would fain imitate when death puts an end to our mortal existence.—*Spurgeon.*

PSALM XLIV.

The meaning and drift of parts of this psalm have been frequently, if not generally, misunderstood: the result has often been a misapprehension of the spirit of the whole. Ver. 20, 21 appear in our English version (and, indeed, in most versions) as a mere assertion that God cannot be deceived. They contain in reality a solemn protestation of steadfastness, with an appeal to God for the truth of it. *We have not forgotten the name of our God, nor stretched out our hands to a strange god; lo, God shall search this out, and he knoweth the secrets of the heart.* Yet, again, it must not be supposed that either these words or any others in the psalm necessarily involve any assertion of *past* innocence. They simply imply that the suppliants are not at the present time in the condition of persons who have forgotten or denied God, and who therefore no longer remember or acknowledge him. Such present faithfulness, whether asserted or not, would be a necessary condition of actual prayer. The subject of this particular psalm brings the assertion of it into unusual prominence. Lastly, it would appear from the ordinary versions of the psalm as though ver. 9–16 were the language of direct complaint, and as though, in the subsequent verses, the church were upbraiding God for afflicting her, and were praying to be delivered for her own merits' sake. But this is not so. The word rendered *but* at the beginning of ver. 9 should rather be rendered *even though, what though;* and its force should be carried on through the succeeding verses. These verses thus form a lengthened protasis, which is summed up in the beginning of ver. 17, and to which then follows the apodosis. The whole is therefore a resolute profession of steadfastness: "What though all this be come upon us, yet will we continue faithful." And while this faithfulness of the worshippers necessarily forms the condition of their prayers being heard, their supplication is, nevertheless, "Redeem us for thy mercies' sake."—*Thrupp.*

3. *They got not the land in possession by their own sword.* Here it is necessary to observe the mode of reasoning which the prophet employs when he argues that it is by the free gift of God that the people obtained the land in heritage, seeing they had not acquired it by their own power. We then truly begin to yield to God what belongs to him, when we consider how worthless our own strength is. And certainly the reason why men, as it were through disdain, conceal and forget the benefits which God has conferred on them, must be owing to a delusive imagination which leads them to arrogate something to themselves as properly their own. The best means, therefore, of cherishing in us habitually a spirit of gratitude towards God is to expel from our minds this foolish opinion of our own ability. There is still in the concluding part of the verse another expression which contains a more illustrious testimony to the grace of God, when the psalmist resolves the whole into the good pleasure of God: *Thou hadst a favour for them.* The prophet does not suppose any worthiness in the person of Abraham, nor imagine any desert in his posterity, on account of which God dealt so bountifully with them, but ascribes the whole to the good pleasure of God. His words seem to be taken from the solemn declaration of Moses: "The Lord did not set his love upon you, nor choose you, because ye were more in number than any people (for ye were the fewest of all people); but because the Lord loved you," Deut. vii. 7, 8. Special mention is here made of the land of Canaan; but the prophet has stated the general principle why it was that God vouchsafed to reckon that people for his flock and peculiar heritage. And certainly the source and origin of the church is the free love of God; and whatever benefits he bestows upon his church, they all proceed from the same source. The reason, therefore, why we are gathered into the church, and are nourished and defended by the hand of God, is only to be sought in God. Nor does the psalmist here treat of the general benevolence of God, which extends to the whole human race; but he discourses of the difference which exists between the elect and the rest of the world; and the cause of this difference is here referred to the mere good pleasure of God.—*Calvin.*

5. *Through thee will we push down our enemies.* The fight was very close; bows were of no avail, and swords failed to be of service; it came to daggers drawing, and hand-to-hand wrestling, pushing, and tugging. Jacob's God was renewing in the seed of Jacob their father's wrestling. And how fared it with faith then? Could she stand foot to foot with her foe and hold her own? Yea, verily, she came forth victorious from the encounter, for she is great at a close push, and overthrows all her adversaries, the Lord being her helper.

Through thy name will we tread them under that rise up against us. The Lord's name served instead of weapons, and enabled those who used it to leap on their foes and crush them with jubilant valour. In union and communion with God, saints work wonders. If God be for us, who can be against us? Mark well that all the conquests of these believers are said to be "through thee," "through thy name." Never let us forget this, lest going a warfare at our own charges we fail most ignominiously. Let us not, however, fall into the equally dangerous sin of distrust, for the Lord can make the weakest of us equal to any emergency. Though to-day we are timid and defenceless as sheep, he can by his power make us strong as the firstling of his bullock, and cause us to push as with the horns of unicorns, until those who rose up against us shall be so crushed and battered as never to rise again. Those who of themselves can scarcely keep their feet, but like little babes totter and fall, are by divine assistance made to overthrow their foes, and set their feet upon their necks. Read Christian's fight with Apollyon, and see how

> "The man so bravely played the man
> He made the fiend to fly."
>
> —*Spurgeon.*

23. *Awake, why sleepest thou, O Lord?* God sleepeth not, but the psalmist puts it so, as if on no other theory he could explain the divine inaction. He would fain see the great Judge ending oppression, and giving peace to the holy, therefore does he cry "Awake." He cannot understand why the reign of tyranny and the oppression of virtue are permitted, and therefore he inquires, "Why sleepest thou?" *Arise.* This is all thou needest to do; one move of thine will save us. *Cast us not off for ever.* Long enough hast thou deserted us. The terrible effects of thine absence are destroying us; end thou our calamities, and let thine anger be appeased. In persecuting times men are apt to cry, Where is the God of Israel? At the thought of what the saints have endured from their haughty enemies, we join our voices in the great martyr cry, and sing with the bard of Paradise:—

> "Avenge, O Lord, thy slaughtered saints whose bones
> Lie scattered on the Alpine mountains cold;
> Even those who kept thy truth so pure of old;
> When all our fathers worshipped stocks and stones,
> Forget not: in thy book record their groans
> Who were thy sheep."
>
> —*Spurgeon.*

PSALM XLV.

The forty-fifth is another Messianic psalm belonging to this period (the age of Solomon). It was not written by Solomon, but by "the sons of Korah"—the same Levitical family who had made such precious contributions to the Psalter in the preceding reign. Its theme—its primary and proper theme—is the glory of the Lord Christ and the church's marriage to him; and this is celebrated with gorgeous imagery, which reminds us of the reign of king Solomon at every turn. The king's house is an ivory palace, fragrant with myrrh and aloes and cassia. The queen is arrayed in gold of Ophir, and the daughter of Tyre brings in her hand the wealth of the nations for a wedding gift. The parallel between the Song of Solomon and the psalm cannot escape any reader, and we may very confidently attribute them both to the brilliant age of the son of David. . . .

The psalm is a nuptial song—the epithalamium of some great king of Israel, who has fixed his love on a Gentile maiden, the daughter of a princely house, and is being united in marriage to her in his own palace. The glories of the king are first described, his superhuman beauty and gracious words, the everlasting stability of his throne, his martial achievements, and the mild equity of his administration. Then follows a description of the marriage. The queen-consort is at the king's right hand, in gold of Ophir; she is conducted—she and her maidens—into the king's palace; and the daughter of opulent Tyre, who has come to grace the day with her presence, brings in her hand a wedding gift. It is a song resplendent with the richest ornaments of oriental poetry. Respecting its ultimate and proper intention, there has been from the first an unfaltering consent among all devout readers. The opening verse—

> "My heart poureth forth a goodly matter:
> I speak the things which I have made touching the king:
> My tongue is the pen of a ready writer:"

—this verse, I say, in their judgment, is strictly parallel to that of the apostle: "This is a great mystery; but I speak concerning Christ and the church," Eph. v. 32. There are, no doubt, differences of opinion in regard to what may be called the *theory* of the psalm; some understanding it to refer to Christ and the church directly and exclusively, while others think there is an immediate reference to Solomon (or some other Hebrew king) and his Gentile wife. But this difference is quite immaterial, so far as our present purpose is concerned; for those who think there is an immediate reference to an earthly marriage agree with the others in holding that there are many things in the psalm which, in their full and proper sense, apply only to Christ, and that it was designed from the first to lead men's thoughts to him.—*Binnie.*

6. *Thy throne, O God, is for ever and ever.* Referring to the Unitarian rendering here, viz. *God is thy throne*, i.e. the support of thy throne, Dr. J. P. Smith justly remarks: "The use of a metaphor so harsh, and apparently repugnant to good taste and to piety, should have been justified by ample proofs of the same or a similar usage. No such proofs are produced. God is often denominated a rock, a tower, a fortress, a shield, a refuge to his faithful servants; but in all these and similar metaphors there is an obvious superiority in strength and dignity preserved to the Divine Being. The reader immediately associates with these expressions the ideas of power and grandeur in a PROTECTING Being, and of his pre-eminence above the objects protected. But it is the reverse in the case brought before us. A *throne* is merely a seat; and it derives its dignity altogether from the character and dominion of the person who sits upon it. To call the Eternal Majesty *the throne of a creature* shocks all taste and good feeling; and it grossly violates the reverence which is ever to be maintained towards him. That heart-touching reverence is amongst the most distinguishing characters of the Scripture style."—*Scripture Testimony.*

10–15. *Hearken, O daughter*, &c. The Psalter, which sets forth so much truth respecting the person and work of Christ—truth more precious than gold, and sweeter than the honey-comb—is not silent respecting the bond subsisting between him and his people—THE MYSTICAL UNION BETWEEN CHRIST AND THE CHURCH. When a prince sets his affections on a woman of lowly rank and takes her home to be his wife, the two are so united that her debts become his, his wealth and honours become hers. Now, that there is formed between Christ and the church—between Christ and every soul that will consent to receive him—a connection, of which this most intimate of all natural relations is the analogue and type, we have already found to be not only taught in the Psalms, but to be implied in the very structure of many of them. He takes his people's sins upon him, and they receive the right to become the sons of God; the One Spirit of God wherewith he was baptized without measure, dwells in them according to the measure of the grace that is given them. I will only add further, that this union, besides being implied in so many places, is expressly set forth in one most glorious psalm—the nuptial song of Christ and the church—which has for its peculiar theme the home-bringing of Christ's elect, that they may be joined to him in a union that shall survive the everlasting hills.—*Binnie.*

12. *And the daughter of Tyre shall be there with a gift*, Hengstenberg renders—*So will the daughter of Tyre implore thee with gifts*—and adds, The object of the earnest entreaty is reception into the community of the people of God, comp. Is. xliv. 5; Ps. xlvii. 9. That Tyre should seek, with fervent supplication and presents, to gain the favour of the queen, and to make her inclined to fulfil her desire, is inexplicable on the literal interpretation. The proud island-city never stood in a relation of dependence to Israel; she always held it to be beneath her dignity to make a humble suit for his favour: Israel's king and queen had nothing which she could have sought from them with imploring earnestness. In this view also one does not see how the humble solicitations could be made dependent on the place the queen had in the heart of the king. On the other hand, every difficulty vanishes with the figurative interpretation. Only when the church of God really occupies the *position* of the church of God, can prayer be directed to her for reception into her society. The church exercises a drawing power toward those that are without, in exact proportion to her own internal connection with the Lord. Her surrender to the Lord forms the ground of the heathen's surrender to her. According to other passages also, the church of God in Messianic times is the object of earnest desire, as generally of the whole heathen world, which brings its riches to her, comp. Ps. lxxii. 10; Is. lx. 6, ss.; Hag. ii. 7, 8, so in particular of proud Tyre; in the likewise Korahite Psalm lxxxvii., Tyre, ver. 4, is

expressly named among other powerful nations for reception into the kingdom of God, and according to Is. xxiii. 18, the gain of Tyre shall one day become holy to the Lord.—עשירי עם, as apposition to בת צר, not the rich of the peoples, but of the people, or among the people, *q. d.* the richest persons, indicates why it is, that precisely Tyre's solicitations for favour are promised to the queen, viz. that she is singled out of the mass of the other heathen nations, whose homage is promised to the queen in and with hers, only as being the richest city of the old world.

PSALM XLVI.

The historical occasion of the psalm cannot with certainty be determined. It was called forth by a catastrophe which befel the kingdom of Judah (comp. in ver. 8: come, *behold* the works of the Lord), and has for its immediate object Judah's deliverance. Otherwise the *particular* in the last strophe would not serve as a foundation for the *general* in the two first strophes; especially this: "God helps her at the break of morning," would not be comprehensible, as it presupposes a heavy oppression on Judah. The admonition also in ver. 10: "Leave off and know that I am God," has only then a motive laid for it, when the desolation effected upon the earth, ver. 8, and the cessation of war in ver. 9, could be recognized by all as done in behalf of Israel's salvation; for only then was the fact a dissuasive for the heathen against fighting with Israel, a demonstrative proof of the godhead of his God. In like manner it is then only that ver. 11 appears as properly explained. But at the same time this catastrophe was an important event in the *world's history*, the annihilation of the power of a world-conqueror: with Judah the *whole circle of the earth* also is delivered, in so far as it could be surveyed from Palestine, ver. 9, and the Lord has thereby glorified himself through all the *earth*, ver. 10. By observing these distinctive marks, hypotheses, such as those of De Wette, who thinks the psalm refers to *foreign* wars, which God had silenced, and of Hitzig, who refers it to a sudden scaring of the Syrians and Ephraimites from the Jewish territory, are entirely set aside. In the whole Israelitish history there is *only one event*, of which we can here think, the destruction of Sennacherib's army before the gates of Jerusalem, Is. xxxvii. 36. That whole chapter and ch. xxxvi. must be read, if we would come to the full understanding and enjoyment of the psalm. After the exodus from Egypt there was no occasion more appropriate than this for bringing vividly out the leading idea in this psalm. The entire might of the world, which, as formerly in Egypt, so then was concentrated in Assyria, the most powerful of kingdoms, up till that time resistless in its march of conquest, came against Jerusalem. To the words: "Let not Hezekiah deceive you, saying, The Lord will deliver us; hath any of the gods of the nations delivered his land out of the hand of the king of Assyria?"—there was an equally impressive answer given then, as formerly to the question of Pharaoh: Who is Jehovah? When all seemed already to be lost, the holy city was, by an immediate exercise of divine omnipotence, delivered, without any co-operation on the part of its feeble inhabitants, without even any interruption to the undertaking of the Assyrians from their chief enemies, the Egyptians. Then, when real greatness was great also in appearance, when the power of the world had assumed a dazzling splendour, at such a time it was, that it was said to the possessors thereof, as is done here in ver. 10, "Cease and know that I am God." . . . It is self-evident that the subject of the psalm upon which Luther's "Ein' feste Burg ist unser Gott," rests, is no Old Testament idea. There is only *one* church of God through all ages, and to it this idea belongs. When Christ supports his church, the gates of hell may rage: this is only the New Testament form for the general fundamental truth.—*Hengstenberg*.

There is sufficient evidence in the psalm now before us to show that it was composed in the reign of Hezekiah, on the occasion of the destruction of the Assyrian host of Sennacherib. For the mercy which it celebrates is evidently the preservation of the holy city, before the walls of which the Assyrian army perished: and the psalmist purposely avoids any allusion to the Jewish territory, through which, according to the prophecy of Isaiah, the king of Assyria had been permitted to pass, overflowing and going over, and reaching even to the neck, though discomfited before he could succeed in crushing the capital. In the mention, however vague, in mountains being carried into the midst of the sea, we have a manifest reference to the previous overthrow by the Assyrian power of the kingdoms of Syria and Israel, and of Hamath, Arphad, and other northern states; mountains being continually used in Scripture as the emblems of kingdoms, and the swelling waves of the sea representing the formidable advance of the great heathen empire. In contrast to the roaring and blustering of this Assyrian ocean, the divine grace by which Jerusalem was preserved is compared to the springing streams of the fountain of Gihon, which, by the formation of a new channel or conduit, Hezekiah had, in preparation for resisting the anticipated siege, lately introduced into the heart of the city. A similar contrast had been drawn in the reign of Ahaz by the prophet Isaiah, when he compared the divinely established dominion of the house of David, representing the kingdom of God, to the softly going waters of the fountain of Siloah, and the opposing might of the Assyrian monarchy, representing the tyranny of the world, to the overflowing stream of the Euphrates. In the words which form the refrain of the psalm, "The Lord of hosts is with us," there is a reminiscence of the name Immanuel, "With us God," on which the recent prophecies of Isaiah had dwelt. Ver. 11, "Be still and know that I am God," is particularly appropriate in reference to the destruction of the Assyrian host, which was accomplished by the arm of the Lord, without the intervention of any associated human willing agency. Hardly less worthy of note are the concluding words of ver. 5, "right early," or "at dawn of morning," in allusion to the same event, when, as has been justly observed, there intervened but one night between the highest pitch of distress and the most complete deliverance: "When they arose early in the morning, behold, they were all dead corpses." And in thorough keeping with what actually occurred is the mention also of the desolations which the Lord had made in the earth, of his breaking the bow, and cutting the spear in sunder, and burning the chariot in the fire. There is, in fact, hardly a psalm in the Psalter reflecting so manifestly as this the circumstances of the period at which it was written.

As the destruction of Sennacherib's host is the most signal historical instance of the issue of the outward conflict between God and the powers of the world, so in the present psalm, the basis of Luther's "Ein' feste Burg ist unser Gott," the Christian church has found the readiest expression of her confidence in God in the midst of surrounding dangers. That the psalmist avowedly spoke in the name of the universal church of all time may be gathered from the first clause of ver. 9, "He maketh wars to cease unto the end of the earth;" words of essentially prophetical import, which must wait to the end for their full accomplishment.—*Thrupp.*

1. *God is our refuge and our strength.* Not our armies, or our fortresses. Israel's boast is in Jehovah, the only living and true God. Others vaunt their impregnable castles, placed on inaccessible rocks and secured with gates of iron, but God is a far better refuge from distress than all these: and when the time comes to carry the war into the enemy's territories, the Lord stands his people in better stead than all the valour of legions or the boasted strength of chariot and horse. Soldiers of the cross, remember this, and count yourselves safe, and make yourselves strong in God. Forget not the personal possessive word "*our;*" make sure each one of your portion in God, that you may say, "He is *my* refuge and strength." Neither forget the fact that God is our refuge just now, in the immediate present, as truly as when David penned the word. God alone is our all in all. All other refuges are refuges of lies, all other strength is weakness, for power belongeth unto God: but as God is all-sufficient, our defence and might are equal to all emergencies. "*A very present help in trouble,*" or *in distresses, he has so been found,* he has been tried and proved by his people. He never withdraws himself from his afflicted. He is their help, truly, effectually, constantly; he is present or near them, close at their side and ready for their succour, and this is emphasized by the word "*very*" in our version, he is more present than friend or relative can be, yea, more nearly present than even the trouble itself. To all this comfortable truth is added the consideration that his assistance comes at the needed time. He is not as the swallows that leave us in the winter; he is a friend in need and a friend indeed. When it is very

dark with us, let brave spirits say, "Come, let us sing the forty-sixth Psalm."

"A fortress firm, and steadfast rock,
Is God in time of danger;
A shield and sword in every shock,
From foe well-known or stranger."
—*Spurgeon.*

2. *Though the earth be removed.* The sentiment of Horace on the just man: Si fractus illabatur orbis, impavidum ferient ruinae, appears excellent at first sight. But since such a person as he draws has never been found, he merely trifles. *This* greatness of soul, on the other hand, is based solely on the *protection of God*, and on the promises which he has made to his own people, and in this way easily overcomes the terror which threatens destruction to all creatures.—*Calvin.*

6. *The heathen raged.* The nations were in a furious uproar, they gathered against the city of the Lord like wolves ravenous for their prey; they foamed, and roared, and swelled like a tempestuous sea. "*The kingdoms were moved.*" A general confusion seized upon society; the fierce invaders convulsed their own dominions by draining the population to urge on the war, and they desolated other territories by their devastating march to Jerusalem. Crowns fell from royal heads, ancient thrones rocked like trees driven of the tempest, powerful empires fell like pines uprooted by the blast: everything was in disorder, and dismay seized on all who knew not the Lord. "*He uttered his voice, the earth melted.*" With no other instrumentality than a word the Lord ruled the storm. He gave forth a voice, and stout hearts were dissolved, proud armies were annihilated, conquering powers were enfeebled. At first the confusion appeared to be worse confounded, when the element of divine power came into view; the very earth seemed turned to wax, the most solid and substantial of human things melted like the fat of rams upon the altar; but anon peace followed, the rage of man subsided, hearts capable of repentance relented, and the implacable were silenced. How mighty is a word from God! How mighty the Incarnate Word! O that such a word would come from the excellent glory even now to melt all hearts in love to Jesus, and to end for ever all the persecutions, wars, and rebellions of men!—*Spurgeon.*

PSALM XLVII.

The occasion of the psalm was, according to ver. 3, an overthrow of several *heathen peoples*, accomplished by the visible interposition of God, who had leagued themselves against Israel, and who, according to ver. 4, had set out with the purpose of expelling Israel from his *land*. The only thing that suggests itself as a fit reference is the victory of *Jehoshaphat* over the combined Moabites, Ammonites, Edomites, and Arabians, in 2 Ch. xx. Several nations were then united against Israel; they were set upon nothing less than driving Israel wholly out of his land, comp. 2 Ch. xx. 11; the overthrow of the enemies followed under circumstances which caused the hand of God to be clearly discerned. Surprised by an attack in the rear from a host of freebooting sons of the wilderness, the enemies fled in a *panic*, and as the spirit of mistrust fell upon them, and each people thought itself betrayed by the other, they turned their arms one against another. So Israel obtained a victory without a battle. The reference to that event is favoured by the circumstance that then, according to 2 Ch. xx. 19, the Korahites are expressly mentioned as having been present in the army; that the immediately following psalm refers to the same event, as also Ps. lxxxiii. (these three psalms perfectly suffice for a defence of 2 Ch. xx. against the attacks of modern criticism); finally, that on this supposition we obtain a suitable situation for ver. 5, from 2 Ch. xx. 26, "On the fourth day they assembled themselves together, in the valley of praise, for there they praised the Lord." Before the people left the field of slaughter, to return back to Jerusalem, they held a solemn service in that valley of praise: from that valley God made, as it were, his ascent to heaven, after having achieved redemption for his people. As the army returned into the holy city, so the leader of the host returned to heaven. This psalm was sung in the valley of praise, as the following one in the service of the temple. So *Hengstenberg.*—But whatever the occasion of the psalm, there can be no doubt that these carnal conquests were but shadows of the victories of the Messiah and the future triumphs of the church. "The psalm, says Calvin, "chiefly magnifies the favour which, according to the state of things at that time, God had graciously vouchsafed to the offspring of Abraham: and salvation to the whole world was to proceed from this source. It however contains at the same time a prophecy of the future kingdom of Christ. It teaches that the glory which then shone under the figure of the material sanctuary will diffuse its splendour far and wide; when God himself will cause the beams of his grace to shine into distant lands, that kings and nations may be united into fellowship with the children of Abraham."

1. *O clap your hands, all ye peoples.* As the psalmist requires the nations, in token of their joy and of their thanksgiving to God, to clap their hands, or rather exhorts them to a more than ordinary joy, the vehemence of which breaks forth, and manifests itself by external expressions, it is certain that he is here speaking of the deliverance which God had wrought for them. Had God erected among the Gentiles some formidable kingdom, this would rather have deprived all of their courage, and overwhelmed them with despair, than given them matter to sing and leap for joy. Besides, the inspired writer does not here treat of some common or ordinary blessings of God; but of such blessings as will fill the whole world with incredible joy, and stir up the minds of all men to celebrate the praises of God. What he adds a little after, that all nations were brought into subjection to Israel, must therefore be necessarily understood not of slavish subjection, but of a subjection which is more excellent and more to be desired than all the kingdoms of the world. It would be unnatural for those who are subdued and brought to submit by force and fear to leap for joy. Many nations were tributary to David, and to his son Solomon; but while they were so, they ceased not at the same time to murmur, and bore impatiently the yoke which was imposed upon them, so far were they from giving thanks to God with joyful and cheerful hearts.—*Calvin.*

5. *God is gone up with a shout.* There is here an allusion to the ancient ceremony which was observed under the law. As the sound of trumpets was wont to be used in solemnizing the holy assemblies, the prophet says that God *goes up*, when the trumpets encourage and stir up the people to magnify and extol his power. When this ceremony was performed in old time, it was just as if a king, making his entrance among his subjects, presented himself to them in magnificent attire and great splendour, by which he gained their admiration and reverence. At the same time the sacred writer, under that shadowy ceremony, doubtless intended to lead us to consider another kind of going up more triumphant—that of Christ when he "ascended up far above all heavens," and obtained the empire of the whole world, and armed with his celestial power, subdued all pride and loftiness. You must remember what I have adverted to before, that the name *Jehovah* is here applied to the ark; for although the essence or majesty of God was not shut up in it, nor his power and operation fixed to it, yet it was not a vain and idle symbol of his presence. God had promised that he would dwell in the midst of the people so long as the Jews worshipped him according to the rule which he had prescribed in the law; and he actually showed that he was truly present with them, and that it was not in vain that he was called upon among them. What is here stated, however, applies more properly to the manifestation of the glory which at length shone forth in the person of Christ. In short, the import of the psalmist's language is, When the trumpets sounded among the Jews, according to the appointment of the law, that was not a mere empty sound which vanished away in air; for God, who intended the ark of the covenant to be a pledge and token of his presence, truly presided in that assembly. From this the prophet draws an argument for enforcing on the faithful the duty of *singing praises to God.* He argues that by engaging in this exercise they will not be acting blindly, or at random, as the superstitious, who, having no certainty in their false systems of religion, lament and howl in vain before their idols. He shows that the faithful have just ground for celebrating with their mouths and with a cheerful heart the praises of God; since they certainly know that he is as present with them as if he had visibly established his royal throne among them.—*Calvin.*

PSALM XLVIII.

Expositors take as the historical occasion of the psalm, either the victory of

Jehoshaphat, or the deliverance from the Assyrians under Hezekiah. To the latter hypothesis it is to be objected, 1. That the discourse here is of many independent kings, who had leagued themselves in a common undertaking against Jerusalem. It is nothing to allege, on the other hand, the saying of the king of Assyria, in Is. x. 8, "Are not all my princes kings?" For that here the discourse is not of such as possibly once were called kings, appears from נועדו in ver. 4, as also from the fact, that here it is always kings that are spoken of, never a king of kings. We never find it thus in the numerous passages which refer to the Assyrians. 2. That here the discourse is of troubled *flight*, not of utter destruction. On the other hand, everything is in perfect accordance with the victory of Jehoshaphat. Then in reality several kings were gathered together against Jerusalem. They came into the immediate neighbourhood of the city, into the wilderness of Tekoa, which is certainly not further than a journey of three hours from Jerusalem, which commands an extensive prospect, and in particular of the environs of Jerusalem,—comp. *Robinson*, P. ii. p. 407 (upon the march of the Moabites and Ammonites, comp. *ib.* p. 426). Their anxious and troubled flight is described quite similarly in the Chronicles. With: "We think, O Lord, on thy loving-kindness in the midst of thy temple," in ver. 9 here, which bespeaks the psalm to have been sung as a song of praise in the temple, as the preceding one on the field of slaughter, comp. 2 Ch. xx. 27, "All Judah and Jerusalem returned, and Jehoshaphat in the forefront of them, back to Jerusalem with joy: and they came to Jerusalem with harps, and cytharas, and trumpets to the house of the Lord." A special reference to Jehoshaphat's time is also found in ver. 7. The omnipotence with which the Lord destroys the enemies, is there placed beside that with which he breaks the ships of Tarshish. The occasion that gave rise to this comparison is recorded in 1 Ki. xxii. 49; 2 Ch. xx. 36, 37. Jehoshaphat had united with Ahaziah in getting ships of merchandise, but the ships were wrecked, נשברו. The internal connection between the two events was the greater, as in that annihilation of the ships of Tarshish there was discerned, according to 2 Ch., a judgment of God.—*Hengstenberg.*

The psalms we owe to the reign of Jehoshaphat are not many. Of only *two* are we quite certain: there may be perhaps *four* or *five*. Some think Ps. xlvi. and xlvii.—both of them Korahite psalms—belong to the period. Certainly we owe to it Ps. xlviii. and lxxxiii.—the former a Korahite psalm, the latter "a song or psalm of Asaph." The character of these odes reminds us that it was a storm of danger that at this epoch awoke for a short time the harps of the Levitical seers. They make mention of an invasion which, as we learn from the historical books, for a while threatened to sweep away Jehoshaphat's throne, and even annihilate the kingdom. The nations bordering on Judah to the east and south, Moab, Ammon, Edom, entered into a coalition against it, and secured the alliance of several more distant powers. They invaded the land from the south, and marched without check till they reached the wilderness of Tekoa, within ten miles of Jerusalem, whence, looking northwards, they could descry the battlements of the city, and the glittering pinnacles of the temple. In this extremity of danger Jehoshaphat and the people betook themselves to prayer. Having received, through one of the prophets, the promise of deliverance, king and people sallied forth in a solemn procession, in the van of which there marched a band of Levites, singing and praising the Lord. When they came in sight of the enemy, they found that God had sown mutual suspicions in the motley host, so that they had turned their swords against each other, and were utterly discomfited. It deserves to be remarked in connection with our subject, that the prophet by whom God's comfortable message was delivered to the king, was Jahaziel, the son of Zechariah, "*a Levite of the sons of Asaph;*" and that among the Levites who sang praise to the Lord, mention is made of a band "of the children of the Korahites," 2 Ch. xx. 14-19. It is an interesting and significant coincidence, that of the two psalms known to date from this epoch, one is marked in the superscription as an Asaph-psalm, and the other is assigned to "the sons of Korah." The Asaph-psalm is Ps. lxxxiii., and is the prayer of the congregation when the danger was at its height. It speaks of a confederation of "the tabernacles of Edom and the Ishmaelites; of Moab and the Hagarenes; Gebal, and Ammon, and Amalek;" and, among the more distant allies, mention is made of Tyre, and of Assyria itself. Their cry is, "Come, let us cut them off from being a nation; that the name of Israel may be no more in remembrance." The cry of Judah in response is towards heaven: "O my God, make them like a wheel;" or, as Milton translates the prayer—

"My God, oh make them as a wheel,
No quiet let them find;
Giddy and restless let them reel,
Like stubble from the wind.

"As when an aged wood takes fire,
Which on a sudden strays,
The greedy flame runs higher and higher,
Till all the mountains blaze;

"So with thy whirlwind them pursue,
And with thy tempest chase."

Such was the prayer. The answer which God gave, in the flame of discord that consumed the confederate host, is celebrated by the sons of Korah in Ps. xlviii.—*Binnie.*

The Mighty One is King, has entered on his dominion, is seated on his throne, is ruling in righteousness. But where is his capital? It is at *Jerusalem.* Here he manifests himself; and by the glory of his presence being shed over that "City of the great King," brighter than the light of seven days, yet far more mellow and tranquillizing than the sweetest hues of evening, *Jerusalem* becomes

"*The joy of the whole earth,*
(The joy) *of the sides of the north.*"

She has become the joy of the earth, far and near, the source of joy to earth's remotest bounds. Now is fulfilled Is. xxiv. 23. Now is Jerusalem made "beautiful for situation," or, set aloft on its hills in beauty, in another sense than formerly. Now is Zion exalted above the mountains, and obtains established pre-eminence above the hills. And if associations are needed to make the place completely interesting, these are not wanting here. Such deeds have been done here, that Sennacherib's overthrow is in a manner cast into the shade. The gathered kings of earth came up, "they passed" in all the pomp of battle, and the Lord scattered them; and writes here his "*Veni, vidi, vici,*" to all nations:—"*They saw! They marvelled! They were troubled! They hasted away!*" It was as when an east wind hurls the ships of Tarshish on the rocks. It comprised in it all that is recorded as wonderful in the achievements of former days; present events now come fully up to the measure of former good deeds, "*As we have heard, so have we seen, in the city of the Lord of hosts.*" The solemn *Selah-pause* occurs here; and then we look out on a peaceful scene, God known in all the earth, ver. 10. "*Thou art praised wherever thy name is known,*" or rather, now at last thou art getting praise worthy of thy glorious name. Zion is glad, Judah's tears are wiped away, while a voice invites all men to come and survey the bulwarks of the city of the great King, that they may tell it from age to age. The bulwarks are strong, for the Lord's presence, *Jehovah Shammah,* is the wall of fire, on whose battlements the happy citizens walk in security, singing,

"*This God is our God for ever and ever;*
He is our God even over death" (Tholuck:
"even beyond death").

—*A. A. Bonar.*

4-6. *Lo, the kings were assembled,* &c. Neither the multitude nor the greatness of the church's foes need alarm her friends. Men can do nothing but play the fool and the coward, if God be against them. "As the east wind shatters the ships of Tarshish, so the divine power strikes terror and astonishment" into the hearts of sinners. All the imaginations that fill the minds of the foes of God and of truth will vanish like the mist of morning. Montgomery beautifully versifies a part of this ode:—

"At the sight of her splendour the kings of the earth
Grew pale with amazement and dread;
Fear seized them like pangs of a premature birth;
They came, they beheld her, and fled.
Thou breakest the ships from the sea-circled clime
When the storm of thy jealousy lowers:
As our fathers have told of thy deeds in their time,
So, Lord, have we witnessed in ours."

Dickson: "Such as come to bring trouble to God's church come to catch trouble to themselves."—*Plumer.*

PSALM XLIX.

Among the psalms which assert the hope of eternal life, an eminent place belongs to the forty-ninth. . . . The psalms which are introduced with a formal preface are very few in number, and they are all psalms of principal note in their several kinds. . . . And this, . . . instead of being addressed to the Hebrew church, . . . is expressly and emphatically addressed to the church catholic, to "all peoples," even "all the inhabitants of the world." . . . Although indited by a Hebrew pen, it is a Christian psalm, and was from the first inscribed to the Christian church. . . . The theme (like that of Ps. xvii. and lxxiii.) is the mystery of God's providence towards the righteous and the wicked; and the aim of the psalmist is the same, namely, to encourage God's people to take "for an helmet the hope of salvation," when they are shaken in mind at the sight of prosperous ungodliness. The grand lesson intended to be inculcated is worked out in each of the two stanzas of which the body of the psalm consists. In the first it is worked out partially, in the second more perfectly. The psalmist has been himself perplexed by the problem to which he summons the attention of the world. Like Asaph, in Ps. lxxiii., he has been shaken in mind by seeing vile men rich, powerful, prosperous. Reflecting on that sight, the first consideration impressed on his mind is the vanity of riches. These men trust in their wealth. . . . Yet, after all, how helpless are they! . . . Death prevails over all. . . . The redemption of a man's life is too precious to be accomplished with silver and gold. The attempt is vain. It must be let alone, and cease for ever. Thus the psalmist is conducted to the sentence with which the first stanza is wound up: "*Man that is in honour hath no continuance; he is become like to the beasts that are destroyed.*" The reflection is a salutary one; . . . but, after all, it is not a bright or consolatory one. There is no glory of heavenly hope upon it. Heathen moralists were as familiar with it as the psalmist. . . . The verses that follow lift us up beyond these clouds into a serener air. The sentence into which the argument of the first stanza was gathered up is set down a second time at the close of the psalm. But this time with an important variation. Here it is the man "that hath no understanding" who is compared to the beasts that are destroyed. We are thus reminded that there are some who, by God's grace, have understanding: men who "fear the Lord, which is wisdom, and depart from evil, which is understanding." . . . They do not perish like the beasts, but are taken up into God's presence, to dwell there like angels. What is thus taught by implication in the refrain is set forth explicitly in the body of the stanza. Two declarations claim special attention. After describing the death of the ungodly as their being "driven by the stern shepherd, Death, into the unseen world," as sheep are driven unwillingly into a pen, he declares his belief that a day is coming—a bright morning—in which the saints shall have dominion (ver. 14); an announcement which carries forward the mind to the morning of the resurrection, when "the saints shall judge the world," 1 Cor. vi. 2. Then, coming home to his own case, he makes profession of his hope in words of strong assurance: "*God will redeem my soul from the power of the unseen world; for he shall take me.*" The former part of this profession of the psalmist's faith is best illustrated by the parallel text in Hosea: "I will ransom them from the power of the grave" (*i.e.* "I will redeem them from the power of the unseen world:" the words in the original are the same as in the psalm); "I will redeem them from death. O death, I will be thy plagues! O grave, I will be thy destruction!" Hos. xiii. 14. The believer has faith in God that, when he dies, he shall not be shut up in darkness, but shall be received into the presence of God, and be raised up in glory at the last day. That victory over death, which the worldling's wealth cannot purchase for his dearest friend, is made sure to every one who puts his trust in God. The words that follow, "for he shall take me," correspond to those of Asaph, "Thou shalt guide me with thy counsel, and afterwards take me to glory;" and, in both places, there is an allusion to the language of the sacred history in relating the translation of Enoch: "He was not, for God took him," Gen. v. 24. Not that Asaph or the writer of Ps. xlix. expected to be translated like Enoch; but the "taking up" of the antediluvian saint suggested to their minds a world of precious truth respecting the future life, and strengthened in their hearts the hope of eternal glory in the presence of God. We have before us, therefore, a clear and strong declaration of hope; for, after all, what more can the believer say even now? The highest attainment our faith can reach, in the prospect of dissolution, is to lay hold on the promise of Christ and say, "Thou wilt come and receive me to thyself, so that where thou art, there I shall be also;" and what is this but to repeat the profession of hope that is embedded in Ps. xlix.?---*Binnie.*

8. *The redemption of their soul is precious.* If riches are capable of many good uses, as the Bible admits, so in a multitude of cases they are utterly powerless. They cannot buy talent, or any excellence of mind or heart. They cannot give a good constitution, nor prolong life for a day. They rather increase than diminish fears. "The abundance of the rich will not suffer him to sleep." They cannot quiet an uneasy conscience. They cannot cool a fever or drive away a chill. They cannot soothe a pain in the head or an ache in the heart. Towards one's salvation they can contribute nothing whatever. Nor can they aid our kin or our friends more than they can ourselves. *Tholuck:* "A rich man may buy much with his money—goods of every kind, pleasures, honours; but he cannot buy eternal life."—*Plumer.*

15. *He shall receive me.* He shall take me. This short half-verse is, as Böttcher remarks, the more weighty, from its very shortness. The same expression occurs again, Ps. lxxiii. 24: "Thou shalt take me," the original of both being, Gen. v. 24, where it is used of the translation of Enoch, "He was not, for God *took* him." We have, then, in this passage again (comp. Ps. xvi. 11; xvii. 15) the strong hope of eternal life with God, if not the hope of a resurrection. In the preceding verse, in the very midst of the gloomy picture which he draws of the end of the ungodly, there breaks forth one morning-ray of light, the bright anticipation of the final triumph of the good over the evil. This is the inextinguishable hope which animates the church of the Old Testament as well as that of the New. Righteousness *shall* eventually, must in its very nature, reign upon the earth. The wicked shall find their end in Sheôl (see Ps. ix. 17), and the righteous shall trample on their graves. This, and not more than this, seems to have been the meaning originally of the psalmist in the words, "And the righteous have dominion over them in the morning." But now that he comes to speak of himself, and his own personal relation to God, he rises into a higher strain. He who knows and loves God has the life of God, and can never perish. That life must survive even the shock of death. "God," says the psalmist, "shall redeem my soul from the hand of Hades, for he shall take me," as he took Enoch, and as he took Elijah, to himself. We are not, of course, to suppose that the sacred poet himself expected to be taken up alive to heaven; but those great facts of former ages were God's witnesses to man of his immortality, and of the reality of a life with him beyond this world. It is a hope based on facts like these which here shines forth. It is a hope, not a revealed certainty. It rests on no distinct promise; it has not assumed the definite form of a doctrine. But it was enough to raise, to cheer, to encourage those who saw ungodliness prospering in this world. The end of the wicked, after all, was a thick darkness which had never been penetrated; the end of the righteous, life with God. —*Perowne.*

18. *While he lived he blessed his soul.* The death which, according to ver. 17, deprives the ungodly of all his glorious privileges, is to be thought of, according to the preceding context, as near at *hand.* In ver. 18 the reason is given why God does not permit the glory of the wicked to follow him, why it comes to so sudden and complete an end. His whole life was set on enjoyment; he has already enjoyed enough, already has he treated himself luxuriously enough, and he cannot complain if he should now come to want. We may compare Lu. xvi. 25, a passage resting upon ours, and serving as a commentary to it: "But Abraham said, Son, remember that thou in thy lifetime receivedst thy good things, and likewise Lazarus evil things; but now he is comforted, and thou art tormented." On this, for he blesses his soul in his life, is to be compared the address of the rich man to his soul, Lu. xii. 19.—*Hengstenberg.*

PSALM L.

Title. The prepositional prefix rendered "*of*" in the present superscription is the same (ל) that is given as "*for*" in that of the preceding psalm. The same considerations are therefore here applicable, and incline us to conclude that the psalms which bear the name of Asaph were written by him. Asaph is frequently mentioned in the historical books as the chief, or one of the chiefs, of the choirs of Israel in the time of David. The psalms ascribed to him are twelve (l.; lxxiii.-lxxxiii.). Two of these, however (lxxiv. lxxix.), could not have been written by him or in his time, as their contents evidently assign them to the period of the captivity. The subject of Asaph's psalms are doctrinal or preceptive: their style, though less sweet than that of David, is much more vehement, and little inferior to the grandest parts of the prophecies of Isaiah and Habakkuk. The present psalm in particular is characterized by a very deep strain of thought and lofty tone of sentiment.—*Kitto.*

If David is, without controversy, the prince of the psalmists, Asaph stands next to him in honour. The psalms in which the Levites sang praise to the Lord in the days of Hezekiah are called "the words of David and of *Asaph the seer*," 2 Chr. xxix. 31. The emphatic manner in which the prophetic title is here annexed to Asaph's name, suggests that he was favoured with a larger measure of the prophetical spirit than any of the Levitical prophets who were his contemporaries. The facts known respecting him are briefly told. He was a Levite, of the family of Gershon. He was one of the three presidents of the Levitical singers, standing at Heman's right hand, as Ethan-Jeduthun did at his left. His four sons presided, under him, over four companies. Their descendants continued to minister in the service of song as long as the first temple stood, and are mentioned in this connection in the histories of Jehoshaphat and Hezekiah, 2 Chr. xx. 14; xxix. 13. They mustered, to the number of 128, among the exiles who returned to Jerusalem with Zerubbabel, and are found ministering in the second temple before the cessation of prophecy. When Zerubbabel and Jeshua laid the foundation of the house, amidst the tears and shoutings of the remnant who had returned, it was the sons of Asaph who "praised the Lord with cymbals, after the ordinance of David king of Israel. And they sang together by course in praising and giving thanks unto the Lord; because he is good, for his mercy endureth for ever toward Israel," Ezra iii. 10; Neh. xi. 22.

There must have been several members of this family who inherited at once their father's name and his gift of minstrelsy; for of the twelve Asaph-psalms, several are of a date long subsequent to David's reign. It deserves to be noticed, however, as confirmatory of the testimony of the superscriptions in prefixing the name to all the twelve, that they constitute a class by themselves. They are the following: Ps. l., and Ps. lxxiii. to lxxxiii. inclusive. Dr. Delitzsch of Erlangen, who was the first to call attention to the peculiarities which characterize these Asaph-psalms, remarks, among other things, that "they are distinguished from the Korahite psalms by their prophetical and judicial character. Like the prophetical books, they frequently introduce God as the speaker. After the manner of the prophets, they contain lengthened representations of God as the Judge of all, as well as somewhat lengthened discourses spoken by him in that character, Ps. l. lxxv. lxxxii. Besides their predictive aspect, the Asaph-psalms present a historical aspect also, frequently commemorating facts pertaining to the ancient times; and one of them, the seventy-eighth, is altogether devoted to holding forth the ancient history of the nation as a mirror for the present generation to look into. The consecutive perusal of the twelve Asaph-psalms brings to light this other curious peculiarity, that Joseph, and the tribes descended from him, are mentioned more frequently in them than in any other." The reader may easily verify this last remark by turning to Ps. lxxvii. 15; lxxviii. 9, 67; lxxx. 1, 2; lxxxi. 5.

Of the Asaph-psalms which we have reason to suppose were written by David's illustrious contemporary himself, three may be named as worthy of special notice. The seventy-eighth claims notice as one of the earliest of the great historical odes. It recapitulates the history of the chosen people from the exodus till the reign of David; and it comes behind no psalm of its class for depth of insight into the treasures of instruction which the Spirit of God has stored up in the sacred history for the edification of all generations. Ps. lxxiii. is another of Asaph's; and it is one for which God's people will never cease to cherish his memory. It is a kind of lyrical epitome of the book of Job. It delineates the trial and triumph of grace in a believer, whose faith, after staggering at the sight of prosperous wickedness, recovers on observing the sudden destruction of the ungodly, and especially on recollecting (what he feels he ought never to have forgotten) that the chief end and felicity of man is, after all, to be found in God—not in worldly prosperity, but in the participation of God's favour.

Ps. l. is from the same pen. It is remarkable for this, that although written at the time when the Levitical ritual was celebrated with its utmost splendour, and by a Levite, whose office called him to act a principal part in some of its most splendid services, it contains as energetic a protest as the apostle Paul ever uttered, against the imagination that ceremonies are in themselves well-pleasing to God. It preaches, from the midst of the ritual magnificence of the age of David and Solomon, the very doctrine which our blessed Lord unfolded to the astonished woman of Samaria at Jacob's well, that God is a Spirit, and they that worship him must worship him in spirit and in truth. What could be plainer or bolder than these words (ver. 7-12)? These last (ver. 14, 15) are golden sentences! The hecatombs that Solomon and the congregation offered at the dedication of the house were, doubtless, acceptable in God's sight; but they owed their acceptance to the joyful faith and thankfulness that animated the offerers—to their humble reverence and unreserved devotion to the God of Israel. And there is not a poor troubled one on earth this day, there is not a soul crushed beneath a load of sorrow, in whom, if he will but importunately call on God, "making known to him his requests with thanksgiving," Phil. iv. 6, God will not take a higher delight than he did in the costly and magnificent offering of the king.—*Binnie.*

8. *Not because of thy sacrifices,* &c. The reason for this act of judgment is given. First, negatively (*positively*, ver. 14, 15). It is not because the people had neglected the externals of the law, or had forgotten to offer the sacrifices appointed by the law. They had brought them; but they had brought them as if the act were everything, and as if the meaning of the act, and the spirit in which it was done, were nothing. But God demands no service for its own sake, but only as the expression of an obedient will. A thankful heart is more than all burnt-offerings. The prophets are full of the like sentiments (Isa. i. 12; lviii.; lxvi. 3; Mic. vi. 6-8; Hos. vi. 6). And so deep-rooted was this tendency in the people to exaggerate the importance of the dead work, to bring the sacrifice of the dumb animal instead of the sacrifice of the heart, that Jeremiah carries the opposition between sacrifices and obedience even to the extreme of a paradox (Jer. vii. 22, 23).—*Perowne.*

23. *Whoso offereth praise,* &c. The English version, with its rendering, "*offereth* praise," loses sight of the distinct reference to the Mosaic sacrifices, which are not indeed absolutely superseded—the time had not yet come for this—but are put in their true place. The very great prominence again given to thanksgiving is worthy of our careful notice. There is no duty so commonly forgotten. God showers down his benefits upon us with both hands, large and free, and we receive them as a matter of course, and never consider whose love has bestowed them; and thus in our unthankfulness we rob God of his honour.

Further, as thanksgiving is thus dwelt upon because it is so commonly forgotten, so it is also put as the sum of religion, because it, in fact, includes all else. Faith, and prayer, and self-denial, and the endurance of the cross, and all holy exercises are, as Calvin observes, comprised in this one grace. For it is by faith only that we are sensible of God's goodness; therefore he who is truly of a thankful spirit has faith; he who is thankful triumphs over his earthly trials; he who is thankful is accomplishing man's highest end, inasmuch as in all things he gives glory to God. The instruction of the psalm abides: it has not lost its force. The sacraments and ordinances of the Christian church may become to us what sacrifice and offering were to the Jews, a mere *opus operatum;* a man may give all his goods to feed the poor, and yet have no love; a man may be punctual in his attendance at all holy ordinances, and yet cherish iniquity in his heart, and upon occasion secretly practise it. Hence the psalm is truly prophetical, that is, universal in its character. It deals with "the sinners and the hypocrites in Zion;" but it reaches to all men in all places to the end of time.—*Perowne.*

This is the third time that the psalmist has inculcated the truth, that the most acceptable sacrifice in God's sight is praise, by which we express to him the gratitude of our hearts for his blessings. The repetition is not a needless one, and that on two accounts. In the first place there is nothing with which we are more frequently chargeable than forgetfulness of the benefits of the Lord. Scarcely one out of a thousand attracts our notice; and if it does it is only slightly, and, as it were, in passing. And, secondly, we do not assign that importance to the duty of praise which it deserves. We are apt to neglect it as something trivial, and altogether commonplace; whereas it constitutes the chief exercise of godliness, in which God would have us to be engaged during the whole of our life. In the words before us the sacrifice of praise is asserted to form the true and proper worship of God. The words, *will glorify me*, imply that God is then truly and properly worshipped, and the glory which he requires yielded to him, when his goodness is celebrated with a sincere and grateful heart; but that all the other sacrifices to which hypocrites attach such importance are worthless in his estimation, and no part whatsoever of his worship. Under the word *praise*, however, is comprehended, as I have already noticed, both faith and prayer. There must be an experience of the goodness of the Lord before our mouths can be opened to praise him for it, and this goodness can only be experienced by faith. Hence it follows that the whole of spiritual worship is comprehended under what is either presupposed in the exercise of faith, or flows from it.—*Calvin*.

PSALM LI.

The psalms which David wrote on occasion of his great fall have gone home to the hearts of the best and holiest men that ever walked the earth. No sermon of Augustine's betrays more tender emotion, more deep and thrilling sympathy with his subject, than the one he preached to the people of Carthage on Ps. li. Nothing can well be plainer than that psalms which for ages have thus found their way to men's hearts, must have come from the heart.

One who would appreciate the character of the psalmist must remember that he was a man of prodigious energy. What he did, he did with his might. It is to be remembered, moreover, that he was a king, an oriental king, to whom law and universal custom permitted polygamy, and who was thus put in the way of being tempted by the foul sin which was the death of his domestic peace. Nor ought it to be forgotten that the sacred history has narrated David's fall with a judicial severity full of the terror of the Lord. The chapter which records his offence sets down every hateful feature in it with an unextenuating, inexorable circumstantiality, unparalleled in all biography, and, to a thoughtful reader, suggestive of the indictment that might be preferred against a criminal at the bar of the Most High. These considerations are not adduced to cloak David's transgression. Its enormity is undeniable, and is denied by none. He sank to a depth of guilt into which few of God's children have ever been suffered to fall. It is to be remarked, however, that this very fact contributed to fit him to be the psalmist of God's Israel. It was not in spite of his fall, but because of it, that God made choice of him to be the spokesman of the church in penitential song. The church is not a company of angels, but of ransomed men; of men who were sinners, who are often sinning still. David well knew that the record of his fall and his forgiveness would furnish to sin-stricken souls in after-times a strength of encouragement which nothing else could yield. In crying for mercy, this was the plea he urged, "Restore unto me the joy of thy salvation;—then will I teach transgressors thy ways; and sinners shall be converted unto thee" (ver. 12, 13). Being forgiven, he felt, like the converted persecutor of the church, that his God had furnished in him "a pattern to them which should hereafter believe in him to life everlasting." How wonderfully has this anticipation been realized! It is a merciful provision that, however profound may be the depths into which a man may be cast by his sins, he finds that the psalmist has been there before him, and has furnished him with words in which "out of the depths" he may cry to the Lord. There is not a poor publican in all God's temple who, as he smites on his breast and cries, "God be merciful to me a sinner," does not find, on turning to the book of Psalms, that the mercy of God has there provided for him songs that express every feeling of his convicted soul—songs, too, originally written by as great a sinner as himself, in the agony of his repentance. Till the judgment-day it will never be known how many souls, who would otherwise have cast themselves down in despair, have been encouraged by David's example, and assisted by his psalms, to embrace the promise and to hope in the mercy of God.—*Binnie.*

5. *Behold, I was shapen in iniquity,* &c. See the supplementary note under Rom. v. 12–19, where the author's views on the imputation of sin are canvassed. Hengstenberg in his notes on this verse justly remarks—"Allusions to the doctrine of a hereditary corruption are to be found even in the oldest portions of revelation. The account of Adam's fall can be understood in its full compass only if in it the whole human race fell, which can no otherwise be conceived than on the supposition of the propagation of sin by generation. That Adam's fall is the fall of the human family, is implied in the *punishment*, which affects not the individual, but the entire race. Everything which stands immediately connected with the account of the fall, the narrative of Cain's fratricide, &c., is inexplicable, if we limit the fall merely to the individual Adam, and there is a breaking down of the bridge formed in the generation between him and his posterity, to which express allusion is made in Gen. v. 3, 'And Adam begot like him and after his image' (in every respect, and hence also in reference to sin, which had now become a property of his nature). The whole subsequent relation is designed to show how fruitfully the principle of sin implanted in nature through Adam developed itself. According to Gen. viii. 21, the thoughts and imaginations of the heart of man are only evil from his youth."

PSALM LII.

8. *But I am like a green olive-tree,* &c. We have seen that David was enabled by the exercise of faith to look down upon the worldly grandeur of Doeg with a holy contempt; and now we find him rising superior to all that was presently afflictive in his own condition. Though to appearance he more resembled the withered trunk of a tree which rots upon the ground, he compares himself, in the confidence of coming prosperity, to a green olive. I need not say that the destruction of Doeg could only communicate comfort to his mind, in the way of convincing him that God was the avenging judge of human cruelty, and leading him to infer that, as he had punished his wrongs, so he would advance him to renewed measures of prosperity. From his language it appears that he could conceive of no higher felicity in his condition than being admitted amongst the number of the worshippers of God, and engaging in the exercises of devotion. This was characteristic of his spirit. We have already had occasion to see that he felt his banishment from the sanctuary of God more keenly than separation from his consort, the loss of worldly substance, or the dangers and hardships of the wilderness. The idea of an allusion being here made by way of contrast to Doeg, who came to the tabernacle of the Lord merely as a spy, and under hypocritical pretexts, is strained and far-fetched. It is more natural to suppose that David distinguishes himself from all his enemies, without exception, intimating that though he was presently removed from the tabernacle, he would soon be restored to it; and that they who boasted of possessing, or rather monopolizing, the house of God, would be rooted out of it with disgrace. And here let us engrave the useful lesson upon our hearts, that we should consider it the great end of our existence to be found numbered amongst the worshippers of God; and that we should avail ourselves of the inestimable privilege of the stated assemblies of the church, which are necessary helps to our infirmity, and means of mutual excitement and encouragement. By these, and our common sacraments, the Lord, who is one God, and who designed that we should be one in him, is training us up together in the hope of eternal life, and in the united celebration of his holy name. Let us learn with David to prefer a place in the house of God to all the lying vanities of this world. He adds the reason why he should be like the green olive-tree—*because he hoped in the goodness of God;* for the causal particle appears to be understood. And in this he adverts to the contrast between him and his enemies. They might flourish for a time, spread their branches far and wide, and shoot themselves up to a gigantic stature, but would speedily wither away, because they had no root in the goodness of God; whereas he was certain to derive from this source ever renewed supplies of sap and vigour. As the term of his earthly trials might be protracted, and there was a danger that he

might sink under their long continuance, unless his confidence should extend itself far into futurity, he declares expressly that he would not presume to prescribe times to God, and that his hopes were stretched into eternity. It followed that he surrendered himself entirely to God in all that regarded his life or his death. The passage puts us in possession of the grand distinction between the genuine children of God and those who are hypocrites. They are to be found together in the church, as the wheat is mingled with the chaff on the same threshing-floor; but the one class abides for ever in the steadfastness of a well-founded hope, while the other is driven away in the vanity of its false confidences.—*Calvin.*

PSALM LIII.

The name *Jehovah* is not used at all in the psalm before us, but occurs four times in Ps. xiv., and *Elohim* thrice. This difference seems to mark Ps. liii. as the later composition, in which the writer aimed at an external uniformity, which did not occur to him at first. This is a much more natural supposition than that he afterwards varied what was uniform at first. The attempts which have been made to account still more particularly for the use of the divine names in these two psalms have entirely failed.—*Alexander.*

How is this diverse use of the divine names to be accounted for? A century has not yet elapsed since the subject first attracted the study of the learned, little more than twenty years since the facts were accurately noted, yet theories not a few have already been elaborated, some feasible, others not feasible at all. The one best known in this country is associated with the name of Dr. Colenso. It is very simple. He has found out that the name which translators, ancient and modern, have been accustomed reverently to veil under the more general title LORD, was *invented*,—say by the prophet Samuel,—shortly before David came to the throne, and that all the earlier Scriptures in which it occurs are spurious or hopelessly interpolated! The older name *Elohim* continued in use, however, for some time, and accordingly prevails in some of the psalms. After a while it gave place entirely to the newer word. Thus the whole difficulty is resolved into an affair of chronology; the *Elohim* psalms are the earlier, the others are the later. A very simple theory, if the facts would only accommodate themselves to it. However, they absolutely refuse to do so. Two may be named out of the hundreds that are available. The song of Deborah in the book of Judges, which is accounted genuine by all critics of every school, celebrates the praises of God by his name *Jehovah;* whereas Ps. lxviii., written long after, and with marked allusions to Deborah's song, uses the other and less sacred title. Moreover, Dr. Colenso's theory obliges him to make some later psalmist, and not David, the writer of Ps. li. A theory which involves such an obligation is self-condemned.

Nevertheless there must be *some* ground for the usage in question. No one who believes in the inspiration of the psalmists can doubt that there must be some wise reason for it. The appropriate use of the divine names in *prayer* is an excellent aid to faith, helping the supplicant "to take encouragement in prayer from God only;" it is no less excellent, we may be sure, in the kindred exercise of *praise.* It is certain that the psalmists did not vary their usage by accident. It could not be by accident that David, after having given forth Ps. xiv. as a Jehovah-psalm, in giving forth a second edition of it substituted the name Elohim. Yet he has done this in Ps. liii. And the same remark applies to Ps. lxx. in relation to the closing verses of Ps. xl. In all this there must have been some object; but what the precise object was it is hard to tell. None of the explanations yet given will solve the whole problem. A partial solution is, however, to be found in the different import of the divine names. *Elohim* is the more general designation, being occasionally applied to angels, to magistrates, to heathen deities; *Jehovah* is the special and peculiar designation expressing God's covenant relation to his own Israel, and is absolutely incommunicable. This obvious diversity of import goes a good way towards explaining the remarkable manner in which the use of the names is varied throughout all the Old Testament Scriptures. Thus it explains the exclusive employment of *Elohim* in Ecclesiastes, a book which, dealing with the problems lying on the border-ground between natural and revealed religion, could not so fitly use the more sacred name. It explains the repeated employment of the same title in Ps. xiv., although it is a Jehovah-psalm. If it does not perfectly explain the existence of a whole book of Elohim-psalms, it at least furnishes a valuable contribution towards the solution of the difficulty.—*Binnie.*

5. *There were they in great fear where no fear was.* The *rebels* who rose up against David's authority, chiefly because they hated his religion, and were instigated by the spirit of persecution, proved on trial very cowardly; for no doubt God was pleased to impress terror on their hearts when there was no adequate danger. Thus the army of Absalom, which encamped against David, was easily routed; numbers fell in the forests, and being left unburied, their bones were scattered; and because God despised the impotent rage of this abandoned party, his servant easily put them to confusion. They were a sort of type of the Jewish persecutors of Christ and his disciples.—*Scott.*

PSALM LIV.

3. *Strangers.* The Chaldee, instead of זרים, strangers, reads זדים, proud, which Luther also follows. This reading has partly proceeded from an unseasonable comparison of the parallel passage, Ps. lxxxvi. 14, in which זרים is intentionally changed into זדים, and partly from the difficulty which *strangers* presents, when compared with the superscription, according to which the enemies are domestic ones. This difficulty is legitimately removed by the remark, that David here figuratively designates his countrymen as strangers, because they who were united with him by so many ties, his "friends," and his "brethren," according to the law of God, in their behaviour toward him were not different from strangers. Precisely the same figurative representation occurs also in Ps. cxx. 5, where the psalmist, heavily oppressed by his countrymen, complains that he dwelt in Mesech and Kedar, heathenish tribes, *q.d.* among heathens and Turks. Analogous also are the numerous passages in which Israelites either in general are described as aliens or heathens, or are coupled with the name of a particular outlandish people, in order to mark their *degeneracy* and *ungodliness.* The transition to the figurative use of זרים was the more easy, as it almost invariably carries the related idea of *hostile*, comp. Gesen. *Thes.*, who is so candid as to admit here this figurative use.—*Hengstenberg.*

4. *Behold! God is mine helper.* Such language as this may show us that David did not direct his prayers at random into the air, but offered them in the exercise of a lively faith. There is much force in the demonstrative adverb. He points as it were with the finger, to that God who stood at his side to defend him; and was not this an amazing illustration of the power with which faith can surmount all obstacles, and glance in a moment from the depths of despair to the very throne of God? He was a fugitive amongst the dens of the earth, and even there in hazard of his life—how then could he speak of God as being near to him? He was pressed down to the very mouth of the grave; and how could he recognize the gracious presence of God? He was trembling in the momentary expectation of being destroyed; and how is it possible that he can triumph in the certain hope that divine help will presently be extended to him? In numbering God amongst his defenders, we must not suppose that he assigns him a mere common rank amongst the men who supported his cause, which would have been highly derogatory to his glory. He means that God took part with those, such as Jonathan and others, who were interested in his welfare. These might be few in number, possessed of little power, and cast down with fears; but he believed that, under the guidance and protection of the Almighty, they would prove superior to his enemies; or perhaps we may view him as referring in the words to his complete destitution of all human defenders, and asserting that the help of God would abundantly compensate for all.—*Calvin.*

7. *Mine eye hath seen his desire upon mine enemies.* When our cause is the cause of God, and there is full sympathy with him in the triumph of right, this language is justified. Both private parties, however, and nations are in some danger, when they suppose their circumstances to be analogous with those of David. Prof. Alexander's illustration here is therefore in better taste than that of our author. "*Mine eye has looked or gazed*, with an implication of delight, or at least of acquiescence, which is commonly conveyed by this construction. This kind of satisfaction in the execution of God's threat-

enings is sinful only when combined with selfish malignity. Apart from this corrupt admixture, it is inseparable from conformity of will and coincidence of judgment with God. The same kind and degree of acquiescence which is felt by holy angels in heaven may surely be expressed by saints on earth, especially in their collective capacity as a church, in whose name the psalmist is here speaking, and not merely in his own or that of any other individual."

PSALM LV.

8. *I would hasten my escape from the windy storm and tempest.* Such was the language of David—and it may be the language of any other good man in the depth of distress. But is it allowable and proper? There is no perfection here; and there is nothing concerning which we should indulge more tenderness of censure than hasty expressions uttered under the pressure of pain or grief. Perhaps it was to prevent our severity here that the cases of Job and Jeremiah are recorded, both of whom, though eminent in piety, cursed the day of their birth. The Scripture is not harsh upon them; and it is observable, that when James refers to one of these bitterly complaining sufferers, he only says, "Ye have heard of the patience of Job." They who have never been in a state of peculiar distress know little of the feelings of human nature under it. But there are others who can respond to the invitation of sympathy, "Pity me, pity me, O ye my friends, for the hand of God hath touched me!" And the Father of mercies knows our frame, and remembers that we are dust. We are not required to choose suffering for its own sake; or to be indifferent to ease and deliverance. Our Saviour himself had not that fortitude which mocks at pain; but that which felt deeply; and yet submitted. With strong cryings and tears he prayed, "Father, if it be possible, let this cup pass from me: nevertheless not my will, but thine be done." But what allows of excuse, truth does not require us to commend. It was his infirmity that induced David to long for death, to hasten his escape from the stormy wind and tempest; and an old writer tells us it would have been more honourable for him to have asked for the strength of an ox to *bear* his trials, than for the wings of a dove to *flee* from them.—*Jay.*

12-15. *It was not an enemy,* &c. Ahithophel's treachery was peculiarly distressing to David; and it was the more painful for being wholly unsuspected. So far from having been an avowed enemy who now took occasion to reproach him and to exult in his calamities, or menace his life, Ahithophel had been David's counsellor and bosom friend, and had been treated by him as an equal, or as one of his own rank; he had also been his chosen and pleasing companion in the exercise of religion and in pious conversation. Yet this very man, without any affront or previous quarrel, became an apostate and a traitor; and gave Absalom the most malicious and infernal counsel imaginable!—Thus Christ was betrayed by one whom he had honoured as a companion, a disciple, and an apostle; who resembled Ahithophel in his crimes and in his doom: for both were speedily overtaken by divine vengeance in the same dreadful manner. This was foretold by David concerning Ahithophel, and by Jesus concerning Judas; for the words are in the future, and more naturally signify a prediction than an imprecation.—"The sudden destruction of Korah, Dathan, and Abiram, who, for stirring up rebellion against Moses and Aaron, 'went down alive into the pit,' seems here alluded to, as the grand representation of the manner in which the bottomless pit shall one day shut her mouth for ever upon all the impenitent enemies of the true King of Israel and the great High-priest of our profession" (Horne).—*Scott.*

PSALM LVI.

According to the inscription, composed when David was detained in Gath by the Philistines. But on neither occasion when he visited Gath does the history inform us of any such detention, 1 Sam. xxi. xxvii. xxix. Hengstenberg, indeed, and Delitzsch suppose that some seizure or imprisonment is implied in the words he "feigned himself mad *in their hands;*" and the expression at the beginning of chap. xxii., "David therefore departed thence, and escaped to the cave of Adullam," may imply that he had been subjected to some confinement. Hupfeld concludes from the absence of anything in the history corresponding to the title of the psalm, that the title is not to be trusted. Yet it is perhaps more likely on this very account that it rests upon some ancient tradition. A modern compiler would have endeavoured to make the title square better with the history.—*Perowne.*

Only from the poet himself could such a poetical superscription be expected; it was precisely David's custom to prefix such emblematical superscriptions to his psalms; and every one of the very peculiar words is found again in the Davidic psalms—*the dove* in Ps. lv., which, certainly not by accident, our psalm immediately follows—the superscription was to derive its explanation from it,—*the being dumb* in Ps. lviii., *the far-dwelling* in Ps. lxv., *the secret* in Ps. xvi.—The second part of the superscription is to be regarded as an explanation of the first part. The Philistines are the "far-dwelling;" David seized by them, "the dumb dove." The history is given in 1 Sam. xxi. David fled, as he no longer found security in his fatherland, to the Philistines. Alone there he waited for his new danger. He, the conqueror of Goliath, was conducted as a formidable enemy before the king, and only by an artifice delivered his life.—*Hengstenberg.*

4. *In God I will praise his word.* We must understand by the word of God, all his promises, which had hitherto been given to the psalmist through the law (comp. Ps. cxix. 25), through Samuel, through internal communications during his earlier history. This word of God, and God himself, who had therein promised to be his God, the psalmist extols as his firm shield, which is sufficient to protect him against the whole world. *John Arnd:* "As Saul and the potentates of this world boast of their hosts of war, their thousands of men, and their munition, I will glory in God's word and promise, which are my warlike force, my fortress, and support; let them trust in their chariots and waggons, we shall think of the name of the Lord." The psalmist calls man flesh by way of contempt, because where there is corporeity there is no real strength,—comp. Is. xxxi. 3, "The Egyptians are men and not God, their horses are flesh and not spirit;" chap. xl. 6, *John Arnd:* "He sets against each other the mighty God and impotent flesh, which is as grass and as the flower of the field."—*Hengstenberg.*

8. *Put thou my tears into thy bottle.* In the Roman tombs are found small bottles (usually called *lachrymatories*) of glass or pottery, but most commonly glass, and of various forms, but generally with long narrow necks. These are commonly supposed to have contained tears shed by the surviving friends of the deceased, and to have been deposited in the sepulchres as memorials of affection and distress. We might very well suppose that the present text alludes to such a custom; and it would therefore imply that it existed very anciently in the East, and particularly among the Hebrews. It must not, however, be concealed that the use assigned to these phials is a modern conjecture, and that there is no trace of such a custom in ancient writings or sculptures; whence Shoëfflin, Paciaudi, and others, were rather led to conclude that these phials were intended to contain the perfumes used in sprinkling the funeral pile. This is not the place to discuss such a question; but we may add that the representation of one or two eyes which is observed upon some of these vessels, is a circumstance in favour of the common opinion. Whatever be concluded on this point, we have little doubt that the psalmist does refer to some custom then existing of putting tears in small bottles, particularly as there are still some traces of such a usage in the East. Thus, in the annual lamentations of the Persians for the slaughtered sons of Ali, their tears are copiously excited by passionate discourses and tragical recitations. When at the height of their grief, a priest sometimes goes round to each person and collects the tears with a piece of cotton, from which he presses them into a bottle, preserving them with the greatest care. This seems a striking illustration of the present text, which takes its allusion from one person putting the tears of another into a bottle. The Persians believe that there is a peculiar virtue in the tears shed on the occasion mentioned; so that persons at the point of death have revived when a drop has been administered to them. This is the reason why they are so carefully collected.—*Pictorial Bible.*

God will not be unmindful of our tears and sorrows. O no! He puts them in his bottle. He registers them in his book. Trials will bring tears. "But," says Arnd, "here lies a powerful consolation, that God gathers up such tears, and puts them in his bottle, just as one would pour precious wine into a flagon, so precious and dear are such tears before God, and God lays them up as a treasure in the heavens; and if we think that all such tears are lost, lo! God hath preserved them for us a treasure in the heavens, with which we shall be richly consoled in that day," Ps. cxxvi. 5. *Calvin:* "We may surely believe that if God bestows such honour upon the tears of his saints, he must number every drop of their blood. Tyrants may burn their flesh and their bones, but the blood remains to cry aloud for vengeance; and intervening ages can never erase what has been written in the register of God's remembrance."—*Plumer.*

PSALM LVII.

Al-taschith. Few expressions in the Psalter have proved so perplexing as the words *Al-taschith*, i.e. *Destroy not*, which occur in the superscriptions of the three Davidic psalms lvii. lviii. lix., and also in that of Ps. lxxv. The one main feature common to these four particular psalms is that they all imprecate or foretell divine destruction upon the wicked. The "destroy not" cannot therefore well be any part of a prayer to God to spare: it is more probably part of some maxim which David had laid down for himself to observe that he would not take the work of destruction into his own hands, but would await the divine vengeance that must in due time overtake his enemies. It is easily conceivable that some unrecorded incident in David's life may have originally suggested these words, which afterwards continually recurred to his thoughts as a sort of motto for his behaviour, and which, in the spirit of simple faith, we might almost say of playfulness, he perpetuated in the superscriptions of his psalms, as a testimony that his utterances of woe against his persecutors arose from no feelings of private malice or hatred. What, for example, if in one of the earlier interviews in which Jonathan warned David of his father's purpose to kill him, he should have used words similar to those he is related to have used in 1 Sam. xx. 15, and should have said, "Destroy not thou, my father, even though thou believe that God will one day destroy him for thy sake?" What if the words, "destroy not," with some such import as this, should have been once employed as a watchword between Jonathan and David? These are of course merely imaginary instances of the numberless ways in which the words "destroy not," with a particular meaning and particular associations attached, might by some trivial circumstance be indelibly impressed upon David's mind. And it may be observed that these very words were repeated by David to Abishai, when on a subsequent occasion the latter wished to kill Saul, whom they had discovered by night unguarded and asleep in his camp in the wilderness of Ziph.—*Thrupp.*

Ps. lvii. may be referred to as exemplifying a somewhat different aspect of the psalmist's exercise of soul during these years of peril and unrest. We still hear in it a cry for mercy and an appeal to the just judgment of God, but the thing that principally strikes a thoughtful reader is the unwavering confidence expressed in the divine faithfulness. David's faith, soaring above the clouds and tempest, bathes itself in the light of God's countenance.—"I will praise thee among the peoples; I will sing psalms unto thee among the nations." These are remarkable words. They show that David from his early days was filled with the presentiment that he was inditing songs in which not Israel only, but the Gentiles, far and near, would one day praise the God of Abraham. How remarkably has the anticipation been fulfilled! David now "sings to God among the nations," in this very psalm which so many nations have already learned to use.—*Binnie.*

8. *I myself will awake early.* Strictly translated, this clause contains a bold but beautiful poetical conception, that of awakening the dawn instead of being awakened by it, in other words, preventing or anticipating it by early praises. In like manner Ovid says the crowing of the cock *evocat auroram.* We thus obtain the same sense in a far more striking form than is expressed by the inexact and prosaic version, *I will awake early.* The intransitive sense given to the verb and the adverbial sense given to the noun are both without sufficient authority in usage. From this verse some have inferred that the psalm was expressly designed to be an even-song; but he does not say, I will do thus to-morrow. The meaning is rather that he will do it daily. The summons to the harp and lyre may be understood as implying that they have long slept without occasion for such praise as they are now to utter.—*Alexander.*

9. *I will praise thee, O Lord, among the people.* These intimations of mercy in store for the Gentiles do not lie quite on the surface of the early Scriptures; and it is likely that in every generation there would be many among the children of Israel who overlooked them, and, like the Pharisees, took occasion from the covenant with Abraham to despise the Gentiles, instead of learning from it to take an affectionate and prayerful interest in them, and to look forward in hope to a time when they should be enrolled among the fearers of the Lord. But we must not do the Old Testament church the injustice of supposing that all its members were so blind and carnal. Here, as in so many other particulars, the psalms enable us to vindicate the faith of the ancient saints. They show that the intimations we have pointed out were neither overlooked nor forgotten. The church's *missionary* work, it is true, did not begin under the former dispensation; nor indeed did it begin till the day of Pentecost; for even Christ himself was not sent save to the house of Israel. Till the full time came for the great Sacrifice to be offered up and the Comforter to be sent forth, there was no commission given to the church to go into all nations, preaching repentance and the remission of sins. The Hebrew church was neither called nor qualified to be a missionary society. But it never ceased to desire and hope for the conversion of the nations. This is seen in those passages in which the psalmists betray a consciousness that they shall one day have all the world for auditors. How boldly does David exclaim, "I will praise thee, O Lord, among the peoples; I will sing unto thee among the nations," Ps. lvii. 9. In the same spirit a later psalmist summons the church to lift up her voice, so that all the nations may hear her recital of the Lord's mighty acts: "O give thanks unto the LORD; call upon his name: make known his deeds among the peoples," Ps. cv. 1. The full import of this class of texts is often hidden from the English reader by the circumstance that our translators have hardly ever used the word *people* in its plural form. Twice in the Revelation they venture to write *peoples;* everywhere else the singular form has to do duty for both numbers; so that in not a few passages the sense is greatly obscured to those who have no access either to the original or to other versions. In the Psalms, in particular, the mention of the Gentiles is more frequent than the English reader is made aware of. It is to be observed, moreover, that in addition to this strain of indirect prediction, the conversion of the world is articulately celebrated in many glorious psalms. Indeed, so numerous are these, and so generally distributed over the centuries between David and Ezra, that it would seem that at no time during the long history of inspired psalmody, did the Spirit cease to indite new songs in which the children of Zion might give utterance to their world-embracing hopes.—*Binnie.*

11. *Be thou exalted, O God.* The same word which he had used, ver. 5, to sum up his prayers in, he here uses again (and no vain repetition) to sum up his praises in; "Lord, I desire to exalt thy name, and that all the creatures may exalt it; but what can the best of us do towards it? Lord, take the work into thine own hands; do it thyself, *be thou exalted, O God.* In the praises of the church triumphant, thou art exalted to the heavens, and in the praises of the church militant, thy glory is throughout all the earth; but thou art above all the blessing and praise of both, Neh. ix. 5, and therefore, Lord, exalt thyself *above the heavens,* and *above all the earth: Father, glorify thine own name: thou hast glorified it, glorify it yet again."—Henry.*

PSALM LVIII.

3. *The wicked are estranged from the womb.* What makes human corruption so dreadful is the fact of its growing out of original sin, and consequently it has its root in the inmost depths of the heart. Those with whom nature is allowed free scope to develop itself as it will, and who shut out grace from access to their heart, must attain to a ripeness in sinning which would be incredible if nature were originally and still predominantly good. The opposition is not between those who have been corrupt from their mother's womb, and who are not so now, but between those in whom the corruption common to all has uninterruptedly developed itself, and those in whom the development has been hemmed in and broken through. That the inborn depravity is quite a general one, extending over the whole family of man, appears from

Gen. viii. 21, the confession of David himself in Ps. li. 6, and Job xiv. 4. *Arnd:* "The godless are wayward from their mother's womb, from their childhood upwards there is nothing good in them; the godly, although they also are conceived and born in sin, yet live in the new birth, in daily repentance." —*Hengstenberg.*

4. *They are like the deaf adder that stoppeth her ear.* What the ineffectual charms are in reference to the excessively poisonous serpent, that are with the venomous and wicked man the prayers and entreaties of those who suffer injury from him and his friends, as an example of which we have only to think of David's representations to Saul, and Jonathan's intercessions, both so persuasive, that their fruitlessness presents to our view the wickedness of Saul, which is a reflection of man's generally, as a deep abyss. Not only, however, does the resemblance hold in regard to such prayers and entreaties, but also to the admonitions of the servants of God, and last of all, to the reproofs and warnings which God himself brings to bear on men through their conscience. How powerfully these resounded in the dark soul of Saul, may be seen in the conviction often uttered by him, that David, upheld by God, would escape his persecutions and gain the day. But although his conscience called to him aloud that his striving was wrong and to no purpose, the strength of wickedness in him was so great, that he could not desist from it. The subject in יאטם is not the adder (commonly, "which stops its ear"), but the wicked. The *stopping* requires hands, and what is already deaf by nature has no need to stop. It is just by means of stopping that the wicked make themselves like the deaf adder. *Arnd:* "As we see in the history of the holy martyr Stephen. When he made his confession before the ecclesiastical council at Jerusalem, and said, 'Lo, I see the heavens opened, and the Son of man standing on the right hand of God,' to the Jewish prelates that was so insufferable a testimony, that in order to retain their poison, they stopped their ears, and cried aloud."—*Hengstenberg.*

PSALM LIX.

1. *Deliver me,* &c. David prays to be delivered out of the hands of his enemies, and that their cruel designs against him might be defeated. "*Deliver me from mine enemies, O my God;* thou art *God,* and canst deliver me; *my* God, under whose protection I have put myself, and thou hast promised to be a God all-sufficient, and therefore, in honour and faithfulness, thou wilt deliver me. Set me on high out of the reach of the power and malice of them that rise up against me, and above the fear of it. Let me be safe, and see myself so, safe and easy, safe and satisfied. Oh deliver me and save me!" He cries out as one ready to perish, and that had his eye to God only for salvation and deliverance. He prays, ver. 4, "*Awake to help me;* take cognizance of my case, behold that with an eye of pity, and exert thy power for my relief." Thus the disciples in the storm awoke Christ, saying, *Master, save us, we perish.* And thus earnestly should we pray daily to be defended and delivered from our spiritual enemies, the temptations of Satan and the corruptions of our own hearts, which war against our spiritual life.—*Henry.*

7. *Swords are in their lips.* This and similar expressions of Scripture bring to mind the strong poetical phrase of our great dramatic poet, "I'll speak daggers to her." See Ps. lv. 21. —*Pictorial Bible.*

11, 13. *Slay them not.*—*Consume them in wrath that they may not be.* David may seem to contradict himself in praying for the utter destruction of his enemies, when immediately before he had expressed his desire that they might not be exterminated at once. What else could he mean when he asks that God would consume them in wrath, but that he would cut them off suddenly, and not by a gradual and slower process of punishment? But he evidently refers in what he says here to a different point of time, and this removes any apparent inconsistency, for he prays that when they had been set up for a sufficient period as an example, they might eventually be devoted to destruction. It was customary with the victorious Roman generals, first to lead the captives which had been kept for the day of triumph through the city, and afterwards, upon reaching the capital, to give them over to the lictors for execution. Now David prays that when God had, in a similar manner, reserved his enemies for an interval sufficient to illustrate his triumph, he would upon this consign them to summary punishment. The two things are not at all inconsistent; first, that the divine judgments should be lengthened out through a considerable period, to secure their being remembered better, and that then, upon sufficient evidence being given to the world of the certainty with which the wicked are subjected in the displeasure of God to the slower process of destruction, he should in due time bring them forth to final execution, the better to awake, by such a demonstration of his power, the minds of those who may be more secure than others, or less affected by witnessing moderate inflictions of punishment He adds, accordingly, *that they may know, even to the ends of the earth, that God ruleth in Jacob.* Some would insert the copulative particle, reading, *that they may know that God rules in Jacob, and in all the nations of the world*, an interpretation which I do not approve, and which does violence to the sense. The allusion is to the condign nature of the judgment, which would be such that the report of it would reach the remotest regions, and strike salutary terror into the minds even of their benighted and godless inhabitants. He was more especially anxious that God should be recognized as ruling *in the church*, it being preposterous that the place where his throne was erected should present such an aspect of confusion as converted his temple into a den of thieves.—*Calvin.*

15. *Wander up and down for meat.* Dogs may in England do this for amusement, when their essential wants are provided for by their masters; but in the East, where they have no particular masters, they are obliged to do so from necessity. Retaining much of their native habits, as beasts of prey, they do this chiefly by night, as the text intimates, being in general dozy and inactive in the daytime. This contributes to render their presence in an oriental city more formidable, to passengers, at night than by day. In their night prowlings they effectually clear the streets of whatever offal or carrion may be in them; and their want of squeamish appetites is then, as well as by day, evinced to an extent which would alone well account for all the abhorrent allusions which the Scriptures contain. They refuse scarcely anything (except crude vegetables) capable of mastication; and yet are for ever lean, hungry, and unsatisfied: which seems to intimate that the dog was so much intended for and suited to complete domestication, that even while in a position more favourable than that which any other undomesticated beast obtains, it is only in fellowship with man that he can arrive at a prosperous condition of existence.—*Pictorial Bible.*

PSALM LX.

The question has been raised whether of the two should be regarded as the speaker in this psalm—Israel, or Israel's king: in other words, whether the psalm should be treated as strictly national, or as mainly personal. The latter is probably the correct view. The plural pronoun of the opening and concluding verses unquestionably refers to the whole community; but the *I* of the central verses belongs to the king alone. In proof of this, it may be observed that all the other psalms, from Ps. li. to lxiv., are personal; that there is thus no other instance of a national psalm among those Davidic compositions which were excluded by David himself from the first book of the Psalter; and that it is not easy to understand on what principle he should have omitted to consign to the permanent and immediate service of the sanctuary a psalm to which he had given utterance in the name of the whole nation.

But, furthermore, reference is made in ver. 6 to a certain special announcement or promise on God's part. This announcement cannot well be any other than the first part of the message from God to David by the prophet Nathan, 2 Sam. vii. 8–11; which message would appear to have been delivered not long before the wars in the midst of which this psalm was written. With the purport of that message the contents of the psalm sufficiently agree. It had been previously known that David, as king of God's people Israel, was to deliver them out of the hand of the Philistines, and out of the hand of all their enemies, 2 Sam. iii. 18. God now more formally declared that by the hand of his servant David he would give his people Israel rest, that he would plant them that they might dwell in a place of their own, where the children of wickedness should no more afflict them. And therefore, in accordance with this announcement, David's prayer in the psalm is, "That thy beloved (ones) may be delivered; save with thy right hand, and hear me;" *i.e.* "Hear and help me, inasmuch as thou hast chosen me to be the instrument of deliverance to thy beloved." Nor, indeed, can the "banner" which God had given to them that feared him, "to be displayed because of the truth," well be aught else than the Davidic sovereignty, now rendered permanent through the promise given by Nathan, and therefore the sure pledge of the salvation of Israel. Hence such passages as these in the prophecies of Isaiah: "In that day there shall be a root of Jesse, which shall stand for an ensign of the people;" and, "Behold, I have given him (David, *i.e.* Christ, the representative of the Davidic house) for a witness to the people, a leader and commander to the people."

Ver. 1–5 form the opening, ver. 9-12 the concluding portion of the psalm; the central and prominent portion is ver. 6–8, consisting of three verses of three lines each. The opening verses delineate the state of depression hitherto; the concluding verses contain the supplication for help; the centre of the psalm is reserved for the announcement of God's promise, and the anticipation, in glorious detail, of its fulfilment.

And here, as unity at home would be essential to the achievement of victory abroad, the king first speaks in ver. 6, 7 of the submission of all Israel to his sway. In ver. 6 Shechem apparently indicates the districts to the west, Succoth those to the east of the Jordan; or should it be urged that Succoth itself was situated to the west of that river, then Shechem may denote the mountain-range of the land of inheritance, and Succoth its level plains. Both Shechem and Succoth are mentioned in the history of Jacob's return from Mesopotamia. He built, as Hengstenberg observes, a house at the latter place, and an altar at the former. In ver. 7 the territories to the east of Jordan are again denoted by the names Gilead and Manasseh; while Ephraim appears as the representative of the central tribes. The Ephraimites were especially strong in point of numbers. In the blessing of Moses it had been said of Ephraim, "His horns are like the horns of unicorns; with them he shall push the people together to the ends of the earth;" hence in the present psalm Ephraim is appropriately described as the "strength of head" of Israel's sovereign. On the other hand, Judah, the royal and dominant tribe, is the king's "staff of authority;" for the staff was not to depart from between Judah's feet till Shiloh came; and in regard to David, it was the tribe of Judah alone that had, immediately upon Saul's death, anointed him king in Hebron, and acknowledged his authority, while Ishbosheth was reigning over the remaining tribes. But at length all Israel had been for a while reconciled; and at the head of a united nation David was gone forth to subdue the surrounding foes of God's people, and to put an end to that state of depression in which Israel had remained during the reign of Saul, and to which reference is made in the beginning of the present psalm.

And in the prosecution of this career of victory there is meted out to each foe his own appropriate recompense. Moab, the descendant and representative of unholy lust, Moab, who had at Shittim enticed Israel to impurity, becomes at David's hands a mere receptacle of filth. Edom, the proudest and most malicious enemy of Israel, is in contumely reduced to the most menial servitude: or if the casting out of the shoe be regarded as the customary token of the appropriation of an estate, then Edom, who had profanely despised his birthright, beholds the inheritance to which birthright is the title ravished from him. And Philistia, the warrior-foe, who had so long oppressed God's people, and so often triumphed over them in the battle-field, is now at last, in bitter irony, bidden triumph if she can. A stronger than she is come upon her to overcome her, taking from her all the armour wherein she trusted, and dividing her spoils.

It is not without reason that we venture to expound the words of this psalm by those of our Saviour. For as the banner of ver. 4, which was to be "displayed because of the truth," is evidently contemplated in the psalm as something permanent, it is certain that David could not have uttered the psalm in his own individual person so much as in the person of his lineage, and more especially of that Great Representative of his house, the Lion of the tribe of Judah, who, having trodden the wine-press alone, should come from Edom, with dyed garments from Bozrah, speaking in righteousness, mighty to save; and who, himself the author of a new and better covenant, and with the whole of the people of the new covenant united under his sway, should go forth conquering and to conquer, and should reign till all enemies were put under his feet. The Christian church, in repeating this psalm, glories, as in Ps. xviii., in the triumphs of her eternal King; and learns at the same time for herself the important lesson that it is by her own internal unity, and the united obedience of her several members to the true sovereignty of Christ, that she will best prepare herself for a career of victory over her heathen foes. —*Thrupp.*

PSALM LXI.

The question may be asked, whether David composed the psalm for any particular occasion, or merely for his own comfort, and that of his successors on the throne, in disastrous times, and for the purpose of confirming the courage of his subjects. In favour of the first view, we have the clause, "from the ends of the earth," which would seem to intimate that the psalmist was at the time in *exile*, and that therefore the psalm must have been composed during the rebellion of Absalom, when David was beyond Jordan. Comp. Ps. xlii. 6. This special occasion, however, must not lead us to lose sight of the *general* reference. It could only be by keeping this reference in view that David issued the psalm for public use. The psalm, even in our days, has its complete use, inasmuch as the promises in 2 Sam. vii. have undoubtedly their complete fulfilment in Christ. Generally, whenever the kingdom of Christ is in danger, we may, in addition to other considerations, plead with God as the psalmist does, on the ground also of this particular promise which he there made.—*Hengstenberg.*

6. *Thou wilt prolong the king's life,* &c. David cannot be considered as using these words of gratulation with an exclusive reference to himself. It is true that he lived to an extreme old age, and died full of days, leaving the kingdom in a settled condition, and in the hands of his son, who succeeded him; but he did not exceed the period of one man's life, and the greater part of it was spent in continual dangers and anxieties. There can be no doubt, therefore, that the series of years, and even ages, of which he speaks, extends prospectively to the coming of Christ, it being the very condition of the kingdom, as I have often remarked, that God maintained them as one people under one head, or, when scattered, united them again. The same succession still subsists in reference to ourselves. Christ must be viewed as living in his members to the end of the world. To this Isaiah alludes when he says, "Who shall declare his generation or age?" Words in which he predicts that the church would survive through all ages, notwithstanding the incessant danger of destruction to which it is exposed through the attacks of its enemies, and the many storms assailing it. So here David foretells the uninterrupted succession of the kingdom down to the time of Christ.—*Calvin.*

6, 7. These words must be applied to Him of whom it was said by the angel, "The Lord God shall give unto him the throne of his father David, and he shall reign over the house of Jacob for ever, and of his kingdom there shall be no end," Luke i. 32. The ancient church prayed for "his" exaltation and glory, under those of his representative; nay, the Chaldee paraphrast expounds this passage of Messiah only: "Thou shalt add days to the days of King Messias; his years shall be as the generation of this world, and of the world to come." Nor can a better paraphrase be easily devised.—*Horne.*

PSALM LXII.

5. *My soul, wait thou only upon God.* Calvin renders, *Nevertheless, my soul, be thou silent before God*, and remarks that "here there may appear to be a slight inconsistency, inasmuch as he encourages himself to do what he had already declared himself to have done. His soul was silent before God; and where the necessity of this new silence, as if still under agitation of spirit? Here it is to be remembered that our minds can never be expected to reach such perfect composure as shall preclude every inward feeling of disquietude, but are at the best as the sea before a light breeze, fluctuating sensibly, though not swollen into billows. It is not without a struggle that the saint can compose his mind; and we can very well understand how David should enjoin more perfect submission upon a spirit which was already submissive, urging upon himself further advancement in this grace of silence till he had mortified every carnal inclination, and thoroughly subjected himself to the

will of God. How often, besides, will Satan renew the disquietudes which seemed to be effectually expelled? Creatures of such instability, and liable to be borne away by a thousand different influences, we need to be confirmed again and again. I repeat that there is no reason to be surprised, though David here calls upon himself a second time to preserve that silence before God which he might already appear to have attained; for, amidst the disturbing motions of the flesh, perfect composure is what we never reach. The danger is that when new winds of trouble spring up, we lose that inward tranquillity which we enjoyed; and hence the necessity of improving the example of David by establishing ourselves in it more and more. He adds the ground of his silence. He had no immediate response from God, but he confidently hoped in him. *My expectation*, he says, *is from God*. Never, as if he had said, will he frustrate the patient waiting of his saints; doubtless my silence shall meet with its reward; I shall restrain myself, and not make that false haste which will only retard my deliverance."

11, 12. *Power belongeth unto God . . . also . . . mercy*. The man who disciplines himself to the contemplation of these two attributes, which ought never to be dissociated in our minds from the idea of God, is certain to stand erect and immovable under the fiercest assaults of temptation; while, on the other hand, by losing sight of the all-sufficiency of God (which we are too apt to do), we lay ourselves open to be overwhelmed in the first encounter. The world's opinion of God is, that he sits in heaven an idle and unconcerned spectator of events which are passing. Need we wonder that men tremble under every casualty when they thus believe themselves to be the sport of blind chance? There can be no security felt unless we satisfy ourselves of the truth of a divine superintendence, and can commit our lives, and all that we have, to the hands of God. The first thing which we must look to is his power, that we may have a thorough conviction of his being a sure refuge to such as cast themselves upon his care. With this there must be conjoined confidence in his mercy, to prevent those anxious thoughts which might otherwise rise in our minds. These may suggest the doubt, What though God govern the world? does it follow that he will concern himself about such unworthy objects as ourselves? There is an obvious reason, then, for the psalmist coupling these two things together, his power and his clemency. They are the two wings wherewith we fly upwards to heaven; the two pillars on which we rest, and may defy the surges of temptation. Does danger, in short, spring up from any quarter, then just let us call to remembrance that divine power which can bid away all harms, and as this sentiment prevails in our minds, our troubles cannot fail to fall prostrate before it. Why should we fear? how can we be afraid, when the God who covers us with the shadow of his wings, is the same who rules the universe with his nod, holds in secret chains the devil and all the wicked, and effectually overrules their designs and intrigues?—*Calvin*.

PSALM LXIII.

It may have been near the Dead Sea, on his way to the ford of Jordan, that the psalmist first sang this song. It is a psalm first heard by David's faithful ones in the wilderness of Judah; but truly a psalm for every godly man who in the dry world-wilderness can sing, "All my springs are in thee"—a psalm for David—a psalm for David's Son—a psalm for the church in every age—a psalm for every member of the church in the weary land! What assurance, what vehement desire, what soul-filling delight in God, in God alone—in God the only fountain of living water amid a boundless wilderness! Hope, too, has its visions here; for it sees the ungodly perish, ver. 8-10, and *the King* on the throne surrounded by a company who swear allegiance to Jehovah. Hope sees for itself what Is. lxiv.16 describes—every mouth "swearing by the God of truth;" and what Rev. xxi. 27 has foretold, the mouth of "liars" closed for ever—all who sought other gods, and trusted to other saviours, gone for ever. And when we read all this as spoken of Christ, how much does every verse become enhanced? *His* thirst for God! *His* vision of God! *His* estimate of God's loving-kindness! *His* soul satisfied! *His* mouth full of praise! *His* soul following hard after God!

"*O God, thou art my El*"—mighty one. Thou art my omnipotence. It is this God he still seeks. The כֵּן of ver. 2 and of ver. 4 is interesting. In ver. 2 the force of it is this, "No wonder that I so thirst for thee; no wonder that my first thoughts at morning are toward thee: no wonder that my very flesh longeth for thee! Who would not that has seen what I have seen? *So* have I gazed on thee in the sanctuary, seeing thy power and thy glory!" The "so" is like 2 Pet. i. 17, "*such* a voice!" And then if the past has been thus exquisitely blessed, my prospects for the future are not less so. I see illimitable bliss coming in as a tide; "*so will I bless thee while I have being!*" ver. 4. Yes; in ages to come, as well as in many a happy moment on earth, my soul shall be satiated as with marrow and with fatness! And when ver. 7 shows us the soul under the shadow of God's wings, rejoicing, we may say, it is not only like as "the bird sheltered from the heat of the sun amid the rich foliage sings its merry note," but it is the soul reposing there as if entering the cloud of glory, like Moses and Elias.

O world! come and see *the Righteous One finding water-springs in God.—A. A. Bonar.*

Ps. lxiii. is a sunny one, although it comes from the darkest period of David's life. It embalms for the solace of God's people the sentiments that filled the psalmist's heart when Absalom's revolt drove him into the wilderness of Judah. In the day of his distress his soul turns to God as his true portion, and he finds ineffable enjoyment in communing with him. How deeply does the psalmist realize the presence of God—of a personal God—to whom he can speak, whom his heart can trust! How entirely is he persuaded that he may behold, and has often beheld, God's power and glory; and that this beholding of "the beauty of the Lord" is the proper felicity of his soul. It ought not to be thought to derogate from the sincerity or value of this profession of faith, or of the similar professions uttered in the psalms formerly cited, that they were elicited by sharp afflictions and temptations. When we are surrounded with the lights of a city, the stars are unheeded; but when those nearer lights are extinguished, the stars shine out and fill the eye with a superior delight. It is just so with God's people. In a prosperous time earthly enjoyments are apt so to occupy the thoughts and affections as to turn them aside from God. He is wont accordingly to send on his people afflictions and temptations in order to drive them in upon their proper portion, and thus to fill their souls with the deep and tranquil enjoyment which it alone yields.—*Binnie.*

The psalm is aptly described by Clauss as "a precious confession of a soul thirsting after God and his grace, and finding itself quickened through inward communion with him, and which knows how to commit its outward lot also into his hand." Its lesson is, that the consciousness of communion with God in trouble is the sure pledge of deliverance. This is the peculiar fountain of consolation which is opened up to the sufferer in the psalm. The Berleb. Bible describes it as a psalm "which proceeds from a spirit really in earnest. It was the favourite psalm of M. Schade, the famous preacher in Berlin, which he daily prayed with such earnestness and appropriation to himself that it was impossible to hear it without emotion." —*Hengstenberg.*

1. *A dry and thirsty land*, &c. The more recent expositors consider the residence in the wilderness and the being weary as a mere *figure*, descriptive of a miserable condition. This in itself is possible; but the parallel passage in Samuel shows that we must abide by the literal rendering. The particular feature, however, is not to be viewed by itself, but as symptomatic and descriptive of the whole condition in which the psalmist was placed. For this it was singularly suited: a king who could not get even a drink of water to quench his thirst! All human fountains of consolation and happiness were dried up to the psalmist. But he thirsts all the more earnestly after the divine fountain which still remained open to him. It is by this that he is known as a child of God. When the children of the world are in a dry land, and are wearied and without water, the last remains of any desire after God disappear from their souls. But real piety in proportion to the severity of personal suffering becomes all the more intense in its longings after God. By the extent to which a man in severe sufferings can say, "I seek thee," &c., may he decide on the state of his soul. —*Hengstenberg.*

PSALM LXV.

The *object* of the psalm is announced in the concluding verse. It should be sung when "the flocks are covered with lambs, and the valleys are clothed with corn." Hence the whole, from ver. 1–8, is to be considered as an *introduction*. We are led to the same result, by observing that it is only the goodness of God, as seen in the blessings of harvest, that is dwelt upon at length, while everything else is touched upon briefly and slightly; that the whole psalm ends with such a special delineation without returning to those general views with which it opened; and finally, that the ninth verse, with which the description of harvest begins, is of such disproportionate length as to show that in it the psalmist enters for the first time upon his proper subject. . . .

Although the psalm refers to the *harvest*, yet it is incorrect to maintain that it is peculiarly a song of thanksgiving for harvest, and especially to suppose that it was sung at the passover, on the second day of which the first-fruits were presented in the temple, upon which harvest began. Luther says more correctly: he thanks God for "good weather and a propitious season." It was intended to be sung when favourable *appearances* had presented themselves in reference to the harvest, when God had given the former and the latter rain in their seasons, Jer. v. 24, and when, in consequence of this, everything was flourishing and growing luxuriantly. This is manifest from the *concluding* verse, according to which, the psalm was intended to be sung at a time when the valleys *are clothing* themselves with corn (not *have been clothed*), and from ver. 9 and 10, where the psalmist speaks of rain as if he saw it just descending. Hitzig has taken altogether a wrong view, according to whom, the psalm was composed for the feast of tabernacles, "when the fruits of the earth had been gathered in, and the seed, recently committed to the ground, was waiting for the early rain." —*Hengstenberg.*

2. *Thou that hearest prayer.* The title here given to God carries with it a truth of great importance, That the answer of our prayers is secured by the fact, that in rejecting them he would in a certain sense deny his own nature. The psalmist does not say, that God has heard prayer in this or that instance, but gives him the name of the Hearer of prayer, as what constitutes an abiding part of his glory, so that he might as soon deny himself as shut his ear to our petitions. Could we only impress this upon our minds, that it is something peculiar to God, and inseparable from him, to hear prayer, it would inspire us with unfailing confidence. The power of helping us he can never want, so that nothing can stand in the way of a successful issue of our supplications.—*Calvin.*

3. *Iniquities prevail against me.* Calvin gives the translation, *Words of iniquity have prevailed*, but adds, "He does not complain of the people being assailed with calumny, but is to be understood as confessing that their sins were the cause of any interruption which had taken place in the communication of the divine favour to the Jews. The passage is parallel with that in Is. lix. 1—"The ear of the Lord is not heavy that it cannot hear, but our iniquities have separated betwixt us and him." David imputes it to his own sins and those of the people, that God, who was wont to be liberal in his help, and so gracious and kind in inviting their dependence upon him, had withdrawn for a time his divine countenance. First, he acknowledges his own personal guilt; afterwards, like Daniel (ix. 5), he joins the whole nation with himself. And this truth is introduced by the psalmist with no design to damp confidence in prayer, but rather to remove an obstacle standing in the way of it, as none could draw near to God unless convinced that he would hear the unworthy. It is probable that the Lord's people were at that time suffering under some token of the divine displeasure, since David seems here to struggle with some temptation of this kind. He evidently felt that there was a sure remedy at hand, for no sooner has he referred to the subject of guilt, than he recognizes the prerogative of God to pardon and expiate it. The verse before us must be viewed in connection with the preceding, and as meaning that though their iniquities merited their being cast out of God's sight, yet they would continue to pray, encouraged by his readiness to be reconciled to them. We learn from the passage that God will not be entreated of us unless we humbly supplicate the pardon of our sins. On the other hand, we are to believe firmly in reconciliation with God being procured through gratuitous remission. Should he at any time withdraw his favour, and frown upon us, we must learn by David's example

to rise to the hope of the expiation of our sins."

4. *We shall be satisfied with the goodness of thy house.* The psalmist insists upon the fruit springing out of the blessed privilege of which he had spoken, when he adds that believers *would be satisfied* with the fulness of his temple. Hypocrites may go there, but they return empty and unsatisfied as to any spiritual blessing enjoyed. It is noticeable that the person is changed in this part of the verse, and that David associates himself with other believers, preferring to speak upon this subject from personal experience. We are not to understand that believers are fully replenished with the goodness of God at any one moment; it is conveyed to them gradually; but while the influences of the Spirit are thus imparted in successive measures, each of them is enriched with a present sufficiency, till all be in due time advanced to perfection. I might remark here that while it is true, as stated, Ps. ciii. 5, that God "satisfieth our mouth with good things," at the same time it is necessary to remember what is said elsewhere, "Open thy mouth, and I will fill it." Our contracted desires is the reason why we do not receive a more copious supply of blessings from God; he sees that we are straitened in ourselves, and accommodates the communications of his goodness to the measure of our expectations. By specifying particularly the *goodness of the sanctuary*, the psalmist passes an implied commendation upon the outward helps which God has appointed for leading us into the enjoyment of heavenly blessings. In these former times God could have directly stretched out his hand from heaven to supply the wants of his worshippers, but saw fit to satisfy their souls by means of the doctrine of the law, sacrifices, and other rites and external aids to piety. Similar are the means which he employs in the church still; and though we are not to rest in these, neither must we neglect them.—*Calvin.*

9-13. This is the special thanksgiving which is called forth by the refreshing rain which God has sent, and the rich and glorious harvest which is already waving and ripening before their eyes. . . .

The language flows with the thoughts. The bright harvest-scene is before the eyes of the inspired singer. He stands looking on the fields white already to the harvest, and his soul within him rejoices in their golden promise. The poet and the world without him are at one accord. The fulness of joy in his heart, as he sees how his God has poured blessing upon the land, passes as it were by a contagion of sunny gladness into the inanimate creation, and the very corn-fields seem to him to shout together, yea to sing for joy.—*Perowne.*

[*Conclusion of the psalm.*] We should, with wonder, gratitude, and praise, behold and participate the abundance, which, by the wise and kind providence of God, is diffused through the earth: and, while we see year after year crowned with the goodness of the Lord, so that the hills and valleys, covered with corn and cattle, seem to proclaim and rejoice in their Creator's praise; we should remember our unworthiness, be thankful for our portion, and use it to the glory of the Giver; admire and imitate his bounty to the indigent, as we are able, and his goodness to the wicked and ungrateful children of men; and pity and pray for those who abuse these gifts to the dishonour of the giver.—But these temporal mercies to us unworthy creatures, shadow forth more important blessings. The rising of "the Sun of righteousness," and the pouring out of the Holy Spirit, that "river of God" full of the waters of life and salvation, render the hearts of sinners, which before were hard, barren, and worthless, fruitful in every good work; and change the face of nations, far more than the sun and rain do the face of nature. Wherever the Lord passes, by the preaching of his gospel, attended by his Holy Spirit, "his paths drop fatness;" and numbers of every description are taught to rejoice in him and praise him. These blessings have already been extended to many nations which were far off: may we unite in fervent prayers and vigorous, persevering, and self-denying endeavours, that they may descend upon the pastures of the wilderness, the heathen world, and the poor benighted Jews; and that the whole earth may hear and embrace the gospel; and may all who are favoured with the means of grace bring forth abundantly "those fruits of righteousness, which are through Jesus Christ, to the glory of God the Father."—*Scott.*

PSALM LXVI.

10, 12. *Thou, O God! hast proved us,*

&c. We may read, *Though thou, O God!* &c., and then the passage comes in as a qualification of what went before, and is brought forward by the psalmist to enhance the goodness of God, who had delivered them from such severe calamities. But there is another object which I consider him to have in view, and this is the alleviation of the grief of God's people, by setting before them the comfort suggested by the words which follow. When visited with affliction it is of great importance that we should consider it as coming from God, and as expressly intended for our good. It is in reference to this that the psalmist speaks of their having been *proved and tried.* At the same time, while he adverts to God's trying his children with the view of purging away their sin, as dross is expelled from the silver by fire, he would intimate also that trial had been made of their patience. The figure implies that their probation had been severe; for silver is cast repeatedly into the furnace. They express themselves thankful to God that, while proved with affliction, they had not been destroyed by it; but that their affliction was both varied and very severe, appears not only from the metaphor, but from the whole context, where they speak of having been cast into the net, being reduced to straits, men riding over their heads, and of being brought through shipwreck and conflagration. The expression, *laying a restraint* (or *chain*) upon *their loins*, is introduced as being stronger than the one which goes before. It was not a net of thread which had been thrown over them, but rather they had been bound down with hard and insolvable fetters. The expression which follows refers to men who had shamefully tyrannized over them, and ridden them down as cattle. By *fire* and *water* are evidently meant complicated afflictions; and it is intimated that God had exercised his people in every form of calamity. They are the two elements which contribute more than any other to sustain human life, but are equally powerful for the destruction of it. It is noticeable that the psalmist speaks of all the cruelties they had most unjustly suffered from the hands of their enemies as an infliction of divine punishment; and would guard the Lord's people against imagining that God was ignorant of what they endured, or distracted by other things from giving attention to it. In their condition as here described, we have that of the church generally represented to us; and this, that when subjected to vicissitudes, and cast out of the fire into the water, by a succession of trials, there may at last be felt to be nothing new or strange in the event to strike us with alarm. The Hebrew word, רויה, which I have rendered *fruitful place*, means literally *a well-watered land.* Here it is taken metaphorically for a condition of prosperity, the people of God being represented as brought into a pleasant and fertile place, where there is abundance of pasturage. The truth conveyed is, that God, although he visit his children with temporary chastisements of a severe description, will ultimately crown them with joy and prosperity. It is a mistake to suppose that the allusion is entirely to their being settled in the land of Canaan, for the psalm has not merely reference to the troubles which they underwent in the wilderness, but to the whole series of distresses to which they were subjected at the different periods of their history.—*Calvin.*

How grievous the distress and danger were. What particular trouble of the church this refers to does not appear. It might be the trouble of some private persons or families only. But whatever it was, they were surprised with it, as a bird with a snare, inclosed and entangled in it as a fish in a net; they were pressed down with it and kept under as with a load *upon their loins.* But they owned the hand of God in it. We are never in the net but God brings us into it; never under affliction but God lays it upon us. Is anything more dangerous than fire and water? *We went through both*—afflictions of different kinds; the end of one trouble was the beginning of another; when we had got clear of one sort of dangers, we found ourselves involved in dangers of another sort. Such may be the troubles of the best of God's saints; but he has promised, "*When thou passest through the waters, through the fire, I will be with thee,*" Is. xliii. 2. Yet proud and cruel men may be as dangerous as fire and water, and more so. "*Beware of men,*" Mat. x. 17. When men rose up against us, that was fire and water, and all that is threatening, Ps. cxxiv. 2-4; and that was the case here. "*Thou hast caused men to ride over our heads;*" to trample upon us and insult over us; to hector and abuse us: nay, to make perfect slaves of us. They have said to our souls, "*Bow down that we may go over,*" Is. li. 23. While it is the pleasure of good princes to rule in the hearts of their subjects, it is the pride of tyrants to ride over their heads; yet the afflicted church in this also owns the hand of God: "Thou hast caused them thus to abuse us;" for the most furious oppressor has no power but what is given him from above.—*Henry.*

PSALM LXVII.

Prayer for revival at home and prayer for a blessing abroad ought ever therefore to go hand in hand. This is brought out in Ps. lxvii.;—the missionary hymn of the Hebrew church. How admirably balanced are the parts of this missionary song! The people of God long to see all the nations participating in their privileges, "visited with God's salvation, and gladdened with the gladness of his nation," Ps. cvi. 5. They long to hear all the nationalities giving thanks to the Lord, and hallowing his name; to see the face of the whole earth, which sin has darkened so long, smiling with the brightness of a second Eden. This is not a vapid sentiment. The desire is so expressed as to connect with it the thought of duty and responsibility. For how do they expect that the happy times are to be reached? They trust, in the first instance, to the general diffusion of the knowledge of God's way, the spreading abroad of the truth regarding the way of salvation. With a view to that they cry for a time of quickening from the presence of the Lord, and take encouragement in this prayer from the terms of the divinely-appointed benediction. As if they had said, "Hast thou not commanded the sons of Aaron to put thy name upon us and to say, The LORD bless thee and keep thee; the LORD cause his face to shine on thee and be gracious to thee? Remember that sure word of thine! God be gracious unto us, and bless us, and cause his face to shine upon us. Let us be thus blessed, and we shall in our turn become a blessing. All the families of the earth shall through us become acquainted with thy salvation." Such is the church's expectation. And who shall say it is unreasonable? If the little company of a hundred and twenty disciples who met in the upper chamber at Jerusalem, all of them persons of humble station and unconspicuous talents, were endued with such power by the baptism of the Holy Ghost, that within three hundred years the paganism of the empire was overthrown, one need not fear to affirm that, in order to the evangelization of the world, nothing more is required than that the churches of Christendom be baptized with a fresh effusion of the same Spirit of power.—*Binnie.*

2. *Thy way.* The *way* of God is his procedure: from the experience of Israel, the heathen shall know how God *acts,* what are those treasures of salvation which are laid up with him for his people; as even at the present time there are not more powerful means of bringing the world to God than the perception of the gifts which he imparts to the living members of his church: comp. Ps. xxv. 10, "All the *ways* of God are grace and truth;" Ps. ciii. 7, "He has made known his *ways* to Moses, his deeds to the children of Israel." The parallel term, "his salvation," is sufficient against the translation, "his religion;" comp. Ps. xcvi. 2; xcviii. 2. The idea that the blessings of Israel would exert an attractive influence on heathen nations, occurs in the promises made to the patriarchs, Gen. xxii. 18; xxvi. 4, "And all the nations of the earth shall be blessed in thy seed," *i.e.* they wish for, and they earnestly desire for themselves the lot of Israel as the highest good, and this wish shall be the means of their obtaining the blessing (*being blessed,* Niph. Gen. xii. 3; xviii. 18), inasmuch as it will lead them to the Author of the blessing. Is. lx. 3 is also parallel: "and the Gentiles shall come to thy light, and kings to the brightness of thy rising."—*Hengstenberg.*

3. *Let all the people praise thee.* As if she had said, Hitherto indeed, blessed Lord, thou hast thought fit to make me the guardian and keeper of that great deposit, thy true religion, from which the nations revolted and fell; but the time is coming, when, by the gospel of thy dear Son, they shall again be called to the knowledge of thee. Thy glory, impatient, as it were, of any longer restraint, and demanding a larger sphere, shall diffuse itself, like the light of heaven, to the ends of the world. Hasten, then, O hasten the dawning of that happy day when congregations of converted Gentiles shall everywhere lift up their voices, and perhaps in the

words of this very psalm, sing to thy praise and glory!—*Horne.*

PSALM LXVIII.

The title confines itself to the announcement that the psalm was composed by David, and set apart by him for the public service; but is silent as to the occasion on which it was composed. For determining this last point, we have nothing therefore to look to except internal reasons. Many expositors, and latterly Stier, have come to the conclusion that the psalm was written on the occasion when the ark of the covenant was brought to Mount Zion: comp. at Ps. xxiv. Others again have adopted the idea that the occasion must have been the termination of some war, when the ark was brought back to the holy mountain. This last view is the correct one. A strong argument in its favour is drawn from the circumstance that God is throughout celebrated decidedly as the *Lord of battle* and *of victory.* The introductory clause, "God arises, his enemies are scattered, and they who hate him flee before him," gives forth at the very beginning the *fundamental tone,* and the subject of the whole psalm; while at the same time, in a psalm composed for such an occasion, and of such a length, many other subjects would certainly be introduced. Farther, we are led to a *victory* as the occasion by ver. 18, which, like ver. 6 of Ps. lxvii., "The earth gave its increase," announces the matter of fact which called forth the psalm, and which ought to be considered as supplementary to the title, and should properly be printed in large characters. Then we have the epithets which are applied in ver. 17 to Benjamin and Judah, and, finally, the close fitting in to the *victory-song* of Deborah: inasmuch as the author, in ver. 7 and 8, at the very beginning of his chief division, refers verbally to the beginning of the chief division of this song, he declares, as distinctly as possible, that he walks in the *footsteps* of Deborah, and that his song is to be considered as a continuation or resumption of hers, exactly as with manifest design, by the reference in the opening verse of the psalm to the language of Moses, he intimates that the text and the subject of the whole are taken from him.

We have two data to guide us in our inquiry as to what particular battle and victory the triumphal procession in the sanctuary belongs, at which, according to ver. 24–27, the psalm was sung. First, the psalm must have been composed at a time when the sanctuary of the Lord was on Mount Zion (ver. 15, 16, 29, 35). The choice is thus very much narrowed. There remain only two great victories, the Syrian-Edomite and the Ammonitic-Syrian. Second, in the war referred to in this psalm, the *ark of the covenant* must have been in the field according to ver. 1 and 24. It is evident from 2 Sam. xi. 11, that this was the case in the Ammonitic war. We may therefore with great probability conclude that the psalm was composed after the capture of Rabbah (2 Sam. xii. 26–31), which terminated that war, the most dangerous with which David had to do. It was quite in accordance with David's usual manner to celebrate a great religious festival at the close of such a war. The closing character which our psalm so manifestly bears, is in favour of this view. That war was the last important external war in which David engaged, and from existing circumstances he might pretty confidently conclude that it would be so. The name of Solomon, which soon after this he gave to his son, shows that he considered peace as secured for a long time.—*Hengstenberg.*

10. *Thou, O God, hast prepared of thy goodness for the poor.* The acknowledgment refers to the gracious attention of God to Israel, his pensioners, while they sojourned in the wilderness. They were destitute of all ordinary supplies; but "he commanded the clouds from above, and opened the doors of heaven, and rained down manna upon them to eat, and gave them of the corn of heaven. Man did eat angels' food: he sent them meat to the full." We are not to look for miraculous provision; but God has not forsaken the earth, nor forgotten to be gracious. Let us observe the nature of this goodness, and the subjects for whom it is prepared. The goodness of God appears in the produce of the ground even for the brute creation. Indeed man is concerned in their support; and a deficiency with regard to them would materially affect his own welfare. But while the Lord cares for oxen, and causes the grass to grow for the cattle, he provides *corn* for the more immediate service of man. . . . But we are here reminded not only of the nature of his goodness, but the subjects of it:

"Thou, O God, hast prepared of thy goodness for the poor." It is not for them exclusively. "The king is served by the field." A supply for the poor is of course a supply for the rich; and it is easy to see that a suspension of the divine goodness would involve all ranks. The rich can no more create than the poor; and should the course of vegetation be stopped by Him who has power to destroy as well as to produce, what profit would a man have of all the wealth he possessed? Wealth would be nothing if it could not be laid out: and if the time ever came, which the Lord forbid! in which there was neither earing nor harvest, the proprietor, as well as the peasant and the pauper, would perish. But it is spoken in reference to the poor, because, First, they are the larger mass of mankind; and whatever pride may think, in the eye of reason, policy, and revelation, by far the most important, useful, and necessary part. Secondly, they would be more peculiarly affected by deficiency. Dear purchases can be made by the rich, who, as the price of provisions advances, can follow it. But the poor are speedily straitened, and become a prey to scarceness; and every door is shut against them but that of precarious charity. Thirdly, to encourage those in humble and trying life to depend upon him. What he did formerly he does now. He prepares of his goodness for the poor. He may try you, and require proof of your confidence, before he communicates relief: but "the needy shall not always be forgotten, the expectation of the poor shall not perish for ever." "Trust in the Lord, and do good, and dwell in the land, and verily thou shalt be fed." And "a little that a righteous man hath is better than the riches of many wicked." Fourthly, to enforce our attention to them from the divine example. We see how he had his eye upon the poor in the Jewish economy. It is delightful to read the various provisions concerning them in the law of Moses. All the earth spontaneously yielded, the seventh year, belonged to the poor. At harvest the owners were not to cut down the corners of their fields; they were to scatter some handfuls behind them for the gleaner; and if they dropped a sheaf, they were not to go back for it.—*Jay.*

13. *Though ye have lien among the pots,* &c. Professor Alexander renders *when ye lie down between the borders,* (ye shall be like) *the wings of a dove covered with silver and her pinions with yellow gold.* The general idea, he adds, seems to be that when "the land had rest," her condition was one of peaceful prosperity. The common version of the first clause (*though ye have lien among the pots*) is justified neither by rabbinical tradition nor the ancient versions. The Hebrew noun occurs only here, and in Ezek. xl. 43, where it is equally obscure, and the cognate forms in Gen. xlix. 14; Judg. v. 16, are scarcely less so. The only meaning, besides those already mentioned, which has any probability, is that of *folds* or *sheep-cotes,* lying among which might be viewed as a poetical figure for rural or pastoral repose, thus amounting to the same thing with the first translation, which describes the people as residing quietly *between the borders,* i.e. within the boundaries or frontiers of their territory, now once more forsaken by the enemy. The beautiful allusion in the last clause to the changeable colours of a dove's plumage seems intended to suggest the idea of a peaceful but splendid prosperity.

18. *Thou hast ascended,* &c. As the passage is applied by Paul in a more spiritual sense to Christ (Eph. iv. 8), it may be necessary to show how this agrees with the meaning and scope of the psalmist. It may be laid down as an incontrovertible truth that David, in reigning over Christ's ancient people, shadowed forth the beginning of Christ's eternal kingdom. This must appear evident to every one who remembers the promise made to him of a never-failing succession, and which received its verification in the person of Christ. As God illustrated his power in David by exalting him with the view of delivering his people, so has he magnified his name in his only-begotten Son. But let us consider more particularly how the parallel holds. Christ, before he was exalted, emptied himself of his glory, having not merely assumed the form of a servant, but humbled himself to the death of the cross. To show how exactly the figure was fulfilled, Paul notices that what David had foretold was accomplished in the person of Christ by his being cast down to the lowest parts of the earth, in the reproach and ignominy to which he was subjected, before he ascended to the right hand of his Father (Ps. xxii. 7).

That in thinking upon the ascension, we might not confine our views to the body of Christ, our attention is called to the result and fruit of it in his subjecting heaven and earth to his government. Those who were formerly his inveterate enemies he compelled to submission and made tributary—this being the effect of the word of the gospel to lead men to renounce their pride and their obstinacy, to bring down every high thought which exalteth itself, and reduce the senses and the affections of men to obedience unto Christ. As to the devils and reprobate men who are instigated to rebellion and revolt by obstinate malice, he holds them bound by a secret control, and prevents them from executing intended destruction. So far the parallel is complete. Nor when Paul speaks of Christ having *given gifts to men*, is there any real inconsistency with what is here stated, although he has altered the words, having followed the Greek version in accommodation to the unlearned reader. It was not himself that God enriched with the spoils of the enemy, but his people; and neither did Christ seek or need to seek his own advancement, but made his enemies tributary, that he might adorn his church with the spoil. From the close union subsisting between the head and members, to say that God manifest in the flesh received gifts from the captives, is one and the same thing with saying that he distributed them to his church. What is said in the close of the verse is no less applicable to Christ—that he obtained his victories that as God he might dwell among us. Although he departed, it was not that he might remove to a distance from us; but, as Paul says, "that he might fill all things" (Eph. iv. 10). By his ascension to heaven the glory of his divinity has been only more illustriously displayed, and though no longer present with us in the flesh, our souls receive spiritual nourishment from his body and blood, and we find, notwithstanding distance of place, that his flesh is meat indeed, and his blood drink indeed.—*Calvin.*

The ascent of the ark, in which God was present, into Zion, prefigured the ascent of Christ into heaven. As God came down to fight for his people, so Christ had descended to this earth for the salvation of men. As, on the return of the ark, the captives and the spoil appeared in the procession, so on the return of Christ in triumph to heaven (Col. ii. 15), He led captive sin and death, and hell, and all evil powers. As God had *taken* tribute among men, which he, however, as the victorious monarch of Israel, had given to Israel, so Christ also had taken gifts among men (in his human nature and through his work on earth) which he now, as ascended Lord, gave to men. The apostle sees that when a king takes, he takes to give, and therefore substitutes the one word for the other, without at all putting the one word as the *translation* of the other. He seizes the idea and represents it in its true fulfilment. Calvin has some excellent remarks on the principle of interpretation to be followed here.—*Perowne.*

PSALM LXIX.

We are somewhat surprised that our author should have any difficulty in connection with the Messianic character of this psalm, and that he should find it necessary to explain the numerous quotations from it in the New Testament on the principle of accommodation—a principle which he has in so many other places abandoned (ver. 4, 9, 21, 22, 25). We subjoin *Dr. Binnie's* view:—"The frequency with which the Old Testament scriptures are cited by our blessed Lord and the writers of the New Testament, and the marked deference with which the citations are made, have always and justly been regarded as a strong testimony to the plenary authority of the ancient scriptures. Well, it is remarkable that the psalms under discussion have been counted worthy of an eminent share in this honour. Ps. lxix., for example, which bears more of the imprecatory character than any other except Ps. cix., is expressly quoted in five separate places, besides being alluded to in several places more. Among all the psalms there are only some three or four others that have been so largely quoted by Christ and the apostles; and they are all great Messianic hymns (Ps. ii. xxii. cx. cxviii. are the four most frequently quoted in the New Testament). The *nature* of the quotations is even more significant than their number. It would seem that our Lord appropriated the psalm to himself, and that we are to take it as a disclosure of thoughts and feelings which found a place in his heart during the period of his ministry on the earth. In the guest-chamber he quoted the words of the fourth verse: 'They hated me without a cause;' and represented them as a prediction of the people's hatred of the Father and of himself (Jn. xv. 25). When he drove the traffickers from the temple, John informs us that 'his disciples remembered that it was written, The zeal of thine house hath eaten me up' (Jn. ii. 17); which implies that those words of the psalm expressed the very mind that was in Christ. When Peter, after mentioning the crime and perdition of Judas, suggested to the company of the hundred and twenty disciples that they ought to take measures for the appointment of a new apostle to fill the vacant place, he enforced the suggestion by a quotation: 'For it is written in the book of Psalms, Let his habitation be desolate, and let no man dwell therein, and his bishoprick let another take' (Acts i. 20):—manifestly on the supposition that this psalm and the hundred and ninth (for the quotation is from them both) were written with reference to Judas. In the epistle to the Romans, the duty of pleasing, every one of us, our neighbour for his good, is enforced by the apostle with the argument that 'even Christ pleased not himself, but as it is written, The reproaches of them that reproached thee fell on me' (ver. 22 and 23, compared with Rom. xi. 9, 10): an argument which has no weight if David alone is the speaker in the psalm—if Christ be not, in some real sense, the speaker in it also. Finally, we are taught in the same epistle to recognize a fulfilment of the psalmist's most terrible imprecations in the judicial blindness which befell the body of the Jewish nation after the crucifixion of Christ. All this proves that if we are not to reject the authority of the apostles and of Christ himself, we must take this imprecatory psalm as having been spoken by David as the ancestor and type of Christ. I do not say that the circumstance that these psalms are so unequivocally endorsed and appropriated by our blessed Lord explains the difficulty they involve. But I am sure that the simple statement of it will constrain disciples of Christ to touch them with a reverent hand; and rather to distrust their own judgment than to brand such scriptures as the products of an unsanctified and unchristian temper." See also Fairbairn's *Typology*, i. p. 102. *Plumer* gives the following excellent digest:—The psalm is decidedly Messianic. The only question is whether it is directly and fully prophetic or typical-messianic. There is no valid objection to the admission that in some parts David as a sufferer speaks as a type of Christ, and that in others he rises to the height of unqualified prediction respecting Messiah. Ver. 4 is cited in Jn. xv. 25; ver. 9 in Jn. ii. 17; Rom. xv. 3; ver. 21 in Mat. xxvii. 34, 48; Mark xv. 23; Jn. xix. 28, 29; ver. 22, 23 in Rom. xi. 9, 10; and ver. 25 in Acts i. 16, 20. Sound commentators generally admit that it has its fulfilment in Christ. *Theodoret:* "It is a prediction of the sufferings of Christ, and the final destruction of the Jews on that account." *Calvin:* "David wrote this inspired ode, not so much in his own name, as in the name of the whole church, of whose head he was an eminent type." *Vitringa:* "It is admitted among Christians, that in Ps. lxix. Christ, and Christ as a sufferer, is to be placed before our eyes. We add that it refers to Christ crucified as the evangelists Matthew, Mark, and John apply it." *Fabritius:* "In this psalm David is a figure of Christ." *Alexander:* "The only individual in whom the traits meet is Christ." *Hodge:* "This psalm is so frequently quoted and applied to Christ in the New Testament, that it must be considered as directly prophetical." Similar remarks might be cited from Gill, Anderson, Scott, and others. Calvin's first remark on this psalm is: "There is a close resemblance between this and Ps. xxii." Many others have observed the likeness. This is a composition of great beauty and poetic excellence.

5. *O God, thou knowest my foolishness.* The broad principle laid down in the introduction to Ps. xxii. applies here. The history of prophets and holy men of old is a typical history. They were, it may be said, representative men, suffering and hoping, not for themselves only, but for the nation whom they represented. In their sufferings they were feeble and transient images of the great Sufferer, who by his sufferings accomplished man's redemption: their hopes could never be fully realized but in the issue of his work, nor their aspirations be truly uttered save by his mouth. But confessions of sinfulness and imprecations of vengeance, mingling with these better hopes and aspirations, are a beacon to guide us in

our interpretation. They teach us that the psalm is not a prediction; that the psalmist does not put himself in the place of the Messiah to come. They show us that here, as indeed in all Scripture, two streams, the human and the divine, flow on in the same channel. They seem designed to remind us that if prophets and minstrels of old were types of the great Teacher of the church, yet that they were so only in some respects, and not altogether. They bear witness to the imperfection of those by whom God spake in time past unto the fathers, in many portions and in many ways, even whilst they point to him who is the living Word, the perfect revelation of the Father.—*Perowne.*

PSALM LXXI.

I am much inclined to think that David's was a case of infant regeneration—certainly it was a case of early piety. Touching proof of this is found in Ps. lxxi. The psalm, I am aware, is anonymous, and is therefore by many recent critics referred to some later writer; but I am satisfied that Venema and Hengstenberg have adduced sufficient reasons for retaining the opinion of Calvin and the older expositors, that it is from David's pen, and is the plaintive song of his old age. It shows us the soul of the aged saint darkened by the remembrance of his great transgression, and by the swarm of sorrows with which that sin filled all his later years. But he finds comfort in reverting to the happy days of his childhood, and especially to the irrevocable trust which he was then enabled to repose in God. The thoughts and feelings expressed remind one of those which invest with such a solemn, tender interest the second epistle to Timothy—which embalms the dying thoughts of the great apostle. Like Paul, David takes a retrospect of the Lord's dealings with him from the beginning; and, in effect, declares, with the dying apostle; "I am not ashamed; for I know whom I have believed, and am persuaded that he is able to keep that which I have committed to him against that day" (2 Tim. i. 12). Only there is this notable difference between the two, that while Paul gathered confirmation of his faith from the experience of a thirty years' walk with his Lord, David's experience stretched over a tract of more than twice so many years; for it began with his childhood —*Binnie.*

PSALM LXXII.

Solomon is named in the title as the *author* of the psalm. Attempts have been made to no purpose to interpret לשלמה here, as in Ps. cxxvii., in another sense. The ל, when it occurs in the titles, without anything to limit its application, *always* indicates, as here, the author. . . . In favour of the announcement in the title, we have first the remarkably *objective* character of the psalm, common to it with the other writings of Solomon, and in striking contrast to that *flow of feeling,* which forms such a marked feature in the psalms of David. And, in the *second* place, there is also the fact that it is the circumstances of Solomon's time that form the ground-work of the psalm. The references to these circumstances partake too much of an individual character, as will be seen in the progress of our exposition, to admit of our supposing with Stier again that they are *prophetical.* There are no reasons of any importance against considering Solomon as the author. It is maintained by Stier, that on account of the typical reference to Solomon, the authorship is suitable only to David. But, in reply to this, it is sufficient to advert to Ps. ii. and cx., where David himself, out of the grace imparted to him in his contests against the enemies of the kingdom of God, constructs a ladder, by which he rises to the contemplation of the infinitely more glorious victories to be won in battle by his descendant. Why should not Solomon, in like manner, see in his righteous *reign of peace,* a type of the kingdom of the *Prince of peace?*—*Hengstenberg.*

Two psalms bear Solomon's name in their titles. One of these is the hundred and twenty-seventh, entitled *A Song of Degrees, of Solomon.* . . . Solomon's other psalm is the seventy-second, and here also the traces of his pen are unequivocal. A mistaken interpretation of the note appended to it —"the prayers of David, the son of Jesse, are ended,"—led most of the older commentators to attribute the psalm to David, and to suppose that it is a prayer offered in his old age "for Solomon," as the peaceful prince who was to succeed him on the throne. However, it has long been known that the note in question refers to the whole of the preceding portion of the psalter, —much of which was written by Asaph and the sons of Korah; and there can be no doubt that the title can only be translated "*of* Solomon." So clear are the traces of Solomon's pen, that Calvin—whose sagacity in this kind of criticism has never been excelled—although he thought himself obliged, by the note at the end of the psalm, to attribute the substance of it to David, felt Solomon's touch so sensibly, that he threw out the conjecture that the prayer was the father's, but that it was afterwards thrown into the lyrical form by the son. This is not the place for detailed exposition; I will therefore content myself with remarking that, properly speaking, the psalm is not "for Solomon" at all. If it refers to him and his peaceful reign, it does so only in as far as they were types of the person and kingdom of the Prince of peace. The psalm, from beginning to end, is not only capable of being applied to Christ, but great part is incapable of being fairly applied to any other.—*Binnie.*

Remarking on the opening part of the psalm (ver. 1-4), *Dr. Binnie* again says—"Solomon is certainly here. The psalm is the joint prayer of prince and people, entreating that the new reign may be wise and just, long and happy. But we cannot read it to the end without feeling that, even when it was first sung, the thought of every reflective Israelite must have been carried beyond the young king, who had just entered upon the government, with such honourable aspirations and such a rich dower of wisdom and diversified accomplishment. In Hebrew the optative and future run so much into each other that it is hard to say whether the psalm ought to be translated throughout as a prayer, or ought not rather to be thrown, in the latter part, into the form of a prediction, as it is in the English version. Some, like Hupfeld, make it a prayer throughout, and read it thus:—

Let the kings of Tarshish and the isles render gifts,
Let the kings of Sheba and Saba offer presents.
Yea, let all kings bow themselves down before him,
Let all nations serve him.
For he delivereth the poor when he crieth,
And the afflicted who hath no helper.
—Mr. Perowne's *Translation.*

But even thus rendered, the terms would have been too fulsome for a Bible psalm, if the scope of it had been limited to the person and reign of Solomon. He could not modestly have asked his people to unite with him in offering to God requests of such far-reaching and glorious import, unless he had intended them to be offered in behalf of THE KING in the most comprehensive sense of the term, as including the seed of David for ever, and especially the greater Son of David who was promised to succeed upon the throne. The reference to Christ is of course still more pointed and obvious, if (as seems preferable) the latter part of the psalm be rendered as a prediction. And if those who first made use of the psalm may be presumed to have looked beyond Solomon, what shall we say regarding those who lived to see the kingdom divided and the house of David represented by men like Rehoboam? The psalm, let it be remembered, was not a mere coronation anthem sung once and then forgotten. It was a new song added to the church's Psalter, and continued to be sung in divine worship. We may be sure, therefore, that even if it could be supposed that the people, in the bright morning of Solomon's reign fixed their hopes on him as they sang the psalm, they would cease to do so when their hopes from him and his were so cruelly disappointed. The type would more and more recede from their view, as the temporal glory of David's house waned; and they would come to sing the psalm, very much as we do, with an entire concentration of the thoughts on the Prince of peace."

3-6. *The mountains shall bring peace,* &c. The hills and mountains prominent in Israel's land, the hills and mountains, too, of earth at large, generally so barren, hills and mountains on which the feet of other messengers have often stood (Is. xl. 9), but never any messengers so blessed as those that visit them now; these hills and mountains display the signs of peace, viz. abundant produce, "*because of righteousness*"—because the righteous One has come to dwell in this new earth. Antichrist and all oppressors are overthrown (ver. 4); earth's thick-peopled regions fear him, and shall go on fearing him in peace, so long as sun and moon remain, that sun and moon which at creation's dawn were appointed to light up earth and guide men to keep holy festivals to the Lord. The Lord Jesus is there. Like "plenty-dropping showers" that reach the very roots of the mown grass (ver. 6), so is he to the earth after it has been shorn by the scythe of war, and every form of ruin and wrath. He revives it, as summer's genial rains cause grass to spring up in new vigour, clothing the soil with a richer and thicker mantle of verdure than before—as Layard tells us how in the season of spring the dusty soil of Mesopotamia will change its aspect, in one night the tame plains turning to a bright scarlet, or to deepest blue, through the burst of flowers, while the meadows put on the emerald green of the most luxuriant pastures, causing even the wild Bedouin, as he riots in the rich herbage and scented air, to exclaim, "What delight has God given us equal to this!"—*A. A. Bonar.*

15. *He shall live.* On ver. 15 a modern translator of the Psalter has appropriately indicated that that which was said to other kings in flattery shall be said to the Messiah in truth: "O King, live for ever." The best commentary on the words "he shall live" is however to be found in the declaration of the glorified Saviour himself in the Apocalypse, "I am he that liveth and was dead; and behold, I am alive for evermore, Amen; and have the keys of hell and of death." In the words "to him shall be given of the gold of Sheba," it is implied that rich offerings shall be made to him by men of their substance as a testimony of the devotion of their hearts. That "prayer shall be made for him continually," has been verified in the supplications which are being continually poured forth by all Christians for the advancement of his kingdom: and the universal worship of the Christian church has already set the seal of truth to the words, "daily shall he be praised."—*Thrupp.*

Prayer shall be made for him. But *what* should we pray for on his behalf? Our prayers should vary with the state of his cause; but we should always bear four things upon our minds. *First,* the degree of its resources; that there be always a sufficiency of suitable and able instruments to carry on the work. To this the Saviour himself directs us: "The harvest truly is great; but the labourers are few; pray ye therefore the Lord of the harvest that he would send forth labourers into his harvest." *Secondly,* the freedom of its administration; that whatever opposes or hinders its progress may be removed. "Pray ye for us," says the apostle, "that the word of the Lord may have free course and be glorified." *Thirdly,* the diffusion of its principles; that they may become general and universal; spreading through every family, neighbourhood, and province, and realm. So prayed of old the pious Jews: "That thy way may be known on earth; thy saving health among all nations. Let the people praise thee, O God; yea, let all the people praise thee." *Fourthly,* the increase of its glory, as well as its extent; that it may abound more in wisdom, purity, spirituality, charity, and zeal; that the light of the moon may be as the light of the sun; and the light of the sun be sevenfold as the light of seven days; that for brass he would bring gold; and for iron, silver; and for wood, brass; and for stones, iron. Thus they that make mention of the Lord are to "give him no rest," not only until he "establish," but make Jerusalem a *praise* in the whole earth.—*Jay.*

PSALM LXXIII.

The psalm is very nearly related to Ps. xxxvii. and xlix. as far as its contents are concerned. Amyraldus took quite a correct view as to what *distinguishes* it from these psalms and forms its individual physiognomy. "In Ps. xxxvii. the prophet merely shows how believers ought to conduct themselves when they perceive the prosperity of the ungodly: he himself did not stumble at it. But here Asaph, though a great and pious man, acknowledges that the providence of God in this respect did sometimes appear to him mysterious, and that he felt great difficulty in justifying it. Yea, from the beginning of this psalm we see how he merged out of the deep thoughts into which his spirit, agitated and vexed by doubts, had sunk, until in the end better views obtained the ascendency. . . . He has adopted this method in order that believers might contemplate, as in a picture, the conflict to which at times they are exposed, and might see what weapons they have to seize against the assaults of the flesh."—*Hengstenberg.*

This is one of the twelve psalms which bear the name of Asaph, and we have seen reason to conclude that it came from the pen of Asaph the seer, the great contemporary of David. The theme of it is one to which the prophets and psalmists often revert—the mystery of God's providence towards the righteous and the wicked. Asaph's faith staggers at the sight of the prosperity of the wicked. They get on in the world. Their forgetfulness of God seems no bar to their success. Beholding them, the saint is tempted to exclaim, My pains have been thrown away; verily I have cleansed my heart in vain, and washed my hands in innocency. Indeed, he is only restrained from venting these dark atheistic doubts by the apprehension that he may thereby undermine the dearest hopes of some whom he knows to be the generation of God's children. Such is his temptation. He recovers himself in some measure when, retiring from the din and glitter of the world, he goes into the sanctuary of God, and contemplates things as they appear in the serene light that shines there. He now perceives what he had before failed to observe, the goal to which the prosperity of the wicked tends; how they are brought into desolation as in a moment; how their felicity passes away like a dream and gives place to consuming terrors. But the consideration which banishes all envy from his heart is not that of the sad end of the ungodly. It is by a loftier thought that his heart is purged of the perilous stuff with which it is overcharged:—

"Yet as for me, I am continually with thee:
Thou hast holden me by my right hand," &c.

What a high estimate of the soul underlies these words with which the saint emerges from the cloud of his temptation! It is as if he had said, "Why should I envy because of the prosperity of the foolish? Why should my faith stagger because a full cup of temporal felicities is occasionally bestowed on them? Wealth, and health, and honour—these are not the objects in which it was ever intended that my soul should find rest and supreme enjoyment. God himself is my soul's fit portion. Seeing then that I have, in the Lord's great mercy, been made heir of that portion, I will make my boast in him, whatever my earthly lot may be. I shall be satisfied with his likeness." It is thus that God would have us arm ourselves against unbelieving thoughts. It is well to be restrained from uttering unworthy suspicions of God by regard to the peace of our Christian acquaintances; it is better to curb envious thoughts by recollecting that godless prosperity is only a smooth road to hell; but it is best of all to be raised above the reach of Satan's fiery darts by the assured persuasion that we possess in God's favour a portion that is richer than a thousand worlds.—*Binnie.*

17. *Until I went into the sanctuary of God.* In ver. 17 several explain, "till I pressed into the divine secrets." But this explanation is altogether an arbitrary one. The word מקדש signifies always the sanctuary, and is the constant one for the tabernacle and the temple; comp. in reference to the plural, Ps. lxviii. 35. There is no occasion whatever for departing from the fully ascertained and literal sense if we only look upon the sanctuary with the eyes of the pious Israelites of the Old Testament dispensation. The substance of the temple to them was the presence of God, and just on this account, according to their view, any man could externally repair to the temple without being truly in it, and in like manner a man could be truly in it, even when outwardly at a distance from it: compare at Ps. lxiii. 2, and the passages quoted there. The psalmist thus goes here also with *the feet of his heart* into the sanctuary, draws near to God, and gets from this clear fountain the insight which natural reason could not give him.—*Hengstenberg.*

So also *Perowne*, who remarks—"The sanctuary is the place of his teaching; not heaven, as Kimchi and others, but the temple, as the place of his special manifestation, not only by Urim and Thummim, but in direct answer to prayer. There, in some hour of fervent, secret prayer, like that of Hannah (1 Sam. i. 13, comp. Luke xviii. 10), or perhaps in some solemn service, it may have been—who can tell?—through the words of some inspired psalm, a conviction of the truth broke upon him. The word *sanctuary* is in the plural, which is used here, as in Ps. xliii. 3; lxviii. 35, for the singular."

28. *It is good for me to draw near to God.* He was greatly encouraged to cleave to God, and to confide in him. If *they that are far from God shall perish*, then, 1. Let this constrain us to live in communion with God. If it fare so ill with those that live at a distance from him, then it is good, very good, the chief good, that good for a man in this life which he should most carefully pursue and secure. "It is best for me to draw near to God, and

to have God draw near to me." The original may take in both. *But for my part* (so I would read it) *the approach of God is good for me.* Our drawing near to God takes rise from his drawing near to us, and it is the happy meeting that makes the bliss. Here is a great truth laid down—That it is good to draw near to God; but the life of it lies in the application, "It is good for *me*." Those are the wise who know what is good for themselves. "*It is good*," says he (and every good man agrees with him in it), "*It is good for me to draw near to God;* it is my duty, it is my interest.—*Henry.*

PSALM LXXIV.

Asaph is named as the author of the psalm. In those psalms which bear his name, we must, when there are no strong reasons against it, conclude that the person meant is the Asaph who lived in the time of David. For that he occupied a prominent place among the sacred poets; and that therefore there must be some of the psalms of his composition, is evident from 2 Chr. xxix. 30, according to which Hezekiah brought into use, in the worship of God, not only the songs of David, but also the songs of Asaph, and where Asaph is named *the Seer*, or *the divinely illuminated*, and from Neh. xii. 46, where the days of the flower of Israelitish sacred poetry are called the days of David and of Asaph. For these reasons, we are perfectly justified in considering this Asaph as the author especially of Ps. l. lxxiii. lxxviii.; and these are altogether well fitted to have procured for him his poetic fame. But *here* we cannot have the least idea of the authorship belonging to David's time. We must not, however, on this account, convict the title of a mistake; for just in proportion as the contents are decidedly and manifestly inconsistent with David's age, was it unlikely that the title would announce that the psalm was composed at that time. Asaph was the *founder* of a family of singers, who went by the name of the *sons of Asaph*, even in the time of Isaiah, compare 2 Chr. xxxv. 15, yea even in the time of Ezra and Nehemiah, Ezra ii. 41; iii. 10; Neh. vii. 44; xi. 22. That the Holy Ghost, who inspired the founder, continued to exert his influence upon the members of this family from age to age, is manifest from the example of Jehaziel, one of the sons of Asaph in Jehoshaphat's time, on whom the Spirit of the Lord came down in the midst of the assembly, 2 Chr. xx. 14. All the sacred compositions of the different members of this family, from time to time, were designated *songs of Asaph*, just as in the title of Ps. lxii., Jeduthun stands for the Jeduthunic choir. If the family had not possessed a founder so very famous in this department, these psalms, like those which bear the name of the sons of Korah, would have had inscribed on their titles "the sons of Asaph."—*Hengstenberg.*

The Psalms of the Captivity, strictly so called, fall under three heads, according as they were written in the first anguish of the carrying away, or after the exiles had settled down in their new abodes in Mesopotamia, or when the time fixed for the return drew near.

To the first class belong Ps. lxxiv. and lxxix. In reading them we seem to hear the cry of the people ascending up to heaven as the Chaldeans scale the wall, and fire the city, and desecrate the sanctuary. They are both entitled psalms of Asaph; and the vividness with which they describe the desolations wrought by the Chaldeans, with sword and with fire, leaves the impression that they must have come from the pen of Levites who were eye-witnesses of the dismal scene. In the former of the two, the godly complain that there is "no more any prophet among them, nor any that knows how long." This has led some commentators to think that, whatever may be the true date of the psalm, it cannot refer to the Chaldean invasion: for it is certain that at that epoch the congregation enjoyed the ministry of distinguished prophets, and that Jeremiah, who was one of these, foretold how long the captivity was to last. The occurrence of the complaint is indeed, by some, deemed sufficient to show that the psalm belongs to the age of the Maccabees, and has reference to the sufferings inflicted on the Jews by Antiochus Epiphanes. This subject of Maccabean psalms will come up again; meanwhile it is enough to say that the one before us cannot have been written after the captivity, inasmuch as the second temple was never consumed with fire till its final destruction by the Romans. The truth is, that complaints uttered in the first pressure of sore affliction are not to be interpreted too literally. The eye dimmed with sudden tears sees only the dark side of things, and is unable for a while to do justice to the rays of light which mitigate the darkness of its affliction. That the psalmist's words must be taken with some qualification, is apparent from the fact, that the same complaint which he utters is found in the Lamentations of Jeremiah himself. He was certainly a prophet, and never ceased to see the visions of God; yet he exclaims, "The Lord hath cast off his altar: he hath purposed to destroy the wall of the daughter of Zion: the law is no more; her prophets also find no vision from the Lord," Lam. ii. 8, 9. Let us hear the psalmist:—

> "O God, why hast thou cast us off for ever?
> Why doth thine anger smoke against the sheep of thy pasture?"

&c., to ver. 10. Such is the former half of the psalm. The latter half is of a more cheerful tenor. The church remembers God's mighty works in nature and in grace, and her grief is assuaged. With recovered faith she betakes once more to prayer: "Have respect unto the covenant; for the dark places of the earth are full of the habitations of cruelty."—*Binnie.*

9. *There is no more any prophet.* The expression has without good reason been maintained to favour the Maccabean reference: it is rather against it. For it takes for granted that the people of the Lord had a *little while ago* enjoyed the presence of prophets. It is only of fresh wounds that the psalmist complains, not of the loss of something of which the people had been deprived for a hundred years, and with the want of which they had long since become familiar. The words are to be explained from Ezek. vii. 26, where it is threatened, "and they seek (in vain) the face of the prophet," from Lam. ii. 9, "and their prophets find not the face of the Lord," and from 1 Sam. xxviii. 6, 15, according to which Saul got no answer from the Lord through the prophets. Jeremiah did indeed survive the destruction of the temple (and to this reference has been made in support of the Maccabean exposition), but his prophetical office terminated with it. It was assuredly the cessation of his office that more immediately gave occasion to the painful cry: There is no longer any prophet. This standing ruin of the prophetical class proclaimed, even in louder accents than the non-appearance of other prophets, that God was no longer Israel's King. It was necessary, that along with the other signs of the dominion of God, this one also should cease for a long period of time, that the people might be taught how they had treated it, wherein they had offended, and might at the same time be led with tears of repentance to seek its return.—*Hengstenberg.*

PSALM LXXV.

There are very decisive reasons for maintaining that the psalm was composed during the time of the Assyrian distress under Hezekiah. The triumphant tone of the psalm does not allow us to descend to the time of the falling, or rather fallen state. Ver. 4-8 render it quite evident that the psalm was called forth by some severe distress on the part of the church of God; compare especially "the wicked of the earth," in ver. 8. We have here, as in Ps. xlvi., a catastrophe of a universal character: according to ver. 3, the whole circle of the earth is shaken, and the whole circle of the earth shall be calmed by the manifestations of might on the part of God. The catastrophe of the Assyrian invasion was the only one of this kind that ever occurred in all history. According to ver. 2 and 3 the people were quieted in the midst of their trouble by an assurance of divine assistance. This happened at the time of the Assyrian invasion by the prophecy of Isaiah. In ver. 6, the places named, from which Israel might possibly obtain human assistance, are the east, west, and south. The omission of the north indicates that the enemy had come from that quarter;—and the Assyrians did make their entrance into Canaan from Syria. To this we may add, that the psalm is closely related to Ps. xlvi. (compare at Ps. iv.), which undoubtedly belongs to the Assyrian period, and that the following psalm, which is also closely related, and is inscribed with the name of Asaph (compare at Ps. lxxiv.), belongs also to the same era.

The question may be asked, Was the psalm composed before or after the Assyrian invasion? Ewald adopts the latter supposition. The inspiration, he supposes, has descried in it the first visible beginning of a great general judgment of God upon all nations. But there are decisive reasons in favour of the *former* view, which indeed would never have been abandoned, had it not been supposed that there was an incongruity in conceiving of a song of triumph sung by the church *before* the victory, and while the *trouble* was still immediately lying upon her. In the very title, "To the chief musician, destroy not, a psalm of Asaph, a song of praise," the expression, "destroy not" (compare at Ps. lvii. 1), which does *not* occur in Ps. lxxvi., where we find the celebration of the victory, after it had been gained, shows that, under "Lord God, we praise thee," there lies concealed, "Lord, have mercy on us." On the supposition that the psalm was composed after the deliverance had been obtained, there is assuredly too little said about it, and the basis laid for hope in the future is too narrow. The thanksgiving and the praise in ver. 9 are merely promised for *future* assistance—a proof that as yet none had been imparted. Finally, the *following* psalm, which was also composed by Asaph, expresses thanks and joy for the assistance which had been already obtained. The two psalms make up one entire whole, if Ps. lxxv. be considered as a song of triumph over what had been *promised.* —*Hengstenberg.*

The reign of Hezekiah witnessed just such another INVASION and DELIVERANCE as had been seen in Jehoshaphat's time. The facts already noticed remind us that this was the age in which the Assyrian monarchy had attained the highest noon of its splendour. It was at this time that the Assyrian kings were rearing at Nineveh those great palaces, whose sculptured slabs have lately lent a new attraction to the museums of Europe. Shalmanezer, who carried the ten tribes into captivity, had been succeeded by Sennacherib, and the new monarch was resolved to measure his strength with the king of Egypt. That he might leave no hostile fortress to threaten his rear, he determined to capture Jerusalem and remove the people to share the captivity of their brethren. The sacred writers have narrated in great detail the history of this attempt: the impious letter of the Assyrian king; the arrogant pride of Rabshakeh his lieutenant; Hezekiah's prayer as he spread the letter before the Lord in the temple; the comfortable answer sent by Isaiah; the stroke of the angel of the Lord which laid low 180,000 men, the flower of Assyria, in one night; the flight of Sennacherib in shame to his own land. As in Jehoshaphat's time the danger and the deliverance are both of them celebrated in psalms. It is certain that Ps. lxxvi. celebrates the *deliverance;* and Ps. lxxv. bears traces of having been written in the crisis of the *danger.* An unfortunate mistranslation in the second verse of the latter psalm is apt to mislead the reader of the authorized version. The verse expresses *God's* purpose, not the purpose of the psalmist. "When I shall seize the appointed time, I will judge uprightly:" God may hide himself long, but when the fit time, the time of his own appointment, comes, he will make bare his arm in the defence of the oppressed.—*Binnie.*

2. *When I shall receive the congregation, I will judge uprightly:* "For I shall *fix a time* when I shall judge righteously." In ver. 2 and 3 we have the grounds of the confidence which the church expressed in ver. 1: God has promised to her his help. Both verses contain the words of God which are uttered in reply to the address of the church: You may well be thus full of my praise, *for*, &c., מועד is the point of time which God has fixed for executing his purposes: compare Ps. cii. 13, thou shalt arise and have mercy on Zion, for the time to be gracious to her is come, yea the *set time*, Hab. ii. 3; Dan. viii. 19; xi. 27, 35. To this, God's point of time, the eye of faith should, in the midst of suffering, be steadily directed. *Arnd:* "Our God, who governs the world by his omnipotence and wisdom, has appointed to all things a boundary, and has also fixed a time and an hour for his judgment, and when this comes, he reveals his judgments, and no man can hinder them. God withholds punishment for a very long time, but at last it comes with certainty, and makes no delay. Even the heathen have learned this from experience according to the saying: *sera tamen tacitis pœna venit pedibus*, and also in the words of Val. Maximus, *tarditatem pœnæ gravitate compensat.*" That *point of time* comes when the chastisement of the church has been brought to a close: compare Is. x. 12, "And it shall come to pass, that when the Lord hath performed his whole work on mount Zion and on Jerusalem, I will punish the pride of the king of Assyria."—*Hengstenberg.*

6. *For promotion cometh neither from the east*, &c. Although many attain to exalted stations either by unlawful arts or by the aid of worldly instrumentality, yet that does not happen by

chance; such persons being advanced to their elevated position by the secret purpose of God, that forthwith he may scatter them like refuse or chaff. The prophet does not simply attribute *judgment* to God. He also defines what kind of judgment it is, affirming it to consist in this, that, casting down one man and elevating another to dignity, he orders the affairs of the human race as seemeth good in his sight. I have stated that the consideration of this is the means by which haughty spirits are most effectually humbled; for the reason why worldly men have the daring to attempt whatever comes into their minds is because they conceive of God as shut up in heaven, and think not that they are kept under restraint by his secret providence. In short, they would divest him of all sovereign power, that they might find a free and an unimpeded course for the gratification of their lusts. To teach us then, with all moderation and humility, to remain contented with our condition, the psalmist clearly defines in what the judgment of God, or the order which he observes in the government of the world, consists, telling us that it belongs to him alone to exalt or to abase those of mankind whom he pleases.

From this it follows that all those who, spreading the wings of their vanity, aspire after any kind of exaltation, without any regard to or dependence upon God, are chargeable with robbing him as much as in them lies of his prerogative and power. This is very apparent, not only from their frantic counsels, but also from the blasphemous boastings in which they indulge, saying, Who shall hinder me? What shall withstand me? As if, forsooth! it were not an easy matter for God, with his nod alone, suddenly to cast a thousand obstacles in their way, with which to render ineffectual all their efforts. As worldly men by their fool-hardihood and perverse devices are chargeable with endeavouring to despoil God of his royal dignity, so whenever we are dismayed at their threatenings, we are guilty of wickedly setting limits to the sovereignty and power of God. If, whenever we hear the wind blowing with any degree of violence, we are as much frightened as if we were stricken with a thunderbolt from heaven, such extreme readiness to be thrown into a state of consternation manifestly shows that we do not as yet thoroughly understand the nature of that government which God exercises over the world. We would no doubt be ashamed to rob him of the title of Judge; yea, there is almost no individual who would not shrink with horror at the thought of so great a blasphemy; and yet when our natural understanding has extorted from us the confession that he is the judge and the supreme ruler of the world, we conceive of him as holding only a kind of inactive sovereignty, which I know not how to characterize, as if he did not govern mankind by his power and wisdom.—*Calvin.*

PSALM LXXVI.

There are very satisfactory reasons for referring this psalm, as the translators of the Septuagint and the Vulgate saw, to the Assyrian catastrophe. The preceding psalm was composed in prospect of this, and the psalm before us after its actual commencement.

The enthusiastic feeling, the courageous tone which characterizes the prophecies and also the psalms of the Assyrian period (comp. besides, Ps. lxxv., especially Ps. xlvi.), meets us in this psalm. It celebrates, according to ver. 3, a mighty overthrow of the enemies, which put an end at one blow to the war. This overthrow took place, according to the same verse, *before* Jerusalem; on which Jarchi remarks, that within the whole compass of sacred history there occurs no other example of the overthrow of the enemy *before* Jerusalem. The overthrow took place without any co-operation on the part of the people, and by an immediate exercise of divine omnipotence, ver. 3, 6, and 8, God has manifested himself as one who cuts off the breath of princes, ver. 12: the enemies are not only driven away, they are put to death. The catastrophe is an event in the *world's history:* all the meek of the *earth* are delivered through the judgment of God, ver. 9, the tumultuous *earth* is in consequence of it quieted, ver. 8, and God has manifested himself as terrible to the kings of the *earth*, ver. 12. The exhortation to the heathen to honour God by presents, ver. 11, is in accordance with the narrative as given in 2 Chr. xxxii. 23, that they actually did so in consequence of the destruction of the Assyrian army. —*Hengstenberg.*

Ps. lxxvi. was evidently written in the first flush of the grateful joy with which the marvellous discomfiture of the Assyrians gladdened every countenance in Jerusalem. It is rendered with such exquisite skill and spirit in the authorized version (and, I may add, in the Scots metrical version also) that citation is unnecessary. Let the reader compare it with the narrative given in Isaiah and the historical books, and he will not marvel that the critics, divided as they are in opinion regarding the origin of so many other psalms, are almost unanimous in connecting this one with the mysterious discomfiture of Sennacherib's host.

To some it may seem that a psalm which originated in an event so marvellous, and which bears such indubitable marks of its origin, must be little adapted for the subsequent use of God's people, and therefore must be out of place in the hymnal of the church catholic. But facts refute such a notion. Times without number the psalm has been sung, as furnishing the fittest expression of the thoughts and feelings of God's people in view of deliverances wrought for them. When the Covenanters at Drumclog closed their ranks to meet the onset of Claverhouse and his dragoons, they sang the opening verses to the tune of Martyrs:—

"In Judah's land God is well known,
His name's in Isr'el great:
In Salem is his tabernacle,
In Zion is his seat.

There arrows of the bow he brake,
The shield, the sword, the war.
More glorious thou than hills of prey,
More excellent art far.

Those that were stout of heart are spoiled,
They slept their sleep outright;
And none of those their hands did find
That were the men of might."

A century earlier, in 1588, when the first rumour of the discomfiture of the Spanish Armada reached Edinburgh, and the citizens assembled to render thanks to God, Robert Bruce, addressing them in the West Kirk, took this psalm for his text, and the two noble sermons he preached on the occasion were, from beginning to end, little more than a running commentary on the psalm. And every hearer must have felt that the whole was as appropriate to the circumstances as if the psalm had been written for the occasion.—*Binnie.*

5, 6. *The stout-hearted are spoiled*, &c. It must be acknowledged that these two verses seem, in a very particular manner, to point at the miraculous destruction of Sennacherib's army, when the "stout-hearted," who doubted not of taking and spoiling the holy city, were themselves suddenly "spoiled" of strength and life; they "slept their sleep, and found not their hands;" they awaked not again to the use of their powers and faculties; a rebuking blast was sent from the God of Jacob, under which the flower of Assyria withered in the space of a night, and in the morning was no more; "the horse and his rider were cast into a dead sleep;" they slept the sleep of death. How, in a moment, "were the mighty fallen, and the weapons of war perished!" How astonishing the downfal of the tyrant! How complete the triumph of the daughter of Sion! Such will be the destruction of the world; such the salvation of the people of God.—*Horne.*

PSALM LXXVII.

Expositors differ widely on the occasion of the psalm, and the time to which it is to be referred. *Dr. Binnie* refers it to the eve of the captivity. "Ps. lxxvii.—another 'psalm of Asaph'—may with all confidence be likewise referred to the eve of the captivity. From the way in which the psalmist gathers comfort by the recollection of the past, 'the days of old, the years of ancient times,' 'the years of the right hand of the Most High,' it is sufficiently plain that his sorrow, the 'sore which ran in the night and ceased not,' was not a private grief, but flowed from his sympathy with the calamity of Zion. It is pleasant to note here also the continued working of the brotherly love lately rekindled between Israel and Judah. Joseph participated in the redemption from Egypt, and the psalmist calls that fact to mind, that he may comfort himself with the hope that the children of Joseph will be remembered when the Lord shall turn the captivity of his people. 'Thou art the God that doest wonders: thou hast declared thy strength among the 'peoples.' Thou hast with thine arm redeemed thy people, the sons of Jacob and Joseph.'"

[*Close of the psalm.*] There is a day coming when we shall, with Christ our head, sing of the church's safe guidance to her rest, in such strains as these, remembering how often by the way we were ready to ask, "Has God forgotten to be gracious?" We are taught by the harp of Asaph in moments of despondency, to "*remember the days of old,*" and assure ourselves that the God of Israel liveth—the God of the passover night, the God of the Red Sea, the God of the pillar-cloud, the God of Sinai, the God of the wilderness, the God of Jordan—the God, too, we may add, of Calvary, and the God of Bethany, who shall lead us as he led Israel, even when earth shakes again, till that day when he comes to cast some light on "his way that was in the sea, and his paths that were in the great waters, and his footsteps" that were a mystery. Asaph has been the instrument of the Holy Ghost to cheer us here, by bidding us look on this picture of *the righteous One under the cloud recalling to mind the Lord's former doings.—Bonar.*

PSALM LXXVIII.

This psalm appears to have been written after David's elevation to the throne, and perhaps before he was acknowledged by the whole race of Israel, 2 Sam. v. 5. Its design is to impress upon the public mind the true grounds of the transfer which had taken place, of the pre-eminence in Israel, from the tribe of Ephraim to that of Judah, as the execution of a divine purpose long before disclosed, and at the same time a just judgment on the sins committed by the people, under the predominant influence of Ephraim from the time of Joshua to that of Eli. The internal character of the psalm determines its external form, which is simple, and admits of no minute division, beyond that afforded by the historical succession of events, and the logical design of the composition, to prove that the Israelites under the ascendency of Ephraim were similar in character to the elder generation which came out of Egypt.—*Alexander.*

The general object of the psalm is to warn Israel, who had escaped the judgments of God, not to provoke a fresh judgment by a fresh apostasy. The conclusion, however, ver. 65-72, indicates, that besides this general object, the psalmist designed to warn the Israelites against a special sin to which they were peculiarly liable from the circumstances of the times. The danger was, that of not being willing to acquiesce in the divine arrangement, by which the prerogative of Ephraim was transferred to the tribe of Judah, of regarding that as a *usurpation* which was in fact a *divine judgment,* and of rebelling against the sanctuary in Zion and the dominion of David and his tribe. . . .

That the psalm, which in the title is called "An Instruction of Asaph," belonged to the age of David, and was therefore composed by the *famous* Asaph (comp. at Ps. lxxiv.), cannot be considered as doubtful, if we take a correct view of its contents and object. The last matters of *fact* on which the author touches, are the kingdom of David, which by the fut. in ver. 72 is exhibited as still standing, and the settlement of the sanctuary on Zion. His *object* is to warn the people against a *possible* revolt from David and from the sanctuary in Zion; he cannot therefore have possibly composed the psalm after this event had *taken place.* He acts in the prosecution of his object with such great *tenderness*—not naming expressly even once the disruption which it is his purpose to prevent, and making no express mention whatever of any inclination to this, which might exist at the time, but leaving his readers to make for themselves the practical application—that it is obvious that he must have written at a time when it was of importance not to irritate, for fear of increasing the dissatisfaction, by even supposing it to exist, and not to call forth the idea of the disruption, by naming it.—*Hengstenberg.*

64. *Their widows made no lamentation.* This implies the extent of the destruction, and is full of meaning to one who has been in an oriental city during a plague or other devastating calamity. At first the cry of wailing which always follows a death in ordinary circumstances is loud and frequent; but such cries do not increase but subside with the increase of the calamity and desolation. Death becomes a familiar object in every house, and every one absorbed in his own losses has little sympathy to spare for others. Hence the loudest lamentations cease to be noticed, or to draw condoling friends to the house of mourning; and therefore, as well as from the stupefaction of feeling which scenes of continued horror never fail to produce, a new death is received in silence, or only with sighs and tears. In fact all the usual observances are suspended. The dead are carried out and buried without mourning ceremonies, and without the presence of surviving friends, by men who make it an employment to take away the dead, on the backs of mules

or asses, from the homes they leave desolate. We have seen this.—*Kitto.*

70. *He chose David also his servant, and took him from the sheepfolds.* To apprehend the whole force of this passage to the end of ver. 73, we should recollect some of the peculiar conditions of the ancient pastoral life. The Hebrew patriarchs, and in a great measure their descendants, when settled in Canaan, did not usually intrust their flocks to menials and strangers, but either tended them in person, or intrusted them to their sons or near relations. The flock which David himself tended was that of his father Jesse. In later times the increase of the population and of the town life, led to the use of hired shepherds: but the difference of treatment which the flock received under the differing circumstances was most strongly felt by the Jews, and was on one occasion most pointedly indicated by our Saviour, who, in comparing himself to the shepherd-owner of a flock, says, "I am the good Shepherd: the good shepherd giveth his life for the sheep. *But he that is an hireling*, and not the shepherd, *whose own the sheep are not*, seeth the wolf coming, and leaveth the sheep, and fleeth. . . . The hireling fleeth *because he is an hireling, and careth not for the sheep*," Jn. x. 11–13. This position of our Saviour is admirably illustrated by the conduct of David himself, who combated and slew both a lion and a bear in defence of his father's flock, 1 Sam. xvii. 34, 35. If, therefore, the sheep under the shepherd-owner may rest in quiet, confident of lacking nothing which the care of that shepherd can provide, how much more he whose Shepherd is the Lord.—*Kitto.*

PSALM LXXIX.

Perowne inclines to the Maccabean origin of this psalm. But there is great force in the argument below:—

This psalm stands nearly related to Ps. lxxiv.; the situation is the same, and they come a good deal in contact as regards the expression. Both psalms refer to the Chaldean devastation. The psalm before us proceeds on the supposition that Ps. lxxiv. had been previously composed, and *supplements* it. In Ps. lxxiv. the *destruction of the sanctuary* was pre-eminently and almost exclusively brought forward; but in Ps. lxxix. it is referred to very briefly, for the purpose of indicating the passages where that psalm is to be brought in, and the other subjects are put in the foreground. There is no good reason for the assertion which has been made, that the psalm before us must have been composed previously to Ps. lxxiv., as the temple is there spoken of as entirely *destroyed*, whereas it is only its *desecration* that is spoken of here. The desecration does not exclude its destruction; the destruction is one of the forms of its desecration. Had the psalmist designed, in allusion to Ps. lxxiv., to speak of the sanctuary in *one single expression*, he could not possibly have found a stronger term than this: the most dreadful thing that can befall the *sanctuary* is that it be *desecrated.* In saying this everything that can be affirmed of it is said.

Several expositors, both ancient and modern, refer the psalm to the time of the Maccabees. But there are quite decisive grounds against this view. First, as it is so closely allied to Ps. lxxiv., the arguments which were *there* adverted to are of force *here*. There are also no traces here of any reference to the special relations of the times of the Maccabees. And there are two circumstances which are not suitable to those times: *the laying of Jerusalem in ruins*, ver. 1, and the mention of *nations* and *kingdoms* in ver. 6 (compare 2 Ki. xxiv. 2), whereas in the time of the Maccabees Judah had to do only with a *single* kingdom. There are also two weighty external reasons. Jeremiah was acquainted with the psalm, and made use of it—comp. at ver. 6, and in 1 Mac. vii. 16 and 17 it is quoted as forming at that time a portion of the sacred volume. It is thus not necessary here to avail ourselves of the general reasons which may be urged against the existence of Maccabean psalms.

The title, "a psalm of Asaph," is confirmed by the fact that the psalm stands closely related to a whole class of psalms which bear in their titles the name of Asaph. Those critics who reject the titles are unable to explain this similarity admitted by themselves, which obtains among all the Asaphic psalms, even among those which were composed at different eras. If we follow the title the reason of this is clear as day. The descendants of Asaph looked upon themselves as the instruments by which the Asaph of David's time, their illustrious ancestor, *continued to speak*, and therefore they very naturally followed as closely in his footsteps as possible: the later descendants, moreover, would always have the compositions of their more early ancestors before their minds. The unity of the person named in the title limits the unity of character of all these psalms. Any one who composed at his own hand, and did not look at his ancestor, or the early or contemporaneous organs of that ancestor, could not have adopted it.—*Hengstenberg.*

3. *There was none to bury them.* This in the East is no uncommon result of a great mortality, whether from war or from plague. Those who feel the deepest interest in the departed have already died, and strangers are too much absorbed in their own misery to undertake so great a labour. The bodies are therefore left to be devoured by dogs and jackals, or are disposed of by some summary public act. We saw much of this ourselves during the great plague of Baghdad in 1831. At first the people were so shocked at the mortality that they made great efforts to dispose of their dead. We recollect that in one quarter where the dead had accumulated frightfully, all the young men arose, and in one night buried all the dead. But this effort was not repeated; and at length, as the mortality increased, the survivors could not exert themselves further than to put the dead bodies into the street; or they left them in the houses, and withdrew to other houses which the plague had untenanted. This produced many shocking scenes; and at length the government found it necessary to hire men at a high price, to go through the town every day to collect the dead bodies, and—not to bury them, for there was no strength in the city left for that labour—but to cast them into the river Tigris. It was also noticed there at that time, that as the mortality increased, and a man saw all his household thinned off, his anxiety about the disposal of his own body would become very great—greater it seemed to us than with respect to the question of life or death; and many took extraordinary pains and incurred much expense to secure beforehand the chance of a decent interment as soon as the angel of death should smite them down. —*Kitto.*

PSALM LXXX.

The mention of the three tribes, "Ephraim, Benjamin, and Manasseh," may perhaps denote that this is a psalm for the northern kingdom. Some have supposed it to be a prayer of the ten tribes in their captivity in Assyria, and it has been conjectured that the inscription of the LXX., ὑπὲρ τοῦ 'Ασσυρίου, is to be taken in that sense. Calvin, on the other hand, thinks that it is a prayer *for* the ten tribes by a poet of the southern kingdom. He reminds us that even after the disruption prophets were sent from Judah to Israel, and that Amos (vi. 6) rebukes those in Judah who do not "grieve for the wound in Joseph." . . . In the course of time a portion of Benjamin may have become incorporated into the northern kingdom. The children of Rachel, Joseph (=Ephraim and Manasseh) and Benjamin, would naturally be drawn together. Benjamin, the tribe of Saul and Ishbosheth, and at one time the leading tribe, would not readily submit to the supremacy of Judah; a jealousy existed which was not extinguished in David's reign (2 Sam. xix. xx. xxi.), and which may have been revived later. It is moreover in favour of this view, that in the previous verse *Joseph* is mentioned, and not Judah; and hence the whole psalm refers apparently only to the kingdom of Israel.—*Perowne.*

It has long been felt that this psalm must have been written with reference to the gradual desolation of the ten tribes. This was pointed out by Calvin, and he has been followed by the best subsequent expositors. The reference to the ten tribes being evident, the psalm, according to Calvin, is a prayer of Judah for her afflicted sister. There was a time when, as the Lord complains by the prophet Amos (Am. vi. 6), the people of Judah, being "at ease in Zion," were "not grieved for the affliction of Joseph;" there was a time when they would have taken pleasure in the captivity of the northern kingdom, looking upon it as the removal of their rival. But they have been brought to a better mind, and have learned to pray for their brethren. That this represents the general drift of the psalm, is unquestionable. But it would require to be taken with some modification. Those who, like Dr. Hengstenberg, adhere to the letter of Calvin's view, are obliged to maintain that Benjamin, which is named along with Ephraim and Manasseh, belonged to Israel, not to Judah. If the psalm is a prayer for Ephraim, it is a prayer for Benjamin also. We get rid of all this difficulty if we look on the psalm as the joint prayer of all the tribes; *the prayer in which the house of Joseph and the house of Judah, so long estranged from one another, unite once more in calling on the God of Abraham, and Isaac, and Jacob.* The psalm has Asaph's name in the superscription, and is inscribed "to the chief musician." It is therefore a song of the temple. What more likely than that it was first sung in the temple in those early years of Hezekiah's reign, when Benjamin found himself once more associated with Ephraim and Manasseh, his mother's sons, in the solemn worship of the Lord; that it is the prayer in which the whole seed of Jacob, now happily restored to complete religious fellowship, united in spreading before the Lord the calamities of the nation, and prayed him to restore them again and cause his face to shine?—*Binnie.*

17. *Let thy hand be upon the man of thy right hand, upon the Son of Man, &c.* A whole host of expositors unhesitatingly refer this to the Messiah, and among them not a few of distinguished name. We subjoin one or two examples:—

"The man of God's right hand," and "the Son of Man" point out the promised Messiah very clearly.—*Scott.*

Here again the component parts of the name *Benjamin* are introduced as parallels, precisely as in ver. 16 (15). The *man of thy right hand* may either be the man whom thy power has raised up, or the man who occupies the post of honour at thy right hand. That the words were intended to suggest both ideas, is a supposition perfectly agreeable to Hebrew usage. A more doubtful question is that in reference to the first words of the sentence, *let thy hand be upon* him, whether this means in favour or in wrath. The only way in which both senses can be reconciled is by applying the words to the Messiah, as the ground of the faith and hope expressed. Let thy hand fall not on us but on our substitute. Compare the remarkably similar expressions in Acts v. 31.—*Alexander.*

Some think that in ver. 17 they are acknowledging *Messiah*, calling him by the name, "Man of thy right hand," "Branch made strong for thyself." The Chaldee Targum says this is "King Messiah." Others claim these names for Israel; for Israel is God's *Benjamin*, and God's strong rod wherewith to rule the nations. The words are in the original such as surely point to Messiah; for they are not "son of thy right hand," but אִישׁ יְמִינֶךָ, "*Man* of thy right hand," and "*son of man* whom thou hast made strong for thyself," בֶּן אָדָם; in this resembling Ps. viii. 6. Even if the terms were appropriate to Israel as God's favoured people, still there would be here simply an allusion to that fact, while the real possessor of the name is Messiah, God's true Israel. And if so, then ver. 17 is Israel, in the latter day, crying "Hosanna!" to Christ, and so entitled to what his words implicitly promised in Mat. xx. 39—"Thou shalt not see me henceforth TILL thou shalt say, Blessed is he that cometh in the name of the Lord." They pray, "*Appoint him* our captain—*let thy hand be upon him*, designating him to his office, as Moses did Joshua," Num. xxvii. 23. And so they may claim to be gathered and blessed with a fuller blessing than their fathers, who, *by the hand of God* upon them, were led up by Ezra (ch. vii. 9), and Nehemiah (ch. ii. 18); for they claim as their leader Messiah, the true Ezra, "Helper," and true Nehemiah, "the Lord's consolation." Is not Ps. cx. 1 of itself sufficient to justify the name, "The man of *thy right hand?*"

"Jehovah, God of hosts, bring us back! Cause thy countenance to shine on us! and we shall be saved" (נִוָּשֵׁעָה, the response to "Hosanna!" הוֹשִׁיעָה נָּא). May we not sympathize in these appeals? May we not put in our own case with theirs? Appoint, Lord, Messiah to be *our* Captain, our soul's leader, and we individually shall be saved! We cry "Hosanna!" הוֹשִׁיעָה נָּא, and thou wilt give a response that shall make us shout back, נִוָּשֵׁעָה. Yes, thy church in all the earth, Lord God of hosts, with one consent joins in presenting to thee *Israel's pleas for full restoration.*—*Andrew A. Bonar.*

PSALM LXXXI.

A partial reunion gladdened the whole church in the first year of Hezekiah. The recent captivity of two tribes and a half had weakened the northern kingdom; and Hoshea, who was Hezekiah's contemporary and the last of its kings, was led by a sense of duty to break the evil custom which his predecessors had inherited from Jeroboam the son of Nebat, "who sinned, and made Israel to sin." He suspended the law against going up to Jerusalem. Hezekiah's posts were permitted to carry to every part of the kingdom the invitation to unite once more with Judah in celebrating the passover in the city which God had chosen out of all the tribes of Israel (2 Chr. xxx.) The invitation, scorned by many, was gladly accepted by others; and a passover was celebrated the like of which had not been seen in Israel since the days of Solomon and the undivided kingdom.

So happy a reunion—happy in itself, twice happy as the pledge of the time when Ephraim should no more envy Judah, and Judah no more vex Ephraim, but they should be one stick in the Lord's hand—could not fail to call forth new songs. There is, I think, sufficient ground to attribute to it Ps. lxxxi. It is, obviously and by universal consent, a festal song. The reference to the exodus from Egypt shows that, although framed to suit all the three feasts, it had a special connection with the passover; and the emphatic reminder that the feast had been ordained in *Joseph* for a testimony may be fairly interpreted as pointing to an occasion when Ephraim and Manasseh, the sons of Joseph, participated with Judah in the solemn rite. There is an undertone of sadness towards the end which reminds us that the desolation of the northern kingdom was at hand; but it opens as with a blast of trumpets:—

"Sing aloud unto God our strength," &c.

—*Binnie.*

5. *A language that I understood not.* What was this unknown tongue? Two interpretations have been given. It has been explained (1) *Of the language of the Egyptians*, which was a foreign tongue to the Hebrews, who were "strangers in the land of Egypt." Comp. Ps. cxiv. 1, "the people of strange language," with Deut. xxviii. 49; Is. xxxiii. 19; Jer. v. 15. Accordingly this fact is mentioned as one of the aggravations of their condition in Egypt, like the toiling with "the burden" and "the basket." Calvin, who takes this view, remarks that the redemption of Israel from a people of foreign language was a special mark of God's favour, inasmuch as the want of that common language, which is the bond of society, made foreigner and enemy synonymous terms: "Quia enim lingua est veluti character mentis ac speculum, non secus ac sylvestres ferae, invicem alieni sunt qui carent linguae usu." It is no objection to this view that the words of God follow abruptly. See Ps. lxxv. 2. (2) *Of the voice of God*, a voice which the people had heard as uttered in his judgments upon the Egyptians, and in his covenant made with themselves, but had not understood (comp. Acts vii. 25). This language is there given in substance in a poetical form by the psalmist, who seems suddenly to hear it, and to become the interpreter to his people of the divine voice. He here places in a fresh light, gives a new application to the earlier revelation, the meaning and purpose of which were not then understood.

Hupfeld supposes it to be called an "unknown" language, merely because it is divine, unlike the everyday *known* language of men. Ab. Ezra sees a reference to the words of God uttered on Sinai. So also Delitzsch, who would explain the expression by reference to Exod. vi. 2, &c. "It was the language of a known, and yet unknown God, which Israel heard from Sinai. God, in fact, now revealed himself to Israel in a new character, not only as the Redeemer and Saviour of his people from their Egyptian bondage, but also as their King, giving them a law which bound them together as a people, and was the basis of their national existence."

This latter interpretation, which regards the language here spoken of as the voice of God, and as virtually given in the following verses, is now that most commonly adopted. It is that of Mendelssohn, Ewald, Delitzsch, and Hupfeld.—*Perowne.*

6. The words of God follow without any indication of a change of speakers. The prophet identifies himself with, and becomes the organ of, the divine voice. He reminds Israel of that fact in connection with which the festival was instituted. It is as though, amidst all the gladness of the feast, and all the music and the pomp of its celebration, other thoughts arose, not to check, but to guide the current of a holy exultation. The sound of trumpet and timbrel and sacred song must be hushed while Jehovah speaks, to tell his forgetful people the lesson of their past history associated with that festival, the warning and the expostulation

suggested by their own perverseness. If they would praise him aright, it must be with hearts mindful of his goodness, and sensible of their own unworthiness and ingratitude. For the spirit in which all festivals should be kept, see on the offering of the first-fruits, Deut. xxvi. 1-11.—*Perowne.*

At the first clause of ver. 6, comp. Exod. vi. 6, 7, "I, the Lord, bring you out from under the burden of the Egyptians." The basket (דוד) is, according to the parallelism, the *burden-basket.* Baskets of this kind were found in the sepulchral vaults which have been opened in Thebes, of which Rosellini first furnished drawings and descriptions: the Israelites used them for carrying from one place to another the clay and manufactured bricks.—*Hengstenberg.*

The same author, in his *Egypt and the Books of Moses,* has the following remarks illustrative of the allusion in our psalm:—Of the labourers, says Rosellini (describing a picture from a tomb in Thebes), some are employed in transporting the clay in vessels, some in intermingling it with the straw, others are taking the bricks out of the form and placing them in rows, still others, with a piece of wood upon their backs and ropes on each side, carry away the bricks already burned or dried. . . . Their complexion, physiognomy, and beard permit us not to be mistaken in supposing them to be Hebrews. Among the Hebrews, four Egyptians are seen: two of them carry a stick in their hand ready to fall upon two other Egyptians, who are here represented like the Hebrews, one of them carrying on his shoulder a vessel of clay, and the other returning from the transportation of brick, carrying his empty vessel to get a new load.

PSALM LXXXII.

Ewald, De Wette, Hitzig, and others suppose the expostulations of the psalm to be addressed, not to Israelitish but to heathen rulers, satraps, &c., by a poet who lived towards the end of the exile in Babylon, and who, witnessing the corruption which was fast undermining the Babylonish empire, lifted up his voice against it. This view rests mainly upon the appeal to God (in ver. 7) as the Ruler and Judge of *all nations,* not of Israel exclusively. But the psalmists so frequently take a wider range than their own nation, so constantly in a true prophetic spirit recognize the special rule and revelation of God in Israel, as only a part of his universal dominion (comp. for instance, Ps. vii. 6-8), that there is no need to depart from the more common view that Israelitish judges are meant; especially as this is confirmed by the general tenor of the psalm. Besides, as Stier and Hupfeld have pointed out, the names, "gods," and "sons of the Highest," are never given to heathen monarchs in Scripture. The former says, "We look in vain for a passage where a heathen king, or even an Israelitish, except David and Solomon as types of the Messiah, is thought worthy of this name (Son of God)."—*Perowne.*

If the psalm was composed in the time of David, in favour of which supposition may be pleaded the prophetic tone peculiar to the Asaph of that period, and against which no tenable ground can be advanced (even Hitzig must allow that there is no allusion of any kind, no late form or connecting particle, no term which could be pronounced as being decidedly of later origin to betray an author belonging to a later age), the psalmist could not, in the first instance, assuredly have referred to the king—a view which is confirmed by the express mention of "the princes" in ver. 7, as compared with "the ancients of his people and the princes thereof" in Is. iii. Still, though the psalm was in the first instance called forth by existing relations, yet being destined for all ages, it undoubtedly admits of being applied to kings in the discharge of their duty as judges, in so far as they are guilty of that perversion of right here imputed to them. . . .

In the law of Moses all those whose office it is to command, to judge, and to arbitrate, all those to whom in any respect reverence and regard is due, are set apart as the representatives of God on earth. The foundation of this is found in the commandment, "Honour thy father and mother," in the Decalogue. It was shown in the *Beitr.* P. iii. p. 605, that this commandment belongs to the first table—thou shalt fear and honour God, first in himself, second in those who represent him on earth—and farther, that the parents are named in it only in an individualizing manner as representatives of all who are possessed of worth, and are worthy of esteem. The direction in Lev. xix. 32 rises on the foundation of this commandment, where respect for the *aged* appears as the immediate consequence of respect for God, whose eternity was designed to be revered and honoured under the emblem of their old age; also Ex. xxii. 27, according to which we are taught to recognize in governors a reflection of the majesty of God: "thou shalt not revile God, nor curse the ruler of thy people," *i.e.* thou shalt not curse thy ruler (or in any other way dishonour him), for he bears the image of God, and every insult offered to such a representative of God in his kingdom is an insult against God, in him God himself is honoured and revered—comp. 1 Chr. xxix. 23, "and Solomon sat upon the throne of Jehovah." But it was in connection with the office of judge that the stamp of divinity was most conspicuous, inasmuch as that office led the people under the foreground of an humble earthly tribunal to contemplate the background of a lofty divine judgment: "the judgment is God's," Deut. i. 17, whoever comes before it, comes before God, Ex. xxi. 6; xxii. 7, 8.

The position assigned to the office of judge must, when properly considered, have exerted a practical influence of a twofold character. It must have filled those who were brought before its tribunal with a sacred reverence for an authority which maintained its right upon earth in the name of God. And on the part of the judges themselves it must have led them to take a lofty view of their calling, it must have called forth earnest efforts to practise the virtues of him whose place they occupied, him "who does not favour princes, and makes no distinction between rich and poor, for they are the work of his hands," Job xxxiv. 19, and it must have awakened a holy fear of becoming liable to his judgment. For there could be no doubt that as they judged in God's stead, the heavenly Judge would not suffer them to go unpunished should they misuse their office, but would in that case come forth from his place, and utter his thundering cry, "How long!" This last idea is expressly brought forward in the law. In Deut. i. 17 solemn admonitions are addressed to judges, grounded on the lofty position assigned to their office—comp. 2 Chr. xix. 6, 7, where Jehoshaphat, with still greater copiousness of detail, addresses the following admonitions to the judges whom he commissioned:—"Take heed what ye do, for ye judge not for man, but for God, who is with you in the judgment: wherefore now let the fear of the Lord be upon you, take heed and do it, for there is no iniquity with the Lord our God, nor respect of persons, nor taking of gifts."—*Hengstenberg*.

1. *God standeth in the congregation of the mighty.* "God sitteth in the assembly of God." It is unquestionably a very unbecoming thing for those whom God has been pleased to invest with the government of mankind for the common good, not to acknowledge the end for which they have been exalted above the others, nor yet by whose blessing they have been placed in so elevated a station; but, instead of doing this, contemning every principle of equity, to rule just as their own unbridled passions dictate. So infatuated are they by their own splendour and magnificence, as to imagine that the whole world was made only for them. Besides, they think that it would derogate from their elevated rank were they to be governed by moderate counsels; and although their own folly is more than enough to urge them on in their reckless career, they notwithstanding seek for flatterers to soothe and applaud them in their vices. To correct this arrogance, the psalm opens by asserting, that although men occupy thrones and judgment-seats, God nevertheless continues to hold the office of supreme ruler. God has made even a heathen and licentious poet bear testimony to this truth:—

> "Regum timendorum in proprios greges,
> Reges in ipsos imperium est Jovis,
> Clari giganteo triumpho,
> Cuncta supercilio moventis."
> *Horatii Carm.* lib. iii. od. 1.

> "Kings rule their subject flocks; great Jove
> O'er kings themselves his reign extends,
> Who hurl'd the rebel giants from above;
> At whose majestic nod all nature bends."
> *Boscawen's Translation.*

That the potentates of this world may not arrogate to themselves more than belongs to them, the prophet here erects a throne for God, from which he judges them all, and represses their pride; a thing which is highly necessary. They may indeed admit that they owe their elevation to royal power to the favour of God, and they may worship him by outward ceremonies, but their greatness so infatuates them that they are chargeable with expelling and casting him to a distance from their assembly by their vain imaginations; for they cannot bear to be subject to reason and laws. Thus the design of the prophet was to deride the madness by which the princes of this world are bewitched in leaving God no place in their assembly. The more effectually to overthrow this irrational self-confidence with which they are intoxicated, civil order is termed *the assembly of God;* for although the divine glory shines forth in every part of the world, yet when lawful government flourishes among men, it is reflected therefrom with pre-eminent lustre. I indeed grant that it is quite common for the Hebrews to adorn with the title of *God* whatever is rare and excellent. But here it would appear from the scope of the passage that this name of the Divine Being is applied to those who occupy the exalted station of princes, in which there is afforded a peculiar manifestation of the majesty of God; even as Solomon in Prov. ii. 17 calls marriage "the covenant of God," from the peculiar sanctity with which that relation is distinguished. In the second clause of the verse it is not material whether we read, *He will judge in the midst of the gods*, or, *He will judge the gods in the midst.* The first construction, however, is the most easy and natural, that, however much the rulers of the world may exalt themselves, they cannot in the least impair the authority of God by divesting him of his sovereignty over them and of the government of all things, which he will ever retain as his inalienable prerogative. But here, as also a little after, the name *gods* is to be understood of *judges*, on whom God has impressed special marks of his glory. To apply it to angels is a fancy too strained to admit of serious consideration.—*Calvin.*

6. *I have said, Ye are gods.* Luther, after giving a picture of the wickedness and profligacy of the great men of his time, remarks: "There existed also among the Jewish people youths of this character, who kept continually in their mouths the saying of Moses in Ex. xxii. 9. They employed this saying as a cloak and shield for their wickedness against the preachers and the prophets; and gave themselves great airs while they said, Wilt thou punish us and instruct us? Dost thou not know that Moses calls us gods? Thou art a rebel, thou speakest against the ordinance of God, thou preachest to the detriment of our honour. Now the prophet acknowledges, and does not deny, that they are gods, he will not be rebellious, or weaken their honour or authority, like the disobedient and rebellious people, or like the mad saints who make heretics and enthusiasts, but he draws a proper distinction between their power and the power of God. He allows that they are gods over men, but not over God himself. It is as if he said, It is true you are gods over us all, but not over Him who is the God of us all. From this we see in what a high and glorious position God intends to maintain the office of the magistracy. For who will set himself against those on whom God bestows his own name? Whoever despises them despises at the same time the true Magistrate, God, who speaks and judges in them and through them, and calls their judgment his judgment. The apostle Paul, Rom. xiii. 2, points out the consequences of this; and experience amply confirms his statement. But again, just as on the one hand he restrains the discontent of the populace, and brings them, on account of it, under the sword and under law, so does he, on the other hand, restrain the magistracy, that it shall not abuse such majesty and power for wickedness, but employ it in the promotion and maintenance of peace. But yet only so far, that he will not permit the people to lift up their arm against it, or to seize the sword for the purpose of punishing and judging it. No, that they shall not do; God has not commanded it. He himself, God, will punish wicked magistrates, he will be judge and master over them, he will get at them better than any one else could, as he has done from the beginning of the world."—*Hengstenberg.*

Children of the Most High. It may well make one wonder that he calls such wicked individuals as those whom he here rebukes so sharply, by the name of sons of God or sons of the Highest, since children of God is an appellation which in Scripture is applied to holy believers. Answer—It is just as great a wonder that he should bestow upon such wicked people his own name; yea, it is rather a greater wonder that he should call them gods. But it all lies in the word: I have said. For we have often remarked that the word of God sanctifies and deifies all things to which it is applied. Wherefore we may call such situations as have had impressed upon them the word of God, in every respect holy divine conditions, although the persons are not holy. Just as father, mother, preacher, minister, &c., are in every respect holy divine situations, although the persons who are in them may be knaves and rogues. Thus, inasmuch as God stamps the office of magistry with his word, magistrates are correctly called gods, and the children of God on account of their divine condition, and the word of God, although they are really vile knaves, as he complains that they are."—*Luther*.

PSALM LXXXIII.

Among those who ascribe the psalm to the age of Jehoshaphat, as Kimchi, De Wette, Hengstenberg, Alexander, &c., Dr. Binnie has also taken his place; and his remarks show how completely he has entered into the spirit of this grand warlike ode. (See Appendix—Ps. xlviii.)

Title. A *song* and *psalm* by Asaph; lively, yet solemn; for there is in it both victory and vengeance. The appeal of last psalm to the Judge, by Asaph, in the name of Messiah and his people, is of the same spirit with this more lengthened and full prayer by the same Asaph. The times are the same. Whatever were the circumstances of the psalmist that furnished an appropriate season in the view of the Spirit of God for giving it to the church—whether such as those of Jehoshaphat's reign (2 Chr. xx. 14) or not—it seems probable that He who knew men's hearts saw more than once this same hatred to Israel taking the form of a combined conspiracy of all the nations round. Even thus has it been more than once in regard to Britain, the retreat of God's hidden ones; and even thus, were the veil lifted up, might it be found to be true at this hour of the foes of Protestant truth. And yet more shall the latter day bring to view a combination of kings and people against the Lamb and his faithful few—a combination which shall meet with extinction on the plains of Megiddo, most fully realizing the prayer and anticipations of this psalm, ver. 9–11. What a song for days when Antichrist shall be wondered at by all the earth! It is pervaded by a tone of astonishment at the Lord's long-suffering.—*A. A. Bonar*.

3. *Hidden ones.* The safety of God's people does not depend on their number, wit, prowess, or inherent strength, but on him who has made them his *hidden ones*. He that touches them, touches the apple of his eye, Zec. ii. 8. In the time of trouble he shall hide them in his pavilion; in the secret of his tabernacle shall he hide them, Ps. xxvii. 5. They are in no sense hidden from the notice or care of God, Is. xl. 27; Ps. xxxviii. 9; Hos. v. 3; 2 Tim. ii. 19. Nor is their course clandestine or cunning. Their very candour makes them suspected. Though they are not ostentatious, they are not deceitful. Nor do they make a secret of their love to Christ. Nor do they try to hide their sins from the eyes of God, but freely confess and bewail them. They have renounced the hidden things of dishonesty, and do not walk in craftiness. Nor do they pass through life without a mark upon them. The world fixes its stigma, and God puts his name in their foreheads. They are the light of the world. And yet they are God's hidden ones. They are hid in God. The being, the providence, every perfection of God, and every part of his Word, are chambers where the humble find refuge. See Ps. xxxii. 7; lxxxiv. 11; Prov. xviii. 10. They are God's *hidden ones*, because they are secretly nourished, having meat to eat which the world knows not of. Nor is their true character known, 1 John iii. 1. Nor does any roll of church-membership on earth contain a correct list of their names. They are often hidden under the calumnies, suspicions, and outcries of the wicked. Their best acts are misjudged, and their best qualities misnamed. And they are all hid in Christ, Col. iii. 3, 4. They are all hidden under the shadow of Jehovah's wings. Though unknown, they are yet well known, where it is of most importance to be known.—*Plumer*.

5–8. *For they have consulted together*, &c. *Calvin's* remarks on these verses afford a fine specimen of the Christian adaptation of the psalm to the circumstances of the church and people of God when numerous and fierce enemies are banded together against them:—"The multiplied hosts which united their powers together to oppose the church of God, and to effect her overthrow, are here enumerated. As so many nations, formed into one powerful confederacy, were bent on the destruction of a kingdom not greatly distinguished by its power, the miraculous aid of God was indispensably necessary for the deliverance of a people who, in such extremity, were altogether unable to defend themselves. In circumstances apparently as hopeless good king Asa gave utterance to that truly magnanimous reflection: 'Lord, it is nothing with thee to help, whether with many or with them that have no power: help us, O Lord our God! for we rest on thee, and in thy name we go against this multitude,' 1 Chr. xiv. 11. The same Spirit who inspired that pious king with such invincible fortitude dictated this psalm for the benefit of the whole church, to encourage her with unhesitating confidence to betake herself to God for aid. And in our own day he sets before us these words, in order that no danger or difficulty may prevent us from calling upon God. When the whole world may conspire together against us, we have as it were a wall of brass for the defence of Christ's kingdom in these words, 'Why do the heathen rage?' &c., Ps. ii. 1.

"It will be in no small degree profitable to us to contemplate this as an example in which we have represented to us, as in a mirror, what has been the lot of the church of God from the beginning. This, if rightly reflected on, will keep us at the present day from being unduly dejected when we witness the whole world in array against us. . . . When we have once arrived at a settled persuasion that no strange thing happens to us, the contemplation of the condition of the church in old time will strengthen us for continuing in the exercise of patience until God suddenly display his power, which is perfectly able, without any created aid, to frustrate all the attempts of the world.

"To remove from the minds of the godly all misgivings as to whether help is ready to be imparted to them from heaven, the prophet distinctly affirms that those who molest the church are chargeable with making war against God, who has taken her under his protection. The principle upon which God declares that he will be our helper is contained in these words, 'He that toucheth you toucheth the apple of mine eye,' Zec. ii. 8. And what is said in another psalm concerning the patriarchs is equally applicable to all true believers, 'Touch not mine anointed, and do my prophets no harm,' Ps. cv. 15. He will have the anointing with which he has anointed us to be, as it were, a buckler to keep us in perfect safety."

PSALM LXXXIV.

A Korahite psalm. See Ps. xlii. xliii.

3. *Yea, the sparrow hath found an house*, &c. We acknowledge a strong preference for the natural and beautiful rendering of this verse adopted by Calvin, Walford, Thrupp, Bossuet, Adam Clarke, and others—"Even as the sparrow findeth an house, and the swallow a nest for herself where she may lay her young, (so I seek) thine altars, O Lord of hosts." The reader will observe that the English version supplies the particle "*even*," and that the above supplement is equally competent, and furnishes the beautiful idea that the saint is drawn to the house of God with a gracious instinct akin to that which draws the wandering bird home to her nest. We subjoin *Walford's* note:—"The common opinion respecting this verse is that it represents sparrows, &c., as building their nests in some parts of the sacred edifices. No other sense can indeed be drawn from the English translation. But there are serious objections to this view of the matter. It is not in the least degree likely that any such lodgments were permitted within these consecrated precincts; and even if they could have been allowed, there seems to be no reason why these birds should prefer this to other more commodious places, where they would not be liable to the disturbance unavoidable here, as the concourse to the house of God was incessant and very great. It is therefore clear that the psalmist expresses in this poetic imagery, his strong desire to be readmitted to the sacred abode. The particles of similitude, "as" and "so," are not indeed in the original text; but there are many instances in which they are omitted in Hebrew, but where it is necessary to supply them in order to make an intelligible version. The sense of the passage thus taken is, As these birds delight in their appropriate abodes, and frequent them with constancy, so it is my earnest wish to be restored to the enjoyments which I have derived from a continued resort to thy house."

Hengstenberg is not materially different:—"Modern expositors have gone astray in consequence of their having unfortunately taken up the idea that the psalm contains the expression of the earnest longings after the temple of one separated from it. They translate: 'Even the sparrows find an house, and the swallows a nest, for themselves, where they lay their young in thine altars, Jehovah Sabaoth, my King and my God,' and suppose the idea intended to be conveyed is: and are thus happier than I am, who am separated from thy sanctuary. 'But the thought obtained in this way is one, notwithstanding the defence which has been made of it by De Wette and Maurer, of a trivial character, and unworthy the holy earnestness of Israelitish poetry; a bird certainly was in no very enviable situation which had fixed its place of dwelling and its nest in the house of the Lord. The main thing, moreover, *I am less fortunate than they*, is *wanting*, and added to the passage without any reason whatever. The '*with* thine altars,' instead of 'at,' is very strange, and certainly the unusual את would not have been used for the purpose of avoiding the ambiguity. The birds durst build their nest if generally in the sanctuary, yet certainly not in the neighbourhood of the *altars*. Finally, ver. 4 is not at all suitable, if we suppose that ver. 3 contains a lamentation over absence from the sanctuary; and even ver. 2 can only by a false interpretation be brought in this case into harmony with ver. 3."

6. *Through the valley of Baca.* This verse is extremely obscure; so that no version can be given of it which is entirely free from objection. I take the meaning to be in general this, that the truly pious worshippers of God allowed no inconveniences or difficulties, many of which attended on travelling in Judea, to prevent their attendance on the solemn festivals at Jerusalem; but that, on the contrary, their regard for these sacred rites was such, that the most rugged paths through dry and barren deserts were transformed by their affectionate longing for the presence of God into pleasant ways; the thirsty valleys, irrigated by no streams and ornamented by no verdure, yet became fertile, irriguous, and delightful, by means of the associations which were connected with them in the minds of these devout pilgrims, and through the sacred enjoyments which sprung from the divine influence and favour which were vouchsafed to them. A stanza in Addison's beautiful paraphrase of Ps. xxiii. expresses the precise notion of the psalmist's words:—

"Though in a bare and rugged way,
Through devious lonely wilds I stray,
His bounty will my pains beguile;
The barren wilderness shall smile;
With sudden green and herbage crowned,
And streams shall murmur all around."

—*Walford.*

We give the following from *Dickson* on account of the quaintness and beauty of the style, and the spirituality and elevation of the sentiment:—"In the fifth place he looketh upon their condition who dwell farre off from the tabernacle, who might at least thrice a year come from the farthest corner of the land to keep the solemnities appointed of God; and he counteth them blessed, albeit in their voyage they should endure never so much toile in travelling, and should with difficulty drink their water, either rained down from the clouds, or drawn from a well or cistern digged with much labour: for albeit they should sustaine toile and drought in their way, yet having refreshments one after another, and renewed strength for their journey, they should all come at last to the place of publick ordinances in Sion; and here he describeth the true and blessed Israelites, whether proselytes or borne Jews, resolved to come and appear before the Lord in the appointed solemnities by these six properties: First, they encourage themselves for the journey by hope in God to be furnished with strength: *Blessed is the man* (saith he) *whose strength is in thee.* Next, they are resolved in their heart for all the inconveniences they meet with in the journey, to hold on their course: *In whose heart are the wayes of them.* Thirdly, they do hold on their course through dry and comfortlesse places, which may be called places of *Baca*, or weeping: *They passe through the valley of Baca.* Fourthly, they overcome this difficulty of wanting water, either by digging a well, where they may find water; or by finding some already digged cistern wherein God's providence had reserved some quantity of rain-water for them: *Who, passing through the valley of Baca, make it a well: the raine also filleth the pooles.* Fifthly, after refreshment found in their journey, they are encouraged to go on their way, till they need and find some new refreshment, and reparation of their strength: *They go from strength to strength.* Sixthly, these godly travellers all come at length to the place they aimed at, to *Sion*, where they appear before God in the holy feast, chearful and joyful souls: *Every one of them in Sion appeareth before God.* And therefore doth he call them blessed, because at length they come through all the difficulties to have sweet communion with God. These two degrees of blessed Israelites are so painted out in figurative terms, as they may most easily lead the spiritual eye to the blessednesse which the figure is fit to represent, so that the typical words cannot well be understood, except the spiritual blessednesse be taken along: for there are two degrees of really blessed persons; some are at home already dwelling with God, of whom it may be most solidly said: *Blessed are they that dwell in thy house, they will be still praising thee*, which is their perpetual exercise. Others are travellers who are in their way toward heaven, the Lord's house; who indeed despair of their own strength to make out their journey, but their confidence is in God's strength, and their encouragement to set forward is this, that of them it may well be said, *Blessed is the man whose strength is in thee:* such men's journey doth take up their heart, the stream of their affections runs thitherward; *In whose heart are the wayes of them.* Those travellers have a wildernesse to go through, a comfortlesse valley wherein they do find matter of mourning and no solid consolation, save that which God doth provide beyond the nature of the place, which God, one way or other, doth furnish unto them, that they shall not fail to have a timous consolation: *Who, passing through the valley of Baca, make it a well; the raine also filleth the pooles.* So that albeit God suffer them to thirst, yet he suffereth them not to want a sufficient measure for bringing them on their way; a strengthening them to go forward: if they misse a well, they shall have a cistern filled with rain from heaven; the measure furnished unto them reneweth their strength after wearinesse, and sufficeth them till they need and meet with another renovation of their strength: *They go from strength to strength.* Not one of those resolute travellers or self-denying persons, relying on God's strength and furniture, do perish by the way, all are upheld and brought forward, till they come where they would be, to enjoy God's presence in *Sion* which is above: *Every one of them*, without exception, *in Sion appeareth before God.*"

10. *I had rather be a door-keeper*, &c. Comp. 1 Chr. ix. 19, where the Korahites are said to be "keepers of gates of the tabernacle; and their fathers keepers of the entry," and the allusion is seen in its true point and beauty.

10, 12. And now, ver. 10, 12, you are made to hear the report of the place given by those who reach it. *Israelites* would thus commend God's holy place to their fellows; but they who reach the kingdom of which all this was the shadow, what would they not say of the glory, and beauty, and bliss, and peace? If a day in the Lord's typical courts was so satisfying, what would be a day in the kingdom? And if *one* day, what the eternal day,—"*dies sempiternus, cui non cedit hesternus, quem non urget crastinus?*" (*August.*)

> "*For the Lord is a sun and shield:*
> *God giveth grace and glory;*
> *The Lord withholds no good*
> *From them that walk uprightly.*"

The Lord is all brightness and no gloom, and all safety. He gives "honour and glory," see Prov. iv. 9, &c. He leaves not one unsatisfied wish. Not one in that kingdom but ever sings (and O that all on earth heard it now!)—"*O Lord of hosts, blessed is the man that trusteth in thee!*" This is the heartfelt utterance of each one that has travelled thither; the testimony ungrudging and unqualified of "*The Righteous One on his way to the city of the living God.*"—*A. A. Bonar.*

PSALM LXXXV.

It is impossible to determine with anything like certainty the date and occasion of this psalm. Expositors are very much divided. Hengstenberg and Alexander agree in thinking that the time of composition cannot be determined. Perowne and Binnie, however, incline to the date of the return from the captivity in Babylon. This opinion seems to carry much probability with it. We abridge the remarks of the first-named writer:—There seems every reason to conclude that this psalm was written after the return of the exiles from the Babylonish captivity. It opens with an acknowledgment of God's goodness and mercy in the national restoration in terms which could hardly apply to any other event. But it passes immediately to earnest entreaty for deliverance from the pressure of existing evils in language which almost contradicts the previous acknowledgment. First, we hear the grateful confession, "Thou hast turned the captivity of Jacob;" and then we have the prayer, "Turn us, O God of our salvation." If the third verse contains the joyful announcement, "Thou hast withdrawn all thy wrath," &c., the fifth pleads as if no such assurance had been given: "Wilt thou for ever be angry with us? Wilt thou draw out thine anger to all generations?"

The most probable way of explaining this conflict of opposing feelings is by referring the psalm to the circumstances mentioned by Nehemiah (chap. i. 3). The exiles on their return, he learned, were "in great affliction and reproach." And when he obtained leave to go to Jerusalem himself, it was only in the midst of perpetual opposition and discouragement (chap. iv.) that he was able to carry on his work of restoration. The bright prospect which was opening before them had been quickly dashed. They had returned, indeed, but it was to a desolate land and a forsaken city, whose walls were cast down, and her gates burned with fire; whilst jealous and hostile tribes were ever on the watch to assail and vex them. Hence it is that the entreaty for mercy follows so hard upon the acknowledgment that mercy has been vouchsafed. Ps. cxxvi. is conceived in a somewhat similar strain. In the latter portion of this psalm (from ver. 8) the present misery is forgotten in the dawning of a glorious future. The prayer has been uttered; the storm of the soul is hushed; in quietness and resignation the psalmist sets himself to hear what God will say, and the divine answer is given, not in form, but in substance, in ver. 9–12. It is a glowing prophecy of Messianic times, most naturally connecting itself with the hopes which the return from Babylon had kindled afresh, and well fitted to enable those who heard it to triumph over the gloom and despondency of the present.

10. *Mercy and truth are met together*, &c. *Calvin* has no doubt that we have here a prophecy concerning the kingdom of Christ. He does not, however, explain the attributes mentioned in the verse as attributes of God meeting in harmony at the cross, or in the person of Christ. He supposes the natural meaning of the passage to be "that mercy, truth, peace, and righteousness will form the grand and ennobling distinction of the kingdom of Christ;"—in other words, that these four virtues shall flourish and rule supreme on the earth. The great commentator however adds—"If any one would rather understand *mercy and truth* as referring to God, I have no disposition to enter into dispute with him." Such an understanding of the passage has prevailed extensively from the days of Augustine downwards. "These words," says *Ralph Erskine*, "may be applied to the happy meeting of graces in men upon the revelation of Christ in the soul, yet I take it mainly to import the happy meeting of perfections in God, to be glorified in the sinner's salvation by Jesus Christ; which is a gloss that no interpreter I have had occasion to consult does neglect or omit: and if any of them should miss it, I think they would miss the very groundwork and foundation of all other happy meetings: 'Mercy and truth have met together, righteousness and peace have kissed each other.'" *Lowth*, remarking on these two views, justly says that the basis and source of these virtues in the hearts of men on earth is the sacrifice of Christ, by which God is reconciled and his character harmonized in the salvation of men. How admirable is that celebrated personification of the divine attributes by the psalmist! How just, elegant, and splendid does it appear, if applied only according to the literal sense, to the restoration of the Jewish nation from the Babylonish captivity! But if interpreted as relating to that sublimer, more sacred, and mystical sense, which is not obscurely shadowed under the ostensible image, it is certainly uncommonly noble and elevated, mysterious and sublime.

In allusion to this text, the cross of Christ has been quaintly but appropriately styled the *trysting-place* of the divine attributes. The following passage is an earnest and beautiful application of the text in this view:—"Are you afraid that truth and righteousness conspire against you, and hinder mercy and peace from ever meeting with you and embracing you? O no: fear not; only believe that mercy and truth are met together, and that righteousness and peace have kissed each other in Christ. Truth will not stand in the way of mercy, for they have kissed each other. He is indeed an infinitely just God, to take vengeance upon sin: but justice will not hinder mercy from coming to you: only believe that justice and mercy are reconciled in Christ, so as mercy can vent towards you, to the credit of justice. But, O! may such a black-mouthed sinner as I, as black as hell and the devil, expect a kiss from such an infinitely fair Jesus? Is that to be expected, that such opposites should meet in one another's arms? Yea, man, woman, allow me, a black sinner like yourself, to be the happy messenger, to tell you in God's name, that, be ye as black as you will, such a meeting and embracing betwixt Christ and you is more to be expected than ever men or angels could have expected, that infinite justice and mercy should have met together and kissed each other in a God-man: and this unexpected meeting is the very ground upon which your expectation of a meeting with, and embracement of God in Christ, is to be founded."—*Rev. Ralph Erskine.*[1]

PSALM LXXXVI.

There can be little doubt of the Davidic origin of the psalm. Calvin, Luther, Hengstenberg, Alexander, &c., ascribe it to David; and there is no reason for rejecting the title. "The whole psalm," says *Alexander*, "is called a prayer, because entirely made up either of direct petitions, or of arguments intended to enforce them. The tone and substance of the composition are well suited to David's situation in his days of suffering at the hands of Saul or Absalom, more probably the latter, on account of the repeated allusions to deliverance from former trials of the same kind. Some account for the position of this psalm in the midst of a series inscribed to *the sons of Korah*, by supposing that the latter composed it in the person or the spirit of David. The same hypothesis is used by these interpreters to explain the many forms of expression borrowed from other psalms of David, as if the *sons of Korah* meant to comfort him by the repetition of his own consolatory words in other cases. Comp. 2 Cor. i. 4. The psalm admits of no minute or artificial division."

7. *In the day of my trouble I will call upon thee.* This was the wisest thing he could do; and it is the best thing we can do. For, *First*, Prayer is enjoined upon us in trouble. . . . "Is any afflicted? Let him pray." *Secondly*, Prayer is the design of trouble. He does not afflict willingly. . . . It is to bring us to himself. It is to quicken us to pray more frequently, more earnestly—"I will go and return to my place, till they acknowledge their offence and seek my face. In their affliction they will seek me early." *Thirdly*, Prayer is the evidence that trouble is sanctified. It is a great thing not to lose a trial. A trial is never neutral in its effect. It always injures or improves. It is worse than nothing when it sends us to the creature, either in a way of accusation or relief. But when we turn to him that smiteth us, and acknowledge that his judgments are right, and cast ourselves at his feet, resolved, if we perish, *there* to die—we need not say with Job, "I am afraid of all my sorrows;" but confess with David, "It is good for me that I have been afflicted." *Fourthly*, Prayer is the solace of trouble. There is some relief in tears, and therefore nature is provided with them. It eases and soothes the bursting heart to pour our grief into the ear of a friend. . . . But how good it is to draw near to God! . . . to pour out our tears unto him, and resemble the child that sobs himself asleep in his mother's arms! *Fifthly*, Prayer is the medium of our deliverance from trouble. For this release we are allowed to be concerned; but we must seek it from God. And in doing this we have not only his power to encourage us, . . . but his goodness and love. . . . Yea, more: we have his faithfulness and truth that we shall not seek him in vain. He has engaged himself to appear to our joy, in his own time and way. He has bound himself and put the bond into our hand; and we can produce and plead it:—"Call upon me in the day of trouble and I will deliver thee, and thou shalt glorify me." "Because he hath set his love upon me, therefore will I deliver him; I will set him on high, because he hath known my name. He shall call upon me, and I will answer him; I will be with him in trouble; I will deliver him and honour him."—*Jay.*

9, 10. *All nations*, &c. Nothing can well exceed the plainness, directness, and precision with which the conversion of the nations is announced. "All nations whom thou hast made shall

[1] It may be mentioned here, as an interesting fact, that Mr. Barnes himself, who has just (Jan. 1871) passed away, preached his last sermon from this noble text.

come and worship before thee, O Lord; and shall glorify thy name. For thou art great, and doest wondrous things: thou art God alone," Ps. lxxxvi. 9, 10. "All the ends of the world shall remember, and turn unto the LORD; and all the kindreds of the nations shall worship before thee," Ps. xxii. 27. There is no mistaking the meaning of these announcements. They are as unambiguous as anything that can be spoken by the most sanguine advocate of Christian missions in this nineteenth century. Yet they come from the age and the pen of David. By him the Holy Spirit has, for eight and twenty centuries, been bearing witness that God's visible church is destined to embrace all the nations whom God has created on the face of the whole earth. A day is coming when they shall all resort to the Lord's throne, and bow themselves down before him. They have long forgotten him; but they shall one day call to remembrance his claims upon them and will turn to him again, even in the uttermost parts of the earth.—*Binnie.*

11. *Teach me thy way, O Lord.* There is here a beautiful connection. We have a prayer for divine teaching. That prayer springs from a resolute will to walk in the divine truth; otherwise it would be hypocritical and vain. But this walk again can only be secured by unity and simplicity of heart and aim. "*Unite* my heart to fear thy name." The meaning has been well expressed by *Perowne.* He says:—"*Unite my heart*—suffer it no longer to scatter itself upon a multiplicity of objects, to be drawn hither and thither by a thousand different aims, but turn all its powers, all its affections, in one direction, collect them in one focus, make them all one in thee. The prayer derives a special force from the resolve immediately preceding: 'I will walk in thy truth.' The same integrity of heart which made the resolve could alone utter the prayer. The nearest Old Testament parallels are, the 'one heart,' Jer. xxxii. 29; 'And I will give them one heart and one way, that they may fear me for ever;' and the 'whole heart' of love to God, Deut. vi. 5; x. 12. Our Lord teaches us how needful the prayer of this verse is. Compare what he says of 'the single eye;' the impossibility of serving two masters, the folly and wearisomeness of those anxious cares by which men suffer themselves to be hampered and distracted, and in contrast with all this, the exhortation, 'Seek ye first the kingdom of God,' &c., Mat. vi. 19-34. See also the history of Martha and Mary, Luke x. 38-42."

PSALM LXXXVII.

It is difficult, if not impossible, to determine the date and occasion of the psalm. *Alexander* and *Hengstenberg* suppose the historical occasion to be the great deliverance from the power of Assyria in the days of Hezekiah. *Calvin* makes it a post-captivity psalm. *Dr. Binnie* refers it to the eve of the captivity. "An attention to the time when this psalm was composed," says *Calvin*, "will contribute in no small degree to a clear understanding of its contents. Although the people had returned from their captivity in Babylon; although the church of God had been again gathered together and united into one body after a long dispersion; although the temple had been rebuilt, the altar set up, and the service of God restored; yet, as of a vast multitude of people there was only a small portion remaining, which made the condition of the church very low and despised, as the number left was daily diminished by their enemies, and as the temple was far inferior in magnificence to what it originally was: all this being considered, the faithful had hardly any ground to entertain favourable hopes as to the future. It certainly seemed impossible that they would ever again be raised to their former state from which they had fallen. There was, therefore, reason to apprehend that the minds of the godly, both from the remembrance of the overthrow which they had already experienced, and from the weight of the present miseries with which they were oppressed, would faint, and finally sink into despair. That they might not succumb under such heavy adversities, the Lord not only promises in this psalm that they would recover what they had lost, but also encourages them in the hope of an incomparable glory with which the church should yet be invested, according to that prophecy of Haggai, ii. 9, 'The glory of this latter house shall be greater than of the former.'"

4. *I will make mention of Rahab*, &c. The name of *Rahab* is put for Egypt in many other parts of Scripture; and this signification is very suitable to the

present passage, the object of which is to portray the magnificent amplitude of the church, which as yet was only matter of hope. It is therefore said that those who formerly were deadly enemies, or entire strangers, shall not only become familiar friends, but shall also be ingrafted into one body, that they may be accounted citizens of Jerusalem. In the first clause it is said, *I will make mention of Egypt and Babylon among my household.* In the second, it is added that the Philistines, Tyrians, and Ethiopians, who hitherto had been so much at variance with the people of God, shall now be brought into as cordial harmony with them as if they were Jews by birth. What a glorious distinction of the church, that even those who held her in contempt shall come flocking to her from every quarter, and that those who desired to see her completely cut up and destroyed shall consider it the highest honour to have a place among the number of her citizens, and to be accounted such! All of them shall voluntarily renounce their own countries in which they had before proudly boasted. Wherever they may have been born, whether in Palestine, or Ethiopia, or Tyre, they shall profess themselves citizens of the holy city.—*Calvin.*

5. *And of Zion it shall be said, This and that man*, &c. The phrase "This man and that man" is literally "man and man," or every man, or one man after another, in a series indefinitely extended. The idea is that of immense numbers. *Calvin* gives the sense thus:—It is asserted in the fourth verse, that the new citizens shall be gathered into the church of God from different parts of the world; and here the same subject is prosecuted. Another figure is, however, employed, which is, that strangers by birth shall be accounted among the holy people, just as if they were descended from Abraham. It had been stated in the preceding verse that the Chaldeans and Egyptians would be added to the household of the church; and that the Ethiopians, Philistines, and Tyrians would be enrolled among her children. Now, it is added, by way of confirmation, that the number of the new progeny shall be exceeding great, so that the city which had been for a time uninhabited, and afterwards only half filled with a few people, shall be crowded with a vast population. The prophet Isaiah describes more at length what is here promised in a few words, ch. liv. 1: "Sing, O barren, thou that didst not bear! break forth into singing, and cry aloud, thou that didst not travail with child; for more are the children of the desolate than the children of the married wife, saith the Lord. Enlarge the place of thy tent, and let them stretch forth the curtains of thine habitations: spare not, lengthen thy cords and strengthen thy stakes; for thou shalt break forth on the right hand and on the left; and thy seed shall inherit the Gentiles, and make the desolate cities to be inhabited." Also, chap. lx. 4, "Lift up thine eyes round about and see; all they gather themselves together, they come to thee: thy sons shall come from far, and thy daughters shall be nursed at thy side." And in chap. xliv. 5, we meet with almost the same language as in the passage before us, or, at least, what comes very near to it: "One shall say, I am the Lord's; and another shall call himself by the name of Jacob; and another shall subscribe with his hand unto the Lord, and surname himself by the name of Israel."

PSALMS LXXXVIII. LXXXIX.

We maintain, says *Hengstenberg*, that the two psalms together, like Ps. ix. and x., xlii. and xliii., and many other pairs of psalms, form one whole consisting of two parts. He adds that the character of a Song of Praise (title) belongs to the *whole* as soon as it is recognized as a whole. The introductory and concluding portions, dark in themselves, are illuminated by the light of a centre-sun. And the design of the whole then becomes manifest, namely, to give instruction how, in circumstances of great distress, to gain the victory over despair by praising God. If we separate Ps. lxxxviii. from Ps. lxxxix. it stands alone in the whole book of Psalms. All expositors remark with one voice, that such a comfortless complaint nowhere else occurs throughout its entire compass. Stier, for example, says: "The most mournful of all the plaintive psalms; yea, so wholly plaintive, without any ground of hope, that nothing like it is found in the whole Scriptures." The fact is all the more striking, that the psalm begins with the words, "O Lord, thou the God of my salvation!" after which one certainly might expect anything else rather than a mere description of trouble, in which the darkness is thickest at the *close*, contrary to the usual practice; for in all other cases the sun breaks through the clouds at the end, if it had not done so before. The peculiar feature of this psalm is, that it ends entirely in night. The importance of these facts is obvious from the circumstance that *Muntinghe* has been led by them to adopt the idea that the psalm is merely a fragment of a larger one—an idea utterly destitute of probability; for we have no such thing as fragments either in the book of Psalms or indeed within the whole compass of the literature of the Old Testament. As soon as the connection between Ps. lxxxviii. and lxxxix. is acknowledged, the difficulty disappears. The psalmist might, in this case, give free scope in the first part to his pain and lamentation, in obedience to an irresistible impulse of human nature, knowing that in the second part the rising sun of *consolation* would dispel all this darkness.—*Introduction to Ps. lxxxviii.*

The historian of Solomon's reign has preserved the names of some of the sages who graced his court, and who doubtless stood related to him in his studies in much the same way as Asaph and the other Levitical seers to David. The list occurs in the encomium on the wisdom of Solomon, which tells how "he was wiser than all men (that is to say, wiser than all the men of his own age and country); than Ethan the Ezrahite, and Heman, and Chalcol, and Darda, the sons of Mahol; and his fame was in all nations round about," 1 Ki. iv. 31. Questions not a few have been raised respecting the sages here enumerated—the wise satellites who revolved around the wisest king. Were they of the tribe of Judah, the king's own tribe, as the insertion of their names in 1 Chr. ii. 6 has been thought to imply? Or were they not rather Levites, registered among the families of Judah, because their lot had fallen to them within the inheritance of that tribe? These questions must remain unanswered here. I quote the list at present simply to call attention to the fact that two of the names that occur in it are found also in the superscriptions of Ps. lxxxviii. lxxxix. The former has the singular peculiarity of possessing two superscriptions, for it is entitled both "A song or psalm *of the sons of Korah*," and a psalm "of *Heman the Ezrahite*, to give instruction." The latter is entitled "A psalm of *Ethan the Ezrahite*, to give instruction." Is the coincidence of these names with those of Solomon's sages a mere accident? or are the Heman and Ethan of the superscriptions to be identified with the Heman and Ethan of the history? . . . I can only say that I am satisfied Calvin hit the truth when he conjectured that Ps. lxxxix. was written by some prophet of Solomon's time who lived on into the disastrous reign of Rehoboam; and that it was written to give expression to the sorrowful feelings with which the godly in Judah had witnessed the disruption of the kingdom and the collapse of the short-lived glory of David's house. . . . With regard to Ps. lxxxviii., one must speak with more hesitation. Neither author nor date is at all certain. It is a tearful song; indeed, it stands alone in the Psalter in this respect, that no ray of light breaks the gloom of the suppliant. Were it not that he calls upon God, in the opening verse, as "Jehovah, the God of his salvation," the whole might have seemed the cry of despair rather than of struggling faith. Dr. Hengstenberg, and some other commentators of note, are of opinion that the two psalms go together. If so, we may pretty confidently identify the "Heman the Ezrahite" of the one superscription, and the "Ethan the Ezrahite" of the other, with the Heman and Ethan of Solomon's time. Some go further, and identify them with the Heman and Ethan-Jeduthun, the Levitical seers and psalmists whom David appointed, along with Asaph their kinsman, to preside over the service of song. It is just possible they may be the same; but in that case they must have lived to extreme old age. The forty years of Solomon's reign, in addition to some of the last years of David's, intervened between the establishment of the Levitical choirs and the disruption of the kingdom. However this may be, since Ps. lxxxix. is a voice from the calamitous reign of Rehoboam, the circumstances of its origin must ever invest it with a certain melancholy interest, as being the last utterance of the Holy Spirit, in this kind, for a long time—the last pulsation of the mighty tide of inspired psalmody which commenced to flow when David was anointed at Bethlehem —*Binnie.*

PSALM LXXXIX.—There is a very

obvious and important observation to be made on the description of the apparent change that had taken place in the conduct of God towards the family and descendants of David. The extraordinary promises which had been given to that prince were certainly not accomplished in the fortunes of his descendants, the kings of Judah; nor shall we be able to discover how the truth of these promises is to be sustained without an admission of their being given in reference to the Messiah, that spiritual King, who "was born of the seed of David according to the flesh." When we take the assurances which were made to David, and which pledged to him the perpetuity of his kingdom in this sense, the mystery is disclosed, and the difficulty is completely removed: "the loving-kindness of God has not been withdrawn from him, nor has his faithfulness failed." David has still a royal successor, though the genealogy of his posterity is lost upon earth; a successor who will endure for ever, and whose throne will be perpetuated in glory, not merely as long as the sun and the moon continue, but will still be rising in splendour, when these lights of heaven shall be extinguished, and the new heavens and the new earth shall witness the imperishable glories of the Son of David.—*Walford.*

30-33. *If his children forsake my law,* &c. In ver. 30 and 31 the strongest possible descriptions of sin are designedly chosen in order to express the thought that the substance of the covenant is altogether independent of human conditions, that even the greatest unfaithfulness on the part of man does not alter the faithfulness of God.—In ver. 32 the words themselves do by no means convey the idea of a *slight* punishment; and neither can this be said of the fundamental passage, 2 Sam. vii. 14, "If he (the seed of David, his race) errs, I will visit him with the rod of men, and with the stripes of the children of men," *i.e.* with such punishments as all men (because all are sinners) are exposed to, grace shall not remove him from this the common lot of men, he has no commission to sin, contrary to Prov. xxiii. 13, 14, "Withdraw not thy son from chastisement; if thou smitest him with the rod he shall not die, and thou shalt deliver his soul from hell." The alleviating limitation is here first given in ver. 33, as it is in the fundamental passage in ver. 15. The alleviation, however, is not to be misunderstood as if it referred to *individuals* contrary to the nature of the thing, and contrary to the history, according to which annihilating judgments did descend upon the rebellious members of the family of David; but the opposition is of the punishment of sin in the individual, and of grace continually remaining to the *family.* We must not fail to notice that in ver. 33 it is not said: I will not withdraw my mercy from *them,* the sinners, but from *him,* the family as such. Now that the kingdom has passed from the *sinful* to the *holy* seed of David, the direct application of this paragraph has ceased. The case provided for in the promise cannot again occur. Still there exists between Christ and his church a case analogous to that between David and his seed. As David's family was chosen in him (compare 1 Ki. xi. 36; 2 Ki. viii. 19; Is. xxxvii. 35; 2 Chr. vi. 42), so that it always remained in possession of the favour of God, notwithstanding the fall and rejection of many of its individual members, in like manner the church is chosen in Christ, and the sins of its members may hurt *themselves* but cannot injure *it.* Notwithstanding the fall of a whole generation, it always flourishes again, and under the most inexorable judgments which are not removed by the appearance of Christ, but rendered more severe, compassionate grace is always concealed.—*Hengstenberg.*

END OF VOL. II.